THE PRINCETON HANDBOOK OF POETIC TERMS

THE PRINCETON HANDBOOK OF POETIC TERMS

ALEX PREMINGER

EDITOR

FRANK J. WARNKE AND O. B. HARDISON, JR.

ASSOCIATE EDITORS

With a Select Reading List by

T. V. F. Brogan

PRINCETON UNIVERSITY PRESS

PRINCETON, NEW JERSEY

TO

AUGUSTA FRIEDMAN PREMINGER

Published by Princeton University Press,
41 William Street, Princeton, New Jersey 08540
In the United Kingdom: Princeton University Press,
Guildford, Surrey

This book has been composed in Linotron Baskerville

Library of Congress Cataloging-in-Publication Data
Main entry under title:
The Princeton handbook of poetic terms.
Rev. ed. of: Princeton encyclopedia of poetry and
poetics. Enl. ed. 1974.
Bibliography: p.
1. Poetics—Dictionaries. I. Preminger, Alex.
II. Warnke, Frank J. III. Hardison, O. B.
IV. Princeton encyclopedia of poetry and poetics.
PN1042.P75 1986 808.1'0321 85-43380
ISBN 0-691-06659-0 (alk. paper)
ISBN 0-691-01425-6 (pbk.)

The Princeton Handbook of Poetic Terms includes
unrevised and revised entries from the original and enlarged editions
of the *Princeton Encyclopedia of Poetry and Poetics*.
In addition, 10 new entries are included.

Clothbound editions of Princeton University Press books
are printed on acid-free paper, and binding materials
are chosen for strength and durability.
Paperbacks, while satisfactory for personal collections,
are not usually suitable for library rebinding.

Printed in the United States of America
by Princeton University Press,
Princeton, New Jersey

PREFACE

It is the purpose of this *Handbook* to make available a selection of entries in the *Princeton Encyclopedia of Poetry and Poetics*, with emphasis on prosodic and poetic terms likely to be encountered in many different areas of literary study. The idea is to produce a volume that is inexpensive enough to be purchased by students and the general public interested in understanding poetry, yet, at the same time, more useful than previous handbooks and dictionaries in that it offers more detailed treatment than is customary.

To keep the price within the target area, the length of the *Handbook* had to be limited to around three hundred pages. This required a highly selective approach. We reluctantly decided to eliminate articles dealing with the histories of national poetries, with periods, movements, schools, and with most aspects of literary criticism. This meant eliminating many entries that are found in the ENCYCLOPEDIA for critical schools and terms. We have tried, however, to compensate for the loss of these entries with survey articles like POETRY, THEORIES OF, to which cross-references have been supplied. We have intentionally been generous in our policy regarding entries on genres, prosody, rhetorical figures, and related matters. These entries are less readily available in other reference books than entries on critical schools and terms. We felt—and feel—that they constitute one of the special strengths of this HANDBOOK. While we have favored entries relating to English poetry and to foreign influences that are important in its history, we have by no means ignored foreign poetry. We have, for example, included articles on CLASSICAL, CELTIC, GERMAN, OLD GERMANIC, ROMANCE, and SLAVIC PROSODY.

No attempt has been made here to revise all the entries carried over from the *Princeton Encyclopedia*. Many did not need updating. Others clearly required revision and, if at all feasible, have, accordingly, been updated. Some articles that are not in the *Encyclopedia* have been added. In the area of poetic forms, for example, a new entry has been added for CYCLE. Reflecting the growing interest in the Bible as literature there is a new article on PSALM. In the area of prosody, entries on EQUIVALENCE, RELATIVE STRESS PRINCIPLE, RHYTHM, and VERSIFICATION have been added, and GENERATIVE METRICS has been completely rewritten. The entries on GERMAN PROSODY and ROMANCE PROSODY have been revised and updated, as have been, for instance, the articles on LYRIC, METAPHOR, METONYMY, ODE, ORAL POETRY, and SYNECDOCHE. More generally, the entry on MUSIC AND POETRY has been entirely rewritten. To provide an introduction to recent developments in poetics and rhetoric, the articles on POETRY, THEORIES OF and on RHETORIC AND POETICS have been revised and updated.

Updated bibliographies have been provided for new and revised entries. As for the others, it was felt that the usefulness of the *Handbook* to students and general readers would be greater if bibliographical updating were in the form of a Select Reading List, which is included at the end of the volume. This list reflects the current state of theory and knowledge in the areas contained in the *Handbook* better than a large number of small—and, inevitably, mostly invisible—alterations in the bibliographies of individual entries. It also allows for the inclusion of books and articles that are important but that might otherwise have been omitted. We hope that the Select Reading List will be a useful guide for those who are interested in the areas it covers.

Abbreviations used in the *Princeton Encyclopedia* have been retained. As in several continental reference works, the entry word (or words) of an entry are abbreviated to the first letter (or letters) when they occur in the text of the entry. Thus *versification* is abbreviated *v.; metaphor m.*; and so forth. Common abbreviations (*Gr.* for *Greek, c.* for *century*, etc.) are used freely. Finally, authors and works referred to frequently are abbreviated by one or two key words. Full citations of these references will be found in the LIST OF ABBREVIATIONS on page x.

We are grateful to the following for their interest, advice, and concrete suggestions: Aldo S. Bernardo, David Bromwich, Frank Chambers, David Chisholm, Charles C. Dunn, Alfred G. Engstrom, Alvin A. Eustis, Robert O. Evans, Robert Fagles, J. Lionel Gossman, John Hollander, Roger A. Hornsby, Alvin Kernan, Murray Krieger, Michael Levinson, Herbert Lindenberger, A. Walton Litz, Wallace Martin, David A. Masson, Earl Miner, Laurence Perrine, Dorothy Clotelle Clarke Shadi, Michael Sperberg-McQueen, Karl D. Uitti, and, above all, T.V.F. Brogan, whose help went far beyond the boundary of his own contributions. A special note of appreciation is due Samuel Friedman for his assistance. We should also like to thank Herbert S. Bailey, director of the Princeton University Press, and Loren Hoekzema, Assistant to the Director for Special Projects, for their constant support.

THE EDITORS

Publisher's Note

Great care has been taken to trace all the owners of copyright material used in this book. If any have been inadvertently overlooked or omitted, acknowledgements will gladly be made in any future editions.

CONTENTS

LIST OF ABBREVIATIONS
BIBLIOGRAPHICAL

Abrams M. H. Abrams, *The Mirror and the Lamp. Romantic Theory and the Critical Tradition,* 1953.

AJP *American Journal of Philology*

AL *American Literature*

ASch *American Scholar*

ASEER *American Slavic and Eastern European Review*

ASR *American-Scandinavian Review*

AUC *Anales de la Universidad de Chile*

Auerbach E. Auerbach, *Mimesis. The Representation of Reality in Western Literature,* tr. W. R. Trask, 1953.

BA *Books Abroad*

Baum P. F. Baum, *The Principles of English Versification,* 1922.

Beare W. Beare, *Latin Verse and European Song,* 1957.

Behrens I. Behrens, *Die Lehre von der Einteilung der Dichtkunst* (Beihefte zur *Zeitschrift* für Romanische Philologie, 92, 1940).

BHR *Bibliothèque d'humanisme et renaissance*

Bowra C. M. Bowra, *Greek Lyric Poetry from Alcman to Simonides,* 1936, 2d ed., 1961.

Bray R. Bray, *La Formation de la doctrine classique en France,* 1927.

Brogan T. V. F. Brogan, *English Versification 1570–1980: A Reference Guide with a Global Appendix,* 1981.

Brooks and Warren C. Brooks and R. P. Warren, *Understanding Poetry,* 2d ed., 1950, 3d ed., 1960.

Brooks, *Tradition* C. Brooks, *Modern Poetry and the Tradition,* 1939.

BZ *Byzantinische Zeitschrift* (Leipzig)

Cabeen *A Critical Bibliography of French Literature,* general ed. D. C. Cabeen, 1– ; 1947– (in progress).

Cassell's *Cassell's Encyclopaedia of World Literature,* ed. S. H. Steinberg, 2 v., 1954.

CBEL *Cambridge Bibliography of English Literature*

CE *College English*

Chadwick H. M. and N. K. Chadwick, *The Growth of Literature,* 3 v., 1932–40.

CHEL *Cambridge History of English Literature*

CJ *Classical Journal*

CL *Comparative Literature*

CP *Classical Philology*

CQ *Classical Quarterly*

Crane R. S. Crane, *The Languages of Criticism and the Structure of Poetry,* 1953.

Crane, *Critics* *Critics and Criticism, Ancient and Modern,* ed. R. S. Crane, 1952.

Crusius F. Crusius, *Römische Metrik,* 2d ed., 1955.

Curtius E. Curtius, *European Literature and the Latin Middle Ages,* tr. W. R. Trask, 1953.

CW *Classical World*

DAI *Dissertation Abstracts International*

Daiches D. Daiches, *Critical Approaches to Literature,* 1956.

Dale A. M. Dale, *The Lyric Metres of Greek Drama,* 1948.

Deutsch B. Deutsch, *Poetry Handbook,* 1957, 2d ed., 1962.

DVLG *Deutsche Vierteljahrsschrift für Literaturwissenschaft und Geistesgeschichte*

E&S *Essays and Studies by Members of the English Association*

EIC *Essays in Criticism (Oxford)*

EIE *English Institute Essays*

Eliot, *Essays* T. S. Eliot, *Selected Essays,* 1932, rev. ed., 1950.

Eliot, *Wood* T. S. Eliot, *The Sacred Wood: Essays on Poetry and Criticism,* 1920.

Empson W. Empson, *Seven Types of Ambiguity,* 1930, 2d ed., 1947.

FiR *Filologia romanza*

FM *Français moderne*

Frye N. Frye, *Anatomy of Criticism,* 1957.

FS *French Studies*

Gayley and Kurtz C. M. Gayley and B. P. Kurtz, *Methods and Materials of Literary Criticism: Lyric, Epic and Allied Forms of Poetry,* 1920.

Gilbert and Kuhn K. Gilbert and H. Kuhn, *A History of Esthetics,* 1939, 2d ed., 1953.

Hamer E. Hamer, *The Metres of English Poetry,* 1930.

Hardie W. R. Hardie, *Res metrica,* 1920.

HR *Hispanic Review*

HSCL *Harvard Studies in Comparative Literature*

HSCP *Harvard Studies in Classical Philology*

HSS *Harvard Slavic Studies*

JAAC *Journal of Aesthetics and Art Criticism*

JAF *Journal of American Folklore*

Jeanroy A. Jeanroy, *La Poésie lyrique des troubadours,* 2 v., 1934

Jeanroy, *Origines* A. Jeanroy, *Les Origines de la poésie lyrique en France au moyen âge,* 3d ed., 1925.

JEGP *Journal of English and Germanic Philology*

JHI *Journal of the History of Ideas*

JNH *Journal of Negro History*

JWCI *Journal of the Warburg and Courtauld Institute*

ABBREVIATIONS

Kastner L. E. Kastner, *A History of French Versification,* 1903.
Ker W. P. Ker, *Form and Style in Poetry,* 1928.
Kolář A. Kolář, *De re metrica poetarum Graecorum et Romanorum,* Prague, 1947.
Koster W. J. W. Koster, *Traité de métrique grecque suivi d'un précis de métrique latine,* 2d ed., Leyden, 1953.
KR *Kenyon Review*
Krieger M. Krieger, *The New Apologists for Poetry,* 1956.
Langer S. K. Langer, *Philosophy in a New Key,* 1948.
Lausberg H. Lausberg, *Handbuch der literarischen Rhetorik,* 2 v., 1960.
Lehmann A. G. Lehmann, *The Symbolist Aesthetic in France, 1885–95,* 1950.
Lewis C. S. Lewis, *The Allegory of Love,* 1936.
LonM *London Magazine*
Martino P. Martino, *Parnasse et symbolisme, 1850–1900,* 1925, 4th ed., 1935.
MdF *Mercure de France*
MFL *Modern Language Forum*
MLJ *Modern Language Journal*
MLN *Modern Language Notes*
MLQ *Modern Language Quarterly*
MLR *Modern Language Review*
Morris-Jones J. Morris-Jones, *Cerdd Dafod,* 1925.
MP *Modern Philology*
N&Q *Notes and Queries*
Navarro T. Navarro, *Métrica española: Reseña histórica y descriptiva,* 1956.
NED *New English Dictionary*
Neophil *Neophilologus* (Groningen)
Nicoll A. Nicoll, *A History of English Drama, 1660–1900,* 6 v., 1952–59.
Norden E. Norden, *Die antike Kunstprosa,* 5th ed., 2 v., 1958.
OED *Oxford English Dictionary*
OSP *Oxford Slavonic Papers*
Parry T. Parry, *A History of Welsh Literature,* tr. H. I. Bell, 1955.
Patterson W. F. Patterson, *Three Centuries of French Poetic Theory,* 3 v., 1935.
PMLA *Publications of the Modern Language Association of America*
PQ *Philological Quarterly*
PR *Partisan Review*
QQ *Queen's Quarterly*
QR *Quarterly Review*
Raymond M. Raymond, *De Baudelaire au surréalisme,* 1933, 2d ed., 1940.
Reallexikon *Reallexikon der deutschen Literaturgeschichte,* ed. P. Merker and W. Stammler, 4 v., 1925–31; 2d ed., ed. W. Kohlschmidt et al., 1958–84.
Ren *Renascence*
RES *Review of English Studies*
RF *Romanische Forschungen*
RFE *Revista de filología española*
RHL *Revue d'histoire littéraire de la France*
Richards, *Practical* I. A. Richards, *Practical Criticism,* 1929.
Richards, *Principles* I. A. Richards, *Principles of Literary Criticism,* 1925.
RLC *Revue de littérature comparée*
RLR *Revue des langues romanes* (Montpellier)
Rom *Romania*
RPh *Romance Philology*
Saintsbury G. Saintsbury, *History of Criticism and Literary Taste in Europe,* 3 v., 1900–04.
Saintsbury, *Prosody* G. Saintsbury, *A History of English Prosody,* 3 v., 1906–10.
SAQ *South Atlantic Quarterly*
SAWW *Sitzungsberichte der [österreichischen] Akademie der Wissenschaften in Wien.* Phil.-hist. Klasse
SB *Studies in Bibliography: Papers of the Bibliographical Society of the University of Virginia*
Schipper J. M. Schipper, *Englische Metrik,* 3 v., 1881–1888 (abridged and tr. as *A History of English Versification,* 1910).
Schmid and Stählin W. Schmid and O. Stählin, *Geschichte der griechischen Literatur,* 2 v., 1929–48.
Science and Literature International Federation for Modern Languages and Literatures. *Literature and Science. Proceedings of the Triennial Congress held at Oxford 1954,* 1956.
SD *Studi danteschi*
SEER *Slavonic and East European Review* [title changed to: *Slavic Review*]
SFI *Studi di filologia italiana*
Shipley *Dictionary of World Literature,* ed. J. T. Shipley, 1943, rev. ed., 1953.
ShS *Shakespeare Survey*
Smyth H. W. Smyth, *Greek Melic Poets,* 1906.
SOED *Shorter Oxford English Dictionary*
SP *Studies in Philology*
SQ *Shakespeare Quarterly*
SR *Sewanee Review*
SRen *Studies in the Renaissance*
Sutton W. Sutton, *Modern American Criticism,* 1963.
SWR *Southwest Review*
Sym *Symposium*
TLS [London] *Times Literary Supplement*
TPAPA *Transactions and Proceedings of the American Philological Association*
TPS *Transactions of the Philological Society (London)*
TSE *Tulane Studies in English*
Tuve R. Tuve, *Elizabethan and Metaphysical Imagery,* 1947.
UNCSCL *University of North Carolina Studies in Comparative Literature*
UNCSRLL *University of North Carolina Studies in the Romance Languages and Literatures*
UTSE *University of Texas Studies in English*
Weinberg B. Weinberg, *A History of Literary Criticism in the Italian Renaissance,* 2 v., 1961.
Wellek R. Wellek, *A History of Modern Criticism, 1750–1950,* 1955–86.

ABBREVIATIONS

Wellek and Warren R. Wellek and A. Warren, *Theory of Literature,* 1949, 2d ed., 1956.

Wheelwright P. Wheelwright, *The Burning Fountain. A Study in the Language of Symbolism,* 1954.

Wilkins E. H. Wilkins, *A History of Italian Literature,* 1954.

Wilson E. Wilson, *Axel's Castle,* 1931.

Wimsatt W. K. Wimsatt, Jr. and M. C. Beardsley, *The Verbal Icon,* 1954.

Wimsatt, *Versification* W. K. Wimsatt, Jr., ed., *Versification: Major Language Types,* 1972.

Wimsatt and Brooks W. K. Wimsatt, Jr. and C. Brooks, *Literary Criticism: A Short History,* 1957.

WR *Western Review*

YCS *Yale Classical Studies*

YFS *Yale French Studies*

ZDP *Zeitschrift für deutsche Philologie*

ZRP *Zeitschrift für romanische Philologie*

ZSP *Zeitschrift für slavische Philologie*

ZVS *Zeitschrift für vergleichende Sprachforschung*

LIST OF ABBREVIATIONS
GENERAL

Am. American
anthol. anthology
assoc. association
b. born
bibliog. bibliography
c. century; centuries
ca. about
cf. *confer,* compare
ch. chapter
cl. classical; classicism
crit. critical; criticism
d. died
dict. dictionary
diss. dissertation
ed. editor; edited (by); edition
e.g. *exempli gratia,* for example
Eng. English
enl. enlarged
et al. *et alii,* and others
ff. following
fl. *floruit,* flourished
fr., frag. fragment
Fr. French
Gesch. *Geschichte*
Gr. Greek
hist. history, *histoire*
i.e. *id est,* that is
introd. introduction
Ir. Irish
It. Italian
jour. journal
L. Latin
lit. literature(s); literary
LL Late Latin
loc. cit. *loco citato,* in the place cited
ME Middle English
ms(s) manuscript(s)
OE Old English
OF Old French
ON Old Norse
p., pp. page; pages
pr. printed
prep. preparation
proc. proceedings
Prov. Provençal
publ. published
q.v. *quod vide,* which see
qq.v. *quae vide,* both which, or all which, see
Ren. Renaissance
repr. reprint; reprinted
rev. revised
Rus. Russian
s. *siècle*
sc. *scilicet,* to wit
Sp. Spanish
supp. supplement; supplementary
t. tome
tr. translated by; translation(s)
v. volume(s)

LIST OF CONTRIBUTORS

M. H. Abrams, Frederic T. Whiton Professor of English, Cornell University

Robert Alter, Professor of Hebrew and Comparative Literature, University of California (Berkeley)

Robert P. apRoberts, Professor of English, California State University (Northridge)

Arthur J. Arberry, late Sir Thomas Adams's Professor of Arabic, University of Cambridge

George Arms, Professor Emeritus of English, University of New Mexico

William Arrowsmith, Professor of Classics, Emory University

John Arthos, Professor Emeritus of English, University of Michigan

Paull F. Baum, late James B. Duke Professor of English, Duke University

William Beare, late Professor of Latin and one-time Pro-Vice Chancellor, University of Bristol

Richard Beck, late University Professor Emeritus of Scandinavian Languages and Literatures, University of North Dakota

Robert Beloof, Professor of Rhetoric, University of California (Berkeley)

Allen R. Benham, late Professor of English, University of Washington

Aldo S. Bernardo, Professor of Romance Languages, State University of New York (Binghamton)

Jess B. Bessinger, Jr., Professor of English, New York University

T. V. F. Brogan, Assistant Professor of English, University of Hawaii

Huntington Brown, Professor Emeritus of English, University of Minnesota

Frank M. Chambers, former Professor of French, University of Arizona

Seymour Chatman, Professor of Rhetoric, University of California (Berkeley)

Arthur Melville Clark, Reader Emeritus in English Literature, University of Edinburgh

Dorothy Clotelle Clarke, Professor Emerita of Spanish, University of California (Berkeley)

J. E. Congleton, Professor Emeritus of English, Findlay College

Procope S. Costas, late Professor of Classics, Brooklyn College, City University of New York

Jonathan D. Culler, Professor of English and Comparative Literature, Cornell University

Charles W. Dunn, Margaret Brooks Robinson Professor of Celtic Languages and Literatures and Chairman of the Department, Harvard University

Robert C. Elliott, late Professor of English Literature, University of California (San Diego)

Gerald F. Else, late Emeritus Professor of Greek and Latin, University of Michigan

John J. Enck, late Professor of English, University of Wisconsin

Alfred Garwin Engstrom, Alumni Distinguished Professor Emeritus of French, University of North Carolina (Chapel Hill)

Robert O. Evans, Professor of English and Comparative Literature, University of New Mexico

Robert P. Falk, Professor Emeritus of English, University of California (Los Angeles)

Solomon Fishman, late Professor of English, University of California (Davis)

Wolfgang Bernhard Fleischmann, Professor of Comparative Literature, Montclair State College

Richard Harter Fogle, University Distinguished Professor Emeritus of English, University of North Carolina (Chapel Hill)

Stephen F. Fogle, late Professor of English, Adelphi Suffolk College

Tatiana Fotitch, late Professor Emerita of Romance Languages and Literatures, Catholic University of America

Albert B. Friedman, Professor of English, Claremont Graduate School

Norman Friedman, Professor of English, Queens College, City University of New York

Paul H. Fry, Associate Professor of English, Yale University

Northrop Frye, University Professor, Massey College, University of Toronto

Joseph G. Fucilla, late Professor Emeritus of Romance Languages, Northwestern University

Paul Fussell, Donald T. Regan, Professor of English Literature, University of Pennsylvania

Robert J. Getty, late Paddison Professor of Classics, University of North Carolina (Chapel Hill)

Ulrich K. Goldsmith, Professor Emeritus of German and Comparative Literature, University of Colorado

Lewis H. Gordon, Professor of Italian and French, Brown University

Bernard Groom, late Professor of English, McMaster University

Fabian Gudas, Professor of English, Louisiana State University

O. B. Hardison, Jr., University Professor of English, Georgetown University

Samuel Hazo, Professor of English, Duquesne University

Marvin T. Herrick, late Professor of English, University of Illinois

Daniel Hoffman, Professor of English, University of Pennsylvania

John Hollander, Professor of English, Yale University

C. Hugh Holman, late Kenan Professor of Eng-

lish, University of North Carolina (Chapel Hill)
Urban T. Holmes, Jr., late Kenan Professor of Romance Languages, University of North Carolina (Chapel Hill)
Roger A. Hornsby, Professor of Classics, University of Iowa
Leo Hughes, Emeritus Professor of English University of Texas
W. T. H. Jackson, late Villard Professor of German and Comparative Literature and Professor of History, Columbia University
James William Johnson, Professor of English, University of Rochester
Charles A. Knudson, late Professor of French, University of Illinois
Murray Krieger, University Professor of English, University of California (Irvine)
James Craig La Drière, late Professor of Comparative Literature, Harvard University
Stephen A. Larrabee, author and critic
Laurence D. Lerner, Professor of English, University of Sussex, England
Samuel R. Levin, Professor of English, Graduate Center, City University of New York
John L. Lievsay, Professor Emeritus of English, Duke University
Herbert Lindenberger, Avalon Foundation Professor of Humanities in Comparative Literature and English, Stanford University
D. Myrddin Lloyd, late Keeper of Printed Books, National Library of Scotland
Albert B. Lord, Professor Emeritus of Slavic Languages and Comparative Literature, Harvard University
Sverre Lyngstad, Professor of English, Newark College of Engineering
Robert Marsh, late Professor of English, University of Chicago
Wallace Martin, Professor of English, University of Toledo
David I. Masson, former Librarian in Charge of Brotherton Collection, University of Leeds Library
Rigo Mignani, Professor of Romance Languages, State University of New York (Binghamton)
Louis T. Milic, Professor of English, Cleveland State University
Earl Miner, Professor of English and Comparative Literature, Princeton University
Stephen L. Mooney, late Professsor of English, University of Tennessee
Bayard Quincy Morgan, late Professor of German, Stanford University
John M. Munro, Academic Vice-President, Simon Fraser University
William Van O'Connor, late Professor and Chairman of the Department of English, University of California (Davis)
G. N. G. Orsini, late Professor and Chairman of the Department of Comparative Literature, University of Wisconsin (Madison)
Lucy B. Palache, editorial research assistant
Douglass S. Parker, Professor of Classics, University of Texas
Laurence Perrine, Professor Emeritus of English, Southern Methodist University
Alex Preminger, former Associate Professor, Brooklyn College Library, City University of New York
Paul Ramsey, Poet-in-Residence and Guerry Professor of English, University of Tennessee (Chattanooga)
James K. Robinson, Professor of English, University of Cincinnati
Hiroaki Sato, author, translator
Bernard N. Schilling, former Trevor Professor of English and Comparative Literature, University of Rochester
Christoph E. Schweitzer, Professor of Germanic Languages and Literatures, University of North Carolina (Chapel Hill)
Isidore Silver, Rosa May Distinguished Professor Emeritus in the Humanities, Washington University
John Simon, drama and and film critic
A. J. M. Smith, late Professor Emeritus of English, Michigan State University
Barbara Herrnstein Smith, Professor of English and Comparative Literature, University of Pennsylvania
Edward Stankiewicz, Professor of Slavic Languages and Linguistics, Yale University
Martin Steinmann, Jr., Professor of English, University of Minnesota
Roy Arthur Swanson, Professor of Classics and Comparative Literature, University of Wisconsin (Milwaukee)
John Thompson, Professor Emeritus of English, State University of New York (Stony Brook)
Louis Untermeyer, late poet, anthologist, and editor
Frank J. Warnke, Professor and Head, Comparative Literature Department, University of Georgia
Edward R. Weismiller, Professor Emeritus of English, George Washington University
Henry W. Wells, late Curator Emeritus, Brander Matthews Dramatic Museum, Columbia University, Former Professor of English, Columbia University
George Whalley, late Professor and Head of the Department of English, Queen's University
Philip Wheelwright, late Professor of Philosophy, University of California (Riverside)
Harold Whitehall, late Professor Emeritus of English and Linguistics, Indiana University
William Carlos Williams, late poet and author
James A. Winn, Professor of English, University of Michigan
A. S. P. Woodhouse, late Professor of English, University of Toronto
Mabel P. Worthington, late Professor of English, Temple University
Lawrence J. Zillman, Professor Emeritus of English, University of Washington

THE PRINCETON HANDBOOK OF POETIC TERMS

A

ACCENT. The vocal emphasis with which a syllable is spoken relative to the emphasis received by contiguous syllables. Some linguists and prosodists equate a. with stress (q.v.); some maintain that stress is simply one of the constituents of a.; and some hold that the two are quite different things. Disagreement over the nature of a. is traditional in prosodic theorizing. Does an accented syllable have a higher pitch (q.v.) than an unaccented one? Does it have a longer duration (q.v.)? Is it louder? Has it a unique timbre or quality? Or is its emphatic characteristic connected with some sort of mysterious "energy" or "impulsion" which cannot be described in terms of either pitch, length, loudness, or quality? There is little solid agreement about these questions, even though the coarsest sensibility is capable of perceiving that the line

To me the meanest flower that blows can give

consists of alternating "accented" and "unaccented" syllables. Although it is obvious that there are infinite degrees of a. (whatever it is), prosodists frequently discriminate three degrees for purposes of scansion (q.v.): primary a., secondary a., and weak a.

Accents are also classified by kind: etymological or grammatical ("lexical" or "word") a. is the accentual pattern customary to the word because of derivation or the relationship of prefix and suffix to root; rhetorical or logical ("sense") a. is the variable degree of emphasis given syllables according to their sense in context, e.g.

Have you the money? Have you the móney?

and metrical a. is the abstract pattern of more or less regularly recurring emphases in a line of fairly orthodox verse. Most modern prosodic theorists would hold that metrical a. almost always yields to rhetorical except in rare cases of presumably intentional "wrenched a.," as in some popular ballads:

And I fear, I fear, my dear mastér,
That we will come to harm.
(*Sir Patrick Spens*)

On the other hand, conservative prosodists of the 18th and early 19th c. frequently maintained that rhetorical a. yields to metrical.

A., however defined, is the metrical basis of Germanic accentual and accentual-syllabic prosodies (see METER), in which, most frequently, the rhetorical importance of words or syllables in context provides the pattern of metrical accents. See STRESS, PROSODY.

R. M. Alden, *Eng. Verse* (1903); J. B. Mayor, *A Handbook of Modern Eng. Metre* (1903); T. S. Omond, *Eng. Metrists* (1921); R. Bridges, *Milton's Prosody* (rev. ed., 1921); Baum; L. Abercrombie, *Principles of Eng. Prosody: Part I* (1923); P. Fussell, Jr., *Theory of Prosody in 18th-C. England* (1954).

P.F.

ACROSTIC. The most common a. is a poem in which the initial letters of each line have a meaning when read downward. There are many variations among which the following are the most important: an a. might be a prose composition in which the initial letters of each paragraph make up the word or words in question; the a. might use the middle (mesostich) or the final letter (telestich) of each line; finally, the key letters might be distributed by stanzas and not by lines.

According to some, the a. was first used as a mnemotechnic device to ensure completeness in the oral transmission of sacred texts. In ancient times mystical significance was attributed to a. compositions. In the Old Testament all the recognized acrostics belong to the alphabetical type (abecedarian). Psalm 119 offers the most elaborate example. Here the 22 letters of the Hebrew alphabet in their proper order form the initial letters of every other line of the 22 stanzas of the Psalm. Another example of this type of a. is Chaucer's poem *An A.B.C.* Gr. authors of the Alexandrian time as well as L. authors (e.g., Plautus) put the title of their plays in the a. verses of the arguments (as did Ben Jonson in *The Alchemist*). During the Middle Ages the a. often spelled out the name of the author or of a saint. Later also the name of the patron or the beloved was thus designated. Among the more famous poets to use the name of their beloveds are Boccaccio and Edgar Allan Poe. In the case of *Der Ackermann aus Böhmen* and of *La Celestina* the name "a." is important evidence for the identification of Johannes von Tepl and Fernando de Rojas respectively as their authors.

By extension, the forming of words—new or old—from the initials of other words is also called an a. In the early Christian church the famous symbol of the fish is the result of this type of a. The initials of the following five words spell out the Gr. word for fish, *ichthys: Iēsous-CHristos-THeou-(H)Yios-Sōtēr.* These words in turn mean Jesus-Christ-God's-Son Saviour. Modern examples include words like AWOL and CARE.—R. Knox, *Book of Acrostics* (1924); R. Marcus, "Alphabetic Acrostics in the Hellenistic and Roman Periods," *Jour. of Near Eastern Studies,* 6 (1947).

C.E.S.

ADONIC (Adoneus, *versus Adonius*). In Gr. and L. poetry this metrical unit was of the same form as the last 2 feet of the dactylic hexameter and took its name from the cry for the god Adonis:

ō tŏn Ădōnīn. . .
(Sappho, fr. 168 Lobel and Page)

Certain Gr. proverbs were in Adonics, e.g.

gnōthĭ sĕautōn.

The fourth and last line of the Sapphic (q.v.) stanza, as usually printed, was an A., although word-enjambement from the third to the fourth line would suggest that the two lines were metrically one, e.g. Horace's

lābĭtŭr rīpă Iŏvĕ nōn prŏbānt(e) ū-xōrĭŭs
āmnīs

(*Odes* 1.2.19–20, a rare example in that poet). Seneca employed the A. sometimes in longer runs of "lesser Sapphics." Some poets later used it stichically:

nūbĭbŭs ātrīs
cōndĭtă nūllūm
fūndĕrĕ pōssūnt
sīdĕră lūmēn.

Bowra; J. F. García, "La cesura en el verso 11 del carmen XI de Catulo," *Emerita* 9 (1941); Kolář; U. von Wilamowitz-Moellendorff, *Griechische Verskunst* (2d ed., 1958). R.J.G.

AIR. (a) A song, especially a form of strophic song (Eng. "ayre," Fr. *air de cour,* It. *balletto*) in which the upper (melody) line is carried by solo voice or instrument. Because of this arrangement there is greater emphasis on the words, or poetic text, than in such compositions as madrigal or choric song. "A." in the above sense flourished during the 16th c., particularly in the hands of the Eng. lutenist composers like Dowland and Campion. (b) In a strictly musical sense, "a." is used in 17th- and 18th-c. France to refer to dancelike instrumental pieces. (c) In a somewhat recondite sense by Eng. musical writers of the 17th c., "ayre" comes to mean the mode, or key, of a particular musical sequence; thus frequently mentioned are the "aires which the Antiquity termed *Modi*" (Thomas Morley, *A Plaine and Easie Introduction to Practicall Musicke,* p. 147). This usage is supported by that of Charles Butler, Thomas Mace, and other theorists. This sense of the word seems to be the one used by Milton in "Lap me in soft Lydian airs" (*L'Allegro* 1.136).—*The Eng. School of Lutenist Song Writers,* ed. E. H. Fellowes (16 v., 1920–32; 2d ser., 16 v., 1925–27); P. Warlock, *The Eng. Ayre* (1926). J.H.

ALBA (Prov.), *aube, aubade* (Fr.), *Tagelied* (Ger.). A dawn song, ordinarily expressing the regret of two lovers that day has come so soon to separate them. It has no fixed metrical form, but each stanza usually ends with the word *alba.* The earliest examples in Prov. and in Fr. date from the end of the 12th c. The a. probably grew out of the medieval watchman's cry, announcing from his tower the passing of the night hours and the return of day. And in one a. it is a watchman who speaks, a friend of the lover's, who has been standing guard. Others are little dialogues between lover and beloved, with occasional comments from the author. In Eng. poetry, examples can be found in Chaucer's *Troilus and Criseyde* and the *Reeve's Tale.*—A. Jeanroy, *Origines . . .* and *La Poésie . . .* ; R. E. Kaske, "An Aube in the Reeve's Tale," ELH, 26 (1959) and "January's Aube, MLN, 75 (1960). F.M.C.

ALCAIC. Generally a 4-line stanza of Aeolic type, named after the Gr. poet Alkaios (Alcaeus, late 7th and early 6th c. B.C.). The scheme is:

⏓ – ⏑ – ⏓ – ⏑ ⏑ – ⏑ ⏓ (twice) ||
⏓ – ⏑ – ⏓ – ⏑ – ⏓ ||
– ⏑ ⏑ – ⏑ ⏑ – ⏑ – ⏓

Lines 1 and 2 are Greater (or hendecasyllabic) Alcaics; line 3 is a 9-syllable A.; line 4 is a Lesser (or decasyllabic) A. This is the strophe used most frequently—37 times—by the Roman poet Horace (65–8 B.C.). It was adapted in It. by Gabriello Chiabrera (1552–1638), Paolo Rolli (1687–1765), and Giovanni Fantoni (1755–1807). Like Chiabrera, Renaissance metricians in England and France attempted recreation of the A. among other classical meters. In 18th-c. Germany F. G. Klopstock composed 17 A. odes. Hölderlin, von Platen, and others contributed to the tradition of the meter. Tennyson ("O mighty-mouth'd inventor of harmonies, . . ."), A. H. Clough, and Swinburne composed Eng. A. verses. Recent examples of translations from Gr. and L. into Eng. Alcaics are to be found in, e.g., Richmond Lattimore's version of Alcaeus'

Asunnetēmmi tōn anemōn stasin
(*Greek Lyrics,* 1955, p. 27)

and J. B. Leishman's, H. R. Henze's, J. Michie's translations of Horace (1956, 1961, 1963).—For bibliog., see CLASSICAL METERS IN MODERN LANGUAGES. Also, C. H. Moore, *Horace* (1902); H. G. Atkins, *A Hist. of German Versification* (1923); O. Francabandera, *Contribuzioni alla storia dell' alcaica* (1928); G. Highet, *The Cl. Tradition* (1949); Koster; J. P. M. Blackett, "A Note on the A. Stanza," *Greece and Rome,* 2 (1956). R.A.S.

ALEXANDRINE. In Fr. prosody, a line of 12 syllables. The a. has been, since the 16th c., the standard meter of Fr. poetry, in which it has had an importance comparable to that of the quantitative hexameter in L. poetry or blank verse in Eng. poetry; it has been used especially in dramatic and narrative forms. The earliest Fr. alexandrines occur in *Le Pèlerinage de Charlemagne à Jérusalem,* a *chanson de geste* (q.v.) of the early 12th c., which abandons the traditional decasyllabic verse of Fr. epic style for the longer line. However, the a. probably takes its name from a slightly later poem, the *Roman d'Alexandre* (late 12th c.) of Lambert le Tort, a romance based on the legendary exploits of Alexander the Great. Having fallen into disuse in the later medieval period, the meter was revived in the 16th c. by J. A. de Baïf and was widely used by Ronsard and other members of the *Pléiade.* After being perfected by the great dramatists of the 17th c., especially Racine, it became the dominant meter of all serious Fr. poetry. A certain regularity, characteristic of even the earlier a. verse, was intensified by the theory and practice of the 17th c. poets, who developed strict rules for the use of the meter. In particular, the position of the caesura after the sixth syllable tended to become standard:

> Je le vis, je rougis, || je pâlis à sa vue . . .
> (Racine, *Phèdre*)

After the days of Corneille, Molière, and Racine, each of whom was able to impress the meter with his own personality, the a. tended to become excessively mechanical, until the advent of the Fr. romantics revolutionized it by an extensive use of enjambement (q.v.) and a freer practice of the so-called *alexandrin ternaire,* with its two pauses:

> J'ai disloqué | ce grand niais | d'alexandrin . . .
> (Hugo)

The evolution is complete with Verlaine who, by his musical fluidity, deemphasizing of rhyme, and offhand treatment of mute *e,* brings the a. to the brink of free verse. Since symbolism, the a. has oscillated, depending upon the poet, between Malherbian rigidity and symbolist evanescence.

The a. has had great importance in the poetry of several other languages, notably Dutch, in which it was the most widely used meter from the early 17th c. until around 1880. It is a common meter in 17th-c. German poetry—widely used in the school of Opitz because of the sanction lent it by *Pléiade* practice, imaginatively exploited by Andreas Gryphius because of its formal appropriateness to his antithesis-filled style. The a. is also the basis from which developed the *cuaderna via,* the important 14-syllable Sp. meter, as well as the It. meter analogous to it. The Eng. a. differs from the Fr. in being actually longer. Composed of iambic feet, it contains 6 stress accents rather than the fluid 4 accents (occasionally 3) of the Fr. poets. Spenser uses the length of the Eng. a. to good advantage in *The Faerie Queene:* the a. which concludes a Spenserian stanza (q.v.) contrasts with the 8-pentameter lines which precede it and enables the poet to achieve both emphasis and stanzaic continuity. Several Eng. works—Drayton's *Polyolbion,* Browning's *Fifine at the Fair,* Bridges' *Testament of Beauty*—are written entirely in alexandrines, but in general the Eng. a. has proved too unwieldy for continuous use in a long work.—H. P. Thieme, *The Technique of the Fr. A.* (1898); V. Horak, *Le vers a. en français* (1911); G. Lote, *L'alexandrin d'après la phonétique expérimentale* (3 v., 1911–12); A. Rochette, *L'alexandrin chez Victor Hugo* (1911); J. B. Ratermanis, "L'inversion et la structure de l'alexandrin," FS, 6 (1952); M. Burger, *Recherches sur la structure et l'origine des vers romans* (1957). F.J.W.; A.P.

ALLEGORY (Gr. *allos,* "other," and *agoreuein,* "to speak") is a term denoting a technique of literature which in turn gives rise to a method of criticism. As a technique of literature, a. is a technique of fiction-writing, for there must be some kind of narrative basis for allegory. We have a. when the events of a narrative obviously and continuously refer to another simultaneous structure of events or ideas, whether historical events, moral or philosophical ideas, or natural phenomena. The myth and the fable are forms closely related to, or frequently used for, a., and the works usually called allegories are genres of fiction: epic (Dante's *Divina Commedia*), romance (Spenser's *Faerie Queene*), prose fiction (Bunyan's *Pilgrim's Progress*) or drama (*Everyman*). It is continuity that distinguishes a. from ambiguity or simple allusion. Fiction-writing has two aspects: (1) a progression of incidents which are imitations of actions, and (2) elements of meaning or thought which represent a poetic use of ideas. Hence there are two main types of a.: historical or political a., referring to characters or events beyond those purportedly described in the fiction; and moral, philosophical, religious, or scientific allegories, referring to an additional set of ideas. If the allegorical reference is continuous throughout the narrative, the fiction "is" an a. If it is intermittent, if a. is picked up and dropped again at pleasure, as in many works of Ariosto, Goethe, Ibsen, and Hawthorne, we say only that the fiction shows allegorical tendencies. A. is thus not the name of a form or a genre, but of a structural principle in fiction.

A. may be simple or complex. In simple a. the fiction is wholly subordinate to the abstract "moral," hence it often impresses the literary critic as naive. An example is the fable, which is directed primarily at the set of ideas expressed in its moral. Simple historical allegories (simple at least as regards their literary structure) occur in some of the later prophecies of the Bible, such as the a. of the four kingdoms in Daniel. More complex historical and political allegories tend to develop a strongly ironic tone, resulting from the fact that the allegorist is pretending to talk about one series of incidents when he is actually talking about another. Hence there is a close connection between historical or political a. and satire, a connection marked in Spenser's *Mother*

Hubbard's Tale (Prosopopoeia), which uses a beast-fable to satirize a contemporary political situation; in Dryden's *Absalom and Achitophel,* which uses an Old Testament story for the same purpose; in Swift's *Tale of a Tub,* and elsewhere.

Moral allegories are apt to be deeply serious in tone. In these the fiction is supposed to provide entertainment and the a. instruction. The basic technique of moral a. is personification, where a character represents an abstract idea. The simpler the a., the more urgently the reader's attention is directed to the allegorical meaning. Hence simple or naive moral a. belongs primarily to educational literature: to the fables and moralities of the schoolroom, the parables and exempla of the pulpit, the murals and statuary which illustrate familiar ideas in official buildings. Often the allegorist is too interested in his additional meaning to care whether his fiction is consistent or not as a fiction. Bunyan, even Spenser, occasionally drop into naive a. In the First Book of *The Faerie Queene,* the Redcross Knight is being taught by Faith, Hope, and Charity, and Hope urges him to take hold of her anchor, the traditional emblem of hope. It is possible to think of Hope as a female teacher lugging this anchor into the lecture room to make her point—such emblems are still brought into classrooms—but it is simpler to think that the literal narrative is being naively distorted by the allegorical interest.

Allegorical interpretation, as a method of criticism, begins with the fact that a. is a structural element in narrative: it has to be there, and is not added by critical interpretation alone. In fact, all commentary, or the relating of the events of a narrative to conceptual terminology, is in one sense allegorical interpretation. To say that *Hamlet* is a tragedy of indecision is to start setting up beside *Hamlet* the kind of moral counterpart to its events that an a. has as a part of its structure. Whole libraries of criticism may be written on the fictions of *Hamlet* or *Macbeth,* bringing out aspects of their meaning that would not occur to other readers, and all such commentary might be said, by a ready extension of the term, to allegorize the plays. But this does not, as is sometimes said, turn the plays into allegories. A glance at *Hamlet* is enough to show that it is not structurally an a. to begin with. If it were, the range of commentary would be greatly limited, because the presence of a. prescribes the direction in which commentary must go. As *Hamlet* is not an a., it has an implicit relation only to other sets of events or ideas, and hence can carry an infinite amount of commentary. Strictly defined, allegorical interpretation is the specific form of commentary that deals with fictions which are structurally allegories. This leaves considerable latitude still, for there are many fictions, notably ancient myths, where the presence or absence of a. is disputable. In this situation the critic must content himself with offering his allegorical interpretation as one of many possible ones, or—the more traditional method—he may assume that the poet has, deliberately or unconsciously, concealed allegorical meanings in his fiction. The history of allegorical interpretation is essentially the history of typical forms of commentary applied to fictions where a. is present, or is assumed to be so.

Of these, one of the earliest and most important is the rationalization of myth, especially classical myth. The stories about the gods in Homer and Hesiod were felt by many early Gr. philosophers to be not serious enough for religon: as Plutarch urged much later, gods who behave foolishly are no gods. A system of interpreting the gods as personifications either of moral principles or of physical or natural forces grew up, known at first not as a. but as *hyponoia.* The practice is ridiculed by Plato in the *Republic* and elsewhere, but it increased with the rise of the more ethical and speculative cults, notably Stoicism. Judaism had similar difficulties, and the extensive commentaries of Philo on the Pentateuch are the most ambitious of the earliest Jewish efforts to demonstrate that philosophical and moral truths are concealed in the Old Testament stories.

With Christianity a special problem arose, that of typology, of which a. formed a part. To some extent the Old Testament had to be read allegorically by the Christian, according to the principle later enunciated by St. Augustine: "In the Old Testament the New Testament is concealed; in the New Testament the Old Testament is revealed." Certain Messianic passages in the Old Testament were held to refer specifically to Jesus; the Jewish law was abolished as a ceremony but fulfilled as a type of the spiritual life. St. Paul in Galatians, commenting on the story of Abraham, Sarah, and Hagar, explicitly says that the story is an a., though it later became more exact to say that such stories had or contained allegorical meanings. Hence a doctrine of multiple meanings in Scripture was elaborated which could be applied to religious literature as well. Dante has given us the best-known formulation of the medieval scheme in his Tenth Epistle, to Can Grande (also at the beginning of the second part of the *Convito*), partly in explanation of his own practice. We begin with the "literal" meaning, which simply tells us what happened; this narrative illustrates certain principles which we can see to be true (*quid credas,* as a popular tag had it), and this is the a. proper. At the same time the narrative illustrates the proper course of action (*quid agas*), this is its moral meaning, and is particularly the meaning aimed at in the *exemplum* or moral fable used in sermons and elsewhere, and which is also employed a good deal by Dante, especially in the *Purgatorio.* Finally there is its anagogic or universal meaning, its place within the total scheme of Christian economy, the Creation, Redemption and Judgment of the world. These last two meanings may also be called allegorical in an extended use of the term.

The allegorization of classical myth continued throughout the Middle Ages, though the emphasis shifted to L. literature, through the popularity of allegorical commentaries on Virgil and Ovid which remained in vogue for well over a millennium. The use of a. for educational purposes, largely popularized by Martianus Capella's *Marriage of Mercury and Philosophy* (early 5th c.), is still going strong in England in Stephen Hawes's *Passtyme of Pleasure* (ca. 1510). In secular literature, the most popular form of a. was the allegory of Courtly Love, which employed an elaborate system of parallels to religon, its God being Eros or Cupid, its Mother Venus, its great lovers saints and martyrs, and so on. A. also of course pervaded the plastic arts, and the emblem books which became popular in the 16th c. are an example of the literary absorption of pictorial iconology.

The orignal motivation for allegorical systems of commentary had been the defense of the sobriety and profundity of religious myths which appeared, on the face of it, to ascribe capriciousness or indecency to the gods. Hence attacks on Homeric theology by Plato, or on early Christianity by anti-Christian apologists, normally included a rejection, usually with some ridicule, of all such face-saving interpretations. With the rise both of Protestantism and of post-Tridentine Catholicism, the same problem entered literary criticism. Puritans attacked classical mythology as puerile fable, and scoffed at all efforts to allegorize it. In Elizabethan England Gosson's *School of Abuse* was one of the most articulate of such attacks, and was replied to by Sir Philip Sidney and by Thomas Lodge. Lodge concerned himself more particularly with the question of a.: "Why may not Juno resemble the air?" he protested; "must men write that you may know their meaning?" Tasso in Italy also defended his *Jerusalem Delivered* along allegorical lines. The conception of major poetry as concealing enormous reserves of knowledge through an allegorical technique was widely accepted in the Renaissance: the preface to Chapman's translation of Homer expresses it eloquently, and other men of letters discovered their own philosophical interests in classical mythology, as Francis Bacon did in his *Wisdom of the Ancients.*

Gradually the Aristotelian conception of poetry became the main basis for the defense as well as for much of the practice of imaginative literature In the *Poetics,* which influenced criticism increasingly from about 1540 on, poetry is conceived as an imitation of nature which expresses the general and the typical rather than the specific and particular, and which consequently is not to be judged by canons of truth or falsehood. This is obviously far more flexible a principle than the assumption of concealed allegorical meanings, and the latter interpretations fell out of favor. In the romantic period a renewed interest in myth, where the myth became subjective and psychological a part of the poet's own creative processes, developed a new conception of a., expressed in Goethe, Friederich Schlegel, and Coleridge (notably in the *Statesman's Manual*). In this conception a. is thought of as essentially the translating of a nonpoetic structure, usually of abstract ideas, into poetic imagery, and is thereby contrasted with symbolism, which is thought of as starting with the poetic image, and attaching concepts to it. This contrast then becomes the basis of a value-judgment, symbolism being good and a. bad. The distinction is uncritical, because it identifies all a. with naive a., but it became very popular, and helped to rationalize the growing prejudice against a. which still exists The good allegorists such as Dante and Spenser were explained away by other means: readers were taught to think of a. as tedious or pedantic, or were encouraged to read Spenser or Bunyan for the story and let the a. go. Such criticism reflects the romantic conception of a direct firsthand encounter with experience as the key to great literature in contrast to the secondhand approach to it through books. Nevertheless, the allegorical tradition survived fitfully. In criticism, it is found notably in Ruskin, whose *Queen of the Air,* a treatise on classical mythology, practically defines a myth as an allegorical story, and classifies the canonical allegories into the moral and the cosmological. In poetry, more or less straightforward a. is found in the second part of Goethe's *Faust*; in Shelley's *Prometheus Unbound*; in Keats's *Endymion*; in Ibsen's *Peer Gynt.*

The new romantic conception of symbolism is illustrated by such fictions as *Moby Dick, The Scarlet Letter, The Golden Bowl, To the Lighthouse,* and others, where there is a central symbol, usually named in the title, with a great variety of suggestive implications, but which lacks the continuity necessary for genuine a. Hawthorne is frequently allegorical in his technique—some of his stories, such as *The Bosom Serpent,* might almost be called naive allegories—but the 19th and 20th c. are notable for fictions which carry a great deal of conceptual weight, such as *War and Peace,* or are mythopoeic, such as *The Plumed Serpent,* and yet are not strictly allegorical. The use of an archetypal model for a fiction, as Joyce uses the Odyssey in *Ulysses* and Faulkner the Passion in *A Fable,* is closer to traditional allegorical techniques. Continuous a., as we have it in Anatole France's *Penguin Island,* usually favors the historical type, with its natural affinity for satire; but the popularity of Franz Kafka indicates that even serious moral a. still makes a powerful appeal.

Since 1900 two new forms of allegorical interpretation have crowded out nearly all the older ones. Dreams have been from ancient times recognized as close to a., but it was only after the appearance of Freud's *Interpretation of Dreams* that there developed in criticism a technique of reading works of literature as psychological allegories, revealing the latent sexual drives and conflicts either of their authors or of their readers. There is now an extensive bibliography of such allegorical criticism in literature, most of it either Freudian or Jungian in reference. About the same time Frazer's *Golden Bough* began a school of criticism which approaches literature much as Christian typology related the New Testament to the Old. Works of literature, especially of ancient literature, are regarded as myths which contain and at the same time reveal the significance of earlier rituals and ceremonics. This form of allegorical interpretation, like the other, assumes the unconscious rather than the deliberate concealment of the allegorical allusion.

There is no comprehensive work on the subject: an immense amount of scholarly research has been done on classical and medieval a., much of it in areas remote from literature; critical treatments of modern literature usually deal with mythopoeia rather than a. The following studies are helpful: Lewis; R. P. Hinks, *Myth and A. in Ancient Art* (1939); J. Seznec, *The Survival of the Pagan Gods,* tr. B. Sessions (1953); E. D. Leyburn, *Satiric A.: Mirror of Man* (1956); H. Berger, Jr., *The Allegorical Temper* (1957); E. Honig, *Dark Conceit: the Making of A.* (1959); M. P. Parker, *The A. of the Faerie Queene* (1960); A. C. Hamilton, *The Structure of A. in "The Faerie Queene"* (1951); P. E. McLane, *Spenser's Shepheardes Calender: a Study in Elizabethan A.* (1961); A. Fletcher, *A.: the Theory of a Symbolic Mode* (1964). N.F.R.

ALLITERATION. Any repetition of the same sound(s) or syllable in two or more words of a line (or line group), which produces a noticeable artistic effect (see also SOUND IN POETRY). A. may occur involuntarily or by choice. It can produce emphasis and euphony (or cacophony!) comparable to the striking effects of end rhyme. The most common type of a. is that of initial sounds (hence the term "initial rhyme" or "head rhyme"), especially of consonants or consonant groups; a. of initial vowels is less frequent since they do not have the same acoustic impact as consonants. In Germanic alliterative meter (q.v.) or "Stabreim" any vowel can alliterate with any other, probably because the preceding glottal stop constitutes the repetition. A. may, however, include with notable effect the repetition of consonants, vowels, or consonant-vowel combinations in medial or even final position ("That b*ra*ve vib*ra*tion . . . ,"—Robert Herrick). This applies especially in languages which, like Fr., lack stress accent ("J'ai cou*r*u les deux me*r*s que sépa*r*e Co*r*inthe"—Racine). On the other hand, in languages with stress accent, a. is not confined to stressed syllables, but may extend to the unstressed (called "submerged" or "thesis" a., e.g.: "Suppos'd as *for*feit to a con*fin*'d doom"—Shakespeare). Different alliterating sounds can be interwoven to produce intricate patterns extending through the whole or sections of a poem. A. on the one sound or sound combination may be followed by, alternate with or include another alliterative sequence (*parallel* or *crossed* a.)

Other varieties of a.: the grammatical figure or *polytopon,* Fr. *l'annomination* (diverse forms of the same syllable in successive words not necessarily etymologically related: "vi vitam"—Ennius); *homoeoteleuton* (identity of word endings: "au travers . . . divers"—Mallarmé; really a form of identical rhyme), *suspended* a. (reversal of the alliterating consonant and the succeeding vowel: "Herds of fallow *dee*r were *fee*ding"—Longfellow. All these varieties are combinations of a. with assonance (q.v.). So-called eye a. consists in identical spelling only: "Have wrought and worshipped" (Swinburne) or "Careless of censure" (Pope). It is doubtful whether such false a. is ever consciously intended by a poet.

In all literatures where a. is practiced, it is subject to changing literary fashions and tastes, but, generally speaking, it is more prominent in the poetry of languages with stress accent (especially where the accent regularly falls on the first syllable, as in Finnish, Esthonian, and Czech) and in verse which is meant to be spoken rather than sung or chanted. Thus in the medieval Germanic idioms (ON, Old High German, Old Saxon, OE, ME), in Finnish (*kalevala* epic), and in early (7th-c.) Ir., a. served as the chief structural principle and was governed by rigid rules [see ALLITERATIVE METER], whereas in languages with tone systems or quantitative structures it is either completely absent (as in Chinese poetry, which is based on syllable count and tone patterns), or used rarely and only for very special emphasis (as in Sanskrit, e.g., Kalidasa, *Kumarasambhava* 1.18, and in Japanese where an 8th-c. tanka and a 17th-c. kyoka furnish notable but rare examples). In the modern Germanic languages, even after its substitution by end rhyme as a structural principle, a. is still more prevalent than in the chiefly syllable-counting Romance tongues.

Ancient Gr. poetry, based on a quantitative metric, uses a. rarely and only for special onomatopoetic effects. In Roman poetry a. is found throughout, beginning with the Saturnian *carmina* (Latin possesses stress accent, and the quantitative metric was taken over from the Greeks). The Romans used the Gr. term *paromoeon,* while *alliteratio* does not occur until the end of the 15th c. Ennius made ample use of the device and went to absurd extremes. While Cicero disdained it, Lucretius delighted in a. Among the "new" poets, Catullus had a marked preference for alliterative ornament in some parts of his work and practiced abstinence in others. Virgil employed a. with great subtlety as a conveyor of emotions. In late Imperial times and through the Middle Ages a. became a cherished mannerism.

All the troubadour poets of Old Prov. practiced a. (*replicatio*), aiming with great skill at achieving parallelisms between sound and meaning. They favored a. especially at the beginning and at the end of a poem. In the modern Romance literatures It. poets use a sparingly, the Sp. more frequently, though with discretion (a manneristic flowering occurred in the 16th and 17th c.). The Fr. used a. very sparingly until the romanticists, symbolists, and moderns sought to endow the Fr. poetic medium with a new musicality. In Baudelaire's *Fleurs du mal* the use of a. often coincides with the division of an alexandrine into anapaests. Mallarmé and Valéry achieve highly sophisticated alliterative effects.

Ir. (Gaelic) is among the most richly alliterative poetic media of world literature Through the centuries, Ir. verse has preserved an unbroken tradition of decorative a. even though its metric has long since been based on rhyme and syllable count, whereas Welsh poetry uses, even today, the complex, versatile "cynghanedd" (q.v.), an ancient artistic device, involving a. and having a metric function.

In Eng. versification, likewise a. continued as an ornamental device after its eclipse as a structural principle. In the 16th c., under the influence of rhetoric, which encouraged "the figure of like letter" (also called "parimion" or "letter-tagging"), some poets used it to excess. Shakespeare burlesques alliterative practices in *L*ove's *L*abour's *L*ost, but where he chooses, he can use it with superb mastery (e.g. Sonnets 18, 29, 30, 128) During the 17th and 18th c., a. lost its importance somewhat. While it was used as an occasional ornament by some poets, such as Dryden, Richard Crashaw, Oliver Goldsmith, it was largely avoided by others, such as Milton. Pope could skillfully avoid the device through long sections of a poem and then suddenly use it with great effect, as at the end of the *Essay on Criticism*. With the romantic poets a new vogue set in. Effects were achieved which aimed to enhance the musicality of the language rather than to produce rhetorical emphasis. The Victorians, Pre-Raphaelites, and moderns continued the practice with further refinement and subtlety. Swinburne parodied his own alliterative abundance in *Nephilidia*. Gerard Manley Hopkins' use of a. (see CYNGHANEDD) is the most willfully original and strikingly bold (see, for example, *The Wreck of the Deutschland*).

The development of a. in Am. poetry runs parallel with the British vogue. Walt Whitman uses it amply, Melville frequently and effectively. T. S. Eliot tends to use repetition of identical words and whole phrases rather than a. proper. Carl Sandburg, Marianne Moore, H. D. like a.; W. H. Auden's *Voices in the Desert* in *The Flight into Egypt* imitates alliterative verse. Wallace Stevens, schooled by the musicality of the Fr. symbolists, does not depend on a. for his sound harmonies, but he can use it most effectively.

In modern German, aside from the sporadic and ineffectual attempts at resuscitating medieval "Stabreim" (W. Jordan, R. Wagner) a. is common as an occasional ornament. In Goethe it is less numerous than in Schiller and the romantic poets, but he uses it frequently enough to permit the conclusion that he did so deliberately, especially to express high emotional tension (e.g., in *Marienbader Elegie*). After the influence of Baudelaire and the symbolists had quickened the renewal of German poetry, a. became a far more consciously used, almost indispensable, euphonic device ("Hiersein ist herrlich"—Rilke; "Ich bin freund und führer dir und ferge"—Stefan George).

R. L. Taylor, *A. in Italian* (1900); K. Florenz, *Gesch. der japanischen Lit.* (2d ed, 1909); Schipper; M. Scholz, "Die A. in der altprovenzalischen Lyrik," ZRP, 37 (1913) and 38 (1914); A. Heusler, "Stabreim," *Reallexikon*, ed. J. Hoops, iv (1919); E. Sikes, *Roman Poetry* (1923); E. Rickert, *New Methods for the Study of Lit.* (1927); H. Schneider, "Stabreimvers, *Sachuörterbuch der Deutschkunde*, II (1930); E. Wölfflin, "Zur A.," *Ausgewählte Schriften* (1933); M. Grammont, *Le Vers français* (4th ed., 1937), R. E. Deutsch, *The Patterns of Sound in Lucretius* (1939); M. Dillon, *Early Ir. Lit.* (1943); U. K. Goldsmith, "Words out of a Hat? A. and Assonance in Shakespeare's Sonnets," JEGP, 49 (1950); N. I. Herescu, *La Poésie latine: étude des structures phoniques* (1960); W. Kayser, *Gesch. des deutschen Verses* (1960).

U.K.G.

ALLITERATIVE METER. A prominent feature of Old Germanic prosody (q.v.) is initial rhyme, used not for mere ornamentation but structurally, to link and emphasize important words within prescribed metrical units. The beginnings of the alliterative tradition are unknown, though one may guess that alliteration was partly a mnemonic aid to primitive oral recitation. Whatever its origins in Germanic antiquity, alliteration is part of a complex prosodic system, and indeed of the fabric of the Germanic languages themselves. The fondness for alliterative formulas is still noticeable in a language like Eng., which uses them easily and habitually in and out of poetry: "might and main," "time and tide," "to have and to hold."

The a. m. of the oldest poetry of Germany, Scandinavia, and England is superimposed upon the speech rhythms of these languages, with their constituent long and short syllabic quantities, in such a way as to increase the rhythmic emphasis of regular numbers of syllables in a given unit of verse, leaving different numbers of subordinatively stressed and unstressed syllables around them. The following lines from the Old Saxon *Heliand* (2242–2247), despite their varying syllabic totals, are metrically identical in that each typographical line (the arrangement of which on the page is a modern editorial convention) contains 4 heavily stressed syllables and several more lightly stressed or unstressed syllables in different patterns. Marks of vowel quantity are omitted from this and subsequent examples, and no attempt is made to indicate secondary accents

Thuo bigan thes wédares cráft,
úst úp stigan, úthiun wáhsan;
súang gisúerc an gimang; thie séu warð an hrúoru,
wan wínd endi wáter; wéros sórogodun,
thiu méri warð so múodag, ni wanda thero mánno nigén
léngron líbes.

Then the power of the storm, the tempest, became greater; waves grew larger; darkness fell; the sea was stirred up; wind and water contended; the sea raged so that men despaired, nor did one of them expect to live longer.

The long line, it should be noted, is divided into 2 metrically independent verses by a pause, and the verse pairs are linked by the alliteration of 1 or 2 stressed syllables in the first verse with the first stressed syllable of the second verse. Different types of verses will be formed from five possible arrangements of long and short, stressed and unstressed syllables, according to a complex system conventionally described by Eduard Sievers (see bibliog. below). As for the alliteration itself, each consonantal sound rhymes (usually) only with another occurrence of the same sound, but any vowel or diphthong may rhyme either with itself or with another vowel or diphthong.

The basic structure of this meter, it must be emphasized, is not stanzaic or even linear: each of the verses in a verse pair is a metrical unit; a sentence may begin or end in the middle of a line, and the verses may be strung together in long verse paragraphs which bring out a characteristic parallelism of thought and diction, like the sequence which concludes the OE *Battle of Brunanburh:*

Ne wearð wǽl máre
on ðys íglánde ǽfre gýta
fólces gefýlled befóran ðýssum
swéordes écgum ðæs ðe us sécgað béc,
éalde úðwitan, siþþan éastan híder
Éngle and Séaxe úpp becómon
ofer bráde brímu, Brýtene sóhton,
wlánce wígsmiðas Wéalas ofercómon,
éorlas árhwate éard begéaton.

Never yet in this island was a greater slaughter of an army by the sword's edge, as books tell us, ancient scholars, since the Angles and Saxons came hither from the east over the broad waters, sought out Britain, proud fighters defeated the Welsh, warriors keen for glory won a homeland.

Alliteration, then, is a device which associates phrases or individual verses within the verse pairs, but the series of lines which constitutes the poem may be loosely or compactly joined, depending on the syntax and style of the whole work.

In England the comparatively severe, remarkably regular alliterative poetry of the OE period gave way to a less systematic ME verse which tolerated much more freedom in the alliteration itself, and in the treatment of stressed and unstressed syllables: compare the resemblances to and the departures from the OE norm in the 14th-c. *Piers Plowman:*

I seigh a tóure on a tóft tríelich ymáked,
A dépe dále binéthe, a dóngeon there-ínne
With dépe dýches and dérke and drédful of síght.
A fáire félde fúl of fólke fónde I there bytwéne,
Of álle máner of mén, the méne and the ríche,
Wórchyng and wándryng as the wórlde ásketh.

I saw a tower on a raised place, excellently built, a deep valley beneath, a dungeon therein with deep dark ditches, dreadful to look upon. In between I discovered a beautiful plain full of people of all kinds, the common and the rich, working and wandering as the world requires.

Sometimes, as in the 14th-c. *Pearl* or *Sir Gawain and the Green Knight,* intricate patterns of rhyme and elaborate stanzaic forms are combined with a freely treated alliterative line. But with the end of the Middle Ages and the assimilation of Fr. and classical syllabic meters into Eng. poetry, the systematic a. m. disappeared for centuries, and only in modern times have Eng. and Am. poets returned to it as a potentially fresh and vital form. It is a hard meter to use well, or even to use at all, if its rhythmic characteristics are more or less faithfully observed; and the retention or rediscovery of its primitive quantitative rules is more difficult still, but not impossible, as shown by C. S. Lewis in the study mentioned below. Poems by Ezra Pound (*The Seafarer*), C. Day Lewis (*As One Who Wanders into Old Workings*), and Richard Eberhart (*Brotherhood of Men*) could be cited as notable experiments in a contemporary alliterative revival. W. H. Auden's *The Age of Anxiety* (1947) is a major work in which many varieties of the Old Germanic a. m. are displayed with great skill. On the Ir. a. m. see below.

E. Sievers, *Altgermanische Metrik* (1893); Saintsbury, *Prosody,* I; J. P. Oakden and E. R. Innes, *Alliterative Poetry in ME: A Survey of the Traditions* (1935); C. S. Lewis, "The A. M.," in *Rehabilitations* (1939); G. Murphy, *Early Ir. Metrics* (1961); A. J. Bliss, *An Introd. to OE Metre* (1962); M. Borroff, *Sir Gawain and the Green Knight* (1962). J.B.B.

ALLUSION. Tacit reference to another literary work, to another art, to history, to contemporary figures, or the like. A. may be used merely to display knowledge, as in many Alexandrian and medieval poems; to appeal to a reader or audience sharing some experience or knowledge with the writer; or to enrich a literary work by merging the echoed material with the new poetic context. A. differs from mere source-borrowing, because it requires the reader's familiarity with the original for full understanding and appreciation; and from mere reference, because it is tacit and fused with the context in which it appears.

The technique of a. assumes: (1) an established literary tradition as a source of value; (2) an audience sharing the tradition with the poet; (3) an echo of sufficiently familiar yet distinctive and meaningful elements; and (4) a fusion of the echo with elements in the new context. It has analogues in biblical and religious writings, the novel, and elsewhere, and usually requires a close poet-audience relationship, a social emphasis in literature, a community of knowledge, and a prizing of literary tradition.

TYPES. *Topical a.*, normally reference to recent events, is common up to the romantic movement, less frequent thereafter except in humorous poetry or ephemeral *vers de société*. *Personal a.*, reference to facts concerning the poet himself, must be to facts widely known, easily grasped, or made familiar, and varies from Shakespeare and Donne's plays on their own names, to Virgil's lamenting his misfortunes in the *Eclogues,* to Dante's account of his love for an idealized Beatrice; but it should be distinguished from the romantic use of personal experience for subject matter, e.g. Coleridge's discussion of his failing poetic powers in *Dejection: An Ode*. *Metaphorical a.* is more complex in function and richer in interest and meaning. Found chiefly in periods setting value on tradition (e.g., Augustan Rome, China from early times, 11–14th-c., Japan, 17–18th– and 20-c. Europe), this technique uses the echoed element as a vehicle for the poetic tenor that it acquires in the new context (e.g., Dryden's allusion to *Aeneid* 5 and 6 in his poem to Oldham expresses through metaphor the relation between himself and Oldham and also between Roman and Eng. cultural values). Frequent in the older Chinese and Japanese poetry, such a. can also be found in Goethe (to religious services in *Faust*), in Foscolo (to Homer in *Dei sepolcri*), in Baudelaire (to the *Aeneid* in *Le Cygne*), and broadcast in the major works of Eliot and Pound. *Imitative a.* is either specific (Dr. Johnson to Juvenal, *Satire* 3, in *London*), generic (Dryden to epic in *Absalom and Achitophel*), parodic (Philips to Milton in *The Splendid Shilling*) or, commonly, synthetic (Pope's *Rape of the Lock*—at once specific to Milton and others, generic to epic, and parodic). *Structural a.* gives form to a new work by suggesting the structure of an older work; in this it resembles imitative a., but it is identifiably different when the a. is to other genres or arts (e.g., the *Odyssey* is alluded to structurally by Joyce's *Ulysses,* and music is alluded to by Eliot in *Four Quartets*). And in spite of Lessing's strictures, many poets from the 17th c. to the present have alluded structurally to nontemporal graphic and plastic arts (e.g., Auden to Breughel's *Icarus* in his poem *Musée des Beaux Arts*).

No comprehensive study of a. exists, but the following touch upon representative aspects of the subjects. H. J. Rose, *The Eclogues of Virgil* (1942); H. F. Brooks, "The 'Imitation' in English poetry . . . Before the Age of Pope," RES 25 (1949); M. Mack, " 'Wit and Poetry and Pope': Some Observations on His Imagery," *Pope and His Contemporaries* (1949); J. R. Hightower, *Topics in Chinese Lit.* (1950); S. P. Bovie, "Classical Allusions," CW, 52 (1958); R. A. Brower, *Alexander Pope: The Poetry of A.* (1959); R. H. Brower and E. Miner, *Japanese Court Poetry* (1961). E.M.

AMPHIBRACH (Gr. "short at both ends"). A classical metrical foot consisting of a long syllable preceded and followed by a short one:

⏑–⏑; *hăbērĕ*

Rarely used in classical poetry either as an independent unit or in a continuous series. In Eng.

× / ×

×/× : arrangement

the amphibrachic cadence is common in stress-groups.—Koster. P.S.C.

AMPHIMACER. See CRETIC.

ANACREONTIC. Named after Anacreon of Teos (6th c. B.C.), the regular Anacreontic (⏑⏑–⏑–⏑––) was the alteration of the lesser Ionic (q.v.) dimeter (⏑⏑––/⏑⏑––) by anaclasis, whereby the final long syllable of the first foot was interchanged with the first short of the second. That the A. was an Ionic measure is supported by such passages as Euripides, *Cyclops* 495–502; 503–510; 511–518, where a sequence of Anacreontics is varied by lesser Ionics. Another view is that the A. was originally an iambic dimeter catalectic with the initial foot an anapaest (Sappho, fr. 102 Lobel and Page, combines pure iambic dimeters catalectic with Anacreontics), and iambic dimeters were indeed employed by both Anacreon and the authors of the later *Anacreontea* (composed in imitation of Anacreon between 200 B.C. and 500 A.D.). Whatever their origin, Anacreontics were used in L. apparently by Laevius (1st c. B.C.) and by Seneca, Petronius, Claudian, Martianus Capella, and Boethius. Hadrian's famous reply to Florus,

ĕgŏ nōlŏ Flōrŭs ēssĕ̄,

is a notable and particularly good example of the meter, which can be paralleled in Longfellow's *Hiawatha,* e.g., "For a while to muse and ponder/ On a half-effaced inscription."—Kolár; Dale; Koster; Crusius. R.J.C.

The *Anacreontea* or *Anacreontics* comprise about 60 short lyrical poems on wine, love and song—graceful and charming but rather shallow pieces. Edited for the first time by Stephanus (Henri Estienne) in 1554, they had a considerable influence on Renaissance and later European poets, e.g., in 16th-c. France, on Ronsard and Rémy Belleau and, in 16th-, 18th-, and 19th-c. Italy, on Tasso, Parini, Monti, Foscolo, and Leopardi who translated and imitated many of these poems. Anacreontic imitation was even more in vogue in 18th-c. Germany among the so-called *Anakreontiker* (Gleim, Uz, Götz, and their forerunner Hagedorn). In England, Abraham Cowley seems to have first used the term in his *Anacreontiques* (1656), but the probably best known verse translation is *Odes of Anacreon* (1800) by the Ir. poet Thomas Moore, dubbed by Byron "Anacreon Moore."—Schmid and Stählin, I.; E. Merker, "Anakreontik," *Reallexikon,* 2d ed., I.

P.S.C.

ANACRUSIS (Gr. "the striking up of a tune"). One or more initial syllables which are not part of a regular metrical scheme. This term, for which the adjective "procephalous" would be a more descriptive and better attested alternative, was adopted by Bentley in principle and Hermann in fact, as well as by their successors in the 19th c. through analogy with modern music, i.e., when a note or notes occur before the first actual bar of the melody. Classical scholars have largely abandoned the view that a. could be assumed to alter rising (e.g., iambic) to falling (e.g., trochaic) rhythms, or vice versa. For an example in Gr. poetry see LOGAOEDIC. An example in modern stress verse occurs in Blake's *The Tyger:*

> When the stars threw down their spears
> *And* watered heaven with their tears

where classical metricians would not now normally regard the first syllable of the second line as justifying a return to the falling rhythm of the first.—Dale; N. A. Bonavia-Hunt, *Horace the Minstrel* (1954). For a. in OE verse see J. C. Pope, *The Rhythm of Beowulf* (1942).

R.J.G.

ANALOGUE, ANALOGY. See IMAGERY; SYMBOL.

ANAPAEST, anapest (Gr. "beaten back," i.e., either a "reversed" dactyl or a verse begun with a "beat" of the foot). A metrical unit, in quantitative verse, of 2 short syllables followed by 1 long one:

> ⏑⏑–; *dĕĭtās*

Originally a warlike march rhythm, it was widely used, in combinations and pure, in Gr. melic and dramatic verse, particularly by comic choruses:

> *ēx hōu gĕ chŏrōisĭn ĕphēstēkēn trўgĭkōīs hŏ*
> *dĭdāskălŏs hēmōn*

(Aristophanes, *Acharnians* 628; anapaestic tetrameter catalectic, i.e., 7 1/2 anapaests, with normal substitution of spondee for a. in the first foot.) It was adopted by the Romans primarily in drama (Plautus, Seneca). The term has been adopted into Eng. for the accentual foot of 2 unstressed syllables followed by 1 stressed one:

> × × /; interrupt

Used mainly in popular verse until the beginning of the 18th c., it was subsequently employed for serious poetry by Cowper, Scott, Byron, Browning, Morris, and especially Swinburne, who used it in lines of every possible length. While the a. is characteristically the foot of hurried motion and excitement:

> The Assyrian came down like a wolf on the fold
> (Byron, *The Destruction of Sennacherib*)

it can also be slow-moving and effective in conveying mourning or sadness, as, for instance, in Matthew Arnold's *Rugby Chapel.* Pure anapaests are comparatively rare in Eng. and tend to jig unless carefully varied with other feet.—A. Raabe, *De metrorum anapaesticorum apud poetas Graecos usu* . . . (1912); J. W. White, *The Verse of Gr. Comedy* (1912); Baum; Hamer; Crusius.

D.S.P.

ANGLO-SAXON PROSODY. See OLD GERMANIC PROSODY.

ANTHOLOGY. Etymologically a "bouquet"; from Gr. *anthos* (flower) and *legein* (to gather, pick up); originally a collection of poetic epigrams, generally composed in elegiac distichs and referent to specific poets or subjects. Compilations were made as early as the 4th c. B.C. About 90 B.C. Meleager of Gadara collected a *Garland* of short epigrams in various meters, but chiefly elegiac, and on various subjects; some fifty poets from Archilochus (7th c. B.C) to himself were represented. About A.D 40 Philippus of Thessalonica collected a *Garland* of exclusively elegiac epigrams by poets since Meleager. Approximately a century later Straton of Sardis put together some hundred epigrams on a single subject, homosexual love. About A.D 570 the Byzantine anthologist Agathias collected a *Circle* of epigrams in various meters; he included selections, arranged by subject, from both *Garlands* as well as a large selection of contemporary epigrams.

Constantinus Cephalas, a Byzantine Greek who lived during the reign of Constantine VII (912–59), compiled an a. in which he combined and rearranged the collections of Meleager, Philippus, Straton and Agathias. In all, it included 15 divisions: Christian epigrams, descriptions of statuary, temple inscriptions, prefaces (by Meleager, Philippus, and Agathias), erotic poems, dedicatory poems, epitaphs (including Simonides' famous lines on the Spartan dead at Thermopylae), epigrams by St. Gregory of Nazianzus, epideictic epigrams, moral epigrams, social and satirical epigrams, Straton's collection, epigrams in special meters, riddles, and miscellaneous epigrams. The A., or Gr. A., as it is called, was edited, revised, and expurgated in 1301 by the monk Maximus Planudes, His edition was the only available Gr. a. until 1606, when the great Fr. scholar Claude Saumaise (Salmasius) discovered a single manuscript of Cephalas in the Elector Palatine's library at Heidelberg; hereafter it came to be known as the *Palatine A.*; it supplanted the *Planudean A.* but retained a Planudean appendix as a 16th division. The first edition of the *Palatine A.* was published in 13 vols. (1794–1814) by Friedrich Jacobs.

The influence of the *Gr. A.* in the modern world dates from Janus Lascaris' Florentine edition of Planudes in 1494. Translations of the epigrams into L. and later into the vernacular languages multiplied consistently until about 1800, when the enthusiasm for the unpointed Gr. epigram was succeeded by that for the pointed epigram as perfected by the Latin Martial (1st c. A.D). Renewed interest in the *Gr. A.* is apparent today in current translations, e.g., Kenneth Rexroth's, of selections from it. Other anthologies include the 5th c. Stobaeus' Gr. *Eclogae (Selections)* and *Anthologion,* the *Anthologia Latina* (ed. Riese, Bücheler and Lommatzsch, 1894–1926, including otherwise uncollected L. verse and a 6th-c. compilation which contained the *Pervigilium Veneris*), medieval *florilegia,* the *Carmina Cantabrigiensia* (11th c.) and *Carmina Burana* (13th c.), and Erasmus' *Adagia* early 16th c.).

The earliest anthologies in Eng. include: *Tottel's Miscellany* (orig., *Songes and Sonettes, written by the ryght honorable Lorde Henry Haward late Earle of Surrey, and other,* 1557); Clement Robinson's *Very Pleasaunt Sonettes and Storyes in Myter* (1566; surviving *only as A Handefull of Pleasant Delites,* 1584); *The Paradyse of Daynty Devises* (1576); *A Gorgious Gallery of Gallant Inventions* (1578); *The Phoenix Nest* (1593); *Englands Helicon* (1600, 1614); *Davison's Poetical Rapsody* (1602).

Other significant European anthologies are: Jan Gruter's *Delitiae* (It., Fr., Belgian, and German poems in Latin; 1608–1614); J. W. Zinc gref's *Anhang unterschiedlicher aussgesuchter Gedichten* (1624); Thomas Percy's *Reliques of Ancient Eng. Poetry* (1765; an a. of early ballads which proved to be considerably influential); Oliver Goldsmith's *The Beauties of Eng. Poetry* (1767); Thomas Campbell's *Specimens of the British Poets* (1891); Palgrave's *Golden Treasury of Eng. Songs and Lyrics* (1861; *the* a. of lyric poetry in Victorian England); *Le Parnasse contemporain* (1866, 1871–76); Sir Arthur Quiller-Couch's *Oxford Book of Eng. Verse* (1900, 1939).

The popularity of anthologies in the 20th c. is so great as to preclude even a representative listing of titles in Eng. Mention should be made, however, of *The New Poetry* (1917) by Harriet Monroe and Alice C. Henderson because of its influence on modern poets, and of such anthologists as Robert Bridges, Louis Untermeyer, Conrad Aiken, Oscar Williams, Selden Rodman, James Reeves, William Cole, and of the collaborators Cleanth Brooks and Robert Penn Warren, whose *Understanding Poetry* (1938, 1950, 1960) is a pedagogical a.

F. Lachère, *Bibliographie des receuils collectifs de poésies publiés de 1597 à 1700* (1901); A. Wifstrand, *Studien zur griechischen Anthologie* (1926); J. Hutton, *The Gr. A. in Italy to the Year 1800* (1935) and *The Gr. A. in France and in the Writers of the Netherlands to the Year 1800* (1946); A.S.F. Gow, *The Gr. A.: Sources and Ascriptions* (1958).

L.U.; R.A.S.

ANTIMETABOLE. See CHIASMUS.

ANTISTROPHE (Gr. "counterturning"). Originally in Gr. choral dance and poetry the second of a pair of movements or "stanzas" in an ode. It corresponds exactly in meter to the preceding strophe. In rhetoric the term means the repetition of words in reversed order, e.g., "The master of the servant and the servant of the master." It also describes the repetition of a word or phrase at the end of successive clauses. See STROPHE; EPODE.

R.A.H.

ANTITHESIS, *antitheton* (Gr. "opposition"; L. *contentio*). A contrasting of ideas made sharp by the use of words of opposite or conspicuously different meaning in contiguous clauses or phrases, a form of expression recommended as satisfying by Aristotle "because contraries are easily understood and even more so when placed side by side, and also because a. resembles a syllogism, for it is by putting opposing conclusions side by side that you refute one of them" (*Rhetoric* 3.9.8), Some later authorities likewise stress the clarity and force that an a. may impart to any idea (e.g., the anonymous *Rhetorica ad Herennium,* 1st c. B.C, 4.15.21; Johannes Susenbrotus, 1541, on *contentio,* ed. of 1621, p. 63); but the *Rhetorica ad Herennium* sees in it also a means of embellishing a discourse, and this is the idea mainly emphasized by the moderns (e.g. Henry Peacham, "it graceth and bewtifieth the Oration," *The Garden of Eloquence,* 1593, p. 161; John Smith calls it "a Rhetoricall Exornation," *The Mysterie of Rhetorique Unvailed,* 1657, pp. 172–73).

The a. that draws a broad, simple contrast of idea is the pattern of many a verse in the biblical

Rook of Proverbs, e.g., "It is better to dwell in the wilderness, than with a contentious and angry woman" (21.19; Smith quotes a number of examples, p. 175), and such antitheses are fairly frequent in Anglo-Saxon poetry, often pivoting on the adversative "nālaes," e.g., "Waraþ hine wraeclāst, nālaes wunden gold" (His lot is the path of exile, by no means twisted gold—*The Wanderer,* 32).

A. was cultivated more or less by the classical poets, and while these poets sometimes contrive a strict balance of form or a complex opposition of idea, e.g., "Non fumum ex fulgore, sed ex fumo dare lucem / Cogitat" (He aims to fetch not smoke from a flash, but light from smoke, Horace, *Ars Poetica* 142–43), this kind of ingenuity is still more characteristic of the Eng. and Fr. poets of the Age of Reason, e.g., "Je veux et ne veux pas, je m'emporte et je n'ose" (I would and would not, I am on fire yet dare not—Pierre Corneille, *Cinna,* 1640, 1.2.122); "Thus wicked but in will, of means bereft, / He left not faction, but of that was left" (Dryden, *Absalom and Achitophel,* 1681, ll. 567–68); "It is the slaver kills, and not the bite" (Pope, *Epistle to Dr. Arbuthnot,* 1735, l. 106). The convenience of the closed couplet, which had early emerged as the preferred verse form of the Restoration and Queen Anne poets, for balanced expressions probably goes some way toward explaining why these poets were minded to exploit a. as they did, sometimes to the point where it amounts to a major element of their style. They found it, in any case, an ideal resource for the display of their satirical wit.

The antitheses quoted above are among the many forms of expression that exhibit two or more "figures of speech," and may be labeled with one term or another according to the particular feature to be distinguished. Thus the second line of the quotation from Dryden exhibits *chiasmus* (q.v.), *epanalepsis,* and *isocolon* (equality of length in the cola of a period).

In contemporary writing the use of a. is chiefly in humorous verse.—P. Beyer, "Antithese," *Reallexikon,* 1; Sister Miriam Joseph, *Shakespeare and the Arts of Language* (1947); Lausberg. S.F.F.; H.B.

APHAERESIS. See METRICAL TREATMENT OF SYLLABLES.

APOCOPE. See METRICAL TREATMENT OF SYLLABLES.

APOSTROPHE (Gr. "to turn away"). A figure of speech which consists in addressing a dead or absent person, an animal, a thing, or an abstract quality or idea as if it were alive, present, and capable of understanding, e.g., "Quid non mortalia pectora cogis, / auri sacra fames!" (Virgil, *Aeneid* 3.56); "Ahi, serva Italia, di dolore ostello" (Dante, *Purgatorio* 6.76); "O judgment! thou art fled to brutish beasts" (Shakespeare, *Julius Caesar* 3.2.10); "Milton! thou should'st be living at this hour" (Wordsworth, *London,* 1802); "Ring out, wild bells" (Tennyson, *In Memoriam* 106). The term originally referred to any abrupt "turning away" from the normal audience to address a different or more specific audience, whether present (e.g., one person out of the assemblage) or absent. In narrative verse the poet "turns away" from the generality of listeners or readers to address a specific reader, a character in the narrative, or some other person, thing, or idea. The use of a. gives life and immediacy to language, but is also subject to abuse and open to parody. L.P.

ARCHETYPE. Generally speaking, an a. is an original pattern from which copies are made or an idea of a class of things representing the most essentially characteristic elements shared by the members of that class. It is, in other words, a highly abstract category almost completely removed from the accidental varieties of elements contained in any particular species belonging to it. Thus, for example, the "Platonic" idea of a table would comprise a flat horizontal surface propped by vertical supports, and this is the a. of all tables everywhere when considered apart from their peculiar differences of size, height, material, shape, finish, and so on.

So, in poetry, an a. may be any idea, character, action, object, institution, event, or setting containing essential characteristics which are primitive, general, and universal rather than sophisticated, unique, and particular. This generality and universality may refer merely to similarities among various literary or subliterary works, as when scholars discover variants or analogues in time and place of certain types of legends and folk tales, or it may refer more broadly to similarities found outside of literary works, as when critics seek comparisons to things found in a poem among myths, dreams, and rituals. In the case of *Hamlet,* for example, one could either construct an a. of the revenge play on the basis of similarities found between Shakespeare's play and other revenge plays, or fashion an a. of the Oedipal situation on the basis of the similarities found between Shakespeare's play, myths, legends, folk tales, and anthropological and psychological literature. The former method tends to be more direct, as when one studies a series of hero stories and tabulates the characteristics which they share in common, while the latter method tends to be more tenuous, as when one tries to construct hypotheses to interpret the meaning of such recurrences in terms of the racial unconscious, the ritual origins of poetry, the diffusions of culture, or whatever. Needless to say, these methods may overlap.

Either way, when one speaks of archetypes in poetry one usually refers to basic, general, or universal patterns (cf. IMAGERY) of one sort or another: birth, coming of age, love, guilt, redemption, and death are archetypal subjects; the conflict between reason and imagination, free will and destiny, appearance and reality, the individual and society, and so on, are archetypal themes; the tension between parents and children, the rivalry among brothers, the problems of incestuous desire, the search for the father, the ambivalence of the male-female relationship, the young man from the country arriving for the first time in the city, and so on, are archetypal situations; the braggart, the buffoon, the hero, the devil, the rebel, the wanderer, the siren, the enchantress, the maid, the witch, and so on, are archetypal characters; and certain animals, birds, and natural phenomena and settings are archetypal images. Any of these elements in a poem, either alone or in some combination, when treated in such a way as to bring forth its general and universal attributes, forms an archetypal pattern or patterns.

Historically, the archetypal approach seems to have derived around the turn of the century from two sources: (1) the Cambridge school of comparative anthropology issuing from Sir J. G. Frazer (*The Golden Bough* [1890–1915]), and including, loosely speaking, Gilbert Murray, Jane E. Harrison, Jessie L. Weston, S. H. Hooke, Lord Raglan, E. M. Butler, and Theodor H. Gaster; and (2) the psychology of C. G. Jung (*Psychology of the Unconscious: A Study of the Transformations and Symbolisms of the Libido* [1916]) and, to a lesser extent, that of Sigmund Freud (see, for example, "Symbolism in Dreams" [1915–17], *A General Introduction to Psychoanalysis* [1920]), and including the further work in the psychology of ritual and myth of Theodor Reik, Otto Rank, Erich Fromm, and so on. The combination of comparative anthropology with depth psychology (in conjunction with certain ideas of Cassirer regarding the origins of language) has resulted in the following series of hypothetical arguments for the interpretation of literature: since dreams, myths, and rituals are basically disguised, indirect, and nonutilitarian ways of fulfilling universal emotional needs and resolving universal human problems, and since a symbol is a disguised, indirect, and nonutilitarian way of saying or doing one thing while intending another, therefore dreams, myths, and rituals are symbolic; if dreams, myths, and rituals are symbolic ways of fulfilling universal emotional needs and resolving universal human problems, and if an a. derives from what dreams, myths, and rituals share in common, then an a. is a universal symbol; and if an a. is a universal symbol, and if a given pattern in a poem is archetypal, then it too is a universal symbol (cf. MYTH).

Thus, according to Jung, "The primordial image or archetype is a figure, whether it be a daemon, man, or process, that repeats itself in the course of history wherever creative phantasy is freely manifested. Essentially, therefore, it is a mythological figure. If we subject these images to a closer examination, we discover them to be the formulated resultants of countless typical experiences of our ancestors. They are, as it were, the psychic residue of numberless experiences of the same type." A poet using archetypes, he continues, speaks in a voice stronger than his own: "he raises the idea he is trying to express above the occasional and the transitory into the sphere of the ever-existing. He transmutes personal destiny into the destiny of mankind. . . . That is the secret of effective art" (*Contributions*). Such contemporary critics as Knight, Bodkin, Bachelard, Chase, Campbell, Frye, and Auden have worked out, each in his own way, the implications of these assumptions, or similar ones, for the study of Shakespeare, Blake, Yeats, Wordsworth, Poe, Coleridge, Milton, and so on. So Bodkin can claim, "I shall use the term 'archetypal pattern' to refer to that within us which, in Gilbert Murray's phrase, leaps in response to the effective presentation in poetry of an ancient theme. The hypothesis to be examined is that in poetry . . . we may identify themes having a particular form or pattern which persists amid variation from age to age, and which corresponds to a pattern or configuration of emotional tendencies in the minds of those who are stirred by the theme" (*Archetypal Patterns in Poetry*). And so Frye can say, "By archetype I mean an element in a work of literature, whether a character, an image, a narrative formula, or an idea, which can be assimilated into a larger unifying category" ("Blake's Treatment of the Archetype").

An approach which looks in poetry for echoes and reenactments of ancient and ubiquitous patterns—for (in the words of Thomas Mann) a "mythical identification, as survival, as a treading in footprints already made"—finds general types implicit in the specific elements of a given poem, and then interprets those types as symbols of human desires, conflicts, and problems. It thus emerges as a kind of symbolic approach (cf. SYMBOL). One may trace the image of "The Descent into Hell," for example, from early myth and ritual, to Homer, Virgil, Medieval Romance, Dante, and up to Hart Crane's subway section of *The Bridge* and to T. S. Eliot's *The Hollow Men*, and then interpret it as an a. symbolizing the encounter with one's own repressed guilt. It will be observed further that such mythical identification need not depend upon the explicit and conscious presence in a work of actual names, places, and events from mythology—the procedure rests rather upon finding more or less unconscious similarities and resemblances.

An archetypal symbology may be reconstructed, then, based upon the parallels which exist between the cycles of human life and those of the external world, and the patterns which these parallels have caused to appear in myth, ritual, dream, and poetry: "In the solar cycle of the day," says Frye, "the seasonal cycles of the year, and the organic cycle of human life, there is a single pattern of significance, out of which myth constructs a central narrative around a figure who is partly the sun, partly vegetative fertility and partly a god or archetypal human being" ("The Archetypes of Literature").

On the other hand, many critics (see Block and Douglas, for example) have questioned the soundness of the theory and/or of the practice of the archetypal approach. In the first place, many poems contain symbols which are primarily personal, and to interpret them archetypally is to overread them, if not to misread them altogether. Secondly, even if a poem does contain universal symbols, they may not symbolize those kinds of depth-meanings which archetypal critics are looking for. Thirdly, this approach, in emphasizing the universal and general, tends to be reductive in its view of particular and unique works of art; it is an approach which simplifies a complex thing, and while it is capable of yielding exciting and valuable results, it tends to blur the essential distinctions, as Jung, for example, frequently does (although he is against the genetic fallacy in theory), between good poems and bad ones. Finally, anthropological and psychological specialists, especially of the American pragmatic school (A. Irving Hallowell and Margaret Mead, for example), have been issuing repeated warnings that no two cultures are actually alike and that therefore it is dangerous if not false to seek parallels between European rituals and those of Africa, India, and the South Sea Islands.

Thus, while comparative and archetypal studies of poetry have an obvious value in helping the reader to see and perhaps interpret symbolically real and important resemblances among many different works, it is essential to recognize that such studies often rest upon assumptions and hypotheses whose validity and utility need continual reexamination.

C. G. Jung, "On the Relation of Analytical Psychology to Poetic Art" (1922), *Contributions to Analytical Psychology,* tr. H. G. and C. F. Baynes (1928); C. G. Jung, "The Problem of Types in Poetry," *Psychological Types,* tr. H. G. Baynes (1923); G. W. Knight, *The Christian Renaissance* (1933); M. Bodkin, *Archetypal Patterns in Poetry* (1934); T. Mann, "Freud and the Future," *Freud, Goethe, Wagner,* tr. H. T. Lowe-Porter (1939); E. Cassirer, *Language and Myth,* tr. S. K. Langer (1946); G. Bachelard, *La Terre et les Rêveries du Repos* (1948); R. Chase, *Quest for Myth* (1949); J. Campbell, *The Hero with a Thousand Faces* (1949); N. Frye, "Levels of Meaning in Lit.," KR, 12 (1950) and "Blake's Treatment of the A.," *EIE 1950* (1951); W. H. Auden, *The Enchafed Flood* (1950); N. Frye, "The Archetypes of Lit.," KR, 13 (1951) and *Anatomy of Crit.* (1957); H. M. Block, "Cultural Anthropology and Contemp. Lit. Crit.," JAAC, 11 (1952); W. W. Douglas, "The Meanings of 'Myth' in Modern Crit.," MP, 50 (1953); *Lit. Symbolism,* ed. M. Beebe (1960); *Myth and Mythmaking,* ed. H. A. Murray (1960); *Symbolism in Religion and Lit.,* ed. R. May (1960); B. Seward, *The Symbolic Rose* (1960); P. Wheelwright, *Metaphor and Reality* (1962); *Myth and Symbol,* ed. B. Slote (1963). N.FRIE.

ARSIS AND THESIS (Gr. "lifting up" and "setting down"). Corresponding to the "rise" and "fall" of the foot in the march or dance, these terms meant respectively the upward and downward beat in keeping time to the enunciation of Gr. verse. Thus the long syllable, on which the beat naturally fell, of a simple metrical foot like the dactyl (–⏑⏑), anapaest (⏑⏑–), trochee (–⏑), or iambus (⏑–) in meters based on them was regarded as the t. and the remainder of the foot as the a. In the later Roman period a. for a time referred to the first part of a foot and t. to the second, but the grammarians came to think of the raising and lowering of the voice rather than the upward and downward beat, so that the original application of a. and t. among the Greeks was reversed and a. denoted the basically long syllable and t. the rest of the foot. The authority of Richard Bentley (1662–1742) and Gottfried Hermann (1772–1848) has made this meaning of the two words usual, but not universal, in modern works on Gr. and L. meter.—J. Caesar, *Disputatio de verborum "arsis" et "thesis" apud scriptores artis metricae latinos . . . significatione* (1885); E. H. Sturtevant, "The Ictus of Cl. Verse," AJP, 44 (1923); Hardie; Dale; Koster; Crusius; Beare. R.J.G.

ART FOR ART'S SAKE. See POETRY, THEORIES OF (OBJECTIVE THEORIES).

ARTE MAYOR. As a general Sp. metric term a.m. may mean any line of 9 or more syllables. However, a.m. almost always refers to a line of a certain pattern (*verso de a.m.*) or to the strophe composed of such lines (*copla de a.m.*). The line developed from the late med. L. double adonic modified by an increasingly liberal use of anacrusis and catalexis. The late medieval poets borrowed the a.m. directly from the Galician-Portuguese of the 13th and 14th c. The form reached the peak of its development in 15th-c. Sp. poetry and gave way to the Italianate hendecasyllable in the 16th, since which time it has occupied only a minor position in Sp. poetry. Juan de Mena (1411–56) is considered its greatest master. A recitative measure, it was the vehicle for most poetry of weighty or serious subject matter of the 15th c. Unlike most learned Sp. verse, the a.m. was not restricted by syllable count, but depended largely on rhythmic beat. The basic pattern was a 12-beat verse divided into 2 hemistichs of 6 beats each and having triple rhythm, thus:

⏑ –″ ⏑ ⏑ –′ ⏑ | ⏑ –″ ⏑ ⏑ –′ ⏑

The primary (′) and secondary (″) stress beats (the latter occasionally lacking) of each hemistich are supplied by accented syllables; the unstressed beats between these two are supplied by 2 obligatory unaccented syllables; the remaining unstressed beats may each be supplied by 1 or 2 unaccented syllables or a rest beat. The pattern was not always strictly followed. The a.m. was normally arranged in groups of 8 lines to form a stanza called *copla de a.m.*, rhyming abbaacca, less often ababbccb or abbaacac. Although the original a.m. enjoyed great rhythmic and syllabic freedom, the line in later centuries became primarily a 12-syllable or a 6-plus-6-syllable verse with marked amphibrachic rhythm.—R. Foulché-Delbosc, "Etude sur le *Laberinto* de Juan de Mena," *Revue Hispanique*, 9 (1902); J. Saavedra Molina, *El verso de a.m.* (1946); P. Le Gentil, *La Poésie lyrique espagnole et portugaise à la fin du moyen âge. 2ᵉ partie. Les formes* (1953); Navarro; D. C. Clarke, *Morphology of 15th C. Castilian Verse* (1964), "Line Formation in the Galician-Portuguese Poetry of the Cancioneiro Colocci-Brancuti," *RPh*, 35 (1981). D.C.C.

ASSONANCE, sometimes called "vocalic rhyme," denotes vowel identity in the tonic syllables, sometimes supported by the same device in the succeeding unstressed syllables, of words whose consonants differ or, if partly the same, avoid creating rhyme (grave / fate; votive / notice; glory / holy) and which (1) echo each other in the same line or in different portions of a poem, or which (2) appear at the end of successive or alternating lines.

The first type (internal a.) is used exclusively for stylistic effect and often occurs in combination with alliteration and consonance (qq.v.) producing elaborate sound textures (see also SOUND IN POETRY and TONE COLOR). To be noticeable, at least the first two assonances in a sequence must be in close proximity, or in the first and last words of a line. Internal a. is characteristic of poetry in any language. Thomas Gray: "Along the heath and near his favorite tree"; George Herbert: "Onely take this gentle rose." Thomas Hardy's *The Voice* has an assonantal pattern on "u," woven through the whole poem. Baudelaire: "Le gouffre a toujours soif, la clepsydre se vide." Goethe has many subtle internal assonances; for rhyme pair assonances echoing the internal ones see his *An die Entfernte*. Rilke is especially fond of assonances on *a* and *ei* (e.g., *Duineser Elegien* 2. 41–42; 10. 1–5, 73). For an interwoven pattern of alliteration and a. see Shakespeare's Sonnet 12; cf. also Marianne Moore's *Spenser's Ireland*.

The second type represents a device for linking lines or line parts. It is not used by poets of the Eng. language as a deliberate device, except very occasionally (e.g., Marianne Moore: ". . . swiftness /. . . crevices" in *The Fish*). Sometimes an a. has to make up for the lack of a pure rhyme (e.g., the only two certain examples of impure rhyme in Shakespeare's Sonnets: "open / broken," 61.1–3, and "remember'd / tender'd," 120.9–11). In popular verse and folk song ("And pray who gave you that jolly red nose? / Cinnamon, Ginger, Nutmeg, and Cloves") a. appears as the result of "carelessness or blunted ear" (Edmund Gosse). In classical L. Virgil, Cicero, and especially Catullus made subtle use of a. as an alternative to rhyme while in ancient Gr. poetry vocalic rhyme echoes were used effectively within lines (e.g. *Iliad* 1.406). In late Vulgar L. and early romance poetry final a. is part of the verse structure and links contiguous lines of indefinite number. The Sp. romances have up to 50 or 60 lines of *rimas asonantes* with the same a., which never becomes tedious because of the rich vocality of the language. (Note the endless variety of words with *i-a* or *i-o* in the last two syllables.) Both the tonic penultimate and the ultimate are in a. Successful use of a. in modern Sp. poetry includes a. on either the ultimate or the penultimate alone (Mármol, Bécquer) and mere vocalic analogies, as *e/i* and *o/u* (Martinez de la Rosa). In Rubén Dario's *Sinfonia en gris mayor* lines 2 and 4 of all 8 stanzas are in a. Semivowels *i(y)* and *w(u)* preceding a vowel do not destroy the a. (e.g., "universo /. . . ingenuo" or "Fulgencio /. . . esto"). A. is also used in the Sp. drama (Calderón, Antonio Hurtado, etc.).

The early OF *chansons de geste* have a. in place of rhyme. The assonant line groups are called *laisses* or *tirades* and vary greatly in number; in the *Chanson de Roland* the average *laisse* has 14 lines. A. takes place only between final syllables of the same category (i.e., masculine or feminine). In modern Fr. poetry Charles Guérin's attempt to reintroduce a. in place of rhyme in *Le sang des crépuscules* (1895) has found no imitators.

In Ir. poetry, rhyme includes an elaborate system of assonances (called "amus"), since *g-b-d, c-p-t,* or *ch-ph-th* are allowed to "rhyme."

Middle High German poetry uses a. often (but nowhere exclusively) instead of, or intermingled with, rhyme (e.g., in the *Graf Rudolf* fragments 15 per cent of the rhymes are thus "impure"). The German *Volkslied* uses a. occasionally, when at a loss for a rhyme. The attempts of the German romantic poets to reintroduce a. in place of rhyme into German poetry in their translations from the Sp. (the brothers Schlegel) and in their own romances and dramas (Tieck, Arnim, Heine) are *tours de force* rather than genuine artistic successes, since New High German, with its prevalence of the *shva*-sound in final syllables, cannot produce sufficiently strong word echoes without the aid of consonance. Modern poets occasionally use a. with great effect, e.g., Stefan George in *Verschollen des traumes . . .* where identical rhyme is regularly interlaced with a. and in *Der Widerchrist* where assonances tellingly deviate "by a hair's breadth" from full rhyme, just as do the works of the Antichrist from Christ's.

A. W. Schlegel, *Briefe an Tieck*, ed. K. v. Holtei, III (1864), 275ff.; F. Brunetière, "A.," *La Grande encyclopédie* (1886); J. Minor, *Neuhochdeutsche Metrik* (2d ed., 1902); M. Méndez y Bejarano, *La ciencia del verso* (1908); W. Masing, *Sprachliche Musik in Goethes Lyrik* (1910); E. Gosse, "A.," *Ency. Britannica* (11th ed., 1911); A. Fischli, *Über Klangmittel im Versinnern* (1920); P. Habermann, "Assonanz," *Reallexikon*, I; E. Rickert, *New Methods for the Study of Lit.* (1927); L. P. Thomas, *Le Vers moderne* (1943); N. I. Heresu, *La Poésie latine: Étude des structures phoniques* (1960); W. Kayser, *Gesch. des deutschen Verses* (1960); C. C. Smith, "La musicalidad del *Polifemo*," RFE, 44 (1961). U.K.G.

AUBADE, *aube*. See ALBA.

B

BACCHIUS (also called *bacchiacus* or *bacchiac*). A unit of verse composed of 1 short syllable followed by 2 long ones, ⏑ – –. The name supposedly derives from the use of the unit in ancient Gr. religious songs to the god Bacchus. Although comparatively rare in Gr. lyric verse, it appears frequently in L. poetry, especially in the plays of Plautus, e.g.,

nām vōx mē | prĕcānt (um h)ūc | fŏrās

ēx|cĭtāvīt

(*Rudens* 260f.)

where, as sometimes happens, the first syllable is a *longa irrationalis*. In L. verse the unit occurs usually in tetrameters, though sometimes it will be combined with spondees and iambs for a line of verse. The Romans felt it to be especially suitable for a serious and solemn style. Eng. poetry is said to admit the unit in such words as "aboveboard" where the second and third syllables receive about the same amount of stress. But the term is really appropriate to ancient quantitative poetry.—W. M. Lindsay, *Early L. Verse* (1922); P. Maas, *Griechische Metrik* (1929); Dale; G. E. Duckworth, *The Nature of Roman Comedy* (1952); Crusius. R.A.H.

BALLAD. See NARRATIVE POETRY.

BALLAD METER, or common meter (The C.M. of the hymnals is roughly the same as ballad meter, except that the beat is more regular because of the deliberate style of singing and the first and third lines usually rhyme). In the characteristic ballad stanza the first and third lines are iambic tetrameter, the second and fourth lines iambic trimeter. Only the second and fourth lines rhyme. A typical quatrain:

> The ladies cracked their fingers white,
>   The maidens tore their hair,
> All for the sake of their true loves,
>   For them they ne'er saw mair.

It has been conjectured that this stanza is actually a couplet composed of two 7-foot lines, the 7-foot line deriving from the septenary (q.v.) of medieval church poetry. The conjecture is borne out to some extent by the musical phrasing of many ballad tunes, for many phrases round themselves over the 7 feet of two lines, ignoring the 4/3/4/3 arrangement of the text. There are so many exceptions to this musical pattern, however, that the conventional practice of printing the ballad stanza as 4 lines is still justified. The stanza is easily managed and is noted for its buoyancy and tunefulness. Folk singers and minstrels as well as the learned poets who have adopted the stanza vary the accentuation of the shorter lines, weighting the line by spondees and lightening it with extra unaccented syllables. An example of the latter effect is Herrick's famous stanza: "Gather ye rosebuds while ye may, / Old Time is still aflying; / And this same flower that smiles today, / Tomorrow will be dying." Although the 4-line ballad stanza accounts for the form of most folk ballads, some of the more important traditional pieces are sung in tetrameter couplets, usually with an irrelevant refrain weaving among the story lines. F. J. Child, G. L. Kittredge, and other ballad scholars considered the tetrameter couplet the older ballad stanza.—See, for a brief discussion, G. H. Gerould, *The Ballad of Tradition* (1932), 124–30. Fuller is J. W. Hendren, *A Study of Ballad Rhythm* (1936). A.B.F

BALLADE. The most important of the so-called OF forms and the dominant verse form of Fr. poetry in the 14th and 15th c. The most common type of b. is made up of three 8-line stanzas rhyming ababbcbC and a 4-line *envoi* (q.v.) rhyming bcbC. As the capital letters indicate, the last line of the first stanza serves as the refrain, being repeated as the last line of each stanza and also of the *envoi*. In the tightness of its rhyme scheme and in its use of the refrain, the b. is one of the most exacting of verse forms. Some variants of the standard b. utilize 10- or (less often) 12-line stanzas and 5- or 6-line *envois* in place of the more common 8- and 4-line arrangements. The *envoi*, which frequently begins with the address "Prince" (a derivation from the medieval literary compositions at which the judge was so addressed), forms the climactic summation of the poem.

Although the b. may have developed from some Prov. form, it was standardized in Fr. by such 14th-c. poets as Guillaume de Machaut, Eustache Deschamps, and, less so, Jean Froissart. It was carried to perfection in the 15th c. by Christine de Pisan, Charles d'Orléans, and, most of all, François Villon, who made the b. the vehicle for the greatest of early Fr. poetry. Such works as his *B. des pendus* (B. of the Hanged) and his *B. des dames du temps jadis* (B. of Ladies of Times Gone By) achieved an unequaled intensity in their use of refrain and *envoi*. The b. continued in favor until the time of Marot in the early 16th c., but the poets of the *Pléiade*, as well as their neoclassical successors in the 17th c., had little use for the form and regarded it as a barbaric survival. Both Molière and Boileau made contemptuous allusions to the b.

The b. of the great Fr. period was imitated in England by Chaucer and Gower, but it never established itself firmly in that country. In the later 19th c. a group of Eng. poets, including Austin Dobson, Andrew Lang, and W. E. Henley, revived the form with enthusiasm, inspired perhaps by the example of Théodore de Banville in France. But the later b., with the possible exception of a few of Swinburne's, has not even aimed at the grandeur and scope of Villon; it has been essentially a delicate and artificial exercise for light or polite versifiers.

The double b. is composed of six 8-line stanzas or six 10-line stanzas. The refrain is included but the *envoi* is optional.—Kastner; P. Champion, *Hist. poétique du XVe s.* (2 v., 1923); J. Fox, *The Poetry of Villon* (1962).

BARD. A poet among the ancient Celtic peoples, whose function it was to celebrate the heroes, victories, or laws of the nation. By extension, in modern usage, any poet, though the term has often been applied to specific poets, notably Shakespeare and Milton.

The term (Welsh, *bardd;* Ir., *bard*) is used by the later L. writers, Lucan, for example, to describe the poets of Gaul and Britain. The bards, who constituted an entire separate social class with hereditary privileges, became extinct in Gaul at a relatively early date, but their existence in Ireland and Scotland until the 18th c. and in Wales, in some respects, until the present day supplies many details as to their organization.

The 10th-c. Welsh code of *Hywel Dda,* with its division of the bardic class into three categories, the *pencerdd* (chief of song), the *bardd teulu* (household bard), and the *cerddor* (minstrel), suggests the earlier Ir. distinction of *druid, filid,* and *baird.* These groups ultimately fell together under the classification *bard* as their separate functions merged.

The Welsh festivals or contests of poetry, known as *Eisteddfodau* (sing. *Eisteddfod*) continued until the reign of Elizabeth I and were revived in 1822, since which date they have been regularly held. In modern Welsh usage, a bard is a poet who has participated in an Eisteddfod.

The art of the bards was essentially social in function, related to the life, traditions, and ideals of the community. Hence, it is in actuality far removed from the personal, lyric emotionalism connected with the term by the 18th-c. Eng. poets, such as Gray and Beattie, who revived it.—E. C. Quiggin, *Prolegomena to the Study of the Later Ir. Bards 1200–1500* (1914); H. I. Bell, *The Development of Welsh Poetry* (1936); G. Murphy, "Bards and Filidh," *Éigse,* 2 (1940); J. J. Parry, "The Court Poets of the Welsh Princes, PMLA, 67 (1952); J. E. Caerwyn Williams, "The Court Poet in Medieval Ireland," *Proc. British Academy,* 57 (1971). F.J.W.; A.P.

BATHOS (Gr. "profundity" or "height," according to the point of view, cf. L. *altitudo).* 1. Though Longinus made b. a synonym of *hypsos* (the sublime) in *On the Sublime* 2.1, Pope, who can hardly be supposed ignorant of Longinus' meaning, took a new departure and made it an antonym in his parody of Longinus' treatise, *Peri Bathous: or, Martinus Scriblerus His Treatise of the Art of Sinking in Poetry,* 1728. The commonest meaning of the word ever since has been that of Pope, namely, an unintentionally ludicrous because ill-managed attempt at elevated expression, in the 18th c. most often an expression of pathos in its wide Aristotelian sense of passion (i.e., any of the passions or emotions), later, of pathos in its more modern, narrower sense of the sad or pitiable. These meanings are obviously accountable in no small measure to the accidental similarity of the two Gr. words, *pathos* and *bathos.* Pope illustrates with "Ye Gods! annihilate both Space and Time, / And make two Lovers happy" (ed. E. L. Steeves, 1952, p. 52); Elizabeth Barrett Browning ardently recalls "Our Euripides, the human— / With his droppings of warm tears" (*Wine of Cyprus* 89–90); and Tennyson misfires with "He suddenly dropt dead of heart-disease" (*Sea Dreams* 64). A veritable feast of b. is to be enjoyed in "an anthology of bad verse" entitled *The Stuffed Owl,* selected and arranged by D. B. Wyndham Lewis and C. Lee (1930).

2. The use of the word for a deliberately contrived effect of pathos *manqué* or any kind of deliberate anticlimax, in the way of irony, gay or serious, is also current, though less common, and is perhaps best avoided. H.B.

BEAT. Regularly reccurring metrical emphasis in accentual poetic lines. The term is often used instead of "stress" (q.v.) by prosodists who are pressing the analogies between verse and music and who are thinking of the metrical foot (q.v.) as an almost exact parallel with the musical bar. The expression "a 5-beat line" emphasizes the "ideal" or "normal" accentual pattern and suggests that the number of syllables may vary as long as the five structural beats are present. See METER.

P.F.

BLANK VERSE. Unrhymed iambic pentameter lines. Neither originally nor exclusively Eng., b.v. is nevertheless the distinctive poetic form of our language; it is the medium of nearly all verse drama and of much narrative and reflective verse. B.v. was introduced in the mid-16th c. Surrey's b.v. translations of books II and IV of the *Aeneid*, written ca. 1540, were printed by Tottel in 1557. In Tottel's *Miscellany*, also 1557, the work of Nicholas Grimald provided two additional examples of the effectiveness of b.v. for narrative. The first appearance of a far more important variety of b.v.—dramatic b.v.—occurred in 1561 with the premiere of the tragedy *Gorboduc* by Sackville and Norton. In spite of the continuing fondness of British dramatists for other forms (e.g., the fourteener, q.v.), after *Gorboduc*, Eng. drama accepted b.v. as its standard form, and b.v. is the standard verse form of Shakespeare's plays.

The freedom of b.v. is also a challenge. Lacking the extrinsic mark of rhyme, poets must prove themselves in b.v. by their powers of conception and by their deployment of the sound-patterns of the language in interaction with the ideal pattern of the metrical form. The shifts of dominance in this interaction constitute the metrical history of b.v.

Probably borrowing the idea of b.v. from the unrhymed hendecasyllabic *versi sciolti*, q.v. ("freed" verse) of Molza's It. translations from the *Aeneid* (Venice, 1539), and being encouraged perhaps by the dislike of the Eng. classicists Cheke and Ascham for "rude beggarly rhyming," as well as by the tradition of ME unrhymed alliterative verse, he worked closely with both the L. text and with the Scots Vergil of Gavin Douglas, which was in couplets (ca. 1515, publ. 1553). Sometimes he manipulated Douglas' phrases to fit them smoothly into an iambic line.

Clam vp againe in the greit hors maw
(Douglas)

Clambe vp again vnto the hugie horse
(Surrey)

Yet Surrey's lines are not monotonously iambic, his pauses are varied, and as Padelford (Surrey, *Poems* 1928) calculated, run-on lines make up one-fourth of his b.v. In general his sentence structure is Latinate and thus quite different in its effects from Douglas's rather pedestrian line.

Early Elizabethan b.v. shows, in minor works by Turberville, Sackville, Barnaby Rich, Greene, and others, a movement toward strict metrical regularity, culminating in Gascoigne's *The Steele Glas* (1576). Here the stress-pattern is unvaried, run-on lines are rare, and a pause occurs always at the fourth syllable, indicated by punctuation if not by the phrase.

But holla: here, I see a wondrous sight,
I see a swarme, of Saints within my glasse
(783–784)

The regularity demonstrates the capitulation at mid-century of the creative artists to the pedants. The situation would be changed—and decisively—by Christopher Marlowe.

Marlowe's *Tamburlaine* (1587), while not the first Eng. b.v. play (Sackville and Norton, *Gordobuc*, 1562; Gascoigne and Kinwelmarshe, *Jocasta*, 1566), inaugurates the great Elizabethan drama. In metrics, Marlowe exercised originality and freedom in stress and phrasing within the line, but composed his lines as individual units, often balanced in two vivid epithets (H. Baker, *Induction to Tragedy*, 1939); Often, however, he ignored the "rules" of prosody in order to make his dialogue expressive: he did not join his lines in longer rhythms.

See see where Christs blood streames in the firmament,
One drop would saue my soule, halfe a drop, ah my Christ.
(*Faustus*, 1593; 1463–1464)

Many Elizabethan plays contain passages like this which resist the conventions of scansion. One line here has 11, the other 12 syllables; it would not seem profitable to try to rationalize the stresses. Marked as it is above, the scansion may suit some. Yet the excess of syllables alone might indicate that the lines are meant to strain the metrical pattern to the breaking point. Dramatic verse (like satire) never held to the strict metric developed by other Elizabethan verse, although it was based on the same convention.

A line such as

Friends, Romans, countrymen, lend me your ears,

spoken as marked here, strains at the convention. Clearly we are dealing here with verse intended to be spoken as dramatic dialogue rather than verse to be "recited." Shakespeare's metrical system provides that while words of more than one syllable must retain their proper sound, monosyllables may be considered either strong or weak-stressed in a line of verse, regardless of their degree of stress in normal speech. The metrical feet have reference only to syllables; they have nothing to do with the divisions into words or phrases of the sounds of speech. This line would be *scanned*, but surely never spoken, thus:

Friends Romans countrymen lend me your ears.

Beginning with this convention, Shakespeare kept a relation to it throughout his career; yet it is plain that he often wrote lines which were willing, if temporary, departures. The increasing freedom with the line of Shakespeare and the later Elizabethan and Jacobean dramatists, Fletcher, Middleton, Webster, Massinger, Ford, was only one mark, and perhaps not a necessary one, of the progress made in b.v. The movement of rhythm through a series of lines, and the accommodation of every range of subject, idea, and feeling to the pentameter line gave this verse a flexibility unequalled, so it is sometimes said, in any language. It could shift from excited eloquence to prosaic statement; in fact, Eliot has said that the achievement of b.v. at this time was the evolution from the "intractably poetic" medium of Marlowe to one which could "carry the burdens and exhibit the subtleties of prose" (*Poetry in the 18th C.*, 1930).

Milton, it would appear, worked in *Paradise Lost* (1667) to restore to b.v. both a more poetic tone and a strong conventional relation to the iambic line. He was, in other words, consciously writing heroic (narrative) rather than dramatic (dialogue) b.v. To accomplish this, he deliberately distorted the normal syntax and sound-patterns of Eng. speech. He retained the privilege of drastic metrical variation, though by some views he had entirely other principles (F. T. Prince, *The It. Element in Milton's Verse,* 1954). His chief metrical achievement is usually said to be the construction of masterful rhythmic periods and "verse paragraphs," or as he put it in his preface to *PL,* where he maintains that b.v. is the noblest medium for verse, lines with "the sense variously drawn out from one verse to another." In *Paradise Regained* (1671) Milton employed a line generally freer than that of *PL,* and in *Samson Agonistes* (1671) a highly individual form including short lines and rhymes.

During the times of Dryden and Pope, b.v. was practiced by minor imitators of Milton, while the heroic couplet dominated the drama and longer poems. Dryden argued against b.v. (*Essay of Dramatic Poesy,* 1668), although he used it in some later plays, following *All for Love* (1671). When the vigor of b.v. was revived, notably by Thomson in *The Seasons* (1726), some Miltonic mannerisms of diction were retained, and although phrases and sentences were arranged freely to run over the line end, which they seldom did in the 18th-c. couplet, b.v. in this period did not attain the easy colloquial mode of Dryden and Pope's couplets. Later in the century, Young's *Night Thoughts* (1742) and Cowper's *The Task* (1785) are distinguished by a certain departure from the conventionally "poetic" diction of the time; metrically they are composed largely in the style of the "single-moulded" line, as Saintsbury called it, and they maintain regularity in stress and syllable.

Many poets of the 19th c. employed b.v. for their longer poems; some, like Tennyson, wrote lyrics in it (*Tears, idle tears,* 1847). The limits and flexibility of the form were established, and while each poet used it in a manner suitable to his own poetic voice, no basic metrical innovations were made. Wordsworth's *Prelude* (1805–50), Keats's *Hyperion* (1820), Browning's *The Ring and the Book* (1868), demonstrate much the same qualities in phrasing and stress-groupings that mark their poetry in other forms.

In contrast with the experimental meters favored by many 20th-c. poets, b.v. for the first time appears as a conservative force. Thus the b.v. in Eliot's *The Waste Land* (1922) appears ordered and traditional in its context, as do Stevens' b.v. poems among his free-verse works. Poets who have maintained the older forms, like Frost and Auden, use b.v. in idioms little different from those of their rhymed poems.

S. Johnson, "Milton," *Lives* (1781); R. Bridges, *Milton's Prosody* (1894); J. A. Symonds, *B.V.* (1895); R. M. Alden, *Eng. Verse* (1903); Saintsbury, *Prosody;* F. G. Hubbard, "A Type of B.V. Line Found in the Earlier Elizabethan Drama," PMLA, 32 (1917); T. Brooke, "Marlowe's Versification and Style," SP, 19 (1922); M. Robertson, "The Evolution of Eng. B.V.," *Criterion,* 2 (1924); H. Baker, "Some B.V. Written by Thomas Norton Before *Gorboduc,* MLN, 48 (1933); T. S. Eliot, *Elizabethan Essays* (1934); G. K. Smart, "Eng. Non-Dramatic B.V. in the 16th C.," *Anglia,* 61 (1937); C. S. Lewis, "The 15th-C. Heroic Line," E&S, 24 (1938); H. Baker, *Introduction to Tragedy* (1939); A. Swallow, "The Pentameter Line in Skelton and Wyatt," MP, 48 (1950); G. L. Trager and H. L. Smith, Jr., *An Outline of Eng. Structure* (1951); F. T. Prince, *The It. Element in Milton's Verse* (1954); J. Thompson, *The Founding of Eng. Metre* (1961). J.T; O.B.H.

IN OTHER LANGUAGES. B.v. (*versi sciolti,* q.v.) originated in Italy. Its derivation is disputed between those who consider the It. *endecasillabo,* in rhymed form used as early as 1135, an offshoot of the Fr. rhymed decasyllable (later called *vers commun*), and those who trace both these metrical lines to a common double source: L. dactylic tetrameter catalectic and Horatian sapphic.

B.v. came into being in response to the need of It. tragedians for a metrical form that would match as closely as possible the iambic trimeter of Gr. tragedy. By adopting unrhymed hendecasyllables, or *versi sciolti,* for his tragedy *Sofonisba* (1515; publ. 1524), Trissino—incidentally, not the first to use b.v.—made this meter the standard one for It. drama. Though b.v. was brought from Italy to Spain in the early 16th c. by Boscán and Garcilaso, *verso suelto* never became assimilated to the Sp. metrical tradition; and the attempts to accommodate *vers blanc* in France were likewise unsuccessful.

Outside of Italy b.v. celebrated its greatest continental triumph in Germany, which received it from England in the 18th c. Wieland used it in his *Erzählungen* (1752) and in the tragedy *Lady Johanna Gray* (1758). But it was Lessing's *Nathan der Weise* (1779) which established b.v. as the standard metrical form of German drama, subsequently to be used by such poets as Goethe, Schiller, Kleist, Grillparzer, Hebbel, Hauptmann, and others. Broad differences in metrical usage exist from the start, between, say, the predominantly end-stopped lines of Goethe and the typically run-on pattern of Lessing's verse. These divergent practices imply two different theoretical conceptions of b.v.: in the first, the line has preserved its metrical integrity; in the second, it has been replaced by the verse paragraph. Grillparzer is the most conservative in his usage, and his b.v. has a lyrical quality; the verse of Kleist, who most consistently disregards the line as metrical unit, is carried forward by a powerful dramatic impulsion. Schiller's position is an intermediate one. Beginning in *Don Carlos* (1787) with a b.v. much like Lessing's, he adopted from *Wallenstein* (1800) on a more conservative form. Besides Wieland, Liliencron wrote b.v. narrative, and Schiller, Heine, Storm, and George used b.v. in the lyric.

The Scandinavian countries received b.v. from three sources, Italy, England, and Germany, with Germany providing the chief models in the dramatic verse of Goethe and Schiller. With *Balders Død* (1773) Johannes Ewald introduced hendecasyllabic b.v. in Denmark, evidently of It. extraction. Preferring the 10-syllable line with masculine endings, Oehlenschläger created a medium capable of a wider range of dramatic effects; his treatment of b.v. in his numerous historical tragedies is very much like that of the later Schiller. Oehlenschläger's followers in the drama, Ingemann and Hauch, naturally adhered closely to the verse form of their master; more individual is the b.v. used later by Paludan-Müller (in his dramatic poems on mythological subjects) and by Rørdam. In Swedish poetry b.v. was introduced with Kellgren's narrative fragment *Sigvarth och Hilma* (1788), in the It. form acquired from Ewald. Excellent Eng. b.v. appeared as early as 1796 in a few scenes of a projected historical play by the Finn Franzén; but not until 1862 did Wecksell, another Finn, produce the only significant b.v. drama in Swedish, *Daniel Hjort.* Unlike the situation in Denmark and Norway, where b.v. appears infrequently in narrative, didactic, satirical, and reflective poetry, in Sweden b.v. has a long and still living tradition in these genres, with contributions by such poets as Tegnér, Stagnelius, Sjöberg, Malmberg, Edfelt, and Ekelöf. The form of Swedish b.v. is generally conservative, not unlike that of Goethe. Norwegian poets started using b.v. about the same time, but the first significant works in this form are several farces and dramas (beginning in 1827) by Wergeland. Wergeland's metrical usage, modeled on Shakespeare's, is exceedingly free. Neither Andreas Munch's imitations of Oehlenschläger (beginning in 1837) nor Ibsen's *Catilina* (1850) displays a distinctive form of b.v. The rhymed verse intermittently used in *Catilina* is far superior to the b.v.; this may partly explain Ibsen's subsequent preference for such a form. Bjørnson, on the other hand, composed excellent b.v. in his saga dramas, in a free form which points to Shakespeare and Schiller as the chief models.

In Russia b.v. appeared with Zhukovsky's translation of Schiller's *Die Jungfrau von Orleans* (1817–21). It was subsequently used by Pushkin in *Boris Godunov* (1825; publ. 1831) and his "Little Tragedies," and by Mey, Ostrovsky, and A. K. Tolstoy in their historical dramas. Tolstoy's *Czar Fyodor Ioannovich* (1868) has been a popular success up to recent years. B.v. also appears in narrative and reflective poetry. In Russia, as elsewhere, b.v. varies within a certain range, from the conservative line-structured form with constant caesura of *Boris Godunov* to the more loosely articulated verse of "little tragedies" like *Mozart and Salieri* and *The Covetous Knight.* In Poland, the hendecasyllabic b.v. of It. origin used by Kochanowski in his tragedy *Odprawa posłów greckich* (The Dismissal of the Gr. Envoys, 1578) failed to inaugurate a tradition. Rhymed verse became standard for Polish drama, and neither J. Korzeniowski's many b.v. plays (beginning in 1820) nor his persistent theoretical advocacy of the medium greatly modified the situation. Of individual works in b.v. may be mentioned *Lilla Weneda* (1840), one of Slowacki's best tragedies, Norwid's comedy *Miłość czysta u kąpieli morskich* (Chaste Love at the Bathing Beach), and J. Kraszewski's epic trilogy *Anafielas* (1840).

In conclusion, it may be noted that, although b.v. in all these countries, except Italy and Poland, is designated as a 5-stress iambic meter, its lines rarely have 5 full stresses. According to K. Taranovski's computation, in *Boris Godunov* only 22.5 per cent of the lines have 5 stresses, 53.5 per cent have 4, and 24 per cent have 3. This distribution also holds roughly for b.v. in the other literatures here treated.

F. Zarncke, *Über den fünffüssigen Jambus mit besonderer Rücksicht auf seine Behandlung durch Lessing, Schiller, und Goethe* (1865); A. Sauer, *Über den fünffüssigen Jambus vor Lessings "Nathan"* (1878); L. Hettich, *Der fünffüssige Jambus in den Dramen Goethes* (1913); H. G. Atkins, *A Hist. of German Versification* (1923); O. Sylwan, *Den svenska versen från 1600-talets början* (3 v., 1925–34) and *Svensk verskonst från Wivallius till Karlfeldt* (1934); A. Heusler, *Deutsche Versgesch.* (v. 3, 1929); K. Taranovski, *Ruski dvodelni ritmovi* I-II (1953); B. O. Unbegaun, *Russian Versification* (1956; with bibliog.); *Poetyka* III: *Wersyfikacja,* v. 3: *Sylabizm,* ed. M. R. Mayenowa (1956; with bibliog.); P. Habermann, "Blankvers," *Reallexikon,* 2d ed., I; W. Kayser, *Gesch. des deutschen Verses* (1960);

L. J. Parker, "Wielands *Lady Johanna Gray:* Das erste deutsche Blankversdrama," 34 *German Quarterly*, (1961). SL

BOB AND WHEEL. A bob is the refrain of a song or, as first used by E. Guest (*A History of Eng. Rhythms*, 1838), a short line, often only 2 syllables, at the end of a stanza, a device frequently employed in ME romances. A wheel is a set of short lines used at the end of a stanza. Sometimes the first line is very short and is then called a bob and the whole is referred to as a "bob wheel" or "bob and wheel." For example, the unrhymed alliterative stanzas of *Gawain and the Green Knight* each end with a bob of 2 syllables followed by a wheel consisting of quatrains, either in ballad form (8686) or in sixes, rhymed alternately (abab); the bob is rhymed with the second and fourth lines.—Saintsbury, *Prosody*, I. R.P.APR.

BREVE. See PROSODIC NOTATION.

BROKEN RHYME refers to the division of a word (not the rhyme) at the end of a line in order to produce a rhyme: for*get*ful/*debt* (Pope); *tu*-tor/*U*-niversity (George Canning). Poets from Shakespeare to Ogden Nash have used b.r. for comic or satiric effects; yet Hopkins has taken it as a resource for serious poetry, e.g., in *The Windhover* and *To what serves Mortal Beauty?* J. Schipper (*A History of Eng. Versification*, 1910) cites another type of b.r., which, however, is usually referred to as mosaic rhyme.

BUCOLIC. The term is ordinarily used as a synonym of pastoral. Virgil's ten pastoral poems, to which he refers as "pastorem carmen" in the fourth georgic and to which the term "eclogue" is now generally applied, were called "bucolics" by the grammarians. During the Renaissance and 17th c. there was a tendency to reserve the term "b." for Virgil's eclogues and for the imitations of them. The critics argued that in primitive times wealthy men—princes, even—were the keepers of cattle, not the keepers of sheep or of goats. Since pastorals in the Virgilian tradition portray people of culture and refinement, they insisted that it would be more accurate to use the term "b." when referring to poems of this type. In modern Eng. the term has a slightly humorous connotation, though it is too vague to be recorded except in a few dictionaries. See ECLOGUE, PASTORAL. J.E.C.

BURDEN, burthen. (a) The refrain or chorus of a song: "Foote it featly heere and there, and sweete Sprights beare the burthen. *Burthen dispersedly.* Harke, harke, bowgh, wawgh" (Shakespeare, *Tempest* 1.2.380). (b) The chief theme, the leading sentiment, of a song or poem: "The burden or leading idea of every couplet was the same" (L. Hunt, *Men, Women & Books* 1.11.199).—R. L. Greene, *The Early Eng. Carols* (1935). R.O.E.

BURLESQUE. No good purpose can be served by a too rigid insistence upon nomenclature in a discussion of parody, burlesque, or travesty in literature. All three employ the device of incongruous imitation and deflationary treatment of serious themes for satiric purposes. There is some general agreement among authorities that parody (q.v.) is the more exclusively literary and critical method, fixing the attention closely on an individual style or poem, while b. is freer to strike at social or literary eccentricity by employing such established verse conventions as the love-romance, the pastoral, the courtly tradition, or the Homeric manner. More important than such distinctions perhaps is what they have in common. George Kitchin states that parody and b., in modern times, have both represented "the reaction of custom to attempted change" and of established social forces and literary forms to subversive excess. They have increasingly become voices of conservatism. Four main types or genres have become identified with the history of poetic b.: Scarronesque poetry (from Paul Scarron's Fr. *Virgile travestie*, 1648–52); Hudibrastic poetry (from Butler's burlesque poem *Hudibras*, 1663–64); dramatic b. like Gay's *Beggar's Opera*, 1728, a burlesque of It. opera sometimes described as an early forerunner of the operettas of Gilbert and Sullivan; and the straight mock-heroic as practiced by Dryden and Pope. B. poetry has had a long foreground in classic comedy (Aristophanes), in medieval church history and ritual where it usually served as a weapon against hierarchy, in Chaucer who used satire against the medieval romance and mock-heroic technique in "The Nun's Priest's Tale," in the Renaissance when anti-Petrarchans debunked the love and pastoral conventions, and in the 17th c., when metaphysical verse was often burlesqued. About 1650, however, b. began to be used as a conscious critical term derived from the Fr. anticlassical burlesque of Scarron and Boileau (*Le Lutrin*, 1674) in which the primary device was the substitution in a heroic composition of bourgeois for aristocratic manners. Scarron had many Eng. imitators, but it remained for Butler to evolve an original Eng. form of the b. in which jogging couplets and quick turns of mood and line are combined with a central theme parallel to *Don Quixote*, in a broad attack on Puritanism, pedantry, romance, religious bigotry, and superstition.

In the 18th c. the accent shifted from Scarron and Butler to mock-heroic verse in couplets. Leaving aside prose burlesques of Defoe, Swift, and Fielding (and Irving in America), the historian must mention Dryden's burlesque animal fable used for polemical purposes (*The Hind and the Panther*), Pope's vengeful satires in the *Dunciad* vein, and the dramatic b. of which Buckingham's *The Rehearsal* was the archetype. These and other belittling treatments of Augustan modes fall within the class of the older satirical imitations where types and general styles, social and religious practices, or literary rivals are the targets. Modern critical parody of specific poems or poets emerged as a later form leaving b. mainly as a form of popular stage entertainment or a looser form of parody often in prose. Parody and b. existed side by side in the early *Punch* which, under Douglas Jerrold's editorship, was dedicated to liberal social causes. *Punch* later grew conservative becoming an organ of well-bred mid-Victorian complacency.

In modern times b. has most commonly been found on the stage, ridiculing the drama or the fashions of the day. Fielding's and Gay's satiric plays (*The Thumb, The Beggar's Opera*) are early examples. Gay's work anticipates the extremely popular 19th-c. form of musical entertainment exemplified in the work of W. S. Gilbert, G. A. Sala, and F. C. Burnand. In Germany stage b. was a popular way of deflating the romantic vogue of *Sturm und Drang* and the classical tragedy or Wagnerian opera. The names of Platen, Heine, and Johann Nestroy are usually mentioned in accounts of German literary humor. Weber and Fields turned the stage b. into a musical vaudeville successful on the Broadway stage around 1900, and since that time the tendency of b. has been more and more toward light, ribald stage effects or comic operas and away from the critical purpose of literary parody.—K. F. Flögel, *Geschichten des Burlesken* (1794); G. Kitchin, *A Survey of B. and Parody in Eng.* (1931); A. H. West, *L'Influence française dans la poésie burlesque en Angleterre entre 1660–1700* (1931); R. P. Bond, *Eng. B. Poetry, 1700–1750* (1932); E. A. Richards, *Hudibras in the B. Tradition* (1937); V. C. Clinton-Baddeley, *The B. Tradition in the Eng. Theatre after 1660* (1952); F. Bar, *Le Genre b. en France au 17ᵉ s.: Etude de style* (1960).

R.P.F.

BURNS STANZA, or Burns meter (also called "Scottish stanza," "Habbie stanza," and the "6-line stave"). A 6-line stanza rhyming aaabab, lines 1, 2, 3, and 5 being tetrameter and lines 4 and 6 dimeter. It takes its name from the use made of it by Burns in *To a Louse, Holy Willie's Prayer,* and in many of his other vernacular poems. The stanza, however, may be found in Prov. poems of the 11th c., and it occurs commonly in Eng. romances and miracle plays of the Middle Ages. Despite its intricacy, the form is highly effective, especially in the hands of a master like Burns. Following the crescendo of the initial tercet, the short lines lend themselves to effects of irony and epigram:

> Ye ugly, creepin, blastit wonner,
> Detested, shunn'd by saunt an' sinner,
> How daur ye set your fit upon her,
>   Sae fine a lady!
> Gae somewhere else, and seek your dinner
>   On some poor body.
>
> (*To a Louse,* stanza 2)

The meter was also used by Wordsworth in his *At the Grave of Burns.*—A. H. MacLaine, "New Light on the Genesis of the Burns Stanza," N&Q, 198 (1953).

C

CACOPHONY. The quality of being harsh-sounding or dissonant; the opposite of euphony (q.v.). Though poets ordinarily avoid c., they may use it deliberately to reinforce meaning. In the following example, the first and third lines may be considered appropriately euphonious, the second appropriately cacophonous:

> How charming is divine philosophy!
> Not harsh and crabbed as dull fools suppose,
> But musical as is Apollo's lute.
>
> (Milton, *Comus*)

L.P.

CADENCE. (1) the expressive melodic pattern (interrogatory, hortatory, etc.) preceding a pause or at the end of a sentence; (2) the rhythm of accentual phrasal units; (3) a term used to describe the rhythmical flow of accentual free verse, Biblical poetry, and "poetic prose." The term when used in this last sense implies a looser concept of poetic rhythm than that assumed by adherents of orthodox graphic scansion (q.v.). The imagists and the vers librists of the early 20th c. frequently exhorted poets to abandon composition by the traditional foot system and to compose instead in loose cadences; as Ezra Pound told his contemporaries, "Compose in the sequence of the musical phrase, not in sequence of a metronome." Again, Pound warns, "Don't chop your stuff into separate *iambs.* Don't make each line stop dead at the end, and then begin every next line with a heave. Let the beginning of the next line catch the rise of the rhythm wave. . . ." (*Make It New,* 1934). W. C. Williams is another modern who has supported composition in loose cadences over composition in more conventional British prosodies. Williams begins with the proposition that the Am. idiom is unique and that it thus requires a unique rhythmical garment, not one imported without alteration from the very different tonalities of the British language. "We must break down," he writes, "the line, the sentence, to get at the unit of the *measure* in order to build again." Williams suggests that much modern Am. poetry is empty, tired, and unreal because poets have maintained a misplaced allegiance to the traditional accentual-syllabic British line in ascending rhythm. The "stasis" of much modern poetry, he believes, can be broken if Am. poets will examine their own natural idiom and deduce from it cadences to form the basis for a genuinely native prosody. As he writes, "We have had a choice: either to stay within the rules of English prosody, an area formed and limited by the English character and marked by tremendous masterwork, or to break out, as Whitman did, more or less unequipped to do more. Either to return to rules, more or less arbitrary in their delimitations, or to go ahead; to invent other forms by using a new measure" ("An Approach to the Poem," *EIE, 1947* [1948]). This "new measure consonant with our day," Williams makes clear, must be a cadence midway in formality between the regularity of traditional British prosody and the whimsical rhythmical anarchy of totally unmetered free verse. The repeated phrasal rhythms of Gertrude Stein's work seem to exemplify the concept of "c." as employed by Pound and Williams. Whitman is clearly one of the important progenitors of the "c." concept. See also PROSODY.

P.F.

CAESURA (cesura). A rhetorical and extrametrical pause or phrasal break within the poetic line. If the pause occurs near the beginning of the line, it is called initial c.; if near the middle of the line, medial; if near the end, terminal. A c. is masculine if it follows an accented syllable, feminine if it follows an unaccented syllable. Feminine caesuras are of two types: lyric if the syllable before the pause is the normal weak element in the foot (q.v., and see SCANSION), epic if an extra weak syllable occurs at the pause. The c., which is frequently marked by punctuation, corresponds to a breath-pause between musical phrases, and its constant intersection with the more or less constant metrical scheme of the poem provides a form of expressive counterpoint. A line may have no c., and it may have more than one. It may also have one or more briefer or less conspicuous caesuras called (by conventional prosodists) secondary pauses or (by "linguistic" or "acoustic" prosodists) junctures.

In Gr. and L. metrics, the term "caesura" designates a word end within a foot (opposed to diaeresis, coincidence of word and foot ending); the "main c." in a line is usually found within the third or fourth foot. In classical metrics, c. is an important technical element of composition but is wholly metrical and should not be confused with pause in modern prosodies. In prosodic analysis of classical verse, terms such as "penthemimeral" or "semiquinarian" (i.e., after the fifth half-foot) are employed to designate caesura position. For example, c. occurring after the first long syllable of the second foot, that is, after the third half-foot, is called trihemimeral or semiternarian; c. after the seventh half-foot is called hephthemimeral or semiseptenarian, and so on.

The c. is generally used with great regularity in much classical, romance, and OE verse. It is only with the development of the iambic pentameter line that varied and expressive c. placement (as in Chaucer) becomes, in Eng., a subtle prosodic device. Whereas in OE verse the medial c. had been rather mechanically used to separate each line into 2 isochronous hemistichs and to emphasize the regularity of the structure, in modern Eng. the c. is often used as a device of variety, a device whose purpose it is to help mitigate metrical rigors by shifting from position to position in various lines. In formal verse, whether classical, Romance, or OE, the medial position of the c. is frequently predictable; in verse of greater flexibility and informality, the position of the pauses cannot be anticipated.

In the syllabic Fr. alexandrine (q.v.) the predictable medial c. occurs with great regularity:

Trois fois cinquante jours le général naufrage
Dégasta l'univers; en fin d'un tel ragage
L'immortel s'émouvant, n'eût pas sonné si tôt
La retraite des eaux que soudain flot sur flot
Elles gaignent au pied; tous les fleuves s'abaissant.
Le mer rentre en prison; les montagnes renaissent.
(Du Bartas, *La Première Semaine*)

It is also extremely regular in accentual, alliterative OE poetry:

Hige sceal þe heardra, heorte þe cenre,
Mod sceal þe mare, þe ure maegen lytlaþ.
(*The Battle of Maldon*)

In early Eng. blank verse:

O knights, O Squires, O gentle blouds yborne,
You were not borne, al onely for your selves:
Your countrie claymes, some part of al your paines.
There should you live, and therein should you toyle.
(Gascoigne, *The Steel Glass*)

And in much Eng. Augustan poetry:

Careless of censure, nor too fond of fame;
Still pleased to praise, nor yet afraid to blame;
Alike averse to flatter, or offend;

Not free from faults, nor yet too vain to mend.
(Pope, *Essay on Criticism*)

In later blank verse, on the other hand, and particularly in that of Milton, the placement of the c. is extremely flexible:

Thus with the Year
Seasons return, but not to me returns
Day, or the sweet approach of Ev'n or Morn.

And Bush with frizl'd hair implicit: last
Rose as in dance the stately Trees.
(*Paradise Lost*)

Its flexibility is also notable in much modern iambic-pentameter verse:

An aged man is but a paltry thing,
A tattered coat upon a stick, unless
Soul clap its hands and sing, and louder sing
For every tatter in its mortal dress . . .
(Yeats, *Sailing to Byzantium*)

From these examples, one can see clearly that, in general, the c. is used in two basic and quite antithetical ways: (1) as a device for emphasizing formality of poetic construction and distance from colloquial utterance; and (2) as a device for investing fairly strict meters with something of the movememt of informal speech. If the c. occurs regularly in the medial position, one is dealing with a different kind of verse from that in which caesura placement is more varied and unpredictable. The surprisingly unvaried medial caesuras in Frost's *Out, Out,* for example, suggest that Frost is seeking to raise a domestic rural tragedy to the level of formal art; while, on the other hand, the unexpectedly varied caesuras in Eliot's *Journey of the Magi* suggest that Eliot, proceeding in the opposite direction, is interested in giving a colloquial cast to speech which might otherwise seem excessively chill, distant, and artificial.

C. M. Lewis, *The Foreign Sources of Eng. Versification* (1898); Saintsbury, *Prosody;* A. L. F. Snell, *Pause: A Study of its Nature and its Rhythmical Function in Verse* (1918); G. R. Stewart, *The Technique of Eng. Verse* (1930); S. E. Sprott, *Milton's Art of Prosody* (1953). P.F.

CANTO. A subdivision of an epic or narrative poem, that divides and orders the content, like the chapter in a novel. The end of each c., in long epic poems, gave the singer an opportunity to rest for a while or perhaps to defer the rest of the recitation to the following day. The subdivision into cantos may apply to poems of all stanzaic patterns. Although the subdivision into smaller units is found in long epic poems of all times and literatures, the It. word *canto* to indicate such a subdivision was adopted mainly by the Romance and Eng. literatures. It appears in the works of Dante, Ariosto, Tasso, Ercilla, Voltaire, Pope, Byron, etc. R.MI.

CANZONE. Due to the intimate link between poetry and music the term *canzone* (from *cantio*) has come to be applied to quite a number of verse forms with differing metrical patterns. Among the better known types are the *c. epico-lirica* whose center of diffusion was originally the Gallo-It. dialect area. It belongs to the Celtic substratum and is akin to compositions of the same genre in France and Catalonia. More indigenous to the It. soil is the *c. a ballo* or *ballata* and other popular compositions such as the *frottola, barzelletta,* the *canto carnascialesco* and the *laude sacra.* At various times these types have been used by the *poeti d'arte,* but the type exclusively employed for refined artistic expression is the so-called *c. petrarchesca.* It is obscure in origin but bears strong traces of Prov. influence. The *strambotto, ballata* and minnesong are also said to have conditioned its architectonic structure. It takes its beginning among the poets of the Sicilian school is employed extensively by Guittone d'Arezzo and his followers and by the poets of the *dolce stil nuovo,* but acquires fixed patterns and perfection in Petrarch's *Canzoniere,* hence the qualifying adjective *Petrarchesca.* Its greatest vogue in Italy occurred, as one might expect, during the Petrarchistic period. It lasted until the death of Torquato Tasso. While in Eng. the Petrarchistic type of c. was employed by William Drummond of Hawthornden and in German by A. W. von Schlegel and other German romantic poets, Spain and Portugal were really the only countries outside of Italy where it was used to a considerable extent. In this type of poem the division for each of its stanzas is tripartite, consisting of two like parts, *piedi,* and one unlike part, *sirima* or *cauda.* There is usually a single *commiato* at the close of the poem in the form of a valediction to the c. Stanzaic length is indeterminate, varying from a maximum of 20 to a minimum of 7 verses. The lines are normally hendecasyllabic with some admixture of heptameters and pentameters. After Tasso, under the strong influence of the Fr. *Pléiade,* this type was supplanted by new forms labeled *canzoni*—the Pindaric and Anacreontic odes. Chiabrera played a leading rôle in their diffusion. He also revived the *canzonetta* originally employed by the poets of the Sicilian School. This became the favorite type used by Metastasio and the Arcadian school. Toward the close of the 17th c. Alessandro Guidi acclimated the *c. libera* which reached its highest development at the hands of Leopardi.—P. E. Guarnerio, *Manuale di versificazione italiana* (1893); F. Flaminni, *Notizia storica dei versi e metri italiani* (1919); R. Murari, *Ritmica e metrica razionale ital.* (1927); E. Segura Covarsi, *La canción petrarquista en la lirica española del Siglo de Oro* (1949); E. H. Wilkins, "The C. and the Minnesong," *The In-*

vention of the Sonnet and Other Studies in It. Lit. (1959). J.G.F.

CAROL, a light-hearted song of religious joy. The pre-Elizabethan c. was a lyric of definite verse form and reflected stylistically its close connection with the dance, but since the 16th c., the word has come to mean any festive religious song, whatever the metrical or stanzaic form, sung to a tune which in pace and melody follows secular musical traditions rather than those of hymnody. In America the c. is now almost invariably associated with Christmas; this is less true of England, where Easter carols are also widely sung. The Fr. *noël* (from L. *natalis)*, a joyous song of the Nativity, is the counterpart of the Christmas c.; it has been an established song type since the 15th c. An earlier Fr. form, the *carole,* was a dance-song similar in structure and movement to the early Eng. c. and probably its ancestor.

The surviving medieval carols are composed of uniform stanzas interspersed with a refrain, usually a rhymed couplet, which seems to have been sung—or read—also at the beginning of the c. A tetrameter triplet (3 rhyming lines of 4 stresses each) makes up the base of the c. stanza. The stanza is completed by a tag line shorter than the triplet lines and normally rhyming with the refrain. The following example is from a 15th.-c. carol of moral advice; it has been slightly modernized:

Man, beware, beware, beware,
And keep thee that thou have no care.

Thy tongue is made of flesh and blood;
Evil to speak it is not good;
By Christ, that died upon the rood,
So give us grace our tongues to spare.

Commonly the stanza rhymes abab; it may also be extended to 5, 6 or 8 lines and bound together by a variety of rhyme schemes. Refrains, too, are sometimes extended by 1 or 2 lines. Perhaps the most notable single variation from the norm is having the tag line of the stanza identical with a refrain line. This tendency to integrate stanza and refrain frequently sets in when a dance-song ceases to be danced.

In the round dances at which carols were originally performed, the stanza was probably sung by the leader of the dance; the refrain was sung by the chorus as they executed an accompanying dance figure. Modern children's games like "Now We Go 'Round the Mulberry Bush" and "A Tisket, A Tasket" represent corrupt descendants of the medieval round dances—then, of course, an adult pastime. From the violent denunciations of caroling that fulminated from medieval clerics, it is clear that caroling, even though the songs, in most cases, dealt reverently with Christian matter, was regarded as a wicked pagan survival. And, in fact, many of the older specimens are highly erotic and suggest pagan fertility rites. Doubtless the reason why caroling flourished strongest at Christmas and Easter was that these Christian festivals coincided with and supplanted the pre-Christian winter and spring fertility revels. Of some 500 medieval carols extant in manuscript, about 200 deal directly or indirectly with Advent and the Nativity. Easter, the New Year, and Epiphany were less frequently celebrated with caroling. Abundant political, moral, and satirical carols are met with, and there are besides many amorous pieces, some of which are frank to the point of lewdness.

Carols were popular in both courtly circles and among the folk, but most of those that have been preserved show learned influences, such as uncorrupted L. tags, and the various manuscript versions of the same c. do not exhibit the variation that one would expect if carols had been orally transmitted and recreated in the manner of folk song.

With the Reformation the medieval c. began to die out. The decline was mainly due to the more sober fashion of celebrating Christmas and other religious holidays that came to prevail. The formal c. was thus gradually replaced by festive songs learned from broadsides, chapbooks, and devotional songbooks. Some carols of this new kind, like *The Seven Joys of Mary, I Saw Three Ships, God Rest You Merry, Gentlemen* and *The Virgin Unspotted,* are regularly described as "traditional," a term which means only that such pieces were long popular and are anonymous, not necessarily that they are folk songs.

The carols which supplanted the medieval carols were themselves beginning to wither in popularity when musical antiquaries like Gilbert Davies (*Some Ancient Christmas Carols,* 1822) and William Sandys (*Christmas Carols, Ancient and Modern,* 1833) collected and revived them. J. M. Neale and Thomas Helmore in 1852 introduced the practice, since followed in most British and Am. c. books, of plundering Fr., Basque, Dutch, Sp., It., German and Scandinavian collections for tunes to which Eng. words could successfully be adapted. Since 1870 the rural counties of England have been scoured for folk carols and the collectors' discoveries have been impressive. By being made available to school children in excellent arrangements by Cecil J. Sharp, Vaughan Williams, and other folk-music experts, the folk carols have been artificially revitalized among educated people. Folk carols are comparatively rare in America; the only ones widely reported in this century, *The Seven Joys of Mary, Jesus Born in Bethlehem* and *The Twelve Days of Christmas,* are all Eng. imports.

R. L. Greene, *The Early Eng. Carols* (1935) is the definitive collection of medieval carols. Greene furnishes a lengthy crit. introd. His theory of the popular character of the extant carols (also held by E. K. Chambers and W. W. Greg) has been contested by R. H. Robbins in "Middle Eng. Carols as Processional Hymns," SP, 56 (1959), who applies to the Eng. carols current Fr. theories that the *caroles* were composed for ecclesiastical festivals. Carols of the later kind are collected in *The Oxford Book of Carols* (1928 and later ed.). E. Routley, *The Eng. C.* (1959) is a running commentary on the Oxford coll. but includes much information on the reputation of the carols and their modern liturgical use. Sir. R. R. Terry's coll., *Two Hundred Folk Carols* (1933), is notable for preserving the Roman Catholic features of the Continental carols he prints. Folk c. collections of the greatest importance are A. E. Gillington, *Old Christmas Carols of the Southern Counties* (1910), C. J. Sharp, *Eng. Folk-Carols* (1911) and R. Vaughan Williams, *Eight Traditional Carols* (1919). For Am. folk carols, see the *F. C. Brown Coll. of North Carolina Folklore,* II (1952), 199–212, where abundant references to other sources are given. A.B.F.

CARPE DIEM (L. "seize [enjoy] the day"). A motif in poetry which usually advises the enjoyment of present pleasures. The *locus classicus* of the phrase occurs in Horace, *Odes* 1.11, though the fullest treatment of the theme by that poet appears in *Odes* 3.29. The motif, which is found in Gr. poetry (Aeschylus, *Persians* 840–42; Anacreon 4.11.7–10) as well as in L. poetry, arises from the realization of the brevity of life and the finality of death. Hence the injunction to enjoy this life. Such enjoyment ranges in L. poetry from the refined leasures of the mind and spirit (Horace, *Odes* 3.29) to purely sensual and momentary delights (Catullus, *Carmina* 5). Even at the height of the single, joyous experience the motif encourages objectivity and detachment, implying full awareness of the sadness of the human situation. To this basically epicurean thought Ausonius added the rose motif wherein the brevity of life becomes symbolized by the brevity of the rose (*De rosis nascentibus* 35–36). In subsequent goliardic verse as well as Fr. and Eng. poetry the rose and its brevity further symbolized the loss of virginity (*Roman de la rose*). The 15th c. poets used the c.d. theme and the rose to rail against fruitless chastity (Lorenzo de' Medici, *Corinto* 28–31). In this same tradition were the Eng. Cavalier poets such as Herrick ("Gather Ye Rosebuds").

But in Christian writing and poetry the c.d. theme has been used as a persuasion to goodness (J. Taylor, *Holy Dying,* p. 31). Herbert used the motif to emphasize not only the transitoriness of this life but the eternity of the Christian life, especially after death. So also did Spenser in the *Faerie Queene.* The motif in one aspect or another is found in Carew, Thomas, Marvel, Milton, and Blake. It is found also in Persian poetry (Omar Khayyám) and ancient Egyptian poetry (*The Song of the Harper*).—J. A. Symonds, *Essays Speculative and Suggestive* (1893); F. Bruser, "Comus and the Rose Song," SP, 44 (1947); Frye. R.A.H.

CATACHRESIS (Gr. "misuse"). The misapplication of a word, especially in a strained or mixed metaphor or in an implied metaphor. It need not be a ridiculous misapplication as in bad poetry, but may be a deliberate wresting of a term from its normal and proper significance. Sometimes it is deliberately humorous. Quintilian called it a necessary misuse (*abusio*) of words and cited Virgil's *Aeneid* 2.15–16: "equum divina Palladis arte / aedificant" (They build a horse by Pallas' divine art). Since *aedificant* literally means "they build a house," it is a catachresis when applied to a horse. Puttenham, in his *Arte of Eng. Poesie,* called c. a figure of "plain abuse, as he that bade his man go into his library and fetch him his bow and arrows." Two celebrated examples of this figure are found in Shakespeare and Milton: "To take arms against a sea of troubles" (*Hamlet* 3.1.59) and "Blind mouths! that scarce themselves know how to hold a sheephook" (*Lycidas* 119–120). A very effective c. is Shakespeare's " 'Tis deepest winter in Lord Timon's purse" (*Timon* 3.4.15), which suggests comparison with some of the strained metaphors or implied metaphors in more modern poetry, e.g., "The sun roars at the prayer's end" (Dylan Thomas, *Vision and Prayer,* last line).—Lausberg. M.T.H.

CATALEXIS, catalectic. See TRUNCATION.

CATHARSIS. The use of the word c. ("purgation") in connection with the theory of literature, originates in Aristotle's celebrated definition of tragedy in the sixth chapter of the *Poetics.* Unfortunately, Aristotle merely uses the term without defining it (though he may have defined it in a putative second book of the *Poetics*); and the question of what he actually meant is a *cause célèbre* in the history of literary criticism. Insofar as there is no agreement yet, and none in sight, all definitions, including this one, must be regarded as interpretations only.

The essential function of tragedy, according to Aristotle's definition, is a representation (*mimesis*) of an action that is serious, complete, and of an appropriate magnitude; and when such representation is effectively carried out it will succeed "in arousing pity and fear in such a way as to accomplish a purgation (c.) of such emotions." The definition was doubtless framed as an answer to Plato's charge that poetic drama encourages anarchy in the soul by feeding and watering the passions instead of starving them. Aristotle held, on the contrary, that anarchy in the soul is most effectively prevented not by starving and repressing the emotions but by giving them expression in a wisely regulated manner. Tragedy he regarded as a chief instrument of such wise regulation, for it works in a twofold way, first exciting the emotions of pity and fear and then allaying them, thereby effecting an emotional cure.

Aristotle's somewhat technical understanding of c. acquires its overtones of meaning from a double linguistic heritage, in part medical and in part religious. On the one hand the idea of c. finds early expression in the writings of the Hippocratic School of Medicine, where it refers to the discharge of whatever excess of bodily elements has produced a state of sickness, and the consequent return of the body to that state of right proportion which is health. There is, in Hippocratic language, a preparatory process of slow "digestion" (*pepsis*), produced by the body's heat, wherein the bodily elements are recombined and fused in such a way that waste products are generated, ready for discharge at the proper time; and when this discharge, or c., has taken place, the result is a new balance or proportion of bodily elements, which is health. Analogously, Aristotle considers that in its "natural" condition the human psyche is well-balanced and serene, but that it falls readily away from this natural state into intemperance; and that the action of a well-made tragedy strikes pity and fear into the beholder in such a way that these emotions become "digested" (as in the Hippocratic description of returning health), with the result that a new proportion and blend of the emotions is produced, and the residue of superfluous emotional impulses is "catharated." The religious meaning of c., on the other hand, finds a diversity of expressions in the dialogues of Plato, and therefore must have entered into the conversations and teachings which surrounded Aristotle during the intellectually formative period of his young manhood. In the *Phaedo,* for instance, Plato declares that c. consists "in separating, so far as possible, the soul from the body, and in teaching the soul the habit of collecting and bringing itself together from all parts of the body, and in living, so far as it can, both now and hereafter, alone by itself, freed from the body as from fetters."

When Aristotle's definition is reconsidered in the light of these two trends of thought, the medical and the religious, an important corollary stands forth. Since the new blending which is attained in the cathartic process is psychic, not merely physical, it involves a new emotional perspective, and even, arising from that, a new intellectual vision. A wisdom is distilled from tragic suffering: man is *Pathei mathos,* "taught by suffering," as the chorus in the *Agamemnon* sings. The tragic c. and the ensuing emotional calm have produced in the spectator a new insight into what the plot of the drama most essentially represents, what its action—which is to say, its meaning in motion—essentially is. Such insight is what justifies Aristotle's assertion (ch. 9) that "poetry is something more philosophical and more highly serious than history, for Poetry tends to express universals, history particulars."

Subsequent critics, on the whole, have been more inclined to accept than to reject the doctrine of c., although their acceptance has usually involved some degree of reinterpretation. In the It. Renaissance Aristotle's definition was revived by such writers as Minturo (*The Art of Poetry,* 1563) and Castelvetro (*Poetica d'Aristotele volgarizzata e eposto,* 1570), although in the former the emphasis is shifted to the "delight and profit" which result to the spectator from his cathartic experience. In France a century later both Corneille and Racine accept the principle of c. in the fairly plain moral sense of regarding the spectator as purified by the tragedy and thus as deterred from performing such evil acts as he has been witnessing. Corneille, in addition, assumes that either pity or fear might operate separately.

In Germany, Lessing in his influential *Laokoön* (1766) opposed the latter view of Corneille, insisting that the special effect of tragedy must come from the union of the two emotions, from which there emerges the cosmically oriented emotion of *awe,* as the spectator recognizes through the tragedy the sword of destiny that is suspended above us all. Lessing also emphasizes (*Hamburger Dramaturgie,* 1768) the applicability of Aristotle's ethical standard of "due measure" to the principle of c.; for tragedy, if it is to transform our pity and fear into virtue, "must be capable of purifying us from both extremes"—from "too little" by its emotional contagion, and from "too much" by the restraint which its formal pattern imposes. Schiller in his essay "On Tragic Art" (1792) reaffirms the importance of measure, and in "On the Sublime" (1801) he draws two corollaries: that the most perfect tragedy is one which produces its cathartic effect not by its subject matter but by its tragic form; and that it has aesthetic worth only so far as it is "sublime"—i.e., as by representing the indifference of the universe to moral ends it produces in the soul of the spectator an "inoculation against unavoidable fate." Goethe, in his *Nachlass zu Aristoteles Poetik* (1827), sees the main importance of the purgatorial, or cathartic situation, not in reference to the spectator, whose condition is incidental and variable, but in the reconciliation and expiation of the characters in the play. Among later German writers on aesthetics we may note Schopenhauer (*The World as Will and Representation,* 1819), who equates the cathartic principle of tragedy with an idealized and universal experience of fellow-suffering wholly disproportionate to moral deserts; and Nietzsche (*The Birth of Tragedy,* 1872), who interprets the matter through the complementary symbols of Dionysus and Apollo, the unresisting plunge into whatever sufferings and joys life may offer and the calm vision that results from this self-surrender.

Of Eng.-speaking writers, Milton in the Pref

ace to *Samson Agonistes* (1671) interprets Aristotle to mean that tragic c. operates on the homeopathic principle, and he draws an analogy from medicine, wherein "things of melancholic hue and quality are used against melancholy, sour against sour, salt to remove salt humours." Wordsworth, shifting the reference from dramatic to lyric poetry, offers a humanitarian interpretation: that readers are to be "humbled and humanized," and to be purged of the prejudices and blindnesses arising from false sophistication and snobbery, "in order that they may be purified and exalted" (Nowell C. Smith, ed., *Wordsworth's Literary Criticism,* 1905). In our own day I. A. Richards (*Principles of Literary Criticism,* 1925) interprets the cathartic process as a reconciliation and reëquilibration of "Pity, the impulse to approach, and Terror, the impulse to retreat," along with various other groups of discordant impulses, and he affirms the importance of tragedy on the ground that "there is no other way in which such impulses, once awakened, can be set at rest without suppression." Among other contemporaries we might mention Elisabeth Schneider (*Aesthetic Motive,* 1939), who has argued that just because the pity and terror are painfully and utterly irreconcilable in real life, the one always driving the other out, we receive the greatest pleasure from their stylized union in art. So here again, at the end as at the beginning of our survey, we are reminded that c. is not a simple elimination, but always operates hand in hand with a process of stylization and an aesthetic creation of significant form.

Aristotle, *Poetics,* or *The Art of Poetry,* tr. Bywater (1909; Fyfe's commentary on a reissue of this translation in 1940 is helpful), Cooper (1913), Butcher (1917), Fyfe (1927), Epps (1942), Wheelwright (1951). See also Else (1957) for a good comprehensive study but controversial theory.—I. A. Richards, *Principles,* chs. 7, 15, 32; M. T. Herrick, *The Poetics of Aristotle in England* (1930); J. C. Ransom, "The Cathartic Principle," *The World's Body* (1938); E. Schneider, *Aesthetic Motive* (1939); *European Theories of Drama,* ed. B. H. Clark (rev. ed., 1947); F. Fergusson, *The Idea of a Theatre* (1949); F. L. Lucas, *Lit. and Psychology* (1951) and *Tragedy; Serious Drama in Relation to Aristotle's Poetics* (rev. ed., 1957); Wellek; R. Kuhns, *The House, the City and the Judge* (1962; ch. 5). P.W.

CAUDA, coda (L. "tail"). The short line, or tail, which in a stanza of longer lines usually rhymes with another, similar, short line, thus serving to divide the stanza into parts. When the caudae rhyme, the stanza is known as a tailrhyme stanza, characteristic of Romance languages. The use of caudae was especially popular in medieval metrical romances (e.g., *Aethelston, Horn Childe*). A school of tailrhyming romance writers is supposed to have flourished in East Anglia in the 14th c. See TAIL-RHYME. R.O.E.

CELTIC PROSODY. No direct information is available about the nature of the poetry composed by the Celts on the continent of Europe before they settled in the separate areas in which they now live. From Caesar we know that in the 1st c. B.C. students learned verses by memory in the druidic schools of Celt. Gaul, but no actual examples of poetry have survived among the remains of the Gaulish language.

Of the Celt. Poetry composed in Welsh, Cornish, and Breton, and in the Gaelic of Ireland, Man, and Scotland, the earliest remains are Ir. and Welsh. These date back only to about the 7th c. A.D., by which time both the Ir. and the Welsh had begun to use rhyme, familiar to them through the Latin hymns of the church, as their central prosodic device.

Some archaic Ir. texts preserve sporadic examples of an ancient verse form which was presumably the dominant type from prehistoric times down to at least the 6th c. It is derived from the same Indo-European system which can be traced in the gnomic and epic poetry composed in Vedic Sanskrit, Gr., and Slavic. A typical line consists of a free initial colon, a separating break, and a final colon with fixed cadence:

Mo chride crūaid | crēchtnăigthĕr.
(Grievously my heart is wounded.)

In the Ir. poetry belonging to this tradition, lines were regulated to certain syllabic counts. Alliteration provided optional decoration but was not, as in later Celt. poetry (and in Germanic), requisite as a patterning device.

The mainstream of Celtic poetry, however, springs from the time that the Celtic peoples heard rhyming L. hymns such as that composed in the 5th c. by Sedulius, which though nominally composed in quantitative iambic dimeter, foreshadowed the stressed, rhyming verse later to become common in European vernacular poetry:

A solis ortus cardine a
Ad usque terrae limitem b
Christum canamus principem b
Natum Maria virgine. a

From the quarter of the rising of the sun
to the boundary of the earth
let us sing Christ the Prince
born of the Virgin Mary.

The new prosodic systems inspired by rhyme are in many cases so intricate that their indebtedness to L. is far from obvious, but the relationship is undeniable and is substantiated by the sudden emergence of, for instance, an Ir. stanza which like Sedulius' consists of 4 rhyming lines, each exactly 8 syllables in length.

An early example of the impact of rhyme upon the Welsh is afforded by Aneirin's *Gododdin,* the original of which may reach back to about A.D.

600. In the following stanza the old and the new meet together, for each line is linked to the next by a final rhyme (*-ant*), while the traditional Celt. device of alliteration is retained as an optional decoration (*k* in line 1, *g* in 2, *h* in 3, *l* in 4, *g* in 5):

Kywyrein ketwyr, kyuaruuant,
y gyt en vn vryt yt gyrchassant.
Byrr eu hoedyl, hir eu hoet ar eu carant.
Seith gymeint o Loegrwys a ladassant.
O gyvryssed gwraged gwyth a wnaethant,
llawer mam ae deigyr ar y hamrant.
(*Canu Aneirin,* ed. Ifor Williams [Cardiff, 1938], 668–673.)

As one the warriors arose, foregathered, together attacked with single purpose. Short were their lives, long the lament of their kinsmen for them. Seven times their number of English they slew. Through strife they left women widows, many a mother with tears on her eyelids.

Even in a poem as early as the *Gododdin,* there are other, more intricate stanzaic forms; but these are a mere tentative preliminary to the later developments of Welsh *cynghanedd,* q.v. (harmony), in which rhyme becomes an integral part of an extraordinary network of sound effects. At this subsequent stage, a disciple of the 14th-c. poet Dafydd ap Gwilym writes couplets such as the following:

Dyrcha ael fain, d'orchwyl fu
Dristau gŵr dros dy garu.
(Caradar, *Welsh Made Easy,* III. 92. See *Gwaith Dafydd ap Gwilym,* ed. T. Parry [Cardiff, 1952], p. clxxxvi.)

Raise your fine eyebrows! Your achievement has been to make a man sad for love of you.

Here he not only satisfies the requirements of *cywydd* (coupled lines), that each line contain 7 syllables and that each couplet contain an end rhyme between a final unstressed syllable and a final stressed syllable (fu: garu). He has also arranged the *cynghanedd* within the line so that a sequence of as many as 5 or even 6 consonants in the first half of the line recurs in the second half of the line: *d--r--ch--l--f:* (*n*) *d--r--ch--l--f; d--r--s--t--g--r: d--r--s--d*(*t*)*--g--r.* And, at the same time, he has followed the rule that the corresponding vowels should be dissimilar (*dris-: dros,* etc.). And, throughout the remainder of the poem, he has alternated at will four different kinds of *cynghanedd,* each with its own stringent requirements.

In the Gaelic poetry common to Ireland, Man, and Scotland, rhyme was early developed into an equally intricate prosodic system known as bardic verse. Its chief characteristics are the limitation of each line to a fixed number of syllables (often 7 or 8) and the use of what may be called generic rhyme—that is, any member of a particular genus of phonetically similar consonants may rhyme either with itself or with any other member of that genus, provided that the preceding vowels are identical. These six rhyming groups are as follows:

1.	*c*	*t*	*p*				
2.	*ch*	*th*	*ph, f*				
3.	*g*	*d*	*b*				
4.	*gh*	*dh*	*bh,*	*mh*	*l*	*n*	*r*
5.				*m*	*ll*	*ng,nn*	*rr*
6.	*s*						

The source of the syllabic measure, as in Welsh, is obviously the Latin hymn. The development of generic rhyme is less clear. An analogous system appears in early Welsh, involving four consonantal sets—*g:d:b, dd:l:r, 3:f:w,* and certain nasal clusters. This may have been borrowed from Irish, for bards of the two nationalities visited one another; or both systems may have been suggested by the tentative rhymes in early L. hymns. (In Sedulius' stanza quoted above, [*lim*]*item* makes full "Ir. rhyme" in its last two syllables with [*princ*]*ipem,* and [*ca*]*rdine* with [*vi*]*rgine.*)

A typical example of Ir. syllabic prosody is the following stanza composed by an anonymous medieval bard, who is describing an ornate goblet owned by a king of Connaught:

Eoin bas n-dearg 's a n-druim r' a thaoibh,
mar do chuim an ceard go cōir
lucht 'gar chasmhail cleasa ceoil—
eoin 's a sleasa d' asnaibh ōir.
(McKenna, *Aithdioghluim Dána,* no. 9)

Birds red of claw stand backed against its borders, just as the artist deftly shaped them as figures seeming really to sing—birds whose sides are ribbed with gold.

This particular meter, known as *rannaigheacht mhōr* (the Great Versification), requires a stanza of 4 lines which must each contain 7 syllables and end in a stressed monosyllable.

The last words in lines 2 and 4 must show generic rhyme with one another (*ōir:ōir*). The last words in 1 and 3 must consonate but not assonate with these (the consonants *bh* in *aoibh* and *l* in *eoil* both show generic rhyme with the *r* in *ōir,* while the vowels *aoi* and *eoi* are identical with the *ōi* in 2 and 4 only in length).

All the stressed words in 2 other than the final rhyming word show generic rhyme with stressed words in 1—*(ch)uim:(dr)uim, (c)eard:(d)earg.* All the stressed words in 4 other than the final rhyming word must show generic rhyme with stressed words in 3—*eoin:(c)eoil, (sl)easa:(cl)easa, asnaibh:(ch)asmhail.* (In a disyllable such as the last, both syllables must rhyme,—*s:s, n:mh, bh:l.*)

Every line must have at least one alliteration between adjacent stressed words, and in the last line this alliteration must be between the last two stressed words—*dearg, druim; chuim, ceard, cōir;*

chasmhail, cleasa, ceoil; asnaibh, ōir (a consonant alliterates either with itself or with its corresponding form produced by initial grammatical mutation, and a vowel alliterates with itself or any other).

The professional bard was allowed to use measures less cramping than the 7-syllable line. A stanza from a 16th-c. religious poem will illustrate the greater scope available. The meter is *droighneach,* whose lines average from 9 to 13 syllables. In the following quatrain the lines number respectively 11, 15 (exceptionally), 11, and 13 syllables.

Tairm na nēal, foghar na n-uile ainmhidhe, 1
foghar ainglidhe na n-ēan, foghar duille gach
    dhionnmhuighe,— 2
ag soin moladh na n-dūileadh dā
    n-daghruire— 3
būireadh an doimh dhamhghoire, foghar na
    fhiodhbhuidhe. 4

(*Aithdioghluim Dána,* no. 76.)

The crash of clouds, the sound of all animals, the angelic sound of birds, the sound of leaves on every hillside, the belling of the stag among the deerherd, the sound of the forest—through these comes the praise of the elements to their kind King.

Such amplitude as this measure permits does not, however, exempt it from the stringencies of bardic law. To conform to the pattern of *droighneach* each line must end in a trisyllable. The finals in 2 and 4 must make generic rhyme—*(dh)ionnmhuighe: (fh)iodhbhuidhe* (*nn* may rhyme with *dh* in a consonant cluster). The finals in 1 and 3 must consonate and must not assonate with the finals in 2 and 4. All the stressed words in 2 except the last must make generic rhyme with words in 1—*(f)oghar* (twice): *(f)oghar, ainglidhe:ainmhidhe, ēan:(n)ēal, (d)uille:uile* (a permissible rhyme). And, similarly, 4 must rhyme with 3—*(b)ūireadh:(d)ūileadh, (d)oimh:(s)oin, (dh)amhghoire:(d)aghruire, (f)oghar: (m)oladh.* In 2 and 4 at least the last two stressed words must alliterate—*duille, dhionnmhuighe; foghar, fhiodhbhuidhe.* In 1 and 3 at least two of the last three stressed words must alliterate —*uile, ainmhidhe; duileadh, daghruire.*

Since long measures like *droighneach* occur less frequently than the compact 7 or 8-syllable measures such as *rannaigheacht mhōr,* it seems apparent that most bards preferred to work under the more severe limitations of their miniaturist's art. Like the decorators of the *Book of Kells,* they found their satisfaction in challenging their ingenuity to fill each minute space in the most colorful, varied, and exhaustive manner possible.

Medieval Gaelic and Welsh verse was produced by professional poets who were schooled in their art for years. The earliest vernacular manuals of prosody known in Western Europe are the Ir., dating back to the end of the 8th c. (See Thurneysen, in *Göttingen Abhandlungen,* 14, no. 2, 78–89.) It is not surprising, therefore, that the prosodic complexities which the bards evolved have never been matched. Within the realm of European poetry, Norse skaldic verse alone approaches Celt. in intricacy, and the reason for its similarity probably lies in the fact that Norse poets attempted to emulate the traveling Ir. bards.

Aesthetic judgment of such poetry is consequently very difficult for those unused to its requirements. In their use of Eng. near-rhyme both Hopkins and Owen have imitated the resources of Celt. generic rhyme, but they have not really accustomed the modern reader to it, for they use such rhyme merely as an optional decoration, not as an unavoidable necessity, and they do not submit to any systematic rules. (For them *rob* would make an equally good rhyme with either *rod* or *rot*; for the Ir. bard only *rod* would be acceptable.) Mere metrical virtuosity will not make an otherwise poor poem remarkable; but a good poem written in the strict Celt. measures derives much of its force from the subtleties of its workmanship.

With the decline of the bardic orders in the Celt. countries, new and simpler meters emerged. In part these are the products of amateur versification, in part they may represent the dignification of popular and perhaps ancient song-meters hitherto unrecorded, and in part they certainly represent the adaptation of alien measures. When the secret of generic rhyme was lost, the most appealing device seems to have been assonance. Thus, in one of the songs of Geoffrey Keating (17th c.), which is typical of the new Ir. stressed verse known as *abhrān,* not only do the final stressed syllables assonate (as in the OF *laisse*), but all the others assonate in order, each of the first stressed syllables with one another, and each of the second, and the third, and the fourth:

Ōm sgeōl ăr ārd-mhāgh Fāil nī chŏdlāim
    ōidhchĕ,
'S dŏ bhreōdh gŏ brāth mē dāla ă pŏbuīl dīlīs.
Gīdh rō-fhāda atāid 'nă bhfāl rĕ brŏscăr bīodh-
    bhădh,
Fă dheōidh gŭr fhās ă lān dŏ'n chŏgāl trīothă.

(*Dánta. . . Sheathrúin Céitinn,* ed. E. C. mac Giolla Eáin [Dublin, 1900], no. 3; see Hyde, *Irish Poetry,* p. 128.)

Because of what I've heard about Fail's noble plain [Ireland] I cannot sleep at night, and it has crushed me utterly to think of her noble people. Though in the rampart they have stood too long facing a hostile rabble, enough of these tares at last have spread among them.

The assonance thus runs

$\bar{o}$--$\bar{a}$--$\bar{a}$--o--$\bar{i}$

through each line.

Since Keating's time some Gaelic poets have become satisfied to use only a single final assonance. In Wales, though *cynghanedd* is still practiced, many song writers have adopted the patterns familiar to rhymed, stressed Eng. poetry even in such nationalistic songs as the original Welsh version of *Men of Harlech.*

Wele goelcerth wen yn fflamio, a
A thafodau tân yn bloeddio a
Ar i'r dewrion ddod i daro a
Unwaith eto'n un. b
(Caradar, 3.68)

Lo, the beacon brightly flaming, and tongues of fire shouting to the brave ones to go once again to strike together.

Only in its alliteration (which is not fully reproduced in the familiar Eng. version of this song) does its prosody retain any peculiarly Celt. flavor. But the most notable mark of the Europeanizing of Celt. prosody lies in the fact that several of today's outstanding Celt. poets have written their best work in vers libre devoid of any of their traditional devices.

Irish: R. Thurneysen, "Entwicklung der irischen Metrik," *Revue celtique,* 6 (1884; on L. origin of Ir. rhyme), and "Mittelirische Verslehren," in *Irische Texte,* ed. W. Stokes and E. Windisch, III, pt. 1 (1891; cf. Königl. Gesellschaft der Wissenschaft zu Göttingen, Philol.-hist. Klasse, *Abhandlungen,* 14, no. 2, 78–89) (prosodic manuals 8th–11th c.); D. Hyde, *Ir. Poetry* (1902; partly outdated, but imitations in Eng. verse tr. are suggestive); K. Meyer, *A Primer of Ir. Metrics* (1909; still valuable but inadequate—see *Ériu,* 8 (1916), and "Ueber die älteste irische Dichtung," Königl. Preussische Akad. der Wissenschaften, Philos.-hist. Classe, *Abhandlungen,* Jahrg. 1913, nos. 6, 10 (early unrhymed and rhymed poetry 7th–8th c.); O. Bergin, "The Principles of Alliteration," *Ériu,* 9 (1921–23); *Tadhg̊ Dall Ó Huiginn,* ed. and tr. E. Knott (Ir. Texts Soc., 22–23, 1922–26; good introd. to bardic verse); E. Knott, *An Introd. to Ir. Syllabic Poetry* (1928, 2d ed, 1957; thorough and reliable), and *Ir. Classical Poetry* (1957); *Aithdioghluim Dána,* ed. and tr. L. McKenna (Ir. Texts Soc., 37, 40, 1939–40; wide variety of bardic meters, succinctly classified); G. Murphy, *Early Ir. Metrics* (1961); C. Watkins, "Indo-European Metrics and Archaic Ir. Verse," *Celtica,* 6 (1963; important discovery).

Scottish Gaelic: W. J. Watson, *Bardachd Ghaidhlig* (2d ed., 1932; important; though, for bardic rhyme, insufficient).

Welsh: J. Loth, *La métrique galloise* (2 v., 1900–1902; on all W. meters, including comparison with Cornish, Breton, and Ir.); J. Morris-Jones, *Cerdd Dafod* [Poetic Art] (1925; in W., indexed by G. Bowen, *Mynegai i Cerdd Dafod,* 1947); A.S.D. Smith (Caradar), *W. Made Easy,* III (n.d.; very helpful introd.); T. Parry, *A Hist. of W. Lit.,* tr. H. I. Bell (1955; appendices to several chapters discuss meters). C.W.D.

CENTO (L. "patchwork"). A poetic composition made up of passages selected from the work of some great poet of the past. Homer largely served this purpose in Gr. literature from the adaptations by Trygaeus of various lines in the *Iliad* and *Odyssey* (Aristophanes, *Peace* 1090–94) to the *Homerokentrones* of the Byzantine period. Similarly Virgil was the most popular source for centos in later Roman times. The oldest of those extant is the tragedy *Medea* by Hosidius Geta (2d c. A.D), while the *C. nuptialis* of Ausonius and the *C. Vergilianus* of Proba (4th c. A.D) are among others drawn from his work. Renaissance and later works of this kind included the It. *Petrarca spirituale* (1536) and the Eng. *Cicero princeps* (1608), which was a treatise, compiled from Cicero, on government. In the modern era may be mentioned a Shakespearean c. which appeared in *English* (Nov. 1919) and humorous centos which are occasionally published in popular literary reviews.—J. O. Delepierre, *Tableau de la littérature du centon chez les anciens et chez les modernes* (2 v. 1874–75); R. Lamacchia, "Dall'arte allusiva al centone," *Atene e Roma* n.s. 3 (1958). R.J.G.

CHANSO *(canso, chanson).* A love song, the literary genre *par excellence* among the Old Prov. poets. Its distinguishing characteristics are precisely the two great contributions of the troubadours to all subsequent European literature—a new conception of love involving the exaltation of the lady, and a constant striving for perfection and originality of form. It is impossible to draw a sharp line between the ch. and the older *vers;* but by the time the name ch. came into common use (toward the end of the 12th c.), the ideals of courtly love had become generally accepted and the technique of composition more polished, so that the ch. is apt to be more artistic, but also more conventional and artificial, than the *vers.* The typical ch. has 5 or 6 stanzas, of identical structure, plus an *envoi* (q.v.) or *tornada* (q.v.). Far from following any set metrical pattern, every ch. was expected to have a stanzaic structure and a tune that were completely original. This proved too high a hurdle for many poets, but the metrical diversity of the extant *chansos* is still very impressive. Unfortunately, the same cannot always be said for their contents, which often ring the changes on a few well-worn themes and situations. The poet's lady love is almost never named, and she is described in such vague generalities that an identification is ordinarily out of the question. The proper names used in a ch. (commonly in the *tornada)* are for the most part those of friends or patrons to whom the poem is dedicated.—Jeanroy, II. F.M.C.

CHANSONS DE GESTE is the term by which the OF epic poems relating the deeds of Charlemagne and his barons, or other feudal lords of the Carolingian era, were known in their time, principally the 12th and 13th c. "Geste" has, aside from the original sense of "deeds," additional senses of "history" and "historical document," and by further extension it comes to mean "family, lineage." Upward of eighty of the poems survive, in whole or in part, in existing mss., some of them in several redactions. They celebrate heroic actions, historical or pseudo-historical, and the chivalric ideals of a Christian, monarchical, and feudal France. Critics have not succeeded in reaching firm conclusions as to whether the ideological preoccupations are primarily those of Carolingian times or of the period of the Crusades and 12th-c. France. The history is at best considerably overlaid with legend, and many of the epics are largely or wholly fictitious, reworking the themes made popular by the earlier poems. This is particularly true where the taste for the romantic and the fantastic nurtured by the romances imitated from Gr. and L. antiquity, the Arthurian romances, and folklore was carried over into the invention of plots for the epics: this hybrid type is best illustrated by poems like *Huon de Bordeaux, Renaud de Montauban,* and *Le Chevalier au Cygne.*

CYCLES. Several more or less well-defined groups of these poems may be distinguished. The most cohesive of these (24 poems) is the cycle of Guillaume d'Orange, to be identified with the historical Count Guillaume de Toulouse, contemporary of Charlemagne, and in which are recounted his deeds and those of his six brothers, his nephews, particularly Vivien and Bertrand, his father Aymeri de Narbonne, and others of his line. The principal poems of this cycle are *Le Couronnement de Louis, Le Charroi de Nîmes, La Prise d'Orange, Le Couvenant Vivien, La Chanson de Guillaume, Aliscans, Le Moniage Guillaume,* and *Aymeri de Narbonne.*

The so-called cycle of Charlemagne is less extensive and less unified. To it are assigned the poems treating of Charlemagne's wars (*La Chanson de Roland, Aspremont, Les Saxons*) or of his youth (*Mainet*) or of earlier royal heroes such as *Floövant,* son of Clovis. One of these is the partly comic *Pèlerinage de Charlemagne,* which includes the description of a highly fanciful visit to the court of the Emperor of Constantinople.

The third main group has as its common element the theme of a feudal lord's revolt, usually provoked by an act of injustice, against his *seigneur,* who is in several cases Charlemagne, as in *Girart de Roussillon* (the only *chanson de geste* surviving in a dialect of the *langue d'oc*), *La Chevalerie Ogier de Danemarche, Renaud de Montauban,* known also as *Les Quatre fils Aymon,* and *Huon de Bordeaux.* In the oldest poem of this group, the 11th-c. *Gormont et Isembart,* surviving only in a fragment, the renegade Isembart fights against his lord King Louis III. *Raoul de Cambrai* relates the sombre violence of feudal warfare following a forcible dispossession. The unforgiving bitterness of struggle between two great families is the subject of a minor cycle, *Les Lorrains,* of which the principal poems are *Garin le Lorrain* and *Hervis de Metz.*

LA CHANSON DE ROLAND. *La Chanson de Roland* is the masterpiece of the genre and the earliest surviving example, composed most likely in the second half of the 11th c. in continental France and preserved in an Anglo-Norman manuscript of the mid-12th c. (Oxford version). Later versions lengthen the poem and insert additional episodes. The historical event on which the poem is based is the annihilation of Charlemagne's rear guard under Count Roland while recrossing the Pyrenees after an expedition against Saragossa in 778. In the poem the attackers are referred to as Saracens, whereas they were in all probability Basques, and a succession of councils is related, leading to the decision to leave Spain. A traitor Ganelon is introduced, as Roland's stepfather, who urges the Saracens to attack the rear guard in revenge for Roland's having designated him for the perilous embassy to the enemy camp. The disaster is assured when Roland overconfidently refuses to call back Charlemagne by sounding his horn when attacked, in spite of the urgings of his companion Oliver. After the defeat at Roncevaux, the poem ends with another battle in which Charlemagme is victorious, and with the trial and execution of Ganelon.

The *Chanson de Roland* is remarkable for the ideals it exalts—unstinting devotion to God and to feudal lord, and to the fatherland, "douce France,"—for its vigorous and incisive portrayals of great characters, closely knit structure, elevation of tone, and firm, concise language.

FORM, VERSIFICATION, STYLE. The usual line is of 10 syllables, with caesura after the fourth, not counting a possible unstressed syllable with schwa-vowel after the accented tenth syllable or after the accented fourth. Among the earlier epics the 8-syllable or the 12-syllable line may be used (*Gormont et Isembart, Pèlerinage de Charlemagne*). The strophic form is that of the *laisse,* a variable number of lines bound together by the same assonance in the earlier poems, by rhyme in later ones. In the *Chanson de Roland* the *laisses* average 14 lines in length; in later poems they tend to be much longer. In length, the *c.d.g.* range from about a thousand lines (*Pèlerinage de Charlemagne*) to 10,000 lines and over; the *Chanson de Roland* has 4,000 in the Oxford version. As their name would indicate, the *c.d.g.* were sung, and the notation of some music has been preserved.

In coherence of composition, the epics vary greatly, from well-knit poems like the *Chanson de*

Roland or the *Pèlerinage de Charlemagne* to rambling and even self-contradictory successions of episodes. The style is vigorous and stamped with the mark of talent in the best poems, but diffuse and filled with *clichés* ("epic formulas") in the poorer ones. The use of *clichés* has been used by some scholars as an argument for the theory that the epics were improvised orally by the performing *jongleur.*

ORIGINS. The debate over the origins and the prehistory of the *c.d.g.* has been, for three-quarters of a century, the outstanding controversy in Fr. medieval literary history. In the 19th c. it was customary to consider the surviving *chansons* as deriving ultimately from poems inspired by contemporary historical events, constantly altered and expanded in the course of oral transmission through two, three, or even four centuries. At the beginning of the 20th c., J. Bédier denied the continuity of transmission and argued to reduce the historic content of the poems to a few data discovered by jongleur-poets in sanctuaries along the pilgrimage routes in the 11th and 12th c. Bédier's "individualism," as it has been called, has increasingly been subject to massive attack by numerous scholars who have revived the older view and buttressed it with new "traditionalist" arguments. It is principally around the *Chanson de Roland* that controversy wages, according to the degree of originality the critic is willing to ascribe to the author of the Oxford version. Traditionalists see him as a mere arranger of a poem with a long prehistory of collective elaboration, an intermediate group see his sources in medieval L. hagiography or epic, while "individualists" minimize his debt to hypothetical predecessors and credit him with the largest possible measure of creativeness.

DIFFUSION. The *c.d.g.* early became popular outside their own domain of northern France and Norman England, being translated notably into Middle High German and Old-Norse-Icelandic. In Italy they were made accessible in an Italianized Fr. before serving as the inspiration for wholly It. poems. They were known in Spain, where, however, national epic heroes were preferred. In France, the 15th and 16th c. knew the epic legends through prose adaptations, before these in turn were forgotten through two and a half centuries of classicism.

In spite of its age and the obsolescence of many of the views expressed, the best general reference is still L. Gautier's *Epopées françaises,* to be consulted in the 2d ed., 4 v., 1878–92, supplemented by his *Bibliographie des c.d.g.*, 1897. J. Bédier's celebrated *Légendes épiques*, 4 v., 1908–13, repr. 1914–21 and 1926–29, is not a general history of the *genre,* but a series of studies which constitute a sweeping criticism of the theory of historical continuity. M. de Riquer's *C.d.g. françaises* (1957), the 2d ed. and tr. of a work originally publ. in Sp., is a very good recent general study, treating at length the most important poems. P. Le Gentil's concise *Chanson de Roland* (1955) is the best and most recent introduction to the study of this poem. Questions of text and prehistory are extensively examined in J. Horrent, *La Chanson de Roland dans les littératures française et espagnole au moyen age* (1951) and M. Delbouille, *Sur la genèse de la Chanson de Roland* (1954). A compendious *état présent* is furnished by A. Junker, "Stand der Forschung zum Rolandslied," *Germanisch-Romanische Monatsschrift,* 1956.

The arguments for oral transmission with free improvisation of the *c.d.g.* are given by J. Rychner in *La C.d.g.: essai sur l'art épique des jongleurs* (1955), and more briefly in an article in *La Table Ronde* (Dec. 1958). Rychner's views are subjected to close scrutiny and criticism in a study by M. Delbouille, "Les C.d.g. et le livre," in Liège. Université. Faculte de philosophie et lettres. *La Technique littéraire des c.d.g. Actes du Colloque de Liège,* Sept. 1957. (1959). *Les Origines des c.d.g.* by I. Siciliano (1951), the 2d, rev. ed. of the original in It., is a brilliant critique of origintheories. R. Menéndez Pidal's *La Chanson de Roland et la tradition épique des Francs* (1960), a 2d, rev. ed. of a work first publ. in Sp., is a substantial defense of the neotraditionalist view of Roland origins.

In 1955 the Société Rencesvals was founded at Pamplona for the study of the Romance epic. Communications delivered at meetings of the society have been publ. in *Coloquios de Roncesvalles* (Saragossa, 1956), v. 3 of *Cahiers de civilisation médiévale,* and v. 21 of *Cultura Neolatina.* The society publ. an occasional *Bulletin bibliographique* (1958, 1960, 1963–).

Ample bibliographical treatment will be found in *A Crit. Bibliog. of Fr. Lit.* (D. C. Cabeen, general ed.), I, *The Mediaeval Period,* ed. by U. T. Holmes, Jr., 2d ed., 1952, and more fully in R. Bossuat, *Manuel bibliographique de la littérature française du moyen âge* (1951) and its two supplements (1955, 1961). C.A.K.

CHANT (OF *chanter,* L. *cantare,* "to sing"). (1) Any song or melody: the "Chant of tuneful birds," *Paradise Regained* 2. 290. (2) Sometimes the actual melody to which the Psalms, Canticles, etc. are sung. (3) Or the Psalm or Canticle itself. (4) A poem intended to be chanted rather than sung or read, as especially those of W. B. Yeats or Vachel Lindsay:

Booth led boldly with his big bass drum . . .
(*General William Booth Enters Into Heaven*)

Chants are most commonly found in liturgical services. The Anglican chants, which have doubtless influenced secular poetry intended to be recited in a similar fashion, derive from the Gregorian, the plain song or *cantus firmus* used in Roman ritual and named for Pope Gregory.

When a poem is set to music, the rhythm is controlled by the music, but when it is chanted the musical elements are subordinated to the ver bal. Chanting gives verse a "hieratic quality, removing it from the language of common speech, and it thereby increases the exhilaration of poetry, bringing it nearer to the sphere of the heroic . . ." (N. Frye, "Introd.: Lexis and Melos," *Sound and Poetry,* 1957). See also SONG. R.O.E.

CHANT ROYAL. One of the most complex and difficult of the OF verse forms. Related to the ballade (q.v.), the c.r. in its most common form (as described in the 14th c. by Eustache Deschamps) consists of 5 stanzas of 11 lines each, rhyming ababccddedE, followed by an *envoi* (q.v.), rhyming ddedE. It is further distinguished by the use of a refrain—as indicated by the capital letters—at the end of each stanza, including the last line of the *envoi,* and by the fact that, except in the *envoi,* no rhyme words may be used twice. Thus, 60 lines must be rhymed on 5 rhyme sounds, a formidable technical task. Perhaps the technical challenge of c.r. explains the regal element in its name, but it is more likely that it is called "royal" because of its address to the "prince" presiding over a *puy,* or poetic contest. In addition to Deschamps, who composed numerous *chants royaux,* Charles d'Orléans, Jean Marot, and, especially, his son Clément excelled in the use of the form.

Ironically, this most solemn and grandiose of the Fr. forms has had the fate, in the 19th and 20th c., of being employed almost solely as *vers de société* by such light poets as Richard Le Gallienne and Don Marquis.—Kastner; Patterson.

CHIASMUS (Gr. "a placing crosswise," from the name of the Gr. letter X, "chi"; L. *decussatio,* from the symbol X for ten, "decem"). According to the Gr. rhetorician Hermogenes (2d c. A.D), the pattern of a sentence consisting of two main clauses, each modified by a subordinate clause, in which sentence each of the subordinate clauses could apply to each of the main clauses, so that the order of these four members could be altered in several ways without change in the meaning of the whole (*Peri heureseōn,* i.e., *On Invention* 4.3, in C. Walz, *Rhetores Graeci,* 9 v., 1832–36, v. 3, p. 157), e.g. "Pardon me, God, I knew not what I did! / And pardon, father, for I knew not thee!" (*Henry VI,* part 3, 2.5.69–70). C. has been more recently defined as the criss-cross placing of sentence members that correspond in either syntax or meaning, with or without word repetition (*Oxford Dictionary*; Lausberg), e.g., "With comely haveour and count'nance sage" (*The Faerie Queene* 3.12.3.8).

The similar figure *antimetabole* (Gr. "transposition," apparently first recorded in Quintilian), though Quintilian defines it merely as a figure of words "repeated with variations in case or tense," is illustrated by him with examples in which two words of the early part of a sentence are later repeated in reverse order, e.g., "Non ut edam vivo, sed ut vivam edo" (*Institutes of Oratory,* 1st c. A.D, 9.3.85); and it is primarily this symmetrical pattern of word repetition (abba) that the term *antimetabole* is most often made to designate by later authorities, e.g., John Hoskins, *Directions for Speech and Style,* ca. 1599 (ed. of 1935, p. 14), John Smith, *The Mysterie of Rhetorique Unvailed,* 1657, and others, most of whose illustrations are from prose. A clear example from Eng. poetry can be seen in the final line of Shakespeare's 154th Sonnet: "Love's fire heats water, water cools not love."

It would seem convenient to use the term "c." for the criss-cross order and correspondence in meaning or syntax of two pairs of words, whether or not involving word repetition, and restrict *antimetabole* to the narrower meaning of a pair of words repeated (usually with some morphological change) in reverse order. H.B.

"CHICAGO CRITICS, THE." See POETRY, THEORIES OF (OBJECTIVE THEORIES).

CHORIAMB (Gr. "consisting of a choree [i.e., a trochee] and an iamb"). A metrical unit of the structure –⏑⏑–, frequently found in Gr. dramatic choruses and lyric verse and used often by Sappho, Alcaeus and, in L. poetry, by Horace. It is found mostly in combination with other units, e.g., in glyconics and asclepiads (qq.v.) but is sometimes pure as

deīnă mĕn ōun, | deīnă tărāss | eī sŏphŏs ōi |
ônŏthĕtās
(Sophocles, *Oedipus Tyrannus* 484)

Some assign it a far greater role in the rationalization of Gr. lyric, either considering it (with Wilamowitz) the basic element in a widespread "choriambic dimeter" whose first foot can evidently be almost anything, or (with Dale) holding it and its resolutions to be one of the two basic "building blocks" of any lyric. In an accentual form, the c. has been used in modern languages, e.g., in German (Goethe's *Pandora,* written in choriambic dimeters) and in Eng. Its occurrence in Eng. verse is fairly rare, but undoubted, varying from single lines such as Marvell's

/ x x / | / x x /
Lilies without, | roses within

(*The Nymph and her Fawn*) to Swinburne's protracted use in his *Choriambics.*—U. v. Wilamowitz-Moellendorff, *Griechische Verskunst* (1921; 2d ed., 1958); E. W. Scripture, "The Choriambus in Eng. Verse," PMLA, 43 (1928); Hamer; A. M. Dale, "The Metrical Units of Gr. Lyric Verse," CQ, 44 (1950) and CQ, n.s. 1 (1951); Koster; E. Martin, *Essai sur les rhythmes de la chanson grecque antique* (1953). D.S.P.

CHORUS (Gr. *choreuein,* "to dance"). Presumably, Gr. tragedy somehow arose from, or in conjunction with, the lyric and religious performances of a ch. of masked and singing dancers. But despite the crucial bond between tragedy and its characteristic ch. (no extant 5th-c. tragedy lacks a fully developed ch.), our information is lamentably scanty. The following facts, however, deserve mention. (1) The tragic ch., rectangular in formation and often military in movement, is *not* to be confused with the "cyclical" ch. of dithyramb. (2) The early number of the ch. is said (on flimsy evidence and by an improbable analogy with the dithyrambic ch.) to have been 50; Aeschylus (cf. *Agamemnon* 1347–1371) used 12 and Sophocles is said to have raised the number to 15. (3) Choral odes (including *kommoi*) were *sung* by all or part of the ch., while the lines of the *coryphaeus* (or chorus leader) were *spoken.* (4) The expenses of training the ch. were assigned by the state to a wealthy man (called the *choregus*), and the "giving of a chorus" by the archon constituted the poet's official admission to the tragic contest.

Both tragedy and ch. appear to have been religious in origin. However, whereas tragedy and comedy in the later 5th c. became secularized as they lost touch with their ritual origins, the ch. remained the conservative soul of the play, the articulate spokesman for traditional religion and society, clinging stubbornly to the forms and wisdom and even the style of the worshipping group from which it arose. This conservative element is visible not only in the elaborately figured archaic lyrics with their "poetic" syntax and heavy load of Doricisms in sharp contrast to the more colloquial dialogue, but in the traditionalism of its moral beliefs, its conventional theodicy, and its commitment to proverbial social wisdom. And so the normal mode of choral utterance is a characteristic group speech, of great power but often limited precision, rising from sheer banality to the apocalyptic gnomic richness of the Aeschylean ch. Dramatists might adapt the ch. to their practical needs by making it serve such simple functions as spectacle, widening emotional range etc., but they seem to have found it difficult to alter this communal and traditionalizing role of the ch. There is, however, little tension between the nature of the ch. and the dramatist's needs until the time of Euripides. But as Olympian religion declined and the old social order went under in the convulsions of the late 5th c., the ch. lost the context that gave it life as a convention, and in post-Euripidean tragedy appears to have been degraded to ornament. According to Aristotle, it was in the 4th c. that the practice arose of writing choral odes that had little or nothing to do with the play.

Conservatism was strengthened by function. For the ch. attends the action as a dependent society in miniature, giving the public resonance of individual action. Thus the ch. exults, fears, wonders, mourns, and attempts, out of its store of traditional moralities, to cope with an action whose meaning is both difficult and unfamiliar. By so doing, the ch. generalizes the meaning of the action and at the same time the action revives and refreshes the choral wisdom. But almost never is the chorus' judgment of events authoritative; if it is an intruded voice, it is normally the voice of tradition, not the dramatist. In Aeschylus perhaps the ch. is least fallible, but in both Aeschylus and Sophocles the ch. tends to lag behind the meaning implicit in the action; that lag is the secret of the chorus' *dramatic* power and the means whereby the tension between the tragic hero and his society is made clear. Euripides, less easy with tradition and hence self-conscious, tends to rely on his ch. more for poetic intensity than dramatic tension (though in no Gr. play is the ch. so fully and ironically exploited against tradition as in the *Bacchae*).

The power of the choral convention explains why the ch. has been so constantly revived in subsequent literature—in the undramatic virtuoso choruses of Seneca; in Milton's *Samson Agonistes,* formally and dramatically the most perfect Gr. choruses in Eng.; in the quasi-Euripidean ch. of Fr. tragedy; in the cosmic choruses of Shelley and Goethe, and finally in the remarkable ch. of Eliot's *Murder in the Cathedral,* to mention but one of the many modern attempts to resuscitate the choral convention. But with almost all of these revivals, no matter how remarkable the mastery, the choral convention has failed somehow to flourish, or flourished only as a literary and archaic device, deprived of the context and ground that in the Gr. theatre gave it a natural rightness. Only Eliot, by placing his ch. within the context of a religious society in the dramatic act of worship, has overcome the difficulties, but the limits imposed by such a context must prove unacceptable to a living and secular theatre.—A. E. Haigh, *The Tragic Drama of the Greeks* (1896); R. C. Flickinger, *The Gr. Theater and Its Drama* (1916); A. W. Pickard-Cambridge, *Dithyramb, Tragedy and Comedy* (1927) and *The Dramatic Festivals of Athens* (1953); T.B.L. Webster, *Gr. Theater Production* (1956); M. Bieber, *The Hist. of the Gr. and Roman Theater* (2d ed., rev. 1961). W.A.

CHRISTABEL METER. The meter of Coleridge's *Christabel* (free, 4-stress couplets, generally iambic or anapestic, but with frequent substitution). In his preface to the poem Coleridge made three claims: 1. that the meter is based not on a count of syllables, but on a count of accents ("in each line the accents will be found to be only four"); 2. that this is a new principle; 3. that the length of line varies with the passion. As various critics have said, the principle was not new. Coleridge assumed that previous poets had measured their lines by counting syllables (as in Fr. and It. verse), but this is not quite true, for from the earliest times *native* Eng. verse had been accentual, as in the long line of *Beowulf.* With Chaucer there seems to have been a blend of the two systems, accentual and syllabic.

What makes *Christabel* meter different is that in a few places Coleridge went the whole way and reduced the line to 4 syllables only—monosyllabic feet, as in the much-cited *Break, break, break* of Tennyson. As to the success of the handling of the accentual meter in *Christabel*, Bridges' charge seems unanswerable that Coleridge never shook off the tradition of conventional metric stress, as opposed to word or sense stress. Thus, in important respects *Christabel* does not provide a good example of accentual prosody. One might also question the appropriateness of the particular usage of the meter in *Christabel* in relation to its theme and tone. Nevertheless, there is little doubt that the meter was an important milestone on the road to some of the most important accentual experiments and successes of succeeding times.—Saintsbury, *Prosody;* R. Bridges, *Milton's Prosody* (1921); A. R. Morris, *The Orchestration of the Metrical Line* (1923); A.L.F. Snell, "The Meter of Christabel," in *The Fred Newton Scott Anniversary Papers* (1929). R.BE.

CLASSICAL METERS IN MODERN LANGUAGES. The ancient Gr. poet marked his arsis and thesis (q.v.) by variance in voice pitch. The "pitch accent" reflected syllable quantity: a syllable was "long" if its vowel was long or diphthongized or if its vowel was short and followed by two consonants (including, in the case of a final syllable, the initial consonant of a following word); a syllable was "short" if its vowel was short and followed by a single consonant sound (see CLASSICAL PROSODY). Vowel quantity can be illustrated by the word *"ibidem"*: the first *i* is short, the second long (by classical standards); in pronunciation the two sounds would correspond respectively to the first and second *i* of "intrigue." (Similarly using the macron (–) to indicate length and the micron (⏑) to indicate brevity:

> măchine, fāther, mĕt, mēet; ŏbey, mōle, pŭt,
> clūe.)

The Gr. quantitative pitch accent was succeeded by the L. quantitative stress accent, in tune with L. speech and early L. verse patterns, e.g., the Saturnian; this succession partially anticipated the full (nonquantitative) stress accent of medieval L. and modern European poetry.

The stress accent of modern languages, including Fr., makes it practically impossible, except by sheer artifice, to divide syllables into "longs" and "shorts." Modern versification depends upon syllable-counting (syllabic verse: flexible in Eng. and German, rigid in Polish and Fr.) and the occurrence of naturally stressed syllables (accentual verse). In Eng. and German the stressed syllables usually alternate with unstressed syllables; in Fr. they occur at the verse's caesura and end. It is safe to say that no modern language approximation to quantitative verse has been completely successful. The most that can be said for Robert Bridges' experiments with Eng. syllable quantities, in testing the theories of his friend W. J. Stone, is that quantity and stress coincide rather frequently. But "quantity" in Eng. is considerably erratic. Except for accent stress, the sounds *e* and *ie* in "believe" are quantitatively equal. But in a *scazon* verse Bridges scans the word as

> bĕlīeve,

quantitatively invalid, but in keeping with modern stress. Modern language accent stress frequently determines vowel "quantity." In L. and Gr. the reverse is true. Some modern language syllables, when recorded on the kymograph, prove to be six times as "long" as others. Consonant clusters in the modern languages, with the exception of, e.g., It. and Sp., neither regularly render actual syllable quantity (except as in "below" and "bellow") nor regularly determine accent.

Generally, a modern approximation of a cl. meter involves the substitution of stress for quantity. Longfellow's

> ´ × × ´ × × ´ × × ´ × ×
> This is the forest primeval. The murmuring
> ´ × × ´ ´
> pines and the hemlocks

would scan, according to quantitative principles alone, something like this: ⏑–⏑⏑–––– ⏑–⏑––––⏑––. A dactyl, then, in the cl. situation, consists of a long syllable followed by 2 short syllables (–⏑⏑); in the modern situation it consists of a stressed syllable followed by 2 unstressed syllables (´××).

The earliest recorded attempt at quantitative "versing" in Fr. is the elegiac couplet written by Estienne Jodelle in 1558:

> Phēbŭs, Āmoŭr, Cȳprĭs, veut sauvēr, nōurrīr ĕt
> ōrnĕr
> Tōn vērs cuer ēt chēf, d'ōmbrĕ, dĕ flāmmĕ,
> dĕ flēurs.

As in all such modern attempts it is not quantity as such, but coincidence of accent with "quantity" that marks the scheme. In or about 1567 Antoine de Baïf attempted to classify syllables as "longs" and "shorts" in effecting various "quantitative" strophes, such as the sapphic. His effort forced him to adopt phonetic spelling.

In 1555 Conrad Gessner, a German Swiss, produced a *Mithridates* in spondaic hexameters. Phrases like alle die / eere

show how questionable his "quantity" is. But his accent coincidence is quite regular. Dean W. R. Inge quotes Goethe's "pentameter" line,

Rothstrumpf immer gehasst und Violetstrumpf
dazu

and rightly asks "If the vowel of *strumpf* is not long by position [i.e., followed by more than one consonant] what vowel can be?"

The Renaissance *literati,* in exalting, discovering, and reexamining literary products of the cl. world, were seriously concerned with the reproduction of cl. quantitative meters. Successful reproduction was limited, however, to the L. language itself, e.g., Petrarca's unfinished and unpublished *Africa* and the *Davidiad* of Marco Marulo (1450–1524) in 14 books. The vernacular languages did not and could not sustain quantitative distinctions. In Spain Estéban de Villegas produced sapphics and hexameters by substituting stress for quantity. Gabriello Chiabrera similarly attempted cl. meters, including the sapphic, in It. In France Ronsard and the Pléiade imitated Horace and translated his quantitative L. odes into stress-accentual Fr. verse. The Renaissance spirit of classicism is reintroduced into It. by the 19th-c. poet, Giosuè Carducci, whose *Odi barbari* (init. 1887) include cl. meters in stress-accentual modern It.

Rus. poetry does not originate before the post-Renaissance period (ca. 1650). There have not been many attempts made in Rus. to reproduce cl. quantitative meters. The "learned" meters include binary iambics and trochaics and ternary dactylics, amphibrachics (⏑–́⏑) and anapaestics. Rus. verse disallows feet of more than 3 syllables (e.g., the proceleusmatic, ⏑⏑⏑⏑).

Likewise stress-accentual is the meter in the modern Gr. "sequel" to the *Odyssey* by Nikos Kazantzakis. His verse measure comprises 17 syllables and 8 stresses. Traditionally, the modern Gr. verse measure comprises 15 syllables and 7 stresses. Kazantzakis achieved a closer approximation to the Homeric hexameters (5 dactyls and a spondee = 17 syllables) in the matter of syllabism but did not minimize the force of stress.

Early attempts to introduce quantitative verse into Eng. were mediocre at best. (See Thomas Watson's hexameter version of the first two lines of the *Odyssey,* noted by Roger Ascham in *The Scholemaster,* 1570.) In the discussion between Edmund Spenser and Gabriel Harvey the great problem began to appear: Should "length" be determined by cl. rules or by ear? Poetically, a high point of Eng. experiment in cl. meters was reached in the examples (especially "Rose-cheeked Laura") offered by Thomas Campion to illustrate his modified cl. system based on stress-equivalents to cl. feet (1602).

In the middle of the 17th c. John Milton "rendred almost word for word without Rhyme according to the Latin Measure [third asclepiadic strophe], as near as the Language will permit" an Eng. version of Horace's Ode 1.5:

Quis multa gracilis te puer in rosa

His first line, "What slender youth bedew'd with liquid odours," is not "according to the Latin Measure" of the poem, since it is more nearly an accentual approximation of the choliambic line. Possibly "without Rhyme . . . Measure" means simply "without rhyme as in Latin poetry"; but Horace's ode presents skillfully wrought internal rhyme. Milton's impatience with quantitative "versing" is expressed in his sonnet to Mr. H. Lawes. Of the many experiments in Eng. during the 19th c. none fully reproduced its cl. exemplar. Tennyson, intensely concerned with syllable quantity, concluded that the Eng. hexameter was "only fit for comic subjects." He comments accordingly in one of his humorous elegiac distichs:

These lame hexameters the strong-wing'd
music of Homer!
No—but a most burlesque barbarous experiment.

The proper accents of "hexameters" and "experiment" have been sacrificed in the interest of "quantity." A. H. Clough used a stress-accentual hexameter for light effect:

Tea and coffee were there; a jug of water for
Hewson. . . .

Swinburne's stress-accentual choriambics, sapphics, hendecasyllabics, and elegiacs show no concession to quantity. Both Tennyson and George Meredith imitated Catullus' galliambic. Tennyson's version is the more rigidly "quantitative": e.g.,

Mad and maddening all that heard her in her
fierce volubility.

His quantitative alcaic ode to Milton, e.g.

Whose Titan angels, Gabriel, Abdiel . . .
Rings to the roar of an angel onset

is perhaps as close to perfection as any Eng. poet has come in this endeavor. The 20th c. has seen no Tennysonian concern for quantitative cl.-verse equivalents. But accentual cl.-verse equivalents are still, indeed perennially, attempted, primarily in translation, e.g., J. B. Leishman's

Horace, Helen R. Henze's *The Odes of Horace* (1961), and Rolfe Humphries' Ovid (*The Art of Love,* 1957).

STUDIES OF CLASSICAL METRICS: W. Christ, *Metrik der Griechen und Römer* (1874); J.H.H. Schmidt, *Introd. to the Rhythmic and Metric of the Cl. Languages,* tr. J. W. White (1883); Hardie; Dale; W. Rupprecht, *Einführung in die griechische Metrik* (3d ed., 1950); Kolář; Crusius; U. v. Wilamowitz-Moellendorff, *Griechische Verskunst* (2d ed., 1958); G. Thomson, *Gr. Lyric Metre* (2d ed., 1961).—MODERN LANGUAGES: Kastner; Schipper; W. R. Inge, "Cl. Metres in Eng. Poetry," Royal Soc. of Lit. of the United Kingdom, *Transactions,* 3d ser., 2 (1922); R. C. Trevelyan, "Cl. and Eng. Verse-Structure," E&S, 16 (1930); J. Körner, *Einführung in die Poetik* (1949); G. L. Hendrickson, "Elizabethan Quantitative Hexameters," PQ, 28 (1949); V. Turri, U. Renda, P. Operti, *Dizionario storico della letteratura italiana* (3d ed., 1951–52); R. Graves, "Harp, Anvil, Oar," *The Crowning Privilege* (1955); B. O. Unbegaun, *Rus. Versification* (1956); Beare; J. B. Leishman, *Translating Horace* (1958); J. Thompson, *The Founding of Eng. Metre* (1961); W. Bennett, *German Verse in Cl. Metres* (1963). R.A.S.

CLASSICAL PROSODY is, with respect to Gr. and L., the science which deals with the nature of syllables, whereas meter is the technique of their arrangement. In its technical sense Gr. *prosōdia* (L. *accentus*) meant primarily accentuation as determined, in Gr. at any rate, by musical pitch; but the scope of the word was subsequently extended, and prosody is now regarded as describing the facts concerning the "quantities" of syllables, i.e., the time taken to pronounce them. Quantity, not stress, was the basis of cl. Gr. and L. metric, with the possible exception of the Saturnian measure in early L. Syllables were regularly either long (–) or short (⏑), the latter quantity being the time unit (Gr. *chronos*, L. *mora*), and a long syllable was conventionally regarded as equivalent in time value to two shorts (– = ⏑⏑). As variations of this simple "disemic" scheme, syllables with greater or less length than either quantity have been postulated in modern times on the ground that syllabic irrationality was apparently recognized in antiquity, not indeed by metricians, but in rhythmical and musical theory. But while the hypothesis of the existence of such irrational syllables in metric was acceptable to scholars of the 19th c. who tried to explain Gr. lyric meters in the light of their own conjectures about the accompanying music, it has little favor with the modern school which adheres to the "graphic" prosody of the long and short syllables of spoken verse. (See MORA.)

Most Am., British, and German metricians, accustomed as they are to stress accent in their own languages, maintain that the L. accent was similar, and many have held that coincidences or clashes of *ictus* (q.v.) and accent were intentional in certain writers (e.g., Plautus and Virgil). But the existence of a pitch accent is arguable from the testimony of the Romans themselves, and Fr. scholars, with the example of their own language before them, are convinced that such was the nature of the L. accent, at any rate during the literary period. Whichever it was, in cl. and post cl. L. it conformed to the "penultimate law," whereby the accent of a dissyllabic word fell on its first syllable, while a polysyllabic word was accented on its last syllable but one if this was long, and on the syllable before that if the penultimate was short.

A syllable containing a short vowel was normally short if the vowel was followed by a single consonant either in the same word or at the beginning of the next, or by no consonant at all. In L. *qu* was regarded as a single consonant, *h* was ignored metrically as being no more than an aspirate [as in transliterated Gr.], and occasionally, in the republican period, a final *s* preceded by short *i* or *u* was disregarded if the following word began with a consonant, e.g.

mēntĭbŭs[s] cāptī.

On the other hand a syllable was long by nature if it contained a long vowel or diphthong, and long by position if its vowel, being short, was followed either by a double consonant (zeta, xi, or psi in Gr. or *x* or *z* in L.), or by two or more consonants. However, since a mute and a liquid consonant in sequence (like *gr, pl, pr,* etc.) could be pronounced together, a syllable containing a short vowel which immediately preceded such a combination in the same word or at the beginning of the next might remain short or be scanned as long in verse (except that of Gr. comedy and early Roman tragedy and comedy where it was not lengthened), e.g.

ā̆grestis

If, however, the mute and the liquid belonged to separate words or to separate parts of a compound word, the syllable was long by position, e.g.

incumbīt ripis, ōb-ruit

The varying quantity before a mute and a liquid is sometimes referred to as *syllaba anceps* (syllable with two possibilities), but the term is usually applied to the particular case where the final syllable of a verse was permitted to be either short or long.

Metricians and linguists, with the support of ancient authorities like Dionysius of Halicarnassus (1st c. B.C), generally maintain that a syllable with a short vowel is long if it is "closed," i.e., ends with a consonant (or consonants) not belonging to the next syllable. This is so with the first (or more) of a group of consonants which, in their respective languages, cannot normally begin a Gr. or L. word, e.g., the syllables of *am | bo, an | trum,* or *sanc | tus* must be divided as shown. A double consonant is divisible between two syllables (e.g., $x = c + s$) and the combination of mute and liquid in the same word may be divided or not as occasion demands. But a single consonant between two vowels is assumed to belong to the syllable containing the second and (as a rule) at the end of a word to be theoretically transferable to the first syllable of the next word in the same verse, if this word has an initial vowel or diphthong, without regard to the intervening punctuation. Thus in the division of feet within the L. hexameter

ēxsĕquă|r. hānc ĕtĭ|ām, Maē|cēnā|s, āspĭcĕ| pārtēm

the final consonants of the first and fourth words belong respectively to the first syllables of the second and fifth feet. But the occasional retention of the final consonant with the word to which it belongs is at least a mechanical explanation of the not infrequent lengthening in hexameters of short syllables in the first place or "rise" of the feet to which they belong, e.g.

ipse ubi tempus erīt omnis in fonte lavabo.

The treatment in syllable division of the final consonant of a word is thus parallel to the functioning of vowel elision and hiatus. Elision occurred in Gr. when a word which began with a vowel or diphthong was preceded by another which ended with a short vowel other than *y* (or, on occasion, with the diphthongs *ai* and *oi*) and the first vowel (or diphthong) disappeared in the second. In L. verse it was usual for a vowel or diphthong (or for a short vowel followed by *m* which presumably nasalized it) to be likewise elided, although some scholars, particularly in continental Europe, prefer to apply the cl. term *synaloepha* (coalescing) to describe what happens to a long vowel or diphthong in elision. In written Gr., but not L., elision is regularly indicated by omitting the elided vowel and inserting an apostrophe, e.g., *legoim' an* for *legoimi an.* Hiatus on the other hand occurred when the final and the initial vowel or diphthong remained separated each in its own syllable, particularly when there was a recognized metrical division or sense-pause between them. A strong sense-pause, however, was not an obstacle to elision, which might take place even when there was simultaneously a change of speaker in drama. An example, first of elision and then of hiatus, is provided by the L. hexameter:

ūt vĭ|di (elision or *synaloepha* of the final *i*),

ūt pĕrĭ|ī (hiatus), *ūt|mē mălŭ|s ābstŭlĭ|t ērrōr.*

In Gr. metric, when a short initial vowel was absorbed into a long vowel or diphthong at the end of the preceding word, this occurrence is called *aphaeresis* or prodelision and was especially common in dramatic verse. Akin to elision and prodelision are *crasis* and *synizesis* or the combination of two separate vowels within a word into one, e.g.,

dēinde for *dĕīnde.*

In L. the shortening, without elision or *synaloepha,* of a long before a short vowel in the next word, e.g.

an quĭ amant,

was, as a prosodic expedient, much rarer than in the Gr. hexameter or elegiac couplet, where such "correption" of a long vowel or diphthong was convenient for either of the two shorts in the second half of a dactyl (–⏑⏑) and can be illustrated by the shortening of the second element in

āgroŭ ĕp' ēschătĭēs

and of the third in

āndră moĭ ēnnĕpĕ.

This too was a form of elision, inasmuch as the second of the two temporal units into which the quantity of the long syllable could be resolved (–=⏑⏑) was elided to leave the first in its place. Other apparent anomalies of quantity in Homeric verse are often to be explained by the disappearance from the traditional text of consonants which were once valid in pronunciation, especially the digamma, which had the sound of L. *v* or Eng. *w*.

A knowledge of syllabic quantity is the indispensable introduction to any study of the various metrical forms. It is to be acquired in the first place only by means of a thorough acquaintance with vocalic quantity, which of course has to be learned by students of both languages as an essential of pronunciation. But, when this has been done, the laws of cl. prosody are on the whole straightforward.

E. Kalinka, "Griechisch-römische Metrik und Rhythmik im letzten Vierteljahrhundert," Bursian's *Jahresbericht,* 250 (1935), 290–507; 256 (1937), 1–126; 257 (1937), 1–160; A. M. Dale, "Gr. Metric 1936–1957," *Lustrum* 2 (1957), 5–51; P. W. Harsh, "Early L. Meter and Prosody 1935–1955," *Lustrum* 3 (1958), 215–280.—E. H. Sturtevant, *The Pronunciation of Gr. and L.* (2d ed., 1940); Kolář; P. Chantraine, *Grammaire Homérique: Tome I, Phonétique et Morphologie* (1948); J. D. Denniston and J. F. Mountford, "Metre, Gr." and "Metre, L." respectively, *The Oxford Cl. Dict.* (1949), pp. 564–570 (with brief but important bibliog.); M. Platnauer, *L. Elegiac Verse* (1951); C. G. Cooper, *An Introduction to the L. Hexameter* (1952; contains a careful account of syllable division); Koster; Crusius; Beare; P. Maas, *Gr. Metre,* tr. H. Lloyd-Jones (1962). R.J.G.

CLERIHEW. A form of comic poetry invented by Edmund C. (for Clerihew) Bentley (1875–1956). A c. consists of two couplets of unequal length often with complex or somewhat ridiculous rhymes and presents a potted biography of a famous personage or historical character. The humor consists in concentrating on the trivial, the fantastic, or the ridiculous and presenting it with dead-pan solemnity as the characteristic, the significant, or the essential. Actually it celebrates the triumph of the *nonsequitur* and indirectly satirizes academic pedantry as well as amateur inconsequence in biographical research. Bentley wrote his first c. as a schoolboy of sixteen.

Sir Humphrey Davy
Detested gravy.
He lived in the odium
Of having discovered sodium.

Famous as the author of the "perfect" detective novel *Trent's Last Case,* Bentley is honored by a coterie of enthusiastic connoisseurs for three collections of capsule biographies: *Biography for Beginners* (1905), *More Biography* (1929), and *Baseless Biography* (1939). In the "Introductory Remarks" to an omnibus volume, *Clerihews Complete,* the author states and illustrates the nature of his work:

The Art of Biography
Is different from Geography.
Geography is about Maps,
But Biography is about Chaps.

It is clear that this art form, which is not unrelated to the limerick (q.v.), is very British and quite Old School Tie, but it has nevertheless attracted many practitioners in America as well as England, among them being W. H. Auden, Clifton Fadiman, Ellen Evans, Diana Menuhin, and others.—C. Fadiman, "Cleriheulogy" in *Any Number Can Play* (1957). A.J.M.S.

CLICHÉ. A phrase or figure which from overuse, like a dulled knife, has lost its cutting edge; a trite expression. Clichés in verse result when the poet's inspiration arises from other poems rather than from a fresh response to experience. Examples of poetic clichés are: fettered soul, eagle-eyed, break of day, rolling wave, purling brook, whispering breeze, ruby lips, pearly teeth, white as snow. Good poets sometimes use clichés intentionally for ironical purposes.—E. Partridge, *A Dictionary of Clichés* (1947); L. D. Lerner, "Clichés and Commonplace," EIC, 6 (1956) presents a different view. See also T. Y. Booth, "The Cliché: A Working Bibliog.," *Bulletin of Bibliog. and Magazine Notes,* 23 (1960). L.P.

CLIMAX (Gr. "ladder"). (1). As a term of rhetoric, according to the anonymous *Ad Herennium* 25, and Quintilian (*Institutes of Oratory* 9.3.54–57), both of the 1st c. A.D, and the Gr. rhetorician Demetrius (*On Style* 270, 1st c. A.D?), c. is the pattern of a series of sentences or other units of discourse linked chainwise, a meaning of the term now mostly abandoned for fear of confusion with sense 2 below. The opening word or words of each unit after the first repeats a word or words, usually the final ones, of the preceding unit, sometimes with a morphological change. The purpose is commonly to build up a crescendo of force or excitement, e.g., "I will grind your bones to dust / and with your blood and it I'll make a paste, / And of the paste a coffin I will rear / And make two pasties of your shameful heads, / And bid that strumpet, your unhallow'd dam, / Like to the earth swallow her own increase" (Shakespeare, *Titus Andronicus* 5.2.187–92). A c. is known as a *sorites* when the linked elements are truncated syllogisms in a chain of argument, the conclusion of each before the last becoming the premiss of the next (see, e.g., Richard Whately, *Elements of Logic* 2.4.7) (2). The meaning currently designated by c. is the point of supreme interest or intensity of any graded series of events or ideas, most commonly the crisis or turning point of a story or play, e.g., the fall of Adam in *Paradise Lost* or the murder of the king in *Macbeth.* H.B.

COMEDY. See DRAMATIC POETRY.

COMMON METER. See BALLAD METER.

COMMON RHYTHM. See RUNNING RHYTHM.

COMPENSATION. One of several devices used to schematize a basically irregular foot or line (see METRICAL VARIATIONS). A pause (see REST) is sometimes said to substitute (or compensate) for a missing part of a foot or a whole foot. This is one of two main varieties of c. The other kind occurs when an extra syllable in one foot may be said to compensate for a missing syllable in another, or when a missing metrical unit in one line may be compensated for by an extra unit in an adjacent line.—Baum; Deutsch. R.BE.

COMPLAINT. A plaintive poem, plaint. (1) Often the c. of a lover to or about an unresponsive mistress (cf. *Greek Anthology,* Villon, Surrey's *A Complaint by Night of the Lover Not Beloved*); (2) a plaint in which the poet seeks relief from his unhappy state (Chaucer's *A Complaint unto Pity*); (3) a plaint about the sorrows of the world or the poet's affairs (Spenser's *Complaints*); (4) less frequently a c. in a lighter vein about some trivial subject (Chaucer's *The Complaint of Chaucer to his Purse*). Usually the poem is in the form of a monologue in which the poet explains the cause of his sorrow and pleads for a remedy. Ponsonby, the printer, claims Spenser's complaints are more serious than usual, that the book is composed of "all complaints and meditations of the worlds vanitie, verie graue and profitable." Dr. Johnson disliked the form, saying that Cowley's ode, *The Complaint,* "seems to have excited more contempt than pity." Sometimes a mournful c. is indistinguishable from a lament (q.v.).—J. Peter, *C. and Satire in Early Eng. Lit.* (1956). R.O.E.

COMPUTER POETRY. A c. is not only a calculator; it is also a data-processing machine, which can manipulate symbols of any kind. That is, it can be programmed to "generate" graphics (line drawings), musical compositions, and verbal strings such as sentences.

Simply described, a c. poem is one or more sentences generated by a specially designed c. program. One current poetic aesthetic would identify as poetic a sentence such as the following: "What did she put four whistles beside heated rugs for?" Although this sentence is syntactically well formed, it violates some of the semantic rules which govern the combination of words in Eng. Any sentence which is well formed but which is difficult to interpret, or any pair or sequence of sentences whose logical connection is obscure is likely to be interpreted as poetry: "The old horse staggers along the road. Newspapers are on sale in Wall Street. The sun will set again this evening." Although the average reader of prose would consider the sequence incoherent, the reader of modern poetry, conditioned to allusive symbolism, will seek or invent relationships to create coherence from three such random utterances. The reader of Shakespeare, Milton, or Pope, however, would not have responded in the same manner because the poetry of earlier eras was governed by a logic of discourse similar to prose. Evidently, c. poetry is possible only in the age of the c., which happens to be an age that demands more logic from prose than from poetry. For this reason, c. prose is extremely difficult to produce.

C. poems are basically of two kinds: formulary and derivative. Formulary poems consist of strings of generated sentences. A c.-generated sentence at the simplest level is produced by means of a formula (sentence rule) like the following:

SENTENCE = NOUN + VERB + ADVERB

Each word-class in the formula is like a bin containing a pile of cards on each of which a word is written (e.g., VERB = *scavenge, misplace, corrupt, vary, yawn*). When the program runs, it is as if someone had picked the top card from each successive bin and arranged the words so drawn into a sequence. If three bins each contained five cards, according to the rule given above the following sentences would be generated: 1. *Craters scavenge nervously*; 2. *Suits misplace wrongly*; 3. *Messiahs corrupt ably*; 4. *Sentiments vary never*; 5. *Graves yawn hungrily*. It will be noticed that the sentences produced are of quite different orders of regularity: 3 is well formed, 2 is ill formed (*misplace* requires an object), 4 is inverted (*never* normally comes before the verb), both 5 and 1 are well formed but violate semantic rules (*yawn* and *scavenge* both require mammal or animate subjects) and 5 produces an acceptable metaphor, whereas 1 creates something like a nonsense metaphor. To generate more than five of the 625 possible sentences, it is necessary to return the cards to the bins after each use but without preserving the original order. Thus any word has the chance of being drawn during any pass and all combinations will eventually occur.

To create poetic objects by such a process, it is necessary only to devise a variety of sentence rules of greater complexity along with rules for combining them. In addition, it may be desirable to place such constraints on the output as length of line, meter, and rhyme—all of which are possible but difficult. Metrical constraints require the prior syllabification of each word and the location of its stress, if it is polysyllabic. To achieve rhyming, it is necessary to recode letter symbols into phonetic equivalents so that similar sounds rather than letter combinations may be matched, although the same can be achieved on a small scale by storing sets of rhyming words. This is easier in most other languages than in Eng.

The following stanzas result from a formulary generation:

The landscape of your clay mitigates me.
Coldly,
By your recognizable shape,
I am wronged.

The perspective of your frog feeds me.
Dimly,
By your wet love,
I am raked.
(M. Borroff)

These two stanzas, resulting from two sentence rules and one stanza rule (Sentence 1 = Nominal + Prepositional phrase + Verb + Personal Pronoun; Sentence 2 = Adverb + Prepositional phrase + Pronoun + Passive verb; Stanza = Sentence 1, Sentence 2) display the unexpectedness of juxtaposition characteristic of this process. At the same time, the repetitive structure may undermine the poetic effect by betraying the mechanical originator. The most sophisticated efforts provide variety of structure along with unusual juxtapositions.

Although documentation is lacking, it is probable that c. poetry was invented simultaneously at various locations during the 1950's by engineers occupied in language tasks (such as machine translation) who relished the opportunity of engaging in complex word play. The earliest examples appear in the pages of technical journals and represent purely sporadic efforts at entertainment. During the following decade, these developments came to the attention of poets, critics, and scholars interested in poetry with some access to c. techniques and vocabulary. They have been interested both in the possibilities offered by this new tool and by the disturbing implications of its use: its apparently superhuman inventiveness and the inability of the reader to distinguish with certainty between the machine and the human product. At the same time, a curiosity about the discoveries made possible by such activity led to derivative c. poetry.

The basic principle of derivative c. poetry is to take an existing poem or line and to alter it in some systematic way. Hamlet's "To be or not to be, that is the question" might become "To speak or not to speak, that is the riddle," "To know or not to know, that is the struggle," etc. . . . If the line were not so well known, the identification of the original might be uncertain. The following stanza is based on one from Dylan Thomas's *In the beginning* and is the result of marking all the nouns, verbs, and adjectives in the original, arranging them in alphabetical order, and replacing them in the poem. The result is a set of stanzas containing only Thomas's own words yet evidently not his work. Some of the collocations are as unusual as his own. Although the question of which is better need not arise, it is noteworthy that, in a number of experiments, college students have usually failed to identify the original except by chance:

In the beginning was the root, the rock
That from the solid star of the smile
Set all the substance of the sun;
And from the secret space of the signature
The smile spouted up, translating to the stamp
Three-pointed sign of spark and spark.

Dylan Thomas more than most poets strove for the exceptional collocation, even at times using mechanical means to achieve it. According to a friend, Thomas recorded likely short ordinary words in a notebook he carried with him (and called his "dictionary") and which he would consult at random when he was at a loss for a word or phrase in a poem (see bibliog.: Milic, "Possible Usefulness . . . ," p. 172). That it is difficult to distinguish between his own "rooting air," "secret oils," and "letters of the void" and the computer's "rooting imprint," "secret space," and "three-pointed sign of spark and spark" perhaps reveals less about c. poetry than about his. Because words have connections with each other in our minds, certain collocations are regularly inhibited even for poets, who are freer than the norm in this regard. The complete disregard of these inhibitions in c. poetry gives it both its fresh and its outrageous character.

Derivative c. poetry is a species of parody when it is practiced on well-known lines. As such, it calls into question the inevitability of the original: "Spring is the nepenthean desert, scrambling . . . ," "April is the vacuous land, inverting. . . ." T. S. Eliot acknowledged that some of the word combinations in parts of *The Waste Land* were incomprehensible to him. This kind of substitution is the active principle of a program called ERATO (by L. T. Milic), which is based on a dozen opening lines by poets of the last hundred years, each of which is provided with vocabulary alternatives for key words. Cummings's "Darling! because my blood can sing" can take many forms if only the noun and verb are altered: "my mouth [life, soul, spirit, heart, hand] can [wing, play, skip, chime, leap, laugh, jump]." Each poem in the series results from the choice of a number of the original lines in random order with key words permuted, the number of lines in each poem and the degree of repetition being determined by random numbers. One example follows:

HEMS

(1) This is my news to the multitude:
(2) Turn to me in the chaos of the day.
(3) I have suspected what capricious
maidens say,
(4) I strutted upon a loathsome place,
(5) Above the new hems of the sea.
(6) I stopped upon a loathsome station,
(7) Still here lying beneath the roof,
(8) Above the humid hems of the surf.

The lines by E. Dickinson (1), C. Rossetti (2), Yeats (3), S. Crane (4,6), Hart Crane (5,8), and MacLeish (7), altered as they have been, constitute a new whole still somehow related to the originals. The relation of line (1) to Emily Dickinson's "This is my letter to the world" is that of paraphrase, but this is not true of lines (4) and (6) to their original, Stephen Crane's "I stood upon a high place." The grammatical structure, especially that conveyed by the choice and arrangement of function words, signals the kinship between derivations and originals. But the new collocations are unique, even when they depart from the original in predictable ways, as lines (5) and (8) plainly connect with Hart Crane's "Above the fresh ruffles of the surf" in the imagery of the edge of the sea as a garment. ERATO evidently produces new poems, even if only in the legal sense that the publisher has no need to seek permission from the owners of the copyright of the originating poets. (It is noteworthy that existing copyright laws protect only sequences of words, not structures or ideas.)

Needless to say, only a fraction of the output of a c. poetry program is displayed as poetry. Editing is inevitable, especially in view of the mountains of paper produced by the machine. Normal poems, however, also undergo a weeding or pruning process, though c. poetry is not edited by a c., but by a person. Editing poetry by c. is not beyond possibility if the criteria for poetic acceptability could be explicitly stated. This would be not unlike defining "good" poetry.

The peculiar affinity of computers and poetry

is based on the previously noted tendency of the modern reader to puzzle out a sense in the obscurest work that is called poetry. The achievement of c. poetry is in the direction of providing a more accurate notion of the workings of poetry, and especially of poetic language. No important c. poems have been produced and none are likely, though one poet (A. Turner) has found inspiration enough in the RETURNER poems, which were based on an original work of hers, to write further poems based on the derivations. The inevitable question on this subject concerns the identity of the author of c. poetry. It is unquestionable that the poet is not the assemblage of wires, transistors, and print trains called a c. The poet is the programmer, whose ideas of what poetry ought to be, whose choice of structures and of vocabulary determine to a considerable extent what the finished product will be. The poem is both the actual verse object and the program, the abstract structure of instructions and data, of which the actual output is only the incidental product. C. poetry is a new way of producing the poetry of our time. If it should ever develop its own aesthetic and break away from the mainstream, it will become a new kind of poetry.

J. A. Baudot, *La Machine à écrire* (Montreal, 1964); *Cybernetic Serendipity*, ed. J. Reichardt (1969); M. Krause and G. F. Schaudt, *C.-Lyrik* (1969); M. Borroff, "C. as Poet," *Yale Alumni Magazine*, 34 (1971); L. T. Milic, "The Possible Usefulness of Poetry Generation," in *The C. in Lit. and Linguistic Research* (1971), *Erato* (1971) and "The 'Returner' Poetry Program," ITL (Institute of Applied Linguistics), 11 (1971); A. Turner, " 'Returner' Re-turned," *Midwest Quarterly*, 13 (1972). L.T.M.

CONCEIT. An intricate or far-fetched metaphor, which functions through arousing feelings of surprise, shock, or amusement; in earlier usage, the imagination or fancy (qq.v.) in general. The term is derived from the It. *concetto* (concept), and all types of conceit share an origin which is specifically intellectual rather than sensuous. The poet compares elements which seem to have little or nothing in common, or juxtaposes images which establish a marked discord in mood. One may distinguish two types of c.: (1) the Petrarchan, in which physical qualities or experiences are metaphorically described in terms of very different physical objects; it often verges on hyperbole (q.v.):

Quando a gli ardenti rai neve divegno
When I turn to snow before your burning
rays. . .
(Petrarch, *Canzone* 8)

(2) the "metaphysical," in which the spiritual qualities or functions of the described entity are presented by means of a vehicle which shares no physical features with the entity:

As lines, so loves, oblique may well
Themselves in every angle greet;
But ours, so truly parallel,
Though infinite, can never meet.
(Marvell, *The Definition of Love*)

The Petrarchan type, valid for its originator and the more gifted of his followers because of the rich psychological content it often implies, degenerated ultimately into the fanciful and decorative figures of marinism, but it was widely employed by the Elizabethan sonneteers and by Tasso. The metaphysical type, so-called from its use by the metaphysical poets, was characteristic not only of Donne and his followers in 17th-c. England and their contemporaries on the Continent, but also of the Fr. symbolists in the latter 19th c. It has been widely used by contemporary poets.

The metaphysical c. is usually intended in critical discussions of the c. Within this type of c. one may perceive two general forms: (1) the extended, in which the initial analogy is subjected to a detailed and ingenious development, as in Donne's famous figure from *A Valediction: Forbidding Mourning*:

If they be two, they are two so
As stiff twin compasses are two;
Thy soul, the fixed foot, makes no show
To move, but doth, if th' other do . . .

(2) the condensed, in which the ingenious analogy or discordant contrast is expressed with a telling brevity, as at the opening of T. S. Eliot's *The Love-Song of J. Alfred Prufrock*:

When the evening is spread out against the sky
Like a patient etherised upon a table.

The lines of Eliot will serve to typify two important aspects of the c.: its subtle use of controlled connotation to enrich the meaning of the poem, with the associated dependence on the imaginative sensitivity of the reader, and its consistent evocation of paradox (q.v.).

The faculty of wit (q.v.), the capacity for finding likenesses between the apparently unlike, is central to the c., and the presence of this faculty largely determines the success of a given c. For the emotion evoked by a good c. is not simply surprise, or, in Dr. Johnson's terms, wonder at the perversity which created the c., but rather a surprised recognition of the ultimate validity of the relationship presented in the c., which thus serves not as an ornament but as an instrument of vision.

R. M. Alden, "The Lyrical C. of the Elizabethans," SP, 14 (1917) and "The Lyrical Conceits of the Metaphysical Poets," SP, 17 (1920); K. M. Lea, "Conceits," MLR, 20 (1925); E. Holmes, *Aspects of Elizabethan Imagery* (1929); G. Williamson, *The Donne Tradition* (1930); C. Brooks, "A Note on Symbol and C.," *Am. Review*, 3 (1934); M. Praz,

Studies in 17th-C. Imagery, I (1939); G. R. Potter, "Protest against the Term C.," PQ. 20 (1941); Tuve; T. E. May, "Gracián's Idea of the 'Concepto,' " HR, 18 (1950); J. A. Mazzeo, "A Critique of Some Modern Theories of Metaphysical Poetry," MP, 50 (1952); D. L. Guss, "Donne's C. and Petrarchan Wit," PMLA, 78 (1963). F.J.W.; A.P.

CONCRETE POETRY. A mode of graphic art, employing graphemes of a given language and selected typeface, used by themselves, in clusters, morphemes, words, or phrases, and so patterned that an evocative or witty reading of an otherwise minimal utterance may result. Alternatively, a mode of inscription poem—and hence vaguely linked to epigram—embodied totally and (imbedded irretrievably) in a unique typographical instance. In this aspect, c.p. is allied to its contemporary concept of *musique concrète,* in which the musical work—whether synthesized electronically, drawn directly (rather than recorded) on a cinema sound track, etc.—exists not as a text to be performed by an instrumental interpreter, but in a canonical and uninterpretable form. A self-conscious literary movement crystallized around the *Constellations* (1953) of the Swiss Eugen Gomringer. This volume contained minimal inscriptions of words in sanserif type, the words, perhaps significantly, being in various languages (an alienated *Sprachgefühl* being in some way characteristic of most c.p.). Gomringer claimed to be intensifying and authenticating linguistic experience by means of varied spatial presentations of words and other elements (a concern with reading as scanning that goes back to Mallarmé); and he and his followers have drawn elaborate and sometimes labored analogies between spatial, musical, and abstract conceptual patternings. An international movement, reminiscent in its many manifestos and group publications of futurist, surrealist and Dadaist literary parties, has embraced practitioners in Brazil (the so-called Noigandres Group), France, England, the U.S., and other countries. The best known of these include Ian Hamilton Finlay (Great Britain), whose more recent inscriptions on wood or stone have fled the page entirely for the outdoors; Mary Ellen Solt (U.S.), a scholar of the movement; Augusto de Campos (Brazil), Helmut Heissenbüttel (Germany), Carlo Belloli (Italy), and Emmett Williams (U.S.).

Writers on the subject have distinguished among "type poems," "typewriter poems," "object poems," and so forth, and such sub- or related movements as *Spatialisme* or *Lettrisme.* A good rule of thumb for identifying a concrete poem might be to try and read the inscription aloud without describing the format (type style, graphic arrangement, etc.) as one might a print. A poem will yield up its heart to oral reading; if a concrete poem will not, it is because no picture will. Consider, for example, e. e. cummings' poem #1 from *95 Poems* (1958):

l(a

le
af
fa

ll

s)
one
l

iness

A *haiku*-like evaded simile is here so arranged that the vehicle is literally troped into the tenor (q.v.): "loneliness" *contains* the single leaffall, its emblem (q.v.). This might have been done in a single horizontal line, but the vertical format graphically represents the dropping, enforces a slow scanning (and hence, reading), discovers hidden "ones" in the words (with graphis puns based on the identity of the 12th letter of the alphabet with the first arabic numeral in many typefaces), etc. Needless to say, this is more complex and sophisticated than many formal instances of c.p., and developed from cummings' lifelong experiments with format and its relation to poetic form.

There is some debate about how the many varieties of typographical experiment in modern European and Am. poetry constitute actual c.p. The shaped poems (arranged for the typewriter's one-em-per-character) of May Swenson's *Iconographs* (1970) and John Hollander's *Types of Shape* (1969) clearly belong to the tradition of the *technopaignia* or pattern poetry (q.v.) stretching from Hellenistic times through Apollinaire's *Calligrammes*; in all these cases, the poems on being read aloud lose only the accompanying pictorial emblem made up by their shaping. More direct precursors of c.p. are: Mallarmé's *Un Coup de Dés*; Christian Morgenstern's *Fisches Nachtgesang* (composed of the metrical signs "∪" and "—", so arranged as to suggest a gaping fish-mouth); the experiments of Henri Barzun; the posterlike texts of the futurists and of such Dada poets as Richard Huelsenbeck; Valéry's inscriptions for the façade of the Trocadero, etc. Then, too, there was the entire typographic ambience of modernist art, including the aesthetics of the Bauhaus, and the specific work of such designers as Jan Tschichold (in his *Typographische Gestaltung*, 1935). A recent and brilliant development in the area of pictured inscription has been the great graphic artist Saul Steinberg's conceptual maps, wherein groups of related pronouns, auxiliary verbs in different tenses, etc. are diagrammed out in a painted and drawn landscape, in such a way as to depict and schematize their relationship.

ANTHOLOGIES: *Anthol. of C.P.*, ed. E. Williams (1967); *C.P.: A World View*, ed. M. E. Solt

(2d ed., 1970); *Imaged Word & Worded Images*, ed. R. Kostelanetz (1970); *The Word as Image*, ed. B. Bowler (1970); *Kon-krete Poesie*, ed. E. Gomringer (1972).

HISTORY AND CRITICISM: A. Leide, *Dichtung als Spiel* (1963); M. Weaver, "C.P.," *Lugano Review*, nos. 5–6 (1966); E. Lucic-Smith, "C.P.," *Encounter*, 26 (1966); R. P. Draper, "C.P.," NLH, 2 (1971). J.H.

CONNOTATION AND DENOTATION. Contemporary critics who have concerned themselves with the "multi-dimensionalism" of language and who advocate that poets should exploit the full resources of language have found the terms "c." and "d." useful to mark distinctions among these resources. These terms are usually applied only to words, and d. almost always signifies the intension and/or extension of a word; however, c. names a variety of concepts.

C. has been used to designate any or all of the responses which a word in a particular context disposes a reader to make other than his recognition of its denotative meaning. Thus c. may be (1) any sensory or emotional response; (2) any cognitive response which is a consequence of suggestion, association, or inference, or of the look, spelling, or sound of a word, or of some device such as Empsonian ambiguity or the symbolic use of a word. Most critics, however, prefer to call such responses the result of the "extralogical" dispositions of words, and use c. as a name for *one* of these dispositions.

M. C. Beardsley (in his *Aesthetics*, pp. 125–126; see also pp. 116–124, 149–151) has proposed the following terminology: the "signification" of a term is the sum total of its "conceptual" or "cognitive" meaning; the "denotation" is the referent it points to; the "designation" is the set of characteristics that the referent must have to be correctly denoted by that term; and the "connotation" is the "secondary" or "accompanying" meaning. (Empson's "Implication" is another name for such secondary meaning.) Connotative meanings are also characteristics of the referent: "What a word connotes . . . are the characteristics that it does not designate but that belong, or are widely thought or said to belong, to many of the things it denotes" (*ibid.*, p. 125. "Characteristic" is interpreted broadly and includes the effects, uses, etc. of the referent. Beardsley should have added that sometimes some of the most important connotations are characteristics that a speech-community thinks a referent *ought* to have). Beardsley says that the connotations of a term are just as "objective" as its designation, and are to be distinguished from "personal associations" which have little value for the explication of poetry. In literature the connotations of a word are "liberated," especially by the power of metaphor, and the explication of metaphor consists in listing the connotations of the "modifier" that may appropriately be attributed to the "subject."

The value of c. depends on the value of the effects the poet can produce by its use. C. has been praised as one of the means by which poetic language achieves depth, density, thickness, richness, and condensation. Enthusiastic critics have said that the meanings of great poems are infinite and hence inexhaustible. But tastes differ; and although some latent or hidden meaning is present (or can be discovered) in all poetry, even the humblest (see Beardsley's interpretation of *Little Jack Horner, ibid.*, p. 405), the recommendations of critics and the practice of poets show no uniformity with respect to the amount of c. and other implicit meaning that is desirable in an imaginative work (see Bateson and Tillyard). Certainly, "The more connotation, the better!" must not be irresponsibly urged; and, as has often been pointed out (see Sparrow, Tate, and Winters), neglect of d. in favor of c. leads to obscurity and incoherence or, at best, to a very limited range of poetic effects.

L. Abercrombie, *The Theory of Poetry* (1926); G.H.W. Rylands, *Words and Poetry* (1928); W. Empson, *Seven Types of Ambiguity* (1930, rev. ed. 1947), and *The Structure of Complex Words* (1951); F. W. Bateson, *Eng. Poetry and the Eng. Language* (1934); J. Sparrow, *Sense and Poetry* (1934); E.M.W. Tillyard, *Poetry Direct and Oblique* (1934); A. Tate, "Tension in Poetry," *Reason in Madness* (1935); Y. Winters, "Preliminary Problems," "John Crowe Ransom," *The Anatomy of Nonsense* (1943); C. Brooks, *The Well Wrought Urn* (1947); R. B. Heilman, "Preliminaries: Crit. Method," *This Great Stage* (1948); M. C. Beardsley, *Aesthetics* (1958); I. C. Hungerland, *Poetic Discourse* (1958). F.G.

CONSONANCE. Aside from the broader meaning of a pleasing combination of sounds or ideas, it is (1) the counterpart of assonance (q.v.) and refers to partial or total identity of consonants in words or syllables whose *main* vowels differ (e.g., *pressed-past, shadow-meadow*). For c. restricted to sounds following the main vowel, see NEAR RHYME. As a deliberate device to replace rhyme, rich (i.e., total), c. has been used in a number of poems by Wilfred Owen, e.g., "Has your soul sipped / Of the sweetness of all sweets? / Has it well supped / But yet hungers and sweats?" Such poems as his *Strange Meeting* are virtually entirely constructed with this type of impure rhyme, intended no doubt to convey the discordant anguish of war and death. (2) In Ir. poetry there is c. ("uaithne") between words when the corresponding vowels are of the same quantity, the corresponding consonants or consonant groups of the same class, and the final consonants of the same class *and* quality.—See also "Generic Rhyme" in CELTIC PROSODY.

E. Rickert, *New Methods for the Study of Lit.* (1927); W. Owen, *The Poems of W. Owen*, ed. E. Blunden

(1931); E. Knott, *Ir. Syllabic Poetry 1200–1600* (2d ed., 1957). U.K.G.; S.L.M.

CONTESTS, POETIC. See POETIC CONTESTS.

CONTRACTIONS, POETIC. See METRICAL TREATMENT OF SYLLABLES.

CONVENTION. By "c." is meant (1) "rule that, by implicit agreement between a writer and some of his readers (or of his audience) allows him certain freedoms in, and imposes certain restrictions upon, his treatment of style, structure, and theme and enables these readers to interpret his work correctly" or (2) "product of the observance of such a rule." The number of readers who are parties to the agreement (that is, who have knowledge of the c.) may be very small indeed; else a writer could never create a new c. (for example, free verse or sprung rhythm), revive an old (alliterative verse, in the 14th c. and, by Auden, in the 20th), or abandon an old (the heroic couplet). Readers who are not parties to the agreement (that is, who are ignorant of—or, at least, out of sympathy with—the c.) must to some extent misinterpret a work that exemplifies it; and, when the number of such readers becomes large, writers may abandon the c.—though, of course, works that exemplify it remain to be interpreted (or misinterpreted). The conventions of the pastoral elegy are instances of abandoned conventions; and Dr. Johnson is an instance of a reader who misinterprets a work (*Lycidas*) because he is ignorant of or out of sympathy with these conventions. Conventions both liberate and restrict the writer because they usually go in sets, because, therefore, a writer's decision to use a certain c. obliges him either to use certain others or to risk misleading his reader, and because the freedom given him by the set as a whole or by some of its parts may well be restricted by other parts. The conventions of the epic, for example, allow a writer to achieve the sublime but compel him to forgo the conversational idiom of the metaphysical lyric (and thus, of course, to risk, as Milton does, the censure of those modern critics who take the conventions of that lyric to be *the* conventions of all poetry). Some examples of conventions of style are the rhyme scheme of the sonnet and the diction of the ballad; of structure, beginning an epic *in medias res* and representing the subject of a pastoral elegy as a shepherd; and, of theme, the attitudes toward love in the Cavalier lyric and toward death in the Elizabethan lyric.

To break with conventions (or "rules") is sometimes thought a merit, sometimes a defect; but, merit or defect, such a break is never abandonment of all conventions but replacement of an old set with a new. Wordsworth condemns 18th-c. poetry for using poetic diction (Preface to the 2d edition of the *Lyrical Ballads*); F. R. Leavis condemns Georgian poetry for adhering to "nineteenth-century conventions of 'the poetical' " (*New Bearings*, p. 14). But—though conventions come and go and though we may regret the passing of the old or welcome the advent of the new—literature, new or old, cannot escape conventions.

Insistence upon the necessity of knowing what the conventions of a given work are (as in the criticism of E. E. Stoll) does not entail, as some theorists wrongly hold (for example, Wellek and Warren, *Theory of Literature*, pp. 32–33), either judgment of the work by the extent to which it conforms to the conventions of its genre or the "intentional fallacy" (or, if it entails the latter, then insistence upon the necessity of knowing the Elizabethan sense of, say, "passing"—as in "passing fair"—also entails that "fallacy"). The concept of genre nowadays is in some disrepute (or, more exactly, sets of conventions are looser than they used to be); but now as always a c. in Sense 1 is a rule of interpretation; and, to understand a given work, a reader must understand its conventions—not only its linguistic ones, but its more specifically literary ones of style, structure, and theme.

R. S. Crane proposes that the sense of "c." be restricted in such a way that " 'convention' denotes any characteristic of the matter or technique of a poem the reason for the presence of which in the poem cannot be inferred from the necessities of the form envisaged but must be sought in the historical circumstances of its composition . . ." (*The Languages of Criticism*, p. 198, n. 62). In other words, those conventions that all works in a certain genre must, by definition, share are not (in Crane's sense) conventions. Thus he would not count an unhappy ending as a c. of tragedy but does count the chorus in Gr. tragedy as such. But he acknowledges that his proposed sense does not conform to modern usage of "c."—S. Johnson, *Lives of the Eng. Poets* (1779–81); W. Wordsworth, Preface to the *Lyrical Ballads* (2d ed., 1800); J. L. Lowes, *C. and Revolt in Poetry* (1922); E. E. Stoll, *Poets and Playwrights* (1930); F. R. Leavis, *New Bearings in Eng. Poetry* (1932); M. C. Bradbrook, *Themes and Conventions of Elizabethan Tragedy* (1935); Wellek and Warren; Crane. M.S.

COUNTERPOINT (syncopation). A rhythmical effect achieved through metrical variations. C. results from the establishment of a relatively stable metrical structure (e.g., iambic pentameter) and then the occasional departure from this structure so as to create a sense of two metrical patterns, the old and the new, continuing at once. C. is impossible except in moderately regular metrical compositions, for any variation must have something fixed to vary from. In general, at least two contiguous feet must be varied or reversed from the initial metrical pattern if a counterpointed rhythm is to be felt. In the following line by G. M. Hopkins,

The world is charged with the grandeur
of God,

the third and the fourth foot constitute a counterpointed section, for they interrupt and "reverse" the ascending rhythm of the earlier part of the line. See METRICAL VARIATIONS.—"Author's Preface," *Poems of Gerard Manley Hopkins*, ed. R. Bridges and W. H. Gardner (3d ed., 1948). P.F.

COUPLET. Two lines of verse, usually rhymed. Ever since the advent of rhymed verse, the c. has counted as one of the principal units of versification in the Western literatures, whether as a stanzaic form in extended composition, as a subordinate element in other stanzaic forms, or as an independent poem of an epigrammatic nature. The c. composed of two lines of iambic pentameter—the so-called heroic couplet (q.v.)—is the most important c. form in Eng. poetry. As perfected by Dryden and Pope, the heroic c. is "closed"—syntax and thought are fitted neatly into the envelope of rhyme and meter—and in this form it dominates the poetry of the neoclassical period: "Know then thyself, presume not God to scan; / The proper study of Mankind is Man" (Pope, *Essay on Man*). Although the heroic c. is generally associated with its 18th-c. masters, one should recognize that it is a form of great antiquity, used by Chaucer in *The Legend of Good Women* and most of *The Canterbury Tales*, by Marlowe, Chapman, and other Elizabethans, and by Donne, whose free use of enjambement achieves effects utterly different from those of Pope and Dryden.

The iambic tetrameter or octosyllabic c. (see OCTOSYLLABIC VERSE) has a distinguished history in Eng. verse as the form of Milton's *L'Allegro* and *Il Penseroso*, Marvell's *To his Coy Mistress*, and Coleridge's *Christabel* (see CHRISTABEL METER). The 4-beat couplets of Samuel Butler's *Hudibras* really constitute a separate type, known as Hudibrastic couplets. Not all Eng. couplets utilize regular line length. Poets as diverse as George Herbert and Robert Browning have developed verse forms in which the couplet rhyming of irregular lines occurs: ". . . With their triumphs and their glories and the rest. / Love is best!" (Browning, *Love Among the Ruins*.)

The c. of rhyming alexandrines is the dominant form of Fr. narrative and dramatic poetry (see ALEXANDRINE). In the hands of the classical masters—Corneille, Molière, Racine, La Fontaine—the alexandrine c. is end-stopped and relatively self-contained, but a freer use of enjambement is found among the romantics. Under Fr. influence, the alexandrine c. became the dominant metrical form of German and Dutch narrative and dramatic verse in the 17th and 18th c. After being neglected during this period, a more indigenous German c. form, the tetrameter c. called *Knittelvers*, was revived by Goethe and Schiller.

Although the c. ranks as one of the major forms for extended poetic composition, its function as a constituent of more complex stanzaic forms is scarcely less important. The principal stanzaic forms created by the later Middle Ages and the Renaissance—ottava rima and rhyme royal (qq.v.)—both conclude with a c., which may be used for purposes of formal conclusion, summation, or epigrammatic comment. The pithy qualities inherent in c. structure are evident not only in these stanzas but also in the independent epigrammatic c., and in the Shakespearean sonnet (see SONNET), which concludes with a c.

As a unit of dramatic verse the c. occurs in the classical Fr. drama, the older German and Dutch drama, and the "heroic plays" of Restoration England. It also fills an important function in Elizabethan-Jacobean drama as a variation from the standard blank verse; its principal use is at the conclusion of a scene or at a peak of dramatic action. The relative frequency of couplet variation is an important means of determining the chronology of Shakespeare's plays, as he tended, with increasing maturity, to abandon the device.

In Fr., the term *couplet* is sometimes used with the meaning of stanza, as in the *couplet carré* (square couplet), a stanza composed of 8 lines of octosyllabic verse. See also DISTICH.

F.J.W.; A.P.

CRETIC or amphimacer (Gr. "long at both ends"). The cretic foot (– ⏑ –) and verse form are thought to have originated with a Cretan poet called Thaletas (7th c. B.C) and to have been at first a meter for the hyporchema. As is obvious from resolution of either long syllable, the c. is really a form of the paeon (q.v.) and cretic-paeonic measures, though rarely employed in the choruses of Gr. tragedy, are not infrequent in comedy. Cretics occur in early Roman drama and are common in the *clausulae* of Cicero (see PROSE RHYTHM). An example in the former is the song of Phaedromus in Plautus, *Curculio* 147–154:

pessuli, heus | pessuli, | vos salu | to lubens,
vos amo, | vos volo, | vos peto at | que obsecro

the meaning and meter of which G. E. Duckworth thus reproduces: "Bolts and bars, bolts and bars, gladly I greetings bring, / Hear my love, hear my prayer, you I beg and entreat." Imitations of cretics are not common in Eng., but lines composed of single feet are found in Tennyson's *The Oak*. Coleridge imitated and described the c. thus: "First and last being long, middle short, Amphimacer / Strikes his thundering hoofs like a proud high-bred Racer."—E. W. Scripture, "The Choriambus in Eng. Verse," PMLA, 43 (1928); Dale; G. E. Duckworth,

The Nature of Roman Comedy (1952); Koster; Beare. R.J.G.

CYCLE. A connected group of stories, dramas, or poems. Much primitive literature is cyclical. It is related to religious rituals which are themselves cyclical because they mark the recurring rhythms of the year, of the twenty-four hour c. of the day, of death and rebirth, of human life, and of many forms of work. Longer cyclical poems grow up in every civilization by accretions of short poems and stories about the same mythic or legendary person or the same quasi-historical event. China has its *Monkey Epic*, India its *Vedas*, and Babylon its *Gilgamesh*.

Aristotle refers in *Poetics* XXIII to the *Cypria* and the *Little Iliad*, which may be considered along with the *Iliad* and the *Odyssey* parts of an enormous c. of poems relating to the fall of Troy. He also refers in the same passage to eight tragedies made from the *Little Iliad* (he actually lists ten). These tragedies may be considered part of a dramatic c. on the Fall of Troy. The consciously and artfully crafted dramatic c. is illustrated by the *Oresteia* of Aeschylus. The practice of treating the three plays of a dramatic trilogy as three parts of a larger story gradually lost favor in Greece, but it was revived in the 19th c. by—e.g., Richard Wagner's *Ring* tetralogy—and in the 20th by Eugene O'Neill's dramatic trilogy *Mourning Becomes Electra*.

Evidently there was a c. of stories about the marvelous adventures of Odysseus on his return to Ithaca, and the *Odyssey* draws on them in the same way that the *Thousand and One Nights* draws on a similar c. of stories in its recounting of the adventures of Sinbad.

In the same way one can refer to the many stories and poems that circulated during the Middle Ages about King Arthur and his knights as parts of an Arthurian c.; and the conscious artistic use of these materials is illustrated by Sir Thomas Malory's *Morte Darthur*. The *Nibelungenlied* is presumably a loosely unified c. of Germanic myths. In the later Middle Ages, biblical and legendary stories about Christian salvation history were combined into gigantic cycles called *Passion Plays* on the Continent and *Corpus Christi Plays* or "Cycle Plays" in England. A secular equivalent of these plays is provided by Shakespeare's history c., which begins with the reign of Richard II in the 14th century and ends with the death of Richard III on Bosworth Field in 1485.

Ballads and lyric compositions are often cyclic. England's border ballads about the centuries-long feud between the British and the Scots are a case in point. The earliest Western "art cycle" is a c. of hymns written in the 4th century by Paulinus of Nola, to be followed shortly by the more famous c. of poems about martyrs by Prudentius titled *Peristephanon*. Because of the cyclical nature of the medieval church year and the services of the hours, a great many medieval liturgical and lyric compositions are cyclical, a tradition that extends much later than the Middle Ages as can be seen, for example, from J. S. Bach's oratorios for various Sundays throughout the year.

The Renaissance was more or less inaugurated by a great c. of secular poems, the 366 sonnets and *canzoni* of Francesco Petrarca's *Canzoniere*. From Italy the vogue of the sonnet c. (q.v.) spread throughout Europe. Numerous other poetic compositions took the form of c. of poems unified by form, emotion, theme, or a combination of these.

In the 19th century c. of lyrics began to be set to music by prominent composers. The German song c. was christened "Liederkranz"—"song wreath." Famous instances of the form are Franz Schubert's *Die schöne Müllerin* and *Die Winterreise* and Gustav Mahler's *Kindertotenlieder* and *Lieder eines fahrenden Gesell*.

Evidently the c. is an archetypal literary form characteristic of the religious and oral phases of literature. It is also, however, a powerful device for imposing unity on diverse materials and hence a tool for the exploration of complex, fluid psychological states by self-conscious artists. See also CHANSONS DE GESTE.—The primitive and archetypal aspects of c. are discussed by Frye; O. Rank, *The Myth of the Birth of the Hero* (1959); T. H. Gaster, *Thespis* (1961); C. M. Bowra, *Primitive Song* (1963). For the liturgical year see F. X. Weiser, *Handbook of Christian Feasts and Customs* (1958); for the sonnet c., see J. W. Lever, *The Elizabethan Love Sonnet* (1956). See also studies of the individual authors cited for use of c. in relation to specific traditions and works. O.B.H.

CYNGHANEDD. A scheme of sound correspondences peculiar to Welch poetry, involving accentuation, alliteration and internal rhyme. Described by Gerard Manley Hopkins as "chimes," he admitted that they were a main influence on his own formal experiments. In Welsh it was well developed by the 14th c., although not finally codified until the Caerwys Eisteddfod (Bardic Assembly) of 1524. It was, and still is, a main feature of strict-meter poetry, but it has often been practiced, with varying degrees of strictness, in the free-meters, and in our own day even in vers libre.

Cynghanedd is of three kinds: consonantal; *sain*, involving both rhyme and alliteration; and *lusg* (dragging), a form of internal rhyme, which was practiced also in Breton.

Consonantal c. is of three kinds: crossing, leaping, and interlinked crossing. In all examples of the "crossing" type, the alliteration forms a pattern in relation to 2 stressed vowels—the last before the caesura and the last in the line. There are three kinds of "crossing": stressed, unstressed, and "uneven-falling." In the first type, for example, the 2 stressed vowels above-mentioned are not followed by unstressed vowels within the same half-lines. In this type, all consonants within the half-lines which precede the final stressed vowels must be repeated in the same order, e.g.

Yr ydwyf í / ar dy fédd (r d f́ / r d f́).

In the unstressed and "uneven-falling" types, the sound relations, though similar to the above, are more complex. In the "leaping" types, the correspondences are as for the "crossing" types, except that, after the caesura, the repetitions are preceded by one or more unrepeated consonants, and where the "crossing" is interlinked, the repetitions begin before the caesura. In *c. sain* the line is in 3 sections, each with a main stress, the first section rhyming with the second, and the second related to the third as in consonantal c. In *c. lusg,* each line must end with a penultimate stress, the unstressed final syllable bearing the main rhyme, and the preceding stressed syllable rhyming with one of the earlier syllables in the same line, which may be stressed or post-stressed. See also CELTIC PROSODY.

The rules of c. are stated above only in broad outline. Much of the skill and delight of c. poetry is in the variation of types in successive lines, and in the contrasting of vowel sounds alongside the repetition of consonants. It is an art form capable of a very rich, melodious, highly wrought and subtle effect, extensively exploited by Welsh poets.—Morris-Jones; Parry. D.M.L.

D

DACTYL (Gr. "finger"). A metrical unit, in quantitative verse, consisting of a long syllable followed by two short ones:

– ⌣ ⌣; *fīlĭŭs*

In accentual verse, an accented syllable followed by two unaccented ones:

/ × ×; ténd×er×ly

Widely used in classical poetry, especially in the hexameter and the elegiac distich (qq.v.), where it may be replaced by a spondee (– –). Also, in lyric verse, pure or in combination with other forms, such as the epitrite (one short and three long syllables, in any order. Except in imitations of the classical hexameter, the use of the d. as a basis for Eng. verse is infrequent till the 19th c., when Browning, Scott, Swinburne, and others employed it, and is still rarely done well, its prolonged use tending to override the normal word-accent and result in a grotesque jigging. But this very grotesqueness is sometimes what is wanted in modern verse.—Hardie; Hamer; Koster; U. v. Wilamowitz-Moellendorff, *Griechische Verskunst* (2d ed., 1958). D.S.P.

DECASYLLABLE. Line of 10 syllables. Appeared in Fr. verse about the middle of the 11th c. in *La Vie de St. Alexis* and *Le Boéce* (later in *La Chanson de Roland*) as a line of 10 syllables with a pause (*coupe*) after the fourth and 2 fixed accents on the fourth and tenth syllables (M. Burger, *Recherches sur la structure et l'origine des vers romans,* 1957, p. 20). In It. the *endecasillabo* appeared early in the 12th c.: "Li mile cento trenta cenqe nato, fo questo tenplo a san Gogio donato . . ." (*Iscrizione Ferrarese,* / 1135 [*Testi volgari italiani,* ed. A. Monteverdi]) and was used by Dante, Petrarch, and Boccaccio. Chaucer may have discovered the line through their work if he had not already become acquainted with it in Machault, Deschamps, Granson, etc. His influence helped to associate the d. with the 5-stress line, and thus to provide (whether one is syllable- or stress-counting) a line which becomes fundamental to the sonnet, the Spenserian and many other stanza forms, the heroic couplet, and blank verse. The real number of syllables in a d. varies in accordance with fashions in pronunciation and with conventions of prosodic practice: thus the Fr. line frequently has 11 syllables because of the addition of a feminine ending; it may have 12 if a further syllable is added at an epic caesura. The It. d. always has at least 11 because a feminine ending is required. In Eng. feminine endings are also employed, but the d. may have as few as 9 syllables when an initial syllable is omitted, resulting in an acephalous line. Frequently what appear to be extrametrical syllables are suppressed by one form of elision or another: "When such / was heard / declar'd / the Almightie's will" (Milton, *Paradise Lost* 7.181).—B. Ten Brink, *Chaucer's Sprache und Verskunst* (1885); M. Kaluza, *A Short Hist. of Eng. Versification* (1911); P.-E. Guarnerio, *Manuale di versificazione italiana* (1913); R. Bridges, *Milton's Prosody* (1921). R.O.E.

DECONSTRUCTION. See POETRY, THEORIES OF (OBJECTIVE THEORIES).

DECORUM in poetry is propriety, a careful attention to what is proper and becoming in action, character, and style. In a good poem, action should fit situation and character, thought and feeling should fit character, expression should so fit subject matter that weighty matters are treated with dignity and trifling matters with humbleness.

Cicero, in the *Orator* (21), defined the term in its general application to real life, oratory, and poetry. Horace illustrated its specific application to poetry, at least to epic and dramatic poetry. Cicero remarked that *decorum* was the L. equivalent of the Gr. *prepon,* which pointed straight to Aristotle's discussion of propriety of style in the *Rhetoric* (3.7.1–2 and 3.7.6). Aristotle also used *prepon* in ch. 17 of the *Poetics,* wherein he recommended that the tragic poet visualize every scene he composes so that he will devise what is appropriate and avoid incongruities. In an earlier chapter, 15, Aristotle used *harmotton* to define appropriateness of dramatic character, and this term was virtually synonymous with *prepon.* There is no evidence that the Romans knew the *Poetics,* but when the Renaissance rediscovered the treatise Aristotle joined Cicero and Horace as leading arbiters of poetic d. In 1536, Paccius translated *prepon* as *decorum* and *harmotton* as *conveniens;* the terms were interchangeable, but d. became the favorite.

Although Horace never actually used the word *decorum* in his *Ars poetica,* his chief doctrine was literary propriety. The favorite passage for his modern disciples was lines 89–127, wherein Horace argued that each style should keep its proper place since a speaker's words should never be discordant with his station; it makes a great difference whether a god or a hero or a slave is speaking, an old man or a youth, a great lady or a nurse, a merchant or a plowman, an Assyrian or a Greek. Moreover, comic themes are distinct from tragic, and the two should never, or very rarely, be mingled. Throughout the Renaissance and long afterward this doctrine of d. was paramount in the theory of poetry and highly influential in its practice. Milton, in his *Tractate of Education,* spoke of the crowning study of poetry as "that sublime art which in Aristotle's *Poetics,* in Horace, and the It. commentaries of Castelvetro, Tasso, Mazzoni, and others, teaches what the laws are of a true epic poem, what of a dramatic, what of a lyric, what *decorum* is, which is the grand masterpiece to observe." As interpreted by the critics and commentators, d. called for distinct poetic genres, consistent characters, and the careful observance of the classical hierarchy of styles (grand, moderate, plain). Neoclassical d. came to emphasize literary propriety in the sense of elegance and correct taste, a propriety that avoided the vulgar as well as the unconventional.

Even while this neoclassical theory of d. was forming, however, it was being challenged by some poets. As Croce has said in his *Aesthetic,* art is intuitive, the rules of criticism concepts, and intuitive poets are always upsetting the rules. Medieval poets had more often than not either ignored or modified classical d., and many Renaissance poets, influenced by the Bible and Christian literature as well as by the medieval anarchy of forms, flouted fixed genres, conventionalized characters, the hierarchy of styles, and studied elegance of expression. "Right" tragedies and comedies, "true" epic poems and odes were written, but along with these neoclassical productions there also flourished tragical comedies, comical tragedies, tragicomedies, histories, romances, simple narrative poems and lyrics. To name just one example among several notable rebels, the actor-playwright Angelo Beolco (b. 1502), better known as Ruzzante from his favorite role, understood classical d. which fostered "literary" poetry, but argued for a different kind of artistic propriety, namely, simple nature. The characters in his peasant eclogues and farces spoke in their native dialects, using the most naive and sometimes the coarsest expressions.

Ruzzante of Padua was a naturalist, and soon turned from verse to prose as even more appropriate for his representations of pure nature. Naturalism in poetry, however, has always distrusted the conventional and traditional d. Wordsworth's revolt against "false refinement" and "poetic diction" was in large part the revolt of the naturalist against an artificial d. As he explained in his Preface to the *Lyrical Ballads,* he had chosen incidents and situations from "humble and rustic" life, and had related these in a "selection of language really used by men." Although Coleridge, in his *Biographia Literaria,* showed that the very act of "selection" plus the use of meter removed this poetry from rusticity, Wordsworth was demonstrating the truth of Croce's assertion that the intuitive artist is always upsetting the rules. For Wordsworth, not rules but the author's own feelings were his "stay and support."

It should be said, however, that although the neoclassical d. that long governed both critics and poets has fallen into disrepute, the original Ciceronian-Aristotelian concept of d. is still valid. No sensible poet or critic can quibble very much with the admonition that it is unseemly to use high-sounding expressions when speaking of the gutter and equally unseemly to use mean expressions when speaking of the majesty of Rome.—R. K. Hack, *The Doctrine of Lit. Forms* (HSCP, 1916); G. C. Fiske, *Cicero's De Oratore and Horace's Ars Poetica* (1929); J.W.H. Atkins, *Lit. Crit. in Antiquity* (1934); M. T. Herrick, *The Fusion of Horatian and Aristotelian Lit. Crit.* (1946); Wimsatt and Brooks; Weinberg. M.T.H.

DENOTATION. See CONNOTATION AND DENOTATION.

DIAERESIS. See METRICAL TREATMENT OF SYLLABLES.

DICTION, POETIC. See POETIC DICTION.

DIMETER (Gr. "of 2 measures"). A line consisting of 2 metra or measures. In classical iambic, trochaic, and anapaestic verse the metron is a dipody (pair of feet). Thus the trochaic dimeter

> ***blāstănēi kāi | sȳkŏphāntēi***
> **(Aristophanes, *Birds* 1479)**

contains 4 feet. But, as used by Eng. prosodists, "-meter" is synonymous with foot. The Eng. dimeter (a 2-stress line), therefore, consists of 2 feet, the trimeter of 3 feet, etc. P.S.C.

DIPODIC VERSE. Verse constructed rythmically so that, in scansion, pairs of feet must be considered together. That is, the metrical unit is less the individual foot than a dipody (2 related but slightly dissimilar feet, one of which normally has a stronger stress than the other). Crude dipodic verse, of the sort encountered in children's rhymes, nursery songs, and popular ballads, provides simple examples:

> **/ × \ ×**
> **Taffy was a | Welshman,**
> **/ × \ ×**
> **Taffy was a | thief.**

Here the first 4 syllables in each line constitute similar dipodies: to scan as if each line began with a trochee and a pyrrhic would be to underemphasize the force of the "secondary accent" on the word "was"; to scan as two trochees would be to overemphasize the stress on "was." More complex dipodic arrangements are to be found in a poem like Masefield's *Cargoes*.—G. R. Stewart, *Modern Metrical Techniques as Illustrated by Ballad Meter, 1700–1920* (1922) and "The Meter of the Popular Ballad," PMLA, 40 (1925); L. Woody, "Masefield's Use of Dipodic Meter," PQ, 10 (1931). P.F.

DIRGE. The name derives from the beginning of the antiphon in L. of the Office of the Dead ("Dirige, Domine . . ." adapted from Psalms 5.9). As a literary genre it comes from the Gr. *epicedium*, the song sung over the dead, and the threnody (q.v.). sung in memory of the dead, both of which were found in the L. *nenia*. Although in ancient literature it was sometimes influenced by the *consolatio* and closely connected with the elegy, its chief aim was to lament the dead, not console survivors. The meter in L. was the hexameter or the elegiac distich. The subject matter included lamentation and eulogy, often with consolatory reflections, apostrophes, invocations, etc. Not only may human beings be mourned but animals as well (cf. Catullus 3.). Simonides, Pindar, and the Alexandrian poets used the genre in Gr. In L., Calvus and Catullus first used it and Propertius brought it to its greatest perfection (4.11). The medieval writers combined the L. form with the church's lamentation for the dead, employing in the process Christian themes. In Eng., such poems as Henry King's *Exequy* on his young wife or George Meredith's *Dirge in the Woods* are examples of dirges.—G. Herrlinger, *Totenklage um Tiere in der antiken Dichtung* (1930); E. Reimer, *Die rituelle Totenklage der Griechen* (1938). R.A.H.

DISSONANCE. The quality of being harsh or inharmonious in rhythm or sound; akin to cacophony (q.v.). Insofar as the terms may be distinguished, cacophony is what is harsh-sounding in itself, d. is that which is discordant or inharmonious with what surrounds it. By extension the term may refer to poetic elements other than sound that are discordant with their immediate context. Donne and Browning have made notable use of d.—J. B. Douds, "Donne's Technique of D.," PMLA, 52 (1937). L.P.

DISTICH. A couple of metrical lines, usually rhymed and expressing a complete idea (see COUPLET). In classical poetry the most common d. is the elegiac (q.v.), consisting of a dactylic hexameter followed by a dactylic "pentameter." It was very often used by writers of epigrams and is common in modern Gr. poetry.—Koster; G. Soyter, "Das volkstümliche Distichon bei den Neugriechen," *Laographia*, 8 (1925). P.S.C.

DITHYRAMB. Gr. choric hymn, accompanied by mimic gestures, describing the adventures of Dionysus, the god of fertility and procreation. The etymology of the term is not very certain. Many consider it of Thracian or Phrygian origin. It was probably introduced into Greece early in the 7th c. and became very popular among the Dorians. In its earliest form it was led off by the leader of a band of revelers, a group of dancers, probably dressed as satyrs and dancing around a burning altar. Arion of Corinth (ca. 600 B.C.) gave it its regular form and raised it to the rank of artistic poetry. Shortly before 500 B.C. it was introduced into Athens by Lasus of Hermione and was soon recognized as one of the competitive subjects at the various Athenian festivals. For more than a generation after its introduction into Athens the d. attracted the most famous poets of the day and reached its highest point of development in the hands of Pindar and Simonides. By this time, however, it had ceased to concern itself exclusively with the adventures of Dionysus and begun to choose its subjects from all periods of Gr. mythology. Furthermore, even as early as before the middle of the 5th c. the d. had begun to undergo changes which affected seriously its original character. These changes consisted primarily in the abandonment of the antistrophic arrangement of the verses introduced by the Dorians, greater metrical freedom, the preponderance of the music over the words, the introduction of solo songs, and the use of bombastic and affected language. The results of these changes are illustrated in the lyric passages of the poet Timotheus (fl. 400 B.C.). In the 4th

c. and subsequently, the d. continued to lose steadily in importance, even in Athens. But we know that it was performed there as late as the imperial period.

In modern literature pure dithyrambs have been very rare. In Eng. poetry the d. probably finds its best expression in Dryden's *Alexander's Feast* (1697). The adjective "dithyrambic" is often used to describe both an enthusiastic and elevated and a wildly vehement and passionate composition.—Smyth; A. W. Pickard-Cambridge, *D., Tragedy and Comedy* (1927); Schmid and Stählin, I; G. A. Privitera, *Appunti intorno agli studi sul ditirambo* (1957). P.S.C.

DOGGEREL (origin unknown). Rough, poorly constructed verse, characterized by cheap sentiment, triviality, and lack of dignity. Chaucer referred to his burlesque *Tale of Sir Thopas* as *rym doggerel,* and Dr. Johnson stigmatized the vice in the following parody:

As with my hat upon my head
I walk'd along the Strand,
I there did meet another man
With his hat in his hand.
(G. Steevens, *Anecdotes of Johnson*
[Miscellanies], p. 315.)

Northrop Frye (in *The Anatomy of Criticism,* 1957) has characterized d. as the result of an unfinished creative process, in which a "prose initiative" has never assumed the associative qualities of true poetry, revealing its failure in a desperate attempt to resolve technical difficulties through any means which suggest themselves. There are, however, many works of real poetic value in which doggerel-like features are deliberately used for comic or satiric effect. John Skelton, Samuel Butler, and Jonathan Swift are all masters of artistic d., and much German *Knittelvers* also achieves a brilliant parodistic effect. L.B.P.

DRAMATIC POETRY. The limits of genres, upon whose conventions most creativity and surely all criticism in the arts depend, keep shifting from one generation to the next. On the other hand, were the boundaries of poetic categories, such as lyric, narrative, and dramatic, wholly fixed, writing would long since have grown mechanical. The 20th c. has prized the dr. highly, thus its emphasis on *show* rather than *tell* and its addiction to formulae such as, "never apologize, never explain," for authors. Poets, particularly, have taken to dramatization: they speak through interior monologues or assume masks; they liberate minor objects and elevate them as striking symbols; they indulge in contrasts between great and small, or private and public, or ancient and contemporary, or elegant and tawdry—in short, they strive for a heightening, not by connected discourse, but by ellipses. A major advocate for this manner, T. S, Eliot, observed that the past directs the present, which then may modify former orders. Consequently, by the standards of this century works have been resurrected from neglect or undergone revaluation. One criterion for excellence rests on how objective, and therefore dr., poets now sound. It follows that Dante, creating a self and expressing it through concrete figures, enjoyed a revival, and that Milton's reputation resting on vague images and didacticism declined. Donne, with two personalities of sinner and prelate, rose in popularity among readers who appreciated his nervous juxtapositions and vivid contrasts. Baudelaire's creating from a dandy's sensibilities an anxiety and vocabulary more witty and analytic than Tennyson had risked placed the Fr. master of postromantic despair far beyond his Eng. counterpart. Examples might extend for paragraphs. The result of this tendency complicates a definition of dr. poetry: older lines have blurred so that much more poetry now sounds dr., and the word has partly lost its descriptive nature and nearly changed into a standard for evaluation.

The traditional groupings of lyric, narrative, and dr., nevertheless, help delimit basic boundaries. Whether any man ever composed as a man rather than self-conscious poet probably no one can affirm. Certain poems do look almost anonymous, perhaps sincerely naive, as though the author expressed only his direct perception and, in some cases, his audience. With such compositions, however dramatized their images, the lyric attributes stay predominant. The narrative poem (including the epic) tells a story so that the writer speaks in his own person while setting the scene or giving exposition, but he puts on varied personalities and adopts different voices as the episodes require. In the dr., finally, the bare narrative fades away, and a group of characters embodied by actors remains. These distinctions have no fixed historical developments, and some works may partake of all three: Shakespeare's sonnets offer an instance. By itself the sonnet generally belongs to lyric poetry. Taken together the separate parts interact and produce a narrative which tells a kind of story. To the extent that the individual sonnets constitute a unified whole for which the author appends no direct commentary, it may look dr. The frequently explicated sequence lacks the precise lines which dr. poetry needs. One can compare Shakespeare's with other lyric poems and his *Troilus and Cressida,* for all its idiosyncrasies, with other plays, but one can scarcely cite any other dr. composition, however loosely that term is applied, quite like the sonnets. When a word which should describe a genre extends to embrace almost unique titles, it has lost its primary function.

Putting aside the subtleties of aesthetic and subjective prejudices, one might then agree upon the approximate range for dr. poetry. Its origins provide clues for the abiding attributes. In the Western world drama had two origins, one in Gr. festivals and, after nearly disappearing, another in the medieval church. A very early example from the Christian era belongs to the enactment of the Easter story called, after the angel's inquiry, the *Quem Quaeritis* Trope. Drama poses a question whose answer must unfold in human terms and not as abstract theology or a single emotion. For another dimension: the development of plays in Gr. culture depended upon adding to the traditional chorus in Dionysiac festivals a speaker, called the *hypocrites* or answerer. The questioner receives his reply from someone who need not reveal all he knows. Taken together these two (or more) constitute the cast or *dramatis personae.* In its origins *persona* seems associated with the term for mask; those who ask and respond assume a distinct personality and project their special traits through what they say. Finally, drama derives from *dran,* to do or act, so that the development does not occur simply as a dialogue but as a recognizable imitation of a happening. Why these speeches initially appear in poetry causes no uncertainty for the moment; it existed before plays themselves as part of the rites. Prose, although it soon enters in passages or takes over entirely, may represent a decline, just as pieces which deviate too far from the stage may grow overly speculative.

One paradox in evaluating any play depends upon its need for production; until having seen a performance one can scarcely possess a very accurate grasp of it, but, afterwards, that single interpretation may unduly influence one's judgments. This condition marks all drama, but, especially, the poetic will partake of the cast's inflections. A more vexing question hinges upon whether a prose translation of a play in verse distorts it seriously, whether, for example, Yeats's prose rendering of *Oedipus Tyrannus* gets closer to or further from Sophocles than Gilbert Murray's stanzas do. Similar problems hinge upon performances; does a dedicated troupe of students declaiming *The Birds* in the original before a non-Gr. audience commit a greater violence on Aristophanes than a professional company acting *Lysistrata* in translation? Here, again, to emphasize dr. qualities and the primacy of the theater itself at least helps. At present, the Comédie Française in Paris, the Piccolo Teatro in Milan, the R.S.C. of London, and the Burgtheater of Vienna among others keep on their active repertoire Molière, Goldoni, Shakespeare, and Schiller respectively in productions which, with varying degrees, exhibit tradition and experiment. Drama, to a greater extent than most other arts, relies on continued revaluations; every mounting entails another approach and in instances will stress novel aspects. At the same time, since printing, plays also remain available on the page, and, no matter how drenched in atmosphere with scrims, lighting, music, and stylization, dr. poetry needs, self-evidently, its language and not just the shifting tricks which directors, rather than authors themselves, may stumble upon through private predilections.

The kind of verse congenial to the stage varies a good deal from country to country and a bit less from time to time, as does the strictness of its uses. Generally the complete script rather than impressive parts sets the prevalent tone. Some examples might help define these conditions. When Lear realizes that Cordelia is dead, he says, in a moment of tragic recognition, "Thou'lt come no more. / Never, never, never, never, never!" The celebrated line, which out of context hardly looks striking, depends for its effects upon many circumstances: the suffering king whom it describes, his change from irascibility at the opening and rage on the heath, pity for Cordelia, and tragic awe. By itself it is not necessarily poetry, but the dr. rhythm undeniably reaches one of its heights here. In contrast, at the end of *Ghosts,* as Oswald declines into imbecility, he mutters, "Mother, give me the sun.... The sun, the sun," and Mrs. Alving wonders whether she can ever bring herself to poison him. Whatever pathos the scene may arouse, the line, scannable in translation, does not partake of poetry because the play throughout relies upon prose and a more pragmatic level—hence the irony of the title—than verse allows. At another extreme, to close *The Rake's Progress* a quartet sings a warning, "For idle hands / And hearts and minds / The Devil finds / A work to do, / A work, dear Sir, fair Madam, / For you and you." This passage indisputably belongs to verse and also the stage. About its merits opinions may differ, depending perhaps upon how clearly the echo from the end of *Don Giovanni* comes through. Opera, however, does not count as dramatic poetry because it fits more suitably into another genre where music has taken over as the medium and replaced a sustained repetition in the movement of language. For their effectiveness many operas rely upon the simplicity of the words. Finally, when Samson laments his condition, "O dark, dark, dark amid the blaze of noon / Irrecoverably dark, total eclipse / Without all hope of day," the poetry projects a special fervor but does not move rightly on the stage. At least, from a few experimental productions *Samson Agonistes* has not held its own and so fits more suitably with closet drama, dialogue designed only for the printed page. To turn back, finally, to Aristotle for a confirmation of such points—and he, of course, knew only plays in verse and closely associated with festivals—drama must contain plot, character, diction, thought, spectacle, and song. Although Aristotle, like most academicians since, did not rate spectacle highly, to ignore it raises too many extraneous questions.

Dr. poetry seldom exists in its pure state, just as, perhaps, *Oedipus Tyrannus* alone quite fits Aristotle's definition of tragedy. Granted imprecise limits, where it leaves off and turns into something else, basic essentials for its unique attributes do emerge. In addition to the general qualities which distinguish all poetry, metrical language, especially when recited on a stage, sustains the tableaux at a more intense level, whether for grandeur or satire, than prose can. Moreover, every production must establish some kind of rhythm, and, here again, if the voice as well as the body furthers the tempo, the performance gains commensurately. Prose has its own cadences, many brilliantly orchestrated, as in Congreve's comedies, and actors may, indeed, sometimes prefer it because it encourages their own mannerisms to cover a wider range. Over the years poetry has held its own for reasons which no one has yet fully explained; were no mystery connected with it, probably it would long since have vanished. One cause for its continuity may hark back to its origins: the theater retains aspects of participation by a group in an established ceremony. For this reason, among others, poetry has seldom attained prominence in motion pictures or television, which direct their products to frankly commercial ends. To mention individual titles as illustrations will probably pin down the range which poetry can encompass more effectively than added speculation here will. Before a chronological survey, one representative title—not necessarily the greatest within the conventional divisions of comedy and tragedy—will establish bases for noting later deviations.

A neoclassical play, obeying the rules promulgated in 17th-c. France, *Phèdre,* observes nearly impeccable proportions. Racine's language, in the expected couplets, establishes a tragic, elevated tone so that, with its deliberate aloofness, it creates its speakers as both individuals and types. Inside such confines it can, exploiting restricted variations, display much subtlety for both euphony of phrase and nuance. It investigates a persistent problem, that of passionate love, here a woman's for her stepson, but the *dénouement* cannot, by definition, dispel the mystery beyond clarifying the particular circumstances. By restricting himself to his notoriously small vocabulary, Racine manages a full exploration of his complex theme. The concepts must refer to psychological complications, and the fewer purely external interferences, the better: character is fate. Inevitability unfolds with unswerving logic, As Phèdre describes her suffering to the confidante, with a minimum of gestures reinforcing the words and in a functional *mise en scène,* the mind operates upon but fails to quell the emotions, which, expressed through the analytic alexandrines, gather to themselves intensity and amplitude. For an indicative comparison, Robert Lowell's Eng. rendering, with gratuitous figures and intensifying words added, sinks into rant and does not commensurately rise to terror, As with architecture, so with poetry in the theater: less is more. In Fr. the deliberate artificiality of the verse prevents the frenzy from spilling over into mere bombast. *Phèdre* stays a nearly unique example, even for the Fr. theater and Racine, and, like most models, the very lack of singularity may restrict it as less engrossing than others with slightly distorted proportions. To place *Phèdre* at a figurative center will indicate different types of diction in plays on similar themes, not by implication better or worse.

When the emotions no longer quite contain themselves in such simplicity of language, and when the characters fall victim to forces disproportionate to their strength and situations, the effect tends toward melodrama, for instance Dryden's heroic play *Aureng-Zebe.* To sustain mounting tensions the story may swell with improbabilities or collapse in an anticlimax. If a musical accompaniment serves to hold the whole together and make acceptable simplified exaggerations which the poetry by itself can no longer contain, the result grows entirely operatic, Verdi's *Don Carlos* based on Schiller's romantic play. Toward an opposite direction, when Phèdre herself serves as not merely a woman but directly embodies a myth, the situation may call for more than she can say in her own person, particularly if an awareness of her as an archetype emerges for an audience to whom she reveals, partially, a religious mystery. The play may then need a chorus for commentary with ceremonial songs and dances, the difference between Racine's *Phèdre* and Euripides' *Hippolytus.* If, too, as in the Gr. tragedy, the obsessive emotions loom as almost supernatural and Artemis and Aphrodite actually occupy the stage, then the verse may incorporate incantation, verging on the goal of all rituals, which bring knowledge of earth from heaven. If one thinks of these two movements as upward and downward, then toward the left, should Phèdre lose her status as a queen, a woman elevated, and become an unhappy wife, the verse may seek more idiomatic turns, paradoxically often away from directness, the effect in Lope de Vega's *Punishment without Revenge.* Eventually it may terminate with a domestic tragedy in prose, such as *Desire Under the Elms,* set forth through O'Neill's typically choked dialogue. Opposite from this point, to the right, when the characters begin uttering words meant primarily to evoke patterns nearly independent of the tableaux, then the effect approaches closet drama or, ultimately, ballet, where the voice separates from individuals and the poet gives up dramatization through words, such as Cocteau's ballet based on *Phèdre.* These directions are not absolutes, and intricate variations may arise through joining them, but, generally, diction must shape and control the episodes; when it no longer does, then a genre freed from the conventions strictly governing a play in verse has evolved.

If tragedy depicts the analysis of a continuing enigma, comedy explodes false mystification through people who should shun pretensions. The language, consequently, revels in weird extravagances. *Volpone,* for example, like *Phèdre* belongs to the neoclassical pattern of the 17th c. It shows three men bringing presents in order to be named the sole heir of a man who pretends to be dying. Because the characters deceive themselves, their vocabulary has lost touch with reality. Vain ambitions, which they project through their speeches, puff all of them. Commensurately with this bent, their baseless wishes swell as disproportionate and ridiculous. Only Jonson's firmly reined blank verse prevents parts from disintegrating into rant. Whereas tragedy must veil an uncontainable fate, comedy must expose people who deceive themselves. In tone comic diction ranges from satire to benignity, from Aristophanes to Molière. Comedy also expands in four approximate directions. That acceptable examples of tragedies on similar topics come to mind at once, whereas nearly every memorable comedy in verse looks nearly unique, suggests that the ridiculous must examine contemporary failings, which seldom endure. When it reverts to an affirmed joy, that man with all his limits will ultimately triumph, it partakes of its origins in celebrating fertility or harvests, and all may dissolve in songs, feasts, games, and wedding ceremonies.

Comparable with tragedy's approach to opera, comedy may quite yield to spectacle so that in the 17th c. the masque (q.v.), where decor buried the poetry, may supersede it and, in the 20th, musical comedy, where prose ties together a spate of lyrics. Again, parallel with tragedy, if the scene grows domestic and the language idiomatic, then what passes for comedy in popular usage has evolved. Finally, just as tragedy veers toward slighting language, comedy may abandon thought and revert to a clown's pantomime, where a touching tragic admixture occurs in the very inarticulate quality of its performers' lacking eloquence. Although circus and farce do not enjoy very high reputations at the present time (nor, until recently, has the musical comedy as evolved in the United States, nor, except to academic studies, have whatever spring rites may survive), these forms, if they overcome clichés, need not be judged by their natures minor; they simply have left off being instances of dr. poetry.

Such a schematic outline does violence to the wayward growth of the drama itself, and a loosely chronological order will help modify the generalizations. The Gr. theater, to which nearly all western developments owe some debt, arose out of rituals, for tragedy those devoted to Dionysus. The large amphitheaters still remaining attest to its popularity, and authors received official prizes for their works. Drama itself started when a speaker exchanged dialogue with the chorus which sang in a rhythmic movement. Consequently, the poetry attendant upon all religious ceremonies accompanied secular plays from the outset, as did dancing or, at least, formal movement. The very nature of this diction required stylization, and the staging itself corresponded, with the actors garbed for tragedy in high masks. The short lines exchanged between speakers, stichomythia, kept to a rigorous pattern. Varied meters served, particularly for the chorus with its standard turns divided into strophe, antistrophe, and epode, but dialogue stayed chiefly in alexandrines. Plays by three writers of tragedy remain, although in each case far from the total number which they composed. Their styles differ, but all elude translation; recently the challenge has intrigued a number of poets in England and the United States, and their versions remove the seeming falsifications perpetrated by preceding centuries. The problem, of course, plagues all dr. poetry. By its nature it incorporates deliberate artificiality, and, yet, if it sounds only stiffly contrived, it fails to catch living accents. As a result, any translation must adhere to limits acceptable by literary and idiomatic standards for less than a century. Moreover, the Gr. dramatists worked in traditional materials so that their audiences could often respond with a directness to nuances not understandable later. Aeschylus, the earliest, while observing an austerity in plots and actions, can rise to solemnity and exuberance poetically. Sophocles indulged in a more personal vocabulary which favored the ironic implications of words as well as action. The characters' discovering the full implications of their sentences and deeds only with the unfolding of the story constitutes his theatrical effectiveness. With Euripides the tone sounds decidedly more mixed. His tragic figures, the women, especially, reveal psychological suffering in images more tortured than his predecessors'. The action, likewise, draws mixed responses; the puzzling *Alcestis* still causes controversy.

Where and how Gr. comedy originated remains more debatable. Aristophanes has left the first surviving examples, although he clearly drew upon antecedents. Indicatively the oral and physical extravagances which adhere to comedy occur in all his plays, as men search vainly to realize their desires and endure indignities, such as ascending to heaven on a beetle. Somehow, in spite of their bewilderment by an unpredictable world, they ultimately triumph. The language features sharply biting exchanges, and the plots revel in exaggerations unavailable to the stage since. The basically personal bias, using more meters than tragedy, represents old comedy. The need for this mode to depict mainly contemporary foibles restricts it more persistently to an idiom of an obvious verisimilitude than tragedy must observe. As part of this nature, Gr. comedy apparently moved through a middle phase, which stays conjectural, and a late phase called new comedy, with which the works of Menander have become virtually synonymous; the recently discovered *Dyskolos* is the only reasonably complete play extant by which Menander's talents can be judged. Although prized above Aristophanes by some critics, Menander's poetry represents a descent toward mere speech. He specializes in the stereotypes who form so conspicuous a part of comedy and who, themselves unchanging, always mouth the fashionable clichés so that plays featuring them age quickly. Plautus and Terence, the Roman dramatists who copied Menander, fill their plots with similar intrigues and cross purposes. While differences set off these two writers, they treat the same topics: clever slaves, lost children, braggarts, and wayward sons. These complications may copy life, particularly Gr. and Roman life, but for language they necessitate a looseness which no versification can entirely rescue and require those embarrassing notes in which editors translate foreign idioms into the outmoded slang of their own youth. As a whole, such works probably give the social historian more pleasure than the playgoer. Seneca, the author of L. tragedies, barely exceeding closet drama, retains an ambiguous reputation. His tortured syntax and melodramatic twists perhaps deserve mention more for their later influence than achievements on their own; in the 17th c. the Roman dramatists exerted a heavier influence than the Gr.

With the medieval period, almost all drama of any sort disappeared, as far as records can prove, until it sprang again mainly from the churches. For a second time European theater took direction from a religious ceremony. Although some critics make the development one toward secularization, or an intrusion of realistic material, such a theory denies art special attributes and reduces it to mirroring events rather than reinterpreting persistent impulses in human terms. For whatever causes, during the 17th c. both tragedy and comedy reached their most impressive achievements since the classical era. Among the conflicting factors credited—such as a popular and/or aristocratic audience, the appearance of gifted authors and/or actors, a culmination from earlier developments, and simply the historical moment—a large measure indisputably depends upon making and perfecting a native idiom for stage poetry in each country. Without merely copying classical patterns, the stage took over its measures and fitted them to the vernacular so that they display both directness and grace. No single tendency will define all of them, but everywhere the crossing between the native and the classical accounts for the vigor. The proportions vary, with the Fr. theater almost determinedly neoclassical and the Eng. more mixed.

For England, *Gorboduc* in the mid 16th c., whatever its limits, hit upon blank verse, which continues almost the basis in Eng. dr. poetry. Until Marlowe's *Tamburlaine,* with his modulation of the line into a more pliant instrument, stage verse stayed awkwardly stiff. His swelling syllables reinforce a conqueror's vision and emphasize man's despair in containing human wishes. In spite of its seeming freedom, Elizabethan poetry obeyed, while expanding, the formal rules for grammar, rhetoric, and logic formulated by Renaissance rhetoricians, who founded their trivium upon classical models. Nevertheless, later, under less skilled hands, drama may disintegrate into mere melodrama or sensational effects of speech and action, a danger perhaps inherent from the outset in Kyd's *Spanish Tragedy* with its Senecan touches. To count Shakespeare the heir of these earlier writers emphasizes once again how greatly any artistic creation must exceed the source upon which it draws. Indeed, to the astounding degree that Shakespeare excels any other dramatist, at least in the qualities now prized, counting him the measure for excellence may limit one's appreciation of other, not necessarily less interesting, playwrights. In language, as any other theatrical trait, he ranges as he chooses and breaks rules with impunity. This very assurance leads lesser authors to fiascoes, as, for example, the succession of dull plays based vaguely upon *Hamlet* sufficiently proves. His poetic resources can range in tragedy from passages of formal balance to quite simple, idiomatic speeches without disrupting a deeply sustained tone. Because his career traces a consistent development, no single title can wholly exemplify his technique, although the movement in diction strives toward greater freedom with meters and a simplified vocabulary. In the great tragedies, through the metaphors, the exploration of thought and emotions ranges so widely that it almost exceeds containable limits. The presence of running patterns in imagery, which comments upon the story, contributes further to this richness. Passages in prose handle effects from realism to humor which verse by itself probably could not sustain.

In comedy he likewise displays assurance from the tavern scenes with Falstaff to the happy endings for lovers. Shakespeare excels in comedy which relies upon romance, but infrequently, except in early works, does he undertake the grotesque extremes in which Jonson specialized. Jonsonian comedy, as in *Volpone,* already discussed, loses contact with actuality while the vocabulary further distorts the speakers' swollen dreams. Few other writers commanded Jonson's assurance, and comedy, even in the Jacobean period, stressed such pyrotechnics less and relied more upon a kind of realism and prose. Tragedy, while partly leaning toward domestic commonplaces after Shakespeare, became generally more extreme with an emphasis upon nearly pathological states. The verse, unable always to contain these effects, therefore verged upon pathos and grew sentimental except in Webster and, unevenly, Ford. The hiatus in theatrical production for nearly twenty years cleared the way for a different style with the Restoration. Comedy moved almost uniformly into prose and explored the foibles of fashionable society. Tragedy, influenced to a degree by the Fr. theater, abandoned blank verse briefly and copied the foreign couplets. The narrow limits of this mode, and its requiring a simplified diction, could not hold the scene very long. Moreover, by featuring unexpected reversals in plots and reducing psychology to the claims of love and honor, debated at length, the action lay stilted and frozen. Nevertheless, the impetus from which much of this derives, the Fr. theater, yields far richer effects.

In France a group of dramatists devotedly serving restrictions more severe than those which Aristotle promulgated produced tragedies distinguished by lines nearly as clear-cut as the Elizabethan and Jacobean are diversified. With Corneille, not wholly happy in the conventions which he obeyed, the theme of love and honor, more congenial to Fr. than Eng. psychology, took readily to couplets, which heightened the antitheses. The style culminates with Racine, although a criticism sometimes directed at his plays holds that the analyses of emotion grow too rarefied and overly refined. In comedy, on the other hand, Molière often serves as a paragon with his graceful emphasis on common sense, on types who violate social standards, on a genial wit, and on easily conversational movement in his verse. He may in instances skirt dangerously close to prosaic moralizing, but by its nature comedy inevitably runs this risk. How closely dramatists succeed in various modes may attend upon native patterns of language. For example, the Sp. theater of Lope de Vega and Calderón, nearly contemporary with the Fr. and Eng., like the Elizabethan may mix emotions and employ varying styles. The *comedia de capa y espada* drew upon such mixed tendencies with a wider range of versification than contemporary plays elsewhere in Europe employed. After the general flowering of drama throughout Europe during the 17th c., the one following witnessed a decline into wholly stilted plays on classical themes or sentimental domestic pieces. In both cases the diction almost disintegrated into artificiality or cloying affectation.

With the approach of the 19th c., the triumphant romanticism which swept through every country brought along a reemphasis upon the theater based chiefly on the new enthusiasm for Shakespeare, particularly in England and Germany. An anomalous aspect of the romantic temperament often trapped it between the lyric, the desire to express fresh, spontaneous feelings, and the dr., the compulsion to impose novel and generally self-conscious poses. Consequently, nearly every romantic poet sought—or expressed the wish—to write a play and failed in the effort. In plots, despite an earnestness, their plays often touch bathos, and the verse emphasizes more twists of speculation than the stage can contain while action itself languishes for long stretches. In England nearly every major poet of the century set his hand to plays, all of which, to 20th-c. tastes, look unstageworthy. With scarcely more memorable results, the Fr. poets, likewise, assaulted the theater. Despite minor rebellions in style, exciting at the time, Hugo's plays, like most romantic drama, sound operatic, and, significantly, some, such as *Hernani,* have furnished the material for libretti. In Germany, as well, the romantic era encouraged a similar development, but philosophizing nearly predominates over psychology, as in Schiller and Goethe. These two directions, toward a lyric expression and toward a versified metaphysic, pulled in opposite directions and, for the period, reached a symbolic culmination with the interminable mythologies of Wagner's operas and Mallarmé's fragmentary prose-poem *Igitur,* admittedly closet drama. By and large the romantics did not admire intentional comedy, which disintegrated with popular playwrights into mere farce, and the serious theater itself yielded to problem plays, well made in utilitarian prose.

In the 20th c., despite many attempts at revitalization, these two extremes survive to hamper dr. poetry: efforts to project a lyric slightness or to express transcendant generalizations. In Eng. Yeats favored enigmatic material influenced by what he made of the Japanese Nō (q.v.) plays. Hugo von Hofmannsthal in Germany experimented with a similar mode before, largely, turning to the books for Richard Strauss' operas, With both authors purely dr. poetry fell into abeyance. On the other hand, modifying Elizabethan approaches, T. S. Eliot through his own theatrical development almost repeated the historical growth of the drama, starting with a religious pageant, *The Rock,* its choruses using irregular meters, and subsequently working through plays which incorporate themes from Gr. tragedies in modern settings. His language has, similarly, modified blank verse and shuns any self-conscious artificiality. Christopher Fry, with *The Lady's not for Burning,* sporadically achieved the exuberance of an essentially comic verse. An instance of how tragedy demands tighter diction occurs in his *The Dark Is Light Enough,* which tries for greater pathos and fails to encompass the theme convincingly. Unfortunately, a promising departure for plays in verse, one based on the idioms of jazz, has not come into its own apart from musical comedies, where undistinguished prose holds together the songs and dances. The most interesting experiments along such lines, the collaborations between W. H. Auden and Christopher Isherwood, suffer from an excessive indulgence in wit. The two titles of an incomplete work in this vein by T. S. Eliot, originally published as "Wanna Go Home, Baby?" but changed to "Fragment of an

Agon," exemplify the difficulties which this manner imposes. The colloquial sounds only trite, no matter how serious the puns, and the formal a bit too stiff and ironic for its subject. Furthermore, with the disappearance of the authentic sources for this speech, even as expressed in vaudeville and the music hall, the future will have no place from which to draw the raw materials.

Indeed, at present the entire concept of poetry in the theater relies less and less upon language and increasingly on the special contributions from stagecraft. Here, again, the 20th-c. tendency to exploit the unique materials of the arts as expressive in themselves perhaps has had an influence. Thus, painting no longer favors a subject, music has abandoned programmatic notes, and sculpture concentrates upon mass and space. The emotions associated with the arts have, as a result, shifted. In many ways the short story provides the sudden insight once reserved for lyric poetry. On the other hand, the novel since James has taken to dramatizing subjects, and the major novelists in this century have annexed what remains of the epic, if not precisely the heroic. What the theater can best trade upon remains problematic. If the term dr., as applied to poetry, now connotes praise, for the theatre itself it sounds almost pejorative, synonymous with commercial or, nearly, anti-poetic. Works belonging to the "Theatre of the Absurd" with their destructive tendencies drawn from early Dada and later existentialism have sought to destroy conventional language along with other middle-class clichés. Whatever originality such plays exhibit, their dialogue—or, frequently soliloquies even when involving two or more speakers—relies on prose whether sinewy as Beckett's or explosive as Genet's. The efforts of others to sustain a poetry sound puerile and not unfortunately, by design. Dryden started "An Essay of Dramatic Poesy," "It was that memorable day, in the first summer of the late war," but removed his debaters from the conflict so they could discuss their points leisurely. At the moment, caught between the claims of disinterested art and engagement, the theater has not yet hit upon any effective substitute for poetry. No one has recently succeeded in bringing forth any enduring verse for the stage, either.

General: critical prefaces and essays of Aristotle, Sidney, Jonson, Lope de Vega, Corneille, Molière, Racine, Dryden, Johnson, Lessing, Schiller, Goethe, Coleridge, and Hugo; A. Nicoll, *Theory of Drama* (1923); G. Baty and R. Chavance, *Vie de l'art théâtral des origines à nos jours* (1932); E. A. Drew, *Discovering Drama* (1937); Wellek and Warren; M. E. Prior, *The Language of Tragedy* (1947); *Understanding Drama,* ed. C. Brooks and R. B. Heilman (1948); J. L. Barrault, *Reflections on the Theatre* (1951); S. H. Butcher, *Aristotle's Theory of Poetry and Fine Art* (4th ed., rev., 1951); M. McCarthy, *Sights and Spectacles* (1956); Frye; A. Artaud, *The Theater and Its Double* (1958).

Specialized Studies: N. Díaz de Escovar and F. de P. Lasso de la Vega, *Historia del teatro español* (2 v., 1924); W. B. Yeats, *Essays* (1924); H. C. Lancaster, *A Hist. of Fr. Dramatic Lit.* (1929–1942); E. E. Stoll, *Poets and Playwrights* (1930); C. V. Deane, *Dramatic Theory and the Rhymed Heroic Play* (1931); J. S. Kennard, *The It. Theatre* (2 v., 1932); T. S. Eliot, *Elizabethan Essays* (1943), *Poetry and Drama* (1951); H. Granville-Barker, *On Poetry in Drama* (1937); M. Bieber, *The Hist. of the Gr. and Roman Theater* (1939; 2d ed., 1961); U. Ellis-Fermor, *Frontiers of Drama* (1945); A. Nicoll, *The Development of the Theatre* (3d ed., rev., 1946); R. Peacock, *Poet in the Theatre* (1946); F. Fergusson, *Idea of a Theater* (1953); R. Langbaum, *The Poetry of Experience* (1957); R. Lattimore, *The Poetry of Gr. Tragedy* (1958); D. Donoghue, *The Third Voice: Modern British and Am. Verse Drama* (1959).

J.J.E.

DREAM-ALLEGORY is one variety of the vision literature popular in the Middle Ages. The allegory may vary widely in purpose and extent and is often fused with other, frequently more interesting, elements. The framework, however, shows little variety. Springtime commonly provides the season. The poet finds himself in a pleasant wood or garden; falls asleep to the music of birds and brook; dreams; and in the dream beholds either real people performing symbolic actions or, more commonly, certain abstractions personified and going through a set of motions which to the conscious mind will have other significance. The type apparently received a major impulse from Macrobius' commentary upon the *Somnium Scipionis* in Cicero's imperfectly preserved *Republic.* Probably its best known representative, vastly influential, was the *Roman de la Rose.* In Eng., the type is best represented by Langland's *Piers Plowman;* and, among many others, both the anonymous *The Pearl* and Chaucer's *Parlement of Foules* have been considered dream-allegories.—E. Langlois, *Origines et sources du Roman de la Rose* (1891); W. H. Schofield, "The Nature and Fabric of *The Pearl,*" PMLA, 19 (1904); E. Rickert, "A New Interpretation of *The Parlement . . . ,*" MP, 18 (1920); C. S. Lewis, *The Allegory of Love* (1938); A.A.T. Macrobius, *Commentary on the Dream of Scipio,* tr. W. H. Stahl (1952); G. de Lorris and J. de Meun, *The Romance of the Rose,* tr. H. W. Robbins, ed. C. W. Dunn (1962).

J.L.L.

DURATION. The length of time phonetic phenomena (particularly syllables) continue. One of the four characteristics of a spoken sound, the others being pitch (q.v.), loudness, and quality. Since poetry is constructed of spoken sounds, duration of syllables, as well as of feet, lines, and stanzas, is an important consideration in analyzing the phonetic construction of a poem. The shortness of many of the important vowels in Pope's line

Not so, when swift Camilla scours the plain
(*Essay on Criticism* 2.372)

contributes to the effect of rapidity and delicacy which the line conveys. Some prosodists have attempted to explain accent (q.v.) in terms of d.

P.F.

E

ECLOGUE. A short, conventional poem, usually a pastoral, in the form of a dialogue or soliloquy. Ordinarily it is without appreciable characterization or action; the setting, described either by the poet or by one of the characters, is objective; and the highly finished verse is smooth and melodious. Originally the word, derived from *eklegein* (to choose), meant "a choice poem." The spelling *aeglogue* (or *eglog*), popularized by Dante, was based on the false etymology which derived the word from *aix* (goat) and *logos* (speech) and was construed to signify, as "E. K." argued, "Goteheards tales." The term was first applied to Virgil's bucolic poems, and from this association became the designation of a formal pastoral poem following the traditional technique derived from the idylls of Theocritus. Though there are precedents in both classical and Renaissance literature of city and piscatory eclogues, most eclogues are pastorals. The term, however, signifies nothing more than structure. The Renaissance was the heyday of the eclogue. Negligible as a genre in the Middle Ages, it was revived by Dante, Petrarch, and Boccaccio and came to full flower under the culture of the humanists of the 15th and 16th c. Widely studied and of dominating influence (as evidenced by Shakespeare's well-known comment, "Ah, good old Mantuan! . . . who understandeth thee not, loves thee not") were the eclogues of Baptista Mantuanus Spagnuoli. Still considered the best modern examples of the genre are those by Garcilaso de la Vega and Edmund Spenser. Pope's eclogues, though called *Pastorals,* epitomize the neoclassic eclogue and rococo art. In the 18th c. new matter was poured into the mold and a variety of eclogues—town, exotic, political, war, school, culinary, Quaker—was produced. The most celebrated of the nonpastoral eclogues is Swift's *A Town Eclogue. 1710. Scene, The Royal Exchange.* See PASTORAL, GEORGIC.—M. H. Shackford, "A Definition of the Pastoral Idyll," PMLA, 19 (1904); W. W. Greg, *Pastoral Poetry and Pastoral Drama* (1906); W. P. Mustard, "Introduction" to *The Piscatory Eclogues of Jacopo Sannazaro* (1914), and "Notes on *The Shepheardes Calendar,*" MLN, 35 (1920); R. F. Jones, "E. Types in Eng. Poetry of the 18th C.," JEGP, 34 (1925); M. K. Bragg, *The Formal E. in 18th C. England* (1926); D. Lessig, *Ursprung und Entwicklung der spanischen Ekloger* . . . (1962).

J.E.C.

ELEGIAC DISTICH. The Gr. *elegeion* (a word of uncertain derivation which first occurs in Critias frag. 4.31 Diehl) was a distich or couplet which was composed of a heroic or dactylic hexameter followed by a pentameter (q.v.). As is shown by Ovid's address to *flebilis Elegeia* (*Amores* 3.9.3), the word was connected in antiquity with the later meaning of *elegos* ("song of mourning" as in Euripides and Apollonius Rhodius 2.782), but its use for epitaphs and laments is probably not quite so ancient as its beginnings in the 8th or 7th c. B.C. with flute songs (Archilochus, Callinus, Mimnermus), war songs (Tyrtaeus), and dedications. It was used for many purposes in the classical age of Greece and, notably but by no means exclusively, for love poems in the Alexandrian, Roman, and Byzantine periods. In L. the Augustan elegiac poets (Tibullus, Propertius, and Ovid) tended to make the sense coincide with the couplet, whereas in Gr. poetry and Catullus it was often continuous for two or more distichs. Among the refinements which in time became regular in the Roman elegists and particularly in Ovid was the restriction of the final word in the pentameter to a dissyllable.

The classic description and imitation of the elegiac distich in the accentual verse of a modern language is Schiller's couplet:

Im Hexameter steigt des Springquells flüssige Säule,
Im Pentameter drauf fällt sie melodisch herab,

which Coleridge thus reproduced:

In the hexameter rises the fountain's silvery column,
In the pentameter aye falling in melody back.

The form has been imitated in Eng. by Spenser, Sidney, Clough, Kingsley, and Swinburne and, in German, by Klopstock and Goethe in addition to Schiller. (See also CLASSICAL METERS IN MODERN LANGUAGES.)—Hardie; Hamer; D. L. Page, "The Elegiacs in Euripides' *Andromache,*" Gr. *Poetry and Life* (1936); C. M. Bowra, *Early Gr. Elegists* (1938, repr. 1960); M. Platnauer, *L. Elegiac Verse* (1951); Koster; M. L. Clarke, "The Hexameter in Gr. Elegiacs," CR, n.s. 5 (1955); D. A. West, "The Metre of Catullus' Elegiacs," CQ, n.s. 7 (1957).

R.J.G.

ELEGIAC STANZA (also known as elegiac quatrain, heroic quatrain, Hammond's meter). The iambic pentameter quatrain, rhymed abab, has apparently acquired the name of elegiac stanza through its use by Thomas Gray for *Elegy Written in a Country Churchyard* (1751). It is identical in form with the quatrain used in Shakespearean sonnets, where its use has no elegiac connotations, and it was frequently employed without elegiac feeling or intention by other poets, e.g., Dryden in his *Annus Mirabilis*. However, according to W. J. Bate (*The Stylistic Development of Keats,* 1945), the pentameter quatrain was "almost invariably employed for the writing of elegiac verse" from about the middle of the 18th c. until almost a century later, beginning with James Hammond's *Love Elegies* (1743). But even Gray's use of the form in his great poem failed to establish a quatrain tradition, both Shelley's *Adonais* and Arnold's *Thyrsis* being written in more complex stanzas. S.F.F.

ELEGY (from Gr. *elegeia,* "lament"). A lyric, usually formal in tone and diction, suggested either by the death of an actual person or by the poet's contemplation of the tragic aspects of life. In either case, the emotion, originally expressed as a lament, finds consolation in the contemplation of some permanent principle. Any discussion of the origin of the e. is complicated by a shifting of definitions. The term in Gr. literature referred both to a specific verse form (couplets consisting of a hexameter followed by a pentameter line) and to the emotions frequently conveyed by that verse form. Originally, any poem in this distich form (with the exception of the epigram) was known as an e., whether it concerned the dead, was a war song, a political satire, or dealt with love. The pastoral laments, such as those of Theocritus, which seem in subject matter to be prototypes of the modern elegy, were classed by the Greeks as idylls. The distich form of e. was employed by the Alexandrian Greeks chiefly for erotic and suggestive verse. The Latin e. itself was initially distinguished from other literary genres by the distich meter, the tone of complaint, and the theme of love, as in Gallus, Propertius, Tibullus, and their successors. In Ovid the distich and the tone of complaint are already extended to other subjects as in *Tristia* and *Ex Ponto,* although love remains his dominant theme.

In early 16th-c. Italy, when other experiments in the imitation of classic meters were being made, the content and subject matter of the e. were taken over into terza rima by such writers as Bernardo Tasso and Ariosto, whose *Rime* and *Satire* received the label of elegies only after his death. The elegiac strain of extended lyrics expressing melancholy and tender sentiments was represented in the baroque period by Filicaia and continued into 19th-c. It. letters by Leopardi and Carducci. In modern times there have even been metrical experiments with the classic distich by D'Annunzio.

In Spain, the e. began as imitations of It. models, as in Garcilaso de la Vega's *First Eclogue* (ca. 1535) on the death of his lady, in the tradition of the pastoral e. and in some of his other poems modeled upon the work of Bernardo Tasso. Lope de Vega (1562–1635) used octaves and other stanzaic measures in imitation of Tasso for his elegiac verse. In the present century, the prevailing tone of Juan Ramón Jiménez in his *Arias Tristes* and *Elegías* is melancholy and elegiac. The work of Federico García Lorca, in *Elegía a Doña Juana La Loca* and *Llanto por Ignacio Sánchez Mejías* shows a more direct obsession with the presentiments of death.

In France, the first attempt at copying the e. form from the ancients was by imitating the classic distich in alexandrine couplets, alternating masculine and feminine rhymes, later by alternating decasyllabic with octosyllabic lines, an experiment of Jean Doublet in his *Élégies,* 1559. Ronsard, in his *Élégies, Mascarades, et Bergeries,* 1565, abandoned the attempt to reproduce the classical meter and returned to the subject matter of the classical elegists. This treatment of the e. was also adopted by Louise Labé and Malherbe. In *l'Art Poétique,* Boileau insists on themes either of love or death for the e., and the genre comes to deal in the 18th c. with the tender and the melancholy rather than with deep grief. The climax of this tendency was reached with André Chénier, at the end of the century:

> Mais la tendre élégie et sa grâce touchante
> M'ont séduit; l'élégie à la voix gémissante,
> Aux ris mêlés de pleurs, aux longs cheveux épars,
> Belle, levant an ciel ses humides regards.

After Lamartine's *Méditations,* 1820, the elegiac tendency in Fr. literature becomes confused with others, and whole poems in the genre appear only sporadically.

In Germany, the subject matter of the e. has been so little restricted that Sir Edmund Gosse could say that the e. as a poem of lamentation does not exist in Germany. There had been a number of attempts during the Renaissance to write elegies in L., but it remained for Opitz, in the early 17th c., to write elegies in the vernacular. His equivalent for the classic meter was alexandrines in couplets, with alternating masculine and feminine rhymes. Klopstock, with greater metrical freedom, turned to sentimental subjects, general sadness, the troubles of love, as well as the memorializing of actual death. The influence of the "graveyard school" of Eng. poets as well as of Young, Goldsmith, Gray, Ossian, and others was also felt heavily in Germany. The *Römische Elegien* of Goethe, although imitative of the L. elegiac meter, should probably be classed as idylls, his chief elegy being *Metamorphosen der Pflanzen.* Schiller, in his essay, "On Primitive and

Sentimental Poetry," distinguishes the elegiac from the satiric and idyllic, by saying that the elegiac longs for the ideal, while the satiric rails against the present situation and the idyllic represents the ideal as actually existent. His notion of the elegiac is illustrated in his own *Die Götter Griechenlands, Die Sehnsucht,* and *Der Pilgrim.* Hölderlin's elegies also deal with the impossibility of attaining an ideal and the longing for the golden days of youth. Mörike and Geibel produced the only German elegies of note in the remainder of the 19th c. The ten *Duino Elegies* (1912–1922) of Rainer Maria Rilke constitute an important renewal of the genre in modern literature and have been widely influential outside of Germany as well as within.

In England, there were a few Renaissance attempts, as, for example, by Sidney, Spenser, and Harvey, to imitate the quantitative verse of the classical distich, but these, like other attempts to write quantitatively in an accentual language, failed. The term *elegie* was used in the 16th and early 17th c. for poems with a variety of content, including Petrarchan love poetry as well as laments, but the connection between death and e. was made more clear with the use of "funeral elegy" in the title of one section of Donne's *An Anatomy of the World* (1611). Milton's pastoral e., *Lycidas* (1637) helped to establish the e., a lament for the dead, as a separate genre in Eng. Eng. literature has not lacked meditative and reflective verse, but a distinction has grown up between this as "elegiac" and the e. proper, although the boundary is by no means sharp. For examples of the former, see Gray's *Elegy Written in a Country Churchyard* (1750), Young's *Night Thoughts,* Samuel Johnson's *Vanity of Human Wishes,* and Whitman's *When Lilacs Last in the Dooryard Bloomed.* In the e. tradition belong such poems as Pope's *Elegy on the Death of an Unfortunate Lady* and Tennyson's *In Memoriam* (1850). A notable example of the modern e., this one employing three very different metrical patterns, is W. H. Auden's *In Memory of W. B. Yeats.* The pastoral (q.v.) elegy, notably illustrated in Eng. by *Adonais* (1821), Shelley's poem on the death of Keats, and *Thyrsis* (1867), Arnold's monody on the death of Clough, derives from a different tradition, being thought of as a subdivision of the idyll or eclogue. In classical literature, the *Lament for Bion* (traditionally attributed to Moschus but probably by an unknown disciple of Bion) and Virgil's Fifth *Eclogue,* as well as the First Idyll of Theocritus and the Tenth Eclogue of Virgil, both of which combine the themes of love and death, were the chief models.

M. Lloyd, *Elegies, Ancient and Modern* (1903); J. H. Hanford, "The Pastoral E. and Milton's Lycidas," PMLA, 25 (1910); Gayley and Kurtz; H. Hatzfeld, *Die französische Renaissancelyrik* (1924); J. W. Draper, *The Funeral E. and the Rise of Romanticism* (1929); F. W. Weitzmann, "Notes on the Elizabethan *Elegie,*" PMLA, 50 (1935); C. M. Bowra, *Early Gr. Elegists* (1938); F. Beissner, *Gesch. der deutschen Elegie* (1941, 2d ed., 1961); G. Luck, *The Latin Love E.* (1960). S.F.F.

ELISION (L. "striking out") a general (metrical) term for the omission or blurring of a final unstressed vowel (vowel sound) followed by a vowel or mute consonant; cf. Fr. *l'épée, l'heure.* The Gr. equivalents *ecthlipsis* and *synaloepha* (q.v.) nowadays tend to have specialized meanings. In Gr., elision—which is variable in prose but more regular in poetry—is indicated by an apostrophe (') to mark the disappearance of the elided vowel (generally short alpha, epsilon, and omikron as well as the diphthong *ai* occasionally in Homer and in comedy); but, when e. occurs in Gr. compound words, the apostrophe is not used. In L. a final vowel or a vowel followed by *m* at the end of a word was not omitted from the written language, but as a rule it was ignored metrically when the next word in the same measure began with a vowel, diphthong, or the aspirate *h.* In Eng. syllable-counting measures, e. is a kind of fiction, two syllables being reckoned as one to make the line conform to the metrical scheme. Or, as S. E. Sprott (*Milton's Art of Prosody,* 1953, p. 63) has it: e. is the "process by which two syllables are reduced to the prosodical value of one." In accentual meters it gives the appearance or illusion of smoothness. A similar phenomenon, not properly to be called e., occurs in such forms as "we'll" for "we will." Cf. HIATUS, the opposite or avoidance of e. See also POETIC CONTRACTIONS; CLASSICAL PROSODY; ROMANCE PROSODY. R.J.G.; P.F.B.

ELLIPSE (Gr. "leaving out," "defect"; L. *detractio*). A figure wherein a word, or several words, usually of little importance to the logical expression of thought but ordinarily called for by the construction, are omitted. Quintilian (*Institutes of Oratory* 9.3.58) exemplifies with Caelius' denunciation of Antony: " 'stupere gaudio Graecus,' the Greek began to be astonished with joy, for 'coepit,' began, is readily understood." The device may be used for a number of psychological reasons, including, according to Quintilian, considerations of modesty: "Novimus et qui te, transversa tuentibus, hircis, / et quo, sed faciles Nymphae risere, sacello" (You—while the goats looked goatish—we know who, / And in what chapel—but the kind nymphs laughed) Virgil, *Eclogues* 3.8. Gr. rhetoricians permitted omission of substantives, pronouns, objects, finite verbs, main clauses, and (rarely) subordinate clauses; modern poets allow omission of almost any member so long as the meaning remains clear. Quintilian distinguishes e. from aposiopesis on the ground that in the latter it is uncertain what is suppressed. "Where wigs [strive] with wigs, [where] with sword-knots sword-knots strive" (Pope, *The Rape of the Lock* 1.101). In their eagerness not to be diffuse, 20th c. poets (especially

Pound, Eliot, Auden, William Carlos Williams, etc.) are particularly attracted to the device.

R.O.E.

EMBLEM. A didactic device consisting, normally, of three parts: a "word" (*mot* or *motto*), a woodcut or engraving symbolically expressing the "word," and a brief verse *explicatio* or application of the idea expressed in the combination. The e. exhibits varied and close affinities with proverb, fable, and epigram. Emblems were introduced into European literature by the *Emblematum liber* (1531) of Andrea Alciati, and for two centuries thereafter enjoyed an enormous vogue. The first Eng. e. book was Geoffrey Whitney's *Choice of Emblemes* (1586), the most notable probably the *Emblemes* (1635) of Francis Quarles. In recent times the form receives amusing illustration in R. L. Stevenson's *Moral Emblems.* As the form developed it became customary to present the *motto* in one language, the *explicatio* in a different language; and many bilingual or multilingual e. books served incidentally as language manuals. Originally erudite productions, e. books became increasingly instruments of popular education, especially in Jesuit hands during the 17th c. Above all, they were a gold-mine of imagery for poets, Spenser, Shakespeare, Donne, Quarles, and Crashaw being notably thus indebted.—H. Green, *Andrea Alciati and His Books of Emblems* (1872); M. Praz, *Studies in 17th-C. Imagery* (2 v., 1939–47); E. James, "The Imagery of Francis Quarles' *E.*," UTSE (1943); R. J. Clements, "Cult of the Poet in Renaissance E. Lit.," PMLA, 59 (1944), "Condemnation of the Poetic Profession in Ren. E. Lit.," SP, 43 (1946), "Ars emblematica," *Romanistisches Jahrbuch,* 8 (1957) and *Picta Poesis: Lit. and Humanistic Theory in Ren. E. Books* (1960); J. Lederer, "John Donne and the Emblematic Practice," RES, 22 (1946); R. Freeman, *Eng E. Books* (1948).

J.L.L.

ENCOMIUM. A Gr. choral song in celebration not of a god but of a hero, sung at the *komos,* the jubilant or reveling procession which celebrated the victor in the games. While Simonides and Pindar wrote encomia, Aristotle says that both the e. and the myth are parts of all early poetry. In later times the term acquired the meaning of any laudatory composition in verse or prose, but it applied more often to a rhetorical exercise in prose, exalting the virtues of some legendary figure or praising the extraordinary deeds of a human being. Aristotle considers it a subdivision of declamatory oratory (*Rhetoric* 1358 b 18ff.). The best examples of this type of e. in the classical period were written by Isocrates. It became very popular in the time of the New Sophistic and was widely imitated by Roman, Byzantine, and modern writers. Occasionally, however, the contents of this type of e. degenerated into the silliest and most trivial and extravagant of subjects. Erasmus' *Praise of Folly* is perhaps the best known example of the rhetorical kind of e. in modern literature. In the Hellenistic period many encomia were composed in the epic style. Theocritus wrote one in honor of Ptolemy Philadelphus (Idyll 17). In later times this type of composition was imitated by several Roman poets.—G. Fraustadt, *Encomiorum in litteris graecis usque ad Romanam aetatem historia* (1909); A. S. Pease, "Things Without Honor," CP, 21 (1926); H. K. Miller, "The Paradoxical E. with special Ref. to its Vogue in England, 1600–1800," MP, 53 (1956).

P.S.C.

END-STOPPED. A term applied to poetic lines in which both meaning and meter undergo a pause at the end of the line. End-stopped lines, like closed couplets (q.v.), are characteristic of the heroic couplets of Eng. 18th-c. poetry: "Hope springs eternal in the human breast; / Man never is, but always to be, blest" (Pope) and of the alexandrine verse of the Fr. neoclassicists. The term "end-stopped" is opposed to *run-on,* or *enjambé* (see ENJAMBEMENT), terms which are used to describe the free and uninterrupted carryover of the grammatical structure from one line to the other, as in most Eng. blank verse and most romantic poetry. The relative occurrence of end-stopped lines has been used as a means of determining the chronology of Shakespeare's plays and of other works.

ENGLISH PROSODY. It is more accurate to speak of Eng. prosodies than of Eng. prosody, for, historically considered, the phenomena of Eng. versification are too manifold and complex to be explained according to a single metrical system, although some scholars and critics have expended whole careers in unhappy attempts to show that all Eng. verse of whatever period manifests one prosodic principle. Only the following three feeble generalizations would seem to hold true for all Eng. verse: (1) Because Eng. is a more markedly accentual language than the Romance tongues, stress has generally played a more notable part in the structure of Eng. verse than it has in many continental poetries; (2) the Eng. language, when metered by whatever system (see METER), appears to flow most pleasingly and naturally in ascending rhythms; and (3) most Eng. poetry seems naturally to seek a line-length neither short nor long: the most "natural" line-length in Eng. would appear to be one of 4 or 5 isochronous units, as in the O. Eng. 4-stress accentual line or the Shakespearean "iambic pentameter" (it is well to remember that about three-fourths of all Eng. poetry is in this meter). Other than sharing these few common characteristics, the poetries of various periods manifest very few prosodic similarities, and their unique characteristics are best seen if we isolate them philologically.

OLD ENGLISH (ca. 500–ca. 1100). The powerful accents of the OE language supply a natural basis for a heavily accentual prosody (see METER) in which sense rhythm, at every point, provides the meter. The standard OE line consists of 4 strongly stressed syllables arranged, together with any number of unstressed syllables, in 2 hemistichs (or half lines) of 2 stresses each. Stressed syllables frequently alliterate, and stichic rather than strophic structure prevails. The 2 hemistichs are separated by an invariable medial caesura (q.v.). "Rests" and the occasional omission of stressed syllables (especially in the second hemistich) provide a sort of syncopation or counterpoint (q.v.) which keeps the prosodic structure varied and expressive (see Pope, *The Rhythm of Beowulf*). The following example from *Beowulf* (lines 4–7) shows the "normal" line structure (second line) and the possibilities of variation through rest and omission of stress (third and fourth lines):

Oft Scýld Scefing   sceáþena þréatum,
mónegum mǽgþum   méodsetla oftéah,
égsode éorlas   syþþan ǽrest wearþ
féasceaft funden   he þaes frófre gebad . . .

Pope has conjectured that, in recitation, the "normal" position of stresses was signaled by a chord on a harp; this constant "beat" would provide a sort of metrical underpinning against which rhythmical variations dictated by rhetorical emphasis would be strikingly noticeable. Despite its apparent simplicity, OE prosody is an instrument of extremely subtle expressiveness: its variations from the "ideal" meter and its returns to it give the rhythm a constantly shifting surface of great sophistication. (See also ENG. POETRY; OLD GERMANIC PROSODY.)

MIDDLE ENGLISH (ca. 1100–ca. 1500): After the Norman Conquest, the rapid changes in the language (loss of inflection, Romance incursions into what had been primarily a Germanic vocabulary, the multiplication of dialects) quickly complicated the principles of Eng. prosody. Although it persisted for a time in the new language, the OE accentual line, with its varying number of unaccented syllables, is gradually abandoned in favor of a line in which syllabic numeration becomes, for the first time, one of the structural criteria. One can observe the phenomenon of the 2 hemistichs of the OE line transforming themselves into the alternating 4- and 3-stress lines of the ballad meter (q.v.). Strophic construction makes inroads on stichic, and elaborate "tail-rhyme" stanzas begin to appear. The strongly Germanic accentual quality of the language begins to weaken slightly, and instead of a prosody of powerful and emphatic pressures at equal times we find a prosody more conscious of the qualitative similarities between stressed and unstressed syllables. The linguistic complexities of the period created a situation in which many unique prosodies are actually to be found simultaneously. We find (1) a continuation of OE prosody adapted (often by the addition of assonance and rhyme) to an increasingly uninflected language; (2) accentual-syllabic rhyming verse in lines of 4 stresses, gradually lengthening to become the heroic couplet (q.v.) of Chaucer and Lydgate; (3) accentual verse in hexameter line-lengths with a strong pseudo-classical air; and (4) a sort of "sprung rhythm" (q.v.), especially in songs and other lyrical pieces set to music. Out of all this complication, and with the relative stabilization of language and dialects, the decasyllabic, 5-stress line of Chaucer gradually emerged, and this line provides the basis for Renaissance developments.

MODERN ENGLISH (ca. 1500–); *16th and 17th C.*: Three circumstances are of great importance in Renaissance prosody: (1) The Eng. language attained a period of relative stability; (2) the widespread admiration of the classics of antiquity served to focus attention on the apparently unsystematic and occasionally rather coarse quality of earlier Eng. metric; and (3) rhetorical and metrical criticism, in the manner of the ancients, began to be written and to be read. These circumstances gave impetus to that stream of systematic and academic prosodic speculation and dogmatizing which has continued without break to our own times.

The Renaissance admiration for Gr. meters impelled one school to attempt to import into Eng. practice Gr. quantitative theory, and theorists, dilettantes, and poets like Cheke, Ascham, Sidney, Dyer, Drant, Spenser, Greene, Campion, Harvey, and Stanihurst labored, with varying degrees of seriousness and success, to imitate the classical heroic hexameter or the Gr. lyric measures. Since the poet was obliged, however, to remember constantly the predetermined "quantities" of the syllables he was using, composition was a laborious, academic-theoretical business, and little work of any natural virtue resulted (see METER).

Along with this impulse to "refine" Eng. poetry by making it mimic Gr. rhythms went the development of the Chaucerian accentual-syllabic pentameter line as a vehicle for dramatic expression. Both Marlowe and Shakespeare use it with consummate mastery, calmly inventing new tonalities when they have exhausted the old, and even the lesser dramatists of the period reveal, through their instinctive feeling of comfort within it, that this is going to be, for whatever reason, The Eng. Line. In lyric verse, the song writers, often obliged to fit words to preexisting airs, produce free accentual lines which foreshadow the sprung rhythm (q.v.) of Hopkins, and lyric practitioners like Donne, Crashaw, Herbert, and Marvell make of the iambic tetrameter or pentameter line a vehicle for wit, shock, and ecstasy by shifting or adding stresses boldly.

And yet, in the midst of all this freedom and inventiveness, signs of an impulse toward greater regulation and predictability are apparent: Daniel's *Defense of Rhyme* (?1603) is a conservative document which anticipates the practice of Denham and Waller, and 20th-c. students (Bridges, Sprott) have shown that Milton, in *Paradise Lost,* despite the expressive variation or omission of stresses, was adhering consciously to a fixed decasyllabic limitation. The end of the Renaissance thus sees a movement away from the metrical spontaneity of the Elizabethans; prosody, both in theory and practice, is now moving toward an ideal of strict syllabic limitation and relative predictability of stress placement.

18th C.: Post-Restoration prosody reveals strong Fr. syllabic influence: the number of syllables instead of the number of stresses becomes the essential criterion of the poetic line. Theorists like Edward Bysshe, Richard Bentley, and Henry Pemberton are to be found advocating rigid regularity in the heroic line, and poets like Richard Glover are to be seen composing strictly "ideal" (i.e., regular) accentual-syllabic verse. This lust for regularity and "smoothness" is clearly one expression of the orderly and rationalistic impulses of the age.

Soon after 1740, however, a reaction to metrical rigidity manifests itself in the prosodic writing of Samuel Say, John Mason, and Joshua Steele. These theorists point out that monotony results from iambic lines long continued without trisyllabic substitution, and that the shifting or omission of stresses is an expressive tool which the poet who wishes to tap all resources of poetry cannot do without. The writings of this "preromantic" school advocate a return to "sense rhythms" after the predominance of "metrical rhythms" earlier in the century, and the positions of this school issue from an early "romantic" aesthetic of impulse, spontaneity, and surprise rather than from an Augustan aesthetic of stability, reason, and quietude. By opposing the poetic contractions (see METRICAL TREATMENT OF SYLLABLES) required by a syllabic prosody, the late 18th-c. theorists sought to create an "expandable" line which could swell or diminish expressively according to the rhetorical pressure within it.

Unlike the sparse prosodic speculation of the Renaissance, that of the 18th c. is copious; it is also relatively systematic, and, under the influence of Locke, remarkably "psychological." Throughout the period, the practice of the poets substantially corroborates the findings of the prosodists: although such masters as Pope and Johnson shift stresses freely and instinctively, even they never violate the strict syllabic limitation, and the lines of most of the lesser manufacturers of the heroic couplet will be found to be strikingly regular in the disposition of stressed and unstressed syllables.

19th C.: The major phenomenon in 19th c. Eng. prosody is a rejection of strict accentual-syllabism and a reaching toward accentualism. Coleridge, in *Christabel,* publicly practiced for a wide audience the principles of trisyllabic substitution advocated a half-century earlier by Say, Mason, and Steele. As a result of this new accentualism, the Eng. pentameter line tends to lose its formal, Augustan oratorical tone and to take on a tone of almost colloquial intimacy (*The Prelude, Fra Lippo Lippi*). In prosodic writing, accentualism soon abetted the rise to fashion of Germanic philology, which helped remind prosodists that Eng. was solidly a Germanic tongue though it was countered by the musical theories of meter (Lanier). The development of "free" or "cadenced" (qq.v.) verse in the middle of the century was generally an expression of impatience with the metrical constraints of the previous century. Triple rhythms, in music as well as in poetry, are attempted more and more in "serious" works (Longfellow, Poe). But despite these new departures, many prominent poets (Tennyson, Arnold) continue to exercise themselves in what is fundamentally the line of the Augustans, with its syllabic limitation and conservative placement of stresses. W. J. Stone, with his *On the use of Classical Metres in English* (1898), attempted to interest the more academic spirits in quantitative prosody once more, but the decay of classical learning and enthusiasm deterred all but Robert Bridges from experimenting seriously with quantitative poems. Gerard Manley Hopkins was moved to revive the medieval and Renaissance technique of overstressing called "sprung rhythm" (q.v.), and it is notable that this technique can be thought of only in a strongly accentual prosodic climate.

The numerous 19th-c. divagations from accentual-syllabic prosody and the general air of quest and experimentation during the period suggest widespread dissatisfaction with the sound of conventional Eng. verse, and this dissatisfaction may have some philological cause. For example, the gradual separation of the Am. from the British language may have had something to do with the new metrical tonalities which the 19th c. sometimes frenetically sought; so may the gradual replacement of classical by modern language studies in schools and universities. Whatever the causes of the dissatisfaction, it is clearly an expression of the age's lust for reform and its commitment to the idea of progress.

20th C.: Most of the prosodic mutations of interest in the 20th c. have been associated with the United States. During the twenties and thirties, the work of Pound and Williams tightened the freely cadenced line of Whitman and made of it a witty instrument in the short poem. Eliot's poetic dramas have used subtle accentual lines with great skill, and Auden has written accentual, accentual-syllabic, and syllabic poems with equal facility. But even after such bold experiments as the "spatial cadences" of E. E. Cummings, the incremental variation of Stein, and the cadenced syllabism of Marianne Moore, 20th-c. poetry still continues the 19th century's quest for new prosodies to express an alarmingly changed social, political, and intellectual order. The failure of many of the experiments of the twenties and thirties to arrive at any very profoundly expressive mode of metric has impelled many post-World War II poets to return to stable lyric measures: Wilbur, Shapiro, Lowell, and others have had happy results with traditional accentual-syllabic lines, and a return to conservatism in metrical structure seems apparent in the pages of little magazines and literary reviews. How closely this return to conservatism in prosody is connected with the similar movement in contemporary politics and intellectual life it would be hazardous to say. It will be obvious, however, to those who have seen in history the intimate alliance between metrics and the general intellectual and emotional tendencies of an age, that no prosodic phenomenon is devoid of wider meaning if only we can learn to read it correctly.

The area of prosodic investigation has been entered in our own time by the so-called acoustic or linguistic prosodists, who, with elaborate machinery (for example, the kymograph and the oscillograph), are trying to discover what actually goes on in the oral delivery of verse. Although this characteristically technological 20th-c. approach to problems which have traditionally been investigated prescriptively or subjectively has yet to demonstrate its full usefulness to metrical study, it has undeniably laid the groundwork for much valuable future study. The very fact that even the machine has finally been called to the assistance of the prosodist helps indicate the continuing pressing interest in the elusive and mysterious prosodies which emerge from Eng. poetry.

Saintsbury, *Prosody;* T. S. Omond, *Eng. Metrists* (1921); R. Bridges, *Milton's Prosody* (rev. ed., 1921); L. Abercrombie, *Eng. Prosody* (1923); G. R. Stewart, *The Technique of Eng. Verse* (1930); G. W. Allen, *Am. Prosody* (1934); E. Olson, *General Prosody* (1938); J. C. Ransom, *The New Crit.* (1941), pp. 254–69, 297–330; J. C. Pope, *The Rhythm of Beowulf* (1942); M. M. Holloway, *Prosodic Theory of Hopkins* (1947); K. Shapiro, *A Bibliog. of Modern Prosody* (1948); G. L. Hendrickson, "Elizabethan Quantitative Hexameters," PQ, 28 (1949); G. L. Trager and H. L. Smith, Jr., *An Outline of Eng. Structure* (1951); P. F. Baum, "Eng. Versification," in Shipley; S. E. Sprott, *Milton's Art of Prosody* (1953); P. Fussell, Jr., *Theory of Prosody in 18th-C. England* (1954); "Eng. Verse and What It Sounds Like," KR, 18 (1956; articles by J. C. Ransom and others); R. Beum, "Syllabic Verse in Eng.," *Prairie Schooner,* 31 (1957); E. L. Epstein and T. Hawkes, *Linguistics and Eng. Prosody* (1959); J. Thompson, *The Founding of Eng. Metre* (1961). P.F.

ENJAMBEMENT or enjambment. The completion, in the following poetic line, of a clause or other grammatical unit begun in the preceding line; the employment of "run-on" lines which carry the sense of a statement from one line to another without rhetorical pause at the end of the line:

> . . . Yet I know her for
> A spleeny Lutheran . . .
> (Shakespeare, *Henry VIII,* 3.2)

The term is also applied to the carrying over of meaning from one couplet or stanza to the next.

E., a device widely used by the Elizabethans and by Milton, fell into disrepute in 18th-c. poetry but was revived by the romantic poets, who saw in it a symbol of liberation from neoclassical rules. Keats's *Endymion* supplies some extreme examples of e.

The technique of e. has been a subject of controversy in Fr. poetry. Rarely found in OF poetry, e. was widely used in the 15th and especially 16th c. (Ronsard and the *Pléiade*). In the 17th c. it was frowned on by Malherbe and, later, by Boileau. These neoclassical authorities, however, allowed its use in certain circumstances—in decasyllabic poetry and in the less "noble" genres such as comedy and fable. Occasionally, e. occurs even in tragedy (e.g., Racine, *Britannicus*). Since André Chénier, e. has been accepted in all genres. The device was exploited to the full by Victor Hugo, whose famous e. at the beginning of *Hernani* ("Serait-ce déjà lui? C'est bien à l'escalier / / Dérobé. . . .") had all the force of a manifesto. E. is a freely used technique of modern poetry.—M. Grammont, *Petit traité de versification française* (5ᵉ éd. revue, 1924).

ENVELOPE. The e. pattern is a special case of repetition (q.v.). A line or stanza will recur in the same or nearly the same form so as to enclose other material. A line or significant phrase may thus enclose a stanza or a whole poem; a complete stanza may be repeated to enclose a poem or a section of a larger poem. The effect of the e. pattern is to emphasize the unity of the enclosed portion, to indicate that elaborations or parallels of statement have not departed from the original focus. Also the repeated words carry an added richness and meaning from the intervening lines, sometimes acquiring an almost incantatory force. The e. pattern is distinguished from the refrain (q.v.) in that the repetitions here affect the enclosed material rather than the material preceding each occurrence. The single-line e., as it applies to a stanza, may be seen in both stanzas of James Joyce's *I Would in That Sweet Bosom Be,* as it applies to an entire poem, in the

Eighth Psalm or Whitman's *Joy, Shipmate, Joy.* A stanza used as an e. for an entire poem may be seen in Blake's *The Tyger* and in Keats's *The Mermaid Tavern.*—R. B. Lewis, *Creative Poetry* (1931); G. W. Allen, *Am. Prosody* (1935). S.F.F.

ENVOI, envoy. (Prov. *tornada;* G. *Geleit*). A short concluding stanza found in certain Fr. poetic forms, such as the *ballade* and the *chant royal.* In the *ballade* it normally consists of 4 lines, in the *chant royal* of either 5 or 7, thus repeating the metrical pattern of the half-stanza which precedes it, as well as the rhyme scheme of that half-stanza. The e. also repeats the refrain which runs through the poem (e.g., Villon's "Mais ou sont les neiges d'antan?"). In its typical use of some form of address, such as "Prince," the e. shows a trace of its original function, which was to serve as a kind of postscript dedicating the Poem to a patron or other important person. However, its true function during the great period of the OF forms was to serve as a pithy summing-up of the poem. For this reason the Prov. troubadours called their envoys *tornadas* (returns). Among the Eng. poets, Scott, Southey, and Swinburne employed envoys. Chaucer wrote a number of *ballades* (e.g., *Lenvoy de Chaucer a Scogan*), in which he departs from the customary form by closing with an e. which is equal in length to a regular stanza of the poem, usually his favorite rhyme royal (q.v.).

EPIC. HISTORY. See NARRATIVE POETRY.

EPIGRAM. A form of writing which makes a satiric, complimentary, or aphoristic observation with wit, extreme condensation, and, above all, brevity. As a poetic form, the e. generally takes the shape of a couplet or quatrain, but tone, which is usually either ironic or gnomic, defines it better than does verse form. An example from Matthew Prior, one of the best Eng. epigrammatists, displays the personal, specific quality which distinguishes the e. from the proverb or the apothegm:

Sir, I admit your general rule,
That every poet is a fool:
But you yourself may serve to show it,
That every fool is not a poet.

The etymology of the term (Gr. *epigramma,* "inscription") suggests the features of pithiness and economy of language which have always characterized the form; from an inscription carved on a monument or statue, the classical Gr. e. developed into a specific literary type, typified by the epigrams contained in the Gr. *Anthology,* which covered a wide range of subjects and attitudes.

The e., as cultivated in the earlier Renaissance in both L. and the vernacular languages, owed more to the coarse, harshly satirical examples of Martial and other Roman writers than to the more polished products of the *Anthology,* but the 17th and 18th c., the greatest periods of epigrammatic writing in England, saw a variety of epigrammatic types, ranging from the brutal thrusts of Donne to the delicate compliments of Herrick.

Epigrams have existed not only as independent poems but also as units in the composition of larger works; Pope's *Essay on Criticism* and *Essay on Man,* for example, are made up of epigrammatic couplets which are often quoted as self-contained observations:

We think our fathers fools, so wise we grow;
Our wiser sons, no doubt, will think us so.
(*Essay on Criticism*)

Although the satiric spirit dominated the 18th-c. e., the 19th c. produced some which, in their delicacy and gracefulness, recall the amatory epigrams of the Gr. *Anthology*:

Stand close around, ye Stygian set,
With Dirce in one boat conveyed!
Or Charon, seeing, may forget
That he is old and she a shade.
(Landor, *Dirce*)

The e. holds an important place in the poetic history of France and Germany as well. In France, where the vernacular e. was initiated by Marot and St.-Gelais in the early 16th c., the satiric and personal e. reached perfection in the hands of Boileau, Voltaire, and Lebrun:

Eglé, belle et poète, a deux petits travers:
Elle fait son visage, et ne fait pas ses vers.
(Lebrun).
Aegle, beauty and poet, has two little crimes;
She makes her own face, and does not make her rhymes.
(tr. Byron).

In Germany, on the other hand, the didactic e., or *Sinngedicht,* has occupied a position of special importance from the time of the *Priameln* of the 13th c. to the time of such masters as Logau, A. G. Kästner, Lessing, Goethe, and Schiller.

The e. is one of the most persistent types of literary expression, as it embodies certain permanent qualities of the human spirit. Such diverse modern epigrammatists as Ezra Pound and Edna St. Vincent Millay in Eng., Christian Morgenstern and Erich Kästner in German, have carried on the tradition, and W. B. Yeats's e. *On Hearing that the Students of our New University Have Joined the Agitation against Immoral Literature* is equal, in bite and precision, to the best of Prior or Voltaire.

COLLECTIONS: *Select Epigrams from the Gr. Anthology,* ed. J. W. Mackail (3d ed., 1911); *The Soul of Wit* (1924) and *Wit's Looking-Glass* (1934; Fr. epigrams tr.), both ed. G. R. Hamilton; *The Hundred Best Epigrams,* ed. E. B. Osborn (1928);

Epigrammata, Gr. *Inscriptions in Verse . . . ,* ed. P. Friedländer (1948).

HISTORY AND CRITICISM: R. Reitzenstein, *Epigramm und Skolion* (1893); T. K. Whipple, *Martial and the Eng. E. . . .* (1925); P. Nixon, *Martial and the Modern E.* (1927); H. H. Hudson, *The E. in the Eng. Renaissance* (1947); O. Weinreich, *Epigrammstudien* (1948); W. Preisendanz, *Die Spruchform in der Lyrik des alten Goethe und ihre Vorgeschichte seit Opitz* (1952). F.J.W.; A.P.

EPISTLE, verse. A poem addressed to a particular patron or friend, written in a familiar style. Two types of verse epistles exist: the one on moral and philosophical subjects which stems from Horace's *Epistles* and the other on romantic and sentimental subjects which stems from Ovid's *Heroides*. Though the verse e. may be found as early as 146 B.C. with Sp. Mummius' letters from Corinth and some of the satires of Lucullus, Horace perfected the form. Employing the hexameter, he used plain diction, personal details, questions, etc. to lend a familiarity to his theme which was usually some philosophical subject. Ovid used the same style for his *Tristia* and *Ex Ponto,* but developed the sentimental e. in his *Heroides* which are fictional letters from women to their lovers. Throughout the Middle Ages the latter seems to have been the more popular type, for it had an influence on the courtly love poets and subsequently inspired Samuel Daniel to introduce the form into Eng. literature, e.g., *Letter from Octavia to Marcus Antonius.* Such also was the source for Donne's copy of the *Heroides* and Pope's *Eloisa to Abelard.* But it was the Horatian e. which had the greater effect on the Renaissance and subsequent poetry. Petrarch, the first humanist to know Horace, wrote his influential *Epistulae Metricae* in L. Subsequently, Ariosto's *Satires* in terza rima employed the form in the vernacular It. In all these epistles Christian sentiment made itself felt. In Spain Garcilaso's *Epístola a Boscán* (1543), and the *Epístola moral a Fabio* in blank verse and terza rima introduced and perfected the form. The Fr. especially cultivated it for its "graceful precision and dignified familiarity." Although others wrote verse epistles, Boileau's twelve (1668–95) in neoclassic couplets are considered the finest examples in Fr. Ben Jonson began the Eng. use of the Horatian form (*Forrest,* 1616) and was followed by others, e.g., Vaughan, Dryden, Congreve. But the finest examples in Eng. are Pope's *Moral Essays* and the *Epistle to Dr. Arbuthnot* in heroic couplets. The romantics did not especially use the e., though Shelley, Keats, and Landor on occasion wrote them. Recent examples are W. H. Auden's *New Year Letter* and Louis MacNeice's *Letters from Iceland.*—H. Peter, *Der Brief in der römischen Lit.* (1901); G. Curcio, *Q. Orazio Flacco, studiato in Italia dal secolo xiii al xviii* (1913); E. P. Morris, "The Form of the E. in Horace," YSC, 1931; J. Vianey, *Les Epîtres de Marot* (1935); E. L. Rivers, "The Horatian E. and Its Introd. into Sp. Lit.," HR, 22 (1954); W. Grenzmann, "Briefgedicht," *Reallexikon,* 2d ed., I; J. A. Levine, "The Status of the Verse E. before Pope," SP, 59 (1962). R.A.H.

EPITAPH (Gr. "[writing] on a tomb"). A literary production suitable for placing on the grave of someone or something, though this need not actually be done or even intended. The e., which is a shortened form of the elegy (q.v.) and which may vary in tone from panegyrical to ribald, indicates in brief compass the outline of a complete life. It attempts to arrest the passer-by, compelling him to read, to reflect on the life of the one commemorated and, by implication, on his own life. The earliest epitaphs are Egyptian, written on sarcophagi and coffins. They have generally the name, the person's descent, his office, and a prayer to some deity. Gr. and Roman epitaphs are often highly personal, sometimes epigrammatic. They may be written in verse (usually the elegiac distich) or in prose. Their details may include the name of the person, his family, the facts of his life, a prayer to the underworld (especially so in Roman epitaphs) and a warning or imprecation against defilement. Rarely are all these details found in a single e. On those from Greece and Rome are found varying concepts of Fortuna and Fate, literary figures such as the thread of life, the removal from light, the payment of a debt as well as various kinds of consolation and lamentation.

The major collection of classical epitaphs is Book 4 of the Gr. *Anthology.* The epitaphs in this collection are of high poetic quality and cover the whole range of the form from satiric and comic to intensely serious. They have influenced subsequent writers of epitaphs from Roman times (e.g., Martial, Ausonius) through the Renaissance (Pontanus, Erasmus, More, Jonson) and on into the present period (Pound, Yeats). Perhaps the single most famous e. from the *Anthology* is that on the dead at Thermopylae: "Go, tell the Lacedaimonians, passer-by, / That here obedient to their laws we lie."

The Middle Ages used the Latin e. both in prose and verse, often leonine verse. Following the themes and practices laid down by the Greeks and particularly the Romans, the Eng. used the form, developing it to an exceptionally high art in the 15th and 16th c., e.g., William Browne on the Dowager Countess of Pembroke, or Milton on Shakespeare. Both Dr. Johnson and William Wordsworth wrote essays on the e. as an art form.

The e. has not always been used to commemorate the dead. It has been put to satirical use against an enemy who is alive, and it has been aimed even at an institution, e.g., Piron's e. on his rejection by the Fr. Academy. As a literary form without a specific occasion it has continued in use into the 20th c., e.g., O. St. J. Gogarty, *Per iter tenebricosum,* W. Stevens, *Death of a Soldier.*—

S. Tessington, *Epitaphs* (1857); H. W. Wells, *New Poets from Old* (1940); R. Lattimore, *Themes in Gr. and L. Epitaphs* (1942); *Epigrammata*, ed. P. Friedländer (1948); Frye; R. W. Ketton-Cremer, "Lapidary Verse," *Proceedings of the British Academy*, 45 (1959). R.A.H.

EPITHALAMIUM (Gr. "at the bridal chamber"). Any song or poem sung outside the bridal chamber on the wedding night; perhaps the intention behind such a song is the encouragement of fertility. Sappho is apparently the first to use it as a distinct literary form, though such a song does appear in Homer's *Iliad* and in Hesiod's *Shield of Herakles*. Brief nuptial songs appear in Aristophanes' *Peace* and *Birds*, but Theocritus is the most significant Gr. poet to have used the form (Eclogue 18 on the marriage of Helen and Menelaus). Among L. writers who used it were Ovid, Statius, and Claudian, but the most important for literary history was Catullus (*Carmina* 61, 62, 64). Medieval literature has devotional poems entitled *Epithalamia*, but these have no connection with the classical genre. The Renaissance revived the form and used it to great advantage: Tasso and Marino in Italy; in France Ronsard, Belleau, Du Bellay; in England Spenser, Sidney, Donne, Jonson, Herrick, Crashaw, Marvell, Dryden. Perhaps the greatest Eng. e. is Spenser's on his own wedding.

The form of the poem as established by the Renaissance poets includes the following conventions: the context is of course a wedding; the characters are the husband and wife who, when not fictional, are upper class, and the poet who is the public celebrator of the couple's private experience; the events of the entire wedding day form the basis of the organization of the poem; and classical allusions and *topoi* are included.—R. H. Chase, *Eng. Epithalamies* (1896); A. L. Wheeler, *Catullus and the Traditions of Ancient Poetry* (1934); A. Gaertner, *Die englische Epithalamienlit. im 17. Jh. und ihre Vorbilder* (1936); T. M. Greene, "Spenser and the Epithalamic Convention, CL, 9 (1957); A. K. Hieatt, *Short Time's Endless Monument* (1960). R.A.H.

EPITHET. See POETIC DICTION.

EPODE (Gr. "sung after"). In the lyric odes of, for example, Pindar, Bacchylides, and the Gr. dramatists, the epode completed an epodic triad by following the strophe and antistrophe (qq.v.), from which it differed in metrical form. In this sense, the Gr. word *epodos* could be feminine in gender, whereas when masculine it also denoted the shorter verse of a couplet, notably an iambic dimeter following an iambic trimeter. (The alternating lines of poems composed in such couplets might, however, be in different meters; for example, a dactylic hexameter might be followed by an iambic dimeter or an iambic trimeter by a dactylic *hemiepes*.) Archilochus seems to have been the founder of this kind of composition which was used for invective and satire. Horace claims to have introduced the form into L. poetry in his "Iambi," which subsequent grammarians called epodes.—Hardie; Koster; B. Kirn, *Zur literarischen Stellung von Horazens Jambenbuch* (1935); E. Fraenkel, *Horace* (1957). R.J.G.

EQUIVALENCE: In the sense used by cl. prosodists e. denotes resolution (q.v.), the metrical rule whereby one *longum* may replace two *brevia* (though not vice versa): so in the epic hexameter spondees may replace certain dactyls, typically in the sixth foot, as Homer does in the first line of the *Odyssey*, or in the sixth and third foot, as in the first line of the *Iliad*. It is the principle or system of metrical e. which justifies this substitution (q.v.) of feet, not any actual temporal ratio of one long equals two shorts, though that belief persisted for centuries. The effect of e. thus allows metrical variety in successive lines while yet ensuring identity in their measure, i.e., conformity to the meter. The term e. has relatively precise reference in cl. metrics, but in the older Eng. metrists it is less clear: some believed the rule applied to Eng. literally, while others seem to use it only by analogy. This latter is roughly the sense adopted by George Saintsbury (trained, like all the older prosodists, in cl. metrics), who uses it with intentional vagueness simply to account for extra syllables in Eng. verse: the metrical "foot or group-system requires *correspondence* of feet or groups, and this . . . at once enjoins and explains . . . the main charm of English poetry" even though such correspondence is "not mathematically" exact: "the elasticity of the system" ensures "its suitableness to the corresponding elasticity of English verse." Other perhaps better terms often used synonymously: *Correspondence, Responsion*.

The modern sense of the term, wholly different and far more central to the very conception of a verse-system itself, is given by Roman Jakobson in 1958 in a classic dictum: "the poetic function [of language] projects the principle of equivalence from the axis of selection into the axis of combination." In communication, language serves a number of functions, only one of which is aesthetic (in epitome, poetic): a message becomes poetic (in function, regardless of whether it is in verse) whenever it focuses on itself, for its own sake, to the extent that e. becomes not merely ornament but "the constitutive device of the sequence." Thus, any given sentence, such as "the child sleeps," is arrayed on two principal axes, one lexical, simultaneous, vertical (the paradigm), the other syntactic, sequential, horizontal (the syntagm). A speaker selects "child" from the register of equivalent nouns ("infant," "baby"), as he does with the verb "sleeps," then combines them in the syntagm to complete the utterance. Items in the paradigm are related by equivalence (similarity-dissimilarity), items in the syntagm by contiguity (cf. the Factors of Similarity and Proximity in Gestalt psychology). In ordinary speech and prose the principle controlling both the selection and arrangement of words is essentially semantic (referential), but in poetry the really constitutive principle is different: poetic language heightens its substantiality (and memorability) by increasing the degree of its *orders*, its patterns of repetition and variation established whenever a certain feature is selected and repeated. Hence the principle of e., which equates the words in the vertical register of speech, can equate other features and be superimposed upon the horizontal sequence as well.

This process is especially evident in metrical verse, where one phonological feature (with its opposite) is deployed systematically. E., however, is not the meter, but the system or convention which *makes the meter possible*: the particular feature the meter will employ (stress, length, pitch) is determined by the language, and the specific pattern the meter will assume is arbitrary. Meter, then, is a synecdoche for e., but e. is a metonym for parallelism (q.v.), and indeed, Jakobson identifies parallelism as "the fundamental problem of poetry." As with the meter, so with all the other formal elements in the text—sound-patterning, rhetorical schemes, lexical echoes, syntactic metaplasm: in every case "equation is used to build up a sequence." E. is thus "the indispensable feature inherent in any piece of poetry." And since the syntagmatic axis presents the sequential unfolding of meaning in language, even as the paradigm represents the axis of simultaneity, e. in poetry serves to embed the atemporal within the temporal: as the lines proceed through their sequent schemes of meaning, e. counterpoises a firm (if subliminal) sense of unchangingness, of the *re*-creation of that which came before in the now. This substratum of identities melds the poem into one seamless whole and becomes, thereby, the very emblem of poeticalness.

R. Bridges, *Milton's Prosody*, 1901 ed., App. F; Saintsbury, *Prosody*, v. I, App. 1; A. W. de Groot, *Algemene Versleer* (1946); R. Jakobson, "Closing Statement: Linguistics and Poetics," *Style in Language*, ed. T. Sebeok (1960). T.V.F.B.

EUPHONY. The quality of having a pleasant and smooth-flowing sound, free from harshness; the opposite of cacophony. E. arises largely from ease of articulation. The vowel sounds, which demand no cessation of breath, are considered more euphonious than the consonants, with the longer vowels being preferred to the shorter. Of the consonant sounds the most euphonious are the liquids and semivowels: *l, m, n, r, y, w.* Poe, considering long *o* the most sonorous vowel and *r* the most reproducible consonant, chose "Nevermore" as refrain word for *The Raven*, a word combining three vowels, four liquids, and a soft *v.* Opinions differ as to the order in which the other consonants follow, but in general those most easily produced are felt to be most pleasing. E. results not only from choice of sounds but from their arrangement. Sounds may be arranged so that they flow easily into each other, or may be placed in difficult combinations, demanding more muscular effort. Meter also will play a role, sometimes clogging a line with heavy accents, sometimes spacing them out more agreeably.

The importance of e. to total poetic effect is a matter of dispute, some finding great pleasure in "linkèd sweetness long drawn out"; others insisting that "mere sound in itself can have no or little aesthetic effect" (Wellek and Warren). Since too much euphoniousness may give the effect of weakness, some poets (e.g., Browning) have reacted against it. In general, however, e. is a desired characteristic, and most poetry is more euphonious than ordinary speech. Nearly all would agree, however, that e. is to be desired chiefly as a means rather than as an end, and that the first test of its desirability is appropriateness. The lines " 'Artillery' and 'armaments' and 'implements of war' / Are phrases too severe to please the gentle Muse" are much more euphonious than those written by Byron in *Don Juan,* but Byron's are much to be preferred as more consonant with their idea: "Bombs, drums, guns, bastions, batteries, bayonets, bullets,— / Hard words, which stick in the soft Muses' gullets." See also SOUND IN POETRY.—G. R. Stewart, *The Technique of Eng. Verse* (1930); A. Spire, *Plaisir Poétique et plaisir musculaire* (1949). L.P.

EXEMPLUM. A short narrative used to illustrate a moral point. The term is applied chiefly to the stories used in medieval sermons, though the illustrative anecdote is still, perhaps, the commonest feature of public speaking. Chaucer's *Pardoner's Tale* furnishes an example; not only the main story but many lesser narratives are used as *exempla* of the Pardoner's text. The most famous source of such stories was the L. prose *Gesta Romanorum* (13th c.), but collections for the use of preachers were also made in poetic form, e.g., *Handlyng Synne* (begun 1303) by Robert Mannyng of Brunne, a treatise on the Seven Deadly Sins with illustrative stories. A secular use is shown in John Gower's poem, *Confessio Amantis* (ca. 1385), where the *exempla* illustrate sins against Venus.—G. R. Owst, *Preaching in Medieval England* (1927) and *Lit. and Pulpit in Medieval England* (1933); J.-Th. Welter, *L'Exemplum dans la litt. religieuse et didactique du moyen âge* (1927). R.P.APR.

EXPLICATION. Also called formal, structural, or textual analysis, e. examines poetry or any work of literature for a knowledge of each part and for the relation of these parts to the whole. For Eng. poetry it begins in the late 1920's with

Laura Riding and Robert Graves's *A Survey of Modernist Poetry* (1928), I. A. Richards' *Practical Criticism* (1929), and William Empson's *Seven Types of Ambiguity* (1930). The relation of these critics to *explication de texte* as practiced in Fr. and British schools seems inescapable, though the educational use seldom went beyond paraphrase. They probably did not know the earlier Rus. formalism; and while e. was implicit in Aristotle, had appeared once in Longinus, and occurred in neoclassical critics, Richards and his associates derived mostly from Coleridge's organic concept of poetry. Cleanth Brooks introduced e. into the United States and brought it a widespread following through *Understanding Poetry* (1939), written with Robert Penn Warren. All the New Critics have made e. the basis of their findings, and so have the Chicago Critics (but with some differences in theory). Such periodicals as *Scrutiny* (1932–1953), *Southern Review* (1935–1942), *Kenyon Review* (1939–), and *Essays in Criticism* (1951–) contain many explications; and *The Explicator* (1942–), which has popularized the term, has been devoted solely to them. Though today few critical essays or books fail to use e., the movement has had many detractors—principally in its early years among literary historians and more recently among proponents of a mythic approach to poetry.

Poetry, as seen by e., is characterized by three major qualities. Self-sufficiency, the first of these, affirms the poem as impersonal and autonomous. Biographical considerations are ignored or at most given slight regard, poetry is detached from its historical context, and the poem is judged for itself rather than for its effect upon a reader. In place of intentional, historical, and affective fallacies, the starting place becomes the point of view within the poem and the tone that develops from it. A second major characteristic, that of unity, is traditional. But e. has insisted upon a comprehensive organicism, has studied the relation of structure and materials, has usually urged the importance of theme, and has occupied itself with the contextuality of poetic truth. A final characteristic is complexity, which stands in antithesis to a simplicity of plainness but not to a simplicity of articulated function. Rather, it senses unity through a *discordia concors* that informs all good poetry and not merely that of the metaphysical school. In its zeal e. has at times attempted too much in revealing ironies, ambiguities, and paradoxes, but whether or not they are the central element of poetry as some have held, the pervasiveness of some kind of countersuggestion in the language and symbols of poetry and in their fusion has won recognition. In treating all these qualities various groups and individuals exhibit differences, and none urge the characteristics as absolute, since to make a poem unmitigatedly unique would not allow a reader to comprehend it in any degree.

E. does not claim to be an act of evaluation, but rather to serve as the basis of literary criticism and history. As W. K. Wimsatt has shown ("Explication as Criticism"), there are serious problems in adjusting the polarities of part and whole, value and disvalue, and value and neutrality. Though he believes that "the extreme theory of explicative criticism cuts apart understanding and value," he also regards successful e. as rising "from neutrality gradually and convincingly to the point of total judgment." When the organic form has been established in its self-sufficiency and complexity, a judgment upon the relationship quite naturally follows.

BIBLIOGRAPHIES: R. P. Basler, C. C. Walcutt, M. Greenhut, *et al.*, "A Checklist of E.," *Explicator* 3—(1945–), June issues; G. Arms and J. M. Kuntz, *Poetry E.: A Checklist* (1950; rev. ed. by Kuntz, 1962).

HISTORY AND CRITICISM: Wellek and Warren, ch. 12; L. Fiedler *et al.*, My "Credo," KR, 12–13 (1950–51); W. K. Wimsatt, Jr., "E. as Crit.," *EIE 1951*, and *The Verbal Icon* (1954); Crane; J. P. Kirby, " 'The Last Verse . . . Is Not Sufficiently Explicated'!" *Va. Librarian*, 2 (1956); Daiches, ch. 15; Krieger; Wimsatt and Brooks, "Epilogue"; G. Arms, "Poetry," *Contemporary Lit. Scholarship*, ed. L. Leary (1958). See also *E. as Crit.*, ed. Wimsatt (1963). G.A.

EYE RHYME. A rhyme which gives to the eye (that is, in spelling) the impression of perfect rhyme but to the ear (that is, in pronunciation) the effect of, at best, an approximation, as in near rhyme (q.v.). In general, eye rhymes represent obsolete or merely regional pronunciations which are inexact in standard modern Eng. or Am. speech. Some prosodists refer to such eye rhymes as *love-prove, flood-brood* as historical rhymes because it is almost certain that these pairs once rhymed perfectly. Note, however, that historical rhymes are not always eye rhymes, e.g., Pope's *tea-away*, words which once echoed each other, "tea" being pronounced "tay" in the early 18th c.—H. C. Wyld, *Studies in Eng. Rhymes from Surrey to Pope* (1923). S.L.M.

F

FABLIAU. A short story in verse, usually in octosyllabic couplets, relating a comic or bawdy incident from middle-class life. The fabliaux, which originated in France, flourished there in the 12th and 13th c., but an 8th-c. warning against them, in Egbert's *Poenitentiale,* shows that they must have existed centuries before. *Richeut* (1159) is regarded by some authorities as the oldest surviving f., but other scholars feel that the *Isopet* of Marie de France is, in effect, an earlier example of the genre.

Opinion is sharply divided as to the origin of the f. and its themes: questions under controversy include whether the genre was bourgeois or courtly in origin, and whether or not its themes derive from oriental sources. It seems likely that all classes of society supplied writers of fabliaux, although the anonymous authorship of so many of them makes this difficult to establish. Writers who can be identified include Rutebeuf, Philippe de Beaumanoir, and Jean Bodel.

The typical f. is realistic in setting, coarse in treatment, and ribald in material. Its favorite theme is cuckoldry, usually achieved through the use of guile, and it frequently contains sharp anticlerical satire. Some critics have seen in its cynical attitude toward women a reaction against the deification of woman implicit in the code of courtly love, which permeated the *lais* and romances of the time.

In the 14th c. the vogue of the f. spread to Italy and to England, where Chaucer imitated the form in his *Miller's Tale* and *Reeve's Tale.* F. tradition continued in the prose *nouvelle,* but the influence of the older form may be noted, centuries later, in the poetry of La Fontaine in France, C. F. Gellert in Germany, and I. A. Krylov in Russia.—J. Bédier, *Les Fabliaux* (5th ed., 1928); P. Nykrog, *Les Fabliaux* (1957); J. Rychner, *Contribution à l'étude des fabliaux* (2 v., 1960).

FANCY. See IMAGINATION.

FARCE. If, following the suggestion of *Rambler* no. 125, we confine ourselves to purpose and ignore the more accidental feature of means, we should have no difficulty in arriving at an acceptable definition of f. Its object is to provoke the spectator to laughter, not the reflective kind which comedy is intended to elicit but the uncomplicated response of simple enjoyment. Its means are often shared by other comic forms, such as burlesque (q.v.), thus giving rise to frequent confusion among them. Once purpose is established these means are not hard to visualize. F. exploits the surprise of sudden appearance or disclosure, the mechanism suggested by many physical actions, repetition, gross exaggeration of character, and so on. Since it does not share with higher comedy the responsibility of commentary on social conduct it may pursue its laughter into a world of fantasy where the unpredictable, even the impossible, is commonplace.

The origins of f. are doubtless hidden somewhere beyond the beginning of recorded literary history since the propensity to horseplay seems as natural to man as the trait of laughter, which is alleged to separate him from the other animals. The presence of f. in Aristophanes and the Roman comic writers and its popularity in the mimes and Atellanan pieces of the Romans suggest an early origin. Something of the crude horseplay common to f. and such kindred forms as burlesque, mime, and satyr play may be observed in surviving vase paintings and statues. The first plays of record to bear the name were Fr., for the name was devised in France from the L. *farcire,* to stuff. The 15th c. reveals Fr. f. at an early peak as it was developed especially by the "joyous societies" who contrived numerous little pieces from the stuff of folklore and fabliau. Usually rendered in lively octosyllabic couplets, these medieval Fr. farces exploited themes of commercial trickery and sexual infidelity, to show a life both coarse and vibrant in which the conventions, particularly the conventional respect for women and the clergy, were flaunted. Two examples of many possible ones may be cited: *Le meunier et le gentilhomme* (ca. 1550), which treats a folk motif traceable back as far as the 7th c. and appearing on four continents, and *Maître Pierre Pathelin* (ca. 1465), most famous of all. F. never quite regained in France the level of popularity it had reached in the Middle Ages, yet it managed to survive and to enjoy a popular esteem, even in the classical period, when Molière as both actor and playwright helped restore it to theatrical recognition. It managed to survive the competition of *drame bourgeois* in the 18th c. and of *mélodrame* and romantic drama in the 19th though perhaps no name greater than that of Labiche came to its support. Italy, Spain, and Germany meanwhile had their f. writers, though *writer* is slightly misapplied in the case of Italy since the bulk of It. f. was supplied by the improvisations of the widely popular and influential *commedia dell'arte* troupes which flourished from the 16th to the 18th c.

The first Eng. f. writer of note—there are farce episodes in the earlier mystery plays—is the 16th-c. John Heywood, a somewhat isolated figure in that he chose to borrow from and imitate Fr. f. and also developed an independent genre. The common practice, following the triumph of classical models just as the professional Eng. theatre was beginning, was to mix farcical episodes in with more serious matter. In Shakespeare's *Comedy of Errors,* for example, or *Merry Wives,* in Jonson's *Silent Woman,* even more in such popular anonymous plays as *Mucedorus,* we find f. scenes mingled with intrigue, romance, and the satirical portraiture of "humours" comedy. Only in the droll of the Commonwealth period was Eng. f. independent of other forms before the coming of the afterpiece at the beginning of the 18th c. With the establishment of the afterpiece and the consequent demand for short pieces in the Eng. repertory f. came into its own as a distinct genre. For much of the next two centuries it thrived vigorously. As taste declined, f. took its place, with sentimental comedy and melodrama, as one of the staples of theatrical fare. Of the hundreds of farces written in this period of its flourishing few worthy of preservation appeared. Only at the very end, with Wilde and Pinero, did f. aspire to be literary, an aspiration usually fatal to the genre. Though it still has its place in the popular theatre and always will have, it no longer enjoys quite the vogue it did a century ago. Even in the cinema, where with Chaplin and other producers of short pieces it had a renewal of life, the more traditional f. with human actors has been displaced by the animated film.

L. Petit de Julleville, *Hist. du théâtre en France* (1880–89); K. Holl, *Gesch. des deutschen Lustspiels* (1923); W. S. Jack, *The Early Entremés in Spain* (1923); K. Lea, *It. Popular Comedy* (1934); W. Klemm, *Die englische F. im 19. Jh.* (1946); I. Maxwell, *Fr. F. and John Heywood* (1946); Nicoll; G. Frank, *The Medieval Fr. Drama* (1954); L. Hughes, *A Century of Eng. F.* (1956); E. Bentley, "The Psychology of F.," *New Republic,* 138 (Jan. 6 and 13, 1958); M. Bieber, *A Hist. of the Gr. and Roman Theater* (2d ed., 1961); B. Cannings, "Toward a Definition of F. as a Lit. Genre," MLR, 56 (1961) L.H.

FEMININE ENDING. See LINE ENDINGS.

FIGURES OF SPEECH are traditionally considered to be words and expressions used in ways that are out of the ordinary, serving primarily as ornament and making their appeal through novelty. Although the distinction between f. of speech and f. of thought was standard in ancient rhetoric, there has never been agreement upon the differentiation. Quintilian, elaborating on Ciceronian rhetoric, provides the simplest and perhaps best test: f. of speech may be changed or removed without changing the sense of what contains them, but f. of thought cannot be so changed (*Institutes* 9.1.17). F. of speech are either grammatical or rhetorical (as aphaeresis, antithesis, isocolon, anaphora). F. of thought are words or expressions used in different senses from those which properly belong to them (as metaphor, metonymy, synechdoche, irony), and these are frequently classified as tropes when they approximate metaphors.

Study of the various f. was originally a branch of rhetoric but came to be included in poetics. Longinus considered that the f. of rhetoric were controlled by what was known to be true and thought to be probable, but the use of similar f. in poetry was to be governed by other considerations, and particularly by their effectiveness in achieving elevation and transport. During the Middle Ages and the Renaissance, partly through the continuing influence of Cicero, the distinction of Longinus was lost, and poetry was very generally thought of as versified rhetoric.

Quintilian divided f. of speech into three classes: those formed by the addition of elements (anaphora, polysyndeton, etc.); those formed by subtracting elements (asyndeton, zeugma, etc.); and those formed through the use of comparable or parallel constructions (antithesis, paranomasia, etc.). Bede, following Isidore of Seville, carried over the classification that had originated in ancient rhetoric in which the major classes were of schemes and tropes (see TROPE). Geoffrey of Vinsauf, the leader in the identification of rhetoric and poetics, listed 34 f. of speech (frequently in the Middle Ages called "colors"), 19 f. of thought, and 10 tropes. Innumerable refinements were developed in the Renaissance, and the classifications were multiplied. In the 16th c, Thomas Wilson listed 19 f. of speech, 27 f. of thought, and 13 tropes. Puttenham changed the basis of the initial classification. He devised three classes of f.: those that made their appeal to the ear (of which there were 21), those appealing to the mind (25), and those that appealed to both (62). In this as in other matters Puttenham was breaking away from the confusion of poetics and rhetoric. Ramus's reform of traditional rhetoric involved the idea that style was the whole of rhetoric, and that f. and tropes, which were the substance of style, should be distinguished from invention and arrangement, which Ramus considered parts of logic.

That f. of speech are ornaments has been a dominant idea in the history of literary criticism. Through many centuries the mastery of f. was considered a sign of virtuosity, and much of the pleasure of reading was thought to depend on the pleasure of discriminating among the devices. Both Longinus and Quintilian argued against the use of f. according to fixed rules, and Thomas Wilson was returning to their position when in his *Art of Rhetoric* (1551) he proposed that they be used according to principles that would justify them in their context, what he called the principles of clearness and fitness and beauty. Puttenham in his *Art of Poetry* (1589) carried this reasoning further: for him poetry took feeling and nature as its guides, decency and decorum were proposed as laws of nature, and

f. of speech, formed according to the demands of feeling and decorum, were employed in order to achieve "good grace." Such theories were an improvement on the medieval doctrine of rhetorical colors but continued to stress the ornamental aspect of the f. By the time of Dryden and Pope the doctrine of decorum (q.v.) and the prevailing rationalism caused the f. to be ever more closely bound to content and argument.

In the later 18th c. the development of psychology supported an emphasis on the criticism of particular poems and particular effects, and with Coleridge there was the beginning of a system in which it may be said that all f. aspired to the state of metaphor and indeed to metaphysical reference. The issues raised by this development have continued to be among the most significant ones for literary criticism in the 20th c. The New Critics and the Chicago Critics have been profoundly concerned with f., as with other phases of the relation of rhetoric to poetics. A paradoxical aspect of some of this interest is that f. of speech are often taken to be the quintessence of poetry when in the past they were primarily valued as ornaments to meaning or the substance of style. See also IMAGERY, RHETORIC AND POETICS, and Trope.—G. Dzialas, *Rhetorum antiquorum de figuris doctrina* (Breslavia, 1896); E. Faral, *Les Arts Poétiques du XIIe et du XIIIe s.* (1923); A. K. Coomaraswamy, *F. of Speech or F. of Thought?* (1946); J.W.H. Atkins, *Eng. Lit. Crit.: The Renascence* (1951); Crane; Wimsatt; W. S. Howell, *Logic and Rhetoric in England, 1500–1700* (1956); Lausberg. J.A.

FIGURES OF THOUGHT. See FIGURES OF SPEECH.

FOOT. A measurable, patterned unit of poetic rhythm. The concept of the f. has been imported into modern accentual-syllabic prosody (see METER) from classical quantitative practice, and disagreement over the nature (and even the "existence") of the f. has been traditional since the late Renaissance. The Eng. f. is customarily defined by the orthodox as a measure of rhythm consisting of 1 accented (stressed, "long") syllable (or 2, as in the spondee) and 1 or more unaccented (unstressed, "short," "slack") syllables. The poetic line in a more or less regular composition, say the traditional prosodists, consists of a number of feet from 1 to 8; conventionally, the feet are to be roughly of the same kind, although metrical variations (q.v.), produced by the occasional "substitution" of different feet, are permissible so long as these substitutions do not efface for long the repeated pattern of the prevailing f.

In traditional Eng. accentual or accentual-syllabic verse (see ENG. PROSODY), the following feet are the most common:

IAMB (iambus); iambic, × / as in *destroy*

ANAPEST (anapaest); anapestic × × / *intervene*

TROCHEE; trochaic / × *topsy*

DACTYL; dactylic / × × *merrily*

SPONDEE; spondaic / / *amen*

PYRRHIC × × *the sea* | *son of* | *mists*

Iambic and anapestic feet are called ascending or rising feet; trochaic and dactylic, descending or falling. Feet of 2 syllables are called duple feet; feet of 3, triple. Spondaic (except in sprung rhythm, q.v.) and pyrrhic feet are generally "substitute" feet (see METRICAL VARIATIONS). Some prosodists recognize also a monosyllabic f. consisting of 1 stressed syllable. The exemplification of these feet by single words, above, of course distorts their nature: it is important to remember that f. divisions do not necessarily correspond to word divisions, and that the structure of a f. is determined contextually by the nature of the feet which surround it.

The f. bears a close resemblance to the musical bar: both are arbitrary and abstract units of measure which do not necessarily coincide with the phrasal units which they underlie. The major difference between them is that the bar always begins with a "stress."

It is perhaps unfortunate that the terminology of feet is borrowed from classical quantitative prosody, where practice is in general much more regular than in most Eng. verse and where "substitutions" are largely governed by rule rather than by whim or instinct. In addition to those listed above, the following feet are among those used in Gr. and L. poetry (where, of course, duration of syllables rather than stress determines "long" and "short"):

AMPHIBRACH ⏑ – ⏑
ANTISPAST ⏑ – – ⏑
BACCHIUS ⏑ – –
CHORIAMBUS – ⏑ ⏑ –
CRETIC (or amphimacer) – ⏑ –
DOCHMIAC ⏑ – – ⏑ –
EPITRITE ⏑ – – – (called 1st, 2d, 3d, or 4th according to position of the short syllable)
IONIC
a majore – – ⏑ ⏑
a minore ⏑ ⏑ – –
MOLOSSUS – – –
PAEON – ⏑ ⏑ ⏑ (called 1st, 2d, 3d, or 4th according to the position of the long syllable)
PROCELEUSMATIC ⏑ ⏑ ⏑ ⏑
TRIBRACH ⏑ ⏑ ⏑

See PROSODY, SCANSION, METER, ENG. PROSODY, CLASSICAL PROSODY.

R. Bridges, "On the Use of Gr. Terminology in Eng. Prosody," *Milton's Prosody* (1921); Saintsbury, *Prosody;* Baum; Hamer; Koster. P.F.

FORM in poetry, simply defined, is the manner in which a poem is composed as distinct from what the poem is about. The latter may be called the subject or the substance of the poem, its subject matter or content as distinct from its form or manner. "Form" being a term with a variety of denotations, some of them closely connected with particular systems of philosophy, poetic f. also admits of several meanings, same so divergent from each other that they are contradictory.

To take first one of the commonest meanings, the f. of a poem may be its meter, poetry being usually composed in verse. Modern alternatives to regular verse such as free verse and patterned prose would also constitute the formal element of the poem in this meaning of the term. Alternatively, the words used in the poem, its language and diction, may be considered the f., as distinct from the thought or subject matter of the poem. By extension, f. may be the style in which the composition is written. Most of these meanings are implied when one speaks of the "cult of form" or formalism in poetry, which is making art consist essentially in the skillful handling of words and phrases, verse and rhyme, style and diction. Formalists believe that the value of a poem depends exclusively on the quality of its f., in that sense. They tend to give poets advice such as Horace's to use unsparingly "the labor of the file," revising and polishing the f. until it is perfect, or the injunction from the Parnassian poet who proclaimed that "form is everything": *"Sculpte, lime, cisèle"* (T. Gautier, preface to *Mlle de Maupin,* and *L'art*). Critics of a different persuasion are apt to object that in this meaning f. "is something superficial, general, diagrammatic. We speak of empty form, mere form, formal politeness; it is opposed to the heart and soul of anything, to what is essential, material, and so forth" (B. Bosanquet, *Three Lectures on Aesthetic,* 1916, p. 15).

W. P. Ker pointed out that "from another point of view, however, which is just as common, it is the scheme or argument that is the form, and the poet's very words are the matter with which it is filled. The form is not that with which you are immediately presented, or that which fills your ears when the poem is recited—it is the abstract original scheme from which the poet began. . . . If it is said that a poem is formless—Wordsworth's *Excursion,* for example—what is meant is generally that the argument is not well planned" (*Form and Style in Poetry,* p. 138). In this sense f. is the structure, tight or loose, supple or flaccid, of the whole composition, "this kind of form being in strictness neither prosaic nor poetical, but just as much the one as the other" (p. 139). This brings us to another widely accepted meaning of f., viz. genre or kind of composition. The epic, the lyric, the drama, with all their subdivisions, are said to be the forms of poetry (see GENRES). This meaning of f. as kind may derive from the ancient philosophical meaning of the term (as with Plato's *eidos*), which has been defined: "that which an object has in common with other objects is its form." Accordingly what a poem has in common with other poems—its presentation as dialogue or narrative or as personal effusion—is its f. or kind. The kind or genre is then conceived to determine the structure of the poem, which is the previous meaning of f.

On the other hand, a philosophical meaning which is practically opposite to the last may be defined as follows: "In a broad sense, whatever in the make-up of an object helps one to perceive it as a whole is its form" (V. M. Ames in V. Ferm, ed., *History of Philosophical Systems,* 1950, p. 555). This makes f. the unifying factor in the poem. In this sense we find it applied also to the novel: "Form represents the final unity of a work of fiction, the successful combining of all parts into an artful whole" (R. B. West and R. Stallman, *The Art of Modern Fiction,* 1949, p. 647). It is therefore much more than the "abstract argument" or "original scheme": it is the actual welding of all parts into a whole, the individual organization of a work so that all its constituents, however defined—words, thoughts, diction, style, or meter—cohere and harmonize. In this sense f. is often called organic f. and sharply distinguished from abstract structure, especially as determined by genre. The external and preconceived structure depending on genre is correspondingly named mechanical or abstract f. in contrast with organic. This famous dichotomy of organic vs. mechanical f. found its classical formulation in A. W. Schlegel's *Lectures on Dramatic Literature* (1809–11), where the free and supple f. of Shakespearean tragedy is defended as organic, in contradistinction of the mechanical regularity imposed by the rules and unities of neoclassicism. Thus Schlegel finally solved the problem of the artistic pattern of Shakespeare's plays, which had puzzled critics throughout the 18th c. In Coleridge's felicitous translation Schlegel's formula found its way into Eng. criticism and there fructified and proliferated, until it has now become almost a commonplace, and its original author and application often forgotten. In the 20th c. the organic unity of f. and content was the subject of another classic pronouncement by A. C. Bradley in his famous inaugural lecture of 1901, "Poetry for Poetry's Sake." He formulated a dichotomy of "form and substance" and argued: "If the substance means ideas, images, and the like taken alone, and the form means the measured language taken by itself, this is a possible distinction, but it is a distinction of things not in the poem, and the value lies in neither of them. If substance and form mean anything *in* the poem, then each is involved in the other, and the question in which of them the value lies has no sense. . . . The true critic in speaking of these apart does not really think of them apart; the whole, the poetic experience, of which they are but aspects, is always in his mind; and he is always aiming at a richer, truer, more intense repetition of that experience" (pp. 16–17). Bradley then used the phrase "significant form" for the unified whole (p. 19), a phrase which shortly afterwards became the key term in Clive Bell's theory of art (1913).

This concept of f. as the result of the operation of the plastic and unifying imagination was developed by romantic criticism and aesthetics, although the concept of f. as a dynamic unifying principle is as old as Aristotle. In Book 7 of the *Metaphysics* Aristotle applied to art his ontological concept of f. determining matter, such as the idea of the statue which is the form in the mind of the sculptor and which he then imposes upon some kind of material: the resultant work is thus a synthesis of f. and matter produced by human intelligence, while living beings are a synthesis of f. and matter produced by nature. This f. might therefore be said to be organic by analogy. But unfortunately in the *Poetics* Aristotle was diverted by the Gr. conception of poetry as mimetic (see IMITATION and POETRY, THEORIES OF) from applying this concept of organic f. to poetry. The recognition of the relationship of the quality of Beauty to the inner f. (*éndon eidos*) was Plotinus' constructive contribution to aesthetics. From Kant onward f. assumes an epistemological significance as the active mental factor in the organization of experience from the manifold of sensations. Schiller then made poetic f. a force that controls and transforms blind impulse into the material of art: in that sense (and not in the sense of the superficial formalism mentioned above) he could say that "Art consists in the destruction of matter by form" (*Letters on Aesthetic Education* 22). On the other hand, in Hegel art is defined as the sensuous appearance of the Idea, which makes f. consist of the sensuous element and matter becomes the spiritual element or the Idea, thus showing again the polysemanticism of these terms.

The organic concept of f. and content has as its logical corollary that there is no such thing in art as the same f. with different content: alteration in one produces alteration in the other. Hence the rejection of the common concept of genre or kind as an empty form into which a separate matter is poured, as in a mold or vessel (cf. Schlegel). The ultimate consequence of this argument is the rejection, by Croce and others, of genres and kinds from the domain of criticism, f. being conceived as individual and as unique as matter, or as "the efficient equivalent" of a poem's unity (L. Abercrombie, p. 62).

The concept of Inner F. in German criticism is apparently a variant of organic f. It appears as early as 1776 in young Goethe's criticism of dramatic rules and of the unities (*Jubilaum Ausgabe,* 36.115). It has been traced back to Plotinus through Shaftesbury, and forward into romantic criticism as well as into W. von Humboldt's theory of language, which also makes use of the concept of Inner F. In the present century it has been used by the school of George in biographical studies in which the "Inner F." of a great mind has been investigated.

A. C. Bradley, *Oxford Lectures on Poetry* (1909); B. Croce, *Aesthetic,* tr. D. Ainslie (2d ed., 1922); E. Panofsky, *Idea* (1924); L. Abercrombie, *The Theory of Poetry* (1926); W. P. Ker, *F. and Style in Poetry* (1928); H. Read, *F. in Modern Poetry* (1932) and *The True Voice of Feeling* (1953); R. Schwinger, *Innere F.* (1935); O. Walzel, *Grenzen von Poesie und Unpoesie* (1937); G. McKenzie, *Organic Unity in Coleridge* (1939); H. Cherniss, "The Biographical Fashion in Lit. Crit.," *Univ. of Calif. Publications in Cl. Phil.,* 12 (1943); J. Benziger, "Organic Unity: Leibniz to Coleridge, PMLA, 66 (1951); C. La Drière, "F.," in *Dict. of World Lit.,* ed. J. T. Shipley (rev., 1953); V. M. Hamm, "The Problem of F. in Nature and the Arts," JAAC, 13 (1954); F. Schiller, *The Aesthetic Education of Man,* tr. R. Snell (1954); R. H. Fogle, "Organic F. in Am. Crit., 1840–1870," *Development of Am. Lit. Crit.,* ed. F. Stovall (1955); *Stil und Formprobleme* in der Literatur, ed. P. Bockman (1959); P. Fussell, Jr., *Poetic Meter and Poetic Form* (1965).

G.N.G.O.

FORMULA. See ORAL POETRY.

FOURTEENER. An Eng. meter of 7 iambic feet. See HEPTAMETER and SEPTENARY.

FREE VERSE. Related to *vers libre* (q.v.). A term popularly, but not accurately, used to describe the poems of Walt Whitman and others whose verse is based not on the recurrence of stress accent in a regular, strictly measurable pattern, but rather on the irregular rhythmic cadence of the recurrence, with variations, of significant phrases, image patterns, and the like. F.v. treats the device of rhyme with a similar freedom and irregularity. The following quotation, from Whitman's *Song of Myself,* is fairly typical:

I celebrate myself;
And what I assume you shall assume;
For every atom belonging to me, as good belongs to you

I loaf and invite my soul;
I lean and loaf at my ease, observing a blade of summer grass.

There are two opinions about the form and Whitman's use of it. Some say that his practice is no more than rhythmical prose. Others that it has distinctively "poetic" qualities. Both of these opinions are consistent with the following addition to the definition given above in paragraph one: whenever and however, either by the agency of the eye or ear, a persistent irregularity of the metrical pattern is established in a poem, it can justly be called f.v. The irregularity involves both the eye and the ear. Whether the measure be written down with a view to the appearance of the poem on the printed page or to the sound of the words as spoken or sung is of no consequence so long as the established irregularity is maintained.

Many antecedents have been cited in the attempt to discover the origins of f.v. Gr. and L. "art prose" (cf. Norden, *Die Antike Kunstprosa*) bears obvious resemblances to the modern form, as do the medieval tropes and sequences. Alliterative verse suggests the tendency of the Germanic languages to seek forms other than traditional quantitative or accentual verse. In England, the King James translation of the Psalms and the Song of Songs, based in part on the original Hebrew cadences, provided a powerful and inspiring model for nonmetrical verse, the influence of which is evident in the work of Whitman and his successors. Technically, Milton's verse is regular, but its effect in *Lycidas, Paradise Lost,* and *Samson* is that of extreme freedom, a fact evident in Milton's tendency to make the verse paragraph rather than the line his basic unit. And although Fr. neoclassicists prided themselves on their regularity, certain modern theorists (Robert de Souza, Georges Lote) have demonstrated that the Fr. alexandrine is extremely irregular if scansion is based on reading rather than syllable-counting.

The neoclassic movement hindered the tendency evident in the baroque Pindaric ode to move toward f.v. Interest revived, however, as the romantic movement gained momentum. Macpherson's *Ossian Poems* are in rhythmical prose, and Christopher Smart's *Jubilate Agno* is f.v. in the tradition of the King James Psalms. In Germany Klopstock (*Messias*), Goethe (*Prometheus*), and Novalis (*Hymnen an die Nacht*) show a similar tendency. 19th c. experimenters in f.v. and related forms include Blake and Arnold (f.v.); Lamb, de Quincey, and Poe (prose tending to poetry); Hölderlin, Heine, and Nietzsche (poetic prose, prose poem); Bertrand, Hugo, Baudelaire (f.v., prose poem). Toward the end of the 19th c. the Fr. symbolists had gone far toward establishing the prestige and flexibility of f.v. on the continent.

During the 20th c. f.v. has become so common as to have some claim to being the characteristic verse form of the age. Merely listing the significant poets who have used f.v. would be a tedious and futile task, but among typical practitioners may be mentioned Rilke, Apollinaire, St.-John Perse, T. S. Eliot, Ezra Pound, and William Carlos Williams. It may be noted that the most important Eng. and Am. f.v. poets of the first half of the century were either involved in or influenced by the imagist program formulated by T. E. Hulme and Ezra Pound between roughly 1905 and 1915.

In all modern literatures f.v. has been defended as more "natural" than regular meter, and it has often, though by no means always, been described as innately "democratic" or even revolutionary. In England and America it has been argued (especially by Pound and Williams) that conventional meters, being based on analogies to Gr. and L. quantitative forms, deform the natural speech pattern. This deformity is most marked in Milton—despite the fact that Milton in some ways anticipated the effects of f.v.—and his techniques, minus his talent, helped to create the artificial diction typical of much 18th- and 19th-c. poetry. On the other hand, the Gr. and L. contour of phrase which Milton and the Elizabethans learned in the schools was capable of effects unprecedented in the colloquial idiom. That, in essence, is still the stumbling block to an easy, not to say natural, poetry in Eng.

A language or practice of speaking or writing which will not conform to rigid prosodic rules is forced to break those rules if it is to be retained in its own character. More accurately, it must adopt a new set of rules which it can obey, find another way of speaking and writing. It is the refusal of Eng. (especially Am. Eng.) to conform to standard prosody which has given rise to "f.v." However, the term can be misleading. Being an art form, verse cannot be "free" in the sense of having *no* limitations or guiding principles.

The crux of the question is measure. In f.v. the measure has been loosened to give more play to vocabulary and syntax—hence, to the mind in its excursions. The bracket of the customary foot has been expanded so that more syllables, words, or phrases can be admitted into its confines. The new unit thus created may be called the "variable foot," a term and a concept already accepted widely as a means of bringing the warring elements of freedom and discipline together. It rejects the standard of the conventionally fixed foot and suggests that measure varies with the idiom by which it is employed and the tonality of the individual poem. Thus, as in speech, the prosodic pattern is evaluated by criteria of effectiveness and expressiveness rather than mechanical syllable counts.

T. S. Eliot, "Reflections on Vers Libre," *New Statesman,* 8 (1917); A. Lowell, "The Rhythms of F.V.," *Dial,* 64 (1918) and "Walt Whitman and the New Poetry," *Yale Review,* 16 (1927); H. Monroe, *Poets and Their Art* (1926); E. Pound, *Make It New* (1934); G. W. Allen, *Am. Prosody* (1935); A. Closs, *Die freien Rhythmen in der deutschen Lyrik* (1947); Y. Winters, *In Defense of Reason* (1947); C. A. Allen, "Cadenced F.V.," CE, 9 (1948); W. C. Williams, "An Approach to the Poem," *EIE, 1947* (1948); L. Bogan, "Vers Libre and Avant-Garde," *Achievement in Am. Poetry, 1900–1950* (1951); *Discussions of Poetry,* ed. G. Hemphill (1961).

W.C.W.

FRENCH PROSODY. See ROMANCE PROSODY.

G

GENERATIVE METRICS. The most conspicuous case of linguistic methods applied to traditional lit. problems is "g.m." The cover term applies to three distinctive theories of meter advanced after 1966 and based on developments in transformational syntax and g. phonology. In g. theories, the abstract pattern of the meter is analogous to the deep structure of language, while each particular poetic line constitutes the surface realization of that meter; "correspondence rules" are then given to generate all those lines which a reader would recognize as metrical while filtering out all unmetrical lines. The ordering of these rules then creates a tension index or "scale of delicacy" by which *degrees* of metricality may be assessed. The primary focus of all three theories has thus fallen on but one aspect, establishing the limen of unmetricality.

In the first and most widely discussed theory, proposed by Morris Halle and S. J. Keyser in 1966, the abstract pattern of the Eng. iambic pentameter is defined not as five "feet" but as a series of ten positions,

(W)* S W S W S W S (X) (X),

i.e. an alternating pattern with undefined optional elements on both ends. It is a known fact that rhythmic series, of which meters are a prime example, are least determined at their beginnings and most determined at their ends; here the ends are left variable to avoid infringing the definition of the "stress maximum" (any fully stressed syllable falling between two unstressed syllables in the same syntactic constituent), which is the criterion of unmetricality in H-K. Three "Correspondence Rules" are then adduced in order of increasing constraint or severity: either stressed syllables occur in only and in all S positions (violated by weak syllables in S positions), or in only but not in all S positions (violated by stresses in W positions), or stress maxima occur in only but not in all S positions. Marking violations of each Rule in sequence yields a numeric score of metricality: violations of the first two rules merely indicate metrical "complexity" (compare "tension" in New Criticism), but violations of the third identify a line as unmetrical.

Such a theory was an improvement over the traditional foot theory of Eng. meter in that for the first time it made an effort to formulate in a rigorous way what a theory should do, it seemed to define the line as a series of positions rather than a series of segmented, hypostasized "feet," and it incorporated the recognition that readers do perceive degrees of acceptability in metrical lines. A number of amendments and modifications were subsequently offered by other researchers to account for phenomena such as displaced stress (Beaver) and to extend the theory to other meters (Hascall, Dilligan), older stages of Eng. (Keyser, Sapora), and other languages.

Crit. of the theory came from many directions. The concept of the "stress maximum" seemed to suggest that Eng. heroic verse was somehow deeply amphibrachic, since it was a stress (flanked by unstressed syllables on *both* sides) in a Weak position of the meter which qualified the line as unmetrical. The system was shown not to apply very well in some verse-traditions outside Eng. pentameter, particularly OE and ME. Some critics argued that the g. system, being based solely on stress, could take no account of the role of other intonational features in verse, a subject which had been of much interest in other quarters, though in this the generativists allied themselves with the tradition. Other critics, especially Wimsatt, complained that to predicate the meter and the natural-language patterns as fixed entities allowed no room for the meter to "tilt" or modulate normal stressings. Their stipulation that constraints on stress maxima applied only within major syntactic boundaries, a feature which greatly improved the accuracy of the theory, still seemed an anomaly, in that the metricality of the line was being determined not across the line as a whole metrical unit but within each syntactic component of the line. In traditional metrics "caesuras" were noticed, but phrase-boundaries, like word-boundaries, played no part as indices of unmetricality, which usually had to do with which types of feet appeared in which positions. More significantly, it was noticed that in their account "metricality or unmetricality results from the absence of invariant features, while line complexity results from the absence of variant features" (Harvey). Halle and Keyser's desire for a sharp metrical "rule" which would neatly cleave all metrical lines from unmetrical ones led to numerous problems of admitting bad lines and excluding good lines, leaving critics to question the relevance of such rules to aesthetic perception. No experimental confirmation was ever provided showing that experienced readers of poetry in fact perceived metricality in such degrees of delicacy and for the particular reasons implied by the H-K correspondence rules. Obviously readers do recognize some lines as more complex than others and some as simply unmetrical, but their implicit criteria for making such recognitions are not immediately referable to the "stress maximum," a concept which has no equivalent or analogy whatsoever in the long hist. of Eng. metrical theory, and for which Halle and Keyser provided no justification other than empirical verification, which turned out to be uneven.

The second theory, by Karl Magnuson and Frank G. Ryder in 1970, differs from its predecessor in construing the line not as a series of weak and strong but odd and even positions, a variation interesting because there is some evidence to suggest that odd positions in the line are constrained differentially (and more heavily) as a class than even ones. Magnuson and Ryder also mark the presence or absence of the Distinctive Features (+ or −) of each syllable on a taxic grid—Weak, Strong, Pre-Strong, and Word-Onset; by this last, their system takes account not only of phonological features (stress) but morphological ones as well, i.e. word-boundaries. They write Base Rules to account for four relations between even and odd positions, finding that the most highly constrained is the relation of even syllables to following odds. But serious shortcomings in the architecture of the theory prevented it from having much generality beyond describing a given line. In the most productive application, Bjorklund mapped out striking differences of compatibility between Eng. and German, as linguistic systems, and the abstract pattern of the iambic pentameter.

The third system, broached by Kiparsky in 1975 but revised radically in 1977 based on a seminal analysis of phonology by Liberman and Prince also published in 1977, is very similar in its ultimate effect to H-K, though K. abandons H-K's notion of the "stress maximum" in favor of L-P's simpler treatment and returns, astonishingly, to defining the meter of the iambic pentameter line as composed of five *feet*, which are "bracketed":

∧ ∧ ∧ ∧ ∧
WS WS WS WS WS.

The surface stress pattern of the line, then, is derived via tree-diagrams (like those in transformational grammar) which create another bracketing (of language) corresponding to that of the meter. In the great majority of verse lines, there will be some kind of "mismatch" between the brackets of the language and those of the meter. Linguistic S's in metrical W's that are lexical (polysyllabic) cause unmetricality; those that are not lexical create "labeling" mismatches (an awkward term). "Bracketing" mismatches occur when the two patterns of W and S agree but the brackets to each pattern are out of sync—as with trochaic words in an iambic line. (These will be seen to be very different phenomena.) K. notes, however, that the two types of mismatches never occur simultaneously. Lexical S's in W create unmetricality because the linguistic S is controlled by elements to its left, whereas on the metrical level the W goes with the S following it on the right; at the beginning of syntactic phrases, however, "the bracketing that is necessary for unmetricality can never arise" (K.). His procedure for assessing the complexity of the line is simply to total the sum of mismatches.

Kiparsky's approach is in several respects simpler than H-K's and closer to one's intuitive sense of how words fit themselves to meter. By postulating feet in the meter and then writing rules for closeness of fit, he returns to the view the generativists first derided so freely as archaic. Certainly his conception of meter per se is utterly simple, even classical. The treatment of bracketing would have to be revised radically if the metrical brackets for the feet were removed.

In later developments Hayes supplements K's trees with metrical "grids" for marking relative stress prominence (taken also from L-P's classic 1977 paper) in order to reduce some of the arbitrariness of K's metrical filters. More significant still, Hayes makes explicit assaults on the scope and importance of meter, claiming that virtually all significant distinctions in meter come straight out of processes in the language, while at the same time confounding his own statements by proposing a theory that the rhythmic structure of poetic meters is based on rules that are purely rhythmic and temporal in nature, not linguistic.

M. Halle and S. J. Keyser, "Chaucer and the Study of Prosody," CE, 28 (1966), responded to by W. K. Wimsatt, Jr., "The Rule and The Norm," CE, 31 (1970); further argued by H. and K. in "Illustration and Defense," CE, 33 (1971), with final form in their *Eng. Stress: Its Form, Its Growth, Its Role in Verse* (1971); partial revisions by S. R. Levin in *Language*, 49 (1973); D. C. Freeman, "On the Primes of Metrical Style," *Language and Style*, 1 (1968); J. C. Beaver, "A Grammar of Prosody," CE, 29 (1968), "Contrastive Stress and Metered Verse," *Language and Style*, 2 (1969), "The Rules of Stress in Eng. Verse," *Language*, 47 (1971); D. L. Hascall, "Trochaic Meter," CE, 33 (1971), "Triple Meter in Eng. Verse," *Poetics*, 12 (1974); R. W. Sapora, Jr., *A Theory of M. E. Allit. Meter with Crit. Appl.* (1977); R. Grotjahn, *Ling. und stat. Methoden in Metrik und Textwissenschaft* (1979).

CRITICISM: W. Klein, "Crit. Remarks on G. M.," *Poetics*, 12 (1974); R. Standop, "Metric Theory Gone Astray," *Language and Style*, 8 (1975); A. M. Devine and L. D. Stephens, "The Abstractness of Metrical Patterns," *Poetics*, 4 (1975); R. P. Newton, "Trochaic and Iambic," *Language and Style*, 8 (1975). K. Magnuson and F. G. Ryder, "The Study of Eng. Prosody: An Alternative Proposal," CE, 31 (1970), rev. as "Second Thoughts," CE, 33 (1971); D. Chisholm, "Phon. Patterning in Ger. Verse," *Computers and the Humanities*, 10 (1976), "G. Prosody and Eng. Verse," *Poetics*, 6 (1977); B. Bjorklund, *A Study in Comp. Prosody: Eng. and Ger. Iambic Pentameter* (1978); J. B. Lord, "Syntax and Phon. in Poetic Style," *Style*, 9 (1975). P. Kiparsky, "Stress, Syntax, and Meter," *Language*, 51 (1975), "The Rhythmic Struct. of Eng. Verse," and M. Liberman and A. Prince, "On Stress and Ling. Rhythm," *Linguistic Inquiry*, 8 (1977); M. Barnes and H. Esau, "Eng. Prosody Reconsidered," *Language and Style*, 11 (1978); M. Harvey, "A Reconciliation of Two Current Approaches to Metrics," *Language and Style*, 13 (1980); G. Youmans, "Hamlet's Testimony on Kiparsky's Theory of Meter," *Neophil.*, 66 (1982); B. Hayes, "A Grid-Based Theory of Eng. Meter," *Linguistic Inquiry*, 14 (1983), "The Phonology of Rhythm in Eng.," *Linguistic Inquiry*, 15 (1984).

T.V.F.B.

GENEVA SCHOOL. See POETRY, THEORIES OF (EXPRESSIVE THEORIES)

GENRES. The theory of g. in Western poetics originates from a distinction made by Plato between two possible modes of reproducing an object, thing, or person: (1) by description (i.e., by portraying it by means of words) or (2) by mimicry (i.e., by imitating it). Since poetry according to the mimetic theory (see IMITATION and POETRY, THEORIES OF) was conceived as such a reproduction of external objects, these two modes became the main divisions of poetry: dramatic poetry or the theatre was direct imitation or mimicry of persons, and narrative poetry or the epic was the portrayal or description of human actions. And as this crude division obviously left out too much, a third division was inserted between the two others (*Republic* 3.392 d): the so-called mixed mode, in which narrative alternates with dialogue, as is usually the case of epic poetry which is rarely pure, unadulterated narrative. But no new principle of classification was thereby introduced, so no room was left for the genre of self-expression or the lyric, in which the poet expresses directly his own thoughts and feelings. Such a subjective point of view was outside the purely extrinsic and objective scheme used for the nonce by Plato, and taken up later by Aristotle in the *Poetics*, ch. 3, where it becomes the foundation of his main classification of poetic g. No express recognition of the lyric genre is to be found there, much less in his statement that in the second of these g. the poet "speaks in his own person": that is merely Aristotle's way of saying that the narrative is the poet's own discourse and not a speech by a fictitious character of drama. So the traditional triple division of poetic g. or kinds into the epic, the drama, and the lyric, far from being a "natural" division first discovered by the Gr. genius, is, it appears, not to be found in the creative age that preceded Aristotle or in Aristotle himself. It was rather the result of a long and tedious process of compilation and adjustment, through the repetition with slight variations of certain traditional lists of poetic g., which did not reach the modern formula of the three divisions until the 16th c.

During the great Attic age we do not find a simple, clear-cut division, but a wide variety of terms for specific g.: the epic or recited poetry, the drama or acted poetry, the latter subdivided in tragedy and comedy; then iambic or satirical poetry (so called because written in iambic meter), and elegiac poetry also written in a distinctive meter, the elegiac couplet, with its offshoots, the epitaph and the epigram (all classed together because composed in the same meter). Then there was melic poetry (as it was called later), or poetry sung usually by a chorus to the accompaniment of a flute or of a stringed instrument. Melic poetry comes closest to our concept of the lyric, but still it excluded what we would consider the essentially lyrical genre of the elegy, and the epigram which was to develop into the beautiful lyrics of the later *Gr. Anthology*. In addition, there was the hymn, the dirge or *threnos,* and the dithyramb, the latter a composition in honor of the god Dionysus which could be anything from a hymn to a short narrative or a miniature play. Songs of triumph or of celebration, chorally recited, were paeans, encomia, epinikia, and epithalamia. There was certainly plenty of material in Gr. poetry to make up a concept of lyrical poetry, but the Greeks of the Attic age apparently never took that step and contented themselves with classifying these g. by such criteria as metrical form. Aristotle in the *Poetics* does not even attempt to enumerate all these g., but concentrates on tragedy, comedy, and the epic, with occasional passing references to some others.

After Aristotle, it was Alexandrian scholarship that undertook the first comprehensive stocktaking of Gr. poetry and began the process of grouping, grading, and classifying poems. Lists or "canons" of the best writers in each kind were made, which led to a sharper awareness of g. The first extant grammarian to mention the lyric as a genre was Dionysius Thrax of the 2d c. B.C., in a list which comprises, in all, the following: "Tragedy, Comedy, Elegy, Epos, Lyric, and Threnos," lyric meaning for him and other Greeks "primarily what the name implies—poetry sung to the accompaniment of the lyre" (Smyth). In Alexandrian literature other g. were added to the list, the idyll and the pastoral, not to speak of prose fiction. But the classification which prevailed and which was repeated afterwards for centuries was a mere return to the Platonic modes, found in the grammarian Diomedes of the 4th C. A.D.: the *genus activum, enarrativum,* and *mixtum.*

Gradually the exact meaning of the terms was forgotten, and the closing of the theatres in the Middle Ages obliterated all notion of drama and dramatic performance. "In Byzantine writing, *drama* means the novel; in the West, it means a philosophical dialogue" (Behrens, p. 38). By the time of Dante the notion of the theatre was lost: for him, the *Aeneid* was a tragedy and his own poem was a comedy. The latter is comic because it is a tale that ends with happiness (in Paradise) and because it is composed in the "middle" style, the other two styles being the "noble" and the "humble": the noble being reserved for "tragedy" or the epic, and the humble for "elegy"—a complete confusion of ancient classifications. Of course, the Middle Ages had g. of their own, but no Aristotle to attempt a classification of them. The It. Renaissance achieved a more exact notion of ancient literature, revived the theatre in its classical form, and rediscovered the *Poetics,* which had actually been translated in the 13th c. but completely neglected by medieval writers. The fresh resort to the original text of the *Poetics* early in the 16th c. came as a revelation to critics and produced a host of commentaries and adaptations, and eventually of criticism and rebuttal. The theory of g. was taken as the foundation of the critical system, and elaborate codes of rules were built up, supposedly out of Aristotle, for the epic and the drama. This led to critical controversies about great medieval poems like Dante's which could not be fitted into the classical schemes or the newly fashioned rules, and about Renaissance poems modeled upon the medieval romances, like Ariosto's and Spenser's. It was also impossible to ignore the lyric any longer as a major genre, since Petrarch's love poems had set a standard of poetry for the whole age. At first the Aristotelian critics tried to fit the lyric into the mimetic scheme by arguing that the lyrical poet was also an "imitator"—he "imitated himself." This rather clumsy device was rejected by the more rigorous theorists, some of whom inclined to exclude the lyric from poetry altogether, since it could not be made to fit into the scheme. But there was no lack of critics who came to the defense of the lyric, and in 1559 we find it listed by Minturno as one of the three great g. of poetry. But he still described the third genre, which he called "melic," as "imitating actions" and "now narrating and now introducing some other speaker," falling back into the traditional two modes of Plato. The lyric genre really did not come into its own until the romantic movement.

Even in the Renaissance some of the more independent thinkers rejected the classification of poetry by g., and Bruno roundly declared that "there are as many genres of poetry as there are poets." The greatest damage to the g. system and its correlative rules was produced by the flourishing of irregular drama, such as the Elizabethan or Sp. theatre, composed outside such rules as those of the three unities, and which finally discredited both the rules and the genre system. Other controversies arose in the 17th and 18th c. about minor g. such as the pastoral and the burlesque or mock-epic. The romantic movement inspired a revolt against (first of all) rigid barriers between g., such as comedy and tragedy. Some romantic critics then favored the mingling or interpenetration of all g. into a single, comprehensive poetic form; others argued in favor of new g., such as the historical novel or historical drama or the *Märchen.* Others extolled the lyric, defining it as the essence and animating spirit of all poetry (Herder). Finally some envisaged the abolition of all definitions and classifications by genre, as F. Schlegel in his *Dialogue on Poetry* (1800) and in his essay on Goethe (1828). His brother August William hit upon the idea of fitting the three g., now fixed in the triad of lyric, epic, and drama, into the dialectical trinity of "Thesis, Antithesis and Synthesis: the Epic is objective, the Lyric is subjective, and the Drama is the interpenetration of both" (*Lectures* of 1801–2).

This neat parallel became very popular, and is still the foundation of many current classifications. It can be imagined to what a riot of dialectic it led in Hegel's aesthetic, which should have been a warning, but acted instead as an incentive to the metaphysical aestheticians of the 19th c., each with his own system of the arts and of the g. Evolutionary thinking, claiming to be as scientific as Darwin, took over bodily the classification by g., as it did many other traditional ideas, and built up evolutions of g., a process culminating in the work of Brunetière. This led to viewing the masterpieces of literature as the result of something like "natural selection," proceeding by the gradual accretion of plots, devices, and conventions. G. were also found convenient devices for grouping large numbers of works in the histories of literature, and as such are still in current usage. Attempts are continually being made to invest these traditional formulas with some critical substance, and to achieve a final definition, e.g., of the "tragic spirit" or the "essence of comedy." But the field is littered with the ruins of past definitions which have convinced no one save their author, and the advance of modern writing is so vast and multifarious that all classifications crumble in front of it. The most radical rejection of g. in modern times was made by Croce, who considered them mere abstractions, useful in the construction of classifications for practical convenience, but of no value as aesthetic categories.

F. Brunetière, *L'Evolution des g.* (1892); Saintsbury, II (1900); H. W. Smyth, *Gr. Melic Poets* (1900); R. K. Hack, "The Doctrine of Lit. Forms," HSCP, 27 (1916; against the genre theory); B. Croce, *Aesthetic,* tr. D. Ainslie (2d ed., 1922, pp. 87–93, 436–49), "Per una Poetica moderna," *Vossler Festschrift* (1922); *La Poesia* (1936, pp. 177–83, 333–36), *Poeti e scrittori del pieno e del tardo rinascimento,* II (1945), 109–18; N. H. Pearson, "Lit. Forms and Types; or, a Defense of Polonius," *EIE 1940* (1941; for the genre theory); J. J. Donohue, *The Theory of Lit. Kinds* (2 v., 1943–49); Behrens (best historical account of the development of genre classification in Western lit.); I. Ehrenpreis, *The "Types Approach" to Lit.* (1945; gives an objective account of discussions pro and con on the theory); M. Fubini, *Critica. e poesia* (1956); Fry (reaffirms g.). G.N.G.O.

GEORGIC. A didactic poem primarily intended to give directions concerning some skill, art, or science. In his "Essay on the Georgic" (1697), which is the most important discussion of the genre, Addison specifically distinguished this kind of poetry from the pastoral and crystallized the definition of the g. by pointing out that this "class of Poetry . . . consists in giving plain and direct instructions." The central theme of the g. is the glorification of labor and praise of simple country life. Though this didactic intention is primary, the g. is often filled with descriptions of the phenomena of nature and likely to contain digressions concerning myths, lore, philosophical reflections, etc., which are somehow suggested by the subject matter. The g. begins as early as Hesiod's *Works and Days* (ca. 750 B.C.) and was used by many of the great ancients—Lucretius, Ovid, Oppian, Nemesianus, Columella. Some of the better known poems in the tradition are Tusser's *Five Hundreth Points of Good Husbandry* (1573), Poliziano's *Rusticus* (1483), Vida's *De Bombyce* (1527), Alamanni's *La Coltivazione* (1546), Rapin's *Horti* (1665), Jammes's *Géorgiques chrétiennes* (1912). The finest specimens of the type are the *Georgics* of Virgil. Virgil's purpose is to pay tribute to Augustus for the new security he brought to the empire and to inspire the farmers to take up afresh the industry of the fields long wasted and neglected. Virgil's *Georgics* cast a long shadow over the poetry of the late 17th and 18th c. Dryden called the *Georgics* "the best poem of the best poet." James Thomson, because of his *Seasons*, was known as the "English Virgil," and William Cowper's *Task* resembles the g. in inspiration and execution. Thomson's far-reaching influence was strongly felt, even on the Continent. Though the term "g." does not appear in the title, scores of poems were written which imitate Virgil's *Georgics* in form and content—poems on the art of hunting, fishing, dancing, laughing, preserving health, raising hops, shearing sheep, etc. Sometimes the serious imitation can hardly be separated from the burlesque, as in Gay's *Trivia; or the Art of Walking the Streets of London* (1716). Because Virgil was addressing his emperor and was intent on glorifying rural occupations, he raised the style of his *Georgics*. Attempting to elevate a lowly subject by elegant circumlocutions led many of his 18th-c. imitators to grotesqueries of style which are easy to ridicule.—M. L. Lilly, *The G.* (1919); D. L. Durling, *G. Tradition in Eng. Poetry* (1935). J.E.C.

GERMAN PROSODY. The Germanic type of verse (see OLD GERMANIC PROSODY) was succeeded by meters which used end rhyme, imitated from Church Latin but which still retained the basic 4-stress dipodic (q.v.) form. The number of unstressed syllables was at first indeterminate, but during the 12th c. the line for all narrative verse gradually approached a standard pattern, although complete standardization was never attained. The lines had either 4 main stresses, the last of which fell on the last syllable of the line (*einsilbig voll*) or on a short penultimate syllable (*zweisilbig voll*), or 3 main stresses with a secondary stress on the last syllable (*klingend*). According to Heusler's theory—still widely accepted, but attacked by Kayser, Glier, and others—there are always four 2/4 bars of musical time, since a quarter or even half note may be represented by a pause rather than an actual syllable. The *Nibelungenstrophe* would thus comprise eight 4-stress lines, but it combines two such lines into an 8-stress long line. The last stress of each of the four long lines is represented by a pause, except for the last line which is represented by a syllable. Earlier critics and some modern prosodists think that we may be certain only that the lines in the romances had 3 or 4 beats and that in the *Nibelungenlied* all half lines except the last had 3. Lyric verse forms were probably borrowed directly from the Romance languages and are closely bound up with music. By the end of the 12th c., in imitation of Romance songs with syllable-counting lines, regular alternation of stressed and unstressed syllables as well as regular dactylic rhythms (the so-called MHG dactyls) became accepted patterns. The length of the lines could vary according to the music, but the best poets observe meshing of the lines within each strophe to produce a specific number of beats of musical time for the strophe as a whole. The *Meistergesang* observed only the number of syllables and ignored coincidence of word accent with verse stress. W.T.H.J.

In the 16th c. the dominant form in narrative and drama was the *Knittelvers*, which derived from the rhymed couplet of medieval narrative and which, like the lyric *Meistergesang*, in its so-called strict form noted only the number of syllables and took no account of the coincidence of word accent with metrical stress (a "free" form of the *Knittelvers*, followed by some poets, allowed for an unlimited number of unstressd syllables). The reform in versification effected by Martin Opitz in the early 17th c. restored natural accentuation to G. verse and established a strict alternation of stressed and unstressed syllables. For more than a century after Opitz the dominant line in serious verse was the rhymed *Alexandriner*, a 12-syllable iambic line modeled superficially after the Fr. alexandrine (q.v.), but quite different in effect because of the strongly accentual quality of the G. language.

Certain metrical conventions which have persisted in G. verse for the last two centuries were initiated in the mid-18th c. by F. G. Klopstock, who succeeded in adapting several Gr. and Roman meters to G. and in developing the so-called free rhythms. Searching for a suitable metrical form into which to cast his epic *Der Messias*, Klopstock hit upon the idea, then regarded as revolutionary, of utilizing the unrhymed classical dactylic hexameter. For his odes he adapted the stanzaic forms of Sappho, Alcaeus, and Asclepiades. In each instance this adaptation took place through the substitution of stressed and unstressed syllables for the classical long and short syllables. Klopstock's free rhythms, employed in odes such as *Die Frühlingsfeier,* are essentially what we today mean by free verse; like his classical odes, they dispense with rhyme, yet they do not attempt to follow a consistent metrical or stanzaic scheme. Many major works in G. poetry derive ultimately from Klopstock's metrical forms, e.g., the classical meters of Goethe's *Römische Elegien* and *Hermann und Dorothea* and Hölderlin's odes and elegies; the free rhythms of Goethe's *Prometheus,* Hölderlin's late hymns, Heine's *Nordsee* and Rilke's *Duineser Elegien.*

The example of Lessing's *Nathan der Weise* (1779) established unrhymed iambic pentameter, modeled after Eng. blank verse, as the prevailing line of G. verse drama, but certain notable exceptions can be singled out, above all, Goethe's *Faust,* which revives the "free" form of *Knittelvers* and also employs most of the other metrical forms to be found in G. poetry. As a result of Herder's efforts to arouse interest in the national past around 1770, and through the influence, much later, of Arnim and Brentano's collection of folk songs, *Des Knaben Wunderhorn* (1806–8), G. poets came increasingly to imitate the tone, language, and metrical forms (especially quatrains with 3- and 4-stress lines) of G. folk poetry. Besides this folk strain, which characterizes many of Goethe's early lyrics, as well as the major work of such later poets as Brentano, Eichendorff and Heine, G. poetry during the age of Goethe assimilated an amazing number of foreign forms, among them the It. ottava rima and terza rima, Sp. assonantal forms, and the Persian *ghazel* (though certain importations, e.g., the It. madrigal and sonnet, were revivals of forms prevalent in the 17th c.). During the remainder of the 19th c., G. poets built upon and refined the metrical forms and traditions which they had inherited, but during the naturalist and expressionist periods and again since 1945, G. verse has displayed intense experimentation in free verse (e.g., A. Holz, E. Stadler, B. Brecht), influenced by foreign free-verse movements as well as by native traditions.

During the last two centuries—the period in which G. has achieved the stature of a major world literature—G. verse has probably been characterized by a greater degree of metrical theorizing and conscious metrical experimentation, plus a more systematic adaptation of foreign and earlier native forms, than have the other literatures of Western Europe during this same period. It is significant that the work of individual poets often displays major achievement within quite divergent metrical traditions—classical meters, free verse, and folk song in Goethe and Mörike, complex rhymed forms and free verse in Rilke. Moreover, one could describe the whole history of G. prosody as a continual veering between two central traditions—an "art" tradition based on strict syllable-counting ("strict" *Knittelvers,* classical meters, the various stanzas borrowed from the Romance literatures) and a "native" tradition which does not regulate the number of unstressed syllables per line ("free" *Knittelvers,* free verse, the folk song and its romantic imitations).

Just as G. poets have tended to show a high degree of interest in prosodic matters, so G. literary scholarship has been particularly rich in systematic attempts to describe the history and nature of G. prosody. Among the most notable of these are A. Heusler's *Deutsche Versgesch.* (3 v., 1925–29), O. Paul and I. Glier, *Deutsche Metrik* (1938; 9th ed., 1974) and U. Pretzel and H. Thomas, "Deutsche Verskunst," *Deutsche Philologie im Aufriss,* ed. W. Stammler (2d ed., v. 3., 1962).—See also H. G. Atkins, *A Hist. of G. Versification* (1923); W. Kayser, *Gesch. des deutschen Verses* (1960); H. de Boor, *Kleine Schriften,* ed. R. Wisniewski and H. Kolb (v. 2., 1966); W. Hoffman, *Altdeutsche Metrik* (1967); S. Beyschlag, *Altdeutsche Verskunst in Grundzügen* (6th ed., 1969); G. Storz, *Der Vers in der neueren deutschen Dichtung* (1970); W. P. Lehmann, "German," *Versification: Major Language Types,* ed. W. K. Wimsatt (1972); W. Jost, *Probleme und Theorien der deutschen und englischen Verslehre* (1976); H. J. Frank, *Handbuch der deutschen Strophenformen* (1980). H.L.; B.Q.M.

GHASEL (*ghazal*). Name given to a lyric in eastern literature, especially Arabic, Persian, Turkish, Urdu, and Pashto, from the 8th c. onward. Such a poem, whose theme is generally love and wine, often mystically understood, varies in length from 5 to 12 couplets all upon the same rhyme. The poet signs his name in the final couplet. Hundreds of poets have used this form, most famous among them the Persians Saʿdī (d. 1291) and Ḥāfiẓ (d. 1389). The g. was introduced to Western poetry by the romanticists mainly Fr. Schlegel, Rückert, and von Platen (*Ghaselen,* 1821) in Germany, and was made more widely known by Goethe, who in his *West-östlicher Divan* (1819) deliberately imitated Persian models.—J.H.S.V. Garcin de Tassy, *Hist. de la litt. hindouie et hindoustanie* (2 v., 1839–47); E.J.W. Gibb, *Hist. of Ottoman Poetry* (6 v., 1900–1909); E. G. Browne, *Lit. Hist. of Persia* (4 v., 1928). A.J.A.

GNOMIC POETRY. Term applied to poetry which consists largely of gnomes or which has a strong gnomic content. A gnome is "a short pithy statement of a general truth; a proverb, maxim, aphorism, or apothegm" (OED). An example is provided by the first recorded Germanic gnome, given by Tacitus: "Women must weep and men remember." The name "gnomic" was first applied to a group of Gr. poets who flourished in the 6th c. B.C., Theognis, Solon, Phocylides, Simonides of Anorgos, and others. But ancient Egyptian literature, Chinese literature (the *Shih* and the *Shû* with pieces going back before the 2d millennium B.C.), and the Sanskrit *Hitopadésa* testify to the long-standing and widespread popularity of the gnome. The most familiar collection of gnomic utterance is the Book of Proverbs. Old Ir. provides an example in *The Instructions of King Cormac MacAirt* and ON a particularly interesting one in the *Hávamál.* The popularity of gnomes among the Germanic peoples is also shown by the two collections in OE, the *Cotton* and the *Exeter* gnomes. The term "gnomic" has, however, been extended beyond mere collections of gnomes to apply to any poetry which deals in sententious fashion with questions of ethics. Ancient literature abounds in gnomic passages, e.g., the Gr. tragedies, particularly the choruses, or many passages in the *Beowulf.* Gnomic poetry has been cultivated in more modern times, in England by Francis Quarles (*Emblems,* 1633) and in France by Gui de Pibras whose *Quatrains* (1574) were a direct imitation of the gnomic poets and enjoyed a great success.—B. C. Williams, *Gnomic Poetry in Anglo-Saxon (1914); The Hávámal,* ed. and tr. D.E.M. Clarke (1923); K. Jackson, *Early Welsh Gnomic Poems* (1935); R. MacGregor Dawson, "The Structure of OE Gnomic Poems," JEGP, 61 (1962). R.P.APR.

GOLIARDIC VERSE. A type of medieval poetry, traditionally attributed to the goliards, wandering "scholar-poets" who flourished especially in 12th- and 13th-c. England, France, and Germany. The origin of the term "goliards" is still not clear. There are references to their belonging to the "household of Golias," whose name, in turn, appears in the rubric of about twenty manuscripts. Yet, according to Hanford, Rozhdestvenskaia (Dobïash), Raby, and other scholars, there was no Golias; nor was there an *ordo vagorum,* an order or guild of goliards. It seems that the name was used as a term of reproach, perhaps by analogy with Goliath of Gath—the symbol of lawlessness—or by derivation from the L. *gula* (glutton)—the sin of gluttony—and was attached to poets who attacked the Papal curia and their ecclesiastical superiors.

That wandering clerks existed, Helen Waddell (*The Wandering Scholars,* 1927) has shown, but they were not organized, nor does it seem very likely that they had the thorough knowledge of classical and medieval L. poetry, the familiarity with vernacular poetry (learned and popular), and—last but not least—the technical skill to write the so-called goliardic verse. The real authors of some of these poems are known. They were accomplished and even famous poets, such as Hugh Primas, the Archpoet, and Walter of Châtillon.

Whatever its origin, "goliardic" verse constitutes one of the most vigorous poetic expressions of medieval Europe. Although the so-called goliards wrote a few authentic religious lyrics, their characteristic productions are (1) satiric, directed almost always against the church and the Pope and (2) profane, devoted to the pleasures of the bed and the tavern in a spirit of reckless hedonism. Their underlying theme is the Horatian *carpe diem* (q.v.). The most notable collection of L. lyrics which contains some "goliardic" poems is the *Carmina Burana,* published by Joseph Andrews Schmeller in Germany in 1847 and, in part, translated by John Addington Symonds in *Wine, Women and Song* in 1884.

The term "goliardic measure" refers to a stanza form much favored by these poets—a stanza of four monorhymed lines of 13 syllables each, sometimes ending with a hexameter, called an *auctoritas,* quoted from some classical source.

The only complete text of the *Carmina Burana* is still the one published by Schmeller, 4th ed., 1907. The best ed. is the one by A. Hilka and O. Schumann, but only v. I, pts. 1 and 2 and v. II, pt. 1 were published in 1931–41. J. M. Manly, "Familia Goliae," MP, 5 (1907–8); J. H. Hanford, "The Progenitors of Golias," *Speculum,* 1 (1926); B. I. Jarcho, "Die Vorläufer des Golias," *Speculum,* 3 (1928); O. Rozhdestvenskaia͡ (Dobïash), *Les Poésies des goliards* (1931; includes some texts and a list of mss.); *The Goliard Poets,* ed. G. F. Whicher (1949; texts and Eng. verse tr.); *Hymnen und Vagantenlieder,* comp. and tr. K. Langosch (1954; contains texts of Hugh Primas and the Archpoet); F.J.E. Raby, *Hist. of Secular L. Poetry in the Middle Ages,* II (1957); *The Penguin Book of L. Verse,* comp. F. Brittain (1962; texts and tr.).

A.P.

H

HAIKU (also called *hokku* and *haihai*).This Japanese poetic form was originally the opening section (hence *hokku,* "opening part") of *renga,* which took shape in the 13th and 14th c. as a sequential verse form that alternates up to fifty times 5-7-5- and 7-7-syllabic parts composed in turn by two or more persons. The name *haiku* derives from the variety of *renga* known as *haikai,* "humorous." *Haikai* poets, most notably Matsuo Bashô (1644–1694), rejected the poetic diction and lyricism of court poetry that prevailed in orthodox *renga,* and found "humor" in describing the mundane. But they retained some basic features of orthodox *renga,* among them the inclusion of a *kigo,* a word or phrase that specifies the season of the composition.

Even though the *hokku,* in units of 5-7-5 syllables, was being written more or less independently by the 16th c., it was not completely severed from *renga* until the end of the 19th c. As it became an independent form, largely at the instigation of the reformist Masaoka Shiki (1867–1902), the name *hokku* was replaced by *haiku*. Some poets, such as Ogiwara Seisensui (1884–1976) and Ozaki Hôsai (1885–1926), went further and rejected the two basic requirements of the *hokku*: the syllabic pattern of 5-7-5 and the inclusion of a *kigo*. Some also departed from the one-line printing format, which was adopted as standard in the 19th c.—the adoption which instilled in the *haiku* writers the strong sense that the h. is a "one-line poem." Such departures from the norm, however, have not converted the majority.

Around 1900, h. began to attract the attention of Western poets, the Fr. being among the first to try to take up the form, calling it *haikai*. In the following decades, mainly under the influence of Fr. poets, a good number of poets in the United States, Latin America, and other countries tried the form, writing their pieces mainly in three lines of 5-7-5 syllables. But they did not go much beyond experimentation. Imagism, a literary movement linked with h., produced Ezra Pound's technique of "superposition" and otherwise had a considerable influence on the poetry of the time, as in reducing discursiveness in Western poetry.

Outside Japan, interest in writing h. gained solid ground after World War II, especially among Am. poets, as a result of a sudden increase in the number and quality of translations of Japanese literature and studies in Japanese culture. Three works have been seminal: the four-volume *H.* by R. H. Blyth (Tokyo, 1949–1952); *The Japanese H.* by Kenneth Yasuda (Tokyo, 1957); and *An Introd. to H.* by Harold G. Henderson (1958). Of the three, Blyth's volumes displayed an intimate knowledge of the subject in relating h. to Zen Buddhism, thereby awakening interest in this form among poets, such as those of the Beat Generation, who were pursuing Eastern philosophies and religions during the 50s. Taking a contrasting secular approach, Henderson, along with his roles as adviser to the poets and as guiding hand in the formation, in 1968, of the H. Society of America, greatly advanced the practical aspect of h. writing during the 60s. In 1963 *Am. H.*, the first magazine devoted to h. in Eng., started publication, followed by at least ten h. magazines in the next two decades. In 1974 *The H. Anthol.*, edited by Cor van den Heuvel, was published. A collection of h. by contemporary Am. and Canadian poets, it was the first notable anthol. in a non-Japanese language.

H. is now written in a great many languages, but receptivity to new ideas and experimentation seems the strongest in North America. One indication of this is the writing of one-line h. that began in the mid-70s largely in recognition of the one-line printing format employed by most Japanese h. writers and as a result of translations of such Japanese h. in one line. This and other developments make a definition of h. impractical, although at least the three-line format, if not the 5-7-5-syllable pattern, seems still to be regarded as the norm in many countries outside Japan.

E. Miner, *The Japanese Tradition in British and Am. Lit.* (1958); R. H. Blyth, *A Hist. of H.* (2 v., Tokyo, 1963–64); H. G. Henderson, *H. in Eng.* (Tokyo, 1967); G. L. Brower, *H. in Western Languages: An Annotated Bibliog.* (1972); M. Ueda, *Modern Japanese H.* (Tokyo, 1976); *From the Country of Eight Islands: An Anthol. of Japanese Poetry*, ed. and tr. H. Sato and B. Watson (1981); H. Sato, *One Hundred Frogs* (1983); *H. Review '84*, ed. R. and S. Brooks (1984); J. T. Rimer and R. E. Morrell, *Guide to Japanese Poetry* (2d ed., 1984); S. Sommerkamp, "Der Einfluss des H. auf Imagismus und Jüngere Moderne" (Ph.D. diss., Univ. of Hamburg, 1984); W. J. Higginson, *The H. Handbook* (1985). H.S.

HEMISTICH (Gr. "half line"). A half line of verse divided at the caesura. It usually forms an independent colon. The device is used in drama where at least two characters exchange half lines of dialogue to create an effect of sharp argument. Such a series of half lines is called *hemistichomythia.* In other types of poetry a hemistich may create an effect of great emotional or physical disturbance, e.g., Virgil's isolated half lines in the *Aeneid* (1.534; 2.233). In Germanic verse the h. is the primary metrical structural unit as is shown in the poetry of OE, Old High German, Old Saxon, and ON. Often in modern poetry any metrically incomplete line is called a hemistich. W. H. Auden's *Always in Trouble* uses this device.—J. L. Hancock, *Studies in Stichomythia* (1917); J. C. Pope, *The Rhythm of Beowulf* (1942). R.A.H.

HENDECASYLLABIC (Gr. "11-syllable"), also called *Phalaecean,* after the Gr. poet Phalaikos (4th c. B.C.?). The scheme is ⏑⏑ (or ⏑–; –⏑; ––) –⏑⏑–⏑–⏑–⏓. It is used by Sophocles (*Philoctetes* 136, 151), Aristophanes (*Ecclesiazusae* 942ff.). The Alexandrian poets employed it as the meter for complete poems, e.g., Theokritos (*Epode* 20), Phalaikos (*Anthologia Palatina* 13.6). Catullus (84–54 B.C.?) perfected it in L., e.g.,

Ădēst (e, h) *ēndĕcăsȳllăbī, quŏt ēstis*

Forty of his 113 extant poems are in h. verses, ranging in function from love lyricism to invective. The It. h. line is used in sonnets, terza rima, and ottava rima by e.g., Dante and Petrarca; unrhymed lines (*endecasillabi sciolti*) after the L. are prominent in the tragic and epic poetry of Giangiorgio Trissino (1478–1550), in the poetry of

Gabriello Chiabrera (1552–1638), and in that of Guiseppe Parini (1729–99), Ugo Foscolo 1778–1827), Giacomo Leopardi (1798–1837), and Alessandro Manzoni (1785–1873). The Marquis de Santillana (Iñigo López de Mendoza) adapted the h. to the Sp. sonnet form in 1444. In general, the development of the h. in Spain followed the same pattern as that in Italy. In Germany Heinse and Goethe imitated the It. h. Modern-language hendecasyllabics are "syllabic" rather than "accentual" (see CLASSICAL METERS IN MODERN LANGUAGES); Tennyson, however, attempted the classical-accentual equivalent, e.g.

All composed in a meter of Catullus,

as did Swinburne. W. S. Landor wrote L. hendecasyllabics. For a recent (1957) rendering of this meter, see F. O. Copley's translation of Catullus' 28th poem (*Catullus, The complete Poetry*).—For bibliog., see CLASSICAL METERS . . . Also, W. Thomas, *Le Décasyllable roman et sa fortune en Europe* (*Travaux et mémoires de l'Univ. de Lille*, n.s., I, fasc. 4, 1904); M. Serretta, *Endecasillabi crescenti* . . . (1938); E. Pound, *Lit. Essays* (1954).

R.A.S.

HENDIADYS (Gr. "one through two"). The use of two substantives or sometimes a substantive and attributive genitive or adjective, connected by a conjunction to express a single, complex idea: "chrono kai poliorkia" (by length of time and siege; i.e., "by a long siege"—Demosthenes 19.123); "we drink from cups and gold" (Virgil, *Georgics* 2.192); "nice and warm" (in place of "nicely warm"—Fowler, *Modern Eng. Usage*). Sometimes h. is confused with simple parallelism, in which the substantives are equivalent: "might and main." Some grammarians argue the term is merely descriptive; others claim no such figure exists. E. A. Hahn contends the term "h." is a misnomer when applied to Virgil; that is, when Virgil chose to write as if he had two ideas, "he really did have two." Hence a phrase, "membris et mole valens," really contains two intentionally distinct ideas, "membris valens" and "mole valens," though it is usually translated simply "strong limbs." H. is found at all periods, usually for purposes of increased emphasis:

The heaviness and guilt within my bosom
Takes off my manhood.
(Shakespeare, *Cymbeline* 5.2.1–2)

E. A. Hahn, "H.: Is there Such a Thing?" CW, 15 (1921–22); G. T. Wright, "H. in *Hamlet*," PMLA, 96 (1981).

R.O.E.

HEPTAMETER. A line of 7 feet, metrically identical with the septenary (q.v.) and the fourteener. The meter exists in classical Gr. and L. prosody (chiefly in comic verse in the latter), and has great importance in Eng. prosody. It flourished in the narrative poetry of the Elizabethans, who coined for it the term *fourteener*, but later appearances of the heptameter line, printed as such, are infrequent. Wordsworth's *The Norman Boy*, E. B. Browning's *Cowper's Grave*, and Whittier's *Massachusetts to Virginia* are instances of post-Elizabethan h. On the whole, however, it has proved unsuitable for the long and elevated verse narrative because of its tendency toward monotony, but Chapman's translation of the *Iliad*, and Coleridge's *Rime of the Ancient Mariner* are notable exceptions. When divided into two parts, the h. becomes the familiar ballad meter (q.v.) or common measure (C.M. of the hymnbooks) of alternating 4- and 3-stress lines.—G. Stewart, *The Technique of Eng. Verse* (1930); J. Thompson, *The Founding of Eng. Metre* (1961).

A.P.

HEROIC COUPLET (also riding rhyme, rhymed decasyllables, rhymed 5-beat lines, etc.). Iambic pentameter lines rhymed in pairs; one of the most important meters of Eng. syllabic verse; origin unknown. The Eng. form is often thought to have developed with Chaucer under influence from the Old Fr. decasyllable rhymed in couplets: e.g., "A toy, Henry, dous amis, me complain, / Pour ce que ne cueur ne mont ne plein . . ." (Machault, *Complainte écrite après la bataille de Poitiers et avant le seige de Reims par les Anglais*, 1354–58). Chaucer's *Compleynte to Pitee* was probably written before his It. journey, 1372–73; hence Fr. influence seems prior to It. However, ten Brink has shown that Chaucer's heroic verse, of which there are some 16,000 lines, differs from the Fr. in almost all respects in which the It. does, and Skeat and Lewis have also expressed some reservations about Fr. influence.

Moreover, it now seems Eng. syllabic verse developed naturally from a disintegration of the old alliterative meters (J. P. Oakden, *Alliterative Poetry in Middle Eng.*, 1930), with doubtless some encouragement from Fr. forms. Accordingly couplets may have arisen as the natural result of a strong native tradition. In any case, couplet rhymes, showing little if any continental influence, appear very early in verses of uneven length: "Castelas he let wyrcean. / And earme men swithe swencean. / / Se cyng waes swa swithe stearc, / And benam of his undertheoddan manig marc . . ." (*Rime of King William* in *Anglo-Saxon Chronicle*). For development of an octosyllabic couplet, such verses would need only slight regularization, and the decasyllabic couplet would seem to be a natural extension. Moreover, as Saintsbury points out, sporadic heroic couplets occur fairly frequently in pre-Chaucerian poetry, concealed in stanzas. But credit for development of the form as a medium for sustained expression belongs to Chaucer.

Although Neo-Chaucerians of the 15th c. did not abandon the h.c. (e.g. Henryson, *Orpheus and Eurydice*), they showed distinct preference for stanzaic verse. In the 16th c. there was a steady increase in its use for occasional, reflective, critical, complimentary, and topical verse, the form reaching a high state of development by 1557 (Nicholas Grimald in *Tottel's Miscellany*). Some scholars distinguish between two distinct varieties of h.c., though the differences may be essentially chronological. The first is the Chaucerian type used by Marlowe and Spenser, the latter making it a suitable medium for satire (*Mother Hubberd's Tale*). The other has come to be known as the classical variety, of which Jonson is the most important source: "To draw no envy, Shakespeare, on thy name, / Am I thus ample to thy book and fame . . ." (*To the memory of my beloved the author, Mr. William Shakespeare, and what he hath left us*). Both types exhibited medial pause, balance, antithesis, crisp diction, parallel construction, contrasted clauses, inversions, etc., but the classical type is supposed to have differed somewhat from the Chaucerian in that thought tended to become more, and narrative less important. Sandys, Hall, Drayton, Fletcher, Beaumont, Fairfax, Donne, Waller, Denham, Oldham all made extensive use of the form before Dryden brought it to near perfection.

In the great dramatic verse of the Elizabethan period the h.c. is used sporadically. It is employed sparingly in Shakespeare, in pastoral drama (e.g. Peele's *Arraignment of Paris*), and it often appears as a device for metrical variation, a commonplace means of terminating blank-verse speeches, and, less frequently, as a link between speeches. D'Avenant and Etheredge made use of the form after the Restoration, and Dryden made it the principal medium for dramatic verse (*Tyrannick Love, Aureng-Zebe*, etc.). The critical controversy over rhyme during this period concerns mainly the use of the h.c. as opposed to blank verse, for tragedy: Dryden allows Lisideius to argue, in the *Essay of Dramatic Poesy*, that he prefers rhyme to the Eng. "way of writing in tragedies . . . in blank verse." To Dryden also belongs credit for making the h.c. the principal nondramatic, neoclassical meter; he became a master of the epigrammatic quality now especially associated with the period: "During his office, treason was no crime; / The sons of Belial had a glorious time . . ." (*Absalom and Achitophel*, 597–98). Pope brought this quality to an even higher state of perfection, paying special attention to the use of anticlimax: "Here thou great Anna! Whom three realms obey, / Dost sometimes counsel take—and sometimes tea . . ." (*Rape of the Lock* 3.7–8). Johnson, Goldsmith, Crabbe, Cowper, Byron, Hunt, Keats, Shelley, Browning, Swinburne, and Morris all made notable use of the h.c., though the form began to decline in prominence early in the romantic period.

Many variations of the h.c. are possible, particularly as the caesura is shifted; indeed, excepting the rhyme requirement, the form is nearly as flexible as blank verse (e.g. Browning's *My Last Duchess*). The simplest, formal separation into types is into (1) closed couplets, those in which a semi- or full stop is employed at the end of the second rhyme, and (2) open couplets, in which the thought continues from the second rhyme into the following line. Similar couplets occur in most European languages, excepting Sp., which makes little use of the decasyllable, but the term h.c. is usually reserved for the Eng. meter.

C. M. Lewis, *The Foreign Sources of Modern Eng. Versification* (1898); F. E. Schelling, "Ben Jonson and the Cl. School," PMLA, 13 (1898); B. ten Brink, *The Lang. and Metre of Chaucer* (1901); R. M. Alden, *Eng. Verse* (1903); Saintsbury, *Prosody;* J.S.P. Tatlock, "The Origin of the Closed C. in Eng.," *The Nation,* 98 (April 9, 1914), 390; E. C. Knowlton, "The Origin of the Closed C. in Eng.," *The Nation,* 99 (July 30, 1914), 134; R. C. Wallerstein, "The Development of the Rhetoric and Metre of the H.C., esp. in 1625–1645," PMLA, 50 (1935); W. C. Brown, *The Triumph of Form* (1948), W. Piper, *The H. C.* (1969). R.O.E.

HEXAMETER (6-measure), refers to the classical 6-foot catalectic dactylic line whose scheme is

— ⏕ | — ⏕ | — ⏕ | — ⏕ | — ⏑ ⏑ | — ⏓
1 2 3 4 5 6

Foot 5 may be a spondee, in which case the line is called "spondaic." The last syllable in the line may be long or short and is called *syllaba anceps.* The caesura, or major pause, may occur *within* foot 3 (penthemimeral, i.e., after 5 half-feet), 4 (hephthemimeral), or 2 (trihemimeral); a line may have as many as 2 minor pauses. Diaeresis (coincidence of word and foot endings), e.g.

kūmătă lēipēi

is fairly common in foot 5. Homer tends to avoid it in foot 4 (bucolic diaeresis) and more particularly in a foot-4 spondee or foot-3 dactyl. The L. h. is in general less flexible than the Gr.; it avoids the foot-3 "feminine" caesura (— ⏑ || ⏑), which is frequent in Homer. Coincidence of metrical and word accents is common in Lucretius, avoided in Virgil. The use of a foot-5 spondee became a feature of Alexandrian verse and was imitated by the Romans, often as a mere fashionable trick, e.g., Cicero's parody (*Atticus* 7.2.1):

flauit ab Epiro lenissimus Onchesmites.

The h. in antiquity is used in lyric, gnomic, elegiac, philosophical, and satirical poetry but is primarily the meter of epic, e.g., *Iliad, Odyssey, Aeneid, Pharsalia.* It is also the meter of the "epyllion," an epic-style short poem (ca. 300–500 lines), e.g., *Ciris,* Catullus 64. It is to classical poetry what the alexandrine is to Fr., the iambic pentameter to Eng. poetry. During the early Middle Ages (4th-6th c.) Christian epics were produced in dactylic h. by, e.g., Juvencus, Sedulius, Arator, and Avitus. The quantitative L. h. continued to be used during the Middle Ages (e.g., John of Salisbury's *Entheticus)*, despite the growing preponderance of syllabic, stress-accentual (see CLASSICAL METERS IN MODERN LANGUAGES), and rhymed verses (including especially the leonine), and during the Renaissance, despite the new vernacular-language verse forms.

In the *certame coronario* of 1441, L. B. Alberti and Leonardo Dati introduced experimental *esametri italiani*. In the next century Claudio Tolomei, followed by other poets, experimented with the re-creation of quantitative h. verse.

Richard Burgi, studying early Slavic literature, suggests on the basis of his observations that this literature "produced the first verse rendering of Homer in a non-classical language." Early in the 16th c. Maksim the Gr. made the first attempt in Rus. at a quantitative prosody based on an artificial and arbitrary classification of long and short vowels (*Maksimovskaja prosodija*). According to Burgi the year 1704 "marks the first appearance in print of the standard accentual prosody of classical Russian verse"—a pair of rhymed hexameters in syllabic verse. Accentual hexameters were revived in Russia toward the end of the 18th c. The translation of the *Iliad* into Rus. h. by N. Gnedič is considered one of the great achievements of Rus. literature; it was greatly admired by Pushkin, who himself wrote much h. verse. V. Brjusov, one of the Rus. symbolists, translated the *Aeneid* and I. Račinskij, a philologist, all of Lucretius in hexameters.

When Andreas Arvidi's *Det Svenska Poeteri*, the first Swedish *Ars Poetica*, was published in 1651, the *knittelvers* (doggerel) was being displaced in ballads and chronicles by both the h. and the alexandrine. George Stiernhielm's monumental *Hercules* (1658) was composed in hexameters. Other important h. poems in Swedish include Thomas Thorild's *Passionerna* (1781) and Johan Ludvig Runeberg's *Julkvällen* (1841). Eventually the alexandrine displaced the h. in Swedish poetry.

Notable hexameters in German literature include F. G. Klopstock's *Der Messias* (1748–73), J. H. Voss's *Homer* and *Luise*, and Goethe's *Reineke Fuchs* and *Hermann und Dorothea* (a "pastoral epic"—1798).

The h. is, at best, merely incidental to the traditions of Fr. and Sp. verse (see CLASSICAL METERS . . .). Nicaragua's Rubén Darío (1867–1916) composed his *Salutación del optimisto* in h. verses varying between 13 and 18 syllables, with most verses consisting of heptasyllabic and decasyllabic hemistichs; the verses are marked by many dactylic clausulae, common in Gr. lyric poetry but alien to epic.

Eng. poets since the 16th c. have been perennially ambitious in hexametrical endeavors, both accentual and syllabic, but particularly so in the 19th c. (see CLASSICAL METERS . . .). One of the earliest (16th c.) examples is Thomas Watson's "All travellers do gladly report great praise of Ulysses, / For that he knew many men's manners and saw many cities"—less wretched, perhaps, than Sidney's hexameters, e.g.

O̅pprest with ruino̅us conceits by the help of an outcry

Spenser had seen the root of the problem (viz., **stress-accent vs. quantitative accent**) when he suggested that we retain normal accents for speech but quantitative accents in prosody. This was the problem faced by Southey, Kingsley, Coleridge, Longfellow, Clough, Tennyson, and Swinburne. Robert Bridges' syllabic hexameter is trying, e.g. for

$$\bar{I}bant\ \acute{o}bscuri\ s\bar{o}la\ s\bar{u}b\ n\breve{o}ct\breve{e}\ p\breve{e}r\ \bar{u}mbram$$

he has

Th́ey wer' amíd the shádows by níght in lóneliness óbscure.

C. Day Lewis' translation of the *Aeneid* (1956) is a stress-accentual h. version with lines varying from 12 (alexandrine) to 17 (full Latin-h.) syllables.

Of Scandinavian languages Danish and Swedish are particularly apt for h. verse. In the former, Sophus Claussen's poem *Atomernes Oprør* (1925) is noteworthy; in the latter, Georg Stiernhielm's epic *Hercules* (publ. 1658) and, in the 19th c., Esaias Tegnér's *Fritiof 'tager aru* . . . stand out. H. poetry became also somewhat popular in Icelandic literature during the 19th c., according to S. Einarsson, who notes that Steingrímur Torsteinsson's mock-heroic *Redd-Hannesarríma* (first ed. in 1925) marked the initial use of the h. for a reasonably long narrative poem. Torsteinsson was followed by his contemporaries, Benedikt Gröndal and Matthias Jochumsson, who wrote shorter mock-heroic h. poems.

For bibliography, see CLASSICAL METERS IN MODERN LANGUAGES. Also, R. Bridges, *Ibant Obscuri* (1916); H. G. Atkins, *A Hist. of German Versification* (1923); A. Izzo, "L'esametro neo-classico italiano," R. Accad. . . . dei Lincei. *Rendiconti*, 7 (1932), fasc. 6; J. Saavedra Molina, *Los hexámetros castellanos y en particular los de Rubén Darío* (1935); G. L. Hendrickson, "Elizabethan Quantitative Hexameters," PQ, 28 (1949); G. Highet, *The Cl. Tradition* (1949); C. G. Cooper, *An Introd. to the L. H.* (1952); S. Einarsson, "H. in Icelandic Lit.," MLN, 68 (1953); Koster; R. Burgi, *A Hist. of the Rus. H.* (1954); Navarro; A. Gustafson, *A Hist. of Swedish Lit.* (1961). R.A.S.

HIATUS. (a) A gap which destroys the completeness of a sentence or verse; "A Dunce-Monk, being [about] to make his epitaph . . . left the Verse thus gaping, *Hic sunt in fossa Bedae—ossa,* till he had consulted with his Pillow to fill up the *Hiatus*" (Fuller, *The Church—History of Britain,* II, III). (b) Grammar and prosody: a break between two vowels coming together without an intervening consonant in successive words or syllables to prevent vowel clash, where neither aphaeresis, crasis, nor elision (q.v.) is operative. In Eng. the indefinite article may be altered by addition of a nasal to prevent hiatus: *an action.* Elision to avoid h. is permissible (R. Bridges, *Milton's Prosody,* 1921). In the classical languages (see CLASSICAL PROSODY) h. is common in Gr. epic poetry, rarer in L. In languages in which number of syllables is an important aspect of verse, like Fr., an understanding of h. is essential both for scansion and for writing verse. In Fr. h. was generally permissible until (at least) the 14th c.; there is no elision to prevent h. in *Saint Alexis* (about 1040), but in Froissart (ca. 1337–ca. 1410) there are 132 cases of elision against 5 of h. (G. Lote, *Hist. du vers français,* III, 87). The two phenomena may be observed, with the same words in *Chanson de Roland*: "J*o i* ferrai de Durendal m'espee" (v. 1462)—h.; "J*o i* puis aler, nais n'i avrai guarant" (v. 329)—elision. In Sp., It., and Portuguese, h. is usually eliminated by contraction. R.O.E.

HOMOEOTELEUTON (Gr. "similarity of endings"). See RHYME. HISTORY.

HOVERING ACCENT. A term suggestive of the effect of slowness and rhetorical weight produced by the spondaic foot (q.v.) or by a quasi-spondaic foot consisting of 1 primary stressed syllable and 1 secondary stressed syllable. In the iambic pentameter line

> **Unfriend|ly lamp | light hid | under | its shade, |**
> **(Yeats, *After Long Silence* 3)**

the third foot may be described as consisting of a hovering accent.—Brooks and Warren. P.F.

HUDIBRASTIC VERSE. The distinctive octosyllabic verse, rhyme use, characteristic satirical tone, and frequently impious imagery—widely imitated but never equalled—employed by Samuel Butler (1612–80) in his *Hudibras.* The meter would appear joggingly monotonous were the reader not kept constantly engrossed in the wide-ranging, conversational, sparkling wit; and constantly alert for the unexpected rhymes, many of them feminine, which, as an anonymous writer has remarked, "seem to chuckle and sneer of themselves." Butler speaks, for example, of "Dame Religion,"

> Whose honesty they all durst swear for,
> Tho' not a man of them knew wherefore;

of a time when

> The oyster women picked their fish up
> And trudged away to cry No Bishop;

and of Hudibras:

> He knew the seat of Paradise,
> Could tell in what degree it lies; . . .
> What Adam dreamt of, when his bride
> Came from the closet in his side; . . .
> If either of them had a navel;
> Who first made music malleable;
> Whether the Serpent, at the Fall,
> Had cloven feet, or none at all:
> All this, without a gloss or comment,
> He could unriddle in a moment. . . .
> (Canto 1, Part 1)

Saintsbury, *Prosody;* I. Jack, "Low Satire: Hudibras," *Augustan Satire, 1660–1750* (1952); C. L. Kulisheck, "Swift's Octosyllabics and the Hudibrastic Tradition," JEGP, 53 (1954). L.J.Z.

HYMN. See LYRIC.

HYPALLAGE (Gr. "exchange"). A change in the relation of words whereby a word, instead of agreeing with the word it logically qualifies, is made to agree grammatically with another word; h. is usually confined to poetry: "neikos andron xunaimon" (kindred strife of men *for* strife of kindred men; Sophocles, *Antigone* 794). Quintilian (*Institutes of Oratory* 8.6.23) does not distinguish clearly from metonymy (q.v.): "Cererem corruptam undis" (Ceres by water spoiled; Virgil, *Aeneid* 1.177). Characteristic of Virgil, Spenser, Shakespeare, Milton. Shakespeare not only depends heavily on the device but also uses it with a flavor of parody: "I see a voice. Now will I to the chink, / To spy and I can hear my Thisby's face" (*Midsummer Night's Dream* 5.1.189–90). Cf. Sister Miriam Joseph, *Shakespeare's Use of the Arts of Language* (1947). Lausberg, discussing "die metonymischen Epitheta," distinguishes syntactical and other varieties. R.O.E.

HYPERBOLE. (Gr. "overshooting," "excess"). A figure or trope, common to all literatures, consisting of bold exaggeration, apparently first noted by Isocrates and Aristotle. Quintilian says, "an elegant straining of the truth, and may be employed indifferently for exaggeration or attenuation" (*Institutes of Oratory* 8.6.67): "Geminique minantur / In caelum scopuli" (Twin rocks that threaten heaven—Virgil, *Aeneid* 1.162).

> Not all the waters in the rude rough sea
> Can wash the balm from an annointed King.
> (Shakespeare, *Richard II* 3.2.54)

Any extravagant statement used to express strong emotion, not intended to be understood literally. According to Puttenham, the figure is also used to "advance or . . . abase the reputation of any thing or person" (*The Arte of Eng. Poesie*, 1589). P. called it "overreacher" or "loud liar" equating it with L. *dementiens*.

Grammarians and rhetoricians sometimes consider h. to be among the second order of figures of speech, along with amplification, examples, images, etc. Use of h. in Elizabethan drama, particularly Jonson, with special reference to the development of comic irony, is discussed by A. H. Sackton, *Rhetoric as a Dramatic Language in Ben Jonson* (1948). See also: R. Sherry, *Treatise of the Figures of Grammer and Rhetorick* (1555); H. Peacham, *The Garden of Eloquence Conteyning the Figures of Grammer and Rhetorick* (1577, enlarged 1593); W. S. Howells, *Logic and Rhetoric in England, 1500–1700* (1956); Lausberg. R.O.E.

HYPERMETRIC (Gr. "beyond the measure"). In prosody a line which has an extra syllable or syllables at the end, or a syllable which is not expected in the regular metrical pattern, e.g., a hypercatalectic line (see TRUNCATION). In classical poetry a verse in which the vowel at the end of one line elides with the vowel beginning the following line: "sors exitura et nos in aeternum / exsilium impositura cumbae" (Horace, *Odes* 2.3.27–28). In Old Germanic poetry a verse expanded by means of an additional initial foot, or, according to the rhythmic theory, by means of doubling the time given to it.—E. Sievers, *Altgermanische Metrik* (1893); Hardie; J. C. Pope, *The Rhythm of Beowulf* (1942); Koster. R.A.H.

I

IAMB (Gr. *iambos*, a word of unknown etymology but certainly very ancient). A metrical unit, in quantitative verse, of a short syllable followed by a long:

$$\smile -;\ \breve{a}m\bar{a}ns$$

The iambic rhythm was thought in antiquity to be nearest to ordinary speech; it was in its 6-foot form (see TRIMETER; L. *senarius*) the standard meter for dialogue in drama and for invective. A clear distinction was made between the strong iambic ryhthm and the lighter, more unstable trochaic rhythm ($-\smile$). Catullus gains a special effect in two poems by using pure iambs, unvaried by spondees. Hipponax invented the *scazon*, the "limping" iambic. The iambic dimeter (*quaternarius*, 8-syllabler) sometimes occurs in Plautus; in Horace it sometimes alternates with the trimeter; it is found in a few inscriptions. It came into its glory in the 4th c. A.D., when Ambrose adopted it for his hymns:

$$\overline{aet}\breve{e}rn\breve{e}\ \overline{r}\bar{e}r\bar{u}m\ \overline{c}\bar{o}nd\breve{i}t\breve{o}r$$

Hardy; Dale; Beare. W.B.

The term has been adopted into Eng. for the accentual foot of an unstressed followed by a stressed syllable:

$$\times\ /\ ;\ \text{impose}$$

This alternation, no doubt because it fits the natural patterns of Eng. words and phrases, has become overwhelmingly the commonest type in all Eng. verse. Its use is complemented by secondary accent:

$$\times\ \backslash\ \times\times\ /\ \times$$
personification

and is varied by occasional substitution of the trochee:

$$/\ \times\quad \times\quad /\quad \times\ /\ \times\ \backslash\quad \times\quad /$$
Milton! thou shouldst be living at this hour

or anapest:

$$\times\quad \times\ /\ \times\quad /\ \times\quad \times\ /\ \times\quad /$$
Pure as the naked heavens, majestic, free

By these and similar devices the iambic movement is spared monotony and made capable of almost every kind of metrical effect.—Baum.

ICTUS (L. "beat"). Roman writers like Horace and Quintilian used this word to describe the movement of the foot or the hand in keeping time with the rhythm of a verse. Audible i. is more than dubious in Gr. verse where the accent was one of pitch, not stress, in the classical period and later. In L. the occurrence of i. has been generally assumed in modern times by those who also believe that words were pronounced with stress; but a recent writer (W. Beare, see bibliog.) thinks that such an assumption "may be due merely to our craving to impose on quantitative verse a rhythm which we can recognize." Whatever its nature was, this rhythmical i. is regarded as falling on the long syllable (i.e., the arsis [q.v.] in the currently accepted sense of that word) of a basic foot like the iambus ($\smile -$) or anapaest ($\smile\smile -$) in rising, or the trochee ($-\smile$) or dactyl ($-\smile\smile$) in falling measures; but, with resolution (q.v.), the i. is marked on the first of the two short syllables which replace the long. Thus Terence begins a senarius (see TRIMETER) in rising rhythm with *hīnc īl|lāe lăcrĭ|māe*

and Horace a hexameter (q.v.) in falling rhythm with

hīnc īl|lāe lăcrĭ|māe

See ARSIS AND THESIS and CLASSICAL PROSODY.—W. Beare, *L. Verse and European Song* (1957); P. W. Harsh, "Ictus and Accent." *Lustrum,* 3 (1958); A. Labhardt, "Le Problème de l'I.," *Euphrosyne,* 2 (1959); O. Seel and E. Pöhlmann, "Quantität und Wortakzent im horazischen Sapphiker. Ein Beitrag zum Iktus-Problem," *Philologus,* 103 (1959); H. Drexler, "Quantität und Wortakzent," *Maia* n.s., 12 (1960); R. G. Tanner, "The Arval Hymn and Early L. Verse," CQ n.s., 11 (1961). R.J.G.

IDYL(L). A short poem or prose composition which deals charmingly with rustic life; ordinarily it describes a picturesque rural scene of gentle beauty and innocent tranquillity and narrates a story of some simple sort of happiness. There are no requirements of form, such as are prescribed in the stricter types (limerick, sestina, and sonnet) or even in the looser types (ode and ballad). The earliest commentators used the term to designate a great variety of short poems of domestic life in which description of beautiful rural scenery was an essential element. But, because the scholiasts used the term in connection with the poems of Theocritus, Bion, and Moschus, it has often been considered a synonym for pastoral (q.v.); and Theocritus' ten pastoral poems, no doubt because of their superiority, became the prototype of the i. In the 16th and 17th c., especially in France, there was frequent insistence that pastorals in dialogue be called *eclogues;* those in narrative, *idylls.* Dictionary definitions from Edward Philip's *New World of Words,* 1678, to the *New Eng. Dictionary,* 1888–1929, have emphasized two restrictions; first, that the term derives from *eidyllion,* meaning "little picture" (which was construed to mean "framed picture"); second, the term is used to designate poems of rustic life, such as that in the pastoral poems of Theocritus. Critics and scholars also have tried to confine the subject matter of the i. within those limits. In 1555 Vauquelin de la Fresnaye, comparing the terms i. and pastoral, declared that the name "of idyl seemed to me to be more closely related to my purposes, especially as it signifies and represents only diverse small images resembling those engraved on stone or on chalcedony to serve sometimes as a seal." And as late as 1904 Martha Hale Shackford was contending that the i. is "a picture of life as the human spirit wishes it to be, a presentation of the chosen moments of earthly content." Two biblical selections are customarily referred to as idylls—Ruth and The Song of Songs. Among the major writers in Eng. literature, however, there is scarcely a poem to meet these specifications, unless such poems as Marlowe's pastoral *The Passionate Shepherd to His Love* or Burns's realistic narrative *The Cotter's Saturday Night* are included. Poems bearing this designation may be found in the works of minor poets, such as Salomon Gessner's *Idyls* or Anna Nicholas' *Idyl of the Wabash.* And among many major poems frequently there are episodes which may justly be called "idyllic," like the Nausicaa episode in the *Odyssey,* the Palemon and Lavinia episode in Thomson's *Seasons,* and the Juan and Haidée episode in Byron's *Don Juan.* Typical prose idylls are illustrated by Barrie's *Auld Licht Idyls.* It must be pointed out, however, that writers have often ignored the prescriptions. A notable instance occurred even as early as the 17th c. in Marc-Antoine de Gérard, sieur de Saint-Amant's *Moyse sauvé,* 1653, an "idylle héroique" of 6,000 lines. In more recent times such use, or abuse, of this term has been made by Victor de Laprade, *Idylles héroïques,* 1858, and Tennyson, *Idylls of the King,* 1859. Perhaps Tennyson thought the use of the term was appropriate for his poem; each i. contains an incident in the matter of Arthur and his Knights which is separate (or framed) but at the same time is connected with the central theme; the contents treat the Christian virtues in an ideal manner and in a remote setting. Such freedom led to a wide imitation of the term by poets. For instance, there is little in the matter of Robert Browning's *Dramatic Idylls,* 1879, 1880, which deal for the most part with psychological crises, to place them in the tradition. Obviously, then, the i. cannot be called, either because of form or of content, a definite poetic type. Actually, after such uses of the term as those cited above, it would be rather difficult to say what might not be called an i. The signification of *idyllic,* however, has been more constant. Usually it is applied only to writings which present picturesque rural scenery and a life of innocence and tranquillity.—M. H. Shackford, "A Definition of the Pastoral I.," PMLA, 19 (1904); R. G. Moulton, "The Song of Songs," *Modern Reader's Bible* (1926); P. van Tieghem, "Les Idylles de Gessner et le rêve pastoral," *Le Préromantisme,* II (1930).

J.E.C.

IMAGE. See IMAGERY.

IMAGERY. An image is the reproduction in the mind of a sensation produced by a physical perception. Thus, if a man's eye perceives a certain color, he will register an image of that color in his mind—"image," because the subjective sensation he experiences will be an ostensible copy or replica of the objective color itself. The mind may also produce images when not reflecting direct physical perceptions, as in the attempt to remember something once perceived but no longer present, or in the undirected drifting of the mind over experience, or in the combinations wrought out of perception by the imagination, or in the hallucinations of dreams and fever, and so on.

More specifically in literary usage, *imagery* refers to images produced in the mind by language, whose words and statements may refer either to experiences which could produce physical perceptions were the reader actually to have those experiences, or to the sense-impressions themselves. When Archibald MacLeish says, in *Ars Poetica,* that a poem should be "Dumb / As old medallions to the thumb," he not only *means* that the language of poetry should make important use of i., he also *exemplifies* what he means by expressing it in terms of i.: a poem, he implies, should make its impact upon the imagination rather than upon the intellect, much as a person feels an old coin with his fingers (a physical perception). When, however, he says "A poem should not mean / But be," his meaning is the same but his language is not, for this statement is abstract rather than concrete and imagery-bearing, dealing as it does with an idea or concept rather than a perception or sensation. This combination of meaning and imagery may indicate the confusion which can result when "i." is applied to literary study, for it is used variously to refer to the meaning of a statement involving images, to the images themselves, or to the combination of meaning and images. Thus Miss Downey says, "The image must not be conceived as a material copy or thing but merely as the content of a thought in which attention is centred on sensory quality of some sort." Or Miss Spurgeon says, "I use the term 'image' here as the only available word to cover every kind of simile, as well as every kind of what is really compressed simile—metaphor." Or C. Day Lewis says, "It is a picture made out of words." Or Fogle refers to it as "the sensuous element in poetry."

For the purposes of the present discussion, the various definitions of imagery can be reduced essentially to three: (1) "mental i.," (2) i. as "figures of speech," and (3) i. and image patterns as the embodiment of "symbolic vision" or of "nondiscursive truth." Interest in the first is focused on what happens in the reader's mind (effect), while in the second and third it is focused on the imagery-bearing language itself and its significations (cause). None of these categories, of course, is entirely separate from any of the others, but such a breakdown is helpful in making a beginning.

The first definition emphasizes the relation of the statement on the page to the sensation it produces in the mind, and involves two parallel problems: first, to describe objectively and analytically the sensory capacities of the poet's mind; and second, to test, and perhaps improve, the reader's capacity to appreciate i. in poetry. The analyst reads a given poem and then reports the different images the poem is capable of stimulating, or he asks a subject to read the poem and report similarly on *his* (the subject's) reactions. Interest in this field was apparently first provoked by the early experiments in the psychology of perception of Sir Francis Galton ("Statistics of Mental Imagery," *Mind,* 5 [1880], 301–18), who discovered that people differ in their image-making habits and capacities ("How much of this morning's breakfast-table can you recall to mind and describe now?" the questionnaires ran). While one person may reveal a predominating tendency to visualize his reading, memories, and ruminations (as indeed many people do), another may favor the mind's "ear," another the mind's "nose," or yet another may have no i. at all.

While the study of mental i. concentrates on psychology in the sense of perception, the study of figures of speech concentrates on figures as they appear in language. This can involve the study of all devices called figures of speech or only those in which a relation is posited between a subject and something to which the subject is compared (an analogue). It can support the idea that poetry is an "art" in the sense of the product of conscious and laborious fabrication, or a process of discovery that arises from moments of inspiration or insight.

Finally, i. patterns are concerned with the appearance and significance of groups of interrelated images in a poem. These can be approached in terms of their revelation of facts about the psychology of the artist or in terms of their expressiveness of a central "meaning," or in terms of how they relate among themselves to create the sensation of meaning in the mind of the reader.

Mental i., figurative i., and symbolic i. It may be now asked what is involved in each definition, how each is related to the others, and what the values of each are. Psychologists have identified a number of different kinds of mental images: visual (sight, which can be further subdivided for brightness, clarity, color, and motion), auditory (hearing), olfactory (smell), gustatory (taste), tactile (touch, which can be further subdivided for heat, cold, and texture), organic (awareness of heartbeat, pulse, breathing, and digestion), and kinesthetic (awareness of muscle tension and movement). Obviously these categories, although perhaps somewhat overelaborate for the purposes of literary criticism, are preliminary to the other approaches to i., for they define the very nature of the materials. And several valuable results have emerged from the application of these distinctions to literature (e.g., Downey). In the first place, the concept of mental i. has encouraged catholicity of taste, for once it has been realized that not all poets have the same sorts of sensory capacities, it is easier to appreciate different kinds of poetry. Much of Browning's i., for example, is tactile, and those who habitually visualize are unjust in laying the charge of obscurity at his door (see J. K. Bonnell,

PMLA, 37 [1922], 574–98). Or again, the frequently voiced complaint that Shelley's poetry is less "concrete" than Keats's suffers from a basic misconception of the nature of i., for Shelley's poetry contains just as much i. as Keats's, although it is of a somewhat different kind (see Fogle [Bibliography]). In the second place, the concept of mental i. provides a valuable index to the type of imagination with which any given poet is gifted. To know that Keats's poetry is characterized by a predominance of tactile and organic i., for example, or that Shelley's is characterized by a predominance of the i., of motion, is valuable knowledge and provides important descriptive terms with which to define the achievement of each poet. Thirdly, the concept of mental i. is pedagogically useful, for a teacher or a critic may encourage better reading habits by stressing these aspects of poetry. Thus, because the reader is encouraged to make specific images in his mind as he reads, aesthetic appreciation can be improved in a very literal sense.

The study of mental i., however, has clear limitations. The functioning of T. S. Eliot's famous simile of the "patient etherized upon a table" (analogue, or figurative image) need depend very little upon the question of whether or not either Eliot or the reader has reproduced in his mind the various sensations which this image is potentially capable of stimulating—the sickly sweet smell of the anaesthetic, the feeling of numbness, the buzzing in the ears, the sense of lying prone, the white and silver gleam of the operating room, and so on. This sort of deliberate exploitation may or may not assist the reader in grasping the use of this image in the poem, but to *understand* that this image is one of half-life, half-death, of suspended animation which is the symbol of spiritual debility, and which is therefore highly appropriate not only to the setting of twilight (half-light, half-dark) but also, in terms of revealing Prufrock's state of mind, to the conceptual problem of death-in-life in the speaker's world around which the poem is built, need not of necessity require any such effort. One can therefore best discuss the functioning of a poem's i. without becoming overly involved in the question of the sensations in the reader's or the poet's mind.

And that is where the study of i. as a device of poetic language turned its attention, in the course of time; for i., whatever its sensory qualities may be, may function either literally, figuratively, symbolically, or in some combination. Thus, an investigation of figurative i. involves such problems as that of rhetorical types, that of the kinds of relationships which may obtain between subject and analogue, that of the nature of symbolic expression, and that of the use of figures in poetry, which the study of mental i. either confused or ignored.

Ancient rhetoric divided figures of speech into several types. "Figures of words" included such syntactical figures as repetition, gradation, antithesis, and balance. "Figures of thought" included oratorical strategies such as description, example, characterization, personification, and extended comparison (or contrast). "Tropes" were figures in the more familiar sense of images of explicit or implied comparison—simile, metaphor, synecdoche, metonymy, and the extended metaphor called allegory. This rhetorical approach to i. was discredited during the romantic period because it seemed artificial and opposed to artistic creativity; hence the use of "rhetorical poetry" to mean "bad poetry," particularly, "verbose poetry."

Among the New Critics, I. A. Richards, William Empson, and Cleanth Brooks, especially, became interested in figures like metaphor and paradox, as means of conveying poetic insights for which discursive language is inadequate. They were followed by classical and renaissance scholars (e.g. Rosamund Tuve, L. Sonnino) concerned with the influence of ancient rhetoric on literary style. By 1960 interest in rhetoric had developed in another area. Structuralism, tracing its lineage to Ferdinand de Sausure and Claude Lévi-Strauss, regards meaning as the product of codes—usually codes absorbed by the mind during childhood. The proper study of literature should be the study of the way its linguistic codes or its "games of words" operates. Classical rhetoric anticipates this, and it can be—and is—utilized by structuralists and post-structuralists (e.g., Derrida, Paul de Man), although in ways directly opposed to the aesthetic tradition of the New Critics.

To summarize, from a rhetorical point of view parallelism, balance, allusion, hyperbole, and metaphor are all figures and hence examples of figurative i. From an aesthetic point of view, the true figures are simile, metaphor, metonymy, synecdoche, allegory, and the like—most (though not all) called tropes in ancient rhetoric. They have in common the fact that they posit relationships between two elements. In the simile "My love is like a red, red rose" the two elements are a subject ("love") and an analogue ("rose"). It may be noted that I. A. Richards popularized an alternative terminology: "tenor" (for subject) and "vehicle" (for analogue).

Four positions are common today in describing the relationships between subject and analogue. The rhetorical approach typically asks how they are similar—specifically, how analogue expresses subject (Aristotle, *Poetics*, 1459a5–7). A directly opposed position is taken by André Breton ("First Manifesto of Surrealism" [1924]), who argues that metaphor derives its force not from the similarity between subject and analogue but from their dissimilarity. It is the disruption of standard meaning that makes metaphor a source of illumination, hence surrealist metaphor: "My love is like a metro stop."

The New Critical approach treats the metaphor as a kind of discovery, often of meanings inexpressible in normal language. It is thus related to the theory of Max Müller that man needs metaphor because as he develops he constantly outgrows his language—the literal mode becomes ineffective, inexact, or incomplete. Finally, structuralism and post-structuralism are interested in figures as part of the codes that create meaning (or the sensation of meaning). An approach that fuses traditional rhetorical criticism with such current interests is George T. Wright, "Hendiadys in *Hamlet*" [PMLA, 1981].

It was once common to claim that proper practice precluded mixing one's analogues in any one figure (see Jennings), while critics today argue that no such rule is universally valid, especially in poetry (see Brooks). Or it was once considered good form to teach students to visualize all figures, but it has been repeatedly pointed out that not only are most metaphors constructed on other bases than mental i. but also that much mental i. is other than visual—in fact, persistent visualizing will break down the relationship entirely between subject and analogue in many figures (see Richards). Again, much attention has been focused upon that kind of figure in which the difference between subject and analogue is especially great, and which, since it is believed that such a figure was used mainly by Donne, Herbert, Marvell, Vaughan, Traherne, and so on, has been termed the "metaphysical image" (see Wells, Rugoff, Tuve)—although Miss Holmes has argued that it was derived from Elizabethan drama. Or again, much has been made of the function of the "central" or "unifying image" in a poem, according to which the poet develops a sustained analogy, which serves as the core of his poem.

When these distinctions serve as the basis for various speculations regarding the nature and development of poetic language, or the quality of the poetic imagination, "i." becomes one of the key terms of criticism. If Max Müller thought that primitive man *compared* abstract ideas to concrete things because his conceptions outran his vocabulary, many critics believe that the primitive *identified* the two in a rich and imaginative fashion (Buck and Barfield anticipated this view). Thus "spirit," meaning "breath," was not borrowed as a concrete term to express the abstract concept of "soul," but rather "soul" was identified with "breath." Prescientific man (and that includes everyone up to around 1700), therefore, was supposed to be gifted with a "unified sensibility," and poets are engaged in a mighty struggle to rectify the "dissociation of sensibility" created by science in the imaginations of men.

From these notions, a value-system has been constructed according to which a good poet "reconciles" abstract and concrete, thought and feeling, reason and imagination, and a bad poet, like the scientist, separates them. Thus the good poet aims at wholeness of experience by means of the poetic imagination or "mythic consciousness," whereby he sees facts in terms of values, and continually invents fresh metaphors (myths in little) and symbols (expanded metaphors). The favorable terms are "rich," "complex," "concrete," "ambiguous," "ironic," "symbolic," "mythic," "sensuous," "unified," "wholeness," and so on, while the pejoratives are "sentimental," "prosaic," "didactic," "dissociated," and so on.

As has been noted already, these are assumptions of what might be called the "New Critical moment" in modern criticism. They have all been challenged and are rejected, sometimes passionately, by a variety of critics who believe variously that they are based on an exploded mythology of identity, a misunderstanding of how meaning is generated by language, a strategy to privilege the literature and experience of Western Europe and America, and/or a strategy (conscious or unconscious) to maintain the dominance in society of an upper middle-class, white, predominantly male group.

The implications of such positions for the study of i. obviously vary. In many cases, however, they have proven extraordinarily fruitful. Most obviously, the sensitivity to the strategies whereby poetry expresses meaning revealed in Roman Jakobson's "Linguistics and Poetics" and his classic interpretation (with Lévi-Strauss) of Baudelaire's "Les Chats" (in R. T. and F. M. de George, eds., *The Structuralists* [1972], pp. 85–146) demonstrate the emergence of a powerful modern "rhetoric" at least as aware of the subtleties of poetic i. as the New Criticism. Again, the review of the relation between signified and signifier that figures so largely in the work of Derrida provides a new basis for approaching metaphor: "From the moment that one . . . recognizes that every signified is also in the position of a signifier, the distinction between signified and signifier becomes problematical at its root." ("Semiology and Grammatology," in *Positions* [1981], p. 21.) And again, the development by Jacques Lacan of the idea that metaphor and metonymy are the two "slopes of the effective field of the signifier in the constitution of meaning," and the relation of these devices to the mode of existence of consciousness as understood by Freud, must be considered an important enlargement of traditional theories of figurative language. (See R. and F. de George, pp. 287–322.)

The study of figurative i. anticipates and overlaps the subsequently developed study of symbolic i. Here the essential question is how the patterns of i.—whether literal, figurative, or both—in a work reveal things about the author and/or his poem. The basic assumption is that repetition and recurrences (usually of images, but also on occasion of word patterns in general) are in themselves significant. Hence the method involves an amateur application (and, some times, distortion) of some elementary statistical principles. These patterns may either be within the work itself, or among literary works and myths in general (see ARCHETYPE), or both.

Assuming for the moment that repetitions are indeed significant, the nature of the significance must next be examined. What, exactly, will counting image clusters tell the critic? There are at least five distinguishable answers; they are, in increasing levels of complexity: (1) texts of doubtful authorship can be authenticated (see Smith); (2) inferences can be made about the poet's experiences, tastes, temperament, and so on (see Spurgeon, Banks); (3) the causes of tone, atmosphere, and mood in a poem or play can be analyzed and defined (Spurgeon); (4) some of the ways in which the structure of conflict in a play is supported can be examined (see Burke, *Philosophy of Literary Form* [1941], etc.); and (5) symbols can be traced out, either in terms of how image patterns relate to the author or of how they relate to archetypes, or some combination (Frye, Knight, Heilman).

The first two approaches relate to problems extrinsic to the work itself, although they seek internal evidence. The procedure involves counting all the images in a given work or in all the works of a given poet (and here the various problems of what an image is, what kind it is, and whether it is literal or figurative, must be resolved anew by each critic doing the counting) and then classifying them according to the areas of experience from which they derive: Nature—Animate and Inanimate, Daily Life, Learning, Commerce, and so on. Since these categories and their proportions represent aspects of the poet's imagination and perception, two inferences can be made on the basis of the resultant charts and figures: first, that these patterns are caused by the poet's personal experiences with life and that, therefore, they give a clue to the poet's personality and background; and second, that since they are unique, they offer a means of determining the authorship of doubtful works. Perhaps the second inference is sounder than the first, although both rest upon dubious assumptions, for frequently images appear in a work not because of the poet's personality or experience but rather because of literary and artistic conventions (see Hornstein, Hankins).

The third and fourth approaches relate to problems intrinsic to the artistic organization of the work itself. "One cannot long discuss imagery," says Burke, "without sliding into symbolism. The poet's images are organized with relation to one another by reason of their symbolic kinships. We shift from the image of an object to its symbolism as soon as we consider it, not in itself alone, but as a function in a texture of relationships" (*Attitudes toward History* [1937], v. 2, pp. 154–55). Certain plays of Shakespeare, it was discovered, are saturated with one kind or another of similar images or "clusters" (usually figurative)—the i. of light and dark in *Romeo and Juliet*, for example, or of animals in *King Lear*, or of disease in *Hamlet*, and so on—and it was reasoned that these recurrences, although barely perceptible except upon close examination, are continually at work conditioning the reader's responses as he follows the action of a play. Thus F. C. Kolbe, a pioneer—along with Whiter and Spaulding—of cluster criticism, claimed in 1930: "My thesis is that Shakespeare secures the unity of each of his greater plays, not only by the plot, by linkage of characters, by the sweep of Nemesis, by the use of irony, and by appropriateness of style, but by deliberate repetition throughout the play of at least one set of words or ideas in harmony with the plot. It is like the effect of the dominant note in a melody" (*Shakespeare's Way*). Modern critics have added that clusters may form dramatic discords as well as harmonies.

From this argument it was a small step to classify images according to their relationship to the dramatic conflicts in the work. There are basically two sorts of clusters: the recurrence of the same image at intervals throughout the work, or the recurrence of different images together at intervals throughout the work. If the same image recurs in different contexts, then it (theoretically) serves to link those contexts in significant ways, and if different images recur together several times, then the mention of any one will serve to call the others to mind.

The next and fifth step was to reason once again from inside to outside the work, but this time ostensibly for the sake of returning to it with greater insight. According to Burke, a poem is a dramatic revelation in disguised and symbolic form of the poet's emotional tensions and conflicts, and if, therefore, some idea of these tensions and conflicts in his personal life can be formed, the reader will then be alerted to their symbolic appearance in his works. Thus Burke can make equations among Coleridge's image clusters by comparing the poet's letters with the *Ancient Mariner*, and can conclude that the albatross symbolizes Coleridge's guilt regarding his addiction to opium, and this, he reasons, illuminates the "motivational structure" of that particular poem.

It is not difficult, on the other hand, to equate image clusters in a particular work with larger patterns found in other works and myths instead of with the poet's personal life (a dream is the "myth" of the individual, a myth is the "dream" of the race), as does Northrop Frye, and even Burke himself, for the "action" of which a poem is "symbolic" frequently resembles larger ritualistic patterns such as purgation, scape-goating, killing the king, initiation, and so on, although expressed on a personal level and in personal terms. R. P. Warren sees in the *Ancient Mariner* a symbol of the artist-archetype, symbolized in the Mariner, torn between the conflicting and ambiguous claims of reason, symbolized by the sun, and the imagination, symbolized by the moon: thus the crime is a crime against the imagination, and the imagination revenges itself but at the same time heals the Mariner; the wandering is also a blessing and curse, for the Mariner is the *poète maudit* as well as the "prophet of universal charity." Thus, in large and general terms, the artist is seen as the hero and his art as a sacrificial ritual, and he is seen as dying to his life in order to be reborn in his art as the redeemer (see Otto Rank, "Myth and Metaphor," *Art and Artist*, tr. C. F. Atkinson [1932], pp. 207–31). One may find implicit images of descent, guilt, purification, and ascent running throughout a poem whose literal action may be of quite a different nature. Image clusters are seen, then, as forming a "spatial pattern" or even a "subplot" calling for special attention in itself.

The difficulties with the fourth and fifth approaches are: first, that the concern centers rather exclusively on problems of moral vision, on the assumption that the really important thing about poetry is its way of viewing life and experience, a "mode of apprehension"; second, that, as a result, almost any poem or play is read as an allegorical struggle between Good and Evil, Reason and Imagination, Guilt and Redemption, or any other favored pair of opposites, and this is excessively reductive; third, that many such inferences as those discussed above are made on the basis of insufficient evidence and faulty or incomplete hypotheses (a statistician could point out, for example, that *some* recurrences are accidental, and a logician could point out, for example, that a favored hypothesis, in order to be valid, must be tested against other alternatives); fourth, that the *literal* action of a poem or play, when viewed as an artistic construct, tends to be inordinately deemphasized or even ignored altogether; and fifth, that these approaches tend to be so loosely oriented and vaguely defined as to allow anything and everything in a work to be seen in terms of anything and everything else.

The importance, however, of these approaches to i. in a work is that they do indeed refocus critical concern on the work, and its parts and devices.

Since economy is a fundamental artistic principle, it may be said that usually literal i. is converted into a pseudo-subject, becoming the symbol of something else as a result of the speaker's reflective and meditative activity. Mere scenery, that is, is rarely enough in itself, except in descriptive poems, to justify its presence in a poem. Thus Arnold in "Dover Beach" converts the scene into a symbol as follows: as it begins to signify sadness to the speaker, it reminds him of Sophocles listening long ago by the Aegean and reflecting similarly. Although the literal sea before him at Dover Beach is now at full tide, the "Sea of Faith" now seems to him to be ebbing. Thus the problem which is troubling the speaker (the discord he senses between an apparently meaningful world and an actually meaningless one) finds its image in the contrast between what he sees—the calm sea, the full tide, the fair moon, the bright gleam of lights, the tranquil bay, the sweet night air—and what he hears—the partially submerged and ominous sound of

the grating roar
Of pebbles which the waves suck back, and fling,
At their return, up the high strand,
Begin, and cease, and then again begin,
With tremulous cadence slow, and bring
The eternal note of sadness in.

It will be noted that the language of this passage is set in contrast to that used above: grating roar, suck back and fling, tremulous, slow, and sadness, as opposed to calm, full, fair, glimmering, vast, tranquil, and sweet. Still talking in terms of the pseudo-subject in the second paragraph, the speaker contrasts what Sophocles heard and thought to what he hears and thinks: the great dramatist, long ago and in another place, heard this same "grating roar" and it brought to his mind "the turbid ebb and flow / Of human misery," while the modern Eng. speaker finds "also in the sound a thought, / Hearing it by this distant northern sea." Taken in context, since the meaning is not wholly explicit, this may imply that Sophocles found *some* meaning, however tragic, in the coming and going of the waves, while Arnold's speaker, focusing now not on the rapid motion of the waves but rather upon the slow ebb and flow of the tide (a shift in i. of which some critics have complained), sees only the absence of any meaning whatever. To the ancient Greeks, that is, the world made sense in moral terms (e.g., the catharsis or sense of justice produced by the tragedies of Sophocles), while to the modern European the world is devoid of value. Thus, although the physical tide is full, the moral tide is ebbing, and he can

only hear
Its melancholy, long, withdrawing roar,
Retreating to the breath
Of the night-wind down the vast edges drear
And naked shingles of the world.

At the end, therefore, since the faith of humanity at large is gone, he can appeal to his lady to reaffirm at least their own faith in one another, "for the world, which seems / To lie before us like a land of dreams" (a reference back to the opening description), is really joyless, confused, and without love. Thus does Arnold's sea-imagery function at once as subject and symbol.

It may be asked, finally, what the poet gains by the use of such devices. I., especially of the figurative or symbolic sort, may, in the first place, serve as a device for explaining, clarifying, and making vivid what the speaker is talking about. Arnold was not content with merely locating his speaker geographically, but had him register his awareness of the precise physical details of the scene before him so that the reader would not only know but feel what he (the speaker) is responding to. Secondly, and correspondingly, the terms in which he is making that response serve to reveal implicitly the mood of tempered sadness in which we find the speaker. Thirdly, and consequently, since this scene serves to call up to the speaker's consciousness—and thereby becomes the vehicle of—a problem which has long been troubling him, it stimulates and externalizes further his mental activity. Fourthly, the poet's handling of i., through his selection of detail and choice of comparisons, serves to dispose the reader either favorably or unfavorably toward various elements in the poetic situation. That faith, therefore, the loss of which the speaker mourns, is made to seem worthy of his lament not only because the reader knows in general what the speaker is talking about but also and more particularly because he compares it to a bright girdle, thereby arousing in the reader's mind the connotations of a thing of value and ornament, pleasant, precious, and useful. I. may serve, fifthly, as a way of arousing and guiding the reader's expectations. Thus, since he places "sea" as the second word of his poem, Arnold prepares the reader for the speaker's symbolic lament: "The Sea of Faith / was once, too, at the full."

I., then, may derive from the speaker's subject, if that happens to involve a person, place, object, action, or event; from a symbolic combination of subject and meaning, if his thought happens to find its expressive vehicle in his physical experience; or from exterior analogies, if he happens to use figures of speech. It may be interpreted in terms of whether it functions to vivify the subject, reveal the speaker's mood, externalize the speaker's thought, direct the reader's attitudes, or guide his expectations. See also METAPHOR.

F. I. Carpenter, *Metaphor and Simile in the Minor Elizabethan Drama* (1895); G. Buck, *The Metaphor: A Study in the Psychology of Rhetoric* (1899); J. G. Jennings, *An Essay on Metaphor in Poetry* (1915); H. W. Wells, *Poetic I.* (1924); Richards, *Principles*; S. J. Brown, *The World of I.* (1927); O. Barfield, *Poetic Diction* (1928); J. E. Downey, *Creative Imagination* (1929); E. Holmes, *Aspects of Elizabethan I.* (1929); C. F. E. Spurgeon, *Shakespeare's I. and What it Tells us* (1935); I. A. Richards, *The Philosophy of Rhetoric* (1936); U. Ellis-Fermor, *Some Recent Research in Shakespeare's I.* (1937); I. A. Richards, *Interpretation in Teaching* (1938); M. A. Rugoff, *Donne's I.* (1939); C. Brooks, "Metaphor and the Tradition," *Modern Poetry and the Trad.* (1939); M. B. Smith, *Marlowe's I. and the Marlowe Canon* (1940); L. H. Hornstein, "Analysis of I.: A Critique of Literary Method," PMLA, 57 (1942); E. A. Armstrong, *Shakespeare's Imagination* (1946); C. D. Lewis, *The Poetic Image* (1947); C. Brooks, "The Naked Babe and the Cloak of Manliness," *The Well Wrought Urn* (1947); Tuve; R. B. Heilman, *This Great Stage: Image and Structure in "King Lear"* (1948); R. H. Fogle, *The I. of Keats and Shelley* (1949); Wellek and Warren, ch. 15; D. A. Stauffer, *Shakespeare's World of Images* (1949); T. H. Banks, *Milton's I.* (1950); W. H. Clemen, *The Development of Shakespeare's I.* (1951); K. Muir, "Fifty Years of Shakespearean Crit.: 1900–1950," *ShS*, 4 (1951); F. Marsh, *Wordsworth's I.* (1952); J. E. Hankins, *Shakespeare's Derived I.* (1953); Frye; F. Kermode, *Romantic Image* (1957); C. Brooke-Rose, *A Grammar of Metaphor* (1959); D. C. Allen, *Image and Meaning: Metaphoric Traditions in Renaissance Poetry* (1960, rev. ed., 1968); J. W. Beach, *Obsessive Images: Symbolism in the Poetry of the 1930's and 1940's* (1960); R. Frazer, "The Origin of the Term Image," ELH, 27 (1960); *Metaphor and Symbol*, ed. L. C. Knights and B. Cottle (1960); H. Musurillo, *Symbol and Myth in Ancient Poetry* (1961); P. Wheelwright, *Metaphor and Reality* (1962); L. Sonnino, *A Handbook of 16th-C. Rhetoric* (1968); J. Derrida, *Of Grammatology*, tr. G. C. Spivak (1976) and *Writing and Difference*, tr. A. Bass (1978); *M. and Thought*, ed. A. Ortony (1979).

N.FRIE., rev. O.B.H.

IMAGINATION is derived from L. *imaginatio*, which was a late substitute for *phantasia* (a simple transliteration of the Gr.) from which fancy is derived. The two terms, with their derivatives, long appeared as synonyms designating the image-receiving or image-forming faculty or process. From philosophy they were borrowed by criticism, and in both contexts were subject to different evaluations by different schools. Their history, though far from a simple linear development, falls into fairly clearly marked divisions.

I. CLASSICAL AND MEDIEVAL. (1) The history starts with the elementary recognition, first, of a mental image accompanying sense perception (and viewed by the materialist as real and an impress made by the object, by the idealist as mere appearance, by the dualist with depreciation as dependent on matter and the senses), and, secondly, of images occurring in the absence of any object, and in various combinations, which might be depreciated as fictitious, suspected as proceeding from the passions, valued as divinely inspired, or simply examined as psychological phenomena.

(2) All these attitudes find some reflection in Plato, who further recognizes a connection of art and poetry with i. Initially, he regards the image as illusory, yielding no knowledge of reality (since of the "idea" one can form no image) but confined to appearance and opinion, and a prey to every prompting from the irrational soul; hence in part the limitations of artist and poet. Thus Plato inaugurates a long tradition of distrust, which was little mitigated by his own important second thoughts, namely, that "images answering to true opinions are true," that to form

images from "ideas" was indeed possible to the god, that an image of pure beauty (subsuming the ideas of truth and goodness) while it could not be produced by any activity of the soul, might be passively received from above, or even "remembered" from the soul's earlier state, a process in which earthly images of beauty might be instrumental, and, finally, that provision was perhaps made (in close proximity to the irrational soul) for a reflection, in the form of images, of ideas entertained by the rational soul.

(3) Aristotle's interest, in the *De Anima,* was psychological and free from prejudice. Set in motion by sense perception, phantasy forms images of objects and their relations; and from such images reproduced, reason abstracts its ideas. Thus, in the process of deriving knowledge from experience, images are the intermediaries between sense and thought; and in the act of choice images have an equally essential role. Aristotle's failure, however, to invoke his theory of the reproductive image in expounding, in the *Poetics,* his view of art as an "imitation of nature" at once realistic and philosophical, was to impede the recognition of the imagination's role in poetry (see below 7).

(4) Distrust of phantasy is dominant in the Stoics (despite some inheritance from the *De Anima*). Neoplatonism, as represented by Plotinus, is more ambivalent. His emanationist theory permitted him to distinguish a higher and a lower phantasy: the lower dependent on sense and a function of the irrational soul, the higher reflective of ideas because a function of the rational soul, but with the lower capable of being brought into harmony with the higher because it is indeed its shadow. Further, as soul was an emanation of mind, nature was an emanation of soul, inferior to it because lacking, among other powers, that of phantasy and, consequently, all perception of its own activity, namely, the imposition of forms upon matter (the last and lowest of the emanations). Here was a philosophy with large, if undeveloped, possibilities for poetic theory: for the imaginative reflection of the ideal, and even for something like Coleridge's conception of "poesy or art" (see 15).

(5) Though, in discussing the art of poetry, Horace had ignored i. and thus impeded its recognition (cf. 7), Quintilian, with illustrations from Virgil, recognizes that by *visiones* (or phantasies) absent things seem present, whence the orator can feel and, by his eloquence, arouse emotion; and Longinus, with illustrations from Euripides, recognizes i. as a source of sublimity when "moved by enthusiasm and passion you seem to see the things whereof you speak and place them before the eyes of your hearers." Here as later (cf. 10, 18) i. and passion unite to characterize poetry and eloquence. A further development is adumbrated in Philostratus, when imitation is declared to be inferior to phantasy, since it can represent only what has been seen, but phantasy what has never been seen, fashioning it according to the analogy of the real.

(6) While Christian asceticism, with biblical phrases about vain i., no doubt fortified existing prejudices, St. Augustine distinguished the reproductive from the simple sensory image, reserving to the former the term *phantasia* or *imaginatio.* He recognized its role when, in reading history, or in writing and reading fables, we see in our mind's eye persons and scenes; he further noticed the interdependence of the reproductive image and the will in the hypothetical representations formed by addition, subtraction, or combination of attributes. But for him i. remained inferior to intellect: to the former prophetic vision might be vouchsafed, but its interpretation only to the latter. In the "faculty psychology" of the Schoolmen, where this order is maintained, i., like the other faculties, is given its location and its distinctive function, namely, with or as the *sensus communis,* to produce from sense data the images of objects and their relations, and (sometimes under the designation of *phantasia*) to reproduce and combine images at will. Of the truth of images reason must judge, and from them it abstracts ideas, which memory in turn retains. This is the basic scheme, of which there were many variants. Dante's interest centered on ascent from the image of earthly beauty to intellectual or heavenly love, and on the image divinely bestowed or inspired; but his practice as poet outran his theory: where, in the *Divine Comedy,* he finally declares that i. fails, he is actually making his most effective use of the symbolic image, and in his account of the poem's fourfold meaning he does not refer to i. at all.

II. Renaissance to Romantics. (7) In Pico della Mirandola's *On Imagination,* the early Renaissance combined a renewed reference to classical sources with much from medieval tradition. Those critics who, in the 16th c., commenced to formulate the principles of neoclassicism, built upon Aristotle and Horace and largely ignored imagination in favor of the imitation of nature; and even when Scaliger and Sidney acclaimed the poet as a "creator," they still clung to the doctrine of imitation.

It is not till Bacon that i. really begins to claim a central role in poetry and then with an attendant limitation, for poetry ceases to be knowledge and becomes fiction and play. "History," he writes, "is referred to memory; poesy to imagination; philosophy to reason." With "the primary materials of knowledge" the "mind . . . exercises itself and sometimes sports. For as all knowledge is the exercise and work of the mind, so poesy may be regarded as its sport." For "being not tied to the laws of matter," as are memory and reason, i. "may at pleasure join that which nature hath severed and sever that which nature hath joined" and give thereby "some shadow of satisfaction to the mind of man" by representing "a more ample greatness, a more exact goodness, and a more absolute variety than can be found in the nature of things."

(8) For immediate acceptance this view ran too completely counter to the neoclassical conception of poetry as an imitation of nature. In England, however, neoclassicism early sought its philosophical basis in empiricism, and while it regarded poetry as an imitation of empirical reality (a severely limiting criterion, as seen in Hobbes) and yielded i. only a secondary role, a philosophy which grounded all knowledge in sense experience had less reason to distrust i. than had rationalism in its Cartesian or any other form, and psychological interest prompted a study of its operation. Hobbes sums up his view of poetry in the dictum: "Time and education beget experience; experience begets memory; memory begets judgment and fancy; judgment begets the strength and structure, and fancy begets the ornaments, of a poem."

(9) For Addison all the data of i. are supplied by the sense of sight. Its primary process is to form visual images of objects in their presence. Its secondary is to reproduce their "ideas" (i.e. images) "when the objects are not actually before the eye, but are called up into our memories or formed into agreeable visions of things that are either absent or fictitious." Here indeed are two processes: simple reproduction of images, and "altering and compounding those images . . . into all the varieties of picture and vision . . . ; for by this faculty a man in a dungeon is capable of entertaining himself with scenes and landskips more beautiful than any that can be found in the whole compass of nature." And "because the imagination can fancy to itself things more great, strange or beautiful than the eye ever saw, and is still sensible of some defect in what it has seen, . . . it is the part of a poet to humour the imagination . . . by mending and perfecting nature where he describes a reality, and by adding greater beauties than are put together in nature where he describes a fiction."

(10) To the influence of Addison's *Spectator* papers much of the emphasis on i. in 18th-c. criticism may be traced. "In the fairyland of fancy," wrote Edward Young, "genius may wander wild; there it has a creative power and may reign arbitrarily over its own empire of chimeras." Reynolds, abandoning "ideal form" for "appeal to the imagination" as his criterion in art, declares that its aim "is to supply the natural imperfection of things" and "to gratify the mind by realizing . . . what never existed but in imagination."

(11) Vico's importance lies less in his theory of i. ("imagination is nothing but extended or compounded memory") than in the results which he attributed to it in ancient poetry and myth, thereby anticipating modern anthropological criticism. To Herder and the Germans it chiefly fell to take up and develop Eng. ideas of primitive poetry and the i. of the folk. More central are the interests of Dougald Stewart, who ascribes imagery wholly to "fancy," the power that "supplies the poet with metaphorical language," while i. (freed from its close association with the image) is the power "that creates the complex scenes he describes and the fictitious characters he delineates," as illustrated in Milton's Eden, Harrington's Oceana, and Shakespeare's Falstaff or Hamlet. This is perhaps the final development and utmost reach of the tradition that stops short of making for i. the transcendental claims put forward by the romantics.

(12) Of such claims there were, however, some intermittent premonitions. After basing his early aesthetic on Hobbes, but unlike Hobbes attempting some distinction between i. and fancy (*imagination* connoting the general power whose first activity is "invention or finding of the thought," while its second activity is "fancy or variation . . . of that thought"), Dryden became restive under its limitations and (with liberal quotation from Bellori) advanced the theory that i. could reach to images of the essential ideas of things, which images were the models for painter and poet when they would represent "nature wrought up to a nobler pitch."

In It. criticism attention was being given to the i. with somewhat different results, and notably by Muratori in his defense of the It. poets against the strictures of Fr. neoclassicists. In order to please, poetry must present what appears to be true and beautiful, marvelous but verisimilar. Herein intellect and i. must cooperate and good taste control. If intellect alone works upon the images, the result is philosophical knowledge; if i. alone, dream and delusion. "Simple" or "natural" images appear immediately true to both. Others may appear immediately true to i., but only mediately to the intellect: such are those images, described as "artificial" or "fantastic," which are applied metaphorically under the stress of emotion. Both kinds are approved by Muratori and copiously illustrated from the poets. In German criticism Eng. ideas on poetry and i. were sometimes grafted on the different philosophical stock of Leibniz, as by Bodmer and Baumgarten. But it is to Kant and his followers in Germany and to the romantic poets in England that we must look for the final exalting of i.

III. The Romantics. (13) Blake takes an extreme line. Ultimate reality is spiritual, and the i. is the organ of its perception: "Imagination is spiritual sensation." It is the "first principle" of knowledge, "and all others are derivative." It perceives—almost one might say, confers—form and value: "Nature has no outline, but Imagination has: / Nature has no tune, but Imagination has. / Nature has no supernatural and dissolves: Imagination is Eternity." In his reaction against empiricism and the theories of art based thereon, Blake condemns all those "who pretend to Poetry that they may destroy Imagination by imitation of Nature's Images drawn from Remembrance."

(14) Meanwhile, in the *Critique of Pure Reason,* Kant had emphasized the role of i. (*Einbildungskraft*) in the formation of knowledge, describing it as "an active faculty for synthesis," which unites and unifies the manifold data of sense perception. Without it, no subjective knowledge would be possible, and no ordered knowledge of an objective world. It is "a necessary ingredient of perception itself" and the indispensable mediator between "mere sensibility and understanding"; and, in order to account for these empirical results, Kant has further to infer "a transcendental synthesis of imagination." Nor is this all. In the *Critique of Judgment* he treats i. in another context, which places it in a different relation to understanding and brings into relief free (as opposed to determined) activity. In aesthetic judgment, "we do not refer the representation . . . to the object by means of understanding, with a view to cognition, but by means of imagination (acting perhaps in conjunction with understanding) we refer the representation to the subject and its feeling of pleasure or displeasure." There i. is free: not simply "reproductive" under "the laws of association," but "productive and exerting an activity of its own"; and even when it is restricted by the form of the object of sense represented, and "does not enjoy free play as it does in poetry," the representation is still judged in relation to such a form "as the imagination, if left to itself, would freely project in . . . general conformity to the law of the understanding." In a word, in cognition i. is at the service of understanding; in aesthetic judgment, "understanding is at the service of imagination" in its free activity. Kant's antinomy of the necessary and the free becomes in Schelling that of the real (nature, the finite and determined) and the ideal (mind, the infinite and free) subsisting within the absolute, and the function of art is to mediate between them, to build the infinite into the finite, through the active and intermediary power of "intelligence," which no doubt subsumes i.: "Intelligence is productive in two ways . . . , unconsciously in the perception of the universe, consciously [and, he adds, with freedom] in the creation of an ideal world."

(15) In Coleridge there are elements from both Kant and Schelling. I., he defines as the intermediate faculty which joins the predominantly passive and predominantly active elements in thinking, but as applied to poetry it connotes "a superior degree of the faculty joined to a superior voluntary control over it." And in a more famous passage he writes: "The primary imagination I hold to be the living power and prime agent of all human perception, and as a repetition in the finite mind of the eternal act of creation in the infinite I AM. The secondary imagination I consider as an echo of the former, co-existing with the conscious will, yet still as identical with the primary in the kind of its agency, and differing only in degree and in the mode of its operation. It dissolves . . . in order to recreate or . . . to idealize and to unify." It is thus sharply differentiated from fancy, which is a mere "mode of memory emancipated from the order of time and space" but receiving "all its materials ready made from the law of association." Coleridge is critic as well as philosopher, and one of his concerns is to validate, against empiricism, the productions of the "secondary" i., the creative i. of poet or artist, by identifying it in kind with the "primary" i., the finite counterpart of God's creative act, and thereby to give philosophic ground and content to the traditional idea of the poet as creator. Unlike fancy and understanding, which are confined to the level of the phenomenal, of *natura naturata,* reason and creative i., aspiring to the noumenal, approximate to each other, so that i. becomes (in Wordsworth's phrase) "reason in her most exalted mood." Deliberately Coleridge seeks to unite creative i. with the imitation of nature, properly understood. For "poesy or art" does not "copy" *natura naturata* but "imitates" *natura naturans*; and thus to imitate nature is in effect to interpret it in and by "symbols," "living educts of the imagination, of that reconciling and mediatory power which, incorporating the reason in images of the sense, and organizing (as it were) the flux of the senses by the permanence and self-encircling energies of the reason, gives birth to a system of symbols, harmonious in themselves and consubstantial with the truths of which they are the conductors."

(16) Though still concerned with the image, Coleridge and Wordsworth extend the sway of i. to "thoughts and sentiments," "characters" and "actions": Wordsworth distinguishes the "human and dramatic" i. of Shakespeare from the "enthusiastic and meditative" of the Bible, Milton, and (he adds) Spenser; and Coleridge between the i. of Shakespeare, by which he goes forth and identifies himself with his subject, and Milton's, by which he brings everything to a center in his own experience. But above all i. manifests itself in the unity of the whole: it draws (says Wordsworth, quoting Lamb) "all things to one" and makes them "take one colour and serve to one effect"; it reveals itself, says Coleridge, "in the balance or reconcilement of opposite or discordant qualities; of sameness with difference, of the general with the concrete . . . , the individual with the representative, . . . the sense of novelty and freshness with old and familiar objects, [and] a more than usual state of emotion with a more than usual order. . . ."

(17) Ruskin distinguishes three modes in which i. operates: the "penetrative" (whereby the artist, reacting to the inner "verity" of his subject,

can present it directly, without resort to metaphor or symbol), the "associative" (the instinctive process, contrasted with conscious "composition," whereby he harmonizes every detail so that it may contribute to the effect of the whole), and the "contemplative" (whereby the artist, in treating a subject that transcends nature and the concrete image directly employed, resorts to an analogical or figurative use of image to convey its meaning and suggest the attendant emotion). None of these modes does he regard as "creative," however. For art to create is to depart from truth and produce fiction, and this is the lower activity of three modes of fancy corresponding to the three modes of i. But, despite his characteristic schematism, Ruskin really cares little for terminology, so long as he can assert that great art embodies truth intuitively apprehended and beyond the reach of reasoning.

(18) In Croce's doctrine of art as intuition (where intuition demands expression and expression is art), i., as productive of the unifying image, is in its turn identified with intuition, so that the doctrine might as well be phrased, art as i. The central role here accorded to i. (*fantasia*) implies a sharp distinction from the mere recalling of images in accidental succession or arranging them in constrained or capricious combinations.

(19) R. G. Collingwood, in expounding a not dissimilar theory, treats i. in greater detail. I. is neither mere sensibility, which is passive and below the level of consciousness, nor intellect, whose activity issues in thought, in the formation and ordering of concepts: it is an activity of mind which coexists with full consciousness, and it is the intermediary between the other two. It furnishes "the basis for a theory of aesthetic experience"; and it fills an essential "place in the general structure of experience" since it provides the means whereby "the activity of thought makes contact with the merely psychic life of feeling."

IV. The Twentieth C. (20) In popular criticism the word *imagination* and its derivatives are still encountered, if less frequently. Their meaning is sufficiently vague, connoting most often perhaps sustained fantasy as opposed to realistic writing; but it is largely devoid of the transcendental overtones inherited from the romantics. One could expect no less from the widespread and varied reaction against romanticism in general and transcendentalism in particular. An example of this reaction was seen in Am. humanism, though Irving Babbitt conceded the importance of i., and a distinction between the "ethical" (or classic) i. and the "idyllic" (or romantic) is pivotal in his doctrine. More unequivocally hostile to i. as such was the whole naturalistic movement in thought and letters (which the humanists also opposed). In and beyond its ill-defined boundaries transcendentalism is of course out of fashion. If, for example, Coleridge is to be accepted by I. A. Richards, he must first be divested of his metaphysics. The psychology and aesthetics of the romantics have been in part developed, in part repudiated. Freudians regard poetry as wish-fulfillment and analogous to dreams; cultural anthropologists see it as reducible to archetypal myths and patterns, and other critics regard the poem as a self-contained entity without significant external relations, whose meaning and effect reside in a pattern of interdependent images.

The structuralist/post-structuralist position is hostile to the philosophical traditions out of which the romantic concept of i. developed. With few exceptions, it rejects the idea that i. is a productive force that creates the unique individual consciousness (the "center" of the self), and also the idea that as a result of the work of i., a literary work can have "organic unity" or a "center" or a "privileged ontological status." A classic application of this position is the "decentering" (or "deconstruction") of Balzac's story *Sarrasine* by Roland Barthes (*S/Z*, tr. R. Miller [1974]), in which Barthes claims to show that the story is a mosaic of "five major codes."

The strong positivist strain of such criticism is, however, being challenged from several directions. Paul Ricoeur's phenomenology is sympathetic to earlier concepts of i., and Jacques Lacan insists on the importance of a psychological "center" in spite of his prominence in the post-structuralist camp. Recent speculations by researchers in artificial intelligence like Seymour Papert and Douglas Hofstadter may also contribute significantly to the debate.

References and Bibliography by Numbered Paragraphs (1–6) M. W. Bundy, *Theory of I. in Classical and Mediaeval Thought* (1927); (2) Plato, *Republic* 10 (595–608), *Phaedrus* (245, 247, 250–51), *Philebus* (38–40), *Timaeus* (70–71); (3) Aristotle, *De Anima* 3.3–8 (427–31); (4) Plotinus, *Enneads,* as in Bundy ch. 6; (5) Quintilian, *Institutio Oratoria* 6.2.29–32, 10.7.15; Longinus, *On the Sublime* 35; Philostratus, *Life of Apollonius* 6.19; (6) St. Augustine, *Epistles* 6,7; Bundy ch. 9 (7–12); L. P. Smith, "Four Romantic Words," *Words and Idioms* (1925); J. W. Bray, *Hist. of Eng. Crit. Terms* (1898); A.S.P. Woodhouse, "Collins and the Creative I.," *Studies in Eng.*, ed. M. W. Wallace (1931), "Romanticism and the Hist. of Ideas," *Eng. Studies Today,* ed. C. L. Wrenn and G. Bullough (1951); G. Williamson, "Restoration Revolt against Enthusiasm," sp, 30 (1933); R. S. Crane, "Eng. Neoclassical Crit.," *Critics and Crit.* (1952); D. Bond, " 'Distrust of I.' in Eng. Neoclassicism," pq, 14 (1935), "Neoclassical Psychology of the I.," elh, 4 (1937); W. J. Bate, "Sympathetic I. in 18th C. Eng. Crit.," elh, 12 (1945); W. J. Bate and J. Bullitt, "Distinctions between Fancy and I.," mln, 60 (1945); (7) Puttenham, *Arte of Eng. Poesie;* Bacon, *Advancement of Learning, Descriptio Globi Intellectualis, De Augmentis Scientiarum* 2.1.13, 5.1; Bundy, " 'Invention' and 'I.' in the Renaissance," jegp, 29 (1930), "Bacon's True

Opinion of Poetry," SP, 27 (1930); (8) Hobbes, *Answer to Davenant, Leviathan* 1.2–3,8; C. D. Thorpe, *Aesthetic of Thomas Hobbes* (1940); (9) Addison, *Spectator,* nos. 411–21; C. D. Thorpe, "Addison's Theory of the I.," *Papers of the Michigan Acad. of Science etc.,* 21 (1935); (10) Young, *Conjectures on Original Composition;* Reynolds, *Discourses,* Notes to Mason's tr. of Du Fresnoy; J. Warton, *Essay on Pope, Ode to Fancy*; H. Home, Lord Kames, *Elements of Crit.*; Alison, *Essays on Taste*; (11) Hume, *Treatise of Human Nature*; Adam Smith, *Theory of the Moral Sentiments*; Gerard, *Essay on Genius*; Duff, *Essay on Original Genius*; Blackwell, *Enquiry concerning Homer*; Blair, *Lectures on Rhetoric*; Vico, *Scienza Nuova* (tr. T. C. Bergin, M. H. Fisch, 1948); D. Stewart, *Philos. of the Mind* 1.3, 5, 8; (12) Dryden, Preface to *Annus Mirabilis, Parallel of Poetry and Painting*; Collins, *Ode on the Poetical Character*; Shaftesbury (3d Earl), "Advice to an Author" (in his *Characteristics*); Muratori, *Della Perfetta Poesia Italiana*; J. G. Robertson, *Studies in the Genesis of Romantic Theory* (1923; ch. 3). (13–18) Wellek; Woodhouse, "Romanticism and the Hist. of Ideas" (above); Abrams; (13) Blake, Letter to Trussler, Aug. 23, 1799, *Milton, Ghost of Abel, Marginalia to Wordsworth, Vision of the Last Judgment* (in *Descriptive Catalogue*); (14) Kant, *Critique of Pure Reason* (tr. N. K. Smith), *Critique of Aesthetic Judgment* (tr. J. C. Meredith); E. L. Fackenheim, "Schelling's Philos. of the Lit. Arts," *Philos. Quart.,* 4 (1954); (15–16) Coleridge, *Biographia Literaria* (ed. J. W. Shawcross; see also the 1983 standard ed. by J. Engell and W. J. Bate), *Poesy or Art, Lay Sermon, Table Talk*; Wordsworth, Preface to *Poems* (1815), *Prelude* (esp. Bk. 14); Hazlitt, "Poetry in General" (*Lectures on Eng. Poets*); Hunt, *What is Poetry?*; Shelley, *Defence of Poetry*; Joubert, *Pensées*; (17) Ruskin, *Modern Painters* 3.1.15.2–3; 3.2.1–4 (and see Index); Arnold, "Pagan and Mediaeval Religious Sentiment" (*Essay in Crit.,* 1st ser.); G. H. Lewes, *Principles of Success in Lit.,* ch. 3; (18) Croce, *Aesthetic* (tr. D. Ainslie, 1922); (19) R. G. Collingwood, *Principles of Art* (1938); (20) I. Babbitt, *Rousseau and Romanticism* (1919); I. A. Richards, *Principles of Lit. Crit.* (1924) and *Coleridge on Imagination* (1934); *The Mind's I* (ed. D. Hofstadter and D. Dennett, 1981).—See also R. L. Brett, *Fancy and I.* (1969); M. Warnock, *I.* (1976). T. McFarland, *Originality and I.* (1984). A.S.P.W., rev. O.B.H.

IMITATION. Until very recently, when it was restored to the critical vocabulary by Francis Fergusson, Kenneth Burke, and members of the "Chicago school" (see also Auerbach's *Mimesis*), "i." had been out of favor as a literary term since the 18th c. Its eclipse began with the critical stirrings that led the way to romanticism, when "i." was more and more felt to be out of keeping with the new spirit of spontaneity and self-expression. Its revival today is associated with other manifestations of a reaction against romanticism, a tendency to adopt a more objective view of the poet's relation to his subject.

"I." the Latin *imitatio,* is a translation of Gr. *mimesis.* The original connotation of the latter seems to have been dramatic or quasidramatic. Whether any theory of poetry as i. was developed before Plato is uncertain. Gorgias's notion of tragedy as a "beneficent deception" (*apate*) perhaps anticipated it in part; and Democritus certainly held that the arts in general arose out of imitation of nature: singing, for example, from imitation of the birds. But the first place where we can actually grasp *mimesis* as a critical term is Plato's *Republic,* Books 3 and 10. In Book 3, however, the context is political and pedagogical rather than merely literary. Plato's concern there is with the education of his élite corps of Guards, and he judges poetry strictly by that criterion. "I." is identified almost exclusively with the dramatic mode: i.e., with the direct impersonation of literary characters. This involves an identification of oneself with others which is perilous for the young; it may lead them away from their best selves to an indiscriminate i. of low and unworthy persons. Hence poetry, but especially the drama, must be banished from the professional education of the ideal ruler. In Book 10 Plato renews his attack on a broader front. I. is now identified as the method of *all* poetry, and of the visual arts as well. The poet, like the painter, is incapable of doing more than counterfeit the external appearance of things; Truth, the realm of Ideas, is inaccessible to him. In this second discussion (perhaps written later) Plato's attention has shifted from the method of i. to its object, and i.—i.e., art is condemned not merely for its moral effects but because it cannot break through the surface of Appearance to the reality it ought to reproduce, the Ideas.

This crushing verdict upon "i." does not result, as we might expect, in banishing the term from Plato's world of discourse; on the contrary, it permeates his thinking more and more in the later dialogues. In the *Sophist* (236) he hints at the possibility of a "true i.," which would reproduce the real nature and proportions of its object. Indeed Plato came to think of the whole complex relation of Becoming to Being, Particular to Idea, as a kind of i. Thus the *Timaeus* (27ff.) presents the universe itself as a work of art, an "image" of the world of Ideas made by a divine craftsman. From this it is only a step to conceiving visual art, and then poetry, as a sensuous embodiment of the ideal. The Neoplatonists (see Plotinus, *Enneads* 5.8, and cf. Cicero, *Orator* 2.8–9) took this step, but Plato himself did not. The condemnation of poetry in the *Republic* was never explicitly revised or withdrawn (it is substantially repeated in the *Laws,* Books 2 and 7), and the developments just mentioned remain hints (highly fruitful ones for later thought) rather than a new positive doctrine of poetic i.

Aristotle accepts i. (*Poetics,* ch. 4) as a fundamental human instinct—an *intellectual* instinct—of which poetry is one manifestation, along with music, painting, and sculpture. His real innovation, however, and the cornerstone of his new theory of poetry, is a redefinition of *mimesis* to mean not a counterfeiting of sensible reality but a presentation of "universals." By "universals" he means (ch. 9) not metaphysical entities like the Platonic Ideas, but simply the permanent, characteristic modes of human thought, feeling, and action. It goes without saying, or at least Aristotle does not bother to say, that knowledge of such universals is not restricted to the philosopher. The poet can represent them, and his readers can grasp them, without benefit of metaphysical training. Poetic i. is of *action* rather than simply of men, i.e., characters. Tragedy (and, with certain reservations, the epic) is an i. of a single, complete, and serious action involving the happiness of an important human being. More specifically, the i. is lodged in the *Plot* (*mythos*) of the poem; and by "plot" Aristotle means not merely a sequence but a *structure* of events, so firmly welded together as to form an organic whole. It follows that the poet's most important duty is to shape his plot. He cannot find it already given; whether he starts from mythical tradition, history, or his own invention, he is a poet only so far as he is a builder (*poietes,* "maker") of plots. Thus "i." comes very close to meaning "creation." But the poet's creation is not of some "second nature" existing only in his fancy; it is a valid representation of the actions of men according to the laws of probability or necessity.

Aristotle's concept of i. was subtle and complex. His chief successors in criticism were men of another stamp, more literary than philosophical in their view of poetry. So far as i. remained a key term in the Hellenistic age (actually we do not hear a great deal about it), it seems to have been conceived as meaning the portrayal of standardized human *types*: the hot-headed man, the braggart soldier, the wild Thracian, etc. Aristotle's "probability" (*to eikos, verisimile*), and the even more characteristic concept of "appropriateness" (*to prepon, decorum*), are now tailored to the measure of particular social standards and conventions more than to any permanent principles of human nature. At the same time Aristotle's insistence on action gives way to more relaxed and eclectic views: the object of i. may be character, thought, or even natural phenomena. Anything can be imitated, in accordance with the laws of the *genre* one has chosen, and the object, whether fable, fact, or fiction, is tacitly assumed to have more or less the same status as a natural object.

Alongside the Aristotelian concept of i., thus denatured, another of very different provenience—and still easier to understand—took on increasing importance in the Hellenistic and Roman periods. This was the relatively simple idea of imitating the established "classics" (the word is Roman, the concept Gr.), the great models of achievement in each *genre.* Its origin was rhetorical, but it ended by spreading impartially over prose and poetry. The treatise of Dionysius of Halicarnassus *On Imitation* is lost except for fragments, but we can get some idea of the theme from the second chapter of Book 10 of Quintilian's *Institutio Oratoria.* From these two authors, and more particularly from "Longinus" (see SUBLIME), we can see that the doctrine had its higher side. I. of the great writers of the past need not and should not be merely a copying of devices of arrangement and style, but a passionate emulation of their spirit. Dryden (in the *Essay of Dramatic Poesy*) puts it very well: "Those great men whom we propose to ourselves as patterns of our imitation, serve us as a torch, which is lifted up before us, to illumine our passage and often elevate our thoughts as high as the conception we have of our author's genius." Here i. is united with its apparent opposite, inspiration. Nevertheless, both in antiquity and in the Renaissance, i. in the sense of emulation of models meant chiefly stylistic i., and thus helped to fortify the prevalent understanding of poetry as an art of words.

The Renaissance inherited at least three major concepts of i. from antiquity: (1) the Platonic: a copying of sensuous reality, (2) the Aristotelian: a representation of the universal patterns of human behavior, and of an action embodying these, and (3) the Hellenistic and rhetorical: i. of canonized literary models. But each of these was further complicated by a deviation or variant interpretation: (1) the Platonic by the Neoplatonic suggestion that the artist can create according to a true Idea, (2) the Aristotelian by the vulgarization of Aristotle's "universals" into particular social types belonging to a particular place or time, and (3) the rhetorical by its rather adventitious association with "enthusiasm" and the *furor poeticus* (a good example is Vida's *Ars Poetica* 2.422–444). That this mixed inheritance did not lead to complete critical chaos was due partly to the chronological accident that the *Poetics* did not become known in Italy until well after 1500, partly to the incorrigible syncretism of the humanists, which refused to give up any part of the ancient tradition but insisted on blending it into a new amalgam, and partly to the plain fact that the chief literary creed and inspiration of the It. Renaissance was rhetorical. Humanism was an imitative movement in its very root and essence: the i. of classical, particularly classical Latin, literature was its life-blood. Thus the burning question in the 15th c., and well into the 16th, was not What is imitation? or Should we imitate? but Whom (i.e., which classical author or authors) should we imitate? The fiercest battle was waged over prose style, i.e., over the question whether Cicero should be the sole and all-sufficient model for L. prose or others such as Sallust, Livy, Seneca, Tacitus might be admitted also. Lorenzo

Valla spoke to this issue in a spirit of enlightened Ciceronianism, in his *De Elegantiis Linguae Latinae* (between 1435 and 1444) and about seventy years later (1512) we find Gianfranco Pico della Mirandola, nephew of the more famous Count Giovanni, and the learned Pietro Bembo (later secretary to Leo X, and Cardinal) debating it once more, with references to a previous controversy between Cortesius and Politian (cf. the latter's *Epistles*). Pico takes the eclectic side, Bembo the Ciceronian, as Politian and Cortesius had done before them. The Ciceronian squabble was more or less ended by Erasmus's *Ciceronianus* (1528). Alongside it ran a similar but less acrimonious dispute over poetic i., centering around Virgil and ending in his canonization by Vida (1527) and Scaliger (1561) as the supreme poet and perfect model.

Meanwhile an issue of more theoretical, or at least of more general, interest was presented by the perennial need for a *defense of poetry* against doctrinal and moral objections from the side of the Church. In this struggle it was only natural that Plato's indictment of poetry as mere i. should be pressed into service by the attackers, e.g., by Savonarola in his *De Divisione ac Utilitate Omnium Scientiarum* (1492), while on the other side "Platonic"—actually Neoplatonic ideas of poetry as a showing forth of Truth and Beauty made their appearance on the other side. The younger Pico (see above) invoked such ideas in his plea for a broad view of "i."

A genuine theoretical interest in the concept of poetic i. as such could not arise, however, until Aristotle's *Poetics* had come to light again and begun to be studied: that is, until after the first quarter or third of the 16th c. Vida's *Art of Poetry* (1527) is still innocent of this new trend. It preaches the i. of "nature" (2.455: *nil conarier artem, Naturam nisi ut assimulet propiusque sequatur*), but for no other real purpose than to inculcate the i. of the ancient poets, above all Virgil, who followed her to the best advantage (*hanc unam vates sibi proposuere magistram*). Daniello (*Poetica*, 1536) knows Aristotle's definition of tragedy as i., but hardly knows what to make of it, since he draws only a faltering distinction between poetry and history. Robortelli, in his commentary on the *Poetics* (1548), allows the poet to invent things that transcend nature. Fracastoro (*Naugerius, sive de Poeta Dialogus*, 1555) pieces out Aristotle's concept of i. with the Platonic idea of beauty, identifying the latter with the universal. Scaliger (1561) recommended the i. of Virgil because Virgil had created a "second nature" more beautiful than the first; and Boileau gave the problem its definitive formulation for neoclassical theory: the surest way to imitate nature is to imitate the classics. But the real difficulty and challenge of Aristotle's idea of i. had not been grasped, much less solved. The later Renaissance was as unable as the earlier to make an effective distinction between poetry and history on the one hand, and between poetry and rhetoric on the other, because it could not seize and define any true "universal" as the object of poetic i., except in vague Platonic (Neoplatonic) terms, and so fell back into regarding poetry as essentially a special way of discoursing about "things." As for the treatises *De Imitatione* penned by humanists north of the Alps in the 16th c.—Camerarius (1560), Sturmius (1574), Ascham's discussion of the subject in the *Scholemaster* (1570)—they belong almost entirely to the history of L. pedagogy, not to criticism.

Although i. was implicitly accepted down through the 18th c. as the goal and method of the fine arts in general, including poetry and painting, it began to slip into disrepute after 1770, being felt more and more to imply a derogation of the artist's integrity. Edward Young sneered at "the meddling ape, Imitation," and Coleridge opined that "To admire on principle, is the only way to imitate without loss of originality." The revival of "i." in our own day (see first paragraph above) has very little to do with either the classical or the neoclassical tradition; it goes straight to Aristotle, not through intermediaries, and views i. above all as a structural concept, the principle of organization of poetic wholes.

S. H. Butcher, *Aristotle's Theory of Poetry and Fine Art*, ch. 2 (4th ed., 1911; suggestive, but overmodernizes A.); U. Galli, "La mimèsi artistica secondo Aristotele," *Studi Ital. di Filol. Class.*, n.s., 4 (1926), comprehensive, covers Plato also; J. Tate, " 'I.' in Plato's *Republic*," CQ, 22 (1928) and "Plato and 'I.,' " CQ, 26 (1932); R. McKeon, "Lit. Crit. and the Concept of I. in Antiquity," MP, 34 (1936), enlightening survey, and "I. and Poetry," in *Thought, Action and Passion* (1954); W. J. Verdenius, *Mimesis: Plato's Doctrine of Artistic I. and its Meaning for Us* (1949; prudent, well documented); F. Fergusson, *The Idea of a Theater* (1949), esp. ch. 1 and Appendix; K. Burke, "A 'Dramatistic' View of 'I.,' " *Accent*, 12 (1952); Auerbach; H. Koller, *Die Mimesis in der Antike* (1954; ambitious but unreliable); G. F. Else, *Aristotle's Poetics: the Argument* (1957) and " 'I.' in the 5th C.," CP, 53 (1958). G.F.E.

IN MEMORIAM STANZA. So called from its use in Tennyson's *In Memoriam*. A stanza of 4 lines of iambic tetrameter, rhyming abba:

I hold it true, whate'er befall;
  I feel it when I sorrow most;
  'Tis better to have loved and lost
Than never to have loved at all.
(*In Memoriam*, 27)

Although Tennyson believed he had invented the stanza, it may be found in earlier poetry, notably in that of Ben Jonson (*If Beauty be the Mark of Praise*), Lord Herbert of Cherbury (*Ode upon a Question Moved, whether Love Should Con-*

tinue for ever). It is true however, that Tennyson exploited the inherent formal capacities of the stanza with a greater mastery than did his predecessors. In particular, he utilized its suitability for successive, mutually independent philosophical observations, each enclosed within its "envelope" of stanzaic pattern, and its possibilities for special emphasis through the rhyme of first and fourth lines. Later uses of the stanza are rare. An interesting example is Oscar Wilde's *The Sphinx,* in which the stanza is printed as 2 lines.—H. Corson, *Primer of Eng. Verse* (1892); E. P. Morton, "The Stanza of I. M.," MLN, 21 (1906) and "Poems in the Stanza of I. M.," MLN, 24 (1909); Baum; Hamer.

INCREMENTAL REPETITION. A phrase coined by F. B. Gummere to describe a rhetorical device peculiar to Eng. and Scottish folk ballads. In i.r. a line or stanza is repeated several times with some small but material substitution at the same crucial spot. A sequence of such repetition accounts for the entire structure of some few ballads, among them *Lord Randal* and *Edward.* More usually, however, i.r. spans a passage of only 3 or 4 stanzas, and it is frequently confined to the lines of a single quatrain, as in the following stanza from *Sir Hugh; or, The Jew's Daughter:*

> Then out and came the thick, thick blood,
> Then out and came the thin;
> Then out and came the bonny heart's blood,
> Where all the life lay in.

Suspense is the principal effect achieved by this device, for with each iteration and its substituted element, tension mounts until the climactic substitution, which resolves the pattern, is reached. Gummere interpreted i.r. as another proof of the choric origins of traditional balladry; he argued that it was a certain test of what was and was not a ballad. More recent ballad theorists, like Louise Pound and G. H. Gerould, hold that i.r. is generally rhetorical not structural and that it is not a determining characteristic of the orally transmitted traditional ballad.—I.r. is elaborately illustrated throughout F. B. Gummere, *The Popular Ballad* (1904, 1907), esp. pp. 117–24. For pugnacious crit. of Gummere, see L. Pound, *Poetic Origins and the Ballad* (1921), pp. 121–35. G. H. Gerould, *The Ballad of Tradition* (1932), pp. 105–10, arbitrates the dispute. A.B.F.

INSCAPE AND INSTRESS. Inscape in the aesthetic of Gerard Manley Hopkins, who coined the term, refers to the principle of physical distinctiveness in a natural or artistic object. Rooted in the Scotist concept of *haecceitas* or "thisness," inscape is whatever uniquely differentiates a thing from whatever was, is, or shall be. Hopkins himself somewhat inadequately defined the term in a letter to Robert Bridges as "design" or "pattern" (*The Letters of G. M. H. to Robert Bridges*, ed. C. C. Abbott, 1935, p. 66). In his critical study of Hopkins, W.A.M. Peters gives a more elaborate definition of inscape as "the outward reflection of the inner nature of a thing, or a sensible copy or representation of its individual essence" (*G. M. H.: A Critical Study Toward the Understanding of His Poetry*, 1948, p. 2). W. H. Gardner states simply that inscape is "the name for that 'individually-distinctive' form (made up of various sense-data) which constitutes the rich and revealing 'one-ness' of the natural object" (*Poems and Prose of G. M. H.*, 1953, p. xx).

Inscape and instress are closely related terms—inscape, the principle of individuation, and instress, the force which sustains and emanates from inscape. In the words of Gardner, instress is essentially the "sensation of inscape," the impulse "which acts on the senses and, through them, actualizes the inscape in the mind of the beholder" (*op. cit.*, p. xxi). Peters notes that instress is the force that "holds the inscape together" as well as "the power that ever actualizes the inscape" (pp. 14–15). For Hopkins, instress is the energy by which "all things are upheld" (*Note-books and Papers of G. M. H.*, ed. H. House, 1937, p. 98).—J. Pick, *G. M. H.: Poet and Priest* (1942); *G. M. H.*, ed. J. C. Ransom and C. Brooks (1945); W. H. Gardner, *G. M. H.: A Study of Poetic Idiosyncrasy in Relation to Poetic Tradition* (2 v., 1948–49); *Immortal Diamond: Studies in G. M. H.*, ed. N. Weyand (1949); A. Heuser, *The Shaping Spirit of G. M. H.* (1959). S.H.

INSPIRATION is the urge that sets a poet to work and the devotion that keeps him at it. There have been two theories of the origins of this urge and devotion. The first, more widespread in space and time than the second, is that i. comes from outside the poet; the second, that it comes from within him. The data on which this first concept is based come from literature and anthropology; the data for the second, from psychology.

In a passage from *On the Orator* (2.46.194) Cicero comments: ". . . I have often heard that—as they say Democritus and Plato have left on record—no man can be a good poet who is not on fire with passion and inspired by something like frenzy." And Plato (*Laws* 719c) alludes to the same view. He often refers to it, sometimes at length (e.g., *Symposium* 197A; *Phaedrus* 244–45). One brief dialogue, the *Ion*, is wholly devoted to a discussion of i. There Plato suggests, borrowing from Democritus, that just as iron filings become magnetized through the power of the magnet, so the poet is inspired through divine power, and that that power is conveyed by him to those who recite poetry—the professional rhapsodists—and, in turn, to their audiences. (See R. C. Lodge, *Plato's Theory of Art*, 1953.)

Cicero discussed i. in his *On Divination* (1.18.37), *On the Nature of the Gods* (2.66: "No man was ever great without divine inspiration"), *On the Orator,* and *The Tusculan Disputations* (1.26). In modern Eng. translations of these passages (e.g., in the Loeb Library) the word *inspiration* is used but the words so translated are in Cicero *afflatus, instinctus,* or *concitatio: inspiratio* does not appear until the late Latin period.

Some recent discussions of Aristotle on this point (see A. H. Gilbert, *Literary Criticism, Plato to Dryden,* 1940, pp. 117, 118) conclude that Aristotle rejected i. as the source of the poet's power. (But see Aristotle, *Rhetoric* 3.7). So did Castelvetro in 1570, Dryden in 1679, and William Morris in the 19th c.

Testimony to i. from the poet's point of view occurs as early as *Odyssey* 22.347–48, where the bard, Phemius, says, ". . . the god has put into my heart all manner of lays, and methinks I sing to thee as a god. . . ." Homer, Hesiod, and Pindar invoke divine i. and so does Theocritus, but with the latter perhaps the invocation is just a literary convention. Virgil's address to the muse is well-known, and Ovid also has references to i. (*Ars Amatoria* 3.549; *Fasti* 6.5).

Longinus opens another aspect of the subject. He thinks of i. from the consumer's point of view. When a poem brilliantly imitates the work of another, we think its author inspired (13, 32). Likewise, when we read or hear a poem that is far beyond our experience, we again think it inspired (15).

When Christianity became the official religion of the Roman Empire, a Judaeo-Christian strain was added to the Graeco-Roman tradition that poetic i. came from outside the poet. For the Hebrew contribution consider Joel 2:28–30 and Ezekiel 2:1–10. The Church Fathers—Jerome in particular—often referred to David as the perfect poet-prophet, inspired by *God.*

From the 8th c. through the first quarter of the 19th we have many testimonies to a belief in the idea that poetic i. comes from outside the poet. Consider the following literary references: Bede (*Ecclesiastical History of the Eng. Nation* 4. 24; account of Caedmon); Dante, *Purgatorio* 1. 1–20; Boccaccio, *Genealogy of the Gods* (tr. Osgood), 14, 15.39, 15.99, etc.; J. C. Scaliger, *Poetics* (tr. Padelford), 1. 2; Sidney, *Defence of Poetry* (ed. Cook), pp. 8, 43; Francis Bacon, *Advancement of Learning* (World's Classics edition), p. 90; and Ben Jonson, *Discoveries* (ed. Schelling), pp. 74–76. The most significant, and probably the most serious, expression of the idea of i. in Eng. poetry of the 17th c. is found in Milton's invocations in Books 1, 3, 7, and 9 of *Paradise Lost.* Milton's Muse is not a tired literary convention carried over from classical poetry but a source of enlightenment comparable to the Protestant "inner light" and equated with the spirit from whom Moses received the Ten Commandments.

In the 18th c. i. was suspected of being "enthusiastic," as were the sermons of the more radical Protestant preachers. To classicists, who believed that the artist should rely primarily on conscious craftsmanship, this was undesirable (e.g., Shaftesbury's *Letter on Enthusiasm*); but to preromantics i. remained important: e.g., Edward Young's *Conjectures on Original Composition* (ed. Edith Morley), p. 30; William Blake's letter to Thomas Butts of April 25, 1803; Wordsworth's conclusion to *The Recluse;* Coleridge's account of the origin of *Kubla Khan* (see E. Schneider, *Coleridge, Opium, and Kubla Khan,* 1953, ch. 2); Poe's *Poetic Principle;* Emerson's *The Poet.*

So much for the first theory, the traditional one, that the poet's i. comes from outside himself, usually from the gods or God. Now for the second theory, that i. comes from within the poet. Of this there are two varieties, the first of which, the theory of genius, will serve as a transition between the two main theories of i. The idea of genius, characteristically, was held by the romantic writers (ca. 1760–1840), who were severely taken to task for this view by Irving Babbitt in his essays *On Genius* and *On Being Original.*

Genius is a L. word, probably considered by the Roman as the equivalent of the Gr. *daimon* (demon). Socrates regarded himself as directed by his *daimon.* We still have in common pariance the phrases "good genius" and "evil genius." When Christianity became the official religion of the Roman Empire *daimon* came to be thought of primarily as diabolical. In late L., however, *genius* came to be used as the equivalent of *ingenium* and its operation was transferred from the outer to the inner world of the poet. *Genius* appears in the Eng. language as early as the 16th c. It came to mean *native talent.* By romanticists, however, a distinction was made between *genius* and *talent*; the former being something more significant than talent. (See S. T. Coleridge, *Biographia Literaria,* chs. 2, 15.) Between 1751 and 1774, twelve publications treat the concept *genius.* The most important and influential of these was Edward Young's *Conjectures on Original Composition* (1759) in which one finds most of the romantic ideas which Irving Babbitt attributes to Rousseau and his influence. (See especially E. Morley's edition of Young's essay, 1918, p. 13.) William Hazlitt published two essays on *Genius and Common Sense* (in *Table Talk*) and one on *Whether Genius is Conscious of its Power?* (in *The Plain Speaker*). See also Charles Lamb, *The Sanity of True Genius* (in *Essays of Elia*).

The second variety of the modern notion that the poet's i. comes from inside himself is due to the labors of psychologists who from about 1840 on were trying to make their field a true science. These researches are found in systematic treatises on descriptive or experimental psychology, in accounts of abnormal or subliminal psychology, and in volumes like Th. Ribot, *Essay on the Creative Imagination* (1906) or R. M. Ogden, *Psychology of Art* (1938). They give us many data on, but fail to solve the mystery of, the poetic temperament. The most coherent body of literary theory that has emerged from these researches is that named *surrealism* which draws on Marxist interpretations of Hegel as well as on psychological studies such as those of Freud and Jung. The surrealists believe that i. arises from the poet's observations of his own suppressed desires, but they also stress an objective factor—the observation of conflicts in society and the economic and political conditions from which the poet rebels. Thus the surrealists have reverted to the position of Blake in his *Marriage of Heaven and Hell* and (in fact) of Heraclitus (fl. 504 B.C.). Herbert Read, who describes surrealism as "the resurgence of romanticism" in the essay listed in the Bibliography (below), says that with the aid of Marx and Freud the surrealists have arrived at a scientific basis for creative activity in terms of its own dynamics.

But even in the midst of this, Croce can still refer to the theory of external i.: "The person of the poet is an Aeolian harp which the wind of the universe causes to vibrate." The problem of the poetic mind is still a mystery. See also IMAGINATION, WIT.

G. E. Woodberry, *The I. of Poetry* (1910; Lowell Lectures); F. C. Prescott, *The Poetic Mind* (1922); R. M. Ogden, *The Psychology of Art* (1938); Gilbert and Kuhn (see index); A. H. Gilbert, *Lit. Crit. from Plato to Dryden* (1940; see index); N. K. Chadwick, *Poetry and Prophecy* (1942); J.W.H. Atkins, *Eng. Lit. Crit., Medieval Phase* (1943); R. Harding, *An Anatomy of I.* (3d ed., 1948; a "case book," somewhat similar to Ghiselin's *The Creative Process*); H. Read, "Surrealism and the Romantic Principle," *Crit.*, ed. M. Schorer, J. Miles, G. McKenzie (1948); H.J.C. Grierson, *Crit. and Creation* (1949); W. Fowlie, *Age of Surrealism* (1950); B. Ghiselin, *The Creative Process* (1952; a "case book," testimonies from mathematicians, musicians, novelists, painters, philosophers, poets, psychologists. Dryden and Mozart earliest); Abrams; C. M. Bowra, *I. and Poetry* (1955; see opening article). A.R.B.

INSTRESS. See INSCAPE AND INSTRESS.

INVERSION. (a) Rhetoric: turning an opponent's argument against him; (b) Grammar: reversal of normal word order, for the sake of meter ("Thus ceased she: and the mountain shepherds came" [Shelley]), rhyme scheme, or emphasis ("Down comes the winter rain—" [Hardy]). I. is often frowned upon as a device for securing emphasis, though it is frequently used. (c) Prosody: commonly the turning about of a foot by substituting stressed for unstressed, unstressed for stressed syllables, e.g., using a trochee for an iamb in iambic verse:

Catcht by|Conta|gion, like|in pun|ishment
(Milton, *Paradise Lost* 10.544).

In traditional Eng. verse inversion of stress is a common device for securing variation, occurring most frequently in the initial foot and often immediately after the caesura, only very rarely in the final foot. Efforts by prosodists to limit the term to its meaning in the sense of reversed word order seem unrealistic. R.O.E.

IONIC. The origin of this verse form was associated with the Ionians of Asia Minor who appear to have used it in the orgiastic worship of Dionysus and Cybele. The greater I. foot (*ionicus a maiore*) was composed of 2 long followed by 2 short syllables (– – ⏑ ⏑), whereas in the lesser I. (*ionicus a minore*) the 2 short preceded the 2 long syllables (⏑ ⏑ – –). Ionics were employed by some of the Gr. lyric poets (especially Anacreon) and by the tragedians, particularly Euripides, whether in monometers, dimeters, trimeters, or tetrameters (including galliambics). Horace, *Odes* 3.12, furnishes a good instance of lesser Ionics in a longish sequence:

miserārum est|neque amōrī|dare lūdum|neque dulcī, etc.,

where the frequency of diaeresis may be noted. The use of regular *ionici a maiore* seems to have originated in the Hellenistic period, and in Latin an example is provided by Varro, *Satirae Menippeae* 489. An instance in Eng. poetry of lesser I. trimeter is Browning's "In the midnight, in the silence of the sleep-time."—J. W. White, *The Verse of Gr. Comedy* (1912); Hardie; Hamer; Dale; B. Gentili, "Gli ionici a maiore nella poesia greca," *Maia*, 2 (1949); Koster; P. Habermann, "Antike Versmasse," *Reallexikon*, 2d ed., I. R.J.G.

IRONY. (Gr. *eironeia*, originally, "dissimulation," especially through understatement). The *eiron* of Gr. comedy was the underdog, weak but clever, who regularly triumphed over the stupid and boastful *alazon*. The later usage of the term shows the influence of its origin. In Plato's *Dialogues*, for example, Socrates acts the part of an *eiron*. His questions seem naive, often pointless, and even foolish; in the end, however, it is Socrates' antagonist whose case is demolished. Hence the term *Socratic irony*.

Classical rhetoricians distinguished several varieties of i. In i. proper, the speaker is conscious of double meaning and the victim unconscious; in sarcasm both parties understand the double meaning. Other forms include meiosis and litotes (understatement); hyperbole (overstatement); antiphrasis (contrast); asteism and charientism (forms of the joke); chleuasm (mockery); mycterism (the sneer); mimesis (imitation, especially for the sake of ridicule). Depending on their use, pun, paradox, conscious naiveté, parody, etc. can all be ironic. Renaissance critics inherited the whole cumbersome schema of figures worked out by classical rhetoricians. They added little to the critical understanding of i. during the 16th and 17th c. On the other hand, baroque poets and dramatists exploited i. more fully and more consciously than their predecessors. They bequeathed a generally ironic point of view to the writers of the 18th c. In Voltaire and Addison i. is frequently a device for avoiding commitment—perhaps a reflection of skepticism and rationalism. In Swift, one of the great ironists, it is the masque of a *saeva indignatio* directed against the complacency of the age.

To the German romantics (Schlegel, Tieck, Solger) i. was a means of expressing the paradoxical nature of reality. Since it expressed two meanings simultaneously it could suggest the polarities (e.g., absolute vs. relative; subjective vs. objective; mental categories vs. *Ding an sich*) which post-Kantian philosophy found everywhere in experience. *Romantic i.* is a special form of irony described by Tieck and practiced most notably by Jean-Paul Richter and Heinrich Heine: the writer creates an illusion, especially of beauty, and suddenly destroys it by a change of tone, a personal comment, or a violently contradictory sentiment.

Modern discussions have tended to emphasize two main categories of i.: simulation (verbal i.) and dramatic i.

Verbal i. is a form of speech in which one meaning is stated and a different, usually antithetical, meaning is intended. In understatement the expressed meaning is mild, and the intended meaning intense; as, for example, Mercutio's comment on his death-wound, "No, 'tis not so deep as a well, nor so wide as a church door; but 'tis enough, 'twill serve." In overstatement, a device especially common in Am. folk humor, the reverse is true. Often a statement becomes ironic because of its context. When one looks out of his window at a rain storm and remarks to a friend, "Wonderful day, isn't it?" the statement can only be understood in an ironic sense. When Hamlet rejects the idea of suicide with the remark, "Thus conscience does make cowards of us all," his remark is unconsciously ironic because *conscience* is a sacramental word associated with moral goodness, whereas *coward* has pejorative connotations. The same kind of i. is illustrated in Comus' speech of seduction, where a true principle (natural fertility) is used to prove an untrue doctrine (libertinism). Often, i. can arise from explicit or implicit contradiction, as when Marvell begins his proposition to his coy mistress with the remark that time is short, and ends with the observation that love can make time pass more quickly ("Thus, though we cannot make our sun / Stand still, yet we will make him run.") Finally, foreshadowing is often ironic. Hamlet's speech on the fall of the sparrow has one meaning in its immediate context and a somewhat different one when considered in connection with Hamlet's own "fall" at the end of the scene.

Naiveté is a special form of i. half way between verbal and dramatic i. Basically, it is a pose of innocence or simplicity. Socrates used it; it appears frequently in the literature stemming from St. Paul's remark that the wisdom of God is the folly of this world, and the wisdom of this world is the folly of God. The tradition of ironic naiveté can be traced in *The Praise of Folly,* Shakespeare's fools and clowns, *Gulliver's Travels,* Blake's *Songs of Innocence,* Dickens' *Barnaby Rudge,* Dostoevski's *Idiot,* and Faulkner's *Sound and the Fury.* An extremely rudimentary example of this form of i. is the stanza,

> The golf links lie so near the mill
> That almost every day
> The laboring children can look out
> And see the men at play.
> (Sarah N. Cleghorn)

Dramatic i. is a plot device according to which (a) the spectators know more than the protagonist; (b) the character reacts in a way contrary to that which is appropriate or wise; (c) characters or situations are compared or contrasted for ironic effects, such as parody; (d) there is a marked contrast between what the character understands about his acts and what the play demonstrates about them.

Tragedy is especially rich in all forms of dramatic i. The necessity for a sudden reversal or catastrophe in the fortunes of the hero (Aristotle's *peripety,* which, he said, is found in all true tragedy) means that the fourth form of i. (form d) is almost inevitable. *Oedipus Rex* piles i. on i. For example, form (a) is present because of the fact that the audience becomes increasingly conscious as the play progresses that Oedipus is rushing blindly to his doom. Form (b) is present because of Oedipus' insistence on pursuing his investigation to its bitter climax (and the fact that his basic motivation is a desire for justice and public welfare is a further i.—his fall is in part caused by his nobility). Form (c) is illustrated in the parallel between blind Tiresias (who can "see" morally) and the figure of Oedipus when he, too, has gained "vision" after blinding himself. Form (d) is, of course, present in the contrast between what Oedipus hopes to accomplish and what he finally does accomplish.

Among later ironists, Chaucer, Montaigne, Shakespeare, Voltaire, Swift, Fielding, Flaubert, Henry James, and Thomas Hardy are especially noteworthy, although this list can only suggest the richness and variety of dramatic i. Shakespeare's plays, because of their multiplicity of characters and fluid act and scene structure abound in dramatic i. of form (c); and often several characters are placed in analogous situations, so that their reactions ironically contrast with each other (e.g., the lovers in *As You Like It*). The 19th-c. determinists often emphasize "i. of fate," by which is meant the contrast between the individual's conscious aspirations and what fate (or biology or society or psychology or the "immanent will") eventually makes of him.

Cosmic i. is the contrast between man's feverish efforts and the indifferent universe, as in Hardy's *The Dynasts.*

A variety of reasons can be given for the presence of i. in literature. J. H. Robinson, for example, says that man is a child and a savage, the victim of conflicting desires. Man may talk like a sentimental idealist and act like a brute. "Human thought and conduct, can only," he says, "be treated broadly and truly in a mood of tolerant irony." Certain literary critics in the 20th c., including I. A. Richards, Cleanth Brooks, and Robert Penn Warren, have insisted that the truly good poem or work of fiction employs a method of i., in the sense that a writer is aware that his proposition or belief may be relative to opposed propositions and beliefs and, being aware, he expresses a temper of mind and employs a language that is necessarily ironic. Kenneth Burke has said that i. is especially common in 20th-c. literature, and the reason, as he has it, is that we live with "relativistic sciences," like psychology and anthropology, which have tended to undermine once stable values. Whether Burke is correct or not, it remains true that the ironic attitude is common in modern literature. Possibly it is a safe generalization to say that periods in which religious and social opinions are relatively homogeneous will feel less need for the skeptical and ironic mind, but even in such periods i. functions as an agent of qualification and refinement.

J.A.K. Thomson, *I., an Historical Introd.* (1926); G. G. Sedgwick, *Of I., Especially in the Drama* (1935); C. Brooks, *Modern Poetry and the Tradition* (1939); D. Worcester, *The Art of Satire* (1940); W. Van O'Connor, *Sense and Sensibility in Modern Poetry* (1948); Wellek; Wimsatt and Brooks; G. Dempster, *Dramatic I. in Chaucer* (1959); R. B. Sharpe, *I. in the Drama* (1959); I. Strohschneider-Kohrs, *Die romantische Ironie in Theorie und Gestaltung* (1960); N. D. Knox, *The Word "I." and its Context, 1500–1755* (1961). W.V.O'C.

ISOCHRONISM. The equality of successive temporal units. In prosody, the assumption that meter (q.v.) consists of a succession of equal-time units (feet, lines, stanzas), said to be isochronous. I. is a term frequently employed by accentual and temporal prosodists (as distinguished from syllabic or accentual-syllabic prosodists) and by those theorists who describe the phonetic phenomena of verse in musical terms. Many maintain that Eng. is a naturally isochronous language, characterized by "a tendency to squeeze units into relatively equal time spans, marked by stress pulses" (S. Chatman, "Robert Frost's 'Mowing': An Inquiry into Prosodic Structure," KR, 18 [1956], 421–38). Those committed to i. as a prosodic assumption (these theorists are sometimes called "stress-timers") hold that a dissyllabic and a trisyllabic foot occupy equal intervals of time. See PROSODY. P.F.

ITALIAN PROSODY. See ROMANCE PROSODY.

J

JINGLE. Any verse which pleases the car by catchy rhythm and pronounced sound-repetitions, as rhyme or alliteration, usually at the expense of sense. *Eeny meeny miny mo* and *hickory dickory dock* are jingles. Because they are easily memorized and repeated, jingles are often as enduring as the loftiest poetry. Mark Twain in "Punch, Brothers, Punch" (*Tom Sawyer Abroad, . . . and Other Stories*) humorously describes his "catching" and passing on a contagious newspaper jingle. The term is sometimes depreciatively applied to any poetry which makes pronounced use of sound-effects. Addison (*Spectator* no. 297) criticizes Milton for often affecting "a kind of Jingle in his Words" in *Paradise Lost.*—*The Oxford Book of Nursery Rhymes,* ed. I. and P. Opie (1951). L.P.

JONGLEUR. A wandering musician and entertainer of the Middle Ages, somewhat analogous in function to the Anglo-Saxon scop (q.v.) or to the minstrel, *trouvère,* or troubadour (qq.v.) of a later era. Although the word dates only from the 8th c., jongleurs seem to have existed in France from the 5th c. to the 15th. In the earlier period the name was applied indiscriminately to acrobats, actors, and entertainers in general, as well as to musicians and reciters of verse. From the 10th c, on, however, the term is confined to musicians and reciters of verse, largely because the church favored them.

At one time the terms "j." and "troubadour" seem to have been used interchangeably; later, however, as the gulf between creative and performing artist deepened, the term "j." came to denote an entertainer who presented material not of his own composition. Material drawn from the great *chansons de geste* (q.v.) often formed an important part of the jongleur's repertoire. The jongleurs were of great importance in the transmission of medieval literary forms from one country to another.—E. Faral, *Les Jongleurs en France au moyen âge* (1910); P. Wareman, *Spielmannsdichtung. Versuch einer Begriffsbestimmung* (1951); R. Menéndez Pidal, *Poesía juglaresca* y origenes de las literaturas románicas (6th rev. and enl. ed., 1957); M. Valency, *In Praise of Love* (1958). F.J.W.; A.P.

K

KENNING (pl. *kenningar*). An implied simile in circumlocution for a noun not named; a feature of the diction used with Old Germanic prosody (q.v.). It ranges in kind from stereotyped descriptive compound epithets varying the plain name of a thing (*dispenser of rings*: *lord*) to complex metaphorical periphrases, especially in skaldic verse (*sea of Odin's breast*: *divine mead of inspiration*: *poem*), and thence beyond legitimate poetic functions, through more and more turgid conceits, into affectation and enigma. In such highly formulaic poetry as the Old Germanic, the kenningar were sometimes, understandably enough, petrified expressions which might not be especially appropriate to a given poetic need; but in the best poetry they were more frequently portmanteau devices whose suggestive associations deserve to be unpacked with care. The most familiar k. encase perceptions of some delicacy or power (*God's beacon*: *sun; foamy-necked floater*: *ship under sail; joy of a bird*: *feather*). Very different values are conveyed by these apparently similar k. for "sea, ocean," all used in *Beowulf*: *windgeard* "enclosure or home of the winds": the sea, its storms, its difference from other kinds of "yards" on land, its aspect as an area to be traversed by sailing ships; *ganotes bæo* "bath of the gannet": a shoreward salt-water area where the sea-fowl dips, fishes, sports, bathes; *hronrád* "riding place of the whale": not "the whale's road," but the great open ocean where the whale rides massively, impressively.—R. Meissner, *Die K. der Skalden* (1921); H. Van der Merwe Scholtz, *The K. in Anglo-Saxon and ON Poetry* (1927); M. Marquardt, *Die altenglischen K.* (1938); C. Brady, "The Synonyms for 'Sea' in *Beowulf*," in *Studies in Honor of Albert Morey Sturtevant* (1952); D. C. Collins, "The Kenning in Anglo-Saxon Poetry," E&S, 12 (1959). J.B.B.

KNITTELVERS (also *Knüttelvers, Knüppelvers, Klippelvers*). A derogatory name ("badly knit verse," doggerel) applied by Opitz and other classical poets of the 17th c. to a popular meter of 15th- and 16th-c. German poetry. K. consists of lines of 4 stresses each, rhyming in couplets; in its earlier form (*freier K.*) the meter uses an indeterminate number of unstressed syllables (as in *Christabel* meter, q.v.), but as employed by Hans Sachs and others in the 16th c. the meter (*strenger K.*) contained a regular total of 8 or 9 syllables per line. The reforms of the Opitzian school resulted in the substitution of the French-derived alexandrine (q.v.) for the 4-beat line, but K. was revived in the 18th c. by Gottsched, who restricted it to comic effects, and by Schiller (*Wallensteins Lager*) and most notably by Goethe (*Hans Sachsens poetische Sendung;* the older parts of *Faust* 1.).

Habe nun, ach! Philosophie,
Juristerei und Medizin,
Und leider auch Theologie
Durchaus studiert, mit heissem Bemühn.
Da steh ich nun, ich armer Tor!
Und bin so klug als wie zuvor.
(Goethe, *Faust* 1.354–59).

Later poets who used the meter include Gerhard Hauptmann.—O. Flohr, *Gesch. des Knittelverses vom 17. Jh. bis zur Jugend Goethes* (1893); A. Heusler, *Deutsche Versgesch.*, III (1929); W. Kayser, *Gesch. des deutschen Verses* (1960).

L

LAI (Fr.), lay (Eng.). A short lyrical or narrative poem. (1) The oldest lyric *lais* in OF are by Gautier de Dargies who flourished in the first third of the 13th c. The l. is addressed to an earthly lady, or to the Virgin, but it differs from other poems of this theme by having varying rhymes and syllable counts in its stanzas, without refrain. One of the most interesting by Ernoul le Vieux has no love theme; it is the *Lai de l'ancien et du nouveau testament.* It is not certain that l. and *descort* are the same thing. (2) The oldest narrative *lais,* almost always written in octosyllabic verse, are the *contes* or short romantic tales originated by Marie de France in the third quarter of the 12th c. She had Breton themes for most of these, but a few of them are based on local traditions and folk elements. Later the term "l." became synonymous with *conte.* As for the origin of l., some authorities believe that the word is derived from a Celtic form similar to Old Ir. *loid* (song). (3) The term "Breton lay" was applied in 14th-c. England to poems set in Brittany, written in a spirit similar to that of Marie's, or, often, simply because the poem says so. About a dozen Breton lays are extant in Eng., among them *Sir Orfeo, Sir Launfal, Emare,* and Chaucer's *Franklin's Tale.* Since the 16th c. "lay" has been used for song, and in the early 19th c. the term was sometimes used for a short historical ballad, e.g., Scott's *Lay of the Last Minstrel.—Lais et descorts fr. du XIIIe s.,* ed. A. Jeanroy and others (1901); E. Hoepffner, *Les Lais de Marie de France* (1935) and "The Breton Lais," *Arthurian Lit. in the Middle Ages,* ed. R. S. Loomis (1959). U.T.H.

LAISSE. In the OF epics or *chansons de geste* (q.v.) this is a stanzaic, or paragraph, division of no specified length. The length of each l. depends upon the emphasis which the poet wishes to make. Each of these divisions has its own assonance, or—in later poems—rhyme. Sometimes the content of a l. would be repeated item for item in one or two following *laisses,* with differing assonance or rhyme, of course. Such repetitions are called *laisses similaires.*—A. Monteverdi, "La Laisse epique," Liège Université. Faculté de philosophie et lettres. *La Technique littéraire des chansons de geste* (1959). U.T.H.

LAMENT. A nonnarrative type of poetry, arising as part of oral tradition, expressing profound regret, sorrow, or concern for a loss of a person or, sometimes, position. The l. seems to have arisen alongside heroic poetry and exists in almost all languages, including Hebrew, Chinese, Zulu.

> Ye daughters of Israel, weep over Saul, who
> clothed you in scarlet . . .
> *David's lament for Saul and Jonathan,*
> 1017 B.C.(?)

> Thou hast finished, finished the nations,
> Where wilt thou go forth to battle now?
> J. Shooter, *The Kafirs of Natal* (1857).

In *Deor's Lament* (Anglo-Saxon) the scop regrets his change of status, having been displaced in the favor of his patron by a rival. Many poems which rely heavily on the *ubi sunt* theme are, in a general sense, laments. Also the separate tragedies in the *Mirror for Magistrates,* wherein a ghost relates the story of his fall from fortune, were called laments (e.g., Sackville's "Lament" for the Duke of Buckingham), and so were in Scotch and Ir. folk music the airs used on occasions of mourning. Any dirge or mournful type of complaint (qq.v.). The essential characteristic seems to be the sense of personal loss.—Chadwick; C. M. Bowra, *Heroic Poetry* (1952). R.O.E.

LEONINE RHYME. Strictly used, the term means a disyllabic rhyme of the last syllable of the second foot and the first syllable of the third foot, with the two syllables of the sixth foot of a Latin hexameter. More commonly it indicates the rhyme of the word preceding the caesura with the final word in both hexameters and pentameters. Although known in classical L. (e.g., Ovid, *Ars Amatoria* 1.59), it was not greatly favored. But around the 12th c. writers began to cultivate it assiduously as, for instance, Bernard of Cluny in his *De Contemptu Mundi* (in couplets). It was used in particular as a mnemonic device and for epitaphs, e.g., "Hac sunt in fossa, Bedae venerabilis ossa." It also appears in the OE *Rhyming Poem,* where it contributed to the decline of the long line of alliterative verse by tending to break the verse into two hemistichs. Some attribute the name to Leoninus, canon of St. Victor's in Paris (12th c.); others to Pope Leo.—Schipper; H. G. Atkins, *A Hist. of German Versification* (1923); J. W. Draper, "The Origin of Rhyme," RLC, 31 (1957; finds l. r. in the *Gāthās* and *Yashts* of the *Avesta*); F. J. E. Raby, *A Hist. of Secular L. Poetry in the Middle Ages* (2d ed., 2 v., 1957). R.A.H.

LIGHT VERSE. A name rather loosely given to a wide variety of types or forms of metrical composition, worldly in character and most often witty, humorous, ingenious, or satirical. Among the kinds of poem that fall into this category are *vers de société,* occasional verse, satire, burlesque, the mock heroic, nonsense poetry; such brief forms as the epigram, the comic or ironic epitaph, the limerick, and the clerihew; and all types of tricky and ingenious verse as acrostics, shaped or emblematic poems, alliterative or rhyming *tours de force,* riddles, puns, and other forms of versified trivia. Usually a certain standard of excellence, or at least competence, in the handling of verse forms is assumed in the writer of l.v., and a certain finish or polish is characteristic of this kind of poetry no matter how trivial its subject or frivolous its treatment. Elegance, polish, and refinement of taste can sometimes impart a serious poetic significance to l.v., particularly, for example, in the Petrarchan love poems of the 16th c., the Cavalier lyrics of the 17th. or the satirical heroic couplets of the 18th.

An interesting early attempt to define l.v. was made by Frederick Locker-Lampson in the Preface to his anthology *Lyra Elegantiarum* (London, 1867). This Victorian anthologist limits his consideration to *vers de société* and the elegant classicism of aristocratic poetry mainly in the traditions of Anacreon, Theocritus, or Horace, but his analysis is sound and illuminating as far as it goes. Locker-Lampson begins by distinguishing his collection of l.v. from the many popular collections of "sentimental, heroic, humourous, juvenile, and devotional" poems. He then describes the limits and province of his anthology and in doing so supplies us with an excellent, if necessarily restricted, working definition of l.v. He calls it "another kind of poetry which was more in vogue in the reign of Queen Anne, and, indeed, in Ante-Reform Bill times, than it is at the present day; a kind which, in its more restricted form, has somewhat the same relation to the poetry of lofty imagination and deep feeling, that the Dresden China Shepherds and Shepherdesses of the last century bear to the sculpture of Donatello and Michael Angelo; namely, smoothly written verse, where a boudoir decorum is, or ought always to be, preserved; where sentiment never surges into passion, and where humour never overflows into boisterous merriment." The characteristics of l.v. here distinguished are elegance, decorum, moderation, neatness of expression, perfection of form, and coolness of sentiment and tone. This is the classical respect for the golden mean, an Horatian, or more precisely, an Addisonian ideal, with just an overtone also of Victorian squeamishness. The writers of verse who fit into it most comfortably would be such men as Campion, Herrick, Lovelace, Prior, Goldsmith, Cowper, Oliver Wendell Holmes, W. M. Praed, C. S. Calverley, and Austin Dobson. Many of the Elizabethan miscellanies and song books contain madrigals and other poems that would be considered light either by the standards of Locker-Lampson or of later critics. These can be conveniently sampled in the late 19th-c. collection edited by A. H. Bullen, *Lyrics from the Song-Books of the Elizabethan Age* (London, 1888). The more ribald, but often quite as smoothly turned verse of the 17th c. and the Restoration are represented in two other anthologies edited by Bullen, *Speculum Amantis* (1888) and *Musa Proterva* (1889). The nature of the verses collected by Bullen (or defined by Locker-Lampson) is well described in a prefatory quatrain on the flyleaf of *Musa Proterva:*

Gay, frolic verse for idle hours,
    Light as the foam whence Venus sprang;
Strains heard of old in courtly bowers,
    When Nelly danced and Durfey sang.

The Durfey referred to here is Thomas D'Urfey (1653–1723), one of the earliest and best collectors of l.v., his *Wit and Mirth, or Pills to Purge Melancholy* (1719) being an interesting collection of the comic and erotic songs of the Restoration period.

Locker-Lampson's definition limits itself to *vers de société.* The definition is amplified by some nice discriminations: l.v., the critic wrote, "should be short, graceful, refined, and fanciful, not seldom distinguished by chastened sentiment, and often playful. The tone should not be pitched high; it should be terse and idiomatic, and rather in the conversational key; the rhythm should be crisp and sparkling, and the rhyme frequent and never forced, while the entire poem should be marked by tasteful moderation, high finish and completeness. . . . The poem may be tinctured with a well-bred philosophy, it may be whimsically sad, it may be gay and gallant, it may be playfully malicious or tenderly ironical, it may display lively banter, and it may be satirically facetious; it may even, considered merely as a work of art, be pagan in its philosophy or trifling in its tone, but it must never be flat, or ponderous, or commonplace." Most of this is discriminating and accurate, but the limitations imposed are narrow and, the modern reader may feel, snobbish rather than genuinely aristocratic; and they lead the Victorian anthologist to exclude much that modern anthologists of l.v. (David McCord, Michael Roberts, J. M. Cohen, or W. H. Auden) would wish to include. One poem, for instance, is left out as being too broadly humorous, another as too satirical and savage, others as too pathetic, too serious, too homely, too fragmentary, or too lengthy. Comic poetry, as such, nonsense poetry, and the merely tricky or ingenious are excluded. More important, savage satire and bitter irony, because of their intensity, are outside the pale of l.v. *The Rape of the Lock* is l.v. (indeed, except for its length it might be considered as the ideal exemplar of what l.v. ought to be), but *The Dunciad* is not; the sophisticated urbanity of Prior and Gay is certainly light, but the savage indignation and cool ferocity of Swift is not. Popular folk poetry is excluded as being "low."

Modern criticism has widened (and deepened) the scope of what can be considered l.v. All of the categories excluded by the Victorian anthologist have, under certain circumstances, been considered by 20th-c. anthologists and critics to fall within the scope of l.v. The conditions are that the point of view should be worldly or secular, the finish polished or ingenious, and the attitude objective and superior; but the tone, particularly in satire, may be as intense or coarse as the occasion and purpose demand. Hard-boiled popular poetry and rough invective have been admitted into the canon, and while intellectual brilliance is still demanded of the writer of l.v., his social credentials are not nearly so strictly aristocratic. This wider view of the inclusiveness of l.v., and, indeed, of the "serious" import of kinds of poetry that have usually been thought of as merely casual or frivolous owes something perhaps to Freudian ideas of the significance of the insignificant. As Geoffrey Grigson remarked in the preface to his *New Verse Anthology,* "It is a fact that an epic and a limerick are poems. You cannot suppose a divine or an inspired origin for one against a secular or rational origin for the other. You can only distinguish in them differences of effect and quality." This is what W. H. Auden in the Introduction to the *Oxford Book of Light Verse* set himself to do. Like Grigson, Auden sees no *essential* distinction between the light and serious elements in poetry or between l.v. and serious poetry. The difference—or, more precisely, the source of the difference—lies in the relation between the author and society. "When the things in which the poet is interested, the things which he sees about him, are much the same as those of his audience, and that audience is a fairly general one, he will not be conscious of himself as an unusual person, and his language will be straightforward and close to ordinary speech."

The result is, Auden believes, that the verse of such a poet will be "light." It will fall into one of three categories, which Auden defines as follows: "(1) Poetry written for performance, to be spoken or sung before an audience, e.g. Folk Songs, the poems of Tom Moore. (2) Poetry intended to be read, but having for its subject-matter the everyday social life of its period or the experiences of the poet as an ordinary human being, e.g., the poems of Chaucer, Pope, Byron. (3) Such nonsense poetry as, through its properties and technique, has a general appeal, e.g. Nursery Rhymes, the poems of Edward Lear." Thus Auden seems to equate l.v., or, perhaps, what might better be called "light poetry," with classical poetry (in its more aristocratic aspects) and with popular balladry and folk song (in its more plebeian connections). The conditions postulated in the first two categories above favor the production of unadventurous descriptive verse and simple narrative, of convivial or amorous songs, and Tory satire, any of which may or may not be "light." As a result, the *Oxford Book of Light Verse* is a curious conglomeration of poetry and rhyme, ranging from doggerel street ballads to *The Rape of the Lock* and from medieval carols and Elizabethan madrigals to 19th-c. songs like *She was poor but she was honest.* The only element they have in common is that they are all extremely lively. Their "lightness" is due to the absence of pretentiousness, solemnity, and self-regard; and although the standards of excellence by which each poem must be judged are various, the excellence of each piece *as poetry* is never in doubt for the modern reader. That this should be so is due in part to the impact of the criticism of T. S. Eliot, especially to its emphasis on "unity of sensibility" and its precise analysis of the "wit" of the metaphysical poets. Indeed, the essential characteristic of genuine l.v. has been described by Mr. Eliot in defining the "wit" of Andrew Marvell's *To his Coy Mistress,* as "a tough reasonableness beneath the slight lyric grace" by which the seriousness of the poem is unexpectedly enhanced. "Tough reasonableness"—an absence of squeamishness, hard-headedness, good sense, intelligence, a sense of values, a rational worldliness—these are the qualities of attitude and tone which condition the spirit of l.v.; "slight lyric grace" (*slight* means *unostentatious*), verbal elegance, technical accomplishment, perfect and economical adaptation of means to ends—these are the formal requirements of the art.

L.v. can be regarded as *poetry at play.* Much of it is characterized by ingenuity and displays of technical virtuosity, particularly in the handling of complex meters and polysyllabic rhymes but also in the manipulation of intricate stanza forms and in the exploitation of verbal meanings, as in puns, and of verbal patterns involving tricks with syllables and letters, as in anagrams, palindromes, and *tours de force* of alliteration. Most of these devices have on occasion been used in serious poetry, as in Browning's skillful use of complex and divided rhymes or in some of the conceits of the 17th-c. metaphysical poets, but generally the display of technical and linguistic ingenuity for their own sake or in an unusual degree serves notice that the mind is at play and that what we have before us—if it escapes the abyss of the merely silly—is l.v. Complex and divided rhymes are found often in limericks, a neat example being the one that tells how "a great Congregational preacher" complimented a hen, which immediately laid an egg in his hat, and ends "Thus did the hen reward Beecher." W. S. Gilbert in his *Bab Ballads* and in the Savoy operas is a master of the comic effect of intricate rhymes, while among the moderns, Ogden Nash has added the effect of phonetic spelling to catch the rhyme and distort the word. Leigh Hunt wrote a piece of verse consisting of a series of triplets, the rhymes in each of them being achieved by dropping the initial letter from the word ending the previous line. The most famous and difficult display of ingenuity in alliteration is the poem by Alaric A. Watts that begins

> An Austrian army awfully arrayed
> Boldly by battery besieged Belgrade

and goes on with undiminished vigor through the whole alphabet. Other successful displays of "apt alliteration's artful aid" are found in parodies of Swinburne—Arthur C. Hilton's *Octopus,* Mortimer Collins' *Salad,* and Swinburne's own *Nephelidia,* and in such a quatrain as this from *The Mikado:*

> To sit in solemn silence in a dull dark dock,
> In a pestilential prison, with a life-long lock,
> Awaiting the sensation of a short sharp shock,
> From a cheap and chippy chopper on a big
> black block!

Not only verbal or metrical complexity but demanding stanzaic patterns and formal shapes have proved stimulating to writers of l.v. The strict and sometimes very difficult Fr. or It. forms, such as ballade, double ballade, rondeau, sestina, and the brief, fragile triolet (qq.v.) have all been used with considerable skill by writers of l.v., particularly in the production of *vers de société.* Certain Eng. writers of the 70's, 80's, and 90's of the last century wrote much that has charm and grace in these forms. Among them should be noted C. S. Calverley, W. E. Henley, Andrew Lang, and, most accomplished of all, Austin Dobson. Emblematic verses (verses whose shape on the printed page is imitative of the poem's theme) had been much in vogue among Eng. religious poets in the 16th and 17th c., but in the 20th c. the device came to be used occasionally by experimental poets—Guillaume Apollinaire in *Caligrammes* and E. E. Cummings *passim*—in l.v., that is not the less light because its intention is often serious.

Serious l.v., as it is found in British and Am. poetry in the 20th c., is not, of course, a modern invention nor an Eng. one. It is found at its purest in Horace and at its most intense in Catullus, Ovid, and Propertius. European romanticism proved favorable to one of its most fruitful sources of inspiration—the mixture of egoistic sensibility and ironic self-questioning that can be found in Byron and Heine alike and that came into modern poetry through Fr. poets of the latter half of the 19th c., particularly Théophile Gautier, Tristan Corbière, and Jules Laforgue. The influence of all these on the lighter side of Ezra Pound and T. S. Eliot is clear and unmistakable, while the *Homage to Propertius* and translations of lyrics from *Die Heimkehr* of Heine by Pound transmitted the quality of serious l.v. to later modern poets with inescapable gusto. Serious l.v. flourishes so richly today that one is tempted to see it as the characteristic expression of the modern temper. Among its authors, besides Eliot and Pound, are W. B. Yeats, E. E. Cummings, W. H. Auden, and many lesser figures.

L.v., in the more ordinary sense in which it is understood, as humorous, comic, or ingenious verse, is also very widely and skillfully produced. Among the best of the contemporary writers are Ogden Nash, Richard Armour, Phyllis McGinley, Franklin P. Adams, Morris Bishop, Arthur Guiterman, and David McCord in the United States, and Sir Owen Seaman, A. P. Herbert, and John Betjeman in England.

Anthologies: (nb: Items marked with an asterisk contain valuable critical material): *Wit and Mirth, or Pills to Purge Melancholy*, ed. T. D'Urfey (1719); **Lyra Elegantiarum,* ed. F. Locker-Lampson (1867); *Musa Proterva,* ed. A. H. Bullen (1889); **A Vers de Société Anthol.*, ed. C. Wells (1900); *Poetica Erotica,* ed. T. R. Smith (1921); *A Little Book of Am. Humorous Verse,* ed. T. A. Daly (1926); *An Anthol. of L.V.*, ed. L. Kronenberger (1935); **The Oxford Book of L.V.*, ed. W. H. Auden (1938); **The Faber Book of Comic Verse,* ed. M. Roberts (1942); *The Stag's Hornbook,* ed. J. McClure (2d ed., 1943); **What Cheer,* ed. D. McCord (1945); * *The Worldly Muse,* ed. A.J.M. Smith (1951); *Comic and Curious Verse,* ed. J. M. Cohen (1952); *Verse and Worse,* ed. A. Silcock (1952); *The Silver Treasury of L.V.*, ed. O. Williams (1957); *The Fireside Book of Humorous Poetry,* ed. W. Cole (1959).

General: L. Untermeyer, *Play in Poetry* (1938); R. Armour, *Writing L.V.* (1947). A.J.M.S.

LIMERICK. A verse form composed of 5 lines rhyming aabba, of which the first, second, and fifth are trimeter and the third and fourth dimeter. Occasionally it is written in 4 lines, the third line being in tetrameter with invariable internal rhyme. The dominant rhythm is anapestic, and the final line is often a repetition, or varied repetition, of the first, as in the following example by Edward Lear (*Book of Nonsense,* 1846), the unquestioned master of the form:

There was an Old Man of the Dee,
Who was sadly annoyed by a Flea;
When he said, "I will scratch it,"
They gave him a hatchet,
Which grieved that Old Man of the Dee.

The l. is unique in that it is the only Eng. stanza form used exclusively for light verse. Always comic, it is often nonsensical and frequently bawdy. Theories concerning its origin range from the belief that it was an old Fr. form brought to the Ir. town of Limerick in 1700 by returning veterans of the Fr. war to the theory that it originated in the nursery rhymes published as *Mother Goose Melodies for Children* (1719). What is certain is that the l. may be found in a volume entitled *The History of Sixteen Wonderful Old Women,* published by J. Harris in 1821, and in *Anecdotes and Adventures of Fifteen Gentlemen,* published by John Marshall about 1822 and possibly written by one R. S. Sharpe. The latter volume is cited by Lear as having given him the idea for his l. Whatever its origin, the l. has a secure, if eccentric, place in the history of Eng. verse. In the wake of Lear such notable authors as Tennyson, Swinburne, Kipling, Stevenson, and W. S. Gilbert attempted the form, and by the beginning of the 20th c. it had become a veritable fashion in England. The etymology of the term "l.," never used by Lear, is unknown.

The chief tendency in the modern l., as exemplified in the practice of the Am. light poet Morris Bishop, has been the development of the final line for purposes of surprise or witty reversal, in place of the simply repeated last line of Lear's day. See also LIGHT VERSE, NONSENSE VERSE, CLERIHEW.—*Dict. of Nursery Rhymes,* ed. I. and P. Opie (1951); C. Fadiman, *Any Number Can Play* (1957). F.J.W.; A.P.

LINE. A formal structural division of a poem, consisting of one or more feet arranged as a separate rhythmical entity. The line, as Brooks and Warren point out, is a "unit of attention," but it is not necessarily a unit of sense: in fact, poems are rather rare in which individual lines constitute complete sense units. For this reason, line divisions, unless they happen to coincide with sense pauses (whether indicated by punctuation or not), are often as unrelated to the rhetoric of poetic assertions as foot divisions. Lines are commonly classified according to their length in feet:

monometer	a line of 1 foot	
dimeter	2 feet	
trimeter	3 feet	
tetrameter	4 feet	
pentameter	5 feet	
hexameter	6 feet	(see also ALEXANDRINE)
heptameter	7 feet	
octameter	8 feet	

Because the memory can retain a rhythmical pattern of only a limited duration, heptameters and longer lines tend to receive from reader or hearer an unconscious restructuring: the heptameter commonly breaks into a tetrameter and a trimeter (as in ballad meter, q.v.), the octameter into two tetrameters, and so on. Line divisions frequently function like foot divisions in providing a form of counterpoint (q.v.) to the rhetorical and syntactical design in a poem. Although generalization on this point is traditionally hazardous, it may be suggested that short lines (trimeter and shorter) tend to imply levity of tone, and that the pentameter line (or a line of similar duration, measured by whatever system of scansion) has proved the most flexible in Eng.—Baum; Brooks and Warren. P.F.

LINE ENDINGS. Divided prosodically into two general types depending upon the position of the final stress in relation to the other syllables near the end of the iambic or anapestic line. A *masculine ending* (generally productive of an effect of some force or weight) has the stress on the final syllable of the line:

Upon the moon I fixed my eye
(Wordsworth, *Strange Fits of Passion* 9)

A *feminine ending* has the last stress on the penultimate (or even the antepenultimate) syllable and most often requires terminal extrametrical syllables:

Whatever ails me, now a-late especially,

I can as well be hanged as refrain seeing her
(Middleton, *The Changeling* 2.1)

Feminine ending is very common in the blank verse of the Elizabethan and Jacobean drama, where it is frequently used to give the verse a suggestion of colloquial informality, lightness, or irregularity. The term *weak ending* is sometimes used to describe masculine ending with a secondary (instead of primary) degree of stress. Marianne Moore's *In Distrust of Merits* is full of weak endings. See TRUNCATION.—P. W. Timberlake, *The Feminine Ending in Eng. Blank Verse* (1931). P.F.

LINGUISTICS AND POETICS. The study of a literary work of art, like that of any organized form, requires for its proper conduct a knowledge of the principles according to which such works are constructed and a theory by means of which these principles can be ordered into some rational and consistent whole. Since Aristotle's classic work on the subject, the study of these principles and theories has been designated by the name "poetics." Poetics, so understood, is thus the most general, hence fundamental, discipline of literary criticism in its widest sense. Inasmuch as it is language which lies at the base of literary studies, it is not surprising that scholars and literary theorists of various backgrounds and persuasions have explored the linguistic characteristics of literary works of art in formulating their particular systems of poetics. It would thus be possible in an article on linguistics and poetics to discuss at some length the contributions of Leo Spitzer, Dámaso Alonso, Amado Alonso, and various other scholars and critics. Since, however, this article is concerned primarily with post-Bloomfieldian linguistics, only passing mention can be made of their contributions.

Just as we may say of linguistics that it is the study of language and intend thereby that it is the study of its principles of organization and of explanatory theories, so we may, similarly for reasons of convenience—and also for the purposes of this Handbook, which is limited to poetry—refer to poetics simply as the study of poetry. On these assumptions, it would appear, inasmuch as language is the medium of poetry, that l. and poetics have (at least in part) a common function. But this conclusion requires some consideration. For, granting that language is the medium of poetry, a poem's status as a linguistic production is nonetheless different from the status of ordinary language productions. The task is thus to ascertain whether any but purely linguistic factors contribute to the different status which a poem enjoys and then, to the extent to which the answer to this question is negative, to determine whether the theories and techniques of l., designed as they are to deal with ordinary language productions, are adequate to the linguistic analysis of poetry.

Of the various views that have been advanced concerning extralinguistic contributory factors, only one will be specifically considered here, namely, the view which would attribute the poem's different status to special psychological sets or responses on the part of the reader (or hearer). The discussion of this view, however, may be taken as paradigmatic for all other extralinguistic factors which might be adduced to explain this special quality of a poem.

It is not ordinarily in the province of l. to deal with psychological sets or responses. But if the poem induces psychological responses beyond those of ordinary communication, then one may reasonably expect to find some linguistic feature or features in the poem to correlate with these responses. If such responses occur for which no linguistic correlate is to be found in the poem, then they would seem to constitute data for psychologists, not linguists. If it should be asserted that such responses in fact constitute the given data of poetics, then there can be no argument from the side of l.; l. simply has nothing to say about them. Further, a psychological set, or *Einstellung,* would seem to be significant only if the reading of the poem sustains that set, and here again one might expect to find correlating linguistic features in the poem. In this case, too, if no linguistic correlation can be established, l. gives over to some other line of inquiry. The approach suggested here has the virtue that it implicitly establishes a hierarchy of validity for critical judgments. From the point of view of l., those judgments that can be supported by linguistic correlates naturally occupy a higher rank in the hierarchy than do those that cannot.

According primacy to those critical judgments for which support can be found in the language of the poem resembles the practice in certain contemporary critical approaches which maintain that the poem must be judged in terms of itself alone. But this view of the New Criticism embodies a response to a poem not merely in terms of the reader's linguistic capabilities, but also in terms of his critical faculties and sensibilities. Linguistic analysis of poetry does not insist on this added requirement. Insofar as it is feasible, linguistic analysis of poetry is usually content to accept the judgments of literary critics, to whom superiority of response is accorded, on the basis of their experience, sensitivity, and general critical capacity, and then to set out and find linguistic correlates for these judgments. If such attempts are made and fail, then two inferences are possible: either the critical responses are occasioned by extralinguistic factors, or the failure to find linguistic support for them reflects present inadequacies in linguistic theory or techniques. Only in this way, by more and more intensive linguistic analyses attempting to explain various critical responses, can the question be settled of whether a poem's special status is due exclusively to linguistic factors.

Whether a poem's special status is a function of its language alone thus remains to be demonstrated. Some linguists, however, tend to proceed on the assumption that it is. In doing so they are not necessarily making a factual claim to this effect—although some of them do. It is rather that a good many critical statements that are purportedly historical, cultural, or biographical, or, alternatively, mythic, doctrinaire, or aesthetic are held by linguists to be prompted *immediately* by the language in a poem, and it is the language that thus deserves the most immediate systematic study. In the same way a good many value statements may turn out to have linguistic correlates in the poem and, that being the case, it is certainly advisable to describe the latter. Thus, while the question of whether, ultimately, the impact of a poem can be explained entirely in terms of its linguistic composition is obviously one of great theoretical interest, it is clear that a good deal of significant work can be done in the linguistic analysis of poetry without waiting to see whether and how the question will finally be answered.

From the point of view of l., the more substantive question is whether or not the theories and techniques of linguistic analysis are adequate to deal with the purely linguistic aspects of poetry. The question immediately arises whether a poem is a manifestation of the same grammar as the grammar manifested by ordinary language utterances. This question has nothing to do with the presence in poetry of such conventional features as rhyme, meter, alliteration, etc., inasmuch as these features accompany a language which is independently distinctive. Since, for reasons of convenience and utility, l. has dealt largely with regular utterances, most linguistic descriptions or theories have resulted in or implied grammars such that poetry would fall outside their scope. This would make it appear that, for descriptive purposes at any rate, poetry is written according to grammatical rules that are different from the grammatical rules governing ordinary language utterances. It would of course be possible to revise grammatical descriptions or theories so as to take account of poetic utterances directly, by increasing the scope of the grammar. But such a course would have two disadvantages. In the first place the grammar would lose a good deal of its generality; in the second place, and more important from the point of view of poetics, this course would preclude the use of the grammar as a standard or norm against which to explain the way in which poetic language is distinctive. As a matter of fact, a good deal of recent work in linguistically oriented poetics has adopted the position, explicitly or implicitly, that poetic language is characterized by deviation from grammatical rules.

Another problem derives from the fact that most work in l. has proceeded on the assumption that the sentence is the highest-level linguistic unit about which grammatical statements can be made. L. Bloomfield's statement (*Language* [1933], p. 170) that ". . . each sentence is an independent linguistic form, not included by virtue of any grammatical construction in any larger linguistic form" has, as one of its corollaries, the fact that linguistic forms larger than the sentence, if they are unified at all, are unified by relations that are different from the relation of grammatical construction. Thus, while relations of some sort certainly bind sentences together into larger units, it is not yet sufficiently clear, from the point of view of linguistic analysis, just what these relations are. The measure for intra-sentence relations is grammaticality, for supra-sentence relations, coherence; and linguistic techniques for dealing with the latter are not yet very highly developed. Moreover, those supra-sentence relations which most immediately come to the linguist's mind—features like anaphora, tense sequence agreement, etc.—have little interest for stylistic analysis, inasmuch as they reflect, in the main, obligatory constraints.

There have been a few attempts to discover and account for supra-sentence relations. Z. Harris, in his "discourse analysis," has suggested techniques for judging sameness and difference of structure in the sentences making up a complete discourse ("Discourse Analysis," *Language*, 28 [1952], 1–30, and "Discourse Analysis: A Sample Text," *ibid.*, 474–94). More recently, M. W. Bloomfield and L. Newmark have adapted generative grammar to the generation of complete discourses (not merely sentences); cf. *A Linguistic Introduc. to the Hist. of Eng.* (1963), pp. 240, 260ff. Consistent with these procedures is the definition of style proposed by A. Hill, according to which it ". . . concerns all those relations among linguistic entities which are statable, or may be statable, in terms of wider spans than those which fall within the limits of the sentence" (*Introduc. to Linguistic Structures* [1958], pp. 406ff.). Levin's book (1962) is an attempt to describe the structure of poetry along these lines. It must be admitted, however, that in the area of discourse analysis (a poem being a discourse in this sense) l. has not yet gone very far. What is needed is to develop means for analyzing the linguistic devices which contribute to the coherence and unity of multi-sentence units, to ascertain what sort of inter-sentence relations these devices enter into, and then to determine the status and function of these devices in the general linguistic system. For a start in this direction, see M. Halliday, "The Linguistic Study of Literary Texts," *Proc. of the IXth International Congress of Linguists* (1964).

L. has dealt with poetic language on the levels of phonology, word, and syntax. Phonology is divided by l. into two aspects: segmental and suprasegmental (or prosodic). The former aspect deals with those phones (sounds) that appear in morphemes, words, and longer sequences composed of these units, whereas suprasegmental phonology deals with the dynamic features—stress, pitch, and juncture (pausal and transition phenomena)—that accompany the segmental units in the speech act. In actual language utterances, of course, segmental and suprasegmental features occur simultaneously. A morpheme, word, or longer stretch is accompanied by stress(es), pitch(es), and junctures. For purposes of analysis, however, these co-occurring features must first be separately isolated before their mutual relations and their function with the segmental material can be properly evaluated. In general, the study of segmental phonology in poetry is relevant to the question of sound-texture, and the study of suprasegmental phonology is relevant to the question of meter.

In this discussion sound-texture is understood as the texture imparted to a poem by various patterns and configurations of its segmental phones. The standard forms of such patterns and configurations are of course rhyme and devices like alliteration and assonance. Frequently, however, it is possible to discern less obvious phonological patterns in a poem, patterns which similarly play a constructive role in its organization. An attempt at codifying many such patterns is D. Masson, "Sound-Repetition Terms," *Poetics. Poetyka*, pp. 189–99. Analyses of the latter kind—in which vowels, consonants, diphthongs, and even distinctive features have been shown to pattern in some nonrandom way—have been carried out by Firth, Fónagy, Masson, Oras, and others. Findings of phonic pattern-regularity have a rather obvious bearing on the question of poetry's higher degree of textural density as well as on questions of greater organizational unity. On the assumption that sounds possess phonaesthetic properties, attempts have also been made to correlate such findings with judgments of a poem's tone or affective address. Other studies (J. Lynch, "The Tonality of Lyric Poetry: An Experiment in Method," *Word*, 9 [1953]; D. Hymes, "Phonological Aspects of Style: Some Eng. Sonnets," *Style in Language*, pp. 109–31) have gone further and have attempted to show that in certain sonnets and other short poems the phonic patterns thus found frequently converge in a single "summative" word occupying a strategic place in the poem. This pattern thus represents one mode in which form and meaning may be fused in poetry.

Metrics has been one of the most significant areas of convergence for l. and literary analysis. Concerned as it is with the phonological tissue of poetry—an isolatable and measurable thing—it has long attracted literary scholars who like exactness of statement and linguists who have aesthetic yearnings. At the turn of the present century, a great search was made for precision in metrics by means of what some might consider the ultimate sacrilege, the machine. The development of devices for analyzing speech sounds, like the Marey tambour (sometimes called the kymograph) and later the oscilloscope, led to mechanical displays of verse like those of Scripture and Schramm. Earlier workers (like Warner Brown, Ada Snell, P. Verrier, and Amos Morris) had exploded long-believed fictions like the literal equality of feet and the long-short dichotomy, but Scripture was the first to outline an entire theory of meter on a mechanical basis. Recognizing the phonetic complexity of metrical elements, he discarded the traditional identification of ictus with "stress," substituting the concept of "centroid" instead. The centroid was the sum of features like greater auditory impressiveness, intenser loudness, pitch change, slowed transition, and more precise pronunciation. Scripture's basic unit of description was the line: "a stretch of the verse-stream that coincides with the printed line." He denied the existence of feet, since they could not be found in the phonetic trace. Nor, for that matter, could one discover syllables in a trace—all that exists, he contended, is syllabicity. He developed an elaborate terminology to describe linear kinds, inventing such terms as "nucretic," "nudiambic," "nuclydonic," etc. His entire emphasis was to discover the vast variety of phenomena occurring in recited verse, and he was all too successful in his search.

Schramm also presented a visual display or "score" of verse performance, although his terminology was somewhat more conventional ("accent," "stress," etc.). Intonational curves, calibrated to the musical scale, were marked on one staff, and intensity was presented on a cotemporal one. Time was divided by vertical bars at one-second intervals. Unlike Scripture, Schramm continued to use the concept of foot—although he recognized its purely formal mode of existence—as a convenient tool of analysis.

Recent developments in acoustic phonetics (frequency and intensity analyzing machines) have made the mechanical analysis of verse performance much easier and more exact. But, at the same time, the rise of phonemic theory has shown the need to correlate physical data with the *system* that language is today universally recognized to be. Thus—and especially for metrical analysis—not raw phonetics but functional phonology, the system of linguistic sounds that mark semantic differences, must be consulted. The need was recognized as early as 1933 by Jakobson in words which laid the groundwork for modern metrics. Jakobson pointed out that meter could not be studied as a purely phonetic object: "Not the phone, but the phoneme as such is utilized as the cornerstone of verse." Although work had been carried on by European linguists like Mukařovský, Lotz, and de Groot, the first recognition and practical application of this notion to Eng. meter came in the 1950's in work by Whitehall, Hill, Chatman (1956), Epstein and Hawkes, and Smith. Whitehall, alone and in collaboration with Hill, first suggested the utility of structural linguistics to metrics and pointed to the Trager-Smith description of the Eng. stress system as an excellent vehicle for precision in metrical statement (G. L. Trager and H. L. Smith, Jr., *An Outline of Eng. Structure* [1951]). Chatman attempted the first application by analyzing a variety of recitations of a given poem to show how variously meter is actualized in performance. Epstein and Hawkes presented what might be called the orthodox Trager-Smith metrics, elaborating the concept of "relative strength" and providing a somewhat too vast inventory of foot-types, although only four basic feet were recognized, spondees and pyrrhics being declared impossible on the contention that one syllable must always be louder than the other. They postulated 6,236 kinds of iambs, 2,376 kinds of trochees, and a vaster number of three-syllabled feet. The most suggestive concept educed by Epstein and Hawkes was that of the foot as the *simplest* recurring unit, on principles of homogeneity and regularity. Smith reviewed and elaborated upon some of the Epstein-Hawkes procedure. Wells (*Style in Language,* pp. 197–200), coming to the subject from a slightly different angle, applied a technique of "logical construction" to the Trager-Smith system, distinguishing the abstract meter from (1) the orthographic record, (2) a recitation of the poem (a more adequate record), and (3) the phonemic system itself. He also suggested the possibility of considering metrics as a derivational or extractional process based upon operational (not prescriptive) rules, the most important being the "maximization principle": one picks the interpretation which gives the maximally regular meter. Thompson (*Poetics. Poetyka,* pp. 167–75) wrote essentially a historical treatment, showing how the Trager-Smith analysis could help to understand how Eng. meter as we know it today was substantially formed in the 16th c.

A different analysis of Eng. intonation, stress, and related features—that of Bolinger ("A Theory of Pitch Accent," *Word,* 14 [1958])—formed the basis of the linguistic metrics by Chatman (1964). Distinguishing on purely rhythmical grounds between *event* and *prominence* features in the metrical construct, he identified the syllable as the linguistic actualizer of the former, but found the latter more complex; metrical prominence could be actualized by one of several features: linguistic stress, or accent, or linguistic zero (no overt performance feature at all). He asserted the need to distinguish between performance (a purely linguistic record), scansion (the reduction of linguistic data to the metrical system in one performance), and metrical analysis (the sum of all reasonable scansions), demonstrating these distinctions by analyzing in acoustic and phonemic depth several recorded performances of Shakespeare's eighteenth sonnet. He developed the concept of simplicity suggested by Epstein and Hawkes, presenting formal guidelines for defining the metrical concepts and procedures in terms of efficiency of metrical design.

These assertions of the utility of l. for metrics have not gone uncontested. A significant critique of linguistic procedure (as well as other procedures) was offered by Wimsatt and Beardsley, who objected chiefly to what they considered an excessive concern for linguistic as opposed to metrical detail in some of the early studies. A defense was made by Pace ("The Two Domains: Meter and Rhythm," PMLA, 74 [1959]), who suggested that not all linguists would agree to the formulations already presented. It is undeniable that there exists nothing so monolithic as *the* linguistic position. Further, it is to be hoped that Wimsatt and Beardsley's very perceptive criticism has been or will be successfully answered in later work. Happily, at least three literary scholars who are not primarily linguists—Thompson, Hollander, and Halpern—have used the linguistic approach without apparent injury to their critical sensibilities.

A matter related to but not to be identified with meter is that of verse performance. Modern techniques of phonological analysis, particularly as they apply to stress, intonation, and related phenomena, have made it possible to discuss problems of oral recitation in increasingly finer detail. One subject of interest has been the analysis of the various components of the ultimate performance—what identifies the reader's concept of the *persona* of the poem (an old man, a neurotic, a duke who has had his wife put to death, etc.) and of the *persona's* attitude (anger, fear, etc.)—particularly as these relate to unavoidable carryovers of the reciter's own speech (his general intonational range, voice quality, etc. [Chatman, 1962]). Another concerns the normative problem of reading: what is the proper interpretation of a line? And how does that interpretation relate to meter? Chatman's argument that meter could be used to assist in interpretation and that performance and meter are cross-revealing (1956, 1957) was criticized by Wimsatt and Beardsley as a confusion between meter and intonation, and his argument that metrical ambiguity is more apparent than real and that performances usually demand resolution was contested by Levin ("Suprasegmentals and the Performance of Poetry," *Quarterly Jour. of Speech,* 48 [1962]), who argued that certain syntactic ambiguities cannot be resolved in performance and that forced oral resolutions may do a serious disservice to poetry's richness.

Grammatical studies of poetic language may be divided according as the emphasis is on words, and according as it is on grammatical sequences of words. Under the first subdivision fall those studies that are concerned with a poem's diction, and under the second those that are concerned with a poem's syntax. Diction studies may in turn be divided into those that deal with the meanings of words and thus lend themselves to statements of a poem's content or import, and those that deal with words primarily as grammatical entities and leave semantic considerations aside. Because words as grammatical entities are much more susceptible to properly linguistic statements, it is with diction in the latter sense that linguistic analysis of poetry has been chiefly concerned. Assuming that part-of-speech membership is given—either tacitly or by analysis—then the words occurring in poetry lend themselves readily to quantitative analysis, and such analysis can be used as a linguistic correlate for certain judgments about a poet's style or aesthetic orientation. Thus, using the data presented by Josephine Miles in an earlier article ("Eras in Eng. Poetry," PLMA, 70 [1955]), in which she distinguished quantitatively between verbal style and substantival style in several centuries of Eng. poetry, A. Kroeber showed that it is in the work of "reasoning" poets like Jonson, Donne, Coleridge, etc. that verb forms predominate, whereas in the work of sensory or visually imagistic poets like Spenser, Milton, Tennyson, etc. the adjectival forms predominate ("Parts of Speech in Periods of Poetry," PMLA, 73 [1958]). Studies with more highly developed statistical techniques have been conducted by Yule and Herdan. In the work of these men there is a greater concern with the problem of establishing adequate statistical procedures, but here also the statistics are used to determine stylistic indices on the basis of the frequencies with which word-classes are represented in literary works. Herdan in fact is interested in establishing a field of "stylo-statistics." Although worthwhile results may be expected from statistical analyses, certain methodological difficulties remain to be overcome. Two problems mentioned by Plath ("Mathematical L.," *Trends in European and American L.* [1961], pp. 21–57) are that of deciding on the optimal size and nature of the sample to be used, and that of finding statistical measures which will hold no matter what the sample size, so that results obtained from texts of different lengths may be compared directly. Both Yule and Herdan have suggested techniques for dealing with these difficulties, and no doubt statistical procedures will ultimately be refined to the point where such quantitative studies will yield more important results for stylistic analysis.

The language of poetry is referred to in various ways that attest to its distinctive character. Aristotle noticed this property of poetic language, and much later, in the 1920's, the Prague School aestheticians signalized it, referring to the "foregrounded" or "deautomatized" expressions of poetry. Attempts to explain these effects have usually centered on the notion of deviation from the norm. The problem has been, however, to characterize the norm. In eras governed by normative dicta, there may be in effect certain linguistic conventions binding literary forms, and transgressions of these conventions would constitute deviations. From the linguistic point of view, however, such norms are artificial, grafted upon antecedent and more fundamental, genuinely linguistic norms. According to traditional descriptive grammar deviant sentences could be simply listed as exceptions to the stated rules. This of course amounts to a rather trivial explanation of deviation. The corresponding decision in a generative grammar would be made where the sequence or sentence in question was not an output of the grammar. *Ipso facto* such a sequence would constitute a deviation. But using a generative grammar as a norm does not limit one simply to absolute decisions of this kind. Since a generative grammar consists of a finely articulated set of grammatical rules, one can test the deviant sequence against these rules and in this way determine in just what particular respect the sequence is deviant. Generative grammar thus makes it possible to arrive at decisions on kinds and degrees of deviation.

A generative grammar, at least in most versions, comprises a transformational level. On this level sentences are transformed from one grammatical shape into another; e.g., actives into passives, statements into questions, and sentences into nominalizations. In addition to these transformations, various other and more complex grammatical structures can also be shown to stand in the transform relation to each other. This formalized technique for showing relations between different sequence and sentence forms can be put to use in bringing to light certain regularities that lie, as it were, beneath the linguistic surface of the poem. If the grammatical structures occurring in a poem are similar or identical to any appreciable extent, that is a stylistic fact of some importance. But even if such similarities or identities are not discoverable in the actual language of a poem, it may turn out that various of the sequences in the poem are related to each other transformationally. See also GENERATIVE METRICS.

E. W. Scripture, *Grundzüge der englischen Verswissenschaft* (1929); R. Jakobson, "Über den Versbau der serbokroatischen Volksepen," *Archives néerlandaises de phonétique expérimentale,* 7–9 (1933); W. Schramm, *Approaches to a Science of Eng. Verse* (1935); G. U. Yule, *The Statistical Study of Lit. Vocabulary* (1944); H. Whitehall, "From L. to Crit.," KR, 13 (1951); S. Chatman, "Robert Frost's 'Mowing': An Inquiry into Prosodic Structure," KR, 18 (1956) and "L., Poetics, and Interpretation: The Phonemic Dimension," *Quarterly Jour. of Speech,* 43 (1957); J. R. Firth, "Modes of Meaning," *Papers in L. 1934–1951* (1957); B. Havránek, "The Functional Differentiation of the Standard Language," *A Prague School Reader on Esthetics, Lit. Structure and Style,* ed. P. Garvin (1958); J. Mukařovský, "Standard Language and Poetic Language," *A Prague School Reader;* H. Whitehall and A. A. Hill, "A Report on the Language-Lit. Seminar," *Readings in Applied Eng. L.,* ed. H. B. Allen (1958); E. L. Epstein and T. Hawkes, *L. and Eng. Prosody* (1959); M. Riffaterre, "Criteria for Style Analysis," *Word,* 15 (1959): H. L. Smith, Jr., "Toward Redefining Eng. Prosody," *Studies in L.,* 14 (1959); W. K. Wimsatt, Jr. and M. Beardsley, "The Concept of Meter: An Exercise in Abstraction," PMLA, 74 (1959); G. Herdan, *Type-Token Mathematics* (1960); R. Jakobson, "L. and Poetics," Conference on Style, Indiana Univ., 1958. *Style in Language,* ed. T. A. Sebeok (1960); M. Riffaterre, "Stylistic Context," *Word,* 16 (1960); S. Saporta, "The Application of L. to the Study of Poetic Language," *Style in Language* (1960); International Conference of Work-in-Progress Devoted to Problems of Poetics. 1st, Warsaw, 1960. *Poetics. Poetyka . . .* (1961; see the various articles dealing with l. and poetics); S. Chatman, "Linguistic Style, Lit. Style and Performance: Some Distinctions," *Georgetown Monograph Series on Language and L.,* 13 (1962); S. R. Levin, *Linguistic Structures in Poetry* (1962); S. Chatman, *A Theory of Meter* (1965). S.C.; S.R.L.

LITOTES (Gr. "plainness," "simplicity"). A figure, related to meiosis (q.v.), employing deliberate understatement for purposes of intensification, or affirmation by the negative of the contrary, usually used to secure emphasis or irony; however, according to Lausberg, "Die Ironie ist in der Litotes nicht total, sondern nur graduell" (*Handbuch der literarischen Rhetorik* 586). Servius, commenting on Virgil's *Georgics* 2. 125 says, "non tarda, id est, strenuissima: nam litotes figura est" (not slow, that is, most brisk: for the figure is litotes), though in fact it seems to be hyperbole. The figure is used so frequently in *Beowulf,* and other OE poetry, that it has become (with kennings) a distinguishing mark of that literature: "þæt wæs god cyning" (that was a good king), following a passage telling how the king flourished on earth, prospered in honors, brought the neighboring people to obey him and pay him tribute. "Nor are thy lips ungraceful, Sire of Men, / Nor tongue ineloquent" (Milton, *Paradise Lost* 8). Effects vary from the obvious ironies of *Beowulf* to the sophisticated subtleties of Pope; l. is also an effective satiric instrument: "He was nat pale as a forpyned goost. / A fat swan loved he best of any roost" (Chaucer, *The Canterbury Tales.* Gen. Prol. 205–6). As an affirmation by negative of the contrary: "I'll bet you won't" meaning "I'm certain you will."—O. Jespersen, *Negation in Eng. and Other Languages* (1917); A. Hübner, *Die "MHD Ironie" oder die L. im Altdeutschen* (1930); F. Bracher, "Understatement in OE Poetry," PMLA, 52 (1937); L. M. Hollander, "L. in Old Norse," PMLA, 53 (1938); Lausberg. R.O.E.

LOGAOEDIC (Gr. "prose-poetic"). Term invented by metricians of Roman imperial times as a general description of mixed anapaestic and iambic or dactylic and trochaic cola (ascending and descending rhythm respectively) in Gr. lyric verse. L. anapaestic cola may be composed of 2 or more anapaests followed by an iambic dipody catalectic or, more usually, by a single iambus, and l. dactylic cola of 2 or more dactyls followed by a trochaic dipody (the last syllable being *anceps*), or by a trochaic dipody catalectic. Anacrusis (q.v.) sometimes is postulated in the latter category, e.g., in Pindar's famous description of Athens:

–| – ⏑ ⏑|– ⏑ ⏑|– ⏑ ⏑|– ⏑ ⏑|– ⏑ | –
o tai liparai kai iostephanoi kai aoidimoi

To the varieties of l. dactylic cola belong the Ibycean (–⏑⏑|–⏑⏑|–⏑|–) and Praxillean (–⏑⏑|–⏑⏑|–⏑⏑|–⏑|–⏓), and with both anacrusis has been assumed. Some modern metricians abhor the name "logaoedic," e.g., A. M. Dale, CR, 62 (1948), 124, who prefers to speak of "prosodiac-enoplian."—T. D. Goodell, *Chapters on Gr. Metric* (1901); J. W. White, *The Verse of Gr. Comedy* (1912); Kolář; Dale; Koster. R.J.G.

LONG METER (L.M. of the hymn books). In effect a variant of ballad or common meter, for if the trimeters of that 4343 pattern are lengthened, the 4444 pattern of l.m. results. The foot pattern is sometimes trochaic, but usually iambic as in Burns's

> Ye banks and braes o' bonnie Doon,
>   How can ye bloom sae fresh and fair?
> How can ye chant, ye little birds,
>   And I sae weary fu' o' care?

Instead of the abcb rhyme scheme, l.m. is frequently found in abab, and even in aabb, the latter differing from octosyllabic couplets in thought development and by being printed as quatrains on the page. The aabb pattern gives a different "turn" to the ideas and is especially well suited, although not limited, to poems of light compliment. L.J.Z.

LYRIC. The term used to designate one of the three general categories of poetic literature, the others being narrative and dramatic. Although the differentiating features between these arbitrary classifications are sometimes moot, l. poetry may be said to retain most pronouncedly the elements of poetry which evidence its origins in musical expression—singing, chanting, and recitation to musical accompaniment. Though the drama and epic as well as the l. may have had their genesis in a spontaneously melodic expression which soon adapted itself to a ritualistic need and thus became formalized, music in dramatic and epic poetry was secondary to other elements of the works, being mainly a mimetic or mnemonic device. In the case of l. poetry, however, the musical element is intrinsic to the work intellectually as well as aesthetically: it becomes the focal point for the poet's perceptions as they are given a verbalized form to convey emotional and rational values. The primary importance of the musical element is indicated in many generic terms which various cultures have used to designate nonnarrative and nondramatic poetry: the Eng. "l.," derived from the Gr. *lyra* or musical intrument; the classical Gr. *melic,* or *mele* (air, melody); the Chinese *shih,* or "word song."

To speak of the "musical" qualities of l. poetry is not to say that such poetry is written always to be sung. Neither does the appellation of "musical" indicate that l. poetry possesses such attributes as pitch, harmony, syncopation, counterpoint, and other mechanical characteristics of a tonal, musical line or sequence. To define the quality of lyricism in this way is to limit a l. poem to the manner in which it is presented or to its architectonic aspects. This is largely the approach which classical criticism and its followers have taken in their treatment of l. poetry. On the other hand, an equation of poetic lyricism with the nonarchitectural or "emotional" qualities of music is even less profitable from the critical point of view, because it leads to such question-begging definitions of the l. as "the essence of poetry," "pure poetry," or, most vaguely, "poetry." To declare that "the characteristic of the l. is that it is the product of the pure poetic energy unassociated with other energies, and that l. and poetry are synonymous terms" (Drinkwater) is as extreme a definition of lyricism as to claim that a passage is lyrical simply because it possesses "the quality of metrical construction or architecture" (Gilbert Murray).

Most of the confusion in the modern (i.e., 1550 to the present) critical use of the term "l." is due to an overextension of the phrase to cover a body of poetic writing that has drastically altered its nature in the centuries of its development. The first critical use of the word *mele* by the Greeks was for the purpose of broadly distinguishing between various nonnarrative and nondramatic types of poetry: the melic poem was intended to be sung to musical accompaniment, as contrasted with the iambic and elegiac poems, which were chanted. The first general use of "l." to characterize a selection of poetic literature encompassing several genres did not come until the Alexandrian period. Then "l." became a generic term for any poem which was composed to be sung, and this was the meaning which it largely retained until the Renaissance. The preoccupation of pre-Renaissance critics with the metrics of melic or l. poetry was entirely appropriate to the principle upon which the category was established.

But with the Renaissance, poets began suiting their work to a visual rather than an auditory medium; even while such critics as Minturno, Scaliger, Sidney, and Puttenham were formulating their discussions of l. poetry, the l. was becoming something quite different from the classical melic poem. No longer a performing bard, scop, or troubadour, the poet ceased to "compose" his poem for musical presentation but instead "wrote" it for a collection of readers. The l. poem, nominally successor to a well-established poetic method, inherited and employed specific themes, meters, attitudes, images, and myths; but in adapting itself to a new means of presentation, the l. found itself bereft of the very element which had been the foundation of its lyricism—music.

At the time the l. was undergoing this important metamorphosis, critics of the 15th and 16th c. chose either to ignore the genre or to treat it in the same quantitative or metrical fashion as the classicists had done. Until the end of the 17th c., therefore, critics failed to distinguish between the true or melodic l., such as the "songs" of Shakespeare, Campion, and Dryden, and the nonmusical, verbal lyrics of Donne, Marvell, and Waller. Both the straightforward, clear song-poem and the more abstrusely phrased print-poem were called "l.": to refer to the "sweetness of numbers" in Waller or Dryden was the critic's substitute for precision of terms in distinguishing poems intended for musical accompaniment from those not so designed. The neoclassical critical concern in 18th-c. France and England with the tragic and epic genres was sufficiently overwhelming to permit the l. to become somehow lost as a subject for discussion; and when the romantic movement came with its championing of lyrical modes, terminological confusion continued in the equation of "l." with "poetry" by Wordsworth, Goethe, Coleridge, Poe, and other literary theorists. The 19th-c. development of a scientific methodology, with consequent insistence on accuracy of terms and precision of generic distinctions, translated itself in the field of literary criticism into a concern with the intrinsic and characteristic nature of the l. The definitions by Drinkwater and Murray were the overinclusive and overexclusive criteria which resulted from this concern; and critical attempts to reestablish the melodic or musical substance of l. poetry were a third, and equally unsuccessful, method of dealing with the paradoxical nature of a "musical" poetry which was no longer literally "melodic." Such, in greatly simplified lines, is the background of the verbal ambiguity with which post-Renaissance critics concealed their basic failure to define exactly the nature of the l. genre which distinguishes it from narrative and dramatic poetry and which includes all the disparate types of poem commonly called "lyrical."

Critical attempts to define l. poetry by reference to its secondary (i.e., nonmusical) qualities have perhaps suffered by being descriptive of various historical groupings of lyrics rather than definitive of the category as a whole. Among the most well-known and popularly cited proscriptions regarding the l. are that it must necessarily be brief (Poe); "be one, the parts of which mutually support and explain each other; all in their proportion harmonizing with, and supporting the purpose and known influence of metrical arrangement" (Coleridge); be "the spontaneous overflow of powerful feelings" (Wordsworth); be an intensely subjective and personal expression (Hegel); be an "inverted action of mind upon will" (Schopenhauer); or be "the utterance that is overheard" (Mill).

Though the attributes of brevity, metrical coherence, subjectivity, passion, sensuality, and particularity of image are frequently ascribed to the l. genre, there are schools of poetry obviously l. which are not susceptible to such criteria. Milton's mood poems, *L'Allegro* and *Il Penseroso,* as well as the most famous of the Eng. elegies are "brief" in only the most relative sense. Much of the vers libre of the present age contradicts the rule of metrical coherence. Imagist lyrics are hardly "empassioned" in the ordinary sense of the word. The "lucubrations" of the metaphysicals are something less than sensual in the romantic meaning of the term. The problem of subjectivity must always plague the critic of the Elizabethan love l. And, finally, the common artistic admission that the universal can be expressed best, and perhaps solely, through the particular image largely invalidates any distinction between the l. and non-l. on a metaphoric or thematic basis.

The irreducible denominator of all l. poetry must, therefore, be those elements which it shares with the musical forms that produced it. Although l. poetry is not music, it is representational of music in its sound patterns, basing its meter and rhyme on the regular linear measure of the song; or, more remotely, it employs cadence and consonance to approximate the tonal variation of a chant or intonation. Thus the l. retains structural or substantive evidence of its melodic origins, and it is this factor which serves as the categorical principle of poetic lyricism.

Contemporary critics, predicating the musical essence of the l. as its vital characteristic, have come close to formulating an exact, inclusive definition of the genre which eliminates semantic contradictions. "Words build into their poetic meaning by building into sound . . . sound in composition: music" (R. P. Blackmur). "A poet does not compose *in order to* make of language delightful and exciting music; he composes a delightful and exciting music in language *in order to* make what he has to say peculiarly efficacious in our minds" (Lascelles Abercrombie). Lyrical poetry is "the form wherein the artist presents his image in immediate relation to himself" (James Joyce). "Hence in lyrical poetry what is conveyed is not mere emotion, but the imaginative prehension of emotional states . . ." (Herbert Read). It is "an internal mimesis of sound and imagery" (Northrop Frye). Thus, in contemporary critical usage it may be said that "l." is a general, categorical, and nominal term, whereas in the pre-Renaissance sense it was specific, generic, and descriptive. In its modern meaning, a l. is a type of poetry which is mechanically representational of a musical architecture and which is thematically representational of the poet's sensibility as evidenced in a fusion of conception and image. In its older and more confined sense, a l. was simply a poem written to be sung; this meaning is preserved in the modern colloquialism of referring to the words of a song as its "lyrics."

However useful definitions of the l. may be, they cannot indicate the great flexibility of technique and range of subjects which have helped this category to comprise the bulk of poetic literature. There are literally dozens of l. genres, ranging from the ancient *partheneia* to the modern vers libre; and no topic, whether a cicada or a locomotive, has been neglected by the l. poets. Though it is manifestly impossible to say everything about the historical development of the l. in a short summary, certain general facts prove interesting as pieces in an evolving pattern of theories about and treatment of the lyrical mode between various ages, cultures, and individuals.

The l. is as old as recorded literature; and its history is that of human experience at its most animated.

It is logical to suppose that the first "lyrical" poems came into being when men discovered the pleasure that arises from combining words in a coherent, meaningful sequence with the almost physical process of uttering rhythmical and tonal sounds to convey feelings. The instinctive human tendency to croon or hum or intone as an expression of emotional mood is evidenced in the child's babbling; and the socialization of this tendency in primitive cultures by the chanting or singing of nonsense syllables to emphasize tribal rites is a well documented phenomenon. At that remote point in time when the syllables ceased to be nonsense and became syntactically and connotatively meaningful, the first l. was composed but in what Cro-Magnon or Neanderthal cave this took place, no one will ever know, though speculations about the folk origins of literature range from those of Herder to Jung to A. B. Lord and Andrew Welsh. The earliest recorded evidence of l. poetry would indicate that such compositions emerged from ritualistic activity accompanying religious ceremonies and were expressive of the mystical experience which the "poet" or speaker was undergoing. The dividing line between the nonsense babblings of the Pythoness at Delphi and the transliteration by the priests into a coherent unit of thought is indicative of the fashion in which many of the early religious lyrics came into existence. Scholars have found evidence to support this theory of the religious derivation of poetry in general and the l. in particular in such literatures as the Sanskrit, Celtic, and Japanese, as well as the Gr.

The most complete written evidence of early l. activity is the Egyptian: the Pyramid Texts (ca. 2600 B.C.) includes specimens of the funeral song (elegy), song of praise to the king (ode), and invocation to the gods (hymn); and tomb inscriptions from the same period include the work songs (*chansons de toile*) of shepherds, fishers, and chairmen. Also among the earliest l. writings of the Old Kingdom are the dialogue, the proverb, and the lament (complaint). Works from the New Kingdom (ca. 1555 B.C.) include the love song, the song of revelry and the epitaph. Although relatively unsophisticated, the Egyptian l. contained in nascent form many of the elements which were to become characteristic of later l. poetry. The poetic lines were probably some form of free rhythm without rigid meter. Alliteration and parallelism were devices frequently used, as was paronomasia or punning. Irony and paradox were present in a primitive form; and these first of all lyrics were already treating such subjects as death, piety, love, loneliness, jealousy, martial prowess, and happiness. Furthermore, the personal tone of the l., though not ubiquitous, was apparent in such poems as those enclosed in *The Dispute with His Soul of One Who Is Tired of Life*.

Remains of such other ancient literatures as the Babylonian and the Assyrian are too fragmentary to disclose much in the way of advancement over the Egyptian l. poems, which the inhabitants of the Fertile Crescent appear to have imitated in certain obvious ways. The most complete of the ancient bodies of lyric poetry is the Hebrew, which, while owing something to Egyptian and Babylonian sources, nevertheless marked positive improvement in the l. technique. These lyrics, well known to modern readers because of their religious associations and highly important because of their effect on the patristic lyricists of the Middle Ages, are among the most strikingly beautiful ever written. Though textual evidence indicates that some Hebrew l. poetry was written as early as the 10th c. B.C. (notably the *Song of Deborah*), many poems were of a later date; and the earliest Jewish literary criticism dealing with the l. was as late as the time of Christ. Philo Judaeus (ca. 20 B.C.-A.D. 50) indicated the Egyptian origin of some Hebrew lyric techniques by declaring that Moses was taught "the whole theory of rhythm, harmony, and meter" by the Egyptians; and Flavius Josephus (ca. A.D. 37–95), dealing with the famous hymn of Moses in Exodus 15:1–2 ("I will sing unto the Lord, for he hath triumphed gloriously") said that it was written in hexametric verse. The hymns and songs of David, Josephus also wrote, employed various meters, including trimeter and pentameter. Later discussions of Hebrew meters were carried on by Origen, Eusebius, and Jerome; but it is questionable how applicable to Hebrew lyrics the Gr. metric nomenclature was in fact, and it must be conceded that very little is known even yet about the nature of ancient Hebrew l. meters. It is known, however, that the lyrics were accompanied by such instruments as the harp, sackbut, and cymbals; and suggestions of the manner in which hymns, elegies, songs of rejoicing, and songs of triumph were composed and performed may be found in the story of David in I Samuel 16:23 and II Samuel 1:17–27, 6:5, 15–16.

The ancient Jewish poets were proficient in the use of parallelism and alliteration, perfecting these devices and using them in a variety of ways. Parallelism is obvious in such lyrics as Psalm 19 ("The heavens declare the glory of God, and the firmament sheweth his handiwork") and in Proverbs 21:17 ("He that loveth pleasure shall be a poor man: he that loveth wine and oil shall not be rich"); but it is also, more subtly, used as in Jeremiah 6:24 ("Anguish hath taken hold of us, and pain, as of a woman in travail"). The use of tropical devices is highly developed in Hebrew l. poetry, with similes and metaphors predominating; the apostrophe and hyperbole increase the personal tone of the l. far beyond the Egyptian. Many of the lyrics indeed appear intensely subjective, as Psalm 69 ("Save me, O God; for the waters are come in unto my soul. I sink in deep mire, where there is no standing"); but even these poems reflect what Frye has called "the sense of an external and social discipline." Yet the personal tone remains and is essential to the lyricism of such passages as those in Isaiah 5:1 ("Now will I sing to my well beloved a song of my beloved touching his vineyard"); Psalm 137 ("By the rivers of Babylon, there we sat down, yea, we wept, when we remembered Zion"); and II Samuel 1:19 ("The beauty of Israel is slain upon thy high places: how are the mighty fallen!").

The Hebrew lyricists developed a number of types and subtypes of the l. genre, which are classified by method of performance, source of imagery, or subject matter. These include the psalm (derived from the Gr. *psallein,* "to pull upon a stringed instrument"); the pastoral, which draws heavily upon the agrarian background of Hebrew culture; and the vision or apocalyptic prophecy, which employs the indirection of the trope to imply its perceptions. Other types include the proverb, the epigram, and similar forms of "wisdom" literature; the descriptive love l.; the triumph; various sorts of threnody; panegyrics of different kinds; and even a lyrical dialogue (or "drama") in the Book of Job. Some overlapping of these types is obvious (the triumph was frequently a panegyric on some hero, and the threnody or elegy was often pastoral); but the ambiguity is an historical one and terminological distinctions have yet to be drawn. Viewed as descriptions, the types are helpful in understanding the characteristics of the variations of the l. expression.

Like the Egyptian and Hebrew, the Gr. l. had its origins in religious activity; the first songs were probably composed to suit an occasion of celebration or mourning. Gr. lyrics were chanted, sung, or sung and danced; each of these lyrical methods of presentation is traceable to some form of religious practice. The dithyramb, for example, may have been composed to commemorate the death of some primitive vegetable god or the birth of Dionysus; in any case, it was originally sung to the accompaniment of the flute playing a melody in the Phrygian mode, which the Greeks considered the most emotional. In time, the dithyramb took on a more particular form involving formalized dance steps corresponding to passages in the text: these rhythmical and thematic patterns conceivably were the prototype of the fully developed ode, or song of celebration, with its divisions of strophe and antistrophe as written by Pindar, Sophocles, and others. Similar tracings of the development of other lyrical modes in Greece from the Heroic Age to the Homeric to the Periclean may be made, though it must be remembered that all are largely hypothetical.

The essential element of the Gr. l. was its meter, which was of two kinds: the stichic, that spoken or recited; and what may be termed the melic, that suited for singing or singing and dancing. Stichic meters were well demarcated lines of equal length and repetitive rhythm that can be broken into equivalent feet or metra. Melic meters were composed of phrases of varying length or movement, the cola, which were combined into a unit rhythmically complete or rounded, the *periodos.* Some cola are rhythmically repetitious in themselves and may be broken into dimeter or trimeter; but in the melic poems, it was the *periodos* or stanza that constituted the l. unit. Melic meters were obviously subject to wide adaptation by individual writers, and most of the best known Gr. lyrical meters are named for the poets who developed and customarily used them: the Alcaic, Anacreontic, Pindaric, and so on. The earliest Gr. lyrics were folk in origin, but even in the works of Homer and Hesiod there is evidence of an artistic concern with the lyrical mood and subjects, if not the lyrical form. In the *Iliad,* for instance, there are such embryonic lyrics as Helen's laments, Achilles' speech at the death of Patroklos, and the elegiac statements at Hector's funeral. The hymn was among the first developed of the definably l. genres, being composed in significant numbers before 700 B.C. The Homeric Hymns date from this period and indicate the religious nature of the first lyrics: they are addressed to Artemis, Dionysus, Heracles, Helios, Selena, *et al.,* and the pattern of some became a distinct type of l. hymn (i.e., the "paean" was a hymn to Apollo). The hymns employ devices appropriate to the apostrophe but are not very expansive in their tropes, chiefly using the attributive epithet, as in the hymn to Hera, XII (Evelyn-White trans.): "I sing of golden-throned Hera, whom Rhea bare. Queen of the immortals is she, surpassing all in beauty."

The Homeric epigrams are attributed to this period, also, thereby setting up an archetype for the later iambics: "Thestorides, full many things there are that mortals cannot sound; But there is nothing more unfathomable than the heart of man." The period from 700–500 B.C. saw the rise of elegiac and political verse, written by Solon among others, and the personal lampoon in iambics, by Archilochus, Hipponax, and Simonides of Amorgos. After 660 B.C., melic poetry developed, primarily in two strains: the Aeolian, or personal, lyrics written at Lesbos by Sappho and Alcaeus; and the Dorian, or objective, by Alcman, Arion, Stesichorus, and Ibycus. This group of lyrics may also be categorized by method of performance as solo or choral, but the dividing line is not sharp, as Gr. scholars have pointed out. Although the ancient distinctions of melic poetry on the basis of metrics may have indicated separate categories, the modern definition of the l. would be hard pressed to differentiate between such poems as those of Ibycus, Sappho, and Alcman (Lattimore tr.):

Blessed is the man who blithely
winds out all days of his life
without tears. But I must sing the
light of Agido. O see her

like the sun that Agido
summons up to shine upon us.
(Alcman)

Now in this season for me
there is no rest from love.
Out of the hard bright sky,
a Thracian north wind blowing
with searing rages and hurt—dark,
pitiless, sent by Aphrodite—Love
rocks and tosses my heart.
(Ibycus)

Throned in splendor, deathless, O Aphrodite,
child of Zeus, charm-fashioner, I entreat you
not with griefs and bitternesses to break my
spirit, O goddess. . . .
(Sappho)

The 5th c. in Greece produced some of the best of the l. poets: Simonides, Pindar, and Bacchylides; it was then that the l. found such magnificent expression in the choral odes of Sophocles, Aeschylus, and Euripides. Melic poetry became national in tone, with the Dorian mode prevailing; there was an abundance of such l. types as the hymn, paean, dithyramb, processional, dance song, triumph, ode, and dirge. Other popular genres were the *partheneia* (songs sung by virgins to flute accompaniment); *nomos* (ode or war song); *kommos* (a mournful dirge sung in Attic drama by an actor and the chorus alternately); *prosodion* (processional song of solemn thanksgiving); *hyporcheme* (a dance song); *epinicion* (song of victory); *threnos* (a dirge); wedding songs for men; and the *scolion* (a banquet song accompanied by the lyre and supposedly originated by Terpander).

The Gr. critics were less concerned with l., or melic, poetry than with the tragedy and the epic; the few extant comments which they made predicate the musical nature of the genre. Plato's denunciation of all poetry, especially the "representational" tragedy, included the melic, which Plato considered "untrue" or false in its depiction of reality. Stripped of musical coloring and laid bare as ideas, the melic poems revealed the ignorance of the poet, which clothed itself in "rhythm, meter, and harmony." (*The Republic* 10.4) Aristotle, in the *Poetics* (1–4) observed the absence of a generic term which might denote such nonepic and nondramatic kinds of poetry as the works in iambic, elegiac, and similar meters, which imitated "by means of language alone" as contrasted with the melic poems, which used rhythm, tune, and meter "all employed in combination." This statement indicates the existence of poetry, l. in the modern sense, which was not melic in the Gr. sense; but the Alexandrian use of "l." to indicate such disparate types as the dithyramb, iambics, elegies, and sapphics, while a broad attempt to repair the deficiency noted by Aristotle, was inexact and confusing.

Roman critical remarks on the l. would indicate that the term was used in the sense of melic poetry or poetry sung to the tune of the lyre. Horace indicated a belief that l. poetry was less substantial in content than epic poetry, being the *iocosa lyra;* and Quintilian concurred in the view that l. poetry was less weighty than epic though the ode might be worthy of more significant themes. To Horace's mind, the "dainty measures" were suited to "the work of celebrating gods and heroes, the champion boxer, the victorious steed, the fond desire of lovers, and the cup that banishes care"; they included the iambic, trimetric, and elegiac distich. These general criteria for form and content were adopted by most of the commentators following Horace—Ovid, Petronius, Juvenal, Pliny the Younger—so that, in l. theory, the Romans were little advanced beyond the Greeks.

In practice, Roman poets tended to imitate the Alexandrian l. writers, who composed works primarily meant to be read rather than performed. Moses Hadas has pointed out that this practice tended to produce l. poems more enigmatic and allusive than earlier "sung" poems had been; and it may be generally noted that Roman l. poets are more subject to examination as formulators of a "personal" or subjective poetry than the Greeks. The extent to which the lyrics of Sappho and the Aeolian school reflected the true feelings of their authors must be largely postulated; but with the Roman l. poets, sufficient internal detail in the poems plus objective evidence recorded of the poets' lives tempts the critic to speculate on the relationship between the nature of the l. mode and the private feelings of the lyricist. Thus, while they modeled their poems on the hymns of Callimachus, the Idyls of Theocritus, the epigrams of Anacreon, the elegiac laments of Bion and Moschus, and the later Gr. lyrics, Roman poets adapted the l. to produce a more subjective or autobiographical utterance. Conventional and minor Roman lyricists were content with the school of "fastidious elegance" which kept them copying the Greeks, and which Catullus mocked, but the Roman genius emphasized his particularized experiences: Propertius in his observations, Catullus in his amours, Virgil in his rustic pleasures, Ovid in the sorrows of his exile, Tibullus in his love pangs, Martial and Juvenal in their private asperities, and so on.

The private insight, the subjective focusing of experience is more keenly apparent in Roman lyrics than in other ancient works: in Ovid's *Tristia* 1.8. ("To their sources shall deep rivers flow"); Martial's *Epigrams* 1.8 ("Thou hast a name that bespeaks the season of the budding year, when Attic bees lay waste the brief-lived spring"); Catullus' *To Hortalus* 65 ("Though I am worn out with constant grief and sorrow calls me away"); and Tibullus, *To Delia* 1.2 ("More wine; let the liquor master these unwonted pains"). Coincidentally, there are many more "occasional" lyrics among the Roman poets which celebrate private rather than public festivals, with a greater proportion of such genres as the prothalamium and epithalamium (wedding songs), the *vale* or farewell, the epigram, the satire, and the epistle. Topicality is a notable element in many L. lyrics.

The formalistic approach to meter which typifies the l. writers of the pre-Augustan and Augustan periods of Roman literature began to weaken by the middle of the 1st c. A.D. and a greater flexibility of form resulted. The rigid preoccupation of the Horatian and Virgilian schools with the exact meters dictated by the system of quantitative verse was probably a classical attempt to substitute precision of metrics for the abandoned melodies of the true l. In any case, the lyrics of Petronius, unlike the imitative formal measures of the Statian odes, were experimental in form; and during the 2d c., definite steps were made by writers of L. lyrics toward a nonquantitative or accentual form of verse. In the 3d c., the completely new principle of rhyme could be found in the verse of the patristic lyricist, Commodian; it was then that the principles which were to guide medieval L. verse—rhyme and accent—were established.

As in the case of the Jews and the Greeks, the patristic critics of literature were an Epimethean lot, choosing to discuss forms and practices long established rather than treating contemporary practices. Eusebius and Jerome were concerned with examining Hebrew l. modes in terms of Gr. meters; Origen's comments were similarly analytical of metrics; and the anthologer, Isidore of Seville, discussed Hebrew and Gr. meters in conventional fashion, noted the musical element of l. poetry, but still failed to make any distinctions between the various genres. Patristic l. criticism throws little light on the practice of the times.

The first church lyrics were, not surprisingly, hymns which were patterned on the Hebrew Psalter and the Gr. hymns. The earliest verse hymns were those of St. Hilary, who probably used meter for its mnemonic effectiveness and who employed the meter that was to become a favorite with Prudentius, Fortunatus, and Thomas Aquinas as well as the basis for several of the medieval sequences: the *versus popularis* or trochaic tetrameter catalectic. St. Ambrose developed the use of iambic dimeters grouped in quatrains (the "Ambrosian" stanza); St. Jerome made L. more flexible as the language of poetry; and Augustine wrote a didactic poem which Brittain has said to contain in embryo the three elements of Medieval L. versification: accentual rhythm, isosyllabism, and rhyme. The Rule of St. Benedict, drawn up in the 6th c., required hymns to be sung at all the canonical hours, and this edict spurred on the writing of numerous lyricists. It should be noted that once more lyrics were composed to be sung or chanted; the indissoluble connection between the L. words and meters and the melodic line must not be forgotten. The Sequence depended on the repetition of phrases, both verbal and musical; and the involved meters as well as the simple rhymes of the hymns which Abelard wrote for Heloise and her nuns to sing were due to their avowedly musical nature:

> Christiani, plaudite,
> (Resurrexit Dominus)
> Victo mortis principe
> Christus imperat.
> Victori occurite,
> Qui nos liberat.

The church lyrics of the 12th and 13th c. are among the most perfect produced in the centuries of liturgical literature: the *Stabat Mater* and *Dies Irae* must be included in any list of the world's great lyrics, and there are numerous other examples of accomplished l. art: sequences, *cantiones,* nativities, and hymns of various kinds. The importance of patristic songs cannot be exaggerated in the history of the l.: not only is the body of church lyrics significant in itself, but it presages most of the metric and tropic techniques which are the foundation of the modern l.

Related to the development of patristic l. poetry was the Mozarabic poetry of Spain. Mozarabic writers inherited from the Visigoths the hymns of various Church Fathers—Hilary, Prudentius, Ambrose—transcribed into Gothic characters. Maurico, the compiler of Mozarabic l. in the 10th and 11th c., collected a large number of the hymns and songs written by Mozarabic poets of earlier periods and patterned on the Gothic and L. copies of patristic l. The Mozarabic l. include hymns, psalms, pleas, and such occasional poems as arose from the ordination of bishops, the building of churches, and the births and deaths of nobles. Though in time the Mozarabic l. adapted itself to accommodate characteristic cultural themes and attitudes of its era of Sp. history and came to be written in the vernacular, it remains one of the least known of all bodies of European l. poetry. Doubtless its claim to being the earliest vernacular poetry of the postclassical period in Europe will lead to its fuller investigation and evaluation in the future

The centuries between A.D. 300 and A.D. 1200 also produced two separate traditions which must be noted in any tracing of l. development. One of these, the Anglo-Saxon, was Western; the other was Eastern. Anglo-Saxon poetry is interesting as an example of a community literature with ancient religious origins. The verse form, composed to be sung and presented by bards or scops, consisted of a heavily accentual rhythm of a 4-beat line with a caesura; thematically, the poetic lines, redolent of Egyptian and Hebrew poetry in their parallelism and alliteration, were developed through the kenning (metaphor). The range of Anglo-Saxon lyrics, subjected to various influences, includes the gnomic verse, the rune, the lament, the complaint, the elegy, and the hymn. In lyric mood and subject matter, *The Wanderer* and *The Seafarer* touch on the highly emotional and personal; *The Phoenix* is an example of descriptive allegory; *The Wife's Lament, Deor,* and *Widsith* represent differing experiences and attitudes; and the Caedmonian hymns display the superimposition of the patristic tradition of hymn-writing on the Anglo-Saxon. The Anglo-Saxon l., long ignored except by such rare commentators as Sir William Temple, has come in for great enthusiasm in recent years because of the efforts of such imitators as G. M. Hopkins, Ezra Pound, and W. H. Auden.

Chinese poetry is almost entirely lyrical: although the earliest lyrics, folk in origin, were composed before the 6th c. B.C., the perfection of the Chinese l. came during the Tʻang Dynasty (A.D. 600–900) when such lyricists as Yüan Chieh, Li Po, and Po Chü-i lived. The ancient folk ballads and odes for sundry occasions were replaced in the 4th c. B.C. by the lyrics of Chʻu Yüan, author of the *Li Sao.* From the first types of "art" l.—the lament, the nostalgic complaint, the pastoral description—the Chinese poem developed into other areas: the political allegory ("The Liberator" by Wu-ti), the marching song ("Song of the Men of Chin-ling" by Hsieh T'iao), the satiric song ("Tchirek Song"), and, finally, the controlled descriptive or mood poems of Li Po. In the 8th c. A.D., Po Chü-i adapted the l. to instructive purposes, writing with the utmost stylistic simplicity in describing scenes which served as the basis for serious reflection.

> Unrewarded, my will to serve the State;
> At my closed door autumn grasses grow.
> What could I do to ease a rustic heart?
> I planted bamboos, more than a hundred
> shoots. . . .
> (tr. Arthur Waley.)

The succinct quality of these Chinese lyrics, as well as their visual effects, has had a decided effect on the imagists of the 19th and 20th c.

Though roughly contemporaneous with Chinese poetry, Japanese l. poetry is a completely separate tradition. The first Japanese l. poetry was reputedly composed by the god Iza-nagi and his descendants, and it is reasonably certain that a few kinds of folk l. were composed in the centuries before Christ: the war song, drinking song, and ballad. It is impossible to date the origins of what are apparently the earliest regular forms of Japanese poetry—the *chōka* (also, *nagauta*); the *tanka,* which was used either autonomously or as envoys to *chōka*; and the *sedōka.* The first extant anthology to include them was the *Man'yōshū* (compiled late 8th c. A.D.), after which the *chōka* and *sedōka* died out as vehicles of great poetry. The tanka, the most popular of Japanese l. forms for centuries, is composed of 31 syllables, and the haiku (or hokku) is composed of 17 syllables; each has alternating lines of 5 and 7 syllables. Though a relative latecomer to Japanese poetry, the haiku has been perfected since its inception in the 15th c. by a long line of masters: Sōkan, Moritake, Teitoku, and the great Bashō. Fusing in its brief span references to nature, human emotion, time, mood, infinity, the haiku is perhaps the most concise kind of l. poetry ever devised.

Another oriental l. tradition which should be mentioned is the Persian, ancient in origin but flourishing in the 12th through the 15th c. Persian lyrics, originally religious and objective in nature, became more personal in the works of Omar Khayyam, Sʻadi, and Hafiz: the famous Rubáiyát of Omar being a specimen of the Persian philosophical wit poem. Other highly developed l. types included the *qasida* (hymn), *hajw* (satire), *marthiya* (elegy), *qitʻa* (a fragment characterized by its prosody), *ghazal* (ode), and learned and descriptive poetry. The vogue for oriental literature in 18th and 19th c. England served to reveal Persian l. poetry to Eng. writers and thus to cause the oriental l. to affect directly the western lyric tradition.

In Europe, the 12th and 13th c. saw the growth in popularity of the wandering minstrel: the quasi-ecclesiastical goliards, who wrote secular songs in L.; the trouvères in northern France, and the troubadours in the south; the Minnesinger in Germany. The l. was sung, or sung and danced, widely. The troubadours, composing in the vernacular, produced the *chanso* (song, often of love), *sirventes* (topical songs of satire, eulogy, or personal comment), the *planh* (complaint), *tenso* (debate), *pastorela* (account of a pastoral episode), *alba* or *aubade* (dawn song), and some songs designed for dancing *(balada* and *dansa).* Much has been said about the differences between the *chansons courtois* and *chansons populaire,* the *caroles* and *rondets* for dancing and the chansons designed for singing only, the *chansons de toile* (work songs) and their subspecies in a number of excellent studies. Few areas of l. history have been as thoroughly dealt with as the medieval.

Medieval lyrics remain in abundance and they exert a special charm for the modern reader in their mixture of naïveté and sophistication. They range from the slapstick "macaronic" songs (a jumble of languages) to the simple understatement in "Foweles in the frith," from the obvious but delightful "Sumer is icumen in" to the complex rondeau of Chaucer's "Now welcom somer, with thy sonne softe" and his ballade, "Hyd, Absalon, thy gilte tresses clere." Although this period produced such masters of the written "art" l. as Chaucer, Bertrand de Born, Chrétien de Troyes, Walther von der Vogelweide, Rutebeuf, Pierre Vidal, and Sordello, l. poetry was still a thing of the people, composed to be sung and enjoyed. The melodic element of the l. genre in the medieval period has not been equalled since the dawn of the Renaissance.

This is not to say that after 1400 the l. and music were immediately and completely disassociated; but in time, the divorcement became more apparent with the rise of such primarily melodic forms as the madrigal, glee, catch, and round which subordinated words to the musical line. In spite of the later efforts of writers primarily poets and not composers—Swinburne, Hopkins, Yeats, Vachel Lindsay, and Edith Sitwell—the l. genre since the Renaissance has remained a verbal rather than a musical discipline and the traces of a melodic origin have become largely vestigial. The influence of the Roman metricians on the It. and Fr. lyrical theorists of the Renaissance may have helped to produce the latter-day emphasis on meter as a substitute for melody. Or Renaissance lyricists, writing for an aristocratic audience of readers, may simply have unconsciously adapted their forms to a different medium. In any event, the l. suffered a sea change after the 15th c. with the consequences noted above.

Renaissance lyrics, diffused as they are through several countries and centuries, nevertheless share certain general characteristics which are evidence of their common origin in the earlier Prov. lyrics. In Spain, l. poets fused their Mozarabic and Prov. traditions to perfect some older forms (the *cantiga* and possibly the *cossante)* and to develop some new ones (the *bacarola, bailada,* and others). After its inception in the Sicilian court of Frederick II, the *sonetto* rose to full perfection in Dante's *Vita Nuova* and Petrarch's *Sonnets to Laura.* The *Canzoniere,* the prototype of It. l. poetry, contained sonnets, sestinas, ballatas, and even a few madrigals. In such sonnets as nos. 33 ("Già fiammeggiava l'amorosa stella") and 35 ("Solo e pensoso i più deserti campi"), Petrarch struck the thematic chords that were to echo in the lyrics of countless imitators in Italy and England in the following centuries. In spite of excellent *canzoni* written by Ariosto and others, it is Petrarch whose name remains synonymous with Renaissance It. art lyrical verse. More popular vernacular verse in Italy—the *strambotto* and *rispetto*—was also composed in great numbers.

What Petrarch was to lyric poetry in Italy, Ronsard was to the poetry of Renaissance France. The leader of the *Pléiade,* a stellar group of poets including Joachim Du Bellay, Ronsard published his version of the sonnets to Laura in *Les Amours* in 1552, and a later collection of sonnets, the *Sonnets pour Hélène,* in 1578. In addition to writing sonnets, Ronsard also composed odes, mythological and philosophical *Hymnes,* and elegiac and pastoral poems. Scorning the older forms of the rondeau and rondelle, Ronsard explored the whole range of lyric images and emotions in his sonnet collections. Though the earlier sonnets contained frank Petrarchan notes (e.g. "Cent et cent fois penser un penser mesme"), the later works were perfectly Ronsard's own ("Adieu, cruelle, adieu, je te suis ennuyeux"). The later ages of Fr. literature have traced Fr. lyricism back to Ronsard just as often as they have traced its antithesis back to Malherbe.

In England, the publication of *Tottel's Miscellany* in 1557 marked the beginning of the most lyrical of England's poetic eras. A collection of "songs," sonnets, and other kinds of verse, the *Miscellany* evidenced the musicality of Eng. poets of earlier periods and set up a form of anthology to be imitated by scores of compilations from *The Phoenix Nest* and *England's Helicon* to the eventual *Broadside Ballads* and Bishop Percy's *Reliques.* Wyatt and Surrey were among the first in England to test the possibilities of the sonnet's thematic and metrical subtleties; and dozens of Eng. sonneteers—Sidney, Daniel, Spenser, Shakespeare *et al.*—published lengthy sonnet sequences, more or less directly patterned on Petrarch's. Certain Cl. forms of the lyric were redeveloped in England, e.g. the prothalamium and epithalamium; and adulation for Horace and other L. lyric poets caused the vogue of the ode to become widespread. The song remained popular, both in its melodic and ballad forms, being written by such experts as Campion, Sidney, Ben Jonson, and Shakespeare.

In general, it may be said of Renaissance l. poetry that it was a succinct example of the philosophy of humanism. The lyric's preoccupation with the subjective self dovetailed neatly with the humanistic interest in the varied forms of human emotion; and the new geographical concerns of the Renaissance supplemented the pastoralism of the traditional l. to produce an imagery that enforced a fusion of the scientific and poetic perspectives. The effect of printing on the lyrical poets has already been touched on; and though the shifting nature of l. poetry was not apparent to those Renaissance critics who discussed that "divine" art—Minturno, Scaliger, Torquato Tasso, Sibilet, Gascoigne, Sidney—its aftermath was important in poetic practice as well as theory.

Although the past 300 years in the history of the l. may be divided into certain chronological "periods" (i.e., the Renaissance, Restoration, Augustan, *Fin de siècle*) or certain distinctive "movements" (metaphysical, neoclassical, romantic, symbolist, expressionist, naturalist, hermeticist, and so forth), these terms reveal little about the true nature of lyrical poetry and practice. Far more accurate is the designation of all l. poetry after 1600 as "modern." The range of this body of lyrics from the most objective or "external" to the most subjective or "internal" may be included in three chief l. types: the Lyric of Vision or Emblem, the Lyric of Thought or Idea, and the Lyric of Emotion or Feeling.

The L. of Vision or Emblem, although it has its antecedents in classic, Anglo-Saxon, and Chinese poetry, is nevertheless fundamentally the product of the Age of Type. It is this sort of lyric that Ezra Pound has discussed as "Ideograms" and Apollinaire has called "calligrammes." This is the most externalized kind of l., utilizing the pictorial element of print to represent the object or concept treated in the context of the poem itself: it is a literal attempt to follow MacLeish's admonition that "a poem should not mean, but be." The optical l. exists, therefore, in itself without need of reference to a private sensibility, whether of poet or reader. The first use of the visual in the modern l. came in the Elizabethan Age with the experiments of Gascoigne and George Puttenham, who wrote critical appraisals of the technique. Renaissance poets printed poems in the shape of circles, spires, and pillars. Later, George Herbert showed wings, altars, and floor patterns in poems on the subject; and the prevalence of pictorial lyrics among Fr. and Eng. poetasters of the 17th and 18th c. drew Dryden's scorn in *Macflecknoe* and Addison's laughter in *The Spectator.* The imagists of the 19th and 20th c., under Chinese influence, revived the practice; the symbolists were influenced by it; and the more recent practitioners of lyrical emblemism include the Fr. dadaists of the 1920's, Amy Lowell, H. D., William Carlos Williams, E. E. Cummings, May Swenson, and John Hollander.

Somewhat more personal but still objective in tone and method is the L. of Thought or Idea, which may be divided into the Expository or Informative and the Didactic or Persuasive (critics like Drinkwater believe "l." and "didactic" to be contradictory terms). This school of lyricists is classically oriented, believing with Horace that poetry must be *utile* as well as *dulce* and consequently emphasizing musicality of form to balance prosaic content. The Expository l. writers include Boileau, Dryden, Cowper, Schiller, and Tennyson in former years; and such modern poets as Rainer Maria Rilke in his early descriptive works, the Sp. "naturalists" (Juan Ramón Jiménez, Jorge Guillén, Rafael Alberti), St. John Perse, T. S. Eliot, Robert Lowell, and Elizabeth Bishop are formulators of a lyrically expositional verse. The preoccupation of 19th- and 20th-c. poets with "sound" and verse form has produced vers libre, which is an obvious effort to accompany poetic statement with musical techniques just as the rigid heroic couplets of the neoclassical poetry of statement were.

The Didactic or Persuasive L. includes the allegorical, satiric, exhortatory, and vituperative species. L. allegory is apparent in the animal myths of La Fontaine, Herrick's use of Cupid, Mandeville's bees, Heine's Atta Troll, Arnold's merman, Davidson's dancers in the house of death, and Frost's departmental ants. The satiric l. includes, of course, the l. parody, such as Lewis Carroll's burlesques of Wordsworth and Swinburne's mockery of Tennyson; but it also includes directly satiric verse: Donne's verses on women, Mayakovsky's *Bedbug,* Bertolt Brecht's acrid observations on romantic love. The exhortatory l. is often patriotic or moralistic as in the Elizabethan panegyrics on England, Burns's call to the Scots, Gabriel D'Annunzio's fervent championing of life and freedom, or Kipling's tributes to Britannia. The vituperative l. aims its darts everywhere: against critics (Pope's *Epistles*); convention (Rimbaud's *Illuminations*); war (Owen and Sassoon); poverty and suffering (Antonio Machado's Del Camino); a parent (Sylvia Plath's *Daddy*); or the world in general (Allen Ginsberg's *Howl*). No discussion of the Didactic L. can ignore Ezra Pound's *Cantos,* which combine all of the subtypes—allegory, satire, exhortation, and vituperation—in a unique manner.

The most subjective or "internal" strain of modern l. poetry is the L. of Emotion or Feeling. It is this lyrical type which has become synonymous with "poetry" through the criticism of the romantic school and which is the prototype of the "personal" or "experienced" l. expression. The L. of Emotion comprises three major groups: the sensual l., the "imaginative" l. which intellectualizes emotional states, and the mystical l. The mystical l. is antipodal to the lyric of emblem: these two varieties of "vision" l., one literal and the other metaphorical, mark the extreme limits of objectivity and subjectivity which confine the l. genre.

The sensual l. enjoys an unbroken continuity from the 16th c. to the 20th in the sonnets of Ronsard and the *Pléiade,* the love poetry of the Elizabethans and metaphysicals, the erotica of the restoration and 18th c., the synaesthetic images of Keats and the romantics, the symbolist glorification of the self and its peculiar sensations, the neurotic sensualism of the Yellow Nineties, and the "new" sensualism of the Lost Generation, the Existentialists, and the Beat Generation. Ranging from the *carpe diem* to the *memento mori,* the sensual tradition is sustained in differing forms by Shakespeare, Donne, Collins, Herder, Heine, Baudelaire, Mallarmé, Whitman, D'Annunzio, Millay, and Dylan Thomas.

The "imaginative" or "intellectualized" l. of emotion furnishes a host of examples. The German lyricists provide a large number of these (notably Goethe and Schiller with Rilke, Hauptmann, and Stefan George as more recent examples). The "verbalized feelings" of the Eng. romantics and the Fr. symbolists have their modern counterparts in the lyrics of Apollinaire and Valéry, as well as in the poetry of Garcia Lorca and the It. hermeticists, Ungaretti and Montale. Many of the lyrics of Pushkin and Boris Pasternak fall in this category. Writers of British lyrics of this type are Auden, MacNeice, Empson, and Spender; Americans include Emerson, Emily Dickinson, Frost, Jeffers, MacLeish, Wallace Stevens, and Marianne Moore. Finally, the poetry of mysticism is significant in modern l. history, possibly being an attempt to find some substitute for the Gr. myths which provoked the classic lyrics, or for the Christian mythology which stimulated the medieval l. Foremost among the mystical lyricists are Herbert, Vaughan, Smart, Blake, Hopkins, Baudelaire, Claudel, Yeats, and Rilke.

The popularity of l. poetry in the modern period has increased with its employment in the causes of Feminism, Racial Equality, and self-expression. The abundance of l. writing has been accompanied by a plethora of critical analyses and theories. The German l. has commanded the critical notice of Behrens, Rauch, Closs, Ermatinger, von Wiese, and Witkop; more recent commentators include Burger, Leonard, Lehnert, Naumann, Haller, and Bircher. Staiger, Petsch, Friedrich, Heselhaus, Fechner, Iser, K. Pestalozzi, and Goheen have contributed broader, more theoretical studies. In France, the academic critics (Henri Bonnet, Gaetan Picon, Jean Frappier) have been joined by writers-turned-critic such as Maurice Blanchot, Jean Rousselot, Seghers, Cocteau, Sartre, and the existentialist critics. Ortega y Gasset and the German critic Siebermann have examined the Spanish l.; and the Russian l. has claimed the interest of Lidiia Ginsburg as well as Zhirmunskii and Gorodetskii. The Eng. tradition of poets writing about poetry has become the backbone of criticism in England and America. Practicing poets (Eliot, Auden, Spender, Day-Lewis, Empson, Thomas, Ransom, Tate, Warren, Jarrell, and Shapiro) have doubled as critics of their own and others' work. There are also those who are critics first and foremost: Wilson, Brooks, Richards, Winters, Deutsch, Hartmann, Vendler. The interested reader must go to the original works by these writers to differentiate their distinguishing posits and applications. The critical collection of Hošek and Parker (1985; see bibliog.) is a convenient guide to post New Critical approaches to the l. by the Phenomenologists, Structuralists, Modernists, and Deconstructionists.

Thus, from its primordial form of the song as the embodiment of an emotional reaction, the l. has been expanded, discussed, altered, and developed through the centuries until it has become one of the chief literary instruments which focus and evaluate the human condition. In flexibility, variety, and polish, it is perhaps the most proficient of the poetic genres. In the immediacy and keenness of its expression, it is certainly the most effective. These qualities have caused the 19th and 20th c. to look upon the l. as largely their own work, but l. poetry has belonged to all ages.

General and Bibliographical Works: F. B. Gummere, *The Beginnings of Poetry* (1901); J. Drinkwater, *The L.* (1915); Gayley and Kurtz; J. Pfeffer, *Das lyrische Gedicht als aesthetisches Gebilde* (1931); M. R. Ridley, "The L.," E&S, 19 (1933); G. Benn, *Probleme der Lyrik* (1954); Frye; C. Day-Lewis, *The L. Impulse* (1965); *Lyrik 25 Jahre: 1945-1970*, ed. H.-J. Schlütter (1974-1983); B. Hardy, *The Advantage of L.* (1977); W. R. Johnson, *The Idea of L.: L. Modes in Ancient and Modern Poetry* (1982).

Specialized Studies: J. Erskine, *The Elizabethan L.* (1903); F. E. Schelling, *The Eng. L.* (1913); A. Erman, *The Lit. of the Ancient Egyptians*, tr. A. M. Blackman (1927); P. S. Allen and H. M. Jones, *The Romanesque L.* (1928); H.J.C. Grierson, *Lyrical Poetry of the 19th C.* (1929); G. Murray, *The Cl. Tradition in Poetry* (1930); K. Kar, *Thoughts on the Medieval L.* (1933); A. L. Wheeler, *Catullus and the Traditions of Ancient Poetry* (1934); Bowra; R. Brittain, *The Medieval Latin and Romance L.* (1937); G. Errante, *Sulla Lirica Romanza dalle Origine* (1943); E. K. Chambers, *Early Eng. Lyrics* (1947); C. M. Ing, *Elizabethan Lyrics* (1951); J. Wiegand, *Abriss der lyrischen Technik* (1951); N. Maclean, "From Action to Image: Theories of the L. in the 18th C.," in Crane, *Critics*; H. Friedrich, *Die Struktur der modernen Lyrik* (1956); J. L. Kinneavy, *A Study of Three Contemporary Theories of L. Poetry* (1956); L. Nelson, *Baroque L. Poetry* (1961); E. Muir, *The Estate of Poetry* (1962); J. M. Cohen, *The Baroque L.* (1963); M. H. Abrams, "Structure and Style in the Greater Romantic L.," *From Sensibility to Romanticism*, ed. F. W. Hilles and H. Bloom (1965); R. Grimm, *Zur Lyrik-Diskussion* (1966); F. Golden, *The Mirror of Narcissus* (1967); *Forms of L.*, ed. R. Brower (1970; see for instance, Paul de Man's essay on the "L. and Modernity"); J. Mazzaro, *Transformation in the Ren. Eng. L.* (1970); W. Killy, *Elemente der Lyrik* (1972); H. M. Richmond, *Ren. Landscapes* (1973); J.J.Y. Liu, *Major Lyricists of the Northern Sung* (1974); P. Dronke, *The Medieval L.* (1977); A. Welsh, *Roots of L.* (1978); D. Woolf, *The Concept of the Text* (1978); *Interpretation of Medieval L. Poetry*, ed. W.T.H. Jackson (1980); O. Sayce, *The Medieval German Lyric 1150-1300* (1982); I. H. Levy, *Hitomaro and the Birth of Japanese Lyricism* (1983); D. Albright, *Lyricality in Eng. Lit.* (1985); R. Alter, *The Art of Biblical Poetry* (1985); *L. Poetry: Beyond New Criticism*, ed. C. Hošek and P. Parker (1985).

J.W.J.

M

MACARONIC VERSE incorporates words of the writer's native tongue in another language and subjects them to its grammatical laws, thus achieving a comic effect. The traditional basic language for m.v. is L. Tisi degli Odassi seems to have been the inventor of m.v.; he interspersed L. with It. (*Carmen maccaronicum,* 1488). Teofilo Folengo, however, using the same mixture, lent m.v. its renown through his famous mock-epic *Maccaroneae* (1517–21). Its anonymous Fr. translator (1606) describes Folengo as the "prototype of Rabelais." According to Folengo, the name "m.v." indicates a crude mixture—like that of flour, cheese, and butter in macaroni—and its burlesque appeal. The Fr. m. classic was Antoine de la Sablé. Priests (or Protestants) and literati were the favorite targets of m. satire. The wealth of German m. production (*Nudelverse*) is second only to that of the Italians, but, prior to Folengo's influence, it may have originated independently in Germany, that is, in student circles and with the mere intent to amuse. One of the rare examples of true m.v. in Eng. is the short 17th-c. epic *Polemo-Middinia,* ascribed to W. Drummond, in which L. terminations are skillfully tacked on to the Lowland Scots vernacular.

Loosely speaking, the term "m.v." has also been applied to any verse mingling two or more languages together, as in the OE *Macaronic Poem* (Krapp-Dobbie VI, 69–70), Máel Ísu Úa Brolchán's *Deus Meus* (*Early Ir. Lyrics,* ed. G. Murphy, 1956), the poems by J. Skelton, R. Brathwait's *Barnabae itinerarium* (1638), and, more recently, in the humorous verse of the American J. A. Morgan.

F. W. Genthe, *Gesch. der maccaronischen Poesie* (1829); J. O. Delepierre, *Macaronéa ou mélanges de litt. macaronique des différents peuples de l'Europe* (1852); J. A. Morgan, *M. Poetry* (1872); *Die Floia und andere deutsche maccaronische Gedichte,* ed. C. Blümlein (1900); *Anglo-Saxon Poetic Records,* ed. G. P. Krapp and E. V. Dobbie (6 v., 1931–53); W. O. Wehrle, *The M. Hymn Tradition in Medieval Eng. Lit.* (1933); U. E. Paoli, *Il latino maccheronico* (1959); B. Ristow, "Maccaronische Dichtung in Deutschland," *Reallexikon,* 2d ed., II.

U.K.G.

MACRON. See PROSODIC NOTATION.

MADRIGAL. A short monostrophic, polyphonic song form. It originated in northern Italy in the 14th c.; those with texts written by Petrarch are good examples of the early type. Revived in the 16th c., the m. underwent a tremendous vogue which extended as far as England, where it was assiduously cultivated by the Elizabethan poets and composers.

In its metrical form the m. displays considerable variety, particularly in its later manifestations. The m. of the 14th c. was usually composed of 2 or 3 tercets followed by 1 or 2 rhyming couplets, the lines generally being of 7 or 11 syllables. By the time of its 16th-c. revival, however, its metrical form had become so free that Bembo, himself a composer of madrigals, wrote that it is bound by no rule concerning number of lines or arrangement of rhymes. But the last 2 lines almost always rhymed, and madrigals seldom exceeded 12 or 13 lines.

The following song from Shakespeare's *Measure for Measure* is a good example of the type of verse to which the term "m." was applied in the later Renaissance:

Take, O, take those lips away,
  That so sweetly were forsworn,
And those eyes, the break of day,
  Lights that do mislead the morn;
But my kisses bring again, bring again,
Seals of love, but seal'd in vain, seal'd in vain.

The echoing device in the final couplet is a characteristic refinement of the later m. verse.

The content of the earlier madrigals is generally pastoral, and the consistent themes of the form, throughout its history, remained nature and love. Verse of the m. type was written in the 19th c. by Carducci and D'Annunzio in Italy, by Goethe and Platen in Germany. The 20th c. has seen a great revival of m. singing in both England and America.—E. H. Fellowes, *Eng. M. Verse, 1588–1632* (1920), *The Eng. M. Composers* (1921) and *The Eng. M.* (1925); A. Einstein, "It. M. Verse," Musical Ass., *Proc.,* 63 (1937), *The It. M.* (3 v., 1949); B. Pattison, *Music and Poetry in the Eng. Renaissance* (1948).

MASCULINE ENDING. See LINE ENDINGS.

MASQUE. The m. developed in the Renaissance as an entertainment in which a procession of masqued or otherwise disguised figures represented a highly imaginative action interspersed with speeches and songs. Many native and foreign traditions contributed to its various forms—morris dancing, mummers' pageants, *ludi,* "disguisings," "triumphs," ballets, morality plays, etc. In Italy, where the m. first acquired a distinctive form, the splendor of the spectacle was of the greatest importance to the presentation of the mythological or similarly fantastic subjects that provided the usual themes. Settings were designed by the greatest artists, Brunelleschi and Leonardo among them, according to the most sophisticated and imaginative taste, and machines were invented to incorporate fountains, artificial clouds, and fire in the production. A single setting might include several scenes in which more than one action or dance would be performed, concurrently or in sequence. The court masques of England equalled these in magnificence and taste even when they were being developed towards a more definite dramatic structure.

Circe, a *ballet de cour* produced in Paris in 1581, exerted a great influence on Eng. masques in providing the example of greater dramatic and thematic unity than had previously been usual. Ben Jonson's and Inigo Jones's *The Masque of Blacknesse* in 1605 moved still further toward establishing dramatic unity as a principle governing the structure of masques by fixing a single concentrated scene for the action upon a stage erected at one end of the hall.

Jonson conceived of the m. as primarily the work of a poet. In the preface to *Hymenaei* (1606) he argued that the design and the words of the m. are its soul, the spectacle and mime and dancing its body. He was thus proposing for the m. a fixed principle, Neoplatonic not merely in declaring the "body" of the m. to be the expression of the "soul," but in claiming the invention itself to be the expression of ideal beauty and truth. To Jonson is also due the credit of inventing the antimasque, a briefer m. to accompany the main one, ordinarily preceding it. This would represent grotseque or comic figures to contrast with the mythological or allegorical personages that were the staple of the main m. For both parts Jonson supplied erudite illustrations in marginalia, partly to point to the philosophic and emblematic nature of the very conception of the works.

Jones, Jonson's collaborator from 1605–31, regarded the spectacle as the main thing, and his own work, after the separation from Jonson, continued to give the greatest scope to visual magnificence. The means for such productions was made available from time to time during the reign of Charles I (Shirley's *Triumph of Peace* [1634] was as lavishly produced as anything under Henry VIII), but with the fall of the Stuarts and the destruction of the conditions that had made the court m. possible, the interest in masques was absorbed in various theatrical and operalike productions.

There had been some place for masques on the Elizabethan stage. The informal, improvised kind that seems to have been very popular in actuality is briefly shown in *Romeo and Juliet.* The more elaborate forms are rather fully presented in *Cymbeline, The Winter's Tale* and *The Tempest.* In the Jacobean and Stuart periods the establishment of the proscenium arch advanced a special form of the m. that has been called "the substantive theatre masque." After the Restoration, masques were sometimes assimilated in the new operatic forms, but in independent productions they appear to have been offered as special kinds of opera, as one may think the 18th-c. productions of *Comus* were regarded.

Whatever the variations, one might say that a m. always derives its form from the initial conception of royalty assuming the role or joining the company of the allegorized divinities of classical belief and, after the fable and dancing are concluded, reverting to its own splendor. Such a combining of dynasty and fancy and moralizing expresses the highest aspirations of a humanist society, the partnership of power and culture in a sententious and joyful entertainment. In the concluding dance, when the masquers, now unmasqued, take their partners from the audience, there is the culminating recognition of the ease and grace and blessedness of the society the actors and dancers in their true selves govern. The spirit of the m. is the opposite of that of the carnival, being royal and noble and classical.

The anti-m. is the other side of the coin, the comic treatment of the unruly, of the forces and elements royalty subdues. To remain true to the tone of the m., the anti-m. opposes it not in satire, which would be alien to the assurance of the rulers, but in the grotesque, the wicked, useless, and amusing imaginings of the ignoble and unworthy.

The combining of music and dancing with drama and spectacle was directed toward a balance that excluded the tensions of drama, and much of the controversy between Ben Jonson and Inigo Jones relates to the problem of how much the burden of meaning and the presentation of character may be allowed to challenge the primarily choreographical and musical movement. Similarly, the spectacular effects were important as much for their variety and their changes as for their dramatic propriety.

R. Brotanek, *Die englischen Maskenspiele* (1902); A. Solerti, *Musica, Ballo e drammatica alla corte Medicea dal 1600 al 1637* (1905); P. Reyher, *Les Masques anglais* (1909); H. Prunières, *Le Ballet de cour en France avant Benserade et Lully* (1914); L. B. Campbell, *Scenes and Machines on the Eng. Stage During the Renaissance* (1923); *Designs by Inigo Jones for Masques and Plays at Court,* ed. P. Simpson and C. F. Bell (1924); E. Welsford, *The Court M.* (1927); A. Nicoll, *Stuart Masques and the Renaissance Stage* (1938); D. J. Gordon, "Poet and Architect: The Intellectual Setting of the Quarrel between Ben Jonson and Inigo Jones," JWCI, 12 (1949); J. Arthos, *On A Mask Presented at Ludlow-Castle, by John Milton* (1954); E. Haun, *"An Inquiry into the Genre of Comus,"* in *Essays in Honor of Walter Clyde Curry* (1954); *Les Fêtes de la Renaissance,* ed. J. Jacquot (1956).

J.A.

MEASURE. A metrical group or period. The m. may consist of the dipody as in classical iambic, trochaic, and anapaestic verse, or of the foot as in Eng. verse. In the so-called musical theories of versification the m. is usually the time sequence consisting of syllables beginning with a main accent and running to the next: "Night's / candles / are burnt / out, and / jocund / day" (*Romeo and Juliet* 3.5.9). In this example the initial word is an example of anacrusis (q.v.); there follow 4 measures of 2 syllables each, of relatively equal time; the final word belongs to the m. ended in the initial syllable of the following line. R.O.E.

MEDIEVAL ROMANCE. The meaning of the term "r." is obscured by the fact that both in medieval and modern times it has been used so loosely. In France, where it originated, it was applied at first to vernacular Fr. (versus L.) literature. Later it came to refer to imaginative works in verse whose subject matter was felt to be fictional or nonhistorical. By the 13th c., however, this distinction was becoming blurred. Any tale of adventure, whatever the origin of its matter, could be a r., and the adventure could be chivalric or merely amorous. Furthermore, r. soon began to be written in prose. Most modern critics distinguish r. from narrative poems treating national themes such as the *Volksepos* in Germany, the *chanson de geste* in France, and the national epic in Spain, even though the treatment of these subjects in the later Middle Ages can hardly be distinguished from that of r. There are several important r. cycles, such as those of Arthur and Alexander, which are associated more by a common background than the presence of a particular character.

The cycles are usually divided by scholars according to their subject matter: (1) "The Matter of Britain" (subdivided into "Arthurian Matter"—r. derived from Breton lays—and "English Matter," e.g., *King Horn*). (2) "The Matter of Rome" (stories of Alexander, of the Trojan War and its heroes, of Thebes, and of the Orient). (3) "The Matter of France" (titles of Charlemagne and his knights).

In general, r. is distinguished from the older *chanson de geste* (q.v.) and epic forms by its less heroic tone, its greater sophistication, its fondness for the fantastic, its more superficial characterization, (often) looser structure, and unity of action. The sources of r. are legion, and there is controversy over which is primary. According to one influential school (e.g., W. P. Ker), the form is the result of the sentimentalization of the earlier heroic materials which occurred when they were combined with such typically high medieval ideals as chivalry and courtly love. Others stress classical sources and/or such late classical r. as *Daphnis and Chloe* by Longus and the *Aethiopica* (3d c. ?) of Heliodorus. Arthurian r. has received particularly full treatment. The theory of Celtic origins has been most vigorously propounded by Roger Sherman Loomis. An opposing school of thought, best represented in America by Urban T. Holmes, Jr., argues with equal vehemence that Chrétien de Troyes must be regarded as the inventor of Arthurian r. Other theories have also been advanced, but an early settlement of the controversy seems unlikely.

Although it is not confined to r., the courtly background is virtually indispensable to them. It is not a realistic background of contemporary courts but an ideal of chivalry, with stress on mercy to an opponent, good manners, and artistic sensitivity as well as the virtues of bravery, loyalty, and preservation of honor. The milieu of r. is tournaments, adventures, and particularly love. The winning of a lady is an essential part of all early r., and it is achieved by "love service," that is by worship, formal courtship, and unremitting attention to her wishes. In its highest form this love ennobles a man and makes him capable of deeds beyond his normal powers. A man truly in love lives a full life, both for his lady and for adventure. Such love may be between man and wife, as it is, after trials, between Erec and Enide, Yvain and Laudine, Parzival and Condwiramurs. It may be adulterous, as between Lancelot and Guinevere and Tristan and Isolde. Married love holds together society, adulterous love destroys it. In both the power of love is predominant over everything else. Later r., although they often paid lip service to the power of love, tended to regard it as merely one more adventure.

Although Arthurian r. are by far the most famous and influential, the earliest extant r. do not belong to this cycle. They are r. of antiquity, rather misleadingly called the "Matter of Rome." An anonymous *Roman d'Enée* was written about 1150. Virgil's *Aeneid* was its source but its tone is emphatically medieval. The work becomes a love adventure with destructive love (Dido) spurned and true love (Lavinia) finally triumphant. The characters behave like medieval knights. A reworking by the Germanic Heinrich von Veldeke (*Eneide,* ca. 1180) retains these characteristics. The greatest of Troy r., the *Roman de Troie* of Benoît de Ste.-Maure (ca. 1165), tells the full story of the Trojan War, based on the L. account by "Dares Phrygius." Again love interests predominate, particularly that of Achilles and Polyxena and—probably Benoît's own invention—of Troilus and Cressida. Here the code of chivalry is applied fully to the warriors of Troy.

Although not originated by him, Arthurian r. is closely associated with Chrétien de Troyes. Chrétien's works are the earliest and greatest of the r. in Fr. Nothing is known of the author except that he was associated with the court of Marie de Champagne. He may have been a cleric. His r. appeared in the order *Erec et Enide, Lancelot* or the *Knight of the Cart, Yvain,* and *Perceval* or *Li Contes del graal. Cligès,* written after

Erec, is an Eastern r. with Arthurian elements. Common to all these is the acknowledged superiority of Arthur's court as a center of civilized behavior, a high standard of manners, courage, and love of service, of which Gawain is the perfect type and Sir Kay the antitype. The world outside is full of uncouth creatures and is fit only for adventure. *Erec* and *Yvain* handle two facets of the same problem, the maintenance of equilibrium between love and adventure. In both cases married love is fulfillment and true adventure is possible only in the service of love. *Lancelot* shows this love carried to absurdity, for the lover, a brave knight, is made to obey every whim, however foolish, of his lady. Chrétien did not finish the work, and it is hard to deny that it is ironical. *Perceval* was clearly intended to show a knightly service higher than that of Arthur's court, for the foolishly simple Perceval is destined for the service of the Grail, which is definitely a religious symbol however mysterious it may be otherwise. The parallel adventures of the perfect secular knight Gawain again express the theme of the higher destiny. Chrétien did not finish the work but Wolfram von Eschenbach about 1210 used his work and other material as a source for *Parzival.* Here the Grail, a precious stone, becomes the gift of Paradise, the center of a band of religious knights whose king must be above the love-adventure morality of Arthur's courts. Parzival's pilgrimage takes him through innocence, error, pride, despair, and repentance, to humility. It is the way of the Christian man but not of any Christian man, for Parzival is a chosen king, an Arthurian warrior on his father's side, a grail warrior on his mother's. In *Parzival* r. reaches its highest spiritual manifestation while maintaining the essential characteristics of the type—adventure, love, and ideal background of chivalry.

If *Parzival* is the noblest romance, Gottfried von Strassburg's *Tristan and Isolt* (ca. 1210) is the most polished and in some ways the most intellectually satisfying. Gottfried used the fine courtly r. of Thomas of Britain (ca. 1180) as a source but his hero is in fact more a minstrel and artist than a knight. The love episodes are courtly only on the surface, for Gottfried shows that courtly love is empty. His lovers seek a deeper, more spiritual, less attainable love which destroys both them and society.

With few exceptions the history of the r. in the 13th and 14th c. is one of decline. The chief characteristic is loss of form and purpose. The Alexander r., for example, the earliest of which date from ca. 1120, were capable of indefinite expansion by increase of incident; and the prose versions of Arthurian r. become highly involved adventure stories in which characters appear and disappear. New and voluminous r. were written about minor Arthurian knights and on persons hitherto hardly known. Two exceptions stand out. *Sir Gawain and the Green Knight* by an anonymous writer of the Eng. Midlands is a superb study of the moral problem of courage. Gawain undertakes a test of courage which he feels is his duty as the model Arthurian knight. He survives a planned assault on his virtue by a lady in the castle where he is staying. Yet he cannot resist the temptation of accepting a charm against wounds, even though it is dishonorable for him to do so. Sir Thomas Malory's misnamed *Morte d'Arthur* is best known in the form in which Caxton rearranged it. It is a final accounting of the Arthurian cycle, with a strong feeling for the fate which the sin of adultery brought to the ideal world of chivalry.

The traditions of r. lingered on, though often in distorted and even parodied form, to the Renaissance. Ariosto's *Orlando furioso,* the *Teuerdank* of Maximilian I, *Amadis de Gaule* all show the conventions of chivalry, and the humor of *Don Quixote,* as well as its tragedy, depends on a recognition of r. conventions.

Collections: *ME Metrical Romances,* ed. W. H. French and C. B. Hale (1930); *Medieval Romances,* ed. R. S. and L. H. Loomis (1957).

History and Criticism: W. P. Ker, *Epic and R.* (1897); W. Golther, *Tristan und Isolde in der Dichtung des Mittelalters und der neuen Zeit* (1907); G. Schoepperle, *Tristan and Isolt* (2 v., 1913); M. Wilmotte, *De l'origine du roman en France* (1923); E. K. Chambers, *Arthur of Britain* (1927); R. S. Loomis, *Celtic Myth and Arthurian R.* (1927) and *Arthurian Tradition and Chrétien de Troyes* (1949); C. B. Lewis, *Classical Mythology and Arthurian R.* (1932); R. R. Bezzola, *Les Origines et la formation de la litt. courtoise, 500–1100* (2 v., 1944–60); U. T. Holmes, Jr., *A New Interpretation of Chrétien's Conte del Graal* (1948); E. Neumann, "Der Streit um 'das ritterliche Tugendsystem,' " *Festschrift für Karl Helm* (1951); G. Cary, *The Medieval Alexander* (1956); J. Frappier, *Chrétien de Troyes* (1957); *Arthurian Lit. in the Middle Ages,* ed. R. S. Loomis (1959); L. A. Hibbard, *Medieval R. in England* (rev. ed., 1961); M.J.C. Reid, *The Arthurian Legend: A Comparison of Treatment in Medieval and Modern Lit.* (1961); R. S. Loomis, *The Development of Arthurian R.* (1963) and *The Grail* (1963).

W.T.H.J.

MEIOSIS (Gr. "lessening"). A figure employing ironic understatement, usually to convey the impression that a thing is less in size, or importance, than it really is; generally synonymous with *litotes* (q.v.), though sometimes considered more generic in application. Quintilian discusses m. as an abuse or fault of language which characterizes obscure style rather than one lacking ornament, but he indicates that deliberately employed m. may be called a figure, and promises to discuss it later, though he neglects to do so (*Institutes of Oratory* 8.6.51). Puttenham distinguishes m. more particularly: "If you diminish and abbase a thing by way of spight . . . , such speach is by the figure *Meiosis* or the disabler" (*The Arte of Eng. Poesie*). "Long for me the rick will wait, / And long will wait the fold, / And long will stand the empty plate, / And dinner will be cold" (A. E. Housman, *A Shropshire Lad* 8.21–24). A singularly persuasive literary device which may dominate an entire poem, as Auden's *Musée des Beaux Arts* or *The Unknown Citizen.* M. may also occur with startling simplicity as part of a longer narrative; e.g., Dante's famous "quel giorno più non vi leggemmo avante" (We read no more that day) from the Paolo and Francesca episode (*La Divina Commedia: Inferno 5*), or the concluding lines of Wordsworth's *Michael.* Note also Shakespeare's later tragedies, especially *Lear,* wherein simplicity and understatement often mark the most dramatic moments. R.O.E.

MELIC POETRY (Gr. "connected with music," "lyric"). Poetry sung or sung and danced. In the classical period the Greeks applied the name to all forms of lyric poetry in which music played a very important part. However, it did not include elegiac, iambic, and epic poetry because in these genres the musical accompaniment was not particulariy significant. M. poetry was chiefly developed by the Aeolians and the Dorians and was written in a great number of meters. Its most brilliant period was between the 7th and the 5th c. B.C. It was divided into two classes, monodic or solo lyric and choral lyric. The monodic lyric was sung by a single voice and expressed the emotions and feelings of one individual. Its stanzas, usually made up of 4–5 lines, were repeated without interruption. Its chief representatives were Sappho, Alcaeus, and Anacreon. The choral lyric expressed the emotions of the group and was sung by a chorus. Its strophes were arranged in triads (strophe, antistrophe, epode) repeated several times. It was chiefly written by Alcman, Stesichorus, Simonides, Pindar, and Bacchylides. The main subdivisions of m. poetry as given by the Alexandrian scholars were: hymns, paeans, dithyrambs, *epinicia, scolia,* epithalamia, and *partheneia.* In Alexandrian and subsequent times this type of poetry is referred to as lyric.—Smyth; Bowra; J. M. Edmonds, *Lyra Graeca* (3 v., 1952). P.S.C.

METAPHOR. A condensed verbal relation in which an idea, image, or symbol may, by the presence of one or more other ideas, images, or symbols, be enhanced in vividness, complexity, or breadth of implication.

The nature and definition of metaphorical terms and of the relations between them have both been matter for much speculation and disagreement. It is unlikely therefore that a more specific definition will at first be acceptable. The metaphorical relation has been variously described as comparison, contrast, analogy, similarity, juxtaposition, identity, tension, collision, fusion; and different views have been held regarding the nature, operation, and function of metaphor in poetry. In recent years the view has gathered weight that m. is the radical process in which the internal relationships peculiar to poetry are achieved; some critics maintaining that m. marks off the poetic mode of vision and utterance from the logical or discursive mode; others, usually on anthropological evidence, that all language is m. The traditional view, however, is that m. is a figure of speech, or a family of tropes, involving two (occasionally four) operative terms, and that it is used for adornment, liveliness, elucidation, or agreeable mystification.

The view of m. as tropical may be considered first. For this view Aristotle is taken to be the prime authority, particularly in his statement that "metaphor consists in giving the thing a name that belongs to something else; the transference being either from genus to species, or from species to genus, or from species to species, or on grounds of analogy" (*Poetics* 1457b). Some of these instances of "transference" have been classed by grammarians under such names as synecdoche, metonymy, catachresis, and so on—the terms not coinciding with Aristotle's division.

Grammarians since Cicero and Quintilian, again on Aristotle's authority (though based upon the *Rhetoric* where the discussion is limited to prose), have insisted upon the harmony or congruity of metaphorical elements, and upon a measure of visual clarity. Hence the traditional condemnation of "mixed metaphor" and the limiting of m. to a descriptive or expository function: so that, for example, George Campbell (*Philosophy of Rhetoric,* 1841) writes: "In metaphor the sole relation is resemblance." Grammarians, noticing some logical incongruity between the elements in m., have also suggested that m. not only transfers and alters meaning but may also pervert it; and this suspicion is preserved in the single definition offered by SOED: "Metaphor. The figure of speech in which a name or descriptive term is transferred to some object to which it is *not properly applicable*" (cf. NED: ". . . some object different from, but analogous to, that to which it is properly applicable"). Philosophers particularly have indulged the suspicion that m. is an "improper" connection of terms, regarding m. as a decorative but inexact alternative to what honest and forthright consideration would disclose in a literal form, and implying that the use of m. is a mark of carelessness, haste, or intellectual unchastity (cf. *Poetics* 1458b 17 which, if read out of context, might seem to support this view).

Traditionally, m. has been represented as a trope of transference in which an unknown or imperfectly known is clarified, defined, described in terms of a known. This is exhibited as an overt or implied predication of the form (*a*) A is [like] B, or (*b*) A is as B—that is, A is [like X] as B [is like Y]. In this scheme a m. is explicated by translating it into a predicative form that will reveal the relation of resemblance. For example: (*a*) 1. "Love is a singing bird" = "Love is like a singing bird" or "Love makes you feel like (or, as though you were listening to) a singing bird"; 2. "the proud nostril-curve of a prow's line" = "a prow's line with the same curve as a proud man's nostril"; 3. "Her head . . . with its anchoring calm" = "Her head that, with its air of calm, makes you feel as secure (? and hopeful) as an anchor would in a ship"; 4. "a Harris-tweed cat" = "a cat that looks (smells, feels) as though it were made of Harris tweed"; (*b*) 5. "My love is . . . begotten by despair upon impossibility" = "My love is conceived as though its father were despair and its mother impossibility"; 6. "Hatred infects the mind" = "Hatred is like an infection in the mind"; 7. "Admiral earth breaks out his colours at the forepeak of the day" = "The earth discloses its colors in the morning with the same abrupt brilliance as the breaking-out of an admiral's colors (ensign) at the forepeak of his flagship."

An unprejudiced examination of the examples given above suggests that although analysis by resemblance may be suitable for analyzing resemblance, it is inadequate—even irrelevant—in most of these cases if we take into account not merely some notion of semantic equivalence but the actual sensation these metaphors induce. First, the apparently simple metaphors 1 and 4 have at least two or three simultaneous meanings; and this occurs not because of a variety of resemblances but because of a substantial though paradoxical coincidence of terms: each term preserves its distinctness, yet in the momentary coincidence—or identity (to use a term applied at least as early as 1930 by Bowra)—each term is changed. Second, examples 3 and 6 show that what appears to be a simple two-term relation can be a condensed four-term relation. Third, the function of the transitive verb in analogical m. (A is to X as B is to Y) is very important (with "hatred infects the mind" cf. "hatred is [like] an infection in the mind" or "hatred works in the mind as infection works in the body"); to reduce or expand an analogical m. to predicative form destroys its vitality. These results may be tentatively consolidated. The radical form of m. is either A is B (a momentary or hypothetical identity being involved), or simply A-B (parataxis, the juxtaposition of two terms, e.g., "sphinx-woman" and 2, 3, 4 above). The analogical m. achieves strength and avoids a simple relation of resemblance by forming itself around a transitive verb (e.g., "bright chanticleer explodes the dawn," "the ship ploughs the waves").

Historically, however, the view of m. as primarily a figure for extending description, comparison, and exposition reflects literary usage rather than critical obtuseness. Rosamund Tuve, for example, has pointed to the 16th-c. emphasis, in handbooks and in practice, upon the delight roused by deft and sustained *translatio*, the exploration by metaphorical means of minute similarities within clearly defined fields of relationship (see *Elizabethan and Metaphysical Imagery*, 1947, pp. 121ff., 223–24). Guided by a clear notion of the didactic and explicatory function they wished m. to serve, writers of that period saw no reason to extend or explore the outer reaches of m. And Milton's use of epic simile, as compared with the Homeric use, is a refined development of *translatio* in the direction of multiple logical resemblances (see SIMILE below). Although at practically all periods we find instances of m. serving important poetic functions outside the scope of the received grammatical definition, these were evidently not thought important enough to modify the definition.

In fact, Aristotle's doctrine of m., though fragmentary, was far more comprehensive than his successors had reason clearly to recognize. He had also said that "the greatest thing by far is to be a master of metaphor. It is the one thing that cannot be learnt from others; and it is also a sign of genius, since a good metaphor implies an intuitive perception of the similarity in dissimilars" (*Poetics* 1458b; cf. *Rhetoric* 1405a); and that "from metaphor we can best get hold of something fresh [new]" (*Rhetoric* 1410b), that "Liveliness [?energy] is specially conveyed by metaphor" (*Rhetoric* 1412a), and that "of the four kinds of Metaphor the most taking is the proportional [4-term analogical] kind"—e.g., "The sun sheds its rays" (*Rhetoric* 1411a). He had not only implied a sharp distinction between the uses of m. in prose and in poetry, but had also emphasized the energetic character of m. by choosing examples, not in predicative form, but as formed around vigorous verbs. In showing the relation between riddle and m. he had in a sense anticipated the doctrine of paratactic m. But tradition, and many later critics, neglected these niceties.

The view that the term m. could legitimately be extended was encouraged by the work of Max Müller (1862–65) and by a succession of anthropologists, linguists, and psychologists who have studied the genesis and history of language. These have produced conflicting and even misleading hypotheses, and by customarily neglecting the evidence of developed literature have provided results not always serviceable to literary criticism. But they have helped to confirm the conclusion, drawn with increasing insistence from literary evidence, that in m. we see that "most vital principle of language (and perhaps of all symbolism)" (Susanne K. Langer, *Philosophy in a New Key*, 1953 ed., p. 112; here discussing Philip Wegener), and that "The genesis of language is not to be sought in the prosaic, but in the poetic side of life" (Otto Jespersen, *Language*, 1933). Shelley incidentally had already noticed this in a luminous if isolated passage: "Language is vitally metaphorical; that is, it marks the before unapprehended relations of things and perpetuates their apprehension, until words, which represent them, become, through time, signs for portions or classes of thought instead of pictures of integral thoughts: and then, if no new poets should arise to create afresh the associations which have been thus disorganized, language will be dead to all the nobler purposes of human intercourse" (*Defence of Poetry*).

The link with a rhetorical past was not easily broken. Much effort—both before and since the 1920's—has been spent on contriving terms suitable for describing how m. works: with distinctions between "what was said" and "what was meant," between "literal" and "metaphorical" meaning, between "idea" and "image," "form" and "figure," and so on. But it is dangerous to assume a readily distinguishable external datum of literality, for the literal meaning in each case is determined *within* the context; and the way Richards' terms "tenor" and "vehicle" fluctuated, even in his own hands (1936), arises from his attempt to answer both the question "*how* does metaphor work?" and the much more profitable question "what happens in a metaphor?" Richards stated in 1925 that m. is "the supreme agent by which disparate and hitherto unconnected things are brought together in poetry for the sake of the effects upon attitude and impulse which spring from their collocation and from the combinations which the mind then establishes between them. There are few metaphors whose effect, if carefully examined, can be traced to the logical relations involved" (*Principles of Literary Criticism,* 1925, p. 240). Richards' *Philosophy of Rhetoric* (1936) emphasized the "organizing" activity in some kinds of m., pointed out that a word may be simultaneously "literal" and metaphorical, and introduced Coleridge into the discussion—a man who had already made at least a perceptive route-traverse of the country with the eye of a psychologist and linguist as well as of a poet and critic.

Max Black's analysis provides a useful summary. He wished to assail the philosophical commandment "Thou shalt not commit metaphor" and in looking for a use of m. acceptable in philosophical discourse analyzed previous accounts of m. into three "views": *substitution, comparison,* and *interaction.* The first two he dismissed (with qualifications), but found that the third, as represented chiefly by Richards (though again with some qualifications), offered "some important insight into the uses and limitations of metaphor." He starts with Richards' definition: "In the simplest formulation, when we use a metaphor we have two thoughts of different things active together and supported by a single word, or phrase, whose meaning is a resultant of their interaction" (*Philosophy of Rhetoric,* p. 93); but rejects the word "interaction" in favor of the image of a *filter.* The metaphor-word—the *focus*—calls up a system of "associated commonplaces" which are in turn related with various aspects of the principal subject: e.g., "Man is a wolf." "The metaphor [in this case] selects, emphasizes, suppresses, and organizes features of the principal subject by implying statements about it that normally apply to the subsidiary subject." Although Black recognizes that the elements of m. are "systems of things" rather than "things," and insists that these metaphors are untranslatable and that the secondary implications of a m. can be extremely intricate, his illustrations—as one would expect of a philosopher—are stated in propositional form. The outcome then is actually a comparison-metaphor, though of a much more highly organized and finely controlled kind than the comparison-metaphor recognized by tradition. Richards had clearly intended to go beyond his point, as some of his uses of the terms "tenor" and "vehicle" show. He wanted to talk about the "total meaning" of m. as arising from the *interaction* of elements. He had quoted Coleridge with approval: "A symbol is characterized by the translucence of the special in the individual . . . It always partakes of the reality which it renders intelligible; and while it enunciates the whole, abides itself as a living part in that unity, of which it is the representative." He seems to have chosen the word *interaction* with care: it allowed him to think of the metaphorical elements as preserving their integrity, and to think of the "total meaning" as the outcome of the impact of elements rather than as a derivative by comparison, fusion, or combination. If he had written his book ten years later he might have said that "interaction" was not like chemical combination but like nuclear fission. Richards' view is not definitive, but it either represents or has stimulated much of the more recent discussion.

Every innovative critical theory of the past two decades has generated a new delineation of m.—either as the "other" of its own conceptual domain, or as the very ground of its new insights. One of the most influential innovations has been Jakobson's opposition of m. to metonymy (q.v.). Though they often cross disciplinary boundaries, recent theories of m. can be classified as (1) linguistic or semiotic (based on intralinguistic relationships, or relations between signs of any sort); (2) rhetorical or pragmatic (involving a difference between sentence meaning and speaker meaning); (3) philosophical (emphasizing relations between words and reality, or sense and reference); and (4) extended (a general category for those theories that apply the concept of m. to non-linguistic interrelationships in other disciplines).

(1) *Linguistics and semiotics.* The most ambitious recent attempt to identify linguistic features of m. appears in *A General Rhetoric,* produced by the "Group μ" of the University of Liège. They treat all unexpected suppressions, additions, repetitions, or permutations of linguistic elements, from phonemes to phrases, as figures, the non-figurative being a hypothetical "degree

zero" discourse from which rhetoric deviates. M. results from an implicit decomposition of words into their semes (lexical features), some of which will be cancelled, and others added, when one word is substituted for another. The natural route for such substitutions is through species and genus, as Aristotle noted, and the Group μ concludes that a m. consists of two synecdoches, the progression being either species—genus—species (the intermediate term being a class that includes the first and last terms) or whole—part—whole (here the central term is a class formed where the first and last overlap). Using a more flexible scheme for the transfer and deletion of semantic features, Samuel Levin, in *The Semantics of M.*, shows that there are six ways to interpret a m. (his example is "the stone died"). He points out that the grammatical structure of many metaphors allows for the transfer of features in two directions: "the brook smiled" can humanize the brook, or add sparkling and liquidity to the idea of smiling. Although he analyzes m. as an intralinguistic phenomenon, Levin recognizes that Aristotle's fourth type, analogy, often depends upon reference to reality—a fact that the Group μ overlooked. Thus m. appears to escape formalization within a system. Umberto Eco's semiotic solution to this problem is to imagine an encyclopedia that describes all the features of reality which are not included in the semanticist's dictionary. For Riffaterre, mimetic reference is only a feint that the literary text makes before refocusing itself in a network of semiotic commonplaces.

(2) *Pragmatics.* Speech-act theorists hold that m. cannot be explained through reference to relationships between words and their linguistic contexts. They make a categorical distinction between "word, or sentence meaning" and "speaker's utterance meaning." M., in their view, arises from a disparity between the literal meaning of the words used and what is intended by the speaker or writer. Words always retain their invariant "locutionary" definitions; when used to request, warn, or make metaphors, the hearer notices that there is something odd about them and infers unstated suggestions or meanings ("illocutions"). As evidence for this theory, Ted Cohen says that a speaker's intention may lead us to infer that a literally true sentence is a m. (e.g., "no man is an island"). As evidence against it, L. J. Cohen points out that speech acts lose their speaker-meaning in indirect discourse ("Tom told George he was sorry" is not an apology), but metaphors remain such when repeated ("Tom said George was a fire-eater")—indicating that the meaning of a m. is in the words, not in the occasion of their use. Grice's theory of "conversational implicature" provides a set of rules and maxims for normal talk that, when violated, may alert us to the fact that someone is speaking figuratively. His theory, like Searle's, locates m. in a difference between utterance meaning and speaker meaning—the area of "pragmatics"—and is subject to the same sort of criticism that speech-act theory has elicited (see Sadock).

(3) *Philosophy.* Searle and Grice are philosophers, but their theories entail empirical claims of relevance to linguists. Donald Davidson's treatment of m. is more strictly philosophic. Meaning, in his view, involves only the relationship between language and reality, apart from speakers and contexts of use. He is willing to accept the interaction account of how m. works, and the pragmatic "distinction between what words mean and what they are used to do," but he denies the existence of anything that can properly be called speaker or metaphoric meaning: "metaphors mean what the words, in their most literal interpretation, mean, and nothing more." If we did not realize they were patently false, we would not know they were figurative. Recognizing them as such, we may discover truths about the world, but this is not a consequence of some meaning inherent in the words. Nelson Goodman disagrees. In *Languages of Art*, he shows that the use of m., like many other activities, can be conceived as exemplification. Rather than applying a label to a thing, we can use the thing as a sample or example of the label, as when the lively appearance of the literal brook is seen as an instance of smiling (cf. Levin, above). This reverses the direction of denotation: the example refers to the word, rather than vice versa, and the word may bring with it a whole schema of relationships that will be sorted anew in the metaphorical context. Goodman concludes that m. is "no more independent of truth or falsity than literal use" (1979).

Many philosophers remain committed to the premise that meaning exists only in propositions (in Austin's terminology, "locutions" or "constatives"); examples, presuppositions, questions, and hypothetical instances are from this point of view deviations from the norm. They take "A is B" as the canonical form of m., since it is obviously a false predication. Most metaphors are in fact of the form "the B of A" or "the B (adjective) A," which presuppose rather than assert a conjunction (see Brooke-Rose).

(4) *Other disciplines.* Postponing discussion of deeper philosophic differences that divide theorists, one cannot help but note that they tend to privilege different moments in the process of interpretation. At first glance, or outside time, m. is false (Davidson). Realizing that the creator of a m. means something else, one might pause and create a theory of the difference between sentence and speaker meaning (Searle; Grice). When engaged in deciphering, a reader exemplifies the interaction theory—discovering new meanings—and the falsity of m. is left behind, as the mere stimulus of the quest. Truth usually results from testing many examples to find one

rule; in m., meaning emerges from repeated consideration of a single example, uncovering all its possibilities, and a hypothesis or generalization is the product of the process, not its inception. In accordance with information theory, the low probability of a word or phrase in a particular context implies that it carries a great deal of meaning.

The improbable interaction of conceptual domains in m. has attracted the attention of theorists in other disciplines and led them to transport the figure outside its proper limits. Like metaphors, scientific models serve heuristic functions when familiar structures are used to map uncharted phenomena. Mary Hesse and Thomas Kuhn have extended Black's discussion of this subject, which has also attracted the attention of Fr. philosophers of science. Citing the work of Bachelard and Canguilhem, Derrida suggests that the function of m. in science is not merely heuristic; Boyd argues that "metaphors are *constitutive* of the theories they express, rather than merely exigetical," and that metaphorical terms can be referential in theoretical contexts. In *Metaphors We Live By*, Lakoff and Johnson show how pervasive they are in organizing personal and social experience. In such cases the occurrence of a particular m. is less significant than the model ("frame," "schema," "system of commonplaces") that it evokes. When employed to order understanding of the past or to plan for the future, metaphoric analogies take on a narrative dimension (see Schön and Sternberg *et al.*, for discussion of their influence on social policy). Stephen Pepper's *World Hypotheses*, which treats most philosophic systems as elaborations of four "root metaphors," proved useful to Hayden White, who argues that a poetic "prefiguration" based on one of the four basic tropes (metonymy, synecdoche, metaphor, and irony, according to Ramus and Vico) underlies the methods of explanation used by modern historians.

Summary. The figural use of "m." in modern theory, through which it assimilates not only all other tropes (as in Aristotle) but models, analogies, and narrative methods as well, leads to the question of whether the literal and figurative can properly be distinguished from one another. The simplest and in some ways most logical answers are that all linguistic meaning is literal (Davidson), or that it is all figural (Nietzsche). Children do not discriminate between the two in language acquisition, and there is little evidence that adult comprehension of literal and metaphorical usage involves different psychological processes (Rummelhart). Vico contests Rousseau's thesis that m. preceded literal usage in the development of language, on the grounds that this distinction, once made, cannot legitimately be projected back on earlier linguistic history (*New Science*, par. 409). This historical argument has an analogue in recent semantic theory. Rather than attempting to identify rules capable of accounting for literal usage, and then explaining figures as transformations or deviations from this set, one can begin from an inclusive set of semantic features, from which literal and figurative usage can be derived through imposition of further constraints (Weinreich; van Dijk; see Levin).

While contributing to an understanding of its linguistic features and conceptual implications, recent theories of m. show that it is not simply one critical problem among others, distinguished only by the number of disagreements it happens to stimulate. As that which lies outside the literal, normal, proper, or systematic, m. serves as the topic through which each system defines itself: m. is not simply false, but that which marks the limits of the distinctions between true and false, or meaningful and deviant. As Derrida says (1972), "each time that a rhetoric defines metaphor, not only is *a* philosophy implied, but also a conceptual network in which philosophy *itself* has been constituted." Thus agreement about the status of m. will be deferred until all other philosophic issues have been resolved. In *The Rule of M.*, the best available survey of the subject, Paul Ricoeur integrates many of the views discussed above in an all-encompassing theory that preserves while subsuming the oppositions on which they are based. To do so, he is forced to assign literary m. (despite its virtues) to a subordinate position in relation to the "speculative discourse" of philosophy, within which m. can reveal the nature of being. Thus showing how little has changed since Plato described the quarrel between philosophy and rhetoric, Ricoeur helped stimulate a more penetrating analysis of the conceptual operation that gives rise to the distinction between being and textuality, and hence to that between the literal and the figurative (Derrida, 1978).

The Works of Aristotle, ed. W. D. Ross, XI (*Rhetoric*, tr. W. Rhys Roberts; *Poetics*, tr. I. Bywater) (1924); M. Müller, *Lectures on the Science of Language*, 2 ser. (1862, 1865); A. Biese, *Die Philosophie des Metaphorischen* (1893); J. G. Jennings, *An Essay on M. in Poetry* (1915); H. Werner, *Die Ursprünge der Metapher* (1919); I. A. Richards, *Principles; Coleridge on Imagination* (1934), *The Philos. of Rhetoric* (1936); O. Barfield, *Poetic Diction* (1928); H. Konrad, *Etude sur la métaphore* (1939, 2d ed., 1958); S. Pepper, *World Hypotheses* (1942); Langer; M. Foss, *Symbol and M. in Human Experience* (1949); W. Empson, *The Structure of Complex Words* (1951); R. Jakobson, "Two Aspects of Language and Two Types of Aphasic Disturbances, (v): The Metaphoric and Metonymic Poles," in R. Jakobson and M. Halle, *Fundamentals of Language* (1956); Frye; C. Brooke-Rose, *A Grammar of M.* (1958); *M. and Symbol*, ed. L. C. Knights and B. Cottle (1960); M. I. Baym, "The Present State of the Study of M.," *BA*, 35 (1961); M. C. Beardsley, "The Metaphorical Twist," *Philos. and Phenomenological Research*, 22 (1962); M. Black,

Models and Metaphors (1962); C. M. Turbayne, *The Myth of M.* (1962); P. Wheelwright, *M. and Reality* (1962); J. Cohen, *Structure du langage poétique* (1966); M. Hesse, *Models and Analogies in Science* (1966); H. Weinreich, "Explorations in Semantic Theory," in *Current Trends in Linguistics*, III (1966); M. B. Hester, *The Meaning of Poetic M.* (1967); N. Goodman, *Languages of Art* (1968); Group μ, *Rhétorique générale* (1970, tr. *A General Rhetoric*, 1981); W. A. Shibles, *M.: An Annotated Bibliog. and Hist.* (1971); J. Derrida, "La mythologie blanche," *Marges de la philosophie* (1972, tr. *Margins of Philos.*, 1982); T. A. van Dijk, *Some Aspects of Text Grammars* (1972) and "Formal Semantics of Metaphorical Discourse," *Poetics*, 4 (1975); H. White, *Metahistory* (1973); *New Literary History*, 6 (1974); P. Ricoeur, *La métaphore vive* (1975, tr. *The Rule of M.*, 1977); T. Cohen, "Figurative Speech and Figurative Acts," *Jour. of Philos.*, 71 (1975); S. R. Levin, *The Semantics of M.* (1977); D. Davidson, "What Metaphors Mean," and P. de Man, "The Epistemology of M.," *Critical Inquiry*, 5 (1978); J. Derrida, "The *Retrait* of M.," *Enclitic*, 2 (1978); M. Riffaterre, *Semiotics of Poetry* (1978); M. Black, "How Metaphors Work," and N. Goodman, "M. as Moonlighting," *Critical Inquiry*, 6 (1979); M. Black, R. Boyd, L. J. Cohen, T. S. Kuhn, S. R. Levin, M. J. Reddy, J. M. Sadock, D. A. Schön, J. R. Searle, R. J. Sternberg *et al.* in *M. and Thought*, ed. A. Ortony (1979); P. de Man, *Allegories of Reading* (1979); G. Lakoff and M. Johnson, *Metaphors We Live By* (1980); J. Culler, "The Turns of M.," in *The Pursuit of Signs* (1981); M. Johnson, "Selected Annotated Bibliog.," in *Philosophical Perspectives on M.* (1981); A. Haverkamp, "Bibliographie" (for ca. 1870–1981), in *Theorie der Metapher* (1983); U. Eco, "The Scandal of M.," *Poetics Today*, 4 (1983) and 5 (1984). G.W.; rev. W.M.

METER. More or less regular poetic rhythm; the measurable rhythmical patterns manifested in verse; or the "ideal" patterns which poetic rhythms approximate. If "m." is regarded as the ideal rhythmical pattern, then "rhythm" becomes "m." the closer it approaches regularity and predictability. The impulse toward metrical organization seems to be a part of the larger human impulses toward order: m. is what results when the rhythmical movements of colloquial speech are heightened, organized, and regulated so that pattern emerges from the relative phonetic haphazard of ordinary utterance. M. is thus one of the fundamental and most subtle techniques of order available to the poet, like rhyme, line division, stanza form, and over-all structure.

Most theorists agree that poetic m., even when most primitive, produces a pleasant effect, but there is widespread disagreement among critics and scholars over the reason for the universal popularity of metered compositions. According to some theorists (mostly rationalists), m. is pleasant because it focuses attention and refines awareness; according to others (mostly romanticists), on the contrary, it is pleasant because it produces a lulling, drugging, or hypnotic effect. One theory holds that, since the beat in most accentual poetries is slightly faster than the normal heartbeat, the apprehension of poetic m. produces a physically exhilarating effect on hearer or reader: his heartbeat, the theory contends, actually speeds up to "match" the slightly faster poetic rhythm. The pleasure universally resulting from foot-tapping and musical time-beating seems to suggest that the pleasures of m. are definitely physical and that they are as intimately connected with the rhythmic quality of man's total experience as are the similar alternating and recurring phenomena of breathing, walking, and love-making. Perhaps one could untangle some of the disagreements about the pleasures of m. by suggesting that the quality of the apprehender will determine the nature of the pleasure in each case: children and the unsophisticated receive from m. primarily physical pleasure which manifests itself in foot- or finger-tapping, head-nodding, and the like; on the other hand, the more experienced and sensitive reader will probably derive most of his metrical pleasure from the higher level of rhetorical attention which m. enforces ("Meter keeps the mind on the stretch," one critic has observed), or from an intellectual delight in witnessing order and containment brought out of chaos and flux. Medieval theories of m., in fact, frequently assume that the pleasure man takes in m. is an image of the pleasure he takes in the observation of the principle of order in a universe which is itself will and order incarnate.

"M." derives from the Gr. term for "measure," and one way to investigate various meters or metrical systems is to examine what is being measured in each. On this basis, four metrical systems are generally—if not quite adequately—discriminated: the syllabic, the accentual, the accentual-syllabic, and the quantitative.

Syllabic prosody measures only the number of syllables per line: hence the term "numbers," frequently used as a synonym for "versification" by syllabic metrical theorists. In syllabic m. stress or accent is usually only a device of embellishment and not a criterion of the basic metrical "skeleton" of the line. Poetry in the Romance languages and in Japanese is fundamentally syllabic in construction. Some Eng. poetry after the Restoration became markedly syllabic (perhaps as a result of Fr. influence) until about 1740, but since that time syllabism has seldom been revived except as an experimental novelty: Robert Bridges, Dylan Thomas, W. H. Auden, and Marianne Moore are some of the recent poets who have experimented with syllabism. It would probably be agreed that syllabism is not a natural m. in a Germanic language so accentual as Eng., although interesting (if perhaps hypersubtle) effects can result from it (here and below, all examples are of poetry in Eng. for purposes of comparison):

Mid the squander'd colour
    idling as I lay
Reading the Odyssey
    in my rock garden
I espied the cluster'd
    tufts of Cheddar pinks
Burgeoning with promise
    of their scented bloom . . .

(R. Bridges, *Cheddar Pinks* [6- and 5-syllable lines alternating; stress used as embellishment])

One clear disadvantage of syllabic construction is that the reader, to sense the form of the poem, must halt unnaturally at line endings: the reader naturally measures by stresses, not by number of syllables, and he finds it almost impossible to grasp the metrical shape of the poem without an elaborately unnatural pause at the end of each line.

In accentual m., on the other hand, only the accents are measured; syllables may vary in number, it being assumed that 3 or 4 syllables can be uttered in the same time as 1 or 2. Most Germanic poetries, including OE, are based on accentual meter, as are most Eng. poems in which the number of syllables varies (through trisyllabic substitution, for example) from line to line:

Why should not old men be mad?
Some have known a likely lad
That had a sound fly-fisher's wrist
Turn to a drunken journalist;
A girl that knew all Dante once
Live to bear children to a dunce;
A Helen of social welfare dream,
Climb on a wagonette to scream.

(W. B. Yeats, *Why Should not Old Men be Mad?* [4 stresses per line, with number of syllables varying from 7 to 9])

I sit in one of the dives
On Fifty-Second Street
Uncertain and afraid
As the clever hopes expire
Of a low dishonest decade:
Waves of anger and fear
Circulate over the bright
And darkened lands of the earth
Obsessing our private lives.

(W. H. Auden, *September 1, 1939* [3 stresses per line, with number of syllables varying from 6 to 8])

Sometimes accentual meters like the two above are called "loose iambic."

The third metrical system, the accentual-syllabic, represents really a tightening of the accentual. Here, both number of accents and number of syllables are measured (frequently through the measuring of "feet" [see FOOT] of stated patterns). Variations in accent placement, addition, or omission are much more readily "allowed" than variations in number of syllables per line. The result of this strictness is a metrical container of some rigidity and inflexibility, but, at the same time, of great compressive power. Fairly strict accentual-syllabic m. will generally be found used by conservative practitioners in Eng.: Dryden, Pope, Swift, and Johnson are examples. One may conjecture that accentual-syllabic m. has been fashionable in Eng. primarily during periods marked by an interest in classical rhetoric and by a commitment to the maintenance of a sense of order and limitation, for of all Eng. metrical systems, it is the one most hostile by nature to impulse, irregularity, and unrestrained grandiosity:

Creatures of every kind but ours
Well comprehend their natural powers;
While we, whom reason ought to sway,
Mistake our talents every day.

(Swift, *The Beasts' Confession to the Priest* [octosyllables with 4 stresses; "natural" in line 2 reduced to a dissyllable by syncope])

In a slightly looser form, sometimes tending, that is, toward accentualism, the accentual-syllabic system is the basis for the standard Eng. meters, such as iambic pentameter (blank verse), or iambic and trochaic tetrameter. The presence or absence of trisyllabic substitution often determines whether a given meter is to be classified as strictly accentual or accentual syllabic.

In quantitative m., finally, durational rather than accentual feet are measured, and each foot consists of a particular pattern of "long" and "short" syllables. Sanskrit, Gr., and later Roman poetries are quantitative, and there have been attempts (particularly during the Renaissance) to write Eng. verse according to the principles of duration rather than stress: "Unhappy verse, the witness of my unhappy state, / Make thyself flutt'ring wings of thy fast flying / Thought, and fly forth unto my love, wheresoever she be: / Whether lying restless in heavy bed, or else / Sitting so cheerless at the cheerful board, or else / Playing alone careless on her heavenly virginals" (Spenser, *Iambicum Trimetrum* [quantitative imitation of classical iambic trimeter]). Inspired by the theorizing of William J. Stone, Robert Bridges, among others, has performed some interesting experiments in our own time with quantitative Eng. verse. It must be said, however, that despite occasional successes with the quantitative principle in Eng., the language seems to be so heavily accentual by nature that no other characteristic can serve adequately as a basis for m. Bridges has testified to the difficulty of thinking in quantities instead of accents, and his experience suggests that a m. customary in a given language is customary just because it "measures" the most characteristic quality of the language.

In poetry, which is the most organic and "total" mode of verbal expression, m. (like the other formal elements) serves as one of the primary correlatives of meaning: since m. is an indispensable contributor to meaning, it follows that the m. of a poem, in and by itself, means something, and even that the m. maintains a portion, at least, of its meaning whether symbolic sounds are attached to it or not. A good illustration of this basic alliance of m. with meaning (perhaps through association only) is the function of m. in the limerick, where the short anapestic lines are themselves expressive of light impudence. The fact that a "translation" of a limerick into another m. (say, iambic tetrameter) seriously impairs the comic tone which is a part of the total expression indicates the large burden of meaning which m. alone carries. In the same way, most sensitive Eng. poets have discovered that triple meters (anapestic, dactylic) tend to have something vaguely comic, light, or superficial about them (some, like Longfellow in *Evangeline*, apparently have made the discovery too late), and they tend to eschew such meters in favor of duple rhythms for the treatment of more or less serious subjects. Taking a somewhat more complex illustration than a limerick, we can see the relationship of m. to meaning in Shakespeare's 129th sonnet:

Th'expense of spirit in a waste of shame
Is lust in action; and till action, lust
Is perjur'd, murd'rous, bloody, full of blame,
Savage, extreme, rude, cruel, not to trust;

Here the metrical disorder and violence of the 4th line is intimately allied with the violence and extremity of the statement, and indeed both creates and is created by that violence. One has only to imagine the same statement expressed in a regular anapestic m. to perceive how m. and meaning are indissolubly married here. In a good poem, thus, limerick or sonnet, rhythmical pattern (together with expressive variations from it) is a constituent and a source of significance; it is never a mere embellishment, appliquéd from the outside onto what would otherwise be "prose" utterance; it issues from the pressure of feeling and reasoning at every point in the poem (see METRICAL VARIATIONS).

In addition to serving as a major technique for the reinforcement of meaning, m. performs more general functions in a poem. It often establishes a sort of "distance" between both poet and subject and reader and subject by interposing a film of unaccustomed rhythmical ritual between observer and experience. It can thus help to control emotion and inhibit cliché responses in both poet and reader. This ritual "frame" in which m. encloses what is often perfectly everyday experience resembles the frame or artificial border of a painting. It reminds the apprehender unremittingly that he is not experiencing the real object of the "imitation" (in the Aristotelian sense) but is experiencing instead that object transmuted into symbolic form. M., as a device of artificiality and unnaturalness, is thus a primary technique of artifice in poetry, just as similar conventions (the palpably artificial stone flesh of statues, for example) are primary techniques of artifice in the other arts. M. also tends to suggest (since ordinary people don't speak in meter) the vatic rôle of the poet, just as it tends to invest with a mysterious air of permanence and authority the words which are cut to its pattern. The strange power of m. to burnish the commonplace has even tempted some thinkers to regard metrical patterns as Platonic forms, themselves inherently and permanently beautiful, which the poet perceives unconsciously and towards which he constantly impels his own utterance.

If one regards absolutely regular m. (as some Platonists do) as the "ideal," then one becomes extraordinarily sensitive to those points in the poem where the "sense" pattern of the language rhythm lies at some distance from the normal or "base" abstract rhythm of the presumed metrical scheme. Prosodists and critics who have studied closely this frequent distance between a poem's "ideal" and "real" m. have developed a theory of prosodic "tension": these theorists maintain that one of the sources of metrical power and pleasure is just this tension between perfect and imperfect metrical patterns. To these theorists, the perpetual tension between "metrical" and real rhythms constitutes the sort of "play" or "suspension" (or even the Coleridgean reconciliation of opposites) which is the secret source of illumination and delight in all art.

A complete discussion of the nature of m. would require not only a consideration of the function of poetic m. in general, but also some investigation of the unique functions of m. in different kinds of poetry. Except for its most obvious offices, it is apparent that m. does not do the same things in lyric that it does in poetic drama; nor does it do the same things in narrative poetry that it does in satiric. Its function is mnemonic in "Thirty days hath September" and in the metered genealogies of epic; musical and hypnotic in *Kubla Khan*; and oratorical and analytically pedagogic in the *Essay on Man*. See PROSODY; ENG. PROSODY; LINGUISTICS AND POETICS; GENERATIVE METRICS.

T. S. Omond, *Eng. Metrists* (1921); E. A. Sonnenschein, *What is Rhythm?* (1925); P. Barkas, *A Critique of Modern Eng. Prosody* (1934); Y. Winters, "The Influence of M. on Poetic Convention," *Primitivism and Decadence* (1937); J. C. Ransom, *The New Crit.* (1941), pp. 254–69, 297–330; D. A. Stauffer, *The Nature of Poetry* (1946); K. Shapiro, *A Bibliog. of Modern Prosody* (1948); Wellek and Warren; A. Stein, "A Note on M.," KR, 18 (1956); J. C. Ransom, "The Strange Music of Eng. Verse," KR, 18 (1956).

P.F.

METONYMY (Gr. "change of name," "misnomer." L. *denominatio*). A trope in which one word is substituted for another on the basis of some material, causal, or conceptual relationship. Quintilian lists the kinds usually named: container for thing contained ("I'll have a glass"); agent for act, product, or object possessed ("reading Wordsworth"); cause for effect; time or place for their characteristics ("a bloody decade"); associated object for its possessor or user ("the crown" for the king).

Because m. and synecdoche involve some literal or referential connection between tenor and vehicle (q.v.), they are often contrasted with metaphor, in which no such relationship is apparent. Distinctions between the former two often dissolve when examined carefully: why should "a fine tenor" be synecdoche for a singer, but m. for a saxophone player (part—whole vs. attribute—agent)? Many theorists call both tropes m., some treating species—genus synecdoche as one of its subclasses.

Drawing on K. Bühler and R. Jakobson, Wellek and Warren divided tropes into two groups: figures of similarity (metaphor) and figures of contiguity (m. and synecdoche). As revised and extended by Jakobson (1956), this distinction applies to all semiotic processes, from cognition, linguistics, and psychoanalysis to movies and the visual arts. Metaphor thus becomes a figure for any type of substitution: given a chain of words or a visual space, the act of replacing one element with another is "metalinguistic." The positioning of elements is on the other hand metonymyic, a matter of contiguity. This opposition cannot be equated with that between word-choice (paradigm) and word-order (syntagm), nor is it rhetorical (m. loses its traditional meaning as a trope of substitution).

Beginning from Jakobson's and Freud's comments on condensation, displacement, and secondary revision in dreams, Lacan proposed that the psychoanalyst could conceive the chain of discourse as a continuous m., displaced from the real, in which metaphoric, unconscious signifiers sometimes appear (see Vergote). Attempts to clarify or revise the m.—metaphor opposition as conceived by Jakobson and Lacan have taken several forms. Henry defines m. as the result of a psychological focus that substitutes the name of one of a word's linguistic features (semes) for the word itself; metaphor in his view is a combination of two metonymies. Le Guern argues that the "contiguity" of Jakobson's m. involves reference to reality, whereas metaphor is the product of a purely linguistic or conceptual operation. De Man pushes this difference further, seeing m. not only as referential, but as contingent or accidental, in opposition to the pull toward unification of essences that underlies most uses of metaphor. Bredin agrees that m. refers to the world, but sees such "extrinsic relations" as "a kind of ontological cement holding the world together," not as contingencies. Metaphor is also referential in his view (cf. Ricoeur), both figures being opposed to the "structural" or intralinguistic relations underlying synecdoche (see the latter entry for further discussion of this problem).

In seeking a logic underlying m. and other tropes, theorists are forced to redefine them, reassigning some of the examples they traditionally include to other tropes, and discarding others. In so doing, they define the tropes stipulatively, or figuratively. The theoretical clarity thus obtained results from treating rhetoric as a branch of philosophy, linguistics, or poetics. See also METAPHOR; RHETORIC AND POETICS.

Quintilian, *Institutio Oratoria*, with an Eng. tr. by H. E. Butler (4 v., 1921–22); R. Jakobson, "Two Aspects of Language and Two Types of Aphasic Disturbances, (v): The Metaphoric and Metonymic Poles," in R. Jakobson and M. Halle, *Fundamentals of Language* (1956); J. Lacan, *Ecrits: A Selection* (1977, orig. publ. 1966); A. Henry, *Métonymie et métaphore* (1971); M. Le Guern, *Sémantique de la métaphore et de la métonymie* (1973); P. Ricoeur, *The Rule of Metaphor* (1977); P. de Man, "Tropes (Rilke)," in *Allegories of Reading* (1979); J. Culler, "The Turns of Metaphor," in *The Pursuit of Signs* (1981); A. Vergote, "From Freud's 'Other Scene' to Lacan's 'Other,' " in *Interpreting Lacan* (1983); H. Bredin, "M.," *Poetics Today*, 5 (1984). R.O.E.; rev. W.M.

METRICAL TREATMENT OF SYLLABLES. Most meters are based on a count of recurring features of language. Thus, the Old Germanic meters require the occurrence in each line of four syllables carrying major stress (there are of course accompanying requirements), while the number of syllables in the line is relatively less constrained; the Romance meters, in comparison, regulate the number of syllables more strictly. The accentual-syllabic or syllabo-tonic meter adapted to Eng. first by Chaucer and again by Wyatt and Surrey from Fr. and It. syllabic models was during the first centuries of its use in England principally a syllable-counting meter with subsidiary constraints on stress.

The concept of the "syllable" is somewhat theoretical and conventional, a point which may be illustrated in the words "higher" and "hire" (hardly distinguishable in pronunciation, though the first is usually considered of two syllables, the second of one). Nonetheless the native speakers of a language tend to feel that they know how many syllables there are in a given word, and therefore how many syllables a given line of verse contains. The time-honored definition of the syllable as a cluster centered in a vowel that may be preceded or followed by a consonant or consonants, provided that the whole remains capable of articulation in a single impulse of the breath, is not, perhaps, technically exact, but it will provide us with a reasonably satisfactory background against which we may view the syllable-counting practice of Eng. poets from, say, the mid-16th c. to the beginning of the Romantic period. During this time span verse writers were as part of their craft counting syllables, and in this they were affected by the state of the language in their time and by conventions that had arisen or were arising having to do with what was thought correct or appropriate or aesthetically pleasing in the handling of syllables.

Gr. and L. quantitative meters, based on a count of *times* (two short syllables being held equal in time to one long, the nature of shorts and longs being conventional), provided Western verse with models for the—somewhat artificial—metrical treatment of syllables. The next-to-the-last foot of the L. dactylic hexameter, for example, is always a dactyl, a long followed by two short syllables; the last foot is always a (potential) spondee, two long syllables—though the final syllable may be treated conventionally as long "by position" even though nothing follows. The first four feet of the hexameter may be either dactylic or spondaic, in any combination, so that the line, always twenty-four "times," will contain no fewer than thirteen syllables (eleven long, two short), and no more than seventeen (seven long, ten short).

To see how a strict count of syllables functions formally in the syllabo-tonic line of a vernacular poetry, we may consider the It. *endecasillabo*, a line intermediate between the L. iambic trimeter and the Eng. decasyllable (or iambic pentameter), and a line the most significant property of which is, as its name makes clear, that it is of eleven syllables. (The line also requires stress on the tenth and on either the fourth or the sixth syllables.) In the first dozen lines of Dante's *Inferno*, for example, the first line—but only the first—is of eleven syllables without adjustment; in the other lines, various kinds of metrical compression or other artifices are required to reduce the number of syllables to eleven or to bring them into the required stress pattern.

Many of the syllable-adjusting devices of It. were adaptable to Eng., and—at first by Chaucer, later by Early Modern Eng. poets from Wyatt and Surrey through Milton—were so adapted. What may in general be referred to simply as ELISION (L. "striking," cognate to Gr. synaloepha) is familiar to readers of 16th- to 18th-c. verse in such forms as "gainst," "twixt," "th'eternal," "th'art," "t'advance," "t'have," "see'st," "fly'st," "low'st," "dev'lish," "pois'nous," "murm'ring," "med'cine," and the like; the first two of these are examples of aphaeresis (the dropping of a word-initial vowel or syllable), the last four (at least) of syncope (suppression of a word-internal vowel), and such (early) forms as monosyllabic "i'th'," "o'th'," "to th'," and "by th' " are fairly clear examples of apocope (excision of a word-final vowel), which is illustrated also, if less familiarly, in such a line as Spenser's

> Callèd *Fidess'*, and so supposd to bee
> (*Fairie Queene* 1.4.2.4).

But the terminology, the elaborate technical vocabulary, would seem useful only if identification of the nature or means of achieving syllabic loss in a given instance were absolutely crucial. Terms such as "aphaeresis," "apocope," "synaeresis," "synizesis," "synaloepha" no doubt have their application to Eng. forms; all things considered, however, the ordinary reader is perhaps better off using a simple explanatory vocabulary as accurately as he can, and no more precisely than the situation requires.

Coalescence of contiguous vowels, the first stressed, is illustrated in Early Mod. Eng. verse in such forms as monosyllabic "prayer," dissyllabic "deity," "piety," "poesy." the fact that primary stress in Eng. has tended to move back toward the beginnings of plurisyllables perhaps accounts for the paucity in Eng. of dissyllabic forms such as "Bianca" and "Iago" (*Shrew* 2.1.346; *Othello* 4.1.3); but Milton gives us tetrasyllabic "humiliation" in *Paradise Lost* and *Paradise Regained*; and the situation may arise between words, as in monosyllabic "the eare" (if the first *e* is not elided), trisyllabic "any other," monosyllabic "to have," etc. The blending of adjacent vowels neither one of which is stressed is very common in Eng.; everywhere in Early Mod. Eng. verse one finds such forms as dissyllabic "hideous," valiant," "worthiest," "glorying," "many a" (in all of which [ɪ] is converted to consonantal [j] before a following vowel, the two together being pronounced [jə] or [jɪ] as well as "echoing," "follower," "shadowy," "sensual," "influence" (in which *o* or *u* is assimilated or converted to consonantal [w] before a sequent vowel). Poets from Chaucer through Milton imitated this process by blending into a single syllable a final syllabic liquid or nasal and a vowel beginning a following word: e.g., dissyllabic "temple and," "open his," "river of."

In syllable-counting verse, forms that may be contracted may equally, of course, be used in full, and forms normally short may be extended; diaeresis, that is, is as much a resource of the poet as synaeresis. When Milton writes

> 8 9 10
> Whispering new joyes to the milde Ocean
> (*On the Morning of Christ's Nativity*, 66),

having prepared us for trisyllabic "O-ce-an" with its rhyme word "began" in line 63, we find contraction and extension in the same line; and, indeed, many 16th- and 17th-c. poets thought it a beauty of verse to use the same word twice in a single line or in adjacent lines, once contracted, once in full. Contraction (or extension) may or may not be signalled by spelling in 16th- to 17th-c. Eng. verse; often it cannot be. When Spenser uses "air" and "fire" as dissyllables, it is true, he spells them "aier" and "fier"; but with some obvious exceptions, specifically metrical spellings (even where these would be possible) are less and less common in the work of later poets.

Considering that in any event not all words are now pronounced as they were pronounced by the great poets of the past, inevitably we ask ourselves whether, and how, to perform the metrical compressions and extensions of earlier poetry, some of which now fall very oddly on the ear. Such instances as Milton's *Nativity Ode* rhyme, however, or Spenser's unusual spelling, suggest that the extensions illustrated were *meant* to be read, were intended to preserve the meter *actually*, not merely theoretically. As for contractions, many of those found in verse of the 16th to 18th cs. occur in prose as well, and so are not specifically "poetic," the motivation for their use being not solely metrical. Alternative linguistic forms such as "wandring," "threatning" are not contractions at all. Genuinely contracted forms used commonly by educated speakers and writers of formal verse must have been thought appropriate to such verse, and it is scarcely to the point for irrelevant modern tastes to decree them, retrospectively, inappropriate, and thus unlikely to have been performed. In general, the unexpected full forms and the metrical compressions of 16th- to 18th-c. verse seem either to have come from speech at an appropriate level or to be phonologically analogous to attested speech forms, and must have been written to be pronounced—though readers of a later period may shudder, or refuse, to think so.

Of course, pronunciations change, usage changes. Speech contractions, after the language discards them, become "poetic" if they continue to be used in verse—e.g., "o'er," "e'en," "ope." Less obviously—but more importantly—the model used by Eng. poets from Wyatt through Milton to regulate number of syllables was basically It.; after the Restoration the model was, rather, Fr. Italianate synaloepha (the blending or coalescence of vowels at the end of one word and the beginning of the next, as in "the͡ eare," "only͡ in," "yellow͡ as") and the Eng. imitation of this process involving syllabic semivowels dropped out of use after Milton. From Dryden on, the syncopations and other contractions lying within the narrowed range considered acceptable were on the whole required, so that one finds in late 17th- to 18th-c. verse relatively far fewer alternative metrical forms than appeared in, or indeed characterized, earlier verse.

Late 20th-c. prosodists, concerned with meter primarily as an abstraction, tend to argue that the Eng. "iambic pentameter" is a line with a base of ten positions alternately weak and strong, and that any of these positions may be occupied by one *or* two syllables—or in exceptional circumstances by none—and that one may read apparent contractions or not, as one chooses, whatever the period of the verse in question. Doubtless it does not matter greatly if one reads "Whispering" as a light trisyllable in Milton's "Nativity Ode," line 66, and doubtless most of us would forgive the actor who, delivering *Julius Caesar* 3.2.101–3,

I thrice presented him a kingly crown,
Which he did thrice refuse. Was this ambition?
Yet Brutus says he was ambitious,

reads the last line as of nine syllables—a tetrameter with a feminine ending—as the previous line is a pentameter with a feminine ending. A modern audience is likely to be put off by [am-bi-si-əs] or [am-bi-ši-əs]. Yet Shakespeare's verse contains thousands upon thousands of lines which are clearly decasyllables, and few textually certain lines of nine syllables. One view of meter is precisely that it tells us *how to read* where otherwise varying possibilities would exist.

But the subject is complex and poses more problems than can be solved here. We *can* say that, from the time of the Romantics on, Eng. poets increasingly admitted to the familiar decasyllabic line extra unstressed syllables which did not allow of contraction:

Migration strange for a stripling of the hills
(Wordsworth, *Prelude* 3.34)

Like the skipping of rabbits by moonlight—
three slim shapes
(Browning, *Fra Lippo Lippi* 59);

whereas poets of the 16th, 17th, and 18th cs.—nondramatic poets, at any rate—seem on the whole not to have written lines containing extra syllables (the feminine ending excepted) which could not be resolved phonologically. This probably says something about the intended performance, the intended *sound*, of the earlier verse. And sound, including tautness or relaxation of rhythm, is sufficiently a part of the meaning of verse that we do well to take seriously the apparent intentions of the poet regarding it.

The basic music of verse in the great Eng. tradition, the verse of Chaucer, of Spenser, of Shakespeare, of Milton, of Dryden, of Pope, and of all the other poets who have used consciously the meter they used, depends to a significant degree upon the artifices for metrical treatment of syllables described above. They reflect the language of their times. And to the degree that the difference between that language and our own is of importance, we must do what we can to understand them.—E. J. Dobson, *Eng. Pronunciation 1500–1700* (2d ed., 2 v., 1968); H. Kökeritz, *Shakespeare's Pronunciation* (1953); A. C. Partridge, *Orthography in Shakespeare and Elizabethan Drama: A Study of Colloquial Contractions, Elision, Prosody, and Punctuation* (1964). E.R.W.

METRICAL VARIATIONS. A term covering the techniques of departing from metrical regularity for the purposes of either sheer variety or rhetorical reinforcement. Strictly speaking, m.v. are possible only in verse composed with a more or less regular base rhythm; they do not exist as such in cadenced or free verse.

"Substitution" (according to conventional graphic scansion) is the most frequent technique of metrical variation. Here, once a basic metrical pattern has been established, the rhythm may be varied by the introduction of a "substitute" foot to replace one or more of the normal ones. In the following example,

An aged man is but a paltry thing,
A tattered coat upon a stick, unless
Soul clap its hands and sing, and louder sing
For every tatter in its mortal dress, . . .
(Yeats, *Sailing to Byzantium*)

each line uses a substitution for one of the "expected" iambic feet: line 1 has a pyrrhic in the third position; line 2 a pyrrhic in the third, line 3 a trochaic (or spondaic) substitution in the first position; and line 4 a pyrrhic in the third. These substitutions serve both to alleviate the metrical monotony of the long-continued iambic pentameter and to allow the metrical structure to "give" and shape itself according to the rhetorical pressures of the statement. In the following lines by Matthew Arnold,

Listen! you hear the grating roar
Of pebbles which the waves draw back, and fling,
At their return, up the high strand,
Begin, and cease, and then again begin, . . .
(*Dover Beach*)

one can see substitutions used with even stronger intentions of sense reinforcement. Against an iambic background, the initial trochaic substitution in line 1 constitutes an unexpected reversal of the metrical movement which emphasizes a shift in the address; in line 2, the spondaic substitution in the fourth position suggests the slowness of the sea wave as it coils back upon itself, gathering force to shoot itself up the beach; in line 3, the pyrrhic substitution in the 1st position suggests the speed with which the wave "flings" itself up the sand; and in line 4, the return to iambic regularity, after these suggestive variations, transmits a feeling of the infinite, monotonous continuance of the wave's process. In Eng. verse, the most common substitution is the replacement of the initial iamb by a trochee, as in the first line of the Arnold example. This initial trochaic substitution is usually found even in the most metrically regular poems, for the unvaried iambic foot becomes insupportably tedious after very many repetitions. In fact, a failure to employ m.v. is one of the stigmata of the bad poet. In the following example: "I know that Europe's wonderful, yet something seems to lack: / The Past is too much with her, and the people looking back. / But the glory of the Present is to make the Future free— / We love our land for what she is and what she is to be" (Henry Van Dyke, *America for Me*) the absence of an instinct for meaningful m.v. goes hand in hand with the complacent ignorance of the ideas and the fatuity of the rhetoric.

In addition to the device of dissyllabic substitution, lines can also be varied by the addition or subtraction of unaccented syllables, which is frequently accomplished by either trisyllabic or monosyllabic substitution. Trisyllabic substitution is regarded by conservative metrists as a "bolder" form of substitution than dissyllabic, for, in duple measures, trisyllabic substitution increases the syllabic length of the line.

As the examples above help illustrate, the fundamental principles of metrical variation are these: (1) a succession of stressed syllables without the expected intervening unstressed syllables tends to transmit an effect of slowness, weight, or difficulty; (2) a succession of unstressed syllables without the expected intervening stressed syllables tends to suggest an effect of rapidity, lightness, or ease; and (3) an unanticipated reversal in the rhythm (as in the first line of the Arnold passage, above) suggests a new direction of thought, a new tone of voice, or a change in poetic address.

The fact that m.v. such as these can be illustrated by scansion and analyzed dispassionately should not cause the reader to believe that, from the point of view of the poet (at least the good poet), they are anything but instinctual. Many poets whose work can be analyzed metrically according to the foot system would be astonished to be told that they have indulged in "substitution": the genuine poet composes according to the rhythms which his utterance supplies, and, although these rhythms frequently turn out to consist of "normal" and "substitute" feet, they do not necessarily begin that way. See METER, PROSODY, SCANSION, COUNTERPOINT, FOOT.—Saintsbury, *Prosody*; Baum; Brooks and Warren; L. Perrine, *Sound and Sense* (1956). P.F.

MIMESIS. See IMITATION; POETRY, THEORIES OF (MIMETIC THEORIES).

MINNESINGERS, authors of *Minnesang* (the first body of poetry in German to rank as part of world literature), which in its widest sense includes all artistic lyrical poetry of the Middle High German period and was composed to be sung or recited (not read) for the entertainment of courtly society. In the narrow sense it is a specific kind of love poetry, the aim and reward of the man's spiritual devotion to woman (*hohe minne*) being "that your worth be enhanced and you gain a joyous elation therefrom" (Albrecht von Jahnsdorf).

It flourished first in the Rhine regions, then chiefly at the courts of Austria and Southern

Germany for a 200-year period, which may be subdivided into (1). *Minnesangs Frühling* (Spring of *minne* song), middle to end of 12th c. (e.g., Der Kürenberger, Heinrich von Veldeke, Dietmar von Aist, Meinloh von Sevelingen); (2). the great flowering, end of 12th to beginning of 13th c. (hardly more than 20 years, e.g., Hartmann von Aue, Albr. von Johansdorf, Heinrich von Morungen, Reinmar von Hagenau, Walther von der Vogelweide); (3). late *Minnesang,* beginning of 13th to beginning of 14th c. (e.g., Ulrich von Lichtenstein, Neithart von Reuenthal), generally considered a period of decline. The early poets came from the higher nobility, later ones also from the lower (professional or semiprofessional minstrels, or *Spielleute,* under the patronage of great nobles).

Love (*minne*) is the chief theme, although there is much formal treatment of nature and reference to contemporary history: the crusades, the poet's relationship to his princely employer, the state of the Empire (Walther). Love had in earlier eras been condemned by the church as lust (*luxuria*). Since, however, *Minnesang* is court poetry, the relationship between man and woman assumes certain noble characteristics of the lord-vassal relationship. The *man* is vassal to his *frouwe* and he wishes to receive a reward (*lôn*) for his service (*dienest*). As the aim of German court society at the time of the Staufen dynasty was the perfect man, who achieved self-discipline and balance (*mâze*) by constant training (*zuht*), the value of the *minne* relationship shifted from the attainment of possession to the arduous but ennobling way which might lead to it. The woman, by this process, became so idealized that the goal became in fact unattainable, and the whole relationship fictitious. Only thus can one understand the apparent paradox of the poet's praise of the virtue of a married noble lady (often the wife of the minnesinger's own lord) whom he implores to relax her standards in his particular case. *Minnesang,* in the work of its greatest representatives, is an elevation of womanhood. In its quasi-religious praise of the Eternal-Feminine, this poetry reflects elements of the worship of the Virgin Mary. In the hands of the lesser practitioners, especially in the late period, *Minnesang* became a social game or empty conventionality to the point of caricature. There is, however, a more realistic strain; even the great singers around 1200 and certainly the late M. would write of sensual love, attainable from women of the lower classes (*niedere minne*). This poetry bears the marks of personal experience and expresses personal feelings.

Minnesang has strong affinities with the love poetry of the Fr. troubadours, but elements of older G. secular love poetry can also be discerned. It is often less gallant and more spontaneous than its Fr. counterpart. A relationship may, moreover, exist between *minne* song and medieval secular love poetry in L. (*Vagantenpoesie*). Lastly, the Arabic sung strophic love lyrics, placing woman in an exalted position, practiced at the Arabic princely courts of Spain, and antedating the troubadour poetry, must be considered in any attempt at historio-genetic explanation.

Form (1). The principal form used by the M. is the *lied* i.e., the strophic poem (the strophe represents both the poetic and the musical unit, as with the troubadours), a frequent variety (from Walther on) being the *Tagelied.* While metric structure and rhyme patterns were, at first, indebted to Prov. models, variations and innovations were developed from ca. 1180 on. (2). There is also the nonstrophic *leich* with varying length and number of lines, and set to continuous music. (3). For the short (originally 1 stanza) poem, which since Walther may deal with political and religious themes, Simrock and Wackernagel (1833) misleadingly introduced the term *Spruch.* It is really the same as a short *lied*; for it is not spoken, but also sung, and must not be confused with the didactic *Spruch* proper.

COLLECTIONS: *Minnesinger,* ed. v. d. Hagen (4 v., 1838, new printing 1923); *Die Schweizer Minnesänger,* ed. K. Bartsch (1886); *Der Minnesang des 12. bis 14. Jhs.,* ed. F. Pfaff (2 v., 1891–95); *Deutsche Liederdichter des 12. bis 14. Jhs.,* ed. K. Bartsch and W. Golther (8th ed., 1928); *Herbst des Minnesangs,* ed. H. Naumann (1936); *Trouvères et minnesänger,* ed. I. Frank (I, texts, 1952) and J. M. Müller-Blattau (II, music, 1956); *Die Lieder Neidharts,* ed. E. Wiessner (1955); *Deutsche Lyrik des Mittelalters,* ed. M. Wehrli (1955); *Dt. Liederdichter des 13. Jhs.,* ed. C. v. Kraus and H. Kuhn (2 v., 1952–58); *Die Gedichte Walthers v. d. Vogelweide,* ed. C. v. Kraus (12th ed., 1959); *Des Minnesangs Frühling,* ed. K. Lachmann (32d ed. by C. v. Kraus, 1959).

HISTORY AND CRITICISM: A. Lüderitz, *Die Liebestheorie der Provençalen bei den Minnesingern der Stauferzeit* (1904); W. Wilmanns, *Walther v. d. Vogelweide,* ed. V. Michels (4th ed., 1916–24); K. Burdach, "Über den Ursprung des mittelalterlichen Minnesangs," *Berliner Sitzungsberichte* (1918); G. Müller, "Studien zum Formproblem des Minnesangs," DVLG, 1 (1923); L. Ecker, *Arabischer, provenzalischer und deutscher Minnesang* (1934); C. v. Kraus, *Walther v. d. Vogelweide* (1935) and *Des Minnesangs frühling: Untersuchungen* (1939); M. Ittenbach, *Der frühe dt. Minnesang* (1939); M. P. Richey, *Essays on the Mediaeval German Love Lyric* (1943); T. Frings, *Minnesänger und Troubadours* (1949); A. Moret, *Les Débuts du lyrisme en Allemagne* (1951); F. Maurer, *Die politischen Lieder W's v. d. Vogelweide* (1954); H. Kolb, *Der Begriff der Minne und das Entstehen der höfischen Lyrik* (1958); B. Kippenberg, *Der Rhythmus im Minnesang* (1962). U.K.G.

MINSTREL. A professional entertainer of the Middle Ages, successor to the earlier scop (q.v.), gleeman, or jongleur (q.v.). Minstrels flourished particularly in the 13th and 14th c.; their activity decreased in the 15th c., and with the invention of printing their function in society ceased to be meaningful.

As in the case of the jongleur, it is difficult to determine with certainty the nature and role of the medieval m. Some were attached to a court or a noble household; others wandered from town to town; some even performed in the public streets. The social position of the m. presents a similar problem. Sometimes the term is applied to the troubadours and *trouvères* (qq.v.), true poets and often men of education and social standing; on other occasions it denotes the wandering acrobats and buffoons. Some scholars have suggested that the more sophisticated entertainers rose out of their class as a result of their talents.

In any case, the literary productions of the minstrels are clearly distinguished in pace and tone from those of the two other main categories of medieval writers—the clerical and the aristocratic. For the most part, the minstrels retold the familiar stories of tradition, as derived from a variety of sources ranging from the *chansons de geste* (q.v.) and the Germanic legends to the later romances and folk ballads. Independent love lyrics are also attributed to minstrel authors. The romantic writers of the late 18th and early 19th c., influenced by a belief in the virtues of "primitive" poetry, endowed the minstrels with the colorful and picturesque aura which surrounds them, even today, in the popular mind.—E. Faral, *Les Jongleurs en France au moyen âge* (1910); H. Naumann, "Spielmannsdichtung," *Reallexikon,* III; P. Wareman, *Spielmannsdichtung. Versuch einer Begriffsbestimmung* (1951); R. Menéndez Pidal. *Poesía juglaresca y orígenes de las literaturas románicas* (6th rev. and enl. ed., 1957). A.P.

MOCK EPIC, MOCK HEROIC. Terms used in a broad sense to describe a satiric method in poetry and prose and, more specifically, a distinct verse form which seeks a derisive effect by combining formal and elevated language with a trivial subject. The mock-heroic poem *per se* consciously imitates the epic style, follows a classical structure and heroic action for deflationary purposes, and employs some of the standard paraphernalia of the epic—i.e., invocations, dedications, celestial interventions, epic similes, canto-divisions, and battles.

The Homeric *Batrachomyomachia* (Battle of the Frogs and Mice) served as a model for many an 18th-c. battle in mock-epic strain. The 1717 version of this work by Thomas Parnell belongs with many such neoclassic, burlesque battles of pygmies or cranes or rats or hoops or books or sexes. Chaucer had employed the mock-heroic style in *Nun's Priest's Tale,* but Boileau's *Le Lutrin* is commonly mentioned as the most influential modern poem magnifying a trivial subject on an ambitious scale. Dryden's *MacFlecknoe* and Pope's *Rape of the Lock* and *Dunciad* are classic examples of Eng. mock-heroic poetry aiming their shafts at literary pretence and social folly. Mock odes, mock elegiacs (Gray's ode *On the Death of a Favourite Cat . . .*), and mock eclogues abound in Eng. verse, but the mock heroic held supremacy among them until it blended with later burlesque and satiric modes.—R. P. Bond, *Eng. Burlesque Poetry, 1700–1750* (1932); K. Schmidt, *Vorstudien zu einer Gesch. des komischen Epos* (1953). R.P.F.

MONODY. Originally in Gr. lyric poetry an ode sung by a single voice, e.g., by one of the characters in a tragedy. It came to be associated with the lamentation of a single mourner, and hence became a dirge (q.v.) or a funeral song. In metrical form the strophes are repeated without variation. In Eng. poetry, Milton referred to his *Lycidas* as a m., as the epigraph of the poem indicates. Matthew Arnold applied the term to his elegy on A. H. Clough: *Thyrsis, A. M.* R.A.H.

MONOLOGUE. The word "m." is used in several distinct senses all of which have in common the conception of one person speaking alone, who may or may not have an audience. The meaning of the term for poetry is elucidated by its use entirely apart from any art form, where it means simply "the prolonged speech of an individual." In colloquial usage the word often has a prejudicial sense, as a "m." that prevents freedom of conversation. In its more general literary sense it signifies any prolonged utterance in direct speech. There may, for example, be monologues within novels, plays, or poems. It is even correct to describe a work of great length as a m. if it is couched in a framework of direct address. But the speaker should preferably be the principal character. Meditations may in this sense also be called monologues. The common use stresses speech as well as the individual speaking; words uttered constitute a purer form of m. than those merely thought or written. The epistle is not a m., since it is imagined as read, not spoken.

Despite its limitation to a single speaker, the m. naturally assumes a dramatic character. For vocalization itself craves an object—one or many persons to constitute an audience. Thus the audience as well as the speaker becomes a part of the total area of imagination. In Chekhov's play, *Tobacco,* the speaker addresses the theater audience believing it to be a jury sitting in judgment on the morality of his actions. This unusual play becomes a m. on two accounts: because the dramatist imagines his speaker and because the speaker imagines his audience. The m. requires not only a single speaker but an advanced degree of impersonation.

The soliloquy of theatrical tradition becomes a form of m. when sufficiently prolonged. The word applies equally to the soliloquy that is an interior debate, as Hamlet's speech, "To be or not to be," or Falstaff's direct address on honor, delivered downstage to the audience. The m. may be either heard or overheard. Many of the outstanding passages of dramatic poetry are in this form. The overheard m., or the speaker's talking to himself, is a favorite vehicle for self-expression and subjective utterance. Passages of this nature introduce many plays, as Marlowe's *Doctor Faustus,* Goethe's *Faust,* and Byron's *Manfred.* Not only in its theatrical form but in nondramatic poetry it becomes a favorite device of the romantic poets. But the origins of m. are too ancient to be sketched in more than conjecture. As the germ of drama, it may well precede even the dialogue. A lament may be regarded as a tragic form of m.; a clownish harangue, a comic form. In biblical literature the poetic m., usually embedded in larger forms, is brought to a high degree of perfection. Specimens are *The Song of Deborah, The Song of Hannah,* and Jeremiah's lament over Jerusalem. From biblical poetry comes also the soliloquy of the personified city. A variety of m. is the prayer, where the devotee addresses the deity who hears but deigns no reply.

Although the m. as a disinct literary form is inconspicuous in early Gr. poetry, the art is brought to refined development within the drama, epic, and ode. Long speeches in highly cultivated rhetoric appear in most of the longer literary forms. On the stage the convention of a colloquy between a single actor and the chorus considerably reduces the tendency to monologue, but impressive achievements of this nature are nevertheless found, as in Aeschylus' *Prometheus Bound.* M. was prominent in miming, though dialogue enjoyed greater popularity. Admirable examples are found among the idyls, especially those of Theocritus. The classical shepherd is by tradition fond of declamation; pathos discourages question or conversation. Notable instances of m. are found among the poems of Ovid and Propertius.

The subjectivity prevalent in Germanic literature favored m. Some of the finest Anglo-Saxon poems, as *The Wanderer, The Seafarer,* and *The Wife's Lament,* afford good examples. Christian devotional literature abounds in such verse, as in poems where the Virgin addresses the Cross, or where, similarly, the Soul addresses the Body. An advance toward the dramatic appears in poetry of the later Middle Ages and early Renaissance, where the formula of "the complaint," or "the address," appears. This becomes happily conspicuous among the Scots Chaucerians, notably Dunbar, Henryson, and Lyndsay, as well as in the work of John Skelton. Imitations of the Horatian or Ovidian epistle aid the rise of the more dramatic forms of address. This development extends throughout the 16th c., from Wyatt through *The Mirror for Magistrates,* and the work of George Gascoigne to the more refined art of Raleigh and Drayton. It offers an important contribution to the perfection of Elizabethan dramatic verse. M. appears in all periods of Eng. literature, though in some more abundantly than in others. Robert Burns made important contributions to the form partly through his familiarity with the Scottish tradition. Sidney Smith's *Imaginary Addresses* represent an admirable development in humorous verse.

In instances where the speaker is strictly identified with the poet, as in much romantic verse, the absence of impersonation vitiates the achievement of m. in the more usual sense of the word. The highest form of m. is dramatic and is best illustrated by the dramatic monologues of Robert Browning. His works in this kind show two contrasting influences: those in stanzaic forms, which are in the majority, betray inspiration from the popular ballad that often employs a single imaginary speaker; those in couplets or in blank verse derive most clearly from the stage; they may be described as drama in miniature. Browning's dramatic monologues may also be regarded as closet dramas where only one person speaks. Such pieces as *My Last Duchess* may be imagined as scenes with a crowded stage and only one speaker. So powerful are Browning's dramatic monologues that his discoveries in the genre surpass those in the realm of the poetic style.

Some of the most important verse in Eng. since Browning plays variations upon his development of the m. Many of Thomas Hardy's, Rudyard Kipling's, and Ezra Pound's works follow Browning's use closely; T. S. Eliot's *The Love Song of J. Alfred Prufrock* is a m. addressed *in vacuo;* several of E. A. Robinson's finest poems, as *Toussaint L'Ouverture,* are addressed to imaginary hearers. An interesting variation is seen in Robinson's *Rembrandt to Rembrandt,* his own favorite among his poems, where one phase of the painter's soul is imagined as conversing with another in his mirror. Conrad Aiken, Edgar Lee Masters, and Robert Frost have contributed further variations.

The m. becomes an especially enlivening form for poetry in any literature tending to neglect the vital relations of poetry to the spoken voice. With Browning as a pathfinder, it has assumed great value for Eng. verse of the 20th c., as this drastically divorces itself from the comparatively bookish diction of Tennyson and Swinburne. But it may safely be concluded that much of the world's finest poetry has in all ages been in the m. form.—I. B. Sessions, "The Dramatic M.," PMLA, 62 (1947); B. W. Fuson, *Browning and his Eng. Predecessors in the Dramatic M.* (1948); R. Langbaum, *The Poetry of Experience* (1957).

H.W.W.

MONOMETER. A line consisting of one meter, either a dipody or foot. In classical iambic, trochaic, and anapaestic verse the metron is a dipody (pair of feet). As used by Eng. prosodists,

"-meter" is synonymous with foot. The Eng. monometer (a 1-stress line), therefore, consists of 1 foot. Probably the most famous examples in Eng. poetry are by Herrick, *The Bridegroom; Upon his Departure Hence*:

Thus I
Passe by
And die:
As one, . . .

R.O.E.

MONORHYME refers to a passage in a poem, to a strophe, or to an entire poem in which all lines have the same end rhyme. It is often used capriciously as an artificial device for producing satirical or comical effects, or even as a mnemotechnical aid. Aside from this it occurs in various languages as a component part of certain meters and is, in this instance, purely conventional. It is fairly frequent in the Romance and Slavic languages where it may be applied with greater ease than in German or in Eng. It occurs in medieval L. poetry; thus, in the poems of Commodian, in a psalm by St. Augustine consisting of 288 lines all ending in *-e* or *-ae* (tirade rhyme), in the sequences of Notker (echoing the *-a* of the Alleluja), in the *Carmen Mutinense*, and in the poems of Gottschalk. It has also been used by the goliards in strophes of four 13-syllable lines (*Vagantenstrophe*). In Old Fr. m. appears in *laisses* of varying length in the medieval *Alexander Romances* while, later, it is restricted to quatrains and tercets which, in turn, were imitated in Spain (the *cuaderna via* as practiced by Berceo and the *tercetos* of Pedro de Veragüe's *Doctrina cristiana*). In modern Fr. it has been employed by Voltaire, Lefranc de Pompignan, and Théophile Gautier. German examples of m. (*gehäufter Reim*) are rare and so are Eng. In Arabic poetry m. is the rule, and there exists a mystical poem of 700 lines with the same end rhyme. In Welsh poetry, likewise, m. is functional. It appears in the *awdl* (ode) and is sometimes used to link a chain of *englynion* (*gosteg o englynion*). T.F.

MORA (L. "delay" but *mora temporis* "space of time." The Gr. equivalent is *chronos*, literally "time"). Term used to denote the duration of a short syllable, which was the time-unit of Gr. and L. quantitative verse. The normal or "disemic" principle of classical metric was to regard a long syllable as equivalent to 2 morae, while rhythmical theory distinguished "trisemes," "tetrasemes," and "pentasemes" (conventionally indicated in modern times by ∟ or ⅃, ⊔, and ⊔⊔) for syllables of the length of 3, 4, and 5 morae respectively. See CLASSICAL PROSODY. R.J.G.

MUSE. One of the nine Gr. goddesses who preside over poetry, song, and the arts, traditionally invoked by poets to grant them inspiration. ("Sing, Goddess, the wrath of Achilles, Peleus' son . . ." Homer, *Iliad* 1.1). At first indefinite in number, the M., daughters of Zeus and Mnemosyne (goddess of memory), were first celebrated in Thrace near Mt. Olympus and Pieria. Hence that peak was regarded as their home and the Pierian Spring as the fountain of learning. Probably before Homer's time their worship had spread southward to Helicon and thence to Delphi; it eventually became a common feature of Gr. religious culture. By the 3d c. B.C. the festival of the Heliconian Muses at Thespai was patronized by Athens and the important guild of artists of Dionysus; here all the poetic and musical talent of Greece was consecrated. Elsewhere, observance of the M. became attached to the worship of Apollo.

The attribution of particular arts to each M. is a late development, and there is some duplication of influence. The M. are: Calliope (epic or heroic poetry); Clio (history, lyre-playing); Erato (love poetry, hymns, lyre-playing, pantomime); Euterpe (tragedy, flute-playing, lyric poetry); Melpomene (tragedy, lyre-playing); Polymnia or Polyhymnia (hymns, pantomime, religious dancing); Terpsichore (choral dancing and singing, flute-playing); Thalia (comedy); and Urania (astronomy, i.e., cosmological poetry).

With the recovery of classical writings in the later Middle Ages the tradition of invoking the Muse or Muses was revived. In Dante (where Beatrice herself fulfills the Muse's role), there are references to the Muses of antiquity (*Inferno* 2.7f.; 32.10f.; *Paradiso* 2.8; 18.82f.). Milton invokes the pagan M. but transforms her into a specifically Christian inspiring power: "Descend from Heaven, Urania, by that name / If rightly thou art called . . . / . . . for thou / Nor of the Muses nine, nor on the top / Of old Olympus dwell'st, but heavenly-born . . . / Thou with Eternal Wisdom didst converse." (*Paradise Lost* 7.1ff.).

For other Renaissance poets, however, the M. of antiquity could be accepted without relinquishing their pagan attributes. Thus Spenser commences *The Fairie Queene*: "Me, all too meane, the sacred Muse areeds / To blazen broad amongst her learned throng; / Fierce warres and faithfull loues shall moralize my song." (1.7–9). The unnamed "sacred Muse" is either Clio (history) or Calliope (epic). The Petrarchan love poets, too, invoked their inspiring spirit: "Fool said my muse to me, look in thy heart and write" (Sidney, *Astrophel and Stella,* 1.14). The beloved herself sometimes assumed the role of M. The tradition continues into modern times of invoking or referring to the Muse or Muses for inspiratory power (cf. Thomas Gray, *The Progress of Poesy*). For a provocative discussion of poetic homage to the M. from ancient to modern times see Robert Graves, *The White Goddess* (3d ed., 1958).—L. R. Farnell, *The Cults of the Gr.*

States, V (1909); G. Murray, *The Cl. Tradition in Poetry* (1927); G. Highet, *The Cl. Trad.* (1949).

D.H.

MUSIC AND POETRY. Our best evidence about primitive song suggests that melodies and rhythms precede words, that the first step toward poetry was the fitting of words to pre-existent musical patterns. Nor did primitive cultures make the distinctions we now make between m. and p.: the Egyptian "hymn of the seven vowels," for example, appears to have exploited the overtone pitches present in the vowels of any language. In the ancient Gr. linguistic system of pitch accents, two stable pitches, indicated in post-Alexandrian texts by the acute accent and the absence of accent, frame a less well-defined middle area from which the sliding pitch indicated by the circumflex arises; the grave accent may also indicate such a medial pitch. This system is strikingly similar to the tetrachordal system of ancient Gr. m., in which two fixed pitches a perfect fourth apart frame a middle area containing two sliding microtonal pitches. Although the linguistic pitch system was separate from the rhythmic system we now call quantitative meter, the scraps of ancient m. we possess show a general correspondence between pitch-accent and melodic shape, and studies of "accentual responsion" in the lyrics of Sappho and Pindar suggest that the poet's choice of words in an antistrophe may have been constrained by an attempt to have those words correspond to the melodic pitch-pattern established in the strophe.

The Greeks used the same word, *moûsike*, to describe dance, m., p., and elementary education. *Moûsike* was essentially a "mnemonic technology," a rhythmic and melodic way of preserving the wisdom of the culture; alphabetic writing, the next advance in mnemonic technology, forced changes. It was adopted as a musical notation soon after its introduction, with letters of the alphabet written above the vowels in a poetic line to indicate pitches. Thanks to the quantitative conventions of Gr. meter, no separate rhythmic notation was necessary. The visual separation of pitches and words in the new notation began to separate the once unified arts; alphabetic writing led to both rhetorical and musical theory, the latter of which, thanks to Pythagorean mysticism, quickly became concerned with advanced theoretical and mathematical problems virtually divorced from performance.

Roman p., in which the normal word-accents of L. words were arbitrarily distorted as those words were wedged into what had once been the rhythms of Gr. m., was another step in the separation. What began as *moûsike*, an organically unified art, had now become not two but four elements: performed m., m. theory, p., and rhetorical theory. Christian thought altered the relative prestige of the four elements: the Church fathers embraced the elaborate mathematical m. theory of the ancient world and allegorized its numbers; they banished instrumental m. from the Church and sought to alter and control vocal m.; on the literary side, by contrast, pagan p. itself had to be saved by allegory, while rhetorical theory was treated with suspicion. The drift in L. p. away from quantitative verse toward accentual-syllabic verse, in which the hymns of Ambrose and Augustine are important documents, was a motion away from writing L. words to Gr. tunes toward writing L. words to Christian tunes whose origin was probably Hebrew.

In the early Middle Ages, liturgical chant became longer, more complex, and more ornate, despite attempts by Charlemagne and Gregory to arrest its development. When the lengthy melismatic passages sung to the last *a* of the word *alleluia* proved hard to memorize, because church singers had a much less accurate notational system than the now-forgotten letters of the ancient Greeks, monks began writing words for them; the resulting works were called *sequences* or *proses*, though they employ many devices we would call poetic. By fitting new words to a pre-existing melody, such sequence poets as Notker Balbulus (ca. 840–912) again altered p., moving it still closer to modern stanzaic form, including rhyme. The troubadours and *trouvères* (qq.v.), composer-poets writing in the vernacular, took over and extended the formal innovations of the sequence, producing increasingly complex stanzaic forms with elaborate rhyme-schemes. In their art, poetic form was more complex than musical form, and by the time Dante defined p. as a combination of m. and rhetoric, "m." had become a somewhat metaphorical term. Not only were the It. poems in forms derived from the troubadours normally written without a specific tune in mind, but poetic form itself had become sufficiently demanding to occupy the attention once devoted to making words fit a pre-existing tune.

Musicians, who were now increasingly called upon to compose settings of pre-existing words, made an important technical advance in the invention of polyphony. They may have gotten the idea of combining two or more melodies from the literary notion of allegory, realizing that the mystical simultaneity of an Old Testament story and its New Testament analogue could become, in music, actual simultaneity. One result, oddly parallel to the dropping away of m. from the troubadour tradition, was that texts became less audible in polyphonic vocal m. than in the monodic singing of all previous m. In early polyphony, the *tenor* or lowest part often sustained one vowel for many long notes, while the more rapidly moving upper parts sang as many as forty short notes on one vowel. Predictably, these upper parts often picked up new texts, including Fr. texts glossing or commenting ironically on the liturgical L. text being sustained in the low part.

Influenced by Christian versions of the ancient Gr. numerological theory in which the universe was conceived as created and ordered by numbers, medieval poets and composers frequently constructed their pieces by complex, mystical, mathematical formulae. Fr. isorythmic motets, tricky crab canons in which one line is the other sung backwards, anagram poems concealing the names of mistresses—all elaborate forms whose principles of construction cannot be heard in performance—flourished as representations of the numerical mystery of the universe, or (for adepts in both arts) as secret displays of technical ingenuity. In the service of such causes, musicians treated texts as a tailor treats cloth: they cut them up, stretched them out, redistributed their rhythms in ways that entirely destroyed the original poetic form, obscured the rhyme scheme, and made the content impossible to hear—especially in motets where three different texts in two different languages were sung simultaneously. Guillaume Machaut (1300–77), who was at once the leading composer and the leading poet of his period, wrote such motets, but also simpler monodic songs such as *chansons*, *virelais*, and *lais* (qq.v.) in which expression of the text was an artistic concern.

In Ren. p. and m., techniques initially developed as virtuoso modes of construction, such as rhyme in p. and chordal harmony in m., began to acquire expressive values. A new rereading of the ancient poets and rhetoricians, with fresh interest in persuasion, emotion, and the moral force of sounds, was an important factor. Medieval composers had often worked out their m. before pasting in a text, but Ren. composers normally started with a text and worked in various ways at animating or expressing it. Josquin des Prés (ca. 1450–1521), who used dissonant harmonies at painful moments in the text, pointed the way toward the witty rhetorical musical expression of the It. madrigal school, which developed a number of harmonic and melodic "word-painting" conventions for setting words dealing with running, weeping, dying, and so forth. When Cardinal Bembo's edition of 1501 restored Petrarch as a model for lyric p., composers of secular songs were compelled to increase the musical sophistication of their settings, and in searching for musical equivalents of Petrarchan oxymorons (q.v.)—"freezing fires" or "living deaths"—they developed a more expressive use of harmony. Despite this general motion toward expression, the highly elaborate methods of construction typical of medieval art survived, as virtuosity or mysticism, in both arts, especially in England, where the hidden numerical schemes of Spenser's p. and the abstract patterns of John Bull's keyboard fantasias provide extreme examples.

The increased attention to the rhetoric and meaning of p. on the part of composers did not satisfy the literary reformers now called the Musical Humanists (the *Camerata* of Bardi in Florence and the *Académie* of Baïf in Paris). Fired by ancient myths concerning the capacity of m. to arouse various passions, these men concluded that it would do so most effectively by submitting to the rule of the text: they opposed independent musical rhythm, arguing that m. should exactly follow the rhythm of the poem; they opposed the staggered declamation typical of the madrigal, favoring homophonic, chordal singing or monody. Such composers as Monteverdi paid lip service to the aims of this reform program, but did not allow it to deprive their art of the techniques it had developed since the Middle Ages. Operatic recitative is the most familiar legacy of Musical Humanism, but Monteverdi's operas show as much attention to musical construction as to literary expression. By the later 17th c., opera singers had become more important in the public view than either composers or librettists, and arias designed for vocal display became a central part of operatic practice.

While most Ren. poets possessed some technical understanding of m., thanks to the importance of m. in the traditional school curriculum, poets in later centuries often lacked such knowledge, and their mimetic theories of musical expression proved increasingly inadequate. In 18th-c. vocal m., such composers as Bach continued to employ versions of the mimetic "word-painting" techniques of the madrigal; Pope's witty lines on "sound and sense" in the *Essay on Criticism* are a poetic analogy. But composers, unlike poets, were able to use materials that originated in such local mimesis as building-blocks from which to construct a larger structure. Trained by such rhetorically organized texts as Fux's *Gradus ad Parnassum* (1725), a treatise on counterpoint praised by Bach, they were also learning to combine canonic procedures with an increasingly stable tonal grammar; these developments liberated instrumental m., which could now embody several kinds of purely musical meaning. The willingness of later 18th-c. concert-goers to attend purely instrumental performances demonstrated once and for all the inadequacy of Ren. theories that had maintained that music's only legitimate function was to animate texts. Mimetic theorists, however, shifted their ground. No longer able to maintain that composers were imitating words, they now insisted that they were imitating or expressing feelings, a doctrine that led to the *Affektenlehre*, a systematic catalogue of musical formulae for expressing passions.

Two fundamentally opposed conceptions of m. were now coexisting uneasily: poets and philosophers continued to insist on the mimetic function of m., now calling it a language of the passions, but composers and some theorists, by developing the tight musical syntax we now call the tonal system, had given m. a grammar of its own, a meaning independent of imitation that made possible such larger forms as the "sonata-allegro." The Romantic poets, just as ignorant of musical technique as their Augustan predecessors, now embraced m. for the very qualities that had made it unattractive to those older poets, its supposed vagueness, fluidity, and "femininity." They sought in their p. to imitate these myths about m., not the logical, witty m. actually being written by such composers as Haydn. In the cause of a more "musical" p., the Romantics loosened Eng. syntax while Haydn and Mozart were tightening and refining musical syntax. But eventually these Romantic and literary myths about m. began to affect composers, and in the m. of Berlioz, Liszt, and Wagner, all of whom acknowledge literary influences, a similar loosening of musical syntax takes place. Later 19th-c. composers frequently embraced poetic aims: "program" m., the idea of the "leitmotif," the revived claim that m. could express emotions and tell stories.

Wagner's opponent Eduard Hanslick insisted on the autonomy of m., espousing the revolutionary idea that musical structure itself was the real subject of m. Contemporaneous poetic theories of autonomy were somewhat similar in their drive to separate p. from its subject matter. But while Hanslick rejected all attempts to describe m. as a language, the poetic autonomists (Poe, Wilde, Pater) claimed to want to make p. more like m. Fr. Symbolist p., in its fascination with sound and its attempt to maximize the extent to which words in a poem acquire their meaning from that particular poetic context alone, attempts to realize the program announced in Verlaine's familiar declaration: "De la musique avant toute chose." Still, the waning of the tonal system in 20th-c. m. and Schönberg's success in devising a new system for composition suggested again the limitations of attempts to describe m. in linguistic terms. 20th-c. relations between the arts have often followed the old axes of numerical construction: Schönberg was profoundly influenced by the mathematical constructive procedures, in p. and m., of Machaut; in his "expressionist" period, he used poetic line-lengths to determine musical structure; Berg organized his "Lyric Suite" on a sonnet by Mallarmé, but suppressed the text; Auden, in seeking a musical sophistication of technique, invented poetic forms closely related to the serial techniques of modern m. Despite the large differences in the way m. and p. are practiced in the modern world, Pound's cranky insistence that "poets who will not study m. are defective" acknowledges the advantages of a long and fruitful partnership.

G. Reese, *M. in the Middle Ages* (1940) and *M. in the Ren.* (1954); T. S. Eliot, *The M. of P.* (1942); B. Pattison, *M. and P. of the Eng. Ren.* (1948); *Source Readings in M. Hist.*, ed. O. Strunk (1950); A. Einstein, *Essays on M.* (1956); J. Hollander, "The M. of P.," JAAC, 15 (1956) and *The Untuning of the Sky: Ideas of M. in Eng. P., 1500–1700* (1961); G. Springer, "Language and M.: Parallels and Divergencies," in *For Roman Jakobson*, ed. M. Halle (1956); *Sound and P.*, ed. N. Frye (1957); D. Feaver, "The Musical Setting of Euripides' *Orestes*," AJP, 81 (1960); J. Stevens, *M. and P. in the Early Tudor Court* (1961); C. M. Bowra, *Primitive Song* (1962); F. W. Sternfeld, *M. in Shakespearean Tragedy* (1963); D. Mace, "Musical Humanism, the Doctrine of Rhythmus, and the St. Cecilia Odes of Dryden," JWCI, 27 (1964); S. Scher, *Verbal M. in German Lit.* (1968); E. Wahlström, *Accentual Responsion in Gr. Strophic Poetry* (1970); H. Van den Werf, *The Chansons of the Troubadours and Trouvères* (1972); W. S. Allen, *Accent and Rhythm* (1973); J. Hollander, *Vision and Resonance* (1975); J. Caldwell, *Medieval M.* (1978); D. Hillery, *M. and P. in France from Baudelaire to Mallarmé* (Berne, 1980); J. A. Winn, *Unsuspected Eloquence: A Hist. of the Relations between P. and M.* (1981); E. Jorgens, *The Well-Tun'd Word: Musical Interpretations of Eng. P. 1597–1651* (1982); L. Schleiner, *The Living Lyre in Eng. Verse from Elizabeth through the Restoration* (1984). J.A.W.

MYTH may be defined as a story or a complex of story elements taken as expressing, and therefore as implicitly symbolizing, certain deep-lying aspects of human and transhuman existence. This definition is framed in such a way as to avoid two contrary and one-sided views of the matter. The one, represented by Cassirer, treats myth as primarily a kind of perspective, and in this vein Cassirer speaks of "transposing the Kantian principle"—that all knowledge involves, at the instant of its reception, a synthesizing activity of the mind—"into the key of myth." Evidently m. here becomes synonymous with the mythopoeic mode of consciousness; it is simply a basic way of envisaging experience, and carries no necessary connotation of storytelling. At the opposite extreme stands the view that m. is *merely* story. In its popular form this gives rise to the colloquial use of the term "m." to mean a tale that is not according to the facts, and the adjective "mythical" as a synonym for "false." A more reflective development of the same general attitude finds expression in Chase's view that "myth is literature and must be considered as an aesthetic creation of the human imagination"; in other words, that the earliest mythologizers were individual poets—which is to say "makers," or storytellers—constructing out of their especially active imaginations tall tales characterized by a peculiar complication "of brilliant excitement, of the terrific play of the forces natural and human," and eventuating in some deeply desired and socially sharable feeling of reconciliation among those forces. As distinguished from Cassirer's position our proposed definition includes the idea of narrative as an essential part of the meaning of m.; but as distinguished from Chase's position it insists that the original sources of such storytelling lie somehow below or beyond the conscious inventions of individual poets, and that the stories themselves thus serve as partly unconscious vehicles for meanings that have something to do with the inner nature of the universe and of human life.

The partial validity of each of the views mentioned, as well as the variable relationships between m. and poetry, become more evident when we distinguish between the two main senses of m.—as mythopoeia and as mythology. Friedrich Max Müller (*The Science of Religion,* II, 1864) has proposed that the adjective "mythic" be employed for the first meaning, where no clear-cut ideas of true and false have yet emerged, and "mythical" for the second, where some degree of deliberate fable-making is implied.

Giambattista Vico (*La Scienza nuova,* 1725) was the first important writer to emphasize that primitive thought is essentially poetic, in that the endowment of inanimate objects with life, will, and emotion is at once the natural tendency of primitive man and the most sublime task of poetry—a point of view carried on with various modifications by Herder (1744–1803) and by Shelley (*A Defence of Poetry,* 1821). The word "mythopoeia" has come into vogue as designating the human outlook and forms of expression most characteristic of that early stage of culture when language is still largely ritualistic and prelogical in character. Each of these two aspects of the character of primitive language has a decisive bearing upon the formation of both m. and poetry. The relation of ritual to the rhythmic and eventually the metric element in poetry needs no demonstration. The ritualistic basis of m. has been emphasized by a number of anthropologists and classical scholars during the last few decades, notably in such works as: Jane Harrison, *Themis* (1912), Francis M. Cornford, *The Origins of Attic Comedy* (1914), A. B. Cook, *Zeus* (1914), S. H. Hooke, ed., *Myth and Ritual* (1933), Lord Raglan, *The Hero* (1937), and Theodore H. Gaster, *Thespis* (1950). Harrison cites an ancient Gr. definition of m. as "ta logomena epi tois dromenois" (the things that are spoken in ritual acts). The reason why ritual tends to engender m. becomes more evident when we consider that genuine ritual is celebrative and therefore participative. Seasonal ritual (as Gaster has shown with respect to the ancient Near East) expresses something of the worshippers' joyful sense of the coming of spring, or of the summer solstice, or of the gathering of grain, and at such times the worshippers feel themselves to be participating in the great rhythmic movement of nature. Dance and song are the natural expressions of such participation, and the words of the song tend to describe or to address or to enact the personified forces that are being celebrated. From description to address it is an easy step in a culture which does not sharply distinguish between person and thing nor between adjective and noun. When the ancient Canaanites described a storm, "Baal opens a rift in the clouds and gives forth his holy voice," they probably got as close to a naturalistic description as their language would allow them to go; the metaphors that make the description possible are such that Baal is envisaged not as an abstraction but as a superhuman operator, to be addressed and to be ritually enacted. Where a set of linguistic habits is such that virtually no distinction is made between the literal and the figurative there is likely to be just as little distinction between the descriptive and the fanciful. Such psychic and linguistic amalgams are one of the most important factors in the genesis and early growth of m.

The role of metaphor in primitive language is a second factor joining poetry and m. Our reference here must be to primary, or radical metaphor. Metaphor in the familiar sense of "the transference of a name from the thing which it properly denotes to some other thing" (Aristotle, *Poetics*) is rhetorical, not primary, for it is possible only where certain terms with fixed meanings are already available as starting-points; it is, therefore, more characteristic of the post-mythological and sophisticated than of the primitive phase of m. There is a prior semantic activity which operates, perhaps preconsciously, by fusing certain raw elements of experience—qualities, relationships, capabilities, emotional colorings, and whatever else—into a unity of reference which some symbol is taken to represent. Thus in Vedic Sanskrit the word *agni* meant fire in its various culturally important aspects: fire as lord of the sacred hearth, fire as "the spoon-mouthed one" which receives the oblation of sanctified butter from a spoon or ladle, fire as the messenger which crackles and leaps as it bears this offering to the gods on high, fire as the dispeller of darkness and hence of evil, fire which punishes evil-doers by its burning heat, fire as the generative urge in the loins of animals, and Lord Agni as a member of the Vedic pantheon. The hymns addressed to Agni in the *Rig-Veda* are thus able to designate the god with a connotative fullness appropriate to poetry, while they also stir up mythic inquiries by suggesting relations between some of these traits and others. Again, in the ceremony of the Night Chant practiced by the Navajo Indians the giant corn plant growing at the Red Rock House and the giant squash vine growing at the Blue Water House are employed as symbols of the masculine and feminine principles respectively, as symbols of food and therefore of plenty, as magically efficacious healing devices, and hence (through the idea of regeneration implicit in each of these aspects) as symbols of man's aspiration to spiritual rebirth. Such symbols have on the one hand a richness of reference, not overexplicit, that makes them suitable materials for poetry; while on the other hand the jostling of different and sometime incongruous meanings may stimulate the invention of mythic tales to comment upon and partly explain how those meanings are related.

In recent years, particularly through the researches of Dr. Carl G. Jung at his school, a promising line of inquiry has been developed into the collective psychology underlying primary myth-formation. Jung postulates a "collective unconscious" which consists of "primordial images" or "archetypes"—i.e., trans-individual ideas with a strong feeling-tone and with a tendency to find expression in characteristic imagistic forms. The Divine Father, the Earth Mother, the World Tree, the satyr or centaur or other man-animal monster, the descent into Hell, the Purgatorial stair, the washing away of sin, the castle of attainment, the culture-hero such as Prometheus bringing fire or other basic gift to mankind, the treacherous betrayal of the hero, the sacrificial death of the god, the god in disguise or the prince under enchantment—these and many other archetypal ideas serve as persistently recurrent themes in human thought. Since they have furnished story elements to the literature of widely different cultures, Jung and Kerényi have employed Herder's word *mythologem* to designate this aspect of them. Jung holds that they are buried deep in man's psyche, below the suppressed or inchoate memories belonging to the individual, and that the libido has recourse to them "when it becomes freed from the personal-infantile form of transference." The epic poet's invocation of the Muse would represent, in one aspect, the poet's desire to free himself from the "personal-infantile" type of thinking through being borne along by the more deeply expressive power of archetypal thought patterns.

The emergence of a definite mythology, recognized as such, represents on the whole a later and more sophisticated stage of human thought, when the primitive mythopoeic way of envisioning the world has been largely replaced by definite conceptions and a greater reliance upon reasoning, with the result that the older mythic stories have become materials to be embellished, recontextualized, and often reinterpreted by the poet's conscious art. The *Iliad* and the *Odyssey* represent two early phases of the development of mythological out of mythopoeic thought. While they contain many traces of a earlier mythopoeic attitude and of a ritual stylization (which the practice of minstrelsy in Homer's time doubtless did much to preserve), yet the voice and genius of an individual poet are unmistakably present, selecting and regrouping and articulating the older stories according to a freshly conceived design. Aeschylus' *Oresteia,* Virgil's *Aeneid,* Dante's *Commedia,* Shakespeare's *A Midsummer Night's Dream* and *The Tempest,* and Milton's *Paradise Lost,* represent in different perspectives the zenith of literary exploitation of mythology. The mythic ideas of the emergence of divinely sanctioned Gr. law out of tribal vendetta, of the destined founding of Rome, of the faery life of the Eng. countryside, of Neoplatonic hierarchies, and of Christian eschatology are here deliberately reconceived and reformulated through the imaginatively constructed medium of the poem. Yet some degree of positive belief is still operative in each of these works, giving spiritual force to the presentation and integrating without too much apparent artifice the diverse particulars. As the attitude towards mythology becomes more overtly sophisticated—e.g., in Ovid's *Metamorphoses,* Goethe's *Faust,* and Eliot's *The Waste Land*—the problem of finding a stable unifying philosophy by which to interpret a given subject matter becomes of increasing concern to the poet.

The spiritual problems of the poet in contemporary society arise in part out of the lack of myths which can be felt warmly, envisaged in concrete and contemporary imagery, and shared with a wide body of responsive readers. Consequently, since the time of Herder there has been a gradually increasing insistence upon the need of what Friedrich Schlegel (*Gespräch über die Poesie,* 1800) calls "the mother-soil of myth." Unlike Herder, who urged the revival of Teutonic mythology as a rich mine of folk imagination available to German poets, Schlegel looked toward a new and more comprehensive mythology which would combine and blend folk elements with the idealistic philosophy of Fichte and Schelling, the pantheism of Spinoza, and the sacred writings of ancient India, thus achieving a "hieroglyphical expression" of nature conceived as a system of correspondences and symbols. However, Herder was careful to warn (what every good poet knows) that the m. must be related to the poem organically, not by way of a conscious effort to plug a gap. In other words, m. in poetry is not to be conceived merely as a narrative structure, but should enter into the very life-blood of the poem—that is, into its very mode of envisaging and formulating its materials. Accordingly, Friar and Brinnin declare that "the use of metaphysical and symbolist devices has grown out of the modern poet's search for a mythology which might offer him some concrete body for metaphor and metaphysic." Thus in St.-John Perse's *Anabasis* the mythic sense of race, of rootage in the soil, of space as the area in which man moves and settles, of matter as the quarry of his building stones, of time as the cycle of seasons shot through with a firm line of communal action in the erection of cities, all conduces to an archetypal image, concretely and movingly envisaged, of the human caravan as massively operative in man's collective prehistory. Rilke's reenvisagement of the Christian mythos ("Every angel is ringed with terror"), Yeats's gradual construction of a highly individual but nonetheless powerfully expressive mythology out of the marriage of Ir. folklore with gnostic theosophy, and Eliot's synthesis of anthropology, Christian mysticism, and Gr. and Hindu metaphysics are further outstanding examples of the poetic revitalization of m. and the fresh exploration of the philosophical and religious possibilities of mythic experience through the medium of poetry in our time.

G. Vico, *The New Science* (1725; Eng. tr. 1948); T. S. Eliot, "Ulysses, Order, and M.," *The Dial*, Nov. 1923; E. Cassirer, *The Philosophy of Symbolic Forms*, II, "Mythical Thought" (1923–29; Eng. tr. 1955) and *Language and M.* (Eng. tr. 1946); F. C. Prescott, *Poetry and M.* (1927); St.-J. Perse, *Anabasis* (Eng. tr. by T. S. Eliot, 1930); H. Rosenberg, "M. and Poem," *The Symposium*, 2 (April 1931); D. Bush, *Mythology and the Renaissance Tradition in Eng. Poetry* (1932) and *Mythology and the Romantic Trad. in Eng. Poetry* (1937); M. Bodkin, *Archetypal Patterns in Poetry* (1934) and *Studies of Type-Images in Poetry, Religion, and Philosophy* (1951); Langer, ch. 7; M. Schorer, *William Blake* (1946; esp. ch. 2); P. Ure, *Towards a Mythology: Studies in the Poetry of W. B. Yeats* (1946); J. Campbell, *The Hero with a Thousand Faces* (1949); R. Chase, *Quest for M.* (1949); E. Drew, *T. S. Eliot: The Design of his Poetry* (1949); T. H. Gaster, *Thespis: Ritual, M. and Drama in the Ancient Near East* (1950); K. Friar and M. Brinnin, "M. and Metaphysics," pp. 421–43 of *Modern Poetry*, ed. by the same (1951); A. W. Watts, *M. and Ritual in Christianity* (1954); H. Weisinger, *Tragedy and the Paradox of the Fortunate Fall* (1954); Wheelwright, chs. 7–10; *M.: A Symposium*, ed. T. A. Sebeok (1955; separate issue of JAF, v. 68, no. 270); Frye; K. Burke, "Myth, Poetry and Philosophy," JAF, 73 (1960); *Myth and Mythmaking*, ed. H. A. Murray (1960); *M. and Symbol*, ed. B. Slote (1963). See also J. Campbell, *The Masks of God* (1959–68); M. Eliade, *The Sacred and the Profane* (1959) and *M. and Reality* (1963); R. Y. Hathorne, *Tragedy, M. and Mystery* (1962). P.W.

N

NARRATIVE POETRY. A n. poem is one that tells a story. The two basic types are epic and ballad. Although metrical romance is often considered as a third basic type, it is probably rightly to be thought of as a kind of epic, because it shares important recurrent themes with epic and presents them in the same narrative manner. Both epic and ballad have a long history as oral literature before they are recorded and literary forms of each emerge. The history of their literary forms is a matter of record; the origin of oral epic and of ballad is undoubtedly to be sought in the prehistoric past.

Storytelling in verse form is sometimes thought to have its beginning in the chanting of myth relating to ritual. Vestiges of this earlier mythic connection of n. poetry can be seen in: (a) the very fact, that the story is told in verse, not in prose; for the rhythms of verse are associated with "magic" effectiveness (not, as is often stated, because verse is easier to remember than prose!); (b) the pervasiveness of alliterative and assonantal techniques in epic, which are also associated with incantation; (c) the structure of the commonest stories, which coincides with the structure of myths; (d) the association of the singing of epic with religious festivals; and (e) the tradition that the bard is a seer.

In answer to the question of why a story should be told in verse, and in *sung* verse, at that (since both epic and ballad were originally sung or chanted), it is often said that the verse serves a purely mnemonic purpose; the story in verse is easier to remember than that in prose. Actually there is little or no basis for this conclusion. Studies of oral poetry that have appeared in this century and research still in progress show clearly that oral n. poetry is not memorized textually, that, indeed, its style has evolved to make a kind of "improvisation" rather than memorization possible. Moreover, the oral transmission of the tale indicates that prose can be handed on with as great ease as poetry and with almost as great, perhaps even greater, fidelity. It seems more likely that the story sung in verse had a magical purpose and was in some way connected with ritual. Such an origin would explain the pervasiveness of repetitions of sounds (alliteration and assonance) in n. as well as in all other kinds of oral poetry; for such phonetic characteristics are essential to the effectiveness of incantations. This technique later loses its overt magical function, but is preserved first as a device to aid in composition, and later as a convention.

The teller, singer, or poet would have been a kind of magician, a mediator between the other world and this world, a specially marked individual, inspired by the "muses." The listeners would be participants in the rite, sharing both individually and as a group in the benefits to be gained from the ritual myth. Such an origin would also then explain the position of the "bard" in society. It would, moreover, make reasonable the persistence of certain story patterns and details as well as provide a residual or vestigial meaning for them in later epic and ballad.

It seems probable that epic and ballad are both cognate in ritual, rather than, as has been often thought, that the one originated from the other. The ballad would represent the joining of the narrative with the dance; whereas the epic would be the joining of the narrative with incantation. In the drama one would see the survival of the three elements of ritual still in conjunction, namely, n. myth, music in its two aspects of chant and dance, and pantomime, the acting out of the myth either directly or in symbols.

There was perhaps a differentiation in performance between original epic and ballad. Epic would have been performed by an individual as priest or magician; ballad would have been performed by a dancing and singing group of devotees with a choral leader who sang the burden of the tale, while the dancing chorus came in with a refrain. Whether the myth became attached first to the incantation or first to the dance song may be a moot point, but it would seem that we should think of the myth, or n., as being joined to two already existent forms, that is, incantation and dance song, rather than of short forms becoming long or long forms being split into shorter ones.

The commonest form for epic poetry is stichic, nonstanzaic sequence of verses. N. poetry, like all poetry, was originally sung or at the very least chanted in a kind of recitative. It was usually accompanied by a musical instrument, the function of which was to maintain the rhythm of the line and of composition, although in the earliest period it may well be conjectured that the musical accompaniment was also associated with magic. There were, nevertheless, elements sometimes present that led in the direction of stanzaic form. One of these was the tendency to join lines in couplets, a natural result of syntactic parallelism on the one hand and of antiphonal singing, where it existed, on the other. The melodic patterns reflect this tendency as well, because in such couplets the real cadence comes only at the end of the second line. Since the parallelism is not only syntactic but often phonological as well, the linking of lines may go beyond the couplet. In those languages in which morphology and syntax conspire to make a series of lines ending in rhyme, there develops a convention of maintaining this rhyme as long as the singer is able. Albanian epic tradition follows this pattern. It is entirely possible that this practice is the cause of the *laisses* of the *chansons de geste* with their assonantal verse endings.

Yet it may be doubted that this tendency ever led to the development of a true stanza. The origin of the stanzaic form of the ballad must, I think, be sought elsewhere. Stanzaic form presupposes a more complex musical structure with a final melodic cadence coming after three or four lines of verse. Moreover, it may very well, as the derivation of the word "ballad" itself implies [OF *ballade,* a dancing song], have been associated with the dance. On the whole this form is less suited to extended n. than is the nonstanzaic. It is closer to the pantomime of ritual and to the choral ode of drama.

Once the myth is incorporated into epic and ballad, there is great possibility for exchange of subject matter from one to the other, and also, in most languages, even for exchange of some of the formulas, provided the metrics allow. Epic and ballad are then from the beginning two aspects of the same n. ritual impulse.

Probably the most significant shift in the history of n. poetry, second only to the creation of the myth itself and its joining to song, took place when the mythic and overtly magical content was transformed into stories of human beings told for no ostensible magic purpose, but to honor or remember great men. We might explain this by saying that the god of the myth becomes a divine king and the king then loses his divinity and becomes a human hero. The framework or structure of the myth remains but its meaning is reinterpreted on a human level. Conflicts with supernatural beings by supernatural beings become conflicts with supernatural beings by human heroes, and then the opponents of the heroes become the tribal and later the national enemy. This is not to argue that the hero is a "faded god," but that the hero has taken the place of the god in the story and the story has been modified to suit him, and he, in turn, acquires some of the characteristics of his predecessor. Epic is not *born* in a heroic age but rather in such an age it is clothed in a new garment.

It may be supposed that when divine kings, demigods, and finally mortal heroes replaced the gods of the myth, the stories too took on the aspect of human events unrolling in the real world. The secularization of epic leads to that branch known as heroic poetry. The story is told for its own sake and becomes a vehicle for moral and ethical teaching by example. The perseverance of the hero, his defense of his own prestige, his fighting for a cause, in short all those ideals that we commonly group under the concept "heroic" become of primary importance. Here stand the epic of Gilgamesh, the *Iliad,* the *Odyssey, Roland, Beowulf,* and so on. The fantastic element in these epics serves to emphasize the superior qualities of the hero.

There is a possibility that the change just outlined, from ritual myth to history with real heroes as *dramatis personae,* is aided by a concurrent development of n. poetry from a related yet distinctly different source. Myths of origins would be related to ritual myths but their purpose would be the gaining of power by incantation over the thing or person whose origin is told. No ritual drama is involved; the ritual is restricted to the incantation itself. The best examples of these myths of origins are to be found in Finnish epic lore. In order to gain control over an iron axe which has caused a wound, one chants the myth of the origin of iron. The singer of the myth is a magician. When the thing to be controlled is the spirit of a dead man, potentially a hostile force, his origin and deeds and perhaps also his death and vengeance may be sung. Epic has a close connection with the cult of the dead and with another poetic form, the lament (q.v.).

If the emphasis on the hero who has taken the place of the god in mythic material leads in a warlike society to what we call heroic epic, the stressing of the element of fantastic adventure and of the "love interest" leads to what is later termed "romance." These romantic and supernatural elements become the focus of the story and the tale is merely a series of strange adventures told for their own sake as entertainment. Some of the later *chansons de geste,* as *Huon de Bordeaux,* and the Gr. metrical romances, fall into this category. Both heroic elements and romance are found in the oral epic of the Yugoslavs, for example, not as separate genres sung by different singers to different audiences, but in the repertories of all singers for all audiences.

There seem to have been four main periods when oral n. poetry was recorded: (1) ca. 2000 B.C. in Sumer, Egypt, and generally in the Middle and Near East; (2) ca. 1000–400 B.C. in Babylon, Greece, and Palestine; (3) the Middle Ages in Europe; and (4) modern times, beginning about 1750 and coming down to the present day. The best known monuments of n. poetry from the earliest period are the Creation Epic and the Epic of Gilgamesh, preserved most fully in Akkadian texts, but known also from Sumer where they were probably original. The second period of the recording of oral texts yielded the Homeric poems, Hesiod, and the Cyclic epics in Gr. and parts of the Old Testament in Hebrew. In the case of the first period we are not sure whether the texts belong to oral or written literature (although very probably the former); it is just possible that written poetry developed this early. On the other hand, we know that an authentic written tradition of n. poetry eventually emerged in Gr., following the model of the recorded oral material, but no longer part of a living oral poetry.

Our earliest truly written n. texts of any length are the n. odes of Pindar. His choral odes from the early 5th c. B.C. are n. in that they recount a myth or myths associated with the athletic victory they celebrate. Pindar's Fourth Pythian tells the story of Jason and the Argonauts and is our earliest full form of that tale. With Pindar should also be mentioned Stesichorus, Simonides of Ceos, and Bacchylides. Our earliest written epic, the *Argonautica* of Apollonius of Rhodes, had to await the scholarly interests of the Alexandrian period. Apollonius' poem in four books totals 5,834 lines in an age that preferred shorter poems. In fact, he quarreled bitterly with his older contemporary, Callimachus, who is reported to have said that a long book is a great evil. Callimachus (b. ca. 330 B.C.) wrote short epics, *epyllia,* which form a separate division of n. poetry. Two of his epyllia have echoes in Roman times; *Hecale,* which tells how Hecale entertains Theseus on his way to kill the bull of Marathon, is like the story told by Ovid of Philemon and Baucis; and *The Lock of Berenice,* which we know from Catullus' version of it (the original is lost). Callimachus also wrote a work in elegiac meter in four books entitled *Aetia,* a series of narratives concerning the origin of customs and of legends, in form not unlike Ovid's *Metamorphoses.* Theocritus, too, a younger contemporary of Callimachus, wrote epyllia, such as *Helen, Hylas, The Infant Heracles,* and *The Dioscuri.* The epyllion, with its tendency to satire and mock heroic, will continue to cross our path in later centuries.

The written literary tradition thus established in Greece continued through Roman and medieval times to our own day, now and then meeting with a native vernacular oral tradition. Eventually it cast all these into the background, triumphing over and assimilating unto itself local or tribal subjects. Thus, while there was probably a native Italic oral tradition of n. poetry in the Saturnian verse, into which Livius Andronicus translated the *Odyssey* in the 3d c. B.C. and in which Naevius wrote his *Bellum Punicum,* the first L. epic, none of these oral poems seems to have been written down or to have survived. For Ennius, the next epic writer in line after Naevius, in his *Annales* borrows the hexameter from the Greeks, and henceforth the "matter of Rome" is native merchandise carried in foreign bottoms.

Rome has bequeathed to us the first historical epic in Naevius' *Bellum Punicum* and Ennius' *Annales.* Virgil's *Aeneid,* though dealing with early Roman legend and based on the Homeric model, is filled with historical overtones and in Book 6 presents us with a brief panorama of Roman history.

Ovid's *Metamorphoses* in hexameters goes back to the same structural frame as Callimachus' *Aetia,* relating one after another, a series of tales of transformations, something like a string of epyllia. Virgil's *Aeneid* and Ovid's *Metamorphoses* were the most lasting and influential of the n. poems of the Augustan period in Rome. The Empire boasted of Lucan (*Bellum Civile*), Statius (*Thebais* and *Achilleis*), Valerius Flaccus (*Argonautica*), and Silius Italicus (*Punica*). Claudian's *De Raptu Prosespinae* comes after some break in time (late 4th c.) and marks the close of classical L. epic. Lucan's fierce poem distorts history for partisan purposes and disdains the divine machinery of previous epic. In the Silver Age, epic preferences were divided. But the tradition ends with a return to myth in Claudian's poem.

Several centuries elapse before we find Greek epic poetry again in Quintus Smyrnaeus' *Posthomerica* (ca. A.D. 400), Nonnus' *Dionysiaca* (ca. A.D. 420), Tryphiodorus' *Taking of Troy* (ca. 470), Colluthus' *Rape of Helen* (ca. 490), and an anonymous *Argonautica* in a collection called *Orphica* (ca. 400). In the middle of the 6th c. Musaeus wrote the last of classical Greek n. poems, *Hero and Leander.* As striking as the long period of time, from the 3d c. B.C. to the 5th c. of our era, during which epic poetry seems to have been written in Gr. is that the poems which we have or know about are concerned with the ancient pagan myths and legends. Unlike Roman n. poetry, that of ancient Greece never turned to history for its subjects.

THE MIDDLE AGES. L. n. poetry did not die out after the classical period. The tradition of Virgil and Ovid was transformed to some extent by Christianity, or, perhaps better, accepted Christianity. The Gospel story was told in L. hexameters in Juvencus' *Evangeliorum Libri* (ca. 330) some sixty-five years before the poem of Claudian (ca. 395). Juvencus' poem contained more than 3,000 lines. In the first half of the 5th c. Sedulius wrote a *Paschal Poem* in five books. Both these poems of the Christian story became well known in the Middle Ages. At the end of the 5th c. Dracontius treated the Creation in his poem *In Praise of God*; and in the 6th c. Arator wrote a poem on Acts. Thus in these centuries at the dawn of the Middle Ages a Christian n. poetry came into being in the literary tradition of Virgil and in dactylic hexameters (or in other cases in elegiac couplets). These were significant moments; for the new mythology of Christianity was replacing paganism in paganism's literary forms.

We are not surprised to find hagiographic works in verse as well as in prose, although prose antedates verse in this genre. Early in the 8th c. Bede wrote lives of St. Cuthbert in both prose and verse, and the following century saw a number of such lives. Milo of St. Amand (ca. 810–71) wrote a versified life of St. Amandus in 2,000 lines, and Heiric of Auxerre did a life of St. Germanus in 3,400 lines.

Historical poems in L. verse also appeared in the Carolingian period. The Saxon Poet's verse annals of Charlemagne reach nearly 3,000 hexameters and elegiac couplets, and the monk Abbo of St. Germain wrote two books of L. epic (ca. 900) on the Norman attack on Paris in 885–86. Ermoldus Nigellus had celebrated the deeds of Louis the Pious (ca. 826) in something like 2,500 lines of elegiac couplets.

The saints' lives may be regarded as continuations of the tradition of songs about the gods as well as songs about heroes. At about this same time, in the early Middle Ages, there began to appear another vastly important branch of n. poetry, romance; and it is to be noted that, like the saint's life and chronicles or annals, the romance can be either in verse or in prose, or in both. Prose romance seems to antedate versified romance in our manuscripts. The Pseudo-Callisthenes Gr. original of the Alexander Romance seems to belong to the 2d c. of our era, and was translated into L. by Julius Valerius in the 3d c., but the verse tales are much later. The earliest apparently to be found in L. belongs to the 13th c. (1256, *Alexandreis* by Quilichinus of Spoleto) and the earliest vernacular poem in the West is a fragmentary Prov. octosyllabic text attributed to Albéric of Besançon of the late 11th c. The L. prose of Dictys Cretensis goes back to the 4th c. and that of Dares perhaps to around 500. But the first L. poem to come to our notice is in the 12th c. (Simon Chèvre d'Or's poem in leonine elegiacs in the middle of the century, and Joseph of Exeter's *De Bello Trojano* in 1187–88)—the same century in which there appeared Joannes Tzetzes' Gr. hexameter poem *Iliaca,* and also the first poem in the vernacular, the famous 30,000 line *Roman de Troie* of Benoît de Sainte-Maure (ca. 1165).

If we turn to a consideration of n. poetry in Byzantium, or in the Gr. East, we find a somewhat similar situation. Nonnus, who had written the *Dionysiaca* in ca. 420, had also produced a Paraphrase of the Gospel of St. John in dactylic hexameters. Saints' lives, however, in the East seem to be almost entirely in prose. The verse autobiography of Gregory Nazianzus (ca. 329–ca. 89) appears to be *sui generis,* in his own day at least. Historical poems in Gr. are found beginning in the 7th c. with George Pisida, who wrote a description of the campaigns of the Emperor Heraclius against the Persians, another on further exploits of the emperor, and still another on the attack of the Avars on Constantinople in 626. There are but a few scattered poems from then until the 12th c., when the verse chronicle of Constantine Manasses was written and another Constantine, Stilbes, composed two poems on two fires in Constantinople in 1197 and 1198!

In the field of romance we do not encounter metrical tales until the 12th c. when we find fragments of the *Loves of Aristander and Callithea* by the chronicler Constantine Manasses. Early in the same century Prodromus wrote a long poem on *Rhodanphe and Dosicles.* In the 13th c. the famous and anonymous *Belthandros and Chrysantza* appears.

Allegory as a literary form (not merely the rhetorical trope) seems to have appeared comparatively early in n. poetry. Examples of personification are, of course, to be found in Ovid and Virgil and other L. poets, but probably the first full dress allegory is the *Psychomachia* of Prudentius (A.D. 348–ca. 410), which depicts a battle of the virtues and vices. Thus allegory entered the service of morality and religion. Not only was the mythic battle of prehistory, refined by the heroic and by the historic, easily adaptable, as we have seen, but also the other basic mythic material, that of the journey, could easily be suited to Christian concepts, as had already been done in saints' lives and in apocryphal tales. The supreme example of religious allegory, Dante's *Divine Comedy,* is structurally a journey into the other world and a return after the gaining of knowledge. The cult of courtly love, a kind of secular religion, led allegory captive and produced the "allegories of love" of which the *Roman de la Rose,* begun about 1230 by Guillaume de Lorris and completed about 1270 by Jean de Meun, is the best known instance.

Oral epic for the first time since the 8th c. B.C. began again to be written down, now in the vernaculars of the West as well as in Middle Gr. Only one poem in the latter can probably be classed as oral, the *Digenis Akritas.* The hero belongs to the 8th or 9th c. (or possibly the 10th), but the earliest Gr. manuscript is probably of the 14th c. Grégoire refers the formation of the epic to the 10th c. and the Rus. version of it to the 12th. In Old Sp. the *Cid* is said to have been composed about 1140 about a hero, Don Rodrigo Díaz, who died in 1099. Our unique manuscript of the poem is actually dated 1307. The thirty-odd separate poems in the ON collection entitled the *Elder Edda* are thought to have been written down in the 12th c.; they are mythological and heroic in character. The Anglo-Saxon *Beowulf* has been assigned to the middle of the 8th c., but its only manuscript dates from about the year 1000. There are somewhere around a hundred *chansons de geste.* The earliest is the famed *Chanson de Roland,* referring to the battle of Roncesvalles in 778, and earliest preserved is the Oxford manuscript of about 1170. The oldest German poem is a fragment of the *Lay of Hildebrand* in Old High German of ca. 800. Surely the best known of the Middle High German epics is the *Nibelungenlied,* which seems to belong to the early part of the 13th c.

The question as to whether these vernacular poems are oral or written is still being debated. In those cases where there are a number of varying manuscripts over a period of time there is a possibility that some are oral and some written. At any rate it seems very probable that written versions, imitating the oral vernacular songs, appear at least as early as the 14th c. and probably earlier. In German and in OF the appearance of rhyme and the rewriting of some of the stories in rhymed rather than alliterative or assonantal verse seems to indicate a new formal tradition, generally associated with writing, coming into existence.

Contemporary with the vernacular epics and the whole group they represent is another body of n. poems in the vernacular on religious subjects. Thus, in Anglo-Saxon there are poems on Genesis, Exodus, Daniel, Christ, and Andreas, all of which are assigned dates close to that of *Beowulf.* Some of these poems are ascribed to Caedmon, others to Cynewulf, others are of unknown authorship. In Old High German there is a *Liber Evangeliorum* (Book of the Gospels) by Otfrid of Weissenburg in the 9th c., and about 830, the *Heliand* recounts the life of Christ. In other words both religious and secular "epic" are written in vernacular (one might also say "oral") style during this period. Somewhat earlier, it will be remembered, L. was the language (except for Gr. in the East) used for the metrical religious narratives including saints' lives. When history appears in verse in the West it is in L., the language of learning.

In the case of the medieval romances, it may be that some are oral and some written, although it is generally assumed, perhaps correctly, that they are written. Besides the material on Troy and Alexander, that on Arthur and his knights is the most widespread (see MEDIEVAL ROMANCE).

In the 14th c., at the end of the Middle Ages, there appear in England, contemporary or slightly later than Dante in Italy, other n. poems that are neither epic nor romance. One of them, *The Vision of Piers Plowman,* is allegory, and is written in three versions in alliterative verse. Part of it was long attributed to William Langland (ca. 1332–ca. 1400). It is a kind of frame story, in the conceit of a dream. The author says that he went walking and sat down and fell asleep beside a brook, and then he dreamed a succession of things, including the Vision of the Field of Folk, Holy Church, and Lady Meed, and the Vision of the Seven Deadly Sins. Another Eng. poet to grace the 14th c. n. scene is, of course, Geoffrey Chaucer (ca. 1343–1400), whose *Canterbury Tales* is perhaps the most famous frame n. in Eng. literature. Here allegory bows to realism as the first person convention does to the proper third person of n.

Elsewhere than in England in the 14th c. n. poetry was also practiced. In Italy this is the century not only of Dante, but also of Petrarch and Boccaccio. We may think of Petrarch chiefly as a writer of sonnets, but he fancied himself also as an epic poet; his *Africa,* on the theme of Scipio Africanus and Roman history, is in L., it will be noted, not It. Boccaccio is known best for prose n. in the frame tradition, in his *Decameron,* but his metrical romance *Filostrato,* on the story of Troilus and Criseida, drew from the Trojan romance and influenced Chaucer in his n. of *Troilus and Criseyde.* He. also wrote *Teseida* (the story of Arcita and Palemone) in ottava rima. Metrical romance was also being cultivated in Gr., as evidenced by *Callimachus and Chrysorrhoë,* which probably belongs to the 14th c.

THE RENAISSANCE. The great Renaissance tradition of epic poetry begins with Matteo Maria Boiardo (1441–94) and continues with Ludovico Ariosto (1474–1553) in Italy. Boiardo is famous for his *Orlando Innamorato,* an unfinished epic, or perhaps more properly romance, with Roland, the hero of the OF *chanson,* as its principal figure. Ariosto's even more famous *Orlando Furioso* picked up the same theme and completed Boiardo's story. The hero in both these poems is in name only the hero of the older epic; he is in them rather the hero of romance. The older kind of epic might well have died in Italy had it not been for an even greater poet of the following century, that of the "high Renaissance," namely Torquato Tasso (1544–95), who combined the more classical idea of the heroic epic, as it was known in those days from ancient models, with the romance. The result was his *Gerusalemme Liberata* (Jerusalem Delivered). For the heroic part of this epic, as distinguished from its romantic part, Tasso turned to the history of the first crusade, to the fairly distant past, therefore; on the other hand the two chief 16th-c. epics of the Iberian peninsula, *La Araucana,* by Alonso de Ercilla y Zúñiga (1533–94) in Spain, and *Os Lusiadas* by Luis de Camoëns (1524–80) in Portugal treated more recent history. The former deals with the conquest of South America (the Araucanians being a tribe of South American Indians in central Chile) by the Spaniards, and the latter with the voyaging to India by Vasco da Gama in 1497–99. One might say that for the first time since Virgil's day one had again a really national epic. 16th-c. France was not much given to epic, although mention should be made of Pierre de Ronsard's (1524–85) *La Franciade,* unfinished but published in 1572. The theme was obviously national here too, and the return to the decasyllables of early medieval times was an archaism not in keeping with a new age. All three of these epics, in France, Spain, and Portugal, were historical, national, and classical, looking backward to Virgil and to classical mythology, and not, as Tasso, toward romance. There was in France another epic poet in the 16th c., a Huguenot, Guillaume de Salluste du Bartas (1544–90), who turned, or returned, to one of the most ancient of subjects for epic, namely to the creation of the world. In 1578 he published *La Sepmaine,* a poem very popular in its day not only in France but also in England. With his *Judith* (1573) he was employing a theme well liked in Renaissance painting.

With Du Bartas, indeed, we are carried in two directions; one is toward England and ultimately to Milton, the other is toward Dalmatia and to the figure of Marko Marulić (1450–1524) of Split, the "father" of Croatian literature. He was not a Protestant, but he also wrote a *Judita* in his native Croatian, in 1501, which went into three editions during his lifetime (1521, 1522, 1523). Like Du Bartas, Marulić did not approve of the pagan themes and settings, and his L. epic *Davidijada* returns to biblical stories rather than to classical antiquity. It is worthy of note that n. poetry was flourishing also in Dalmatia during the 16th c. under the influence of the It. Renaissance. On the island of Hvar the poet Petar Hektorović wrote a n. poem telling of a fishing expedition, *Ribanje i ribarsko prigovaranje* (1555), partly in imitation of It. models of "fishing pastorals" (fishermen and nymphs instead of shepherds and nymphs), but completely realistic, *sans* nymphs. It included, however, the singing of folk songs, some of them n. ballads. A friend of Hektorović's in Dubrovnik, Mavro Vetranić (1482–1576) wrote an unfinished philosophical-allegorical epic entitled *The Pilgrim,* picturing man as a traveler through the three conditions of sin, repentance, and perfection. Petar Zoranić (1508–?1569) of Zadar on the Dalmatian coast wrote a pastoral romance in verse and prose entitled *Planine,* "The Mountains" (1536, published 1569) in which a shepherd named Zoran goes to the mountains to find herbs to cure him of lovesickness. Among other adventures he encounters a mountain spirit named Croatia, who complains of the lack of interest in the Croatian tongue. This national theme appears again in the later work of two other poets of Zadar, Brno Krnarutić (1520–72) and Juraj Baraković (1548–1628). Krnarutić's fame comes from his epic on a contemporary theme, *The Capture of the City of Sziget,* which fell to the Turks in 1566 after a heroic defense by Nikola Zrinski. And Juraj Baraković published in 1614 his *Vila Slovinska,* devoted to the past and contemporary history of Zadar. It is in the early 17th c. that Dalmatia produces her Tasso, in the person of Ivan Gundulić (1588–1638) of Dubrovnik, whose unfinished epic *Osman* follows Tasso's theory of the combining of the classical heroic with the romantic, with this difference, however, that Gundulić chose a theme from contemporary Balkan history, in the spirit of Christendom's crusade against the Turks with the Polish prince as its heroic champion.

Although the pastoral (q.v.) romance has its roots deep in the past with the idylls of Theocritus and Bion and their descendants (for example, in the *Eclogues* of Virgil) and although one can find examples in the 15th c. such as Boccaccio's *Ameto,* in prose and verse, it is common to date pastoral romance from the publication of J. Sannazaro's *Arcadia* in 1504, also a work combining verse and prose. The pastoral romance is distinguished by the fact that its protagonists are shepherds, its background and scenery are the countryside where shepherds and shepherdesses tend their flocks, and its adventures are in keeping with its protagonists in love. All is ideal and paradisiacal. The limitations of such a form are obvious and its possibilities were exhausted in England actually by the end of the 17th c. The pastoral impulse went elsewhere, into pastoral drama, lyric, and even into the novel.

Eng. n. poetry other than pastoral of the 15th and 16th c. follows patterns well established on the continent. The prolific John Lydgate's *The Fall of Princes* (36,000 lines), for example, is a translation of Boccaccio's *De Casibus Virorum Illustrium,* and his *Troy Book* (1412) was a translation of Guido. Hawes' *Pastime of Pleasure* (1509) was an allegory, a pilgrimage of the soul of the active man. In the same century Spenser's *Faerie Queene* indulged in the allegory of courtly love; and we have at least two historical narratives in Edward Hall's *Chronicle* and Samuel Daniel's (1562–1619) *Civil Wars* (1595). With Michael Drayton it is abundantly clear that we are in a period when forms shorter than the older epic and romance have become attractive. Once again we see appearing what we might call the Ovidian collection of epyllia, that is, Drayton's *England's Heroical Epistles* (1597).

And at the fairs and in the streets of London and throughout the cities of the British Isles appeared in ever greater numbers the cheap broadsides with their n. ballads. In 1520 *Robin Hood* was being sold at Oxford in broadsides. Our oldest copy of *Chevy Chase* is in a manuscript of ca. 1559. The earliest collection of broadsides comes from the first two decades of the 17th c., and the Percy Folio Manuscript of ballads and broadsides is dated about 1650. But it is to the 18th c. that one must turn for the real history of ballad collecting and publishing.

THE 17TH AND 18TH C. TO ROMANTICISM. It has already been seen that the activity in n. poetry in the 16th c. was ebullient, and it welled over into the next. The world was changing, however, in the 17th c., and as the century wore on n. poetry, with certain notable exceptions, gave place to occasional poems and especially to satire. This state of things lasted actually until after the middle of the 18th c., when romanticism brought n. poetry as such back into favor. In Italy and Germany this intermediate period was especially barren. France presents us with some interesting exceptions. We find Nicolas Boileau's *Le Lutrin* (lectern) a mock epic, written in 1673–83; some of the *Fables* of La Fontaine (1621–95) are n. poetry; but more important, two works, one in the 17th c., Fénelon's "prose poem" *Télémaque* (1699), which tells the tale of Odysseus' son in search of his father and his adventures, and the other in the 18th, Voltaire's *Henriade* (1728), a national epic on the religious wars. Actually both these works, one from ancient story and the other from recent history, are used by their authors as platforms from which to expound their educational, social, or political views. In parts they tend to be tracts, or to be mere rhetoric. It almost seems that epic, and, as we shall soon see, the short n. forms, move easily in the direction of satire. The story is amusing, or biting, or formally perfect; it has lost its lure as a story for entertainment.

At the close of the 16th c. in England we might note two links with the past. Christopher Marlowe (1564–93) wrote a poem on *Hero and Leander* (1593), completed and published by George Chapman in 1598. By it we are reminded of Musaeus' epyllion that marked the end of the ancient Gr. epic tradition. And Abraham Cowley (1618–67) wrote a *Davideis* (1656) which remained unfinished, a biblical epic in Virgilian style. This was a different task from the *Davidijada* of Marko Marulić mentioned above, which was a more or less direct paraphrase of the biblical story.

But the picture in the 17th c. is dominated by John Milton and his *Paradise Lost* (1667). Milton went back to the wellsprings of epic for his subject, to religious myth, to the creation, to the war of the gods. He thought to fashion a new hero in Adam, and thus misjudged the tradition of the heroic. Yet his magnificent poem stands as perhaps the last great epic in Western literature. There are examples of the genre later, but they are either *tours de force* or weak in their concept of the hero, as in the Victorian epic.

When the other great poets of these centuries, whose chief fields were either drama or satire, turned to n., it was to translation rather than to original creation, yet their translations became classics. Such are the renderings by John Dryden of Ovid, Virgil, Chaucer, and Boccaccio; that of the Homeric poems by Alexander Pope (1688–1744) and by William Cowper (1731–1800). The best of all translations of Homer, however, in this early period was that of George Chapman (1559–1634).

ROMANTICISM. A new interest in n. poetry began to grow from about the middle of the 18th c., no longer a neoclassical movement (which seemed pretty well exhausted), but a movement in the direction of the songs of the common people. This was, of course, in keeping with the times. The opening gun of this new interest in n. might be said to be the publication in 1765 by Thomas Percy of his *Reliques of Ancient Eng. Poetry*. In this the term "Ballad" was limited to those songs which described action, and the term "Song" was used for those which expressed a sentiment. Actually the publication of Percy's book was preceded by a few years by the "hoaxes" of James Macpherson (1736–96), *Fragments of Ancient Poetry collected in the Highlands of Scotland* (1760), *Fingal, an Ancient Epic Poem in Six Books, together with Several Other Poems composed by Ossian, the Son of Fingal, translated from the Gaelic Language* (1761), *Temora* (1763) and *The Works of Ossian* (1765).

From the point of view of n. poetry and aside from the question of the value of their content, these two books or groups of books exerted influence in three important directions. First, they encouraged through the work of men like Johann Gottfried von Herder (1744–1803) and the brothers Grimm, Jakob and Wilhelm, the collecting and studying of folk ballads and folk epic song throughout Europe. Secondly, they led to the unearthing, publication, and scholarly investigation of medieval manuscripts of epic which were revived during the 19th c. Thirdly, they inspired written ballads in a literary tradition. To these three influences it might be added that they played no small role in the beginning of the romantic movement in general with its theories about the origins, transmission, and composition of poetry, with its new view of the world and of the past, and the revival of some of the themes of epic from antiquity retold in the romantic spirit.

Of the first of these something has been said in the article on oral poetry. Of the second there has been some treatment both in that article and in this. It is of the third that we must speak further here.

Burns and Scott would seem to be the best examples of the impact of the ballad on written n. poetry. They both knew the popular form from an early age. Robert Burns (1759–96) is more given to lyric, but in such poems as *Tam o'Shanter* he exhibited his skill with the ballad spirit. N. was more serious a matter for Sir Walter Scott (1771–1834), whose *Minstrelsy of the Scottish Border* (1802–03), a collection of the ballads of Scotland, prepared him well for his own *The Lay of the Last Minstrel, Marmion,* and *The Lady of the Lake.* Scott's instinct for story, a true n. instinct, expressed itself more genuinely perhaps in his novels, the real successors of epic. Scott is a more veritable follower of the n. genius in Western literature than many another, for the story interests him above all.

And this is the fate of n. poetry after 1750. William Wordsworth (1770–1850) turns to the common folk and tells stories of local events, as in *Goody Blake and Harry Gill,* but it is a self-conscious attempt. *Michael* is more sentimental than the popular ballads, although it has something of their spirit in that the kind of change that comes over Luke in the evil cities of men is not untypical. In *Laodamia* Wordsworth is consciously telling a tale from the past, a tale that touches the heart of epic mythic origins, and one that he retells with perfection. It is not his fault but that of the moment of intellectual history that the perfection of the poet in his craft is more significant than the story of *Laodamia.* We might, I suppose, call *The Prelude* n., but the first person in ballad is pure convention, and to concentrate upon it as the real subject of the tale is contrary to the objectivity of traditional story poetry. True, there are famous examples in epic where a character, as, for example, Odysseus in the *Odyssey,* tells a long tale in the first person, but Odysseus is not Homer. In Samuel Taylor Coleridge (1772–1834), whose *The Rime of the Ancient Mariner* is surely one of the best known n. poems of this period, together with his unfinished, and somewhat less known *Christabel,* we find an artistic sense of and feeling for the ballad situation and an uncanny ability effectively to present weird tales. The ballad manner and the traditional phrasing are lacking, of course, and the intensity of the poet lends an air of its own. The style here, too, and the poet are what count rather than the story.

And what should we say of George Gordon, Lord Byron (1788–1824) and n. poetry? He is closest to storytelling in his oriental tales, in *The Giaour,* for example. Here is storytelling for its own pleasure. *Beppo* is good n. but also an excellent illustration of the use of n. for satire. The Romans were past masters of this genre. In *Don Juan* the story is but a vehicle for all the views of the poet. And *Childe Harold's Pilgrimage,* while ironically enough it takes us back to the tale of a journey, so basic to n. myth, is only veiled autobiography. Perhaps it is truly n. only in its digressions. John Keats (1795–1821) is objective enough to be a master of n., and some might say that his perfection of style serves the n. rather than that the n. serves the style. This certainly seems true for *The Eve of Saint Agnes* and for *Lamia.* Whether he could have sustained this balance to complete the longer epic is doubtful perhaps, to judge from the fate of *Hyperion.*

From the Victorian Age to the Present. N. poetry comes more into its own in the Victorian Age, when writers had greater interest in the story and less in form. It should be sufficient to name the more famous poets and their equally famous works. Alfred, Lord Tennyson's (1809–92) *Idylls of the King* takes us back to the romances of chivalry, and, indeed, it is a revival of old subjects that faces us. Thomas Babington, Lord Macaulay (1800–59) in his *Lays of Ancient Rome* went even further back than Tennyson, to early Roman times. Matthew Arnold (1822–88) follows fashion in his interest in oriental tales, and his *Sohrab and Rustum* drew from ancient Persian history and epic, which lies a bit uneasy in its 19th-c. sentimental cradle. And, finally, William Morris (1834–96) reminds one of Scott in the earlier part of the century; he too had a real instinct for n. and a sense of storytelling of the past, as can be seen from his saga translations, for example. His *Jason* is probably our last telling of the tale of the Argonauts. *The Earthly Paradise* not only returns us to Gr. myth in some of its tales and emphasizes as well the mythic tales of the Scandinavians, but also takes us back to the frame story. And the story for the frame is an ancient mythic one of wanderings. We have thus returned to the beginning of our account. The date was 1866–70, over a hundred years ago.

There has been some n. since then, of course, but our own age has felt that the genius of poetry was lyric, or fashionably dramatic. It has scorned n. poetry in general and sought its stories for entertainment, instruction, or artistic edification in the novel. When poetry is thought of as form and ecstasy, then n. poetry is an anomaly. Rudyard Kipling's (1865–1936) ballads took the fancy of a generation, John Masefield (1878–1967) had a real talent for n., and many will remember his *The Everlasting Mercy* (1911) and *The Widow in the Bye Street* (1912). Stephen Vincent Benet's (1898–1943) *John Brown's Body* (1928) is an interesting almost-epic experiment in n.

Ten years later (1938) in Greece and in Gr. there was published the n. poem that ends our own tale, *The Odyssey, a Modern Sequel,* by Nikos Kazantzakis; the translation into Eng. of this poem, which narrates the further wanderings and adventures of Odysseus, appeared in 1958.

W. P. Ker, *Epic and Romance* (2d ed., 1908) and *Form and Style in Poetry* (1928); G. H. Gerould,

The Ballad of Tradition (1932); Chadwick; Lewis; W. J. Entwistle, *European Balladry* (1939); D. Bush, *Eng. Lit. in the Earlier 17th C., 1600–1660* (1945; 2d ed., 1962); E. K. Chambers, *Eng. Lit. at the Close of the Middle Ages* (1945; especially chap. 3, "Popular N. Poetry and the Ballad"); C. M. Bowra, *From Virgil to Milton* (1948) and *Heroic Poetry* (1952); E.M.W. Tillyard, *The Eng. Epic and Its Background* (1954); R. Poggioli, "The Oaten Flute," *Harvard Library Bulletin*, 11 (1957); K. Kroeber, *Romantic N. Art* (1961). A.B.L.

For further consideration of the epic in the various literatures, see the articles on ASSYRO-BABYLONIAN POETRY ENG., FINNISH, GR., INDIAN, L., OLD NORSE, etc. in the *Princeton Encyclopedia of Poetry and Poetics*. Consult also ORAL POETRY, CHANSONS DE GESTE in this volume, and refer to such bibliographic titles as: E. W. Hopkins, *The Great Epic of India* (1901; the *Mahābhārata*; also some discussion of the *Rāmāyana*); L. Abercrombie, *The Epic* (1914); R. Heinze, *Virgils epische Technik* (3d ed., 1915); H. V. Routh, *God, Man, and Epic Poetry* (2 v., 1927); W. W. Lawrence, *Beowulf and Epic Tradition* (1928); J. M. Parry, *L'Epithète traditionelle dans Homère* (1928) and "Traditional Metaphor in Homer," CP, 28 (1933); C. M. Bowra, *Tradition and Design in the Iliad* (1930); R. Menéndez Pidal, *Historia y epopeya* (1934) and *La epopeya castellana a través de la literatura española* (1945); C. S. Lewis, *A Preface to Paradise Lost* (1942); E. Mudrak, *Die nordische Heldensage* (1943); D. Knight, *Pope and the Heroic Tradition* (1951); U. Leo, *Torquato Tasso* (1951); Auerbach; Curtius; G. R. Levy, *The Sword from the Rock* (1953); A. Heusler, *Nibelungensage und Nibelungenlied* (5th ed., 1955); C. Whitman, *Homer and the Homeric Tradition* (1958); R. W. Chambers, *Beowulf: An Introd.* (3d ed., 1959); A. B. Lord, *The Singer of Tales* (1961); G. S. Kirk, *The Songs of Homer* (1962); T. M. Greene, *The Descent from Heaven: A Study in Epic Continuity* (1963).

NEAR RHYME. The repetition in accented syllables of the final consonant-sound without correspondence of the preceding vowel- or consonant-sounds, and either with or without "feminine" unaccented syllables following (which should be largely identical). E.g., *grope-cup, maze-coze, drunkard-conquered.* It is a special case of consonance (q.v.), and is called by such various names as slant rhyme, half rhyme (also applied to rich consonance), oblique rhyme, para-rhyme. An old device in Icelandic, Ir., and Welsh verse, n.r. appears to have been deliberately used in Eng. first by Vaughan, who was influenced by Welsh practice. Both internally and at line ends such inexact echoes can be found occasionally in all poetry, especially in ballad, folk, and popular song. Swift rhymed "justice" with "hostess," Emily Dickinson "port" with "chart," Osbert Sitwell "war" with "armchair" (which last have *no* true echo in Standard British Eng.). But no major poet in Eng. had used n.r. consistently until Hopkins and Yeats. Hopkins knew George P. March's work in Icelandic and himself studied the Welsh. Yeats, although not a student of Ir., knew of Ir. metrics through Kuno Meyer and others. Once considered an oddity in the work of such poets as Emerson and Emily Dickinson, n.r. is now accepted and used by nearly all 20th-c. poets, not to supplant perfect rhyme but to supplement it, so as to provide a greater range and freedom for the poet. The Am. poet Trumbull Stickney uses n.r. systematically intertwined with regular rhyme in *Mnemosyne.* For examples of n.r. in modern poetry, see Hopkins, Yeats, Ransom, Eliot, Owen, Tate, Wylie, and Auden.—G. P. March, *Lectures on the Eng. Language* (1859; anticipates modern borrowing and experimentation); K. Meyer, *A Primer of Ir. Metrics* (1909); E. Rickert, *New Methods for the Study of Lit.* (1927); T. W. Herbert, "Near-Rimes and Paraphones," SR, 14 (1937); G. Symes, "A Note on Rhyme," *Eng.*, 7 (1949). S.L.M.; U.K.G.

NEW CRITICISM. See POETRY, THEORIES OF (OBJECTIVE THEORIES).

NŌ. This relatively short Japanese dramatic form, employing poetry, prose, patterned movement, dance, and music, was perfected in the 14th c. Adapting with some variations, the traditional syllabic fives and sevens, the poetry is highly allusive and elevated. Such elevated richness, the religious subjects, and the slow tempo of most nō create a drama akin to the Gr., which it further resembles in its use of traditional materials, masks, male performers, and a chorus (that takes no part in the action).

Nō has broadly and rapidly influenced Western drama, nondramatic poetry, and literary criticism since Ezra Pound first received (1914), studied, revised, and published (1916) Ernest Fenollosa's notes and rude translations. Pound felt that nō showed how to write a long Vorticist (i.e., imagist) poem, since he saw in it a technique by which crucial images unified whole plays or passages. He utilized both allusions to nō and this technique of "Unity of Image" in the *Cantos* by employing certain recurring, archetypical images—e.g., light, the literary journey, and the heavenly visitor to earth—to unify his poem. Often these images take on an additional oriental dimension, since the heavenly visitor to earth may be the central character of the nō *Hagoromo* as well as Diana; or it may be the Sino-Japanese character for "brightness" combined with other imagery of light.

Pound had discussed his interests with Yeats, who became so absorbed that he completely reshaped his later dramaturgy in the image of nō. On this Japanese model, he fashioned an "aristocratic form" employing a bare stage, masks, dance, a few rhythmic instruments, a chorus not part of the action, and other characteristics of nō. Some of his "Noh plays," as he called them, have elements borrowed from specific nō: e.g., the blue cloth centrally onstage in *At the Hawk's Well* is modeled on the brocade cloak of Aoi no Ue; and *Words Upon the Window-Pane* and *The Dreaming of the Bones* borrow the *Nishikigi* motif of unmarried ghostly lovers from a distant past. Yeats seems to have come upon the idea of a unifying-image technique in nō independently of Pound, using it to give coherence to such plays as *The Only Jealousy of Emer, Calvary,* and *A Full Moon in March,* through dramatic focus on an object onstage (Cuchulain's body, Christ hanging on the cross) or an imagistic pattern (of moon and cat's eyes). The importance of nō to Yeats can be measured by his use of it to form a new poetic drama, by his use of images and techniques related to it in his nondramatic poems, and by his statement that the Japanese dramatists were more like modern Western man than either Shakespeare or Corneille.

Yeats's enthusiasms, the Fenollosa-Pound adaptations, Arthur Waley's translations and commentaries, and the monumental studies of Noel Peri, *Cinq Nô* (1929) and *Le Nô* (1944) have influenced many other playwrights, especially those concerned with the poetic or semiprivate theater. Yeats induced his friend T. Sturge Moore to write "Noh plays," and such others as Gordon Bottomley and Laurence Binyon soon followed. In Germany, Bertolt Brecht conceived his two didactic plays, *Der Jasager* and *Der Neinsager,* in the light of Waley's translation of *Tanikō;* and in France, Paul Claudel, who had seen nō performed in Japan, borrowed techniques for his marionette plays. Similarly, Thornton Wilder modeled the bare-stage technique of *Our Town* in part upon nō and has adapted the *waki* (deuteragonist) and the chorus of nō into a *raisonneur* for many plays. Such other, lesser known writers as S. Foster Damon and Paul Goodman have written plays modeled on nō, and Stark Young's *Flower in Drama* uses earlier ideas about nō as antinaturalistic dramatic criteria. If haiku (q.v.) has influenced more Western poets than any Japanese or other non-European form in this century, the nō may be credited with having produced a larger amount of first-rate literature, especially in Eng., through its influence upon dramatists and poets.—W. B. Yeats, Introd. to *Certain Noble Plays of Japan* (1916); A. Nicoll, *World Drama* (1949); D. Keene, *Japanese Lit.* (1953); E. Miner, *The Japanese Tradition in British and Am. Lit.* (1958). E.M.

NONSENSE VERSE is, quite simply, a type of verse which does not make sense. Although seemingly obvious, the point is worth making because to most people, including the compilers of many so-called nonsense anthologies, any verse which relates an absurd or improbable story, or makes extensive use of exaggerated parody, far-fetched rhymes and neologisms, is nonsense. Yet, a great deal of this kind of verse depends for its effect not on the reader's willingness to accept it as n. but on a recognition of the writer's ingenuity. This is especially true of many so-called n. limericks, whose appeal lies not so much in their subject matter as in the dexterity of the writer in finding suitable rhymes for the most improbable words. Such a limerick as this cannot rightly be called n.:

> There was a sculptor named Phidias
> Whose statues were perfectly hideous;
> He made Aphrodite
> Without any nightie
> And shocked the ultra-fastidious.

Similarly, parody cannot be called n., because its appeal lies in the writer's ingenuity, in his ability to suggest by means of distorted exaggeration the writer he is parodying. For all its absurdity, a poem such as Cuthbert Bede's *In Immemoriam* is not really n.:

> We seek to know, and knowing seek;
> We seek, we know, and every sense
> Is trembling with the great intense,
> And vibrating to what we speak.
>
> We ask too much, we seek too oft;
> We know enough and should no more;
> And yet we skim through Fancy's lore
> And look to earth and not aloft.

Perhaps closer to n. are those verses which invert the natural order of things, but it is doubtful whether they are really pure n. The very consistency of the inversion suggests that behind the poem lies a rational intellect displaying its skill in a systematic reversal of the expected. The following anonymous poem is typical:

> 'Tis midnight and the setting sun
> Is slowly rising in the west.
> The rapid rivers slowly run.
> The frog is on his downy nest.
> The pensive goat and sportive cow
> Hilarious, leap from bough to bough.

This is not really a n. world: it is simply an inversion of the normal one, and our appreciation is the result of recognizing the deviations from the familiar. Similarly, a poem such as Thackeray's *The Sorrows of Werther,* included in Carolyn Wells's nonsense anthology, is not pure n. either, because here again the effect depends on our recognition of how normal people behave and noting the way Werther and Charlotte contradict the expected:

> Werther had a love for Charlotte
> Such as words could never utter;
> Would you know how first he met her?
> She was cutting bread and butter.
>
> Charlotte was a married lady,
> And a moral man was Werther,

And for all the wealth of Indies
Would do nothing for to hurt her.

So he sigh'd and pined and ogled
And his passion boil'd and bubbled,
Till he blew his silly brains out
And was no more by it troubled.

Charlotte having seen his body
Borne before her on a shutter,
Like a well-conducted person
Went on cutting bread and butter.

None of these verses can properly be called n., because appreciation depends not on a willingness to accept the irrational laws of topsy-turvydom so much as a recognition of the writer's ingenuity or clear-headed common sense. Pure n. is entirely dependent on the rejection of what most people consider logical or even normal and an acceptance of the conventions of a completely different universe.

This fact is convincingly demonstrated in the limericks of Edward Lear. In his verses the Old Men and Old Women persist in a behavior so palpably absurd that it outrages the sensibilities of all those proper and sensible people whom Lear refers to quite simply as "They." Such is the case concerning the

. . . Old Man in a Garden
Who always begged everyone's pardon,
When *they* asked him, What for?
He replied, "You're a bore!
And I trust you'll get out of my garden."

In this instance "They" were apparently sent about their business, but quite frequently "They" make life extremely unpleasant for the eccentrics. The Old Man of Montrose, "who walked on the tips of his toes," was told that his behavior was not at all "pleasant" and that he was "a stupid Old Man of Montrose"; and "They" even went to the extreme of "smashing" the Man of Whitehaven, whose only sin was to dance with a raven. N. simply cannot exist in the world of common sense and the Old Person of Basing who

. . . purchased a steed
Which he rode at full speed
And escaped from the people of Basing

did indeed show "a presence of mind that was amazing," for he realized that freedom for pure n. could only be obtained in a place where the conventions of common sense were completely disregarded.

The world of pure n. is an autonomous world, a world which operates according to its own laws and into which sane people can never really penetrate. It is true that we can make some sense out of Lewis Carroll's "Jabberwocky," but it is doubtful whether we could manage without Humpty Dumpty's gloss in chapter 5 of *Through the Looking Glass*. Consider the opening four lines for example:

'Twas brillig and the slithy toves
Did gyre and gimble in the wabe;
And mimsy were the borogroves
And the mome raths outgrabe.

It may be that we do not need to be told that "slithy" is a "portmanteau" word derived from "lithe" and "slimy," or that "gyre" means "to go round and round like a gyroscope," but certainly, without Humpty Dumpty telling us that "toves" are "something like badgers . . . something like lizards . . . something like corkscrews," or that a "rath" is "a sort of green pig," we would be at a loss to account for their appearance. Although by exercising our ingenuity we can make some sense of Carroll's coinages and even arrive at an approximate meaning of the poem, we cannot go further. The Jabberwocky world remains a rather forbidding place where strange creatures move and behave in an incomprehensible way, and even though the Jabberwock is slain in a most appalling manner we remain quite unmoved by his death, because he bears so little resemblance to anything which is even remotely familiar.

It is one of the characteristics of pure n. that the most violent things can happen without evoking in us the slightest compassion or sympathy, as in this limerick of Lear's, for example:

There was an Old Man who screamed out
Whenever they knocked him about
So they took off his boots, and fed him on
fruits
And continued to knock him about.

The idea of an old man being subjected to such barbarous treatment is discomforting, no matter how flippantly it is expressed. Yet, in this limerick there is not the faintest assault on our sensibilities. However, if for the third line we substitute, "So they averted their eyes and stifled his cries," the result, although not profoundly moving, at least causes us some emotional unease. The reason for the change of effect lies in the substitution of a logical statement for a blatantly illogical one, which focuses the reader's attention on certain elements natural to such a situation—the inability of the knockers about to look at the old man and the necessity they feel for stifling his cries—rather than to the irrelevant taking off of the Old Man's boots and the feeding him fruits.

It is not simply that our sympathy is diverted by the illogical behavior of Lear's knockers-about; we are drawn even further from emotional participation by the writer's choice of two objects, "boots" and "fruits," which carry no emotional significance at all. These two words are, in Coleridgean terms, "fixities and definites" and the poem as a whole is evidently the product of the Fancy. "The Fancy," wrote Coleridge, ". . .

has no other counters to play with, but fixities and definites. The Fancy is indeed no other than a mode of Memory emancipated from the order of time and space; while it is blended with and modified by that empirical phenomenon of the will, which we express by the word CHOICE. But equally with the ordinary memory the Fancy must receive all its material ready made from the law of association." Change "association" to "dissociation" and this is a remarkably just description of the process behind the making of a poem of pure n. All pure n. adopts a similar technique, for it is only by concentrating our attention on "fixed" and "definite" irrelevancies that we can exclude the emotions and so avoid the reader's sympathetic involvement with the events in the poem.

This theory is confirmed by the emphasis on precision and regularity in n. verse. We are reminded in *The Walrus and the Carpenter,* for example, that it would take "Seven maids with seven mops," sweeping for "half a year" to clear away the sand from the beach where the oysters dwell, and the Old Person whose habits "induced him to feed upon rabbits" actually ate eighteen before he turned green. The meticulous regularity of the rhythms of n. verse is another way in which we are reminded of the "fixed" and "definite" nature of the n. world, and of course the fact that so many writers of n. have felt it necessary to support their writing with precise line-drawings so as to indicate the character and appearance of their creations, is still another way by which these writers direct our attention to definite things and keep our imagination and sympathy from intruding.

In some n. verse, however, we see beyond the "fixities and definites" to an emotional reality which transcends the n. Such poems owe more to Coleridge's Imagination than Fancy. Coleridge maintained that the ideal poet ". . . diffuses a tone and spirit of unity, that blends, and (as it were) *fuses* each into each, by that synthetic and magical power, to which we have exclusively appropriated the name of imagination. This power, first put in action by the will and understanding, and retained under their irremissive, though gentle and unnoticed control (*laxis effertur habenis*) reveals itself in the balance or reconcilement of opposite or discordant qualities . . . and while it blends and harmonizes the natural and the artificial, still subordinates art to nature, the manner to the matter; and our admiration of the poet to our sympathy with the poetry."

This definition of what Coleridge considers as the highest kind of poetical activity, also describes quite accurately such a poem as Lear's *The Dong with the Luminous Nose.* Here, in contrast to, say, Lewis Carroll's *The Walrus and the Carpenter,* Lear does indeed "blend" the "natural and the artificial," for he subordinates his ingenuity to the sympathetic portrayal of the "natural" behavior of the forsaken Dong, and while we admire the poet's technical virtuosity we also feel "sympathy" for this unfortunate creature, jilted by his Jumbly girl and ever in search of her.

The essential difference between *The Dong with the Luminous Nose* and *The Walrus and the Carpenter* is that behind Lear's poem we can sense the personality of the poet. Lear was himself a pathetically ugly, restless wanderer who traveled extensively, evidently seeking some kind of repose, and although Carroll, too, was a timid, unhappy man, he did not subconsciously dramatize his predicament as Lear seems to have done. In Carroll's n. world, particularly in the "Alice" stories, the emotions are rigorously excluded and the particulars are presented with an unequivocal precision. On the other hand, Lear, in the "Dong" poem, presents a world of evocative vagueness, similar to that of the Gothic imagination:

> When awful darkness and silence reign
> Over the great Gromboolian plain,
> Through the long, long wintry nights;—
> When the angry breakers roar
> As they beat on the rocky shore;—
> When storm-clouds brood on the towering
> heights
> Of the hills of the Chankly Bore:—
> Then, through the vast and gloomy dark,
> There moves what seems a fiery spark,
> A lonely spark with silvery rays
> Piercing the coal-black night,—
> A meteor strange and bright:—
> Hither and thither the vision strays,
> A single lurid light.

The Dong with the Luminous Nose does, in fact, evoke a natural, sympathetic response, which makes one hesitate to call it n.

Possibly, Lear's poem has as much right to be called surrealist as n. Certainly, the line between n. verse and surrealism is often difficult to distinguish. Influenced by Freudian theories of the unconscious, by the ideal of free association, by Jungian concepts of the archetypal, or perhaps just out of boredom with existing poetic modes, many artists in the 20th c. have produced poetry very similar to n. Such poetry, however, is based on a serious theory of poetic communication. As Sir Herbert Read remarked in an essay occasioned by the London Surrealist Exhibition of 1936, "surrealism is . . . the romantic principle in art" and takes its form and substance from the individual unconscious of the creator; therefore such a poem as the following, which many people might regard as n., has an emotional quality suggesting the workings of the Coleridgean imagination:

> du dubon dubonnet
> the snake laughs brightly
> rumble rumble rumble
> in the infinite womb of dreams
> i in my isolation
> asking the way

Here, the opening line recalls the signs that flash past in the Paris *metro,* and once we recognize this, most of the other details of the poem fall into place. The actual meaning of the poem may still be obscure, but at least the reader is able to discern the controlling image which holds the poem together. It should be noted, however, that in so far as surrealism is a formal program for the exploitation of the unconscious—an idea emphasized by surrealism's chief theoretician, André Breton, in his *First Surrealist Manifesto* (1924)—it differs from n., which is opposed to all programs.

N. then, occupies the narrow ground between wit and humor on the one hand, and surrealism on the other. Although at first sight it has the appearance of being a fairly prolific genre, there is surprisingly little true n. verse. Pure n. is completely negative in its effect. The poet must avoid the temptation to turn an amusing phrase or relate a recognizably humorous anecdote, and he must be equally cautious of allowing his imagination to intrude. It is essentially a poetry of escape, a conscious refusal to communicate anything which could be considered positive, a form which demands unceasing control and a disposition more cerebral than emotional. Hence, it is not surprising that the two most successful n. writers in Eng. were not poets at all, but men engaged in work which demanded precision and exactness—Lear, a professional illustrator of scientific books of natural history, and Carroll, a professor of mathematics.

G. K. Chesterton, *The Defendant* (1902); *A N. Anthol.,* ed. C. Wells (1903); E. Cammaerts, *The Poetry of N.* (1925); L. Reed, *The Complete Limerick Book* (1925); A. L. Huxley, *Essays New and Old* (1927); C. L. Dodgson, *The Complete Works of Lewis Carroll,* illustrated by J. Tenniel (1936); *Surrealism,* ed. H. Read (1936); E. Partridge, *Here, There and Everywhere* (1950); E. Lear, *The Complete N. of Edward Lear,* ed. and introd. H. Jackson (1951); E. Sewell, *The Field of N.* (1952); G. Orwell, *Shooting an Elephant* (1954).

See also the discussion of the German Christian Morgenstern as an intermediate figure between Carroll and Lear and the surrealists in L. W. Forster, *Poetry of Significant N.* (1962).

J.M.M.

NUMBER(S). (a) The prosodical meters of both classic and modern poetry; hence, (b) poems, lines, strophes, etc. As originally applied to quantitatively scanned poetry, the notion of "numbers" involved the idea of metrical *proportion,* and was thus linked to the proportions of musical harmonies (and, in the Middle Ages, of musical rhythm). In the Renaissance, "numbers" simply means poetry in general, although the extension to music and musical compositions may also be invoked, as in "In full harmonic number joined . . ." (Milton, *Paradise Lost* 4.687); the most general sense of musico-mathematical proportion is preserved in such commonplace references to Plato as one affirming that he held that "the mynd was made of certaine harmonie and musicall nombers" (E. K., *Gloss to Spenser's Shepheardes Calender* "October" 27). Ing argues for an Elizabethan distinction between "number," or mere syllable-count, and "numbers," used in its traditional sense for quantitative prosody.—St. Augustine, *De Musica; Elizabethan Crit. Essays,* ed. G. G. Smith (1904); C. M. Ing, *Elizabethan Lyrics* (1951).

J.H.

NURSERY RHYMES. A nursery rhyme may be defined as a rhyme or verse preserved in the world of children. Examples are:

Humpty Dumpty sat on a wall,
Humpty Dumpty had a great fall—
All the King's horses and all the King's men
Couldn't put Humpty Dumpty together again.

Rain, rain, go away,
Come again another day.

The origins of the r. are manifold, but except for lullabies and those verses which accompany infant games ("This little piggy") very few originated in the nursery. Material from adult life was introduced to children either for reason or by accident, often simply because of its memorability; that material which proved popular with the children survived, and with surprisingly little alteration, despite the fact that some of it disappeared from print for two centuries at a time.

Peter Opie estimates that at least one-fourth, and probably one-half, of the r. known to Eng.-speaking children today are more than 200 years old. It is impossible to be precise about the age of most of the verses. "White bird featherless" appears in L. in the 10th c.; "Two legs sat upon three legs" in Bede, "Thirty days hath September" in Fr. in the 13th c., "Matthew, Mark, Luke, and John" in German in the 15th c.; but it is likely that these r. existed many, perhaps hundreds, of years before they were set down. References in Gr., Roman, and Oriental literatures would indicate that children's games and verses analogous to ours were known in these cultures, and some scholars believe that some "classic" r. (e.g., "Buck, buck," "Humpty Dumpty") are thousands of years old. The theory would be supported by the prevalence of a number of the r. or their analogues throughout Europe. One cannot of course ignore the likelihood that many were carried from country to country by armies, travelers, missionaries, and, in latter days, translators; many Eng. r. have been translated into Hindustani, Malayan, Russian, etc. But the possibility exists that some of the lore came down in an unbroken line from the ancient world.

It is possible to trace the sources (or define the types) of many of the later r.—those of the last 300 years. Some of these sources are: (1) *Songs.* These include ballads and folk songs ("One misty moisty morning"); drinking songs ("I've got sixpence"); war songs ("The King of France went up the hill"); songs from plays ("There was a jolly miller"—but probably this song existed before it was incorporated in *Love in a Village*); romantic lyrics ("Where are you going, my pretty maid?"); popular songs of recent date ("Where, o where has my little dog gone?"); lullabies proper ("Rockabye, baby"). (2) *Street cries* ("Hot Cross Buns"). (3) *Riddles* ("Little Nancy Etticoat"). (4) *Proverbs* ("Needles and Pins"). (5) *Custom and ritual* ("London Bridge"). (6) *Religious and antireligious matter* ("Matthew, Mark, Luke, and John," "Good morning, Father Francis"). (7) *R. about historical personages* ("Lucy Locket," Robin Hood rhymes). (8) *Poems by recent authors* ("Twinkle, twinkle, little star," by Jane Taylor). (9) *Words accompanying games* ("Here we go round the mulberry bush"). (10) *Counting out r.*, many of which seem to have derived from old Celtic numbers preserved among primitive people in England and still used for counting sheep, fish, stitches in knitting, etc. ("Eena, meena, mina moe," "One-ery, two-ery," and originally "Hickory Dickory Dock"). The above classifications are rough and do not account for all the r.; they will serve, however, to show from what a variety of sources the lore of the nursery is culled.

The first published collection of nursery songs was *Tommy Thumb's Pretty Song Book* (1744); there is a single extant copy of the second of its two volumes, containing about 40 songs, in the British Museum. In ca. 1765 appeared *Mother Goose's Melody, or Sonnets for the Cradle;* in 1784 came *Gammer Gurton's Garland.* In America, in 1719, appeared *Songs for the Nursery, or Mother Goose's Melodies for Children;* no copies are extant. There is a story that the printer named the book after his mother-in-law, née Elizabeth Goose. The r. are usually called "Mother Goose R." in America, but the origin of "Mother Goose" seems to be Fr. The term "Nursery R." was not used in England until the 19th c.; before that they were "Tommy Thumb's songs." During the past century and a half hundreds of collections of the r. have been issued.

The first scholar to concern himself with the material was James Orchard Halliwell, whose collection of 300 r., most of them still popular today, was published by the Percy Society in 1842. His work has been superseded by that of Iona and Peter Opie, whose *Oxford Dictionary of Nursery R.* contains 550 entries, with many variants, important notes, and a valuable introduction.

During the 20th c., scholars and other interested persons have proffered various theories concerning the r. One of these, the *historical* theory, tries to identify the "real personages" of the verses: e.g., Old King Cole is a British king of the 3d c.—or the father of St. Helena—or the father of Finn McCool; Georgie Porgie is George I—or the Duke of Buckingham; the Queen the pussy-cat went to see is Elizabeth I. Although some of these "identifications" must be described as wild surmise, there is evidence for the historicity of a number of the characters: Elise Marley was a famous alewife, Lucy Locket and Kitty Fisher courtesans of the time of Charles I, and Jack Horner probably a steward of the Abbot of Glastonbury, whose "plum" was a deed to valuable property still in the Horner family.

Henry Bett believes that the r. (as well as many children's tales and games) reflect nature myths ("Jack and Jill" is about the tides), custom ("London Bridge" echoes the old rite of human sacrifice necessary to appease the water over which a bridge was built), and history ("John Ball"). James Joyce owned a copy of Dr. Bett's book and apparently found much to agree with in it. Joyce's *Finnegans Wake* contains a multitude of references to about 70 rhymes; the author uses them to reinforce his concept of ever recurrent motifs in human existence; he sees the r. as embodying myths which express the experiences of the human race. In this use of the r. Joyce illustrates what may be called the *psychoanalytic* theory, a theory recently put forth (not specifically about nursery r., but about folk material in general) by Joseph Campbell, in *The Hero with a Thousand Faces.*

J. O. Halliwell, *The Nursery R. of England* (1842); H. C. Bolton, *The Counting Out R. of Children* (1888); L. Eckenstein, *Comparative Studies in Nursery R.* (1906); H. Bett, *Nursery R. and Tales* (1924); D. E. Marvin, *Historic Child R.* (1930); V. Sackville-West, *Nursery R.* (1947); I. and P. Opie, *The Oxford Dict. of Nursery R.* (rev. ed., 1952; best general survey) and *The Oxford Nursery R. Book* (1955); P. Opie, "Nursery R.," in Cassell's; M. P. Worthington, "Nursery R. in Joyce's *Finnegans Wake,*" JAF, 70 (1957); P. H. Evans, *Rimbles* (1961).

M.P.W.

O

OCCASIONAL VERSE. Any poem, light or serious, good or bad, written for a special occasion and with a special purpose, as, for example, the memorial pieces in honor of Edward King, among which *Lycidas* was one; the birthday odes expected of a poet laureate; tributes to a poet placed at the beginning of his volume particularly in the 16th and 17th c.; epithalamia, such as those by Spenser and Donne; funeral elegies, respectful or ironic; sonnets or odes memorializing some state occasion or historic event; or the prologues and epilogues to 17th- and 18th-c. plays. O.v. is public poetry and has a practical social function to perform.

Certain modern poets, e.g., W. B. Yeats, Ezra Pound, William Carlos Williams, have written a good deal of o.v. Some modern occasional poems are Hardy's *On an Invitation to the United States,* Yeats's *Easter, 1916,* and Auden's *September 1, 1939.* A characteristic brief example is Yeats's epigram *On Those that Hated 'The Playboy of the Western World,' 1907*:

Once, when midnight smote the air,
Eunuchs ran through Hell and met
On every crowded street to stare
Upon great Juan riding by:
Even like these to rail and sweat
Staring upon his sinewy thigh.

A.J.M.S.

OCTAMETER. A line of 8 measures or feet, rare in classical poetry; rarer still in Eng., though Poe claimed some lines of *The Raven* were in o. acatalectic. The most noteworthy, if not the only true, example in Eng. is found in Swinburne's *March,* from *Poems and Ballads.*

OCTAVE, octet. A group of 8 lines, either a stanza (ottava rima, q.v.) or part of a stanza, as the first 8 lines of a sonnet (usually rhyming abbaabba) are called the octave, or octet. "I Have finished the First Canto, a long one, of about 180 octaves," Byron, *Letter to Murray.* R.O.E.

OCTOSYLLABIC VERSE. Tetrameter verse in iambs or trochees, with variants limited to prevent "tumbling verse." It forms the structural line of several stanzas (long meter, *In Memoriam* stanza, etc.) but is more commonly associated with couplets. Byron's reference to "the fatal facility of the octo-syllabic meter" recognizes the danger of sing-song monotony, a danger offset, however, by the feeling of rapid movement inherent in the pattern which makes it an excellent medium for narrative verse. In the hands of a skilled craftsman monotony is not difficult to avoid, as is evident in Milton's *Il Penseroso:*

Come, pensive Nun, devout and pure,
Sober, steadfast, and demure,
All in a robe of darkest grain,
Flowing with majestic train,
And sable stole of cypress lawn
Over thy decent shoulders drawn.
Come; but keep thy wonted state,
With even step, and musing gait . . .

The o. couplet derived from late medieval Fr. poetry (with a fusion of L. verse elements) in the chronicles, romances, and legends of the 12th c. (Wace, *Roman de Brut*); the romance of manners, *lais,* and *dits* in the 13th c. strengthened its position. In the course of time its association with verse essentially frivolous or gay marked its use in France, and even as late as the 18th c. Le Sage, Peron, and Voltaire employed it thus for popular appeal. The form (normally in varied rhyme schemes rather than couplets) reached Spain in the 14th c. (Ruiz, *Libro de Buen Amor*) from the Prov. troubadours by way of Galician-Portuguese sources, and strengthened a native tendency toward it in earlier Sp. poetry. By the 15th c. it was firmly established through collections of courtly lyrics (e.g., *Cancionero de Baena*), and since that time has come to be "the national meter par excellence."

In England the influence of Fr. o. verse in the 12th and 13th c. (through Anglo-Norman poets like Gaimar, Wace, Benoît) led to refinement on the common accentual 4-stress Anglo-Saxon structure for narratives, with evidence of growing syllabic regularity as the couplet developed through a flexible use in Chaucer (*The Boke of the Duchesse,* etc.), monotonous regularity in Gower (*Confessio Amantis*), and so to miracle and morality plays and a lessening Elizabethan use. The vehicle next of shorter poems, descriptive or philosophical, by Jonson, Milton, Dyer, Parnell, Gay, Swift, Collins, and others, its most notable 17th-c. narrative use was in the widely imitated *Hudibras* of Samuel Butler (1612–80), the individuality of whose jogging satiric verse with its ingenious rhymes has distinguished it as "Hudibrastic verse" (q.v.). Serious or whimsical narrative was again written in the form as Burns, Wordsworth, and Coleridge, but especially Byron, Scott, and later, Morris, brought the couplet to its height in the 19th c. Other more varied patterns have tended to overshadow if not to replace the o. couplet in modern poetry, although an occasional distinctive use will be found, as in Edna St. Vincent Millay's popular *Renascence.*—Saintsbury, *Prosody*; Schipper; Hamer; E.N.S. Thompson, "The O. Couplet," PQ, 18 (1939); D. C. Clarke, "The Sp. Octosyllable," HR, 10 (1942); J. Saavedra Molina, *El octosílabo castellano* (1945); M. D. Legge, *Anglo-Norman Lit. and Its Background* (1964). L.J.Z.

ODE (Gr. *aeidein* "to sing," "to chant"). In modern usage the name for the most formal, ceremonious, and complexly organized form of lyric poetry, usually of considerable length. It is frequently the vehicle for public utterance on state occasions, as, for example, a ruler's birthday, accession, funeral, the unveiling or dedication of some imposing memorial or public work. The o. as it has evolved in contemporary literatures generally shows a dual inheritance from classic sources, variously combining the measured, recurrent stanza of the Horation o., with its attendant balance of tone and sentiment (sometimes amounting to a controlled ambiguity, as in Marvell's *Horation O.* on Cromwell), and the regular or irregular stanzaic triad of Pindar, with its elevated, vertiginously changeable tone, as in

Collins' *O. on the Poetical Character* and in interesting recrudescences as late as Coventry Patmore, Robert Bridges, and Paul Claudel. Both forms have frequently been used for poems celebrating public events, but both have just as frequently eschewed such events, sometimes pointedly, in favor of private occasions of crisis or joy. The serious tone of the o. not only calls for the use of a heightened diction and enrichment by poetic device, but thus lays it open, more readily than any other lyric form, to burlesque. A third form of the modern o., the Anacreontic, is descended from the 16th-c. discovery of a group of some sixty poems, all credited to Anacreon, although the Gr. originals now appear to span a full thousand years. In general the lines are short and, in comparison with the Pindaric o., the forms simple, with the subjects being love or drinking, as in the 18th-c. song "To Anacreon in Heaven," whose tune has been appropriated for "The Star-Spangled Banner."

In Gr. literature, the odes of Pindar (522–442 B.C.) were designed for choric song and dance. The words, the sole surviving element of the total Pindaric experience, reflect the demands of the other two arts. A strophe, a complex metrical structure whose length and pattern of irregular lines varies from ode to ode, reflects a dance pattern, which is then repeated exactly in an antistrophe, the pattern being closed by an epode, or third section, of differing length and structure. Length of the o. itself (surviving examples range from fragments to nearly 300 lines) is achieved through exact metrical repetition of the original triadic pattern. These odes, written for performance in a Dionysiac theater or perhaps in the Agora to celebrate athletic victories, frequently appear incoherent through the brilliance of imagery, abrupt shifts in subject matter, and apparent disorder of form within the individual sections. Modern criticism has answered such objections, which date from the time of Pindar himself and range through Gr. and L. to modern times, by discerning dominating images, emotional relationships between subjects, and complex metrical organization. The tone of the odes is emotional, exalted, intense, and the subject matter whatever divine myths can be adduced to the occasion being celebrated.

Apart from Pindar, another pervasive source of the modern o. in Gr. literature is the cult-hymn, which derived from the Homeric hymns and flourished during the Alexandrian period in the work of Callimachus and others. This sort of poem is notable not for its form but for its structure of argument: an invocation of a deity (later of a personified natural or psychological entity) followed by a narrative genealogy establishing the antiquity and authenticity of the deity, followed by a petition for some special favor and concluding with a vow of future service. A complete modern instance of this structure is Keats's *O. to Psyche*. Yet another source of the modern ode's structure of prayerful petition is the Psalms and other poems of the Hebrew Bible, which increasingly influenced Eng. poetry by way of Milton, the criticism of John Dennis, the original and translated hymns of Isaac Watts, and Bishop Robert Lowth's *Lectures on the Sacred Poetry of the Hebrews*. In L. literature, the characteristic o. is associated with Horace (65–8 B.C.), who derived his forms not from Pindar but from less elaborate Gr. lyrics, through Alcaeus and Sappho. The Horatian ode is tranquil rather than intense, contemplative rather than brilliant, and intended for the reader in his library rather than for the spectator in the theater. Horace himself wrote commissioned odes, most notably the *Carmen Saeculare* for Augustus, all of which more closely approximated the Pindaric form and voice, but his influence on modern poetry is felt more directly in the tradition of what might be called the sustained epigram, especially in the period between Jonson and Prior. Among the Eng. poets of note, only Mark Akenside habitually wrote odes in the Horatian vein.

Throughout Europe the history of the o. commences with the rediscovery of the classic forms. The humanistic o. of the 15th and earlier 16th c. shows the adaptation of old meters to new subjects by Fifelfo, in both Gr. and L., and by Campano, Pontano, and Flaminio in neo-Latin. The example of the humanistic o. and the publication in 1513 of the Aldine edition of Pindar were the strongest influences upon the vernacular o. In Italy, tentative Pindaric experiments were made by Trissino, Alamanni, and Minturno, without establishing the o. as a new genre. More successful were the attempts in France by members of the *Pléiade*, where, after minor trials of the new form by others, Pierre de Ronsard in 1550 published *The First Four Books of the Odes* with stylistic imitations of Horace, Anacreon, and (in the first book) Pindar. Influenced by Ronsard, Bernardo Tasso and Gabriele Chiabrera later in the century succeeded in popularizing the form in Italy, where it has been used successfully by, among others, Manzoni, Leopardi (in his *Odi-canzone*), Carducci (*Odi barbare,* 1877), and D'Annunzio (*Odi navale,* 1892). In France, the example of Ronsard was widely followed, notably by Boileau in the 17th c., and by Voltaire and others in formal, occasional verse in the 18th. The romantic period lent a more personal note to both form and subject matter, notably in the work of Lamartine, Musset, and Victor Hugo. Later, highly personal treatments of the genre may be found in Verlaine's *Odes en son honneur,* 1893, and Valéry's *Odes,* 1920.

The o. became characteristically German only with the work of G. R. Weckherlin (*Oden und Gesänge,* 1618–19), who, as court poet at Stuttgart, attempted to purify and refashion German letters according to foreign models. In the middle of the next century Klopstock modified the classic models by use of free rhythms, grand abstract subjects, and a heavy influence from the Lutheran psalms. Later Goethe and Schiller returned to classical models and feeling, as in Schiller's *O. to Joy,* used in the final movement of Beethoven's Ninth Symphony. At the turn of the century Hölderlin in his complex, mystical, unrhymed odes united classic themes with the characteristic resources of the German language. Since Hölderlin, few noteworthy odes have been written in German, with the possible exception of those of Rudolph Alexander Schröder (*Deutsche Oden,* 1912).

The few attempts at domesticating the o. in 16th c. England were largely unsuccessful, although there is probably some influence of the classical o. upon Spenser's *Fowre Hymnes, Prothalamion* and *Epithalamion.* In 1629 appeared the first great imitation of Pindar in Eng., Ben Jonson's *O. on the Death of Sir H. Morison,* with the strophe, antistrophe, and epode of the classical model indicated by the Eng. terms "turn," "counter-turn," and "stand." In the same year began the composition of Milton's great o., *On the Morning of Christ's Nativity,* in regular stanzaic form. The genre, however, attained great popularity in Eng. only with the publication of Abraham Cowley's *Pindarique Odes* in 1656, in which he attempted, like Ronsard and Weckherlin before him, to make available to his own language the spirit and tone of Pindar rather than to furnish an exact transcription of his manner. With Dryden begin the great formal odes of the 18th c.: first the *O. to the Memory of Mrs. Anne Killigrew,* and then, marking the reunion of formal verse and music, the *Song for St. Cecilia's Day* and *Alexander's Feast.* For the 18th c. the o. was the perfect means of expressing the sublime. Using personification and other devices of allegory, Gray and Collins in the mid-18th c. marshall emotions ranging from anxiety to terror in the service of their central theme, the "progress of poetry," making the o. a crisis poem that reflects the rivalry of modern lyric with the great poets and genres of the past. The romantic o. in Eng. literature is a poem written on the occasion of a vocational or existential crisis in order to reassert the power and range of the poet's voice. It begins with Coleridge's *Dejection: An O.* (1802) and Wordsworth's *O. on Intimations of Immortality* (written 1802–4, publ. 1815). Wordsworth's *O.*, with its varied line lengths, complex rhyme scheme, and stanzas of varying length and pattern, has been called the greatest Eng. Pindaric o. Of the other major romantic poets, Shelley wrote the *O. to the West Wind,* and Keats wrote the *O. on a Grecian Urn, O. to a Nightingale,* and *To Autumn,* probably the most brilliant group of odes in the language. Since the romantic period, with the exception of a few brilliant, isolated examples, such as Tennyson's *O. on the Death of the Duke of Wellington,* the o. has been neither a popular nor a really successful genre in Eng. Among modern poets, the personal o. in the Horatian manner has been revived with some success, notably by Allen Tate (*O. to the Confederate Dead*) and W. H. Auden (*In Memory of W. B. Yeats, To Limestone*).

G. Carducci, "Dello svolgimento dell'ode in Italia," *Opere,* xvi (1905); R. Shafer, *The Eng. O. to 1660* (1918); K. Viëtor, *Gesch. der deutschen O.* (1923); Bowra; G. N. Shuster, *The Eng. O. from Milton to Keats* (1940); G. Highet, *The Cl. Tradition* (1949); N. Maclean, "From Action to Image: Theories of the Lyric in the 18th C.," in Crane, *Critics;* C. Maddison, *Apollo and the Nine: A Hist. of the O.* (1960); A. W. Pickard-Cambridge, *Dithyramb, Tragedy and Comedy,* rev. T.B.L. Webster (1962); S. Commager, *The Odes of Horace: A Crit. Study* (1962); K. Schlüter, *Die Englische O.* (1964); J. Heath-Stubbs, *The O.* (1969); G. Hartman, "Blake and the Progress of Poetry," *Beyond Formalism* (1970); J. D. Jump, *The O.* (1974); J. Culler, "Apostrophe," *Diacritics,* 7 (1977); P. H. Fry, *The Poet's Calling in the Eng. O.* (1980); K. Crotty, *Song and Action: The Victory Odes of Pindar* (1982). S.F.F.; rev. P.H.F.

OLD ENGLISH PROSODY. See OLD GERMANIC PROSODY.

OLD GERMANIC PROSODY. The Teutonic peoples of the early Middle Ages had a remarkably homogeneous prosodic system, specimens of which have survived in runic inscriptions and poetic manuscripts. The majority of these are in the Old English (OE) and Old Norse (ON) languages, but enough survives also of the Old Saxon (OS) and Old High German (OHG) poetic documents to allow some generalizations about a large corpus of poetry.

No matter what its theme or place of origin, and in spite of the comparatively late time at which most of it was copied into written form, Old Germanic (OGc.) poetry is highly formulaic and formalistic, so that its techniques are comparable from century to century and from one linguistic area to another. The material versified is of many kinds: legal texts, mnemonic lists of rulers and peoples, heroic epics and religious narratives, reflective or elegiac lyrics, sober collections of maxims, encomiastic pieces, and others besides, including a variety of satirical and erotic verses.

The most important key to the governing style of OGc. poetic composition is the fact that the poetry was so largely an oral phenomenon prior to the introduction of Christianity and the Latin alphabet into the Gc. area. That is, oral composition upon traditional themes helped create and perpetuate a leisurely, formulaic, periphrastic, and repetitious style, with considerable freedom in syntax, and an elaborate poetic diction in which the kenning (q.v.) is a conspicuous feature. This flow of verse (spoken, chanted, or sung) is rhythmically organized into a series of short, metrically independent phrases or verses.

The verses contain 2 stressed syllables which are long in quantity, and differing numbers of syllables in addition which are relatively unstressed and may be long or short in quantity. A "resolved stress" sometimes occurs when two short syllables, only the first of which is accented, replace a single long accented syllable. The quantitative and accentual unit thus formed will resemble one of five metrical "types"—patterns of long and short, stressed and unstressed syllables—analytically described by Eduard Sievers (see below) as common to all OGc. verse; a detailed examination of these basic patterns would be beyond the scope of this survey. Finally, this independent basic verse or metrical unit is linked to another by the rhyming of initial sounds in some, not all, of the stressed syllables, and the verse-pairs so created are centrally divided by a pause. In modern editions of the poetry these verse-pairs are printed as a single typographical line. The alliteration within the verse-pairs is systematic, not occasional or ornamental. As a rule, each initial consonantal sound rhymes with itself only; any vowel or diphthong rhymes with itself or with any other vowel or diphthong. Thus an alliterative meter (q.v.), ordering and emphasizing what would be the normal spoken accents of successive phrases, is the conservative foundation upon which most OGc. poetry is built. Side by side with this complex poetic form there may well have existed similar but less exacting popular meters which are now lost beyond hope of recovery. But the written records, faulty as they often are, display a poetic tradition which is at best superb, perhaps especially in the epic recitative of long narrative poems, where with vigorous stresses and sonorous vowel music the linked verses flow, wheel, and clash by turns, moving with a magisterial deliberation proper to the art of the court singer, or, to give him his Anglo-Saxon name, the scop (q.v.). This is an oral poetry not merely in the circumstances of its origins, but also in the sense that it must be heard aloud if justice is to be done to its essential nature.

A passage from the OE *Beowulf* (205–16) will demonstrate the structure and illustrate some of the stylistic features just described. In this and the following examples, marks of vowel quantity are ignored and secondary stresses are also left unmarked.

Hǽfde se góda Géata léoda
cémpan gecórone þára þe he cénoste
fíndan míhte; fíftyna súm
súndwudu sóhte, sécg wísade,
lágucræftig món lándgemýrcu.
Fýrst fórð gewat; flóta wæs on ýðum,
bát under béorge. Béornas géarwe
on stéfn stígon,— stréamas wúndon,
súnd wið sánde; sécgas bǽron
on béarm nácan béorhte frǽtwe,
gúðsearo géatolic; gúman út scufon,
wéras on wílsið wúdu búndenne.

The hero had chosen fighters from the men of the Geats, the boldest he could find; he and fourteen others went to the sea-wood [i.e., ship]; the man skilled in the craft of the sea showed the way to the shore. The time came that the vessel was in the waves at the foot of the cliff. Ready warriors climbed aboard; currents eddied, sea against sand; men brought bright treasure and splendid war-gear into the ship's bosom; mariners pushed off the trim craft on the journey they eagerly sought.

The same basic metrical structure and stylistic manner are evident in the OS *Heliand* (2005–2012):

Wérod blíðode,
wárun thar an lúston líudi atsámne,
gúmon gládmodie. Géngun ámbahtman,
skénkeon mid scálun, drogun skírianne wín
mid órcun endi mid álofatun; was thar érlo dróm
fágar an fléttea.

The troop was in good spirits; people there were happy together; men were cheerful. Servants went around with pitchers; they poured clear wine with cups and vessels; there was a splendid revelry of heroes in the hall.

An equally pronounced repetitive and periphrastic style will be noted in the OHG *Hildebrandlied* (63–68):

Do léttun se ǽrist ásckim scrítan,
scárpen scúrim, dat in dem scíltim stónt.
Do stópun tosámane, stáimbort chlúbun,
héuwun hármlicco húitte scílti,
únti im iro líntun lúttilo wúrtun,
giwígan miti wábnum.

Then first they let fly spears, sharp weapons, so that they stuck in the shields. Then they strode together, split the bucklers, hacked grimly at the bright linden shields until they were cut to bits, destroyed by weapons.

ON verse bears a strong family resemblance to other Gc. national poetry, especially in the narrative stanza known as *fornyrðislag* (old lore meter); but in this example, chosen from the *Darraðarljóð,* it will be noted that the stanzaic form itself (one of several common in ON verse) contrasts with the stichic or nonstanzaic poetry of other Gc. traditions:

Víndum, víndum véf dárraðar,
þars vé váða vígra mánna;
látum éigi líf hans fárask;
éigu válkyrjur váls um kósti.

We weave, we weave the web of the spear, while the brave warrior's standard advances; we shall not let him lose his life; only the valkyries may decide who shall be slain.

The ON stanza, concentrating as it does upon one verse paragraph at a time, lends itself to a less relaxed and flexible style, and easily achieves a greater intensity than will be found, for instance, in OE epic verse. During the 9th c. and afterward in Norway and Iceland, this concentration, accompanied by an elaboation of kenningar, developed into the extraordinary complexity and artifice of the skaldic stanzas, as in the court measure or *dróttkvætt*.

It remains to be said that some technical aspects of OGc. prosody are still disputed even after many decades of study. At present little is known about the partnership of the verse with the vocal and instrumental music which must have been associated with it in early times. Contradictory theories about the exact scansion of the verse itself—for example, the arrangement of strong and subordinate stresses, the scansion of certain expanded verses, and the use of pauses or rests within the verse pairs—continue to be advanced, and cannot be discussed in a short space; a few important and suggestive works are listed below. However, the student who has made a beginning at the languages themselves will find that he can read the verse with pleasure if he is careful to observe and reproduce aloud whenever he can the rhetorical intention of the poet-singer, who based his art upon the natural (that is, the logical and grammatical) patterns of stress in Gc. speech rhythms.

E. Sievers, *Altgermanische Metrik* (1893) and *Zur Rhythmik des germanischen Alliterations-verses* (anastatic reprint, N.Y., 1909); A. Heusler, *Die altgermanische Dichtung* (1923); J. C. Pope, *The Rhythm of Beowulf* (1942); M. Daunt, "OE Verse and Speech Rhythm," Philological Soc., *Transactions*, 1946 (1947); P. F. Baum, "The Meter of the *Beowulf*," MP, 46 (1948–49); F. P. Magoun, Jr., "Oral-Formulaic Character of Anglo-Saxon Narrative Poetry," *Speculum*, 28 (1953); W. P. Lehmann, *The Development of Gc. Verse Forms* (1956); J. C. Pope, *OE Versification* (mimeographed ed., Yale Univ., 1957); A. J. Bliss, *The Metre of Beowulf* (1958) and *An Introd. to OE Metre* (1962). J.B.B.

ONOMATOPOEIA. Strictly, o. refers to the formation or use of words which imitate sounds, such as *hiss, snap, buzz, clash, murmur.* Broadly, the term refers to combinations of words in which any correspondence is felt between sound and sense, whether of sound, of motion, or of mood. In Tennyson's

> The moan of doves in immemorial elms
> And murmuring of innumerable bees,

only *moan* and *murmuring* are strictly onomatopoetic, but their reinforcement by the repeated *m*'s, *n*'s, and *r*'s of *immemorial, innumerable,* and *elms* makes the whole passage onomatopoetic in the broader sense.

Whether sounds of themselves can suggest meaning has been much disputed. Riding and Graves in *A Survey of Modernist Poetry* (1928) point out that the suggestiveness of Tennyson's lines is lost if their sounds are reproduced in a line of different meaning: "More ordure never will renew our midden's pure manure." Experimental evidence, however, indicates that sounds do have limited capacity for suggesting meaning; e.g. agreement will be almost universal as to which of the nonsense words *taketa* or *naluma* should go with a curved diagram and which with an angular one (W. Kohler, *Gestalt Psychology*, 1947). Undoubtedly this capacity has been often exaggerated and many purely fanciful correspondences discovered. Pope's dictum that "the sound must seem an echo to the sense" seems a reasonable view, since an echo comes after rather than before the event it accompanies. Most readers would agree that Tennyson's lines are more appropriate to their meaning than the following revision:

> The moan of doves in stately ancient oaks
> And quiet murmuring of countless bees.

The importance of o. to poetry has also been much disputed, some considering it the crowning technical achievement of the poet, others decrying it as a technical bauble quite removed from the essential nature of poetry. The historical record indicates that great poetry has existed without it, but that great poets in all languages have sought it. In Virgil's "Quadrupedante putrem sonitu quatit ungula campum" has been heard the gallop of a horse, and in Ennius's "At tuba terribili sonitu taratantara dixit" the sound of a trumpet. See also SOUND IN POETRY.—G. R. Stewart, *The Technique of Eng. Verse* (1930); L. P. Wilkinson, "O. and the Sceptics," CQ, 36 (1942); N. C. Stageberg and W. L. Anderson, *Poetry as Experience* (1952); C. R. Woodring, "O. and Other Sounds in Poetry," CE, 14 (1953). L.P.

ORAL POETRY, especially o. traditional p., is poetry composed and transmitted orally, mainly, but not exclusively, by people who cannot read or write. It is traditional when each generation has received it orally from the preceding one back to the dawn of poetry, and transmits it to the next as long as the tradition lives. O. traditional p. has its own method of composition and transmission which differentiates it from written literature. We should, however, exclude from this category poetry composed in the manner of written literature "for o. presentation." Such poetry, although delivered orally, does not differ from written poetry in its manner of composition. The origins of o. p. are those of poetry itself and are to be sought in ritual; for the rhythms, sound patterns, and repetitive structures of poetry help to support and give power to the words and actions of ritual.

There are three general divisions by genre: ritual, lyric, and narrative. The non-narrative types of o. traditional p. include, under ritual: (a) incantation, (b) lullabies, (c) wedding ritual songs, (d) laments, (e) songs for special festivals, and (f) praise poems, or eulogies. Lyric songs are preeminently love songs.

The two main types of o. traditional narrative p. are epic and ballad. The epic is stichic (see STICH), the same metric line being repeated with some variation for the entire song; whereas the ballad is stanzaic. Consequently, the tempo of narration of epic is rapid, but that of the ballad is slower. The epic tends to be longer than the ballad, because it tells its story from beginning to end, often with a fullness of detail which is typical. The ballad concentrates frequently on the most intense or dramatic moment of a story, and some ballads consist entirely of dialogue. Although there are comic ballads, the genre as a whole has an elegiac tone. Some of the great o. traditional epics, such as the *Iliad* of Homer, or the *Chanson de Roland*, are tragic or have tragic overtones, but on the whole o. traditional epic is optimistic; the hero generally triumphs gloriously over the enemy.

The most distinctive characteristic of o. traditional p. is its fluidity of text, but in some cultures a certain degree of word-for-word memorization is reported, particularly in the shorter forms. In the longer songs, such as epics, the absence of a fixed text makes word-for-word memorization impossible, there being nothing stable to memorize. In the shorter songs the text tends to become more stable in the practice of a single singer and in a song which is frequently sung. In the case of magic incantations, it is sometimes said that the exact reproduction of a text is necessary to make the magic effective, but the existence of variants seems to indicate that sometimes only certain sound patterns such as alliteration and assonance, or certain types of words or word-combinations, are preserved rather than an entire poem, however short. When traditional singers tell us that a text must be repeated exactly, word-for-word, we know from comparison of performances that they mean essential characteristic for essential characteristic; for their concept of a word is different from that of lettered people.

In those cultures where fluidity of text is attested beyond any doubt, where the absence of a fixed text is well documented, the singer/poet learns in the course of years a special technique of composition by "formula" and "theme." It would be misleading to call it improvisation, which implies creating a story or song "on the spur of the moment." It would seem, of course, that there are such o. traditional improvisations of both content and text. They are generally topical in nature. Some scholars maintain, however, that even these "improvisations" are traditional and composed in the formulaic technique.

The formula is "a word or group of words regularly used under given metrical conditions to express a given essential idea." The most often used phrases, whole lines, or even couplets, those which a singer hears most frequently when he is learning, establish the patterns for the poetry, its characteristic syntactic, rhythmic, metric, and acoustic molds and configurations. In time the individual practitioner of the art can form new phrases, create formulas, by analogy with the old as needed. When he actually has become proficient in thinking in the traditional patterns, including the traditional phrases and everything else like them, he is a full-fledged singer of o. traditional p. In essence, he has learned to speak—or to sing—the special language of that poetry. He composes naturally in the forms of his tradition, unconsciously, and often very rapidly, as one speaks a language.

O.p., of whatever genre, is paratactic. Its style has been called an "adding" style, because the majority of its lines *could* terminate in a period, insofar as their syntax is concerned; instead, however, another idea is often "added" to what precedes. A comparatively small percentage of necessary run-on lines, in contrast to the number of cases of non-periodic enjambement, is, therefore, another distinctive and symptomatic feature of o. traditional style. This does not mean that the traditional singer only adds ideas; he can develop them as well, and he can return to themes introduced earlier.

Even as the formulas and their basic patterns make composing of lines possible in performance, so the associative use of parallelism in sound, syntax, and rhythm aids the o. poet in moving from one line to another. A line may suggest what is to follow it. Thus clusters of lines are formed, held together by sound, structure, and association of meaning. Such units are easily remembered. At times the complexity of structural interconnections between verses in o. traditional style is so great that it seems that one could have attained it only with the aid of writing. The truth is that these intricate architectonics of expression were developed first in o. traditional verse, establishing in this way from very archaic times the techniques which man with writing inherited and then believed himself to have "invented" with the stylus, the quill, and the pen. The language of o. traditional p., formulaic though it be, is in fact a dynamic, organic language, an organism of man's imaginative life.

Because poems composed in the formulaic style have no fixed text, they are not, and cannot be, memorized, for the text is never the same even in performances by the same singer. There may be changes in the narrative or other context as well. To say that the text remains "essentially the same," or "more or less the same," over time is not to say that the text is fixed.

Although there are many repeated incidents, scenes, and descriptions, these remain flexible, susceptible to expansion or contraction; a journey may be related briefly or with copious details, the description of armor may occupy one line or fifty and still be termed the same "theme," as such repeated incidents and descriptions are called. A "theme" is not merely a repeated subject, however, but a repeated *passage*. It has a more or less stable core of lines or parts of lines, surrounded by various elements adapting it to its context.

The theme is multiform, and has existence only in its multiforms. Habit and frequent use may set its form in the practice of a single singer to some degree of stability, but no given form of it is sacrosanct. Themes are useful, even as the formulas, in any song in which the incident or description may belong. The journey framework may be employed in any number of stories; the assembly of men or of gods is common to many tales in song. In learning a song which the singer hears for the first time he does not think of the text, for he constructs his own. He needs only to remember the names of persons and places and the sequences of events. In formulas and themes he has the building blocks and techniques for rapid composition.

There are "themes" in ritual and lyric songs as well. Recent research has demonstrated that non-narrative o. traditional p. composed formulaically has passages consisting of a more or less stable core of lines and parts of lines that are used in several songs. For such research to be meaningful, it is necessary to have a large body of texts, as many variants of songs as possible, for comparison.

In the o. traditional p. of some cultures in India and Africa there is reportedly more memorization than in those discussed above, although it is said that they too are composed formulaically. An analysis of some sample texts has indicated, however, that they also exhibit a more or less stable core with surrounding variations similar to what has been described in the composition of o. traditional formulaic p.

It is not surprising that a special manner of composition and transmission would influence in a profound way the poetical structure and the poetics of o. traditional p. One of the most obvious ways in which this is manifested is in the repetitions of formulas. Written poetry does not tolerate a high degree of repetition, but nothing is more characteristic of o. traditional p. than repetition, because it is endemic in the method of o. formulaic composition itself. Translators of Homer normally avoid Homer's repetitions of noun-epithet formulas, for example, using several different epithets where Homer used only one. They are tacitly acknowledging the difference between the poetics of written poetry and that of o. traditional p. Another device in some o.p. is on occasion to repeat the second half of a line at the beginning of the next line. This is not acceptable as a regular phenomenon in written poetry, but it is natural to o. traditional p. O. traditional p. has elements of poetics and aesthetics not shared with written poetry. On the other hand, one must stress that rhetorical devices like anaphora, epiphora, and figures of speech such as similes, metaphors, and even ring-composition were used in o. traditional p. before the invention of writing and were inherited by written poetry from its predecessor.

The configuration of themes that forms a song in o. formulaic traditional composition is similar to the single theme in its fluidity. Like the themes that make it up, the song, reflecting the desires of the singer at the moment of performance, may be sung long or short, even as tales can be told at length or in brief. It may be ornamented to a greater or lesser degree. It too has multiforms, which are usually called variants or versions. The term "multiform" is more accurate than "variant" or "version," which imply an "original" that has undergone some kind of change resulting in the text before us.

In o. traditional p. one can distinguish three meanings of the word "song," not only in the narrative genres but also in ritual and lyric songs. The first is that of any performance; for each performance is unique and valid in its own right. The second might be called that of the specific subject matter; for example, the song of the capture of Bagdad by Sultan Selim, which would be designated by a title, "Sultan Selim Captures Bagdad." Combining the first and the second meanings one can say that there will be as many texts of the specific song as there are performances, whether they are recorded or not. The third meaning of "song" could be called the "generic." The story of the capture of Bagdad (the specific song) falls into the category of a number of stories dealing with the capture of cities, just as the *Odyssey*, for example, falls into the generic category of songs recounting the return of the hero after long absence from home. The texts of this generic song are very numerous, of course, and reach far back into the depths of human history.

The generic song is of considerable importance in o. traditional p. It is not merely a convenient method of classification. It represents the significant core of ideas in a song that survive reinterpretation and specific application to "history," a core held together by tensions from the past that give a meaning to the song not apparent on its surface, no matter how lowly or local any given performance may be. Because of this core, one might say that every song in o. tradition retains the essence of its origins within it, in this way reflecting the origin of the very genre to which it belongs.

In o. traditional p. the question of authorship is complicated, yet it is clear, to use the first of the three meanings of song, given above, that the performer, the traditional singer, is the "author" of his particular performance. In this case the performer is composer as well. One has, therefore, multiple authors, even as one has multiple texts, of any specific or generic song. From that point of view there are as many authors as there are performances. But of any given text there is but one author, namely its performer-composer. This is a different concept of multiple authorship from that historically employed in Homeric and other epic criticism since Wolf. Moreover, this concept should not be confused with that of "communal" authorship put forth by scholars of the romantic period.

The date of any text of an o. traditional poem is, consequently, the date of its performance, that being the date of its composition. The date of the specific song would be the date on which some traditional singer for the first time adapted existing themes and configurations to other specific people and events, that is to say it would be the date of the first performance. This is ordinarily beyond our ken. The date of the generic song is lost in prehistory.

In some cultures there are poems, or songs, usually topical in nature, made up on the spot on demand or composed in live contests of poetry. The poems in this category are ephemeral, created for the moment and usually not transmitted to anyone else. Therefore, since they are improvised for a specific circumstance and do not "enter into tradition," they might be called "o. non-traditional" poems. Because the practice of "improvising" such poems has long existed, however, some scholars feel that the style of these ephemeral creations can also be traditional.

O.p. long played an integral role in the life of human beings and social communities; its practice provided that spiritual activity necessary to man's existence; its bonds with everyday life were manifold and close. Its deeper qualities are becoming clear as they are sifted from the transitional periods in which they were first recorded. The knowledge of how o. traditional p. is composed and transmitted has brought with it new modes for its evaluation. And these modes have led back to the symbols and meanings of poetry itself in its origins.

The study of o.p. begun by Milman Parry in the 1930s has engendered many other studies and debate continues. His theory consisted of first making as exact a description as possible of the process of composition and transmission of o. traditional narrative p. in order to determine its basic and necessary characteristics, and then applying that knowledge to texts from ancient and medieval times for which there is little or no information about how they were composed. He concentrated on the living practice of o. traditional epics in Yugoslavia, but he also collected a large number of o. traditional lyric songs as well. A description of the collecting and a digest of the contents of the collection can be found in the introduc. to v. 1 (1954) of *Serbocroatian Heroic Songs*, ed. by Albert B. Lord. More details on singing and collecting are given in David E. Bynum's Prolegomena to v. 6 (1980) and 14 (1979), ed. by him. The music of a selection of the lyric songs was transcribed by Béla Bartók and publ. with a full study of them by him in 1951.

Parry died in 1935 and Lord's book *The Singer of Tales*, publ. in 1960, gave a description of the Yugoslav practice and applied the principles gained from its study to the Homeric poems, the Anglo-Saxon *Beowulf*, the *Chanson de Roland*, and the medieval Gr. epic of *Digenis Akritas*. Later the theory was applied to other poetries as well, including the works of Hesiod and the Homeric Hymns in ancient Gr. tradition, the Middle High German *Nibelungenlied*, the medieval Sp. *Cantar de mio Cid*, Eng. and Scottish ballads, Pre-Islamic and cl. Arabic poetry, Chinese traditional lyrics, the quatrains of Latvian *dainas*, and many others.

Subsequent scholarship focussed largely on the definitions of o.p. and of the formula, the problem of composition by formula and theme vis-à-vis improvisation, memorization, and the context of performance. Ruth Finnegan has advocated a broad definition of o.p. with emphasis on the literal meaning of "o." and on performance. Among reports of o.p. in various parts of the world those of Jeff Opland on praise poetry among the Xhosa in South Africa have contributed to deepening an understanding of the place of that kind of poetry in the general scheme of o.p. Opland has also applied his experience with African o.p. to Anglo-Saxon poems and their possible indebtedness to eulogy.

Biblical and Near Eastern studies have been influenced by the approach of scholars in the field of o. traditional p. Robert C. Culley and William Whallon were among the pioneers in applying o. formulaic theory to the Old Testament, and the work of Werner H. Kelber is a valuable contribution to the study of the Gospels from that same point of view. Ching-Hsien Wang broadened the field to include Chinese traditional lyrics. James T. Monroe has written on the o. composition of Pre-Islamic poetry, and Michael J. Zwettler's book *The O. Tradition of Cl. Arabic Poetry: Its Character and Implications*, 1978, in addition to its main subject, has an excellent introd. on the o.-formulaic theory. A thorough history of the scholarship on the theory and a full introd. to it, with an annotated bibliog., is available in John Miles Foley's *O. Formulaic Theory and Research: An Introd. and Annotated Bibliog.*, 1985.

Parry's work was concerned primarily with o. traditional epic song. He was also interested in the way of life of the people who practiced that kind of poetry, and he was very much aware of the importance of the circumstances of performance and the role of the audience. These aspects of o.p. have been written about by both anthropologists and others concerned with social studies. A special philosophical branch of studies of orality—rather than o. literature—has also developed from Parry's writings. It includes the work of Eric A. Havelock, H. Marshall McLuhan, and Walter J. Ong. These scholars have examined the effect of literacy and mass media on the way in which men view the universe and the world in which they live, as well as how they think. Since their writings have some pertinence to the study of o.p., a representative selection has been included in the bibliog. See also POETRY READING.

B. Bartók and A. B. Lord, *Serbo-Croatian Folk Songs* (1951); R. H. Webber, "Formulaic Diction in the Sp. Ballad," *Univ. of Calif. Publications in Modern Philology*, 34, no. 2 (1951), 175-277; C. M. Bowra, *Heroic Poetry* (1952); A. B. Lord, *The Singer of Tales* (1960); H. M. McLuhan, *The Gutenberg Galaxy* (1962); E. A. Havelock, *Preface to Plato* (1963, repr. 1982); "Perspectives on Recent Work on O. Lit.," in *O. Lit. Seven Essays*, ed. J. J. Duggan (1975); G. S. Kirk, *The Songs of Homer* (1962); R. C. Culley, *O. Formulaic Language in the Biblical Psalms* (1967); J. B. Hainsworth, *The Flexibility of the Homeric Formula* (1968); N. K. Chadwick and V. Zhirmunsky, *O. Epics of Central Asia* (1969); William Whallon, *Formula, Character, and Context: Studies in Homeric, OE, and Old Testament Poetry* (1969); *The Making of Homeric Verse, The Collected Papers of Milman Parry*, ed. A. Parry (1971); J. T. Monroe, "O. Composition in Pre-Islamic Poetry," *Jour. of Arabic Lit.*, 3 (1972); J. Duggan, *The Song of Roland: Formulaic Style and Poetic Craft* (1973); M. N. Nagler, *Spontaneity and Tradition, A Study in the O. Art of Homer* (1974); Ching-Hsien Wang, *The Bell and the Drum. "Shih Ching" as Formulaic Poetry in an O. Tradition* (1974); B. Peabody, *The Winged Word* (1975); *O. Lit. and the Formula*, ed. B. A. Stolz and R. S. Shannon, III (1976); R. Finnegan, *O. P., Its Nature, Significance, and Social Context* (1977); D. E. Bynum, *The Daemon in the Wood, A Study of O. Narrative Patterns* (1978); G. Nagy, *The Best of the Achaeans: Concepts of the Hero in Archaic Gr. Poetry* (1979); V. Vikis-Freibergs and I. Freibergs, "Formulaic Analysis of the Computer-Accessible Corpus of Latvian Sun-Songs," in *Computers and the Humanities*, 12 (1979); J. M. Foley, *O. Traditional Lit.*, (1980, 2d print. 1983); *O. Formulaic Theory and Research, An Introd. and Annotated Bibliog.* (1985); J. Opland, *Anglo-Saxon O. P.* (1980); *Xhosa O. P., Aspects of a Black South-African Tradition* (1983); W. J. Ong, *Orality and Literacy, The Technologizing of the Word* (1982); R. Janko, *Homer, Hesiod and the Hymns: Diachronic Development in Epic Diction* (1982); W. H. Kelber, *The O. and the Written Gospel: The Hermeneutics of Speaking and Writing in the Synoptic Tradition, Mark, Paul, and Q* (1983); V. Vikis-Freibergs, "Creativity and Tradition in O. Folklore or the Balance of Innovation and Repetition in the O. Poet's Art," in *Cognitive Processes in the Perception of Art*, ed. W. R. Crozier and A. J. Chapman (1984); J. F. Nagy, *The Wisdom of the Outlaw, the Boyhood Deeds of Finn in Gaelic Narrative Tradition* (1985). A.B.L.

OTTAVA RIMA. A stanza of 8 iambic lines, rhyming abababcc. Its origin is obscure, being variously attributed to development from the ballade or the *canzone* (qq.v.) or to imitation of the Sicilian *strambotto*. However, it was in use in the religious verse of late 13th-c. Italy, and it was given definitive artistic form by Boccaccio in his *Teseida* (1340–42) and his *Filostrato* (1339–40). Becoming almost immediately the dominant form of It. narrative verse, it was developed by Poliziano, Pulci, and Boiardo in the 15th c. and reached its apotheosis in the *Orlando Furioso* (1516) of Ludovico Ariosto, whose genius exploited its potentialities for richness, complexity, and variety of effect. Later in the same century, Tasso showed his mastery of the form. The poets of Renaissance Spain and Portugal followed It. example in adopting the form for narrative purposes. Notable epics in o.r. are Ercilla's *La Araucana* in Sp. and Camões' *Os Lusíadas* in Portuguese.

Although the form was occasionally used by the Eng. Renaissance poets (e.g., Wyatt, Spenser, and Drayton), it was not until the romantic period that the form found a true Eng. master in Byron, whose translation of a portion of Pulci's *Morgante Maggiore* seems to have made him aware of the stanza's possibilities. He employed the stanza in *Beppo, The Vision of Judgment,* and, with greatest success, in *Don Juan.* Keats and Shelley also wrote poems in o.r.

The work of the great masters of the stanza—Ariosto and Byron—suggests that o.r. is most suited to work of a varied nature, blending serious, comic, and satiric attitudes and mingling narrative and discursive modes. Byron, referring to the work of Pulci, calls it "the half-serious rhyme" (*Don Juan* 4.6). Its accumulation of rhyme, reaching a precarious crescendo with the third repetition, prepares the reader for the neat summation, the acute observation, or the epigrammatic twist which comes with the final couplet:

And Julia's voice was lost, except in sighs,
  Until too late for useful conversation;
The tears were gushing from her gentle eyes,
  I wish, indeed, they had not had occasion;
But who, alas, can love, and then be wise?
  Not that remorse did not oppose temptation:
A little still she strove, and much repented,
And whispering "I will ne'er consent"—consented.

(Byron, *Don Juan* 1.117)

Furthermore, the stanza is long enough to carry the thread of narrative but not so long that it becomes unmanageable.—Schipper; Hamer;

V. Pernicone, "Storia e svolgimento della metrica," in *Problemi ed orientamenti critici di lingua e di letteratura italiana,* ed. A. Momigliano, II (1948); Wilkins; G. M. Ridenour, *The Style of Don Juan* (1960). F.J.W.; A.P.

OXYMORON (Gr. "pointedly foolish"). A figure of speech which combines two seemingly contradictory elements. It is a form of condensed paradox (q.v.): "O heavy lightness! serious vanity! / Mis-shapen chaos of well-seeming forms! / Feather of lead, bright smoke, cold fire, sick health!" (Shakespeare, *Romeo and Juliet* 1.1). Although o. has been a recurrent device in poetry from the time of Horace ("concordia discors rerum"—the jarring harmony of things—*Epistulae* 1.12.19) to the time of Dylan Thomas, it is, *par excellence,* the rhetorical expression of the baroque era. Such poets as Marino in Italy, Góngora in Spain, Crashaw in England made it a primary vehicle of the 17th c. sensibility.

> Welcome, all wonders in one sight!
> Eternity shut in a span,
> Summer in winter, day in night,
> Heaven in earth, and God in man!

As the above quotation indicates, o. is particularly effective in evoking religious mysteries or other meanings which the poet feels to be beyond the reach of human sense. Its popularity in the late Renaissance owes something to the heightened religious concerns of that period and something to the revival of the habit of analogical thinking.

O., which reveals a compulsion to fuse all experience into a unity, should be carefully distinguished from antithesis (q.v.), which tends to divide and categorize elements of experience. Significantly, the latter figure, with its basis in rationality, dominates the poetry of the 18th c., a period which regarded the figures of the baroque poets as examples of "bad taste" or "false wit." But o. is not exclusively suited to religious poetry. Against Milton's use of the figure in *Paradise Lost* to evoke the unimaginable glories of God we may place the lines from Shakespeare quoted earlier, the stock Petrarchan figures for love's contradictions, and many passages in which Keats expresses the paradoxes of man's sensuous experience. See also CATACHRESIS, SYNAESTHESIA.—Lausberg; E. Mc Cann, "O. in Sp. Mystics and Eng. Metaphysical Writers," CL, 13 (1961). F.J.W.; A.P.

P

PAEAN (Gr. *paian*). The earliest mention of a p. is in *Iliad* 1.473, where, after the plague which Apollo had sent upon them, the Achaeans sought to propitiate the god with song. Apollo in his capacity as god of healing came to be invoked as *Paian* ("healer"), whence choral songs in his honor or in that of his sister Artemis were called "paeans." The p. as a literary form was employed by Pindar and others in the classical period of ancient Greece. As time went on, it might also be addressed to a successful general like Lysander or T. Quinctius Flamininus. The p. should be distinguished from the paeon (q.v.) which, however, has the same derivation.—A. Fairbanks, *A Study of the Gr. P.* (1900); Smyth; G. Norwood, *Pindar* (1945). R.J.G.

PAEON. A metrical unit consisting of 1 long and 3 short syllables: first p., –⏑⏑⏑; second p., ⏑–⏑⏑; third, ⏑⏑–⏑; fourth, ⏑⏑⏑–. The first and the fourth p. are, in effect, cretics (–⏑–) by resolution of their last and first syllables respectively. The second and the third p., however, exist only in ancient metrical theory, and the fourth is quite rare. Paeonic verse, especially the first p., is found in Gr. poetry and more frequently in comedy than in tragedy. Cretics and paeons may occur in combination (cf. Aristophanes, *Acharnians* 210ff.). In Eng. poetry all four types have been used in combination with other kinds of feet. While the first and fourth p. are rare, the second and especially the third are not uncommon in modern accentual verse:

> The appeáling | of the Pássion | is ténderer |
> in práyer apárt"
> (G. M. Hopkins, *The Wreck of the Deutschland*).

J. W. White, *The Verse of Gr. Comedy* (1912); Dale; Hamer; B. Ghiselin, "Paeonic Measures in Eng. Verse," MLN, 57 (1942). D.S.P.

PALINDROME (Gr. "running back again"). A word, sentence or verse which reads alike backward or forward. Its reputed inventor was Sotades, a lascivious poet of the 3d c. B.C., from whose name the palindromes are often referred to as Sotadics. There are no examples from the classical Gr. period. The best known p. in Gr. is "nipson anomemata me monan opsin" (wash my transgressions, not only my face), attributed to Gregory of Nazianzus and often inscribed on fonts in monasteries or churches. A familiar one is also the Latin "Roma tibi subito motibus ibit amor." The following line by Camden illustrates a more refined type of p. in which each word reads alike backward or forward: "Odo tenet mulum, madidam mappam tenet Anna, Anna tenet mappam madidam, mulum tenet Odo." Palindromes were popular in Byzantine times. We possess a number of them written by the emperor Leo the Wise (10th c.). In 1802 Ambrose Pamperis published, in Vienna, a pamphlet containing 416 palindromic verses recounting some of the campaigns of Catherine the Great. Among the best known examples in Eng. are perhaps the following: "Madam, I'm Adam" and "Able was I ere I saw Elba," a saying attributed to Napoleon. Also called *carcinoi, versus anacyclici, versus echoici.*—K. Preisendanz, "Palindrom," A. Pauly, G. Wissowa, and W. Kroll, *Real-Encyclopädie der classischen Altertumswissenschaft,* XVIII, 2 (1949).

P.S.C.

PANEGYRIC. A speech or poem in praise of an individual, institution or group. Originally p. was a rhetorical type belonging to the epideictic category of oratory. Its rules are given in the rhetorical works of Menander and Hermogenes and famous examples include the *Panegyricus* of Isocrates, the p. of Pliny the Younger on Trajan, and the eleven other *XII Panegyrici Antici* (4th c.). Much primitive poetry is p. in nature, consisting of the praises of heroes, armies, victories, states, etc. Pindar's odes have been loosely described as panegyrics. After the 3d c. B.C., p. was accepted as a formal poetic type and its rules were given in handbooks of poetry. It became popular during the decadence of classical poetry and like other such forms persisted until the Renaissance. Scaliger gives its rules in his *Poetices Libri Septem* (1561).

P. is almost indistinguishable from encomium, but according to Scaliger it tends to deal with present men and deeds, while encomium deals with the past. Among significant examples of p. poems are Sidonius' poems on the Emperors Avitus, Majorian, and Anthemius; Claudian's on Honorius and on the consulship of Probinus and Olybrius; the p. on the death of Celsus by Paulinus of Nola; Aldhelm's *de Laudibus Virginum*; and innumerable poems in praise of Mary, the cross, the martyrs, etc. In the Renaissance the tradition continued unabated with perhaps more emphasis on the praise of secular figures and institutions. One notable feature of p. is its tendency to develop toward epic, which it heavily influenced in the Renaissance.—T. Burges, *Epideictic Lit.* (1902); Chadwick. O.B.H.

PANTOUM. A poem of indeterminable length, composed of quatrains in which the second and fourth lines of each stanza serve as the first and third lines of the next, the process continuing through the last stanza. In this quatrain the first line of the poem also reappears as the last and, in some Eng. pantoums, the third line of the poem as the second. Thus, the p. begins and ends with the same line. Another distinct feature is that different themes must be developed concurrently in the p., one in the first 2 lines and the other in the last 2 lines of each quatrain, the 2 pairs of lines being connected only by their sound.

A distinct Malayan verse form (*pantun*), the p. was introduced into Western poetry by the Fr. orientalist Ernest Fouinet and was established by the practice of Victor Hugo in his Notes to *Les Orientales.* In Fr. the form was effectively used by Théodore de Banville, Louisa Siefert, Leconte de Lisle, and, with considerable variations, by Charles Baudelaire; in Eng. by Austin Dobson, Brander Matthews, and others. Despite its oriental origin and its relatively late Western adoption, the p. is often listed with the much older Fr. forms, such as rondeau, triolet, ballade, and villanelle (qq.v.).—Kastner; M. Grammont, *Petit traité de versification française* (7th ed., 1930); P. G. Brewster, "Metrical, Stanzaic, and Stylistic Resemblances between Malayan and Western Poetry," RLC, 32 (1958; finds European analogues of the p. in the German *Schnaderhüpfel,* the Russian *chastushka,* the Sp. *copla,* the Latvian and Lithuanian *daina*). A.P.

PARADOX. A statement which seems untrue but proves valid upon close inspection. E.g.: "The longest way round is the shortest way home;" or, "When my love swears that she is made of truth / I do believe her, though I know she lies" (Shakespeare, Sonnet 138). P. was recognized by ancient rhetoricians (Menander, Hermogenes, Cicero, Quintilian, etc.) as one of the standard figures. It was popular during the decadent period of Graeco-Roman literature in such forms as paradoxical encomium, *controversiae,* and *suasoriae.* During the Middle Ages paradoxical arguments were used to train students in rhetoric and for humor or irony in literature, as in the arguments against chastity in the *Romance of the Rose.* The most famous Renaissance example of sustained p. is *The Praise of Folly* by Erasmus; but because of the paradoxical nature of Christian values, p. abounds in both popular and esoteric literature of the later Middle Ages and Renaissance. In literature of the Renaissance, p. is handled with moderation and is merely one of several popular figures. However, during the baroque period, p. became a central poetic figure. It is particularly important in the prose and poetry of Donne. One of his earliest works is the prose collection *Paradoxes and Problems;* and the techniques of paradoxical argument developed in this collection are evident throughout his *Songs and Sonnets* and his sermons. Fondness for p. is evident in poetry of the later 17th c. and the 18th c. However, as in Dryden and Pope, it tends to be verbal p., reflected in the use of balance and antithesis in the heroic couplet, rather than paradoxical argument. Hazlitt called neoclassic poetry "the poetry of paradox" and contrasted it with what he felt was the far richer "poetry of imagination" written by the Elizabethans.

Both Friederich Schlegel and Thomas De Quincey argued that p. is a vital element in poetry, reflecting the paradoxical nature of the world which poetry imitates. DeQuincey wrote in the *Autobiography,* ". . . to speak in the mere simplicity of truth, so mysterious is human nature, and so little read by him who runs, that almost every weighty aspect of truth upon that theme will be found at first sight to be startling, or sometimes paradoxical. And so little need is there for chasing or courting paradox, that, on the contrary, he who is faithful to his own experiences will find all his efforts little enough to keep down the paradoxical air besieging much of what he *knows* to be the truth. No man needs to *search* for paradox in this world of ours. Let him simply confine himself to the truth, and he will find paradox growing everywhere under his hands as rank of weeds."

As a widely employed critical term, p. is peculiar to 20th-c. criticism. The rediscovery of Donne and Marvell undoubtedly played a part in its usage, as well as our general awareness of the need for the ironic mind. It is in Cleanth Brooks' *The Well Wrought Urn* that p. is most closely examined. Brooks says, in "The Language of Paradox," that p. is a form of indirection, and indirection is a general characteristic of poetic language and structure. Brooks brings a good deal of evidence to bear in support of his thesis, showing examples of p. in a poet like Wordsworth, whom one might expect to be a poet of simple, direct statement. An issue that he touches on but probably does not develop sufficiently is the difference between *verbal paradoxes* and *paradoxical situations.* Because he does not sufficiently stress this distinction, Brooks is sometimes accused of reducing poetry to "screaming paradoxes." Obviously, as his analysis of Wordsworth's *Composed upon Westminster Bridge* shows, Brooks does not insist merely on witty paradoxes. He is more concerned, and rightly so, to show that many interesting and good poems are written from insights that dramatically enlarge or in some way startlingly modify our commonplace conceptions and understandings, and these we call paradoxical. A good poet might, for example, take Eliot's p., "Liberty is a different sort of pain from prison," and make it into a full poem. Whether he kept Eliot's own verbal p. or chose to render the idea either by a series of examples or of simple direct statements would be of little significance. His poem would remain paradoxical.—Brooks and Warren; C. Brooks, "The Language of P.," *The Well Wrought Urn* (1947); R. Crane, "The Critical Monism of Cleanth Brooks," *Critics and Crit.* (1952); D. Daiches, "Poetry and P.," *Crit. Approaches to Lit.* (1956); H. K. Miller, "The Paradoxical Encomium . . . ," MP, 53 (1956). W.V.O'C.

PARALLELISM (Gr. "side by side"). In poetry a state of correspondence between one phrase, line, or verse with another. P. seems to be the basic aesthetic principle of poetic utterance. According to B. R. Lewis, *Creative Poetry* (1931), primitive man, "if strongly aroused, and if his emotion was sustained, . . . must have repeated . . . the same sequence of sounds. . . ." Such repetitions as "Nyah eh wa, Nyah eh wa," of the Am. Indian. "Ha-ah, Ha-ah," of the New Zealander, "Wa-la-wa, Wa-la-wa," of the *Beowulf* poet, are parallel refrains of the most elemental, lyrical nature. Tense emotion, such as joy, grief, anger, longing, seems naturally to give rise to parallel utterance, and, doubtless, p. was the basic element of primitive poetry before such refinements as meter and rhyme were invented.

P. of clauses is the central principle of biblical verse, a fact not fully understood by the translators of the Authorized Version. The principle was rediscovered by Bishop Robert Lowth who called it *parallelissimus memborum* and noted several distinct varieties; in fact many structural types have been described, including especially those based on sameness, antithesis, and complement. But in the Bible there seems not only to have been structural and rhythmic p. but also p. on an interpretive level. Thus the significance of a figure may be understood by the envelope or stanzaic pattern formed by the relations of the members. Accordingly the Lord's Prayer might be printed:

Our Father which art in heaven:
  Hallowed be thy name,
  Thy Kingdom come,
  Thy will be done,
In earth as it is in heaven.

Therein all the parallel clauses are connected with both the opening and closing, and the meaning becomes: "Hallowed be thy name in earth as it is in heaven; Thy kingdom come in earth as it is in heaven, etc.," thereby considerably enriching the interpretive value. This principle has been of some importance to modern biblical commentary.

Doubtless p. occurs in all languages in which there is poetry dealing with feelings of a religious or exalted nature or where strong emotion is expressed. But the poet who has certainly made the most use of this device in Eng. is Walt Whitman. G. W. Allen divides Whitman's devices into four main types: (*1*) *Synonymous p.*, where the second line enforces the first by repeating the thought: "I too am not a bit tamed. I too am untranslatable. / I sound my barbaric yawp over the roofs of the world." (*Song of Myself,* Sec. 52). (There may or may not be repetition of the actual words). (*2*) *Antithetical p.*, where the second line denies or contrasts the first. (*3*) *Synthetic or cumulative p.*, where the second line, or several consecutive lines, supplements or completes the first.

(4) *Climactic p.*, or "ascending rhythm," where each successive line adds to its predecessor, usually taking words from it and completing it. However, as C. M. Lewis, *The Foreign Sources of Modern Eng. Versification* (1898) claims, there is no modern poetry of any great importance in which this principle is the only determinant of form."—Bishop R. Lowth, *Isaiah, a New Tr., with a Preliminary Dissertation* (1778); C. A. Smith, *Repetition and P. in Eng. Verse* (1894); R. G. Moulton, *The Lit. Study of the Bible* (1895); G. W. Allen, *Am. Prosody* (1935). R.O.E.

PARODY (Gr. *parōdia*). DEFINITIONS. P. is as old as poetry itself. One fundamental distinction can be made between comic p., which is close to burlesque (q.v.), and literary or critical p., which follows more closely a given author's style or a particular work of art. In the broader sense p. and literary burlesque originated in classic drama where they expressed a basic impulse for emotional counterpoint to tragic themes. From Aristophanes to Shakespeare and into our time the comic interlude, with its ludicrous parallel of the main plot, has functioned as a parody—to provide a breather or the catharsis of laughter. It is, therefore, somewhat beside the point to regard all p. with suspicion or distrust. For, although a parasitic art and written at times with malice, p. is as fundamental to literature as is laughter to health.

Critical p. has been defined as the exaggerated imitation of a work of art. Like caricature it is based on distortion, bringing into bolder relief the salient features of a writer's style or habit of mind. It belongs to the genus *satire* (q.v.) and thus performs the double-edged task of reform and ridicule. Eccentricity, sentimentalism, pedantry, dullness, pompousness, and self-importance are among its major targets, and at its best it is a critical instrument of telling force because it approaches the subject from within rather than from without, and thus avoids the reproach of poets and creative writers that a critic is simply a disappointed artist. P. usually makes its point by employing a serious style to express an incongruous subject, thus disturbing the balance of form and matter. It keeps attention focused on the poem imitated with, in most cases, a deflationary intent.

The best p. surpasses mere imitation. It stands on its own feet, containing enough independent humor to be funny beyond aping of the original. The following brief example of modern p. will illustrate its insistence upon common sense and reality against what Mark Twain termed "girly-girly romance." Bret Harte's sequel to Whittier's sentimental ballad *Maud Muller* details the long connubial years of Mrs. Judge Jenkins and closes with a deft p. of the final familiar couplet by showing us the other half of the coin:

If of all words of tongue or pen
The saddest are 'It might have been,'

Sadder are these, we daily see,
'It is, but hadn't ought to be!'

There are as many different motives for p. as there are parodists. Sometimes, especially in the 18th-c. coffee houses, it was personal spite. More often the parodist employed the style of his original to poke fun at current follies or vices. He might have a social axe to grind or he might wish to expose a certain literary school or mannerism which has hardened into conventionality. Thus Cervantes dealt a classic blow to the fiction of knight-errantry and Fielding punctured the Richardsonian novel of sentiment in *Joseph Andrews*. A familiar example of the double-edged p. in verse is Lewis Carroll's *Hiawatha's Photographing* in which the rhythms of Longfellow are employed to poke fun at the then novel practice of the family photograph. J. C. Squire aped Gray's *Elegy* and at the same time aimed his p. at the Spoon River series of Masters; and E. B. White in *A Classic Waits for Me* has written a fine take-off on the Classics Club selection of best sellers in the rolling lines of Whitman.

HISTORY. P. was originally "a song sung beside," i.e., a comic imitation of a serious poem. The imitation may be of the actual words or of the manner; the comic effect may be achieved by applying high-flown language or meter to trivial themes or by some other form of incongruity or caricature. The instinct to burlesque any lofty or pompous performance is deep in our nature; but with us p. proper is a form of literary criticism which consists in heightening the characteristics of the thing imitated. Aristotle (*Poetics* 1448^a12) attributes the origin of p. as an art to Hegemon of Thasos, because he used epic style to represent men not as superior to what they are in ordinary life but as inferior. Hegemon was, we are told, a comic poet of the 5th c. who was the first to introduce parodies into the theater (Athenaeus 15.699a); he was reciting his p. of the *Battle of the Giants* in the theater when the news arrived of the disaster in Sicily. Athenaeus elsewhere quotes Polemo as saying that p. was invented by the iambic poet Hipponax (6th c. B.C.), who had himself been the victim of caricature at the hands of the sculptors and painters; we have a few lines of his mock-heroic epic on the adventures of a glutton. Athenaeus also refers to Epicharmus and two poets of the Old Comedy, Cratinus and Hermippus. Much earlier than these was the pseudo-Homeric *Margites*, known to Archilochus (Bergk, *Poetae Lyrici Graeci*, Archilochus fr. 117), which set forth in hexameters (with intermingled iambics) the story of a fool. We still have the *Battle of the Frogs and Mice*, which parodies Homer. Athenaeus has preserved a long passage by Matron setting forth in epic style an account of an Athenian banquet.

The supreme parodist in antiquity was Aristophanes, who may be thought to have reached his highest level in the *Frogs,* where he parodies the styles of Aeschylus and Euripides. But almost every page of Aristophanes contains a touch of p. In later comedy this element dwindles. Plato imitates the styles of several prose writers with amusing effect; in the *Symposium* (194e–197e) he puts into Agathon's mouth a speech in the manner of Gorgias. Lucian has a good many touches of p. or burlesque, for example in Dialogue 20, the *Judgment of Paris,* where the comic effect is achieved by making the divine characters talk in the language of ordinary life.

Roman humor had a strong element of satire; the phlyax pots and the performances which they presumably illustrate must have appealed to the Romans. In L. comedy we find occasional burlesque of the tragic manner, e.g., in the prologues to the *Amphitryon* and the *Rudens,* the mad scene in the *Menaechmi,* and Pardalisca's mock-tragic outburst (*Casina* 621ff.)—passages which, whatever the original may have been, owe their effect to the language and the meter. A more delicate irony is shown in Syrus' mocking reply to the sententious words of Demea (*Adelphoe* 420ff.). Lucilius imitates the style of the Roman tragic poets, for example Pacuvius' unusual words and awkward compounds. The fourth poem of Catullus is closely parodied in *Catalepton* 10. Persius ridicules by imitation the styles of Pacuvius and other poets. Petronius (*Satyricon* 119–24) gives us a long hexameter poem on the Civil War, parts of which may be meant as a caricature of Lucan.

In its later days the Roman mime parodied the rites of the Christian church. During the later Middle Ages parodies of liturgy, well-known hymns, and even the Bible were popular. Renaissance authors, when not embroiled in the polemics of the Reformation, preferred to parody the classics or such "gothic" phenomena as romance and scholasticism—e.g., Pulci's *Morgante Maggiore,* Cervantes' *Don Quixote* (p. of romance); Giambattista Gelli's *Circe,* Tassoni's *La Secchia Rapita,* Scarron's *Virgile Travesti* (p. of the classics); Erasmus' *Praise of Folly,* Rabelais' *Gargantua and Pantagruel* (p. of scholasticism). Of these authors Rabelais is the most universal, the richest, and the most difficult to classify.

P. became institutionalized during the 17th c. The existence of academies and distinct literary movements, particularly in Italy, France, and England, encouraged debates in which p. was used as a weapon of satire. Boccalini's *Ragguagli di Parnasso* (1612) was the origin of a whole *genre* employing p. as a device for criticizing contemporary authors.

Eng. p. had its beginnings in ecclesiastical litany and the Mass. It was employed in the Miracle Plays where a scene of common life (the Mak episode in *The Second Shepherd's Play*) provided comic relief. Chaucer's *The Rime of Sir Thopas* parodied the grandiose style of medieval romances. Shakespeare burlesqued his own romantic love plots with *rustic amours,* and John Marston, in turn, wrote a rough, humorous travesty of *Venus and Adonis.* In 1705 John Phillips (*The Splendid Shilling*) used the solemn blank verse of Milton to celebrate ludicrous incidents. One of the best-known 17th c. parodies was the Duke of Buckingham's *The Rehearsal* (1671) which leveled its shafts mainly at Dryden's *The Conquest of Granada* and at the grand manner of heroic drama. In the next century, Sheridan's *The Critic* took a similar target. Exceptions to the general rule that p. rarely outlives the literature parodied, *The Rehearsal* and *The Critic* have been revived in the 20th c.

The Golden Age of p. in Eng. poetry paralleled the rise of romantic and transcendental attitudes, perfect targets for the literary headshrinkers. Canning, Ellis, and John Hookham Frere produced a series of parodies in the *Anti-Jacobin Journal* (1790–1810). Here the Southey-Wordsworth brand of Fr. revolutionary sympathy for knife-grinders and tattered beggars provided good anti-Jacobin sport. Byron's *Vision of Judgment* and Shelley's *Peter Bell* likewise parodied Southey, Wordsworth, and "elemental" poetry. James Hogg in 1816 took on most of the Eng. romantics, and in 1812 James and Horace Smith published *Rejected Addresses,* a landmark in Eng. p., in which the styles of Scott, Wordsworth, Byron, Coleridge, Dr. Johnson, and others were skillfully but not uproariously parodied. In the later 19th c. names and titles continue to multiply. Tennyson, Browning, Longfellow, Poe, Swinburne, and Whitman become the chief targets for such parody artists as J. K. Stephen, C. S. Calverly, J. C. Squire, Lewis Carroll (*Father William* after Southey's *The Old Man's Comforts*), Swinburne (*The Higher Pantheism in a Nutshell* à la Tennyson and *Nephelidia,* a self-parody), Andrew Lang, and Max Beerbohm. In America the names of Phoebe Cary, Bret Harte, Mark Twain, Bayard Taylor, H. C. Bunner, and J. K. Bangs were most prominent before 1900. In the present century *The New Yorker* has carried on the tradition established by *Punch* and *Vanity Fair.* During the 1920's p. found a highly congenial atmosphere when such talented writers as Corey Ford, Louis Untermeyer, Frank Sullivan, Donald Ogden Stewart, Wolcott Gibbs, James Thurber, Benchley, Hoffenstein, and E. B. White persisted in seeing the funny side of the hard-boiled generation in prose and verse. With a history of twenty-five centuries behind it, p., it seems, is here to stay. Like all literature it has had its ups and downs, but at its best it is more than a parasitic art. It has attracted men and women of major stature and at times has shown the capacity to outlive the serious work which has inspired it. See also BURLESQUE.

COLLECTIONS: *Parodies of the Works of Eng. and Am. Authors,* ed. W. Hamilton (6 v., 1884–89); *A*

P. Anth., ed. C. Wells (1904); *A Book of Parodies*, ed. A. Symons (1908); *A Century of P. and Imitation*, ed. W. Jerrold and R. M. Leonard (1913); *Am. lit. in P.*, ed. R. P. Falk (1957); *Parodies, an Anthol.*, ed. D. MacDonald (1960).

History and Criticism: A. T. Murray, *On P. and Paratragoedia in Aristophanes* (1891); A. S. Martin, *On P.* (1896); C. Stone, *P.* (1915); P. Lehmann, *Die Parodie im Mittelalter* (2 v., 1922); E. Gosse, "Burlesque," *Selected Essays, First Series* (1928); G. Kitchin, *A Survey of Burlesque and P. in Eng.* (1931); A. H. West, *L'Influence française dans la poésie burlesque en Angleterre entre 1660–1700* (1931); R. P. Bond, *Eng. Burlesque Poetry, 1700–1750* (1932); G. Highet, *Anatomy of Satire* (1962; chap. on p.).

R.P.F.; W.B.

PARONOMASIA. See PUN.

PASTORAL. History. The p. imitates rural life, usually the life of an imaginary Golden Age, in which the loves of shepherds and shepherdesses play a prominent part. To insist on a realistic (or even a recognizably "natural") presentation of actual shepherd life would exclude the greater part of the compositions that are called p. Only when poetry ceases to imitate ordinary rural life does it become distinctly p. It must be admitted, however, that the term has been and still is used to designate any treatment of rural life, as for instance Louis Untermeyer's speaking of Robert Frost as a "pastoral" poet or John F. Lynen writing on his "P. art." Perhaps most critics agree with Edmund Gosse that the "pastoral is cold, unnatural, artificial, and the humblest reviewer is free to cast a stone at its dishonored grave." But there must be some unique value in a genre that lasted 2,000 years. This long-lived popularity, it seems, derives from the fact that the shepherd—a simple swain, with whom everyone may easily identify himself—deals with a universal subject—something fundamentally true about everyone. Thus the complex is reduced to the simple; the universal is expressed in the concrete.

For all practical purposes the p. begins with Theocritus' *Idyls*, in the 3d c. B.C. Though the canon of his work is unsettled, enough of the poems in the collection made by Artemidorus are certainly his to justify the claim that Theocritus is the father of p. poetry. No. 11, for example, in which Polyphemus is depicted as being in love with Galatea and finding solace in song, becomes the prototype of the love lament; no. 1. in which Thyrsis sings of Daphnis' death, sets the pattern and, to no small degree, the matter for the p. elegy; no. 5 and no. 7 introduce the singing match conducted according to the rules of amoebaean poetry. And no. 7, in the appearance of contemporary poets under feigned names, contains the germ of the allegorical p. Theocritus wrote his pastorals while he was at Ptolemy's court of Alexandria, but he remembered the actual herdsmen of his boyhood and the beautiful countryside of Sicily; so he, like the p. poets who followed him, was a city man longing for the country. But perhaps no other p. poet has ever been able to strike such a happy medium between the real and the ideal.

Virgil's *Eclogues* refine and methodize Theocritus' idyls. Expressing the sentiment inspired by the beauty of external nature in her tranquil moods and the kindred charm inspired by ideal human relationships (love in particular) in verse notable for its exquisite diction and flowing rhythm, they consolidate and popularize the conventions of p. poetry. During the Middle Ages, the p. was chiefly confined to the *pastourelle* (q.v.), a native type of dialogue poem, and to a few realistic scenes in the religious plays. The vast body of the modern p.—elegy, drama, romance, p. poetry in general is a direct outgrowth of Renaissance humanism.

The p. elegy, patterned after such classical models as the *Lament for Adonis*, credited to Bion, the *Lament for Bion*, traditionally ascribed to Moschus but most probably by a disciple of Bion, and Theocritus' first idyl, became conventional in the Renaissance. The traditional machinery with variations was the invocation, statement of grief, inquiry into the causes of death, sympathy and weeping of nature, procession of mourners, lament, climax, change of mood, consolation. Marot and Spenser contributed Renaissance specimens, and numerous other p. poets, including Pope, Ambrose Philips, and Gay, tried their hand at the genre. Milton's *Lycidas* and Shelley's *Adonais* conform rather closely to the classic conventions, and vestiges of them can be seen even as late as Arnold's *Thyrsis*.

The p. drama was latent in the idyls and eclogues, for the brief dialogue was easily expandable. Even as early as Boccaccio's *Ninfale Fiesolano* the dramatic intensity of the eclogue was considerably heightened. With the addition of the crossed love plot and secret personal history, the p. drama emerged and grew in popularity as the medieval mystery plays lost ground. Poliziano's *Favola di Orfeo* (1472), is perhaps more correctly classified as an opera, but p. elements are prominent. Agostino de' Beccari's *Il Sacrificio* (1554), the first fully-developed p. drama, led to the heyday of the p. drama in Italy during the last quarter of the 16th c. Tasso's *Aminta* (1573), an allegory presenting the court of Ferrara, is no doubt the greatest of the kind and has exerted the most far-reaching influence of the tradition. Second only to it is Guarini's *Il Pastor Fido* (1583), the first important tragicomedy. In France, the most famous drama is Racan's *Les Bergeries* (1625), founded on d'Urfé's *Astrée*. It was followed by countless *bergeries*, which, after the mode of *Astrée*, were so filled with *galant* shepherds and beautiful nymphs that the type wore itself out with its own artificiality. England's first noteworthy p. dramas—Lyly's *Gallathea* and Peele's *Arraignment of Paris*—were both published in 1584, and the most excellent—Fletcher's *Faithful Shepherdess* (imitating Tasso's *Aminta*)—in 1610. Because of the constant pressure of Eng. empiricism and the austerity of the Puritan taste, the p. drama in England never reached the extravagant artificiality that it attained on the Continent. The last p. drama in England was the belated *Gentle Shepherd* by Allan Ramsay in 1725. Written in Lowland Scots, picturing particular Scottish scenes, and using "real" shepherds, it was highly praised by the early romantic poets and critics.

The p. romance usually takes the form of a long prose narrative, interspersed with lyrics, built on a complicated plot, and peopled with characters bearing p. names. Anticipated by Boccaccio's *Ameto* (1342), a mixed composition of graceful prose and tuneful verse, the genre is usually dated from Sannazaro's *Arcadia* (1504), a remarkable composition, written in musical prose and filled with characters who live in innocent voluptuousness. Popular imitations are Montemayor's *Diana* (1559?), in Portugal, and Cervantes' *Galatea* (1585), in Spain. In France the indigenous *pastourelle* held back the p. romance; but Rémy Belleau's *Bergerie* (1572), established the type and in d'Urfé's *Astrée* the baroque p. romance found its most consummate example, as nymphs bedizened in pearls and satin cavort with chivalric shepherds. The most celebrated Eng. p. romance is Sir Philip Sidney's *Arcadia* (1590). Its lofty sentiment, sweet rhythm, ornate rhetoric, elaborate description and high-flown oratory, display one aspect of the Italianate style of Elizabethan courtly literature. In spite of the riddle of its plot, in which the strange turns of fortune and love make all the virtuous happy, it is still good reading as a romance of love and adventure. The literary influence of the *Arcadia* was pervasive: Greene and Lodge, for example, imitated it; Shakespeare drew from it for the character of Gloucester in *King Lear;* on the scaffold Charles I recited an adaptation of a Pamela's prayer; in translation the *Arcadia* contributed to the elaborate plots of the Fr. romances; and traces of it may perhaps be seen even in Richardson and Scott. The sustained elaboration of its structure marks another step in the development which distinguished the novel from the short story and the picaresque tale. Robert Greene's *Menaphon* (1589; reprinted as *Greene's Arcadia* in 1590), conventional and imitative, adds little to the genre except some delightful lyrics. Thomas Lodge's *Rosalynde* (1590), in the style of Lyly's *Euphues* but diversified with sonnets and eclogues, was dramatized with little alteration by Shakespeare in *As You Like It.*

Early in the 14th c. the p. eclogue was profoundly influenced by the new learning, when Dante, Petrarch, and Boccaccio wrote L. eclogues after the mode of Virgil. They continued the allegory of their master, extended its political and religious scope, and introduced the personal lament. About the turn of the 15th c. Baptista Spagnuoli Mantuanus exploited the satirical possibilities of the p. by using rustic characters to ridicule the court, the church, and the women of his day. Late in the century Marino (1569–1625) developed a style paralleling gongorism and euphuism. His *Adone* (1623), filled with affected word-play and outrageous conceits, represents a baroque aberration of the genre comparable to the contemporaneous *Astrée.* The *Pléiade* transplanted the classical eclogue into France, and Marot and Ronsard and many imitators produced conventional eclogues. In England, aside from the inferior works of Barclay and Googe, p. poetry may be dated from Spenser's *Shepheardes Calender* (1579). Though Spenser follows the conventions of the classical eclogue, he aims at simplicity and naturalness by making use of rustic characters speaking country language. During the last quarter of the 16th c., England continued to produce much p. poetry in imitation of Spenser. According to modern taste and judgment, those of most merit are Michael Drayton's *Shepherds Garland* (1593), and William Browne's *Britannia's Pastorals* (1613–16). In his *Piscatory Eclogues* (1633), Phineas Fletcher imitated Sannazaro, who may have taken his cue from Theocritus' fisherman's idyl, no. 21.

The swan song of the p. was sung by the Eng. poets of the 18th c. Revived by Pope and Philips, whose rival pastorals appeared in Tonson's *Miscellany* in 1709, the p. attracted a surprising amount of interest. Pope, inspired by Virgil's *Eclogues,* produced one of the showpieces of rococo art—a part of "Summer" being so tuneful that Handel set it to music. Philips, under the rising influence of Eng. empiricism, tried to write pastorals that came closer to the realities of Eng. rural life. The followers of neither poet wrote any p. worthy of mention, and the genre soon died of its own inanition. So artificial and effete had it become that Gay's *Shepherd's Week,* in broad burlesque, was sometimes read as a p. in the true Theocritean style. The outstanding example of the romantic p. is Salomon Gessner's *Daphnis* (1754), *Idyllen* (1756), and *Der Tod Abels* (1758); and Wordsworth's *Michael,* reflecting the empirical element of Eng. romanticism, well marks the end of serious attempts in the genre.

E. Gosse, "An Essay on Eng. P. Poetry," *Complete Works in Verse and Prose of Edmund Spenser* (1882); M. H. Shackford, "A Definition of the P. Idyll, PMLA, 19 (1904); J. Marsan, *La Pastorale dramatique en France . . .* (1905); E. K. Chambers, *Eng. Pastorals* (1906); W. W. Greg, *P. Poetry and P. Drama* (1906); J. Marks, *Eng. P. Drama . . .* (1908); J. H. Hanford, "The P. Elegy and Milton's *Lycidas,* PMLA, 25 (1910); H. M. Hall, *Idylls of Fishermen* (1912); H. A. Rennert, *Sp. P. Romances* (1912); J.P.W. Crawford, *Sp. P. Drama* (1915); H. E. Mantz, "Non-dramatic P. in Europe in the 18th C., PMLA, 31 (1916); J. W. MacKail, "Allan Ramsay and the Romantic Revival," E&S,

10 (1924); M. K. Bragg, *The Formal Eclogue in 18th C. England* (1926); P. van Tieghem, "Les Idylles de Gessner et le rêve p.," *Le Préromantisme,* II (1930); W. P. Jones, *The Pastourelle* (1931); W. Empson, *Some Versions of P.* (1938); T. P. Harrison, *The P. Elegy* (1939); M. I. Gerhardt, *La Pastorale* (1950); J. Duchemin, *La Houlette et la lyre: Recherche sur les origines pastorales de la poésie* (1960–); J. F. Lynen, *The P. Art of Robert Frost* (1960).

THEORY: Sustained criticism of the p. begins with the essays of the Renaissance humanists, the most important being Vida's *Ars Poetica* (1527), Sebillet's *Art Poétique françoys* (1548), Scaliger's *Poetices* . . . (1561), and "E.K.'s" epistle and preface in 1579. The interest of these critics in the p. sprang from their desire to enrich the vernacular by imitating the "ancients" in this genre and to exploit its allegorical potentialities.

But mere imitation of Theocritus and Virgil did not long suffice, as the debate over Guarini's tragicomedy *Il Pastor Fido* illustrates. In his *Discorso* (1587), Jason Denores attacked this play because, he argued, it is a bastard genre, unauthorized by Aristotle. In *Il Verato* (1588), and *Il Verato Secondo* (1593), Guarini secured the new form against his adversary, thereby widening the scope of the genre. D'Urfé, in "L'Autheur à la Bergère Astrée" (1610), further extended the bounds of the p. when he turned critic to defend his baroque romance. Though Marini never expressed his critical ideas, his aberration of the genre in his extravagant p. idyl *Adone* (1623), made him the main target of the neoclassic attack.

In 1659 René Rapin argued that p. poets should return to the ancient models, and to his *Eclogae sacrae* he prefixed "Dissertatio de carmine pastorali." Reaching the apogee of authoritarianism in p. theory, he declares that he "will gather" all his theory from *"Theocritus* and *Virgil,* those . . . great and judicious Authors, whose very doing is Authority enough," and concludes "that *Pastoral* belongs properly to the Golden Age."

The most significant rebuttal to Rapin's theory is Fontenelle's "Discours sur la nature de l'églogue" (1688). Whereas Rapin looked for his fundamental criterion in the objective authority of the ancients, Fontenelle, like his master Descartes, sought a subjective standard in and expected illumination from "the natural light of Reason." Fontenelle's method is deductive. He starts with a basic assumption, the self-evident clarity of which he thinks no one will question: "All men would be happy, and that too at an easy rate." From this premise he deduces the proposition that p. poetry, if it is to make men happy, must present "a concurrence of the two strongest passions, laziness and love."

This quarrel between the ancients and the moderns was transferred directly to England; Rapin was translated by Thomas Creech in 1684, and Fontenelle was "Englished by Mr. Motteux" in 1695. The clash between the objective authority of the classics and the subjective standards of reason divided the critics into two schools of opinion, which are best denominated as neoclassic and rationalistic. The immediate source of the basic ideas of the Eng. neoclassic p. critics, the chief of whom are Walsh, Pope, Gay, Gildon, and Newbery, is Rapin's "Treatise." Pope, in practice as well as in theory, epitomizes the neoclassic ideal, explicitly admitting that his "notions concerning" the p. "were derived from . . . *Theocritus* and *Virgil* (the only undisputed authors of P.)."

The immediate source of the basic ideas of the Eng. rationalistic critics, the chief of whom are Addison, Tickell, Purney, Johnson, and *Mirror* no. 79, is Fontenelle's "Discours." But the Eng. followers of Fontenelle insist that the p. conform to experience as well as to reason. Though Dr. Johnson's *Rambler* essays on the p. in general observe both rationalistic and empirical premises, his "true definition" of a p. poem, in which he asserts that a p. is nothing more than a poem in which "any action or passion is represented by its effects on a country life," is basically empirical.

Romantic p. theory evolved from rationalistic theory. As the critics became more certain of their empirical grounds, they showed more freedom to disregard the form and the content of the traditional p.; to look on nature with heightened emotion; to endow primitive life with benevolence and dignity; and to place a greater value on sentiment and feeling. For example, in *An Essay on the Genius and Writings of Pope* (1756), Joseph Warton, by arguing that Theocritus was primarily a realistic poet and that the Golden Age depicted in his poetry may be equated to 18th-c. rural life, substitutes cultural primitivism for the chronological primitivism of the Golden-Age p. In "Discours Préliminaire" to *Les Saisons,* Jean-François de Saint-Lambert disregards the distinction between the p. and descriptive poetry and speaks with enthusiasm concerning the beauty of fields, rivers, and woods and of the felicity of rural life as he knew it in his childhood. In *Lectures on Belles Lettres,* 1783. Hugh Blair singles out Salomon Gessner's *Idyllen* as the poems in which his "ideas . . . for the improvement of Pastoral Poetry are fully realized." Blair's essay, along with Wordsworth's *Michael* (which exemplifies much of Blair's theory), ends serious consideration of the p. After that poem and Blair's essay, the genre belongs to the academicians.

PASTOURELLE (Prov., *Pastorela*). A short narrative poem of the Middle Ages which relates the encounter of a knight (who tells the story) and a shepherdess. The form was not fixed; only this conventional situation defines the genre. In the typical p., the knight, while riding along one morning, spies a pretty shepherdess beside the road. He proceeds at once to make advances to her, advances backed up by small gifts or greater promises. In some poems the shepherdess yields with pleasure after very little persuasion. In others, the knight takes by force the favors she tries to deny. In still others, she cleverly outwits him by one stratagem or another, or she is rescued by friendly shepherds, and the knight rides away humiliated or even beaten.

The p. was most popular and had its most typical development in OF in the 13th c. Prov. literature offers relatively few examples (though one of these, by Marcabru, is the earliest extant p. in any vernacular literature), and those few depart widely from the standard pattern. In German, Neidhardt von Reuenthal and his successors developed accessory and subsequent details (the mother's attitude, later developments, scenes of rustic revelry, etc.). The genre has been traced back with some show of probability to certain Latin poems slightly older than the vernacular pastourelles; but the characters in these poems are not a knight and a shepherdess, as they always are in the true p. Whatever its ultimate origin, the p. is the aristocratic product of a superficially polished age, which could find humor in the plight of a silly peasant girl seduced by a man of high rank, as well as in the far less probable discomfiture of the knight outwitted by a peasant girl cleverer than he. It is interesting to note that the delightful little play *Robin et Marion* is nothing more than an expanded p. of this second type.—E. Piguet, *L'Evolution de la p. du XIIe s. à nos jours* (1927); J. W. Powell, *The P.* (1931); Jeanroy, II; W.T.H. Jackson, "The Medieval P. as a Satirical Genre," PQ, 31 (1952).

F.M.C.

PATHETIC FALLACY. A phrase coined by John Ruskin and discussed in "Of the Pathetic Fallacy," ch. 12 in *Modern Painters,* III (1856). It describes the tendency of poets and painters to credit nature with the feelings of human beings. This fallacy is caused by "an excited state of the feelings, making us, for the time, more or less irrational." It is the "error . . . which the mind admits when affected strongly by emotion," a "falseness in all our impressions of external things." To illustrate his definition Ruskin quotes from Kingsley's *The Sands of Dee*

> They rowed her in across the rolling foam—
> The cruel, crawling foam

and says, "The foam is not cruel, neither does it crawl. The state of mind which attributes to it these characters of a living creature is one in which the reason is unhinged by grief."

The highest (creative) order of poets (Homer, Dante, Shakespeare) seldom admit this falseness. It is the second (reflective or perceptive) order (Wordsworth, Coleridge, Keats, Tennyson) who "much delight in it." Ruskin puts his two orders of poets in perspective when he includes them in his four "ranks of being," using the reaction of Wordsworth's Peter Bell to the primrose as a touchstone. The nonpoet is "the man who perceives rightly because he does not feel, and to whom the primrose is very accurately the primrose because he does not love it." The second-rank poet is "the man who perceives wrongly, because he feels, and to whom the primrose is anything else than a primrose." The first-rank poet is "the man who perceives rightly in spite of his feelings, and to whom the primrose is for ever nothing else than itself—a little flower, apprehended in the very plain and leafy fact of it." The inspired poet is a strong man who nevertheless is submitted to influences stronger than himself and who sees inaccurately because what he sees is inconceivably above him. Ruskin thus finds the pathetic fallacy in second-rank poets and in inspired poets. In the former the fallacy is to be condemned as a sign of morbid feeling or inaccurate perception. Inspired poets, on the other hand, quite validly resort to the fallacy, for they are ever aware of the fact out of which strong feeling comes. Ruskin's attack on what he considers to be a morbidity of mind in modern painters and poets, the overpowering of intellect by narrow feelings, follows naturally from his moral theory of art, in terms of which the fallacy of this group is to distort truth, to "miss the plain and leafy fact."

Ruskin coined the phrase, the "p.f.," to attack the secular sentimentalism of his contemporaries. It existed, of course, long before Ruskin named it as a traditional figure of speech, a species of personification going back as far as Homer. But the late 18th c. saw its extensive use. There are numerous figures in Gray, Collins, Cowper, Burns, Blake, Wordsworth, Shelley, and Keats which attribute to natural objects human feelings and powers. Mountains mourn, winds sigh, fields smile. Wordsworth justified such expressions by asserting that "objects . . . derive their influence not from properties inherent in them . . . , but from such as are bestowed upon them by the minds of those who are conversant with or affected by these objects."

The morbid use of the p.f., which Ruskin denounced in theory, Tennyson refined and diminished in poetic practice. Not the large natural forms but individual objects with their peculiar characteristics came to be celebrated for their overtones of human emotion. Knowing more about science than any Eng. poet before or since (except possibly William Empson), and being near-sighted to boot, he took a close look at natural objects. His verse from 1842, as Josephine Miles has shown, reveals a markedly less frequent resort to the fallacy than theretofore. Rather than stress the great likeness between man and nature in terms of sympathies of feeling, he heralded a new emphasis on qualitative comparison between objects in terms of sense perception. The old order, then, had already begun to yield to the new when Ruskin named and denounced the morbid use of the fallacy. After Ruskin, and perhaps because of him, use of the fallacy declined markedly. The Pre-Raphaelites, in paint and language, tried to set down what was really there. Hopkins followed them in his concern with "the plain and leafy fact" of the primrose, though, of course, his inscapes are of a vital nature. Among 20th-c. poets use of the p.f. has continued to decline, although Dylan Thomas used it with brilliant effectiveness.

J. Ruskin, "Of the P.F.," *Modern Painters,* III (1856); J. Miles, P.F. *in the 19th C.* (1942); A. H. Warren, Jr., "John Ruskin," *Eng. Poetic Theory: 1825–1865* (1950); B. Morris, "Ruskin on the P.F., or On How a Moral Theory of Art May Fail," JAAC, 14 (1955); J. D. Thomas, "Poetic Truth and P.F.," *Texas Studies in Lit. and Language,* 3 (1961). J.K.R.

PATTERN POETRY. Verse in which the disposition of the lines is such as to represent some physical object or to suggest motion, place, or feeling in accord with the idea expressed in the words. The pattern poem, or "shaped" poem, first appears in Western-world literature in the works of certain Gr. bucolic poets, notably in a few poems of Simias of Rhodes (ca. 300 B.C.), later much imitated. It is unlikely that the form is a Gr. invention; its origin has been thought to be Eastern. The true oriental p. poem (Persian or Turkish) blends several visual arts and bears more relation to acrostics, calligraphy, and illumination than to poetry proper. Among the shapes commonly represented in such poems have been axes, eggs, spears, altars, wings, columns, pyramids, diamonds, and other geometric figures. The chief agent in transmitting p. poetry from antiquity to modern times was the Planudean version of the *Gr. Anthology.* An extravagant instance of figure-poems is the *Musarum libri* (1628) of Baldassare Bonifacio, whose whole volume is devoted to the type. The first Eng. p. poems belong to the 16th c. (Stephen Hawes, 1509; Richard Willes, 1573; George Puttenham, 1589), though the best known is doubtless the *Easter Wings* of George Herbert. Modern practitioners of the form, or of related graphic devices, include Guillaume Apollinaire, Dylan Thomas, and E. E. Cummings. See also CONCRETE POETRY.—G. Puttenham, *The Arte of Eng. Poesie,* ed. G. Willcock and A. Walker (1936; Bk. 2); M. Church, "The First Eng. P. Poems," PMLA, 61 (1946); Wellek and Warren; A. L. Korn, "Puttenham and the Oriental P.-Poem," CL, 6 (1954). J.L.L.

PENTAMETER (Gr. "of 5 measures or feet") should mean a line of 5 measures. The term was actually applied in antiquity to a dactylospondaic line consisting of two equal parts (2½ + 2½ feet):

¯ ˘ ˘ ¯ ˘ ˘ ¯ ¯ ˘ ˘ ¯ ˘ ˘ ¯
In the Pen|tameter | aye || falling in | melody | back
(Coleridge)

The first 2 feet may be either dactyls or spondees; then comes a long syllable; the second half consists of 2 dactyls, followed by a long syllable. The division between the two halves is marked by a break between words; there must not be hiatus, elision, or *syllaba anceps* (short allowed to stand for long) at this position. The p. is normally the second part of the elegiac distich (q.v.), the first part of which is a hexameter. The classical p. should not be confused with the so-called Eng. p. (5-stress line), which is usually iambic and generally regular. See BLANK VERSE; HEROIC COUPLET.—Hardie; K. Rupprecht, *Einführung in die griechische Metrik* (1950); U. von Wilamowitz-Moellendorff, *Griechische Verskunst* (2d ed., 1958). W.B.

PERFECT, TRUE, OR FULL RHYME. The correspondence in accented syllables of the vowel-sound and the following consonant(s) but not of the consonant(s) before the vowel. It is single, duple, or triple: *Keats-beets, Shelley-jelly, Tennyson-venison* (J. C. Ransom's "Survey of Literature"). P.r. is the equivalent of Fr. *rime suffisante* (cf. *rime très riche, vaillant-travaillant,* in which the preceding vowel and consonant are also identical; *rime riche, éclaire-crépusculaire,* in which the preceding consonant is also identical; and *rime pauvre, ami-fini, mont-ton,* where the vowel stands alone or is followed by different unpronounced consonants; if the latter are pronounced, rhyme has weakened to assonance [q.v.]). The designation "perfect" points to the acceptance of varieties of rhyme not perfect, which may have been taken from Ir., Welsh, Icelandic, and other sources into Eng. to make up for the relative scarcity of perfect rhymes in the language, as contrasted with the abundance of such rhymes in other languages; the main varieties are consonance and near rhyme (qq.v.). P.r. has not, however, been displaced by these new devices, which remain still supplemental and not central. S.L.M.

PERIPHRASIS as a round-about way of naming something makes its meaning apparent by approximating a whole or partial definition. Quintilian distinguished two kinds, the euphemistic (as in the phrase "the Lord of Hosts" to signify God) and the descriptive (as in the phrase "the wandering stars" to signify planets. *Institutes* 7.6.59). The distinction is the fundamental one. Of the first kind are also those which are meant to weaken the thought of evil (the *absit omen* motif, as in the phrase "passing away" to signify death); the descriptive kind includes most of those which approximate the two-word definition in the combination of a specific with a general term ("the finny tribe" to signify fish). While widely used in biblical and Homeric literature, the development of p. as a truly important feature of poetic style begins with Lucretius and Virgil, and through their influence it became an important feature of epic and descriptive poetry throughout the Middle Ages and into the Renaissance. Its use in the earlier period, however, was possibly supported by the use of kenning (q.v.) in Germanic poetry. The practice of the *Pléiade* in the 16th c. gave periphrases a new vogue throughout Europe and led directly to the establishment in the late 17th and 18th c. of a whole battery of phrases many of which conformed to the growing interest in scientific definition (as in the phrase "liquid ambient" to signify water). Since the 18th c., the form has lost much of its prestige, and more often than not survives in inflated uses for purposes of humor, as it does in Dickens. In the history of rhetoric p. is most generally characterized as a trope, and its function has been best analyzed by Longinus, who shows how it serves the elevation of thought, and how by unfitting use it becomes gross and turgid (28–29).—E. Krantz, *Essai sur l'esthétique de Descartes* (1882); J. Arthos, *The Language of Natural Description in 18th C. Poetry* (1949). J.A.

PERSONIFICATION, as a manner of speech endowing things or abstractions with life, has been a feature of European poetry since Homer. Psychologically and rhetorically it may be described as "a means of taking hold of things which appear startlingly uncontrollable and independent" (T.B.L. Webster). But the famous personifications of Strength and Force in *Prometheus Bound* parallel and challenge the figures of gods in myths, and according to a theory now current, supported by Cassirer, Cornford, and others, personifications replace mythical figures when rational attitudes supersede the primitive imagination. This theory had an ancient presentation in the Stoic doctrine that abstractions in the form of personifications express demonic force.

In the early Christian and medieval ages the history of p. is closely associated with the rise of allegory (as in the *Psychomachia* of Prudentius, *The Romance of the Rose,* and *Piers Plowman*). It was almost equally important in the mingled development of mythological and romantic poetry in the Renaissance (Poliziano, Spenser). Here, too, as in Ariosto's descriptions of war and in Spenser's *Mutabilitie Cantos,* the personifications aspire to the power and automatism of mythical figures. Such is the central personification of Spenser's *Hymn to Love:*

> For Love is lord of truth and loyalty.

In the 18th c. personifications lost much of their emotional and quasi-mythical power to the degree that poetry subscribed to the vague anthropomorphism of deistic philosophy, but their vogue increased even as they themselves became, as in much nature poetry, barely more than abstractions. The development of symbolist poetry in the 19th c. largely smothered the use of p. as a figure in which the rational element is the determining character. But this kind has returned again to fashion in Auden (*At the Grave of Henry James*), while the more nearly mythological forms have been employed by Dylan Thomas (*The force that through the green fuse drives the flower*).

H. Usener, *Götternamen* (1896); J. Tambornino, *De antiquorum daemonismo* (1909); R. Hinks, *Myth and Allegory in Ancient Art* (1939); B. H. Bronson, "P. Reconsidered," ELH, 14 (1947); E. R. Wasserman, "The Inherent Values of 18th-C. P.," PMLA, 65 (1950); T.B.L. Webster, "P. as a Mode of Gr. Thought," JWCI, 17 (1954); C. F. Chapin, *P. in 18th-C. Eng. Poetry* (1955); N. Maclean, "P. but not Poetry," ELH, 23 (1956); Lausberg. J.A.

PHENOMENOLOGY. See POETRY, THEORIES OF (EXPRESSIVE THEORIES).

PHONETICS AND POETRY. See LINGUISTICS AND POETICS.

PITCH. Highness or lowness of tone. One of the four characteristics of a spoken sound, the others being duration (q.v.), loudness, and quality. P. is measured by the number of vibrations per second (8 to 30,000), is sometimes roughly described by the terms acute (high) and grave (low), and is often indicated by musical notation. A number of authorities hold that p. usually coincides with accent (q.v.) or that it is one of the constituents of accent. Despite controversy over the relation of p. to accent, most prosodists would agree that the management of p., in poetry, is one of the primary means of rhetorical emphasis or intensification.—Baum; K. M. Wilson, *Sound and Meaning in Eng. Poetry* (1930); D. Bolinger, "A Theory of P. Accent in Eng.," *Word,* 14 (1958). P.F.

PLOT may be defined as the pattern of events in a narrative or a drama, either in prose or in verse. *Plot* is the Eng. word commonly used to translate Aristotle's *mythos,* a term used in the *Poetics* to describe one of the six elements of tragedy. Aristotle gives *p.* a precise critical definition, assigns it the place of honor, and calls it "the first principle, and, as it were, the soul of a tragedy." The definition given in the *Poetics* has been the basis of almost all other considerations of p., either friendly or hostile.

The concept of p. has shifted from time to time in the history of criticism, as the critic's concern has been with the making of a work or with the responding to a work, with the creator or the spectator. Viewed in terms of the principles controlling the making of a work of art, p. has referred to action, to pattern, to structure or some variation of these elements; viewed in terms of the psychological and emotional response of the audience or reader, p. has referred to impression, to sense of unity, to purpose, or to some similar response. In terms of the latter view of p., any of many different elements may constitute the controlled affective quality of a work; it is essentially in terms of witness rather than creation that the critics of the contemporary Chicago school have attempted to broaden greatly the concept of p. (See paragraph below on "the Chicago school.") In the common usage of the term p., however, the sense of the making or shaping principle has been dominant in most criticism, and it is in that sense that this article treats the concept of p.

Aristotle called the p. "the imitation of the action (see IMITATION) as well as "the arrangement of the incidents." He demanded that the action imitated be "a whole," i.e., have a beginning: "that which does not itself follow anything by causal necessity, but after which something naturally is or comes to be"; a middle: "that which follows something as some other thing follows it"; and an end: "that which itself naturally follows some other thing, either by necessity, or as a rule, but has nothing following it." He asked that a p. have unity, i.e., that it "imitate one action and that a whole, the structural union of the parts being such that, if any one of them is displaced or removed, the whole will be disjointed and disturbed." These well-knit plots he opposed to episodic plots "in which the acts succeed one another without probable or necessary sequence." He also distinguished between simple and complex plots, a simple p. being one in which a change of fortune takes place without Reversal of the Situation and without Recognition, and a complex p. being one in which the change of fortune is accompanied by a Reversal or by a Recognition or by both. The Reversal is a change by which the action veers round to its opposite, and a Recognition is a change from ignorance to knowledge. These should both arise, he says, from "the internal structure of the plot, so that what follows should be the necessary or probable result of the preceding action." Therefore, Aristotle's test for sound plotting appears to be "whether any given event is a case of *propter hoc* or *post hoc*." This emphasis on causality is central to the Aristotelian concept, yet he also argued against a mechanic art, declaring that "a single action, whole and complete, with a beginning, a middle, and an end will "resemble a living organism in all its unity." There is much to be said for Humphry House's view that the episode or incident is for Aristotle the means by which the plot is realized. Aristotle's statement that, having found his story, the poet "should first sketch its general outline, and then fill in the episodes and amplify in detail," House would translate "should first sketch its general outline, and then *episodize*" (*Aristotle's Poetics,* 1956). Aristotle asserted that the poet "should be a maker of plot . . . since he is a maker because he imitates, and what he imitates are actions." House asserts that "episodizing"—i.e., realizing the plot in terms of incidents—"is the essential activity of the poet as the maker."

The distinction between story and p. is a difficult one to make. E. M. Forster says that ". . . a story [is] a narrative of events arranged in their time-sequence. A plot is also a narrative of events, the emphasis falling on causality" (*Aspects of the Novel,* 1927). Story, he believes, arouses only curiosity; whereas p. demands intelligence and memory. House is illuminating on this distinction; he says: "There is first a rambling and amorphous 'story,' often taken over from tradition or picked up from some other extraneous source . . . and then comes the serious business of *making* it into a play or an epic." This *making* is essentially the making of *story* into *plot.*

The superiority which Aristotle assigns p. over character has been a matter of great debate, with most critics since the early 19th c. defending active character as the dynamic aspect of narrative or drama and p. as the mechanic aspect. Edward J. O'Brien, writing on the short story, says: "The plot of a story is structural. . . . The action of a story, as contrasted with the plot, is a matter of dynamics. . . . Plot is merely a means to an end" (*The Short Story Case Book,* 1935). Probably the best and certainly the most graceful of the mediators between these positions is Henry James, who says: "I cannot imagine composition existing in a series of blocks, nor conceive, in any novel worth discussing at all, of a passage of description that is not in its intention narrative, a passage of dialogue that is not in its intention descriptive, a touch of truth of any sort that does not partake of the nature of incident, or an incident that derives its interest from any other source than the general and only source of the success of a work of art—that of being illustrative. . . . What is character but the determination of incident? What is incident but the illustration of character" ("The Art of Fiction," 1884). James's term *illustrative* appears to be his rough equivalent of *imitation.*

The critics of "the Chicago school" have attempted greatly to extend this organic view of p. Ronald S. Crane says: "The form of a given plot is a function of the particular correlation among . . . three variables which the completed work is calculated to establish, consistently and progressively, in our minds." The variables are: "(1) the general estimate we are induced to form . . . of the moral character and deserts of the hero . . . ; (2) the judgments we are led similarly to make about the nature of the events that actually befall the hero . . . as having either painful or pleasurable consequences for him . . . permanently or temporarily; and (3) the opinions we are made to entertain concerning the degree and kind of his responsibility for what happens to him . . ." (*Critics and Criticism,* 1952). Paul Goodman, also of the Chicago school, considers "Any system of parts that carries over, continuous and changing, from the beginning to the end" a p., and he applies the definition even to short poetry, making it refer to rhythm, diction, and imagery, as well as incidents" (*The Structure of Literature,* 1954).

The various views of p. have in common an attention to arrangement or pattern or structure. For all critics "pattern" seems a minimal definition; and for almost all of them "pattern of events" is a primary description, however much more than this they may also wish to include. Clearly an episode in itself does not make a p.; equally clearly the presence of two or more episodes does not make a p.; the concept of p. refers to a relationship—and an implied causality—among episodes. We may conclude, therefore, that p. is an intellectual formulation about the relationship existing among the incidents of a drama or a narrative, and that it is, therefore, a guiding principle for the author and an ordering control for the reader. It is something perceived by the reader as giving structure and unity to the work. And herein lies, perhaps, one of the greatest difficulties; for, as Percy Lubbock has argued, it is difficult for a reader to hold the pieces of a drama or a narrative in his mind and almost impossible to retain the total work firmly enough in mind to examine its informing and unifying principle (*The Craft of Fiction,* 1921).

This difficulty is illustrated by an examination of a special type of narrative structure, the framework story, i.e., the kind of work in which a narrative or a group of narratives is set within a larger controlling frame. The question of when the frame becomes a p. itself or even a portion of the p. is a delicate one. Boccaccio's *Decameron,* a collection of tales told by a group in special circumstances, has no narrative frame p. at all, for nothing is presented of the circumstances out of which the tales come. Chaucer's *Canterbury Tales* clearly has a narrative in its frame—the pilgrims are realized as persons, the pattern of a journey is given, a contest within this journey is presented, and the tales themselves at least in part grow out of the events which occur in this framework. Yet the *Canterbury Tales* can hardly be said to have a framework p. in the sense in which p. has been described in this essay. In some cases the framework does become a p., as, for example, in Melville's *Moby-Dick,* where the narrator has his own problem and the action dealing with Ahab becomes in a sense an element in this problem. On the other hand, one might argue that the *Faerie Queene,* had it been completed, would have had no real p., but rather a conceptualized allegorical structure. This is a kind of structure which raises another critical question about p.

Many critics have suggested that theme or philosophical concept is or may be the basis of p. Now certainly the action being imitated in a p. should not be stripped of its rich complexity; yet it must be asserted that the raw materials of plots are conflicts and actions, not concepts and philosophical statements. Even in an allegory we do not think of the p. in terms of the conceptualized abstractions represented by the characters but rather in terms of the characters and their actions broadly independent of the conceptualizations that they represent. Thus, if we give a plot summary of *Everyman* similar to Aristotle's summary of the *Odyssey,* in which no names are attached to the actors, we are carried further away from rather than closer to the abstract statement beneath the play. P. may be a formulation by which the author of an allegory translates his concepts into dramatic or narrative terms, but it does not itself partake of the concept which is expressed through it.

Thus we are pointed back toward a view of p. as the controlling and unifying principle of action in a work. It is helpful to think of p. as a "planned series of interrelated actions progressing, because of the interplay of one force upon another, through a struggle of opposing forces to a climax and a *dénouement*" (W. F. Thrall, A. Hibbard and C. H. Holman, *A Handbook to Literature,* rev. ed., 1960). Here the emphasis is on conflict as the unifying principle of action. Basically there are four kinds of conflict which may be made the basis of a p.: man against the forces of nature, man against his fellowman, man against himself, and man against some conceptualized or personalized aspect of the order of things, such as Fate or Destiny or Nemesis.

If viewed in terms of the basic conflict, the elements of a p. are: (1) The *Exposition,* i.e., the establishing of the situation within which the conflict develops. This exposition is frequently delayed until after the conflict has gotten underway and then given piecemeal. (2) The *Initiating Action,* i.e., the event which brings the opposing forces into conflict. (3) *The Rising Action,* i.e., the separate events which advance the conflict to its crucial point at which the protagonist in the conflict takes, consciously or unconsciously, the action which determines the future course of the conflict irrevocably. It is possible for this action of the protagonist to be a failure to act, as in the scene where Hamlet fails to kill Claudius at prayer. This decisive point is called the *crisis,* for upon it the action turns. It frequently, but by no means always, coincides with the *climax,* which is the point of highest interest. Crisis refers to structure; climax to emotional response. (4) The *Falling Action,* i.e., the incidents and episodes in which the force destined to be victorious establishes its supremacy. (5) The *Dénouement* or conclusion, i.e., the incidents or episode in which the conflict called forth by the initiating action is irremediably resolved. The unified p. may be considered to make an upward spiral, in that the resolution of the conflict returns us to a situation similar in its repose or the balance of its forces but not in their exact nature or alignment to that presented in the exposition.

S. H. Butcher, Aristotle's *Theory of Poetry and Fine Art, The Poetics* and ch. 9 (4th ed., 1911); P. Lubbock, *The Craft of Fiction* (1921); E. Muir, *The Structure of the Novel* (1928); C. H. Grabo, *The Technique of the Novel* (1928); J. W. Linn and H. W. Taylor, *A Foreword to Fiction* (1935; ch. 5); W. F. Thrall, A. Hibbard and C. H. Holman, *A Handbook to Lit.* (1936; rev. ed. 1960); H.D.F. Kitto, *Gr. Tragedy* (1939); F. Fergusson, *The Idea of a Theater* (1949); R. A. Brower, "The Heresy of P.," EIE *1951* (1952); R. S. Crane, "The Concept of P. and the P. of Tom Jones," *Critics and Crit. Ancient and Modern* (1952); P. Goodman, *The Structure of Lit.* (1954); H. House, *Aristotle's Poetics* (1956); W. C. Booth, *The Rhetoric of Fiction* (1961); E. Olson, *Tragedy and the Theory of Drama* (1961); J. Jones, *On Aristotle and Gr. Tragedy* (1962); R. Lattimore, *Story Patterns in Gr. Tragedy* (1964). C.H.H.

POET LAUREATE. About to be seized by Apollo, Daphne turns into a laurel tree. Apollo takes the laurel for his emblem, and decrees that its branch or bay shall become the prize of honor for poets and victors. (Ovid, *Metamorphoses* 1.) The line from Apollo to the Eng. poets l. follows the custom of kings and chieftains of maintaining a court poet to sing heroic and glorious achievement. The Scandinavian skald, the Welsh bard, and the Anglo-Saxon scop resembled the poets l. in being attached to a ruler's court and serving his purposes. Professional entertainers like William I's *ioculator regis* or Henry I's *mimus regis* develop into the *versificator regis* who is part of Henry III's royal household in England. The *versificator* suggests an official l. not only by his regular payment in money and wine, but in being ridiculed as were Jonson, Davenant, Eusden, Cibber, Pye, and even Tennyson later on. The actual term "l." arose in the medieval universities which crowned with laurel a student admitted to an academic degree in grammar, rhetoric, and poetry. In time the word applied to any notable poetic attainment, and was used as a standard compliment to Chaucer, and more formally, Petrarch. In a tradition of loosely bestowing the title "l." we find the names of Gower, Lydgate, Skelton, and Bernard Andreas, the Augustinian friar who, under Henry VII, anticipated Dryden's later double appointment as court poet and historiographer royal. Spenser, Drayton, and Daniel shared in various forms of court activity receiving official recognition, while Ben Jonson, a successful court entertainer and panegyrist, thought of himself as a formal l., having received two pensions and much popular acclaim. Davenant seems to have enjoyed a tacit recognition as poet l. under both Charles I and II, but held no official patent. The office was finally authorized with the appointment of John Dryden as the first "poet l." in 1668, and historiographer royal in 1670. The two offices were separated in 1692, and the emolument of l. was fixed at £100 a year where it has in effect remained ever since.

Since Dryden's removal in 1688, fourteen men have been chosen poet l. in succession as follows: Thomas Shadwell, 1689–92; Nahum Tate, 1692–1715; Nicholas Rowe, 1715–18; Laurence Eusden, 1718–30; Colley Cibber, 1730–57; William Whitehead, 1757–85; Thomas Warton, 1785–90; Henry James Pye, 1790–1813; Robert Southey, 1813–43; William Wordsworth, 1843–50; Alfred Tennyson, 1850–92; Alfred Austin, 1896–1913; Robert Bridges, 1913–30; John Masefield, 1930–67. A number of poets have sought the laureateship in vain, including Johnson's friend Richard Savage the "volunteer l.," William Mason, Leigh Hunt, and Lewis Morris when, after Tennyson, a period of four years elapsed without a choice being made. The position has likewise been refused by Gray, Scott, Wordsworth once before accepting it, and Samuel Rogers on the death of Wordsworth.

Traditionally the laureate's duty was to write eulogies, elegies, and other celebrations of important events. In this sense, Tennyson's *Ode on the Death of the Duke of Wellington* (1852) emerges as the ideal performance. In practice, the laureateship from its beginning with Dryden falls into three periods. Dryden, Shadwell and Tate had no stated duties, and could make of the office what they chose. In Dryden's case this was to speak brilliantly and with entire conviction for the royal cause, making *Absalom and Achitophel* in its way the ideal laureate's poem. In the early 18th c., the l. became a member of the royal household, charged with writing annually a New Year's Ode and a Birthday Ode, to be set to music and sung before the king. The office became something of a joke, until the annual odes were abandoned in the tenure of Southey. The modern phase has restored dignity to the position, with Wordsworth symbolically, and Tennyson actively standing for the best that poetry is capable of. Paradoxically, however, the laureateship will suffer until the poet is free of any subservience to the very court that first sustained him; likewise the notion of immediate continuity should be abandoned. If the laureateship ceases to be an office which must be filled as soon as it is vacant, it may gain dignity by waiting until a poet of high order is chosen. Then the difference between what it could be and what in fact it has been will diminish. (See especially E. K. Broadus, *The Laureateship*, 1921, pp. 216–18.)—W. S. Austin, Jr., and J. Ralph, *The Lives of the Poets L.* (1853); W. Hamilton, *The Poets L. of England* (1879); K. West, *The Laureates of England from Ben Jonson to Alfred Tennyson* (1895); W. F. Gray, *The Poets L. of England* (1914); K. Hopkins, *The Poets L.* (1955). B.N.S.

POETIC CONTRACTIONS. See METRICAL TREATMENT OF SYLLABLES.

POETIC DICTION. CRITICAL THEORY. The phrase "p.d." begins to assume importance in Eng. literature about the 19th c., when the Preface to Wordsworth's *Lyrical Ballads* (2d ed. 1800) raised the question whether the language of poetry was essentially different from that of prose. In that Preface Wordsworth is as much concerned to discredit the conventional use of words and phrases long associated with meter as to vindicate the genuine language of passion. P.d. therefore generally means, in Wordsworth's criticism, false p.d., a fact indicated by the author himself in his statement, "There is little in [*Lyrical Ballads*] of what is usually called poetic diction" (*Preface,* 1800). The ambiguity of the phrase has persisted to the present day, for to some writers p.d. means the collection of epithets, periphrases, archaisms, etc., which were common property to most poets of the 18th c., while to others p.d. means the specifically poetic words and phrases which express the imaginative and impassioned nature of poetry. Thus a book entitled *Poetic Diction,* by Thomas Quayle (1924), has the subtitle *A Study of Eighteenth Century Verse,* while in another book, also entitled *Poetic Diction,* by Owen Barfield (1928, 2d ed., 1952), the author says, in his opening passage, "When words are selected and arranged in such a way that their meaning either arouses or is obviously intended to arouse, aesthetic imagination, the result may be described as *poetic diction.*" On a broad view, Barfield's use of the term must appear as the correct one: any special or limited application of it should be indicated by the use of some qualifying word or phrase.

The earliest instance of "diction," given in the OED, in the sense it bears on "p.d." occurs in Dryden's *Fables* (1700): "The first beauty of an Epic poem consists in diction, that is, in the choice of words, and harmony of numbers." "Diction" thus corresponds to the *lexis* of Gr. critics.

The history of the critical theory of p.d. as such is not extensive, for the subject does not much lend itself to discussion in general terms, most of the criticism being found in articles on individual poets. The few sentences of a general nature in Aristotle's *Poetics* are, however, extremely pregnant. The passage, translated by Ingram Bywater, is as follows:

"The perfection of Diction is for it to be at once clear and not mean. The clearest indeed is that made up of the ordinary words for things, but it is mean, as is shown by the poetry of Cleophon and Sthenelus. On the other hand, the diction becomes distinguished and non-prosaic by the use of unfamiliar terms, i.e. strange words, metaphors, lengthened forms, and everything that deviates from the ordinary modes of speech . . . A certain admixture, accordingly, of unfamiliar terms is necessary. These, the strange word, the metaphor, the ornamental equivalent, etc., will save the language from seeming mean and prosaic, while the ordinary words in it will secure the requisite clearness."

It might have been expected that Aristotle's successors among the Gr. critics, many of whom had an acute appreciation of poetic style, would have developed and applied the principles admirably stated in this passage. But instead, this branch of criticism was left to rhetoric, which claimed to offer rules for poetic as well as oratorical diction under the heading of style (*lexis, elocutio*). (*See* RHETORIC AND POETICS.) Rhetoric remained a determining influence on conventional p.d. from about the 1st c. A.D. until the end of the 18th c. The influence of rhetoric is best seen in the long and elaborate lists of figures of speech in works like the *Rhetorica ad Herennium* and Cicero's *De Inventione,* and in their medieval and Renaissance counterparts such as the *Poetria Nova* of Geoffrey of Vinsauf (ca. 1150) or the *Arcadian Rhetorike* of Abraham Fraunce (1590). Generally speaking, rhetoric emphasized the artificial and ornamental aspects of p.d.

In L. criticism there is even less discussion of p.d. than in Gr. The caution of the Roman mind, enforced no doubt by the L. disposition to consider design and general effect rather than the details of execution, led the critics to assume a somewhat aloof attitude towards the ornaments of poetic style. While few of the world's poets have had such skill in the magical use of words as Virgil, the critics, like practical gardeners, concerned themselves with the nature of the soil from which these flowers of speech might best spring. One pronouncement on the subject which might be quoted as the essence of sober classicism was the dictum of Horace: "Cui lecta potenter erit res, nec facundia deseret hunc nec lucidus ordo" (Whosoever shall choose a theme within his range, neither speech will fail him, nor clearness of order—*Ars poetica* 40–41, tr. H. Rushton Fairclough). According to this view, conception is the great thing: execution may be left to take care of itself. There is an almost puritanical austerity in the Horatian critics, who appear as disciplinarians against the inclinaton of poets to luxuriate in verbal extravagance.

The revival of poetry in the Middle Ages was marked by a close concern among poets with the technique of expression. They were interested in general questions of language as well as the art of versification. Short works on these matters by Prov. and Catalan poets survive, and this activity culminates in the L. treatise of Dante, *De Vulgari Eloquentia.* This work is of great importance in the history of both literature and language, and it is highly significant to find the poet discriminating between various Romance dialects, finally giving his preference to Tuscan on the score of euphony and "significance." Yet the very breadth of Dante's view (and its date) precludes that specialized discussion which marks the criticism of p.d. in the strict sense. Dante, like his medieval predecessors, is concerned with the "lingua d'arte," and his view embraces both poetry and rhetoric. He is concerned with the creation of a literary language rather than a specifically poetic one and pays little or no heed to the distinction between prose and poetry which is fundamental to the nature of p.d.

Critical thought during both the Middle Ages and the Renaissance was much concerned with the "lingua d'arte," but it viewed the matter rather in terms of rhetoric than of poetry. During the later Middle Ages and after, poetry came to be regarded as little more than a subdivision of rhetoric, and poets themselves were known as "rethors" or "rhétoriqueurs." This new emphasis fortunately came after the time of Chaucer, whose position as one of the creators of Eng. p.d. is not sufficiently recognized: he was as clearly conscious of the distinction between poetry and prose, as between poetry and rhetoric. The emphasis on rhetoric coincided with a barren period of Eng. poetry, when style was first marked by "aureate" extravagance, and later by the "drabness" (to borrow Professor C. S. Lewis's word) of versifiers who abandoned verbal ornament to their contemporaries in the sphere of prose. Strong traces of the assimilation of poetry to rhetoric appear in much Elizabethan criticism.

For reasons already noticed, the Horatian critics were disinclined to isolate p.d. as an important subject for discussion, though in Johnson's *Lives* there are many acute comments on the diction of particular poets. But in Gray's letter to his friend West (1742), there is a passage indicative of a new approach to the subject: the following sentences are original to an extent not easily appreciated today:

"The language of the age is never the language of poetry; except among the French, whose verse, where the thought or image does not support it, differs in nothing from prose. Our poetry, on the contrary, has a language peculiar to itself; to which almost every one, that has written, has added something by enriching it with foreign idioms and derivatives: nay, sometimes with words of their own composition or invention. Shakespeare and Milton have been great creators this way; and no one more licentious than Pope or Dryden, who perpetually borrow expressions from the former. . . ."

Not long after this a contribution to the *British Magazine* (1762) anticipated a future form of criticism by a detailed examination of verbal effects drawn from many authors. The paper, "On Poetry, as Distinguished from Other Writing," contains some discriminating comments on the "figurative" and "emphatical" qualities of p.d., with apt illustrations from Gr., L., and Eng. poetry.

A revival of interest in the treatise on the Sublime attributed to Longinus had far-reaching effects on poetry and criticism in the 18th c. The treatise was translated into Fr. in 1674 by Boileau, who defined "sublimity" as the quality "qui fait qu'un ouvrage enlève, ravit, transporte." The name of "Longinus" constantly appears in the writings of Eng. critics from Dryden onwards. Addison familiarized his readers with the notion that Milton was the poet of the Sublime, *par excellence*. "Longinus" was frequently appealed to, in the 18th c., against the neoclassical standard of "correctness," and "sublimity" was thus associated with a poetic style and diction which were daring, irregular, romantic. Passages in Thomson's *Seasons* which excited awe or terror were admired as "sublime." The odes of Gray, especially *The Bard,* were "sublime." In critical writings later than the 18th c. the term "sublime" tended to be replaced by others, e.g., the "grand style."

One of the most important documents on our subject is the *Preface* (1800) to Wordsworth's *Lyrical Ballads*, already mentioned. The views of this work are expressed in exaggerated terms and they are at variance with Wordsworth's own practice in most of his best poetry. Yet it remains the most comprehensive and impassioned utterance ever made by a great poet on this vital aspect of his art. Behind the *Preface* lies the conviction of the superiority of the natural to the artificial, and its main doctrines are contained in two theses: that *true* p.d. is natural, and that *false* p.d. is artificial. Wordsworth, who emphasizes the human character of the poet, considers the genuine language of passion to be itself poetical, meter being merely a "superadded" though desirable element. "The poet is a man speaking to men." On the other hand, all the conventional expressions associated with meter (faded classicism, "stock" epithets, verse equivalents for the living words of real emotion) which had accumulated over a century or more of "classical" writing create a barrier between the poet and his audience, and are to be discarded as artificial. Nor have they any justification in theory. "There neither is, nor can be any *essential* difference between the language of prose and metrical composition."

It was principally the implication of this last sentence that impelled Coleridge in his *Biographia Literaria* (chs. 14–22) to complement and correct the views of Wordsworth's *Preface*. Coleridge, with a vast range of reading to support him, appeals to the nature of meter as an outward token that the poet, in accepting its stimulus and discipline, intends to use a language differing in spirit and purpose from that of ordinary life. Poetic language is more nearly universal, more impassioned, more imaginative than other forms of utterance, and its purpose is to give aesthetic pleasure in itself as well as through "what" it expresses. Admitting that there is a "neutral style" common to prose and poetry, Coleridge finds it "a singular and noticeable fact . . . that a theory which would establish the *lingua communis* not only as the best, but as the only commendable style, should have proceeded from a poet, whose diction, next to that of Shakespeare and Milton, appears to me of all others the most *individualized* and characteristic" (*Biographia Literaria,* ch. 20). He makes a further important point in his criticism of some lines by Wordsworth in which the words, considered separately, are admittedly in everyday use; "but," he asks, "are those words *in those places* commonly employed in real life to express the same thought or outward thing? Are they the style used in the ordinary intercourse of spoken words? No! nor are the modes of connections; and still Less the breaks and transitions" (*ibid.*). The whole tendency of Coleridge's arguments is to maintain the right of the poet to create a diction strongly marked by the character of his own mind, within the laws which determine the general nature and use of language.

Wordsworth, in his attacks on false p.d., and Coleridge, in his vindication of true p.d., laid down the principles and prepared the way for much valuable criticism in the 19th and 20th c. Many authors who have written excellent studies of the diction of individual poets, e.g., J. W. Mackail, Walter Raleigh, Oliver Elton, Alfred Noyes, E. de Selincourt, Ethel Seaton, Geoffrey Tillotson, George Rylands, while contributing much from their own studies, have not sought to modify the fundamental principles established by the two poet-critics.

An especially constructive contribution to the theory of p.d. is Owen Barfield's *Poetic Diction.* Barfield holds that there are naturally poetic periods of language before the birth of a distinction between poetry and prose. Language being then predominantly concrete, and meanings not yet split up, there are properly speaking, no "metaphors," which are the revolt "... primary 'meanings' were *given,* as it were, by Nature, but the very condition of their being given was that they could not at the same time be apprehended in full consciousness; they could not be *known,* but only experienced, or lived. At this time, therefore, individuals cannot be said to have been responsible for the production of poetic values. . . . A history of language written, not from the logician's, but from the poet's point of view, would proceed somewhat in the following manner: it would see in the concrete vocabulary which has left us the mythologies the world's first 'poetic diction.' Moving forward, it would come, after a long interval, to the earliest ages of which we have any written record—the time of the *Vedas,* in India, the time of the *Iliad* and *Odyssey* in Greece. And at this stage it would find meaning still suffused with myth, and Nature all alive in the thinking of man. . . . The gods are never far below the surface of Homer's language—hence its unearthly sublimity." Barfield then describes the character of p.d. when meanings are "splitting up . . . and language beginning . . . to lose its intrinsic life." He notes the birth of hitherto unknown antitheses, such as those between truth and myth, between prose and poetry, and again between an objective and a subjective world. "Poetry has now passed from the 'fluid' to the 'architectural' type, and in many characteristic works the aesthetic effect corresponds to a sense of difficulties overcome. . . . In Horace's *Sapphics* and *Alcaics* the architectural element practically reaches its zenith. And again if we turn to the history of English, I do not think that we find this architectural element at all pronounced until the 17th c. It strikes us, for instance, in Milton and the metaphysicals, and frequently afterwards, but hardly in Chaucer or Shakespeare." The whole of Barfield's book is an important challenge to the view of Jespersen, and other philologists, to whom "progress in language . . . is synonymous with an increasing ability to think abstract thoughts."

The Diction of Eng. Poetry. OE poetry possessed an elaborate p.d. which was closely linked with the alliterative meter then in use. It included kennings or periphrases (e.g., *swanrād,* "swan's-road," or "sea"), compound epithets (e.g., *fāmigheals,* "foamy-necked"), and mythological allusions. The new rhyming measures introduced from Fr. after the Norman Conquest fostered the creation of a "verse diction" abounding in clichés. Its worst features are amusingly parodied in Chaucer's *Sir Topas.* But Chaucer also developed in his more serious poetry the elements of a distinctively p.d., e.g., the use of mythological names such as *Flora, Zephirus* (*The Book of the Duchesse,* 402); decorative compound epithets such as *golden-tressed* (*Troilus and Criseyde,* 5.8), *laurel-crouned* (*Anelida and Arcite,* 43); and picturesque metaphorical verbs such as *unneste* ("fly out of the nest") (*Troilus and Criseyde,* 4.305). And sometimes there is a phrase modeled on one from Dante to remind us how the new It. style in poetry (*dolce stil nuovo*) stimulated in Chaucer the ambition to draw higher and more imaginative effects from his native tongue. An example is: "Al the orient laugheth of the light" (*The Knight's Tale,* 1494) adapted from "Faceva tutto rider l'oriente" (*Purgatorio,* i.20).

In the Poetry of Spenser, especially in *The Faerie Queene,* may be found all the chief elements of that nondramatic diction of poetry which has constituted one of the main traditions in Eng. literature. More than any other man Spenser established by the spell of his example the right of poets to draw upon words and phrases outside those of contemporary speech. As E. de Selincourt says: "He cherished words which though still in use were rapidly passing out of fashion, and the sustained colouring and atmosphere of his style is thus given by a constant use of words which are found in Marlowe, Shakespeare, or Sydney, perhaps once or twice. 'Eftsoons,' 'ne,' 'als,' 'whilom,' 'uncouth,' 'wight,' 'eke,' 'sithens,' 'ywis'—it is words like these continually woven into the texture of his diction which, even more than the Chaucerian or romance elements, give it the Spenserian colour" (Oxford *Spenser,* Introduction by E. de Selincourt). Few Eng. poets have been as archaistic as Spenser, but a select number of archaisms have colored the diction of most nondramatic Eng. poets, almost up to the present time. Spenser also cultivated epithets as an enrichment of style, occasionally filling a whole line with them, as in his description of Britain as a

"saluage wildernesse,
Unpeopled, unmanurd, unprou'd, unpraysd"
(*Faerie Queene* 2.10.5)

His compound epithets are more numerous and memorable than Chaucer's, and are of various kinds: the morally serious (e.g., *hart-murdring* love: *F Q.* 2.5.16); the picturesque (e.g., *firie-footed* teeme: *ibid.* 1.12.2); the classical (e.g., *rosy fingred* Morning: *ibid.* 1.2.7). Spenser's epithets were the model and inspiration of much brilliant work in Marlowe, Chatterton, Keats, Tennyson, and others, and are no less important than his conservatism which seemed bent on preserving all from the past that could still be made current.

The greatness of Shakespeare as a poet gives him a primary place in this survey. Dramatic dialogue must above all things appear unpremeditated: the archaic and literary qualities of Spenser's diction remove it far from "the real language of men." Shakespeare as a poet could not escape the influence of Spenser, and some of his earlier work (e.g., *Romeo and Juliet* and *A Midsummer Night's Dream*) contain passages of rich Spenserian "color." But his mature dramatic needs required that he should develop an extreme suppleness of diction answering to a vast range of characters and passions. The grammatical licenses permitted by Elizabethan usage were effectively exploited by Shakespeare at an early date in his career. For instance, we find him using two variations on the word "king" in a couple of lines in *Richard II:* "Then am I king'd again: and by and by / Think that I am unking'd by Bolingbroke." These and similar licenses, when put to the service of Shakespeare's power of metaphor, produce that astonishing flexibility of style which matures in *Hamlet* and reappears again and again as late as *The Tempest.* The vivid metaphor of the noun-as-verb in Horatio's phrase "It harrows me with fear and wonder" is typical of Shakespeare's maturely developed diction.

During the period about 1620–60 Eng. poetry divides into three major schools. The neoclassical school as represented by Ben Jonson revived the Horatian ideals of decorum, restraint, and neatness, or "curiosa felicitas." Donne and his followers among the metaphysicals valued a more elaborate diction marked by complex structure, allusion, and elaborate, often obscure metaphor. The most gifted Spenserian of the age was Milton, but the poems he wrote before 1660, exquisitely worded though they are, could not have given him the commanding place which is his in the history of p.d. In *Paradise Lost* he created a genuine epic diction. Its chief features are: use of Latinate vocabulary and syntax, emphasis on sound effects, use of classical and Hebraic allusions, use of epic simile, and subordination of blank verse line to verse paragraph.

Between 1660 and 1700 the prevailing tendency was toward simplicity seasoned by wit: the powerful secular forces of the age fostered a rational and combative diction, which, as Dryden said, was "fittest for discourse and nearest prose." But in his later years Dryden became more sensitive to the beauty of verbal ornament. In his translation of Virgil and in the *Fables, Ancient and Modern* his links with Spenser are evident. He revives or adapts many old words and expressions for their poetic color. His critical remarks helped to transmit his admiration of Milton and Spenser to the next century.

The complex pattern of 18th-c. poetry includes one dominant motif—the rivalry between the "way of Pope" and the "way of Dryden." Pope, who opened his career with a display of verbal ornament gathered from his reading of Milton and others, achieved his greatest success in the wise and witty *Moral Essays, Satires,* and *Epistles,* in which the diction is close to the best contemporary prose usage. The style and diction of Pope were so congenial to the neoclassical temper of the age that they established themselves, in the eyes of many, e.g., Johnson, as the last word in the art of poetry. Yet even at the height of Pope's reputation there survived a memory of the warmer, more colored, more wayward, and less rigid diction of Spenser, and this was imitated in the work of such professed Spenserians as Thomson, Shenstone, and—somewhat later—Beattie. The fuller and freer tradition of diction was maintained by Gray and by other learned poets such as T. Warton, who had read widely in Eng. poetry and knew how limited was Pope's mastery of diction (however perfect in its way) in comparison with the "pomp and prodigality" of Shakespeare and Milton (Gray, *Stanzas to Mr. Bentley*). The last quarter of the century witnessed the vindication of dialect as a medium of poetry in the work of Burns, and the development of a mixed style, between poetry and rhapsody, undisciplined by meter, in the earlier Prophetic Books of William Blake.

At no time in the history of Eng. poetry does diction play a more vital part than in the work of the romantic poets from Wordsworth to Keats, nor has there ever been more fruitful discussion of the subject. In Wordsworth, two impulses are evident: opposition to the "inane phraseology" of the more lifeless verse of the time—personifications, clichés, trite mythology, and the like; and an impassioned love of simple words and the poetic effects latent within them, as in the celebrated line in *Michael:* "And never lifted up a single stone." Wordsworth's love of plain language, however, does not preclude the frequent borrowing of apt phrases from other poets: his diction is, in fact, more literary than is commonly recognized. Coleridge's original achievement in diction was to raise the style of the ballad to a high poetic level, and in *Kubla Khan* to bring language to the verge of its frontier with music. Byron's diction, in general, is somewhat wanting in precision and the finer qualities, but in *Don Juan* he produced a diction, which has the ease of prose but often rises to brilliant satiric and lyric effects. The diction of Shelley clearly reflects the notions expressed in his *Defence of Poetry*. Two statements are particularly important: that poets are the true creators of language, and that "composition" can never do full justice to "inspiration." Shelley's ideal diction emanates from the primal creative elements of nature, from sunlight and from the ether, but in practice Shelley's writing is often vague and abstract. Keats, on the other hand, stressed concrete, visual description and appeal to sense (especially sight, sound, and smell); and his diction owes much to Spenser and Milton. Keats has no superior in the intense picturesqueness of his best descriptions, and at the same time he often employs language with a mythopoeic power, in which the spirit of Gr. poetry reappears with a subtle modernization.

The achievement in diction by these early 19th-c. writers is the highest attained in Eng. poetry since the age of Shakespeare. Their successors were in a difficult position. Though they were men of high poetic ability, the way to originality was less clear than it had been among the excitements and dangers of the previous age. Tennyson, a consummate artist in diction, had an almost unrivaled versatility. Those who are familiar with the grace, power, and picturesque elegance of his better-known poems should not overlook his equal success in dialect. What is most novel in Browning's diction is his use of a contemporary colloquial idiom in short dramatic lyrics and in the much longer dramatic monologues.

The decline in the poetic quality of "poetic" language in Browning is symptomatic of a change affecting nearly the whole of Eng. poetry for some eighty years. Within that period may be distinguished three main attitudes on the subject of diction. The first is that of the poets to whom the traditional diction of poetry was still a suitable vehicle for poetry. To this group belong such poets as Swinburne, Francis Thomson, Robert Bridges in his earlier work, A. E. Housman, Mrs. Meynell, Rupert Brooke, Walter de la Mare, and John Masefield. The second attitude is that of the poets who respected the traditional diction, but felt that it must be vigorously rejuvenated in a changed and changing world. Fresh vitality might be infused by bold experiments in diction itself, or by novel effects in meter and rhythm. Thus, G. M. Hopkins handled his epithets in a manner suggesting "a passionate emotion which seems to try and utter all its words in one" (Charles Williams); he also enlivened his verse by what he called "sprung rhythm." Robert Bridges, the associate of Hopkins, increasingly felt the need for novel effects of diction and rhythm: in his late poem, *The Testament of Beauty*, he employed "loose Alexandrines" in which scientific and philosophical terms are woven into the older fabric of traditional diction. A concerted but less vigorous effort to rejuvenate the diction of the past was made by the group of writers associated under the title of "Georgian poets." Writers outside Great Britain often revived the older diction by expressions peculiar to their native custom and landscape. Thus Am. poets had long engrafted new local terms of their own on the traditional stock of Eng. p.d., a method used by a succession of writers from Longfellow to Robert Frost. The Ir. school of poets to which W. B. Yeats belonged did the same, with a more considered program. "Rejuvenation" also came to diction through the experiences of World War I, especially in the work of Wilfred Owen. The third attitude cannot be precisely distinguished from the second, but it is connected with the rise of free verse (q.v.). When metrical regularity disappears in an unlimited "freedom," the distinction between the poetic and the nonpoetic is blurred. Whitman's diction, for example, is powerful and original, but it is also crude and (often intentionally) prosaic. The conditions which made Whitman acceptable in 19th-c. America were reproduced in an acute form in postwar England. The revolutionary spirit in diction appears in the work of Eliot and Auden, and, a little later, in Dylan Thomas who (says Anne Ridler, herself a poet) "treats words as though he were present at their creation." Nonetheless, there is a widespread instinct to distrust "revolutionary" writers as models, however much their individual work may be admired. The life of poetry is continuous. There is abundant ground for holding that the consensus of opinion among many good poets now writing is in favor, not of the abandonment of tradition, but of some form of "rejuvenation."

Analogies in Other Literatures. The many varieties of diction found in Eng. poetry are closely paralleled in the chief literatures of the Western world. The parallels are of two kinds: there are the fundamental resemblances between techniques of effective diction in classical, especially Gr., poetry and in Eng. poetry; there are also parallels—with some significant differences—between the history of p.d. in Eng. and its history in other important literatures, such as Fr., It., and Sp.

The metaphorical quality of language in Homer, Aeschylus, and Sophocles as well as in Shakespeare and his greatest successors is well known and scarcely needs illustration. Another parallel, little less significant, is the endeavor of poets in their most energetic moments to find or create (in Coleridge's phrase) *"one word* to express *one act* of imagination." The Homeric phrase "Pēlion einosiphullon" (Pelion with quivering leafage) and Aeschylus' "anērithmon gelasma" (multitudinous laughter, i.e., of the sea) are brilliant examples of this: each produces the effect described by Wordsworth in his poem on the daffodils: "Ten thousand saw I at a glance." This is the imaginative power which Coleridge called "esemplastic." The "embracing" or "extensive" epithet occurs frequently in both literatures. The compound epithets in Gr. beginning with *eury-*, and *tele-*, and *poly-* have their Eng. analogues beginning with *wide-*, *far-*, and *many-*. The *poly-* or "many" group is particularly large. By the side of Gr. epithets having the sense of "rich in flowers," "with many furrows," "with many trees," "with many ridges," "with many glens," "poluphloisbos" (loud-roaring, Homer's epithet for the sea), and many more of the like character, may be placed Milton's "wide-watered" (shore), Keats's "far-foamed" (sands), and Tennyson's "many-fountain'd" (Ida). Such epithets are imaginative in their reduction of multiplicity to unity, of complexity to simplicity. Descriptive diction at its best in both Gr. and Eng. poetry is frequently marked by these two characteristic features—the unifying (or "esemplastic") and the metaphorical.

Parallels between p.d. in Eng. and Fr. are especially instructive. The decline of medieval poetry, marked in England by aureate diction, produced its Fr. counterpart in the affectations of the rhétoriqueurs. Renaissance poetry in France and in England was exposed to similar influences, but the national genius of the two countries reacted differently. Sir Thomas Elyot in England and Joachim du Bellay in France both labored to enrich their respective languages with the wealth of classical Gr. and L. But whereas this movement, in England, led to "exornation" and culminated in the unsurpassed wealth of Shakespeare's poetic vocabulary, in France the critical and negative spirit of Malherbe diverted poetry into another channel. The characteristic triumph which Fr. poetry soon after achieved in the work of Racine was marked not by creative abundance of diction but by restraint, conscious elevation, and a certain economy. "La poésie de Racine," says Ste.-Beuve "élude les détails." It shows "une perpétuelle nécessité de noblesse et d'élégance"; it uses "un vocabulaire un peu restreint." In England, the natural reaction which followed Elizabethan exuberance of diction prepared the way for the neoclassical poetry of the 18th c. which is a close parallel to contemporary poetry in France. The p.d. denounced by Wordsworth has its systematized counterpart in the compilation called *Le Gradus Français* a guide for the use of poets to epithet, allusion, and periphrasis.

The literary revolution of the early 19th c. had, in England, for its principal arenas, lyrical and narrative poetry, and philosophical criticism. In France, the contest was fought out more publicly on the stage, the classical drama being the stronghold of "noblesse" and "élégance" in diction, as it was of the Unities. The claim made in Victor Hugo's celebrated *Préface* to *Cromwell* (1827) to the whole truth as the province of poetry, instead of simply the Beautiful and the Sublime, aimed at removing restraints from language no less than from the handling of dramatic plot and the structure of scenes. Thus a new art of diction was introduced, and language was henceforth to be chosen for its intensity of emotion and descriptive effect, without regard for tradition. In due time romantic fervor cooled into aesthetic precision and the cult of the "mot juste," but the essence of the movement survives in a saying of the brothers Goncourt, valid for more than half the century, "l'épithète rare, voilà la marque du poète."

With the development of the "symboliste" movement some new and valuable thoughts on p.d. have been put forward by Fr. writers, of whom Paul Valéry is an outstanding example. The restricted outlook which haunted the Fr. mind so long after Malherbe is now exchanged for a conception of poetry as entirely free and autonomous. In Valéry the Eng.-speaking reader is reminded of Dryden, of Wordsworth, of Pater, and of Housman, but the breadth of Valéry's generalization is his own. For him literature is simply "un développement de certaines des propriétés du langage . . . les plus agissantes chez les peuples primitifs." Poetry must renew its diction from the "undefiled wells." "Plus la forme est belle, plus elle se sent des origines de la conscience et de l'expression; plus elle est savante et plus elle s'efforce de retrouver, par une sorte de synthèse, la plénitude, l'indivision de la parole encore neuve et dans son état créateur" (Jean Hytier, *La Poétique de Valéry,* p. 70). Valéry's theory of p.d. is an integral part of his conception of "la poésie absolute."

General: Aristotle, *Poetics,* tr. I. Bywater (1909); Dante, *De Vulgari eloquentia,* tr. A. G. Ferrers Howell (1890; a poet's critical contribution to the making of a literary language); Buffon, *Discours sur le style* (1753; for statement of neoclassical point of view); Thos. Gray, *Letter to R. West,* April 1742; "On Poetry, as Distinguished from Other Writing," *British Magazine* (1762); W. Wordsworth, *Lyrical Ballads, Preface* (2d ed., 1800); *Appendix on what is usually called Poetic Diction* (1802); *Essay, Supplementary to the Preface* (1815); S. T. Coleridge, *Biographia Literaria,* chs. 14–22; Ker; F. W. Bateson, *Eng. Poetry and the Eng. Language* (1934, 2d ed., 1961); F. A. Pottle, *The Idiom of Poetry* (2d ed., 1946); J. Miles, *The Continuity of Poetic Language* (1951); O. Barfield, *P.D.* (2d ed., 1952); B. Groom, *The Diction of Poetry from Spenser to Bridges* (1956).

Special Studies: Norden; M. Arnold, *On Translating Homer,* ed. W.H.D. Rouse (1905);

W. Raleigh, "P.D.," *Wordsworth* (1921); *T. Quayle, P.D.: a Study of 18th C. Verse* (1924); J. W. Mackail, "The Poet of *The Seasons*," *Studies of Eng. Poets* (1926; a valuable study of James Thomson's diction); H. C. Wyld, "Diction and Imagery in Anglo-Saxon Poetry," E&S, 11 (1925); O. Elton, "The Poet's Dictionary," E&S, 14 (1928); G. Rylands, "Eng. Poetry and the Abstract Word," E&S, 16 (1930); S. H. Monk, *The Sublime* (1935); B. Groom, *The Formation and Use of Compound Epithets in Eng. Poetry from 1579* (1937; SPE Tract no. 49); C. M. Bowra, *The Heritage of Symbolism* (1943); J. Arthos, *The Language of Natural Description in 18th C. Poetry* (1949); R. F. Jones, *The Triumph of the Eng. Language* (1951; ch. 6); D. Davie, *Purity of Diction in Eng. Verse* (1952); J. Hytier, *La Poétique de Valéry* (1953); D. L. Clark, *Rhetoric in Greco-Roman Education* (1957); G. Tillotson, *Augustan Studies* (1962). B.G.

POETIC LICENSE. A freedom allowed the poet to depart in subject matter, grammar, or diction from what would be proper in ordinary prose discourse. In a broad sense, the poet is exercising p.l. when he invents fictions ("tells lies," as Plato has it) or takes liberties with facts, as when Virgil makes Dido the contemporary of Aeneas. More frequently the term is confined to the poet's freedoms with language: departing from normal word order; using one part of speech for another ("As those move *easiest* who have learned to dance"); employing coined or archaic words; contracting or lengthening words (*'gainst, o'er; beweep, aweary*); altering their pronunciation (*wind* rhymed with *behind*), etc.

P.l. may be used to achieve some special effect or beauty otherwise unattainable, or merely to make the verse conform to the exigencies of meter or rhyme. In general, the freedom allowed the poet in his language varies inversely with the freedom allowed him in his meter. In the 18th c., for instance, when metrical laws were very strict, licenses in language were commonly accepted which would not be allowed today when the poet has much greater metrical freedom. In the 20th c., when most poetry is written in colloquial language and in free verse or irregular meters, p.l. is not a significant issue.

Aristotle and Horace both recognize the right of the poet to coin, lengthen, alter, or import words to give distinction to his language, and Aristotle allows him to invent images or situations that improve upon nature: "For poetic effect a convincing impossibility is preferable to that which is unconvincing but possible." Quintilian (ca. A.D. 95) points out that "poets are usually the servants of their meters and are allowed such license that faults are given other names when they occur in poetry." George Gascoigne (1575) advises Eng. poets to place all words in their usual pronunciation and to frame all sentences in their natural idiomatic order, "and yet sometimes . . . the contrary may be borne, but that is rather where rime enforceth, or *per licentiam Poeticam,* than it is otherwise lawful or commendable." Alexander Pope admits in a famous line that poets often "snatch a grace beyond the reach of art." R. M. Alden (1909) states that "all these licenses are admitted sparingly in modern poetry, and are to be reckoned as blemishes unless . . . the change from the normal choice of words or order of words has a certain stylistic value of its own."—R. F. Brewer, The *Art of Versification and the Technicalities of Poetry* (1925).

L.P.

POETIC MADNESS. In *Phaedrus* 245 Socrates asserts that poets are susceptible to madness and, in fact, cannot succeed without it. In the *Ion* both poet and critic are described as possessed by a frenzy so that they do not consciously control their words. In Aristotle's *Problemata* 30 it is said that poets and philosophers are inclined to excessive melancholy. Roman poets are possessed by spirits or demons (Ovid: "Deus est in nobis / Agitante calescimus illo"—"A god is within us; when he urges, we are inspired"); write best when tipsy (Horace); are filled with the divine afflatus (Cicero); or are literally mad (the tradition that Lucretius was driven insane by a love potion). The concept of p.m., which can be found *passim* in European poetry and criticism, is summed up in two familiar quotations: "The lunatic, the lover, and the poet / Are of imagination all compact" (Shakespeare); and "Great wits are sure to madness near allied / And thin partitions do their bounds divide" (Dryden).

The parallel between poets and madmen is extremely primitive. It apparently goes back to the time when the poet, the prophet, and the priest were one and the same and when madmen were considered the special children of the gods, invested with prophetic and magical powers. By Plato's time we may assume that only a small residue of the primitive attitude survived. Although Plato evidently considered p.m. suspect, to Horace and many Neoplatonic writers it was the special dispensation which made poetry superior to other forms of discourse. In the form of *furor poeticus* it was identified, especially during the 16th c., with inspiration.

The question whether or not there is a scientific basis for the idea of p.m. is hard to answer. Being especially sensitive, poets may be more subject to neurosis than other men. Many poets (e.g., Sappho, Lucretius, Villon, Marlowe, Collins, Smart, Nerval, Nietzsche, Pound) were either insane or exhibited marked personality disturbances. The romantic theory of the artist as tormented outcast was subsumed by Freud in his essay "The Relation of the Poet to Day-Dreaming" and elsewhere. To Freud, the artist is neurotic and his work is a by-product—often a symbolic statement of—his disturbance. In various forms this idea has been restated by Thomas Mann, Kenneth Burke, and Lionel Trilling. It is explored in considerable detail by Edmund Wilson in *The Wound and the Bow,* where "wound" refers to the artist's neurosis, and "bow" to the art which is its compensation. In this theory poetry is a catharsis for the author—the pearl of art forms around the irritant of emotional disturbance. However, the theory is challenged by critics in the aesthetic tradition (e.g., Croce, I. A. Richards), who tend to claim that the creator is not less but more healthy than average. Among psychologists, Jung and his followers assert the health of the artist, since creative activity puts man in contact with the primal source of human vitality, the collective unconscious.—G. E. Woodberry, "P.M.," *The Inspiration of Poetry* (1910); F. C. Prescott, "The P.M. and Catharsis," *The Poetic Mind* (1922). See also L. Trilling, "Art and Neurosis," *The Liberal Imagination* (1950). See INSPIRATION. A.R.B.

POETRY READING. The formal presentation of poetry read aloud either by its author or by an actor-interpreter. Settings for a p.r. can be a literary *salon*, a poetry workshop, an invitational event like Johann Wolfgang von Goethe's (1749–1832) readings from his work before the Court of Weimar, or a quasi-theatrical performance at which a poet, poets, or interpreters of poetry address a wide public. By extension to the electronic media, p. readings can also take place via radio or television broadcasts, as well as through phonograph records and electromagnetic tapes. It is assumed, however, that work presented in a p.r. has been committed to writing and may be available in published form. Thus defined, the p.r. is differentiated from oral poetry (q.v.: "composed *in* oral performance by people who cannot read or write"), from productions of a poet's dramatic works, and from the classroom reading of poetry for teaching purposes.

Occidental p. readings from the Greeks to the 19th c. centered on invitational performances in courtly settings. This tradition appears also in read presentations of Chinese and Japanese poetry and continues in 20th c. Japan. It is likely that p. readings took place at the Alexandrian court of the Ptolemies (ca. 325–ca. 30 B.C.) and in the aristocratic residence of C. Cilnius Maecenas (d. 8 B.C.), who encouraged the work of Vergil (70–19 B.C.), Horace (65–8 B.C.), and Propertius (ca. 47–15 B.C.). Trimalchio, in the fiction of Petronius' (d. A.D. 66) *Satyricon*, first writes, then recites his own "poetry" to the guests at his banquet. Written poetry was recited at the 13th-c. court of Frederick II, in the Florentine circle of Lorenzo de'Medici (1449–92) and, according to La Bruyère (1645–96), in the late 17th-c. *salons* of the Princes de Condé. Within Goethe's long life, the p.r. changed from a courtly to a public function. As a young poet of the late 1770's, Goethe read his work at the Weimar court of Carl August; on the occasion of a production of *Faust* to commemorate his eightieth birthday in 1829, he personally coached the actors in the elocution and delivery of lines. Public recitation of their work by poets and their admirers became commonplace in the 19th c. The format was generally quasi-theatrical. Edgar Allen Poe (1809–49) in America, Victor Hugo (1802–85) in France, and Alfred, Lord Tennyson (1809–92) in England are examples of major poets noted for the dramatic quality of their readings. The work of Robert Browning (1812–89) was recited in meetings of the Browning Society (founded 1881), an organization which produced hundreds of offshoots in the U.S. of the 1880's and 1890's. A *Goethe Gesellschaft* (founded 1885) brought readings from the poet's work to places as distant from each other as St. Petersburg, Manchester, and New York, for each of which an 1890 membership list shows a sizeable potential audience. Richard Wagner's (1813–83) opera *Die Meistersinger von Nürnberg* (musical version, 1867) brought the late medieval German tradition of p. readings by members of craft guilds to the attention of a vast international audience. Centered on the historic figure of Hans Sachs (1494–1576), Wagner's work favors "spontaneous" oral poetry in the tradition of Greek rhapsodists, Provençal troubadours, and German minnesingers (qq.v.) over a reading of poems written by others that the poets. Wagner stresses the superiority of national over foreign idiom, of aristocratic over bourgeois poetic voices (Stolzing vs. Beckmesser), and of desirability of correlation between the physical appearance of the poet and the quality of his work.

Wagner's poetics, as expressed in *Die Meistersinger*, is central to symbolist conceptions of the p.r. Stéphane Mallarmé (1842–98) read his poetry to a select audience of never more than twelve, on designated "Tuesdays" at which the poet himself played both host and reader in quasi-cultic, priestly style. While Mallarmé's poetry was anything but spontaneously written, his oral presentation as part of the dramatic monologue which characterized his "Tuesdays" both personalized and socialized the work. Stefan George's (1868–1933) mode of reading poetry was consciously influenced by Mallarmé's: the audience was restricted to the poet's circle of disciples (*Kreis*) and the occasion of the p.r. was perceived as cultic and sacral. While George read from manuscript, he followed a self-prescribed, strict mode of rhapsodic recitation. His poetry was written to be read aloud. Disciples permitted to participate in the p.r. were obligated to follow George's style of reading both for his and for their own work. As the *Kreis* became, during World War I and after, ever more consciously German and xenophobic in outlook and as the poet's style of dress and demeanor grew increasingly reminiscent of Richard Wagner's, the p. readings approached ideals implied in *Die Meistersinger* even more closely than the practices of Mallarmé's "Tuesdays."

Some of these ideals carried over to modes of p.r. characteristic of the first half of the 20th c. William Butler Yeats (1865–1939) was much concerned with having his work sound spontaneous and natural. Though his style of reading was dramatic and incantatory, he deliberately revised some poems so that they would sound like an ordinary man talking under normal circumstances. By contrast, T. S. Eliot's (1888–1965) p. readings were aristocratic and cultic in style. The Wagnerian prescription of having the reader seem at once spontaneous in expression but, in his person, remote from an audience had its most splendid 20th c. exemplification in the p. readings of Dylan Thomas (1914–53). Thomas's regal, dramatic stance, and sacral incantations offered sharp contrast to the secular, conversational p. readings of Robert Frost (1875–1963) and W. H. Auden (1907–74), in which the poet presents himself as if in dialogue with his audience, to whom he offers commentary and asides in the course of the reading. Auden's and Frost's style of presentation became normative for many modes of p.r. developing in the second half of the 20th c.

Dadaism and surrealism also helped shape the conventions of the later p.r. These vanguardistic European movements of the second and third decades of the century generated presentations in which p. readings were staged simultaneously with music, dance, or film. The at least apparently unplanned, spontaneous character of dadaist and surrealist events influenced p. readings of the 1950's and 1960's in their function as components in both multimedia presentations and random artistic "happenings." P. readings held during World War I and in the decade to follow as vehicles of social protest and as revolutionary proclamations were models for similar presentations in the second half of the century. This was true not only for dadaist and surrealist p. readings but also for those held in early post-revolutionary Soviet Russia. Vladimir Mayakovsky (1894–1930), self-proclaimed "drummer of the October Revolution" sang its praises in lyrics written to be read aloud. Mayakovsky's dramatic p. readings attracted mass audiences not only in the U.S.S.R. but also in Western Europe and in the U.S. His use of the p.r. as a forum of political declamation has been internationally emulated into the 1970's. In the U.S.S.R. itself, the politicized p.r. has been institutionalized through the observance, since 1955, of an official, annual "Poetry Day" held in Moscow, Leningrad, and other large cities. During World War II, the B.B.C. broadcast p. readings by poets exiled from countries then occupied by the Germans for the specific purpose of sustaining national consciousness.

Since the 1950's, the p.r. on the Western side of the Iron Curtain has been overwhelmingly an Am. phenomenon. Its tone is "democratic," ranging from polite conversational idiom to street language. P. readings by one poet only have been increasingly rare; the more usual format ranges from two to six, with marathon p. readings by a multitude not uncommon. The separation of the poet from his audience has all but vanished. Conversation between stage and auditorium in the course of the p.r. is usual; "open p. readings" are events to which anyone may bring his work to read. Locales and audio-visual dimensions for p. readings are diversified: church basements, coffee houses, and public parks serve as often as theaters, college auditoriums, and private homes. In many p. readings the physical presence of either poets or live actors is unnecessary, since cassette tapes, loudspeakers, phonograph records, radios, or television sets can transmit the work presented. Moreover, language is no longer the p. reading's sole medium of communication, since jazz or rock music, electronic visual effects, and spontaneous dramatic presentations ("happenings") may accompany the event. Costumes for poets reading are arbitrary, ranging from business suits and evening dress to coveralls and, occasionally, total nudity. In spite of what may appear a partial merging of the p.r. with a variety of other social and cultural phenomena, it has not lost its sacral character. Many audiences consider the p.r. a cultic group experience, a sharing of special sentiments. Features beyond the presentation of poetry itself (e.g., reading it naked, to the accompaniment of bongo drums) are perceived as reinforcements of this sharing. Consumption of mind-altering drugs and alcohol during the p.r. is not uncommon for the same purpose.

Prominent innovators were the beat poets, notably Allen Ginsberg (b. 1926), Gregory Corso (b. 1930), and Lawrence Ferlinghetti (b. 1919), all participants in an important 1957 San Francisco p.r. to the accompaniment of jazz. In the 1960's and 1970's, New York and San Francisco have been the two major Am. p.r. centers, with London, Amsterdam, and West Berlin constituting European counterparts, these latter marked by contacts and actual p. readings involving Ginsberg, Corso, and Ferlinghetti. The German poet Peter Rühmkorf (b. 1929), the Austrian Ernst Jandl (b. 1925), the Dutch Simon Vinkenoog (b. 1928), and the Russian Andrei Voznesensky (b. 1933) are strongly connected to European p.r. presentations in the San Francisco style.

Whatever the style or era, the problem arises whether the actual audience reception of a work coincides with its intentions (q.v.). As the examples of Dylan Thomas and Robert Frost show, a poet's own staging of his work can make it appear more meaningful and commanding than a reader might gather from the printed page. Whether the poem is read by himself or by another, there is no guarantee that a p.r. audience will hear what was "intended" in the making of the poem. Ways of assessing refraction between poetic intentions and what is heard in a p.r. have only begun to be studied. Widely different approaches to the problem by descriptive linguists (Seymour Chatman, Samuel R. Levin), on the one hand, and by phenomenological critics (Georges Poulet, Wolfgang Iser) on the other, agree that identity between poetic intentions and what emerges from the act of reading is highly unlikely. For phenomenologists a poem achieves a true existence only as it is "animated" within the consciousness of a reader. The principle applies even if the reader is the poet himself: when he approaches his poem at any moment other than that of its inception, he is incarnating the text in a new way. Linguists see the necessary choice of one particular interpretation for reading purposes as a barrier between identity of intention and performance; also, they note that phonetic differences between written text and spoken delivery, constrained by the range and pitch limitations of the human voice often make impossible oral replication of texts in the p.r. The strong 20th-c. popularity of the p.r., which seems greater than general interest in reading poems from the printed page in private, is probably more deeply rooted in the dramatic-sacral character of the event than in the literary quality of poetry presented.

M. v. Boehn, "Faust und die Kunst," in J. W. v. Goethe, *Faust* (Centennial Ed., 1932); H. Mondor, *La Vie de Stéphane Mallarmé* (1941); E. R. Boehringer, *Mein Bild von Stefan George* (1951); K. Wais, *Mallarmé* (2d ed., 1952); E. Salin, *Um Stefan George* (2d ed., 1954); S. Chatman, "Linguistics, Poetics, and Interpretations: The Phonemic Dimension," *Quarterly Jour. of Speech*, 43 (1957); *Evergreen Review*, 1, no. 2 (1957); A. B. Lord, *The Singer of Tales* (1960); *The Penguin Book of Russian Verse*, ed. D. Obolensky (1962); S. Levin, "Suprasegmentals and the Performance of Poetry," *Quarterly Jour. of Speech*, 48 (1962); K. T. Loesch, "Lit. Ambiguity and Oral Performance," ibid., 51 (1965); D. Levertov, "Approach to Public Poetry Listenings," *Virginia Quarterly Review*, 41 (1965); E. Lucie-Smith, "Wild Night," *Encounter*, 25 (1965); *The New Russian Poets 1953–1968*, ed. G. Reavey (1966); *Ein Gedicht und sein Autor*, ed. W. Höllerer (1969); G. Poulet, "Phenomenology of Reading," NLH, 1 (1969); P. Dickinson, "Spoken Words," *Encounter*, 34 (1970); *The San Francisco Poets*, ed. D. Meltzer (1971); *The East Side Scene*, ed. A. De Loach (1972); W. Iser, "The Reading Process: A Phenomenological Approach," NLH, 3 (1972); S. Massie, *The Living Mirror: Five Young Poets from Leningrad* (1972); P. Turner, "Introd." to R. Browning, *Men and Women 1855* (1972). W.B.F.

POETRY, THEORIES OF. There is no uniquely valid way to classify theories of poetry; that classification is best which best serves the particular purpose in hand. The division of theories presented here is adopted because it is relatively simple; because it stresses the notable extent to which later approaches to poetry were expansions—although under the influence of many new philosophical concepts and poetic examples—of Gr. and Roman prototypes; and because it defines in a provisional way certain large-scale shifts of focus during 2,500 years of Western speculation about the identity of poetry, its kinds and their relative status, the parts, qualities, and ordonnance of a single poem, and the kinds of criteria by which poems are to be evaluated. But like all general schemes, this one must be supplemented and qualified in many ways before it can do justice to the diversity of individual ways of treating poetry.

Most theories take into account that poetry is a fabricated thing, not found in nature, and therefore contingent on a number of factors. A *poem* is produced by a *poet*, is related in its subject matter to the *universe* of human beings, things, and events, and is addressed to, or made available to, an *audience* of hearers or readers. But although these four elements play some part in all inclusive accounts of Poetry, they do not play an equal part. Commonly a critic takes one of these elements or relations as cardinal, and refers the poem either to the external world, or to the audience, or to the poet as preponderantly "the source, and end, and test of art"; or alternatively, he considers the poem as a self-sufficient entity, best to be analyzed in theoretical isolation from the causal factors in the universe from which the poem derives its materials, or the tastes, convictions, and reponses of the audience to which it appeals, or the character, intentions, thoughts, and feelings of the poet who brings it into being. These varied orientations give us, in a preliminary way, four broad types of poetic theory, which may be labeled mimetic, pragmatic, expressive, and objective.

MIMETIC THEORIES: In Plato's *Republic* 10, Socrates said that poetry is mimesis, or "imitation," and illustrated its relation to the universe by a mirror which, turned round and round, can produce an appearance of all sensible things. Plato thus bequeathed to later theorists a preoccupation with the relation of poetry to that which it imitates, and also the persistent analogy of the reflector as defining the nature of that relation. But in the cosmic structure underlying Plato's dialectic, the sensible universe is itself an imitation, or appearance, of the eternal Ideas which are the locus of all value, while all other human knowledge and products are also modes of imitation. A poem therefore turns out to be the rival of the work of the artisan, the statesman, the moralist, and the philosopher, but under the inescapable disadvantage of being an imitation of an imitation, "thrice removed from the truth," and composed not by art and knowledge, but by inspiration, at a time when the poet is not in his right mind (*Ion*). Plato thus forced many later critical theorists into a posture of defense, in a context in which poetry necessarily competes with all other human enterprises, and is to be judged by universal criteria of truth, beauty, and goodness.

In Aristotle's *Poetics* the various kinds of poetry are also defined as "modes of imitation" of human actions. Aristotle attributes the origin of poetry to our natural instinct to imitate and to take pleasure in imitations, and grounds in large part on the kinds of subjects which are imitated such essential concepts as the different species of poetry, the unity of a poem (since an imitation "must represent one action, a complete whole"), and the primacy of plot in tragedy (for "tragedy is essentially an imitation not of persons but of action and life"). But Aristotle's use of the term "imitation" sharply differentiates his theory of poetry from that of Plato. In Aristotle's scheme, the forms of things do not exist in an otherworldly realm, but are inherent in the things themselves, so that it is in no way derogatory to point out that poetry imitates models in the world of sense. On the contrary, poetry is more philosophic than history, because it imitates the form of things, and so achieves statements in the mode of "universals, whereas those of history are singulars." Furthermore "imitation" in Aristotle is a term specific to the arts, distinguishing poems from all other activities and products as a class of objects having their own criteria of value and reason for being. And by exploiting systematically such distinctions as the kinds of objects imitated, the media and manner of imitation, and the variety of emotional effects on an audience, Aristotle implements his consideration of poetry as poetry by providing means for distinguishing among the poetic kinds—e.g., tragedy, comedy, epic—and for discriminating the particular parts, internal relations, power of giving a specific kind of pleasure, and standards of evaluation proper to each type of poem.

Later the eclectic Cicero (*Ad M. Brutum Orator* 2) and Plotinus (*Enneads* 5.8) demonstrated that it was possible to assume a world-scheme which includes Platonic Ideas, yet to allow the artist to short-circuit the objects of sense so as to imitate, in Plotinus' phrase, "the Ideas from which Nature itself derives." In accordance with this strategy, later critics used building blocks from Plato's cosmos to construct aesthetic theories which could raise poetry from Plato's inferior position to the highest among human endeavors. The claim that poetry imitates the eternal Forms was developed by It. Neoplatonists in the 16th c., occasionally echoed by neoclassic critics (including, in England, Dennis, Hurd, and Reynolds), and played a prominent part in the writings of German romantic philosophers such as Schelling and Novalis. Diverse cognitive claims for poetry as approximating verities beyond sense-experience are also found in the Eng. romantic critics Blake, Coleridge, and Carlyle. Shelley, in his eloquent *Defence of Poetry,* demonstrates the reductive tendency of an uncompromising Neoplatonic theory. Since all good poems imitate the same Forms, and since these Forms, as the residence of all values, are the models for all other human activities and products as well, Shelley's essay all but annuls any essential differences between poem and poem, between poetic kind and poetic kind, between poems written in various times and in various places, and between poems written in words and the poetry of all other men who "express this indestructible order," including institutors of laws, founders of civil society, inventors of the arts of life, and teachers of religion. In our own day a formal parallel to such critical monism is to be found among the critics who, after Jung, maintain that great poems, like myths, dreams, visions, and other products of the collective unconscious—or else of the generic imaginations compelled by enduring human needs and desires—all reproduce a limited set of archetypal paradigms, and ultimately the whole or part of that archetype of archetypes, the cycle of the seasons and of death and rebirth. (See, e.g., Wheelwright; Frye.)

Among mimetic theorists proper, however, the concept that art reproduces aspects of the sensible world has been much more common than the Neoplatonic or transcendental variant. The doctrine that poetry and the arts are essentially imitations of this world, in a variety of systematic applications, flourished through the Ren. and well into the 18th c. In *Les Beaux Arts réduits à un même principe* (1747), Charles Batteux found in the principle of imitation the "clear and distinct idea" from which he undertook to deduce the nature and the rules of the various arts. The Englishman Richard Hurd declared that "all poetry, to speak with Aristotle and the Greek critics (if for so plain a point authorities be thought wanting) is, properly, *imitation* . . . having all creation for its object" ("Discourse on Poetical Imitation," 1751). And Lessing's classic *Laokoon* (1766), although it set out to substitute an inductive method for the blatantly deductive theories of Batteux and other contemporaries, still discovered the "essence" of poetry and painting to be imitation, and derived the bounds of the subjects that each art is competent to imitate from the differences in their media.

Since the 18th c. the mimetic doctrine has been more narrowly employed by proponents of artistic realism, or in theories limited to the more realistic literary genres. In the Ren. there had been many echoes of the saying Donatus had attributed to Cicero that dramatic comedy is peculiarly "a copy of life, a mirror of custom, a reflection of truth." In the early 19th c., when prose fiction had superseded comedy as the primary vehicle of realism, Stendhal put the mimetic mirror on wheels: "a novel," he said "is a mirror riding along a highway." Since that time representational theories have been voiced mainly by exponents of naturalistic fiction and imagist poetry, as well as by Marxist critics who claim that great literature "reflects" (or at least ought to reflect) the "objective" reality of our bourgeois era.

The mimetic approach to literature, accordingly, has been used to justify artistic procedures ranging from the most refined idealism to the rawest realism. What the various theories have in common is the tendency to look to the nature of the given universe as the clue to the nature of poetry, and to assign to the subject matter which is represented—or which ought to be represented—the primary role in determining the aims, kinds, constitution, and criteria of poems. The key word in mimetic definitions of poetry, if not "imitation," is another predicate which aligns the poem in the same direction: the poem is an "image," "reflection," "feigning," "counterfeiting," "copy," or "representation." The underlying parallel for a poem, which often comes to the surface as an express comparison, is Plato's mirror, or "a speaking picture," or a photographic plate. The focus of attention is thus on the relation between the imitable and the imitation, and the primary aesthetic criterion is "truth to nature," or "truth to reality." In purely representational theories, the patent discrepancies between the world as it is and the world as it is represented in poems tend to be explained, not by reference to the psychology of the poet or the reader, or to the conventions and internal requirements of a work of art, but by reference to the kinds or aspects of reality which are to be imitated. Transcendental theorists maintain that poetry represents the poet's intuitions of models existing in their own supramundane space. This-worldly theorists claim that poetry represents, or should represent, a composite of the beautiful and moral aspects of things, or "la belle nature," or the statistical average of a biological form, or the universal, typical, and generically human, or the quotidian, the particular, the unique, and "the characteristic," or the conditions of bourgeois reality. In all these instances, however opposed, the objects or qualities are conceived to be inherent in the constitution of the universe, and the genius of the poet is explained primarily by his acuity of observation, enabling him to discover aspects of reality hitherto unregarded, and by his artistic ingenuity, enabling him to select and arrange even the more familiar elements into novel combinations which, nevertheless, surprise us by their truth.

PRAGMATIC THEORIES: The pragmatic scheme sets a poem in a means-end relationship, regarding the matter and manner of imitation as instrumental toward achieving certain effects in the reader. "Poesy therefore," declared Sir Philip Sidney in a typical formulation which assimilates mimesis to a pragmatic orientation, "is an art of imitation . . . a speaking picture: with this end, to teach and delight." Ancient rhetorical theory provided the conceptual frame and many of the terms for this approach to poetry, for it was held that the aim of rhetoric is to effect persuasion, and there was wide agreement (e.g., Cicero, *De Oratore* 2.28) that this end is best achieved by informing, winning, and moving the auditor. But the great prototype for the pragmatic view of poetry was Horace's *Ars Poetica,* with its persistent emphasis that the aim of the poet, and the measure of poetic success, is the pleasure and approval of the contemporary Roman audience and of posterity as well. Aristotle has been more often quoted, but Horace has in fact been the most influential critical exemplar in the Western world. For the pragmatic orientation, exploiting the mode of reasoning and many of the concepts and topics presented in Horace's short epistle, dominated literary crit. through the Ren. and most of the 18th c., and has made frequent reappearances ever since.

"Aut prodesse volunt, aut delectare poetae," Horace declared, although pleasure turns out to be the ultimate end, with instruction requisite only because the graver readers will not be pleased without moral matter. Later critics added from rhetoric a third term, "movere," to sum up under the three headings of instruction, emotion, and pleasure the effects of poetry on its audience. Most Ren. humanists, like Sidney, made moral profit the ultimate aim of poetry; but from Dryden through the 18th c. it became increasingly common to subordinate instruction and emotion to the delight of the reader, as the defining end of a poetic composition. Samuel Johnson, however, continued to insist that "the end of poetry is to instruct by pleasing," and that "it is always a writer's duty to make the world better" (*Preface to Shakespeare*). In the 19th c. the influential reviewer, Francis Jeffrey, deliberately justified writing in such a way as to please the least common denominator of public taste, and in this procedure he has been followed by later pedlars of formulae for achieving popular success. Neoclassic pragmatists, however, justified the sophisticated preferences of the classically trained connoisseurs of their own day by the claim that these accorded with the literary qualities of works whose long survival prove their adaptation to the aesthetic proclivities of man in general (Johnson's "common reader"), and that works written in accordance with these principles have the best chance to endure. The renowned masters, John Dennis said, wrote not to please only their countrymen; "they wrote to their fellow-citizens of the universe, to all countries, and to all ages."

We recognize pragmatic critics of poetry, whatever their many divergences, by their tendency to regard a poem as a made object, the product of an art or craft, which (after due allowance for the play of natural talent, inspired moments, and felicities beyond the reach of art) is still, for the most part, deliberately designed to achieve foreknown ends; we recognize them also by their tendency to derive the rationale, the chief determinants of elements and forms, and the norms of poetry from the legitimate requirements and springs of pleasure in the readers for whom it is written. Thus the *ars poetica* looms large in this theory, and for centuries was often codified as a system of prescriptions and "rules." "Having thus shown that imitation pleases," as Dryden summarized the common line of reasoning, "it follows, that some rules of imitation are necessary to obtain the end; for without rules there can be no art" (*Parallel of Poetry and Painting*). These rules were justified inductively as essential properties abstracted from works which have appealed to the natural preferences of mankind over the centuries; in the 18th c., especially in such systematic theorists as Beattie, Hurd, and Kames, they were also warranted by a confident appeal to the generic psychological laws governing the responses of the reader. Through the neoclassic period, most critics assumed that the rules were specific for each of the fixed genres, or kinds, but these poetic kinds in turn were usually discriminated and ranked, from epic and tragedy at the top down to the "lesser lyric" and other trifles at the bottom, by the special moral and pleasurable effects each kind is most competent to achieve. Poetic deviations from the truth of fact, which in strictly mimetic theories are justified by their conformity to objects, forms, and tendencies in the constitution of the universe, are warranted pragmatically by the reader's moral requirements, and even more emphatically, by his native inclination to take delight only in a selected, patterned, heightened, and "ornamented" reality. In 1651 Davenant (*Preface to Gondibert*) attacked the traditional use of pagan machinery and supernatural materials on the mimetic assumption that the poet undertakes to "represent the world's true image"; a point of view which Hobbes at once abetted by proscribing all poetic materials that go "beyond the conceived possibility of nature" (*Answer to Davenant*). To this mimetic interpretation of poetic probability as correspondence to the empirical constitution and order of events, pragmatic critics responded by shifting the emphasis from the nature of the world to the nature of man, and by redefining poetic probability as anything which succeeds in evoking the pleasurable responsiveness of the reader. "The end of poetry is to please," Beattie wrote in his *Essays on Poetry and Music* (1776), and "greater pleasure is . . . to be expected from it, because we grant it superior indulgence, in regard to fiction," than if it were "according to real nature." Later Thomas Twining justified for poetry "not only impossibilities, but even absurdities, where that end [of yielding pleasure] appears to be better answered with them, than it would have been without them" (Preface to *Aristotle's Treatise on Poetry* 1789).

Expressive Theories: The mimetic poet is the agent who holds the mirror up to nature; the pragmatic poet is considered mainly in terms of the inherent powers ("nature") and acquired knowledge and skills ("art") he must possess to construct a poetic object intricately adapted, in its parts and as a whole, to its complex aims. In the expressive orientation, the poet moves into the center of the scheme and himself becomes the prime generator of the subject matter, attributes, and values of a poem. The chief historical source for this point of view was the treatise *On the Sublime* attributed to Longinus. In this treatise the stylistic quality of sublimity is defined by its effect of *ekstasis,* or transport, and is traced to five sources in the powers of the author. Of these sources, three have to do with expression, and are amenable to art; but the two primary sources are largely innate and instinctive, and are constituted by the author's greatness of conception and, most important of all, by his "vehement and inspired passion." Referring the major excellence of a work to its genesis in the author's mind, Longinus finds it a reflection of its author: "Sublimity is the echo of a great soul."

The influence of Longinus' essay, after it became generally known in the third quarter of the 17th c., was immense, and its emphasis on thought and passion, originally used to explain a single stylistic quality, was expanded and applied to poetry as a whole. The effect on poetic theory was supplemented by primitivistic concepts of the natural origins of language and poetry in emotional exclamations and effusions, as well as by the rise to high estate of "the greater lyric," or Pindaric ode, which critics (following the lead of Cowley) treated in Longinian terms. By 1725 the boldly speculative Giambattista Vico combined Longinian doctrines, the Lucretian theory of linguistic origins, and travelers' reports about the poetry of culturally primitive peoples into his major thesis that the first language after the flood was dominated by sense, passion, and imagination, and was therefore at once emotional, concrete, mythical, and poetic. In Vico is to be found the root concept of the common expressive origins and nature of poetry, myth, and religion which was later exploited by such influential theorists as Herder, Croce, and Cassirer; this mode of speculation is still recognizable in the recent theories of Suzanne Langer and Philip Wheelwright, among many others.

In the course of the 18th c. there was a growing tendency to treat poetry, although still within a generally pragmatic frame, as primarily an emotional, in contrast to a rational, use of language, especially among such Longinian enthusiasts as John Dennis, Robert Lowth, and Joseph Warton (see, e.g., Warton's *Essay . . . on Pope,* 1750–82). By the latter part of the century, unqualifiedly expressive theories of poetry as grounded in the faculties and feelings of the poet are to be found in Sir William Jones's "Essay on the Arts Called Imitative" (1772), J. G. Sulzer's *Allgemeine Theorie der schönen Künste* (1771–74), and Hugh Blair's "Nature of Poetry" (*Lectures on Rhetoric and Belles Lettres*, 1783). German romantic theorists such as the Schlegels, Schleiermacher, and Tieck formulated the expressive view in the terminology of post-Kantian idealism; Novalis, e.g., said that "poetry is representation of the spirit, of the inner world in its totality" (*Die Fragmente*). In France Mme de Staël announced the new outlook on poetry in *De L'Allemagne* (1813), and in Italy it manifested itself, later on, in some of Leopardi's speculations on lyrical poetry.

Wordsworth's "Preface" to *Lyrical Ballads* is the heir to a century of developments in this mode of thinking, and became the single most important pronouncement of the emotive theory of poetry. His key formulation, twice uttered, is that poetry "is the spontaneous overflow of powerful feelings." The metaphor "overflow," like the equivalent terms in the definitions of Wordsworth's contemporaries—"expression," "uttering forth," "projection"—faces in an opposite direction from "imitation," and indicates that the source of the poem is no longer the external world, but the poet himself; and the elements which, externalized, become the subject matter of the poem are, expressly, the poet's "feelings." The word "overflow" also exemplifies the water-language in which feelings are usually discussed, and suggests that the dynamics of the poetic process consists in the pressure of fluid feelings; later John Keble converted the water to steam, and described the poetic process as a release, a "safety valve," for pent-up feelings and desires. The poetic process, therefore, as Wordsworth says, is not calculated, but "spontaneous." Wordsworth still allows for the element of "art" by regarding the success of spontaneous composition to be attendant upon prior thought and practice, and takes the audience into account by insisting that "poets do not write for poets alone, but for men." But in the more radical followers and successors of Wordsworth, including Keble, Mill, and Carlyle, the art of affecting an audience, which had been the defining attribute of poetry in pragmatic theory, becomes precisely the quality which invalidates a poem. "Poetry," wrote John Stuart Mill, "is feeling, confessing itself to itself in moments of solitude." And when the utterance "is not itself the end, but a means to an end . . . of making an impression upon another mind, then it ceases to be poetry, and becomes eloquence" ("What is Poetry?" 1833). Later writers adapted the concept of poetry as emotive expression to a communicative, or pragmatic, frame of reference. That poetry is emotional communication is the basic principle of Tolstoy's "infection theory" of art (*What is Art?* 1898), as well as of the earlier writings of I. A. Richards, who claimed that emotive language is "used for the sake of the effects in emotion and attitude produced by the reference it occasions," and that poetry "is the supreme form of emotive language" (*Principles of Literary Crit.* 1924).

Feelings overflow into words, so that it is characteristic of Wordsworth and later emotive theorists, through the school of I. A. Richards, to give to the nature and standards of poetic diction, or "language," the systematic priority which earlier critics had given to plot, character, and considerations of form. In earlier discussions of poetry as an imitation of human actions, the chief instances of poetry had been narrative and dramatic forms, and the usual antithesis to poetry had been history, or the narration of events that have actually happened. But Wordsworth, Hazlitt, Mill, and many of their contemporaries, conceiving poetry as the language of feeling, thought of the lyrical poem, instead of epic or tragedy, as the exemplary form, and replaced history as the logical opposite of poetry by what Wordsworth called "matter of fact, or science." This romantic innovation positing poetry as an antithesis to "science," has become a common theoretical gambit in the 20th c.; and, as we shall see, both Continental Formalists and American New Critics tend to establish the essential nature of poetry by detailed opposition to the features attributed to the language of science.

Among expressive theorists of the 19th c., the old criterion of truth to objective or ideal nature was often reinterpreted as truth to a nature already suffused with the poet's feelings, or reshaped by the dynamics of desire. More commonly still, the criterion was turned around, in the demand that poetry be "sincere"; it was in this period that "sincerity" became a cardinal requirement of poetic excellence. "The excellence of Burns," as Carlyle said, clearly revealing the reversal of the standard of "truth," "is . . . his *sincerity*, his indisputable air of truth. . . . The passion that is traced before us has glowed in a living heart." Or as J. S. Mill asserted, in a phrasing anticipating the theory of later symbolists and expressionists, poetry embodies "itself in symbols which are the nearest possible representations of the feeling in the exact shape in which it exists in the poet's mind." The mirror held up to nature becomes a mirror held up to the poet, or else it is rendered transparent: Shakespeare's works, according to Carlyle, "are so many windows, through which we see a glimpse of the world that was in him." Correspondingly, the elements constituting a poem become in large part qualities which it shares with its author: feelings, imagination, spirit, and (in Matthew Arnold, e.g.) such traits of character as largeness, freedom, benignity, and high seriousness.

As Carlyle shrewdly observed so early as 1827, the grand question asked by the best contemporary critics is "to be answered by discovering and delineating the peculiar nature of the poet from his poetry." Essays on Shakespeare, Milton, Dante, Homer became to a singular degree essays on the temperament and moral nature of the poet as manifested in his work. The most thorough exponent of poetry as self-expression was John Keble in his *Lectures on Poetry* (1832–41), whose thesis was that any good poem is a disguised form of wish-fulfillment—"the indirect expression," as he said in a review of Lockhart's *Scott,* "of some overpowering emotion, or ruling taste, or feeling, the direct indulgence whereof is somehow repressed"—and who specified and applied a complex set of techniques for reversing the process and reconstructing the temperament of the poet from its distorted projection in his poems. In both critical premises and practice, Keble has hardly been exceeded even by critics in the age of Freud who, like Edmund Wilson, hold that "the real elements, of course, of any work of fiction, are the elements of the author's personality: his imagination embodies in the images of characters, situations, and scenes the fundamental conflicts of his nature . . ." (*Axel's Castle,* 1936). Another recent development is that of the Geneva School of "phenomenological crit.," or "critics of consciousness." These critics conceive a literary work, in its elements and form, to be an objectified embodiment of the unique mode of consciousness of its author, and propose that the chief aim of the reader should be to re-experience this immanent consciousness. As Georges Poulet wrote, in "Phenomenology of Reading" (1969): "When I read as I ought . . . my consciousness behaves as though it were the consciousness of another." So early as 1778 J. G. Herder had declared: "This *living reading*, this divination into the soul of the author, is the *sole* mode of reading, and the most profound means of self-development." The quotation reveals the extent to which consciousness-crit., although employing phenomenological concepts derived from the philosopher Husserl, is rooted in the Romantic conception that a work of literature is the expression of a unique self.

The principal alternative, in 19th-c. expressive theory, to the view that poetry is the expression of feelings, or unrealized desires, of an individual personality, was Coleridge's view that "poetry" (the superlative passages which occur both in poems and other forms of discourse) is the product of "that synthetic and magical power, to which we have exclusively appropriated the name of imagination" (*Biographia Literaria,* 1817). The creative imagination of the poet, like God the Creator, is endowed with an inner source of motion, and its creative activity, generated by the tension of contraries seeking resolution in a new whole, parallels the dynamic principle underlying the created universe. Following the lead of post-Kantian German theorists, especially Schelling and A. W. Schlegel, Coleridge opposes the organic imaginative process to the mechanical operation of the fancy; that is, he deals with it, in terms that are literal for a growing plant and metaphoric for imagination, as a self-organizing process, assimilating disparate materials by an inherent lawfulness into an organic unity revealed "in the balance or reconciliation of opposite or discordant qualities. . . ." Coleridge thus inaugurated the organic theory of poetry in England, as well as the aesthetic principle of inclusiveness, or the "reconciliation of opposite or discordant qualities" which became both the basic conception of poetic unity and the prime criterion of poetic excellence in I. A. Richards and many of the New Critics.

One other variant of the expressive theory deserves mention. Longinus had attributed the sublime quality especially to the stunning image, or to brief passages characterized by "speed, power, and intensity," comparable in effect "to a thunder-bolt or flash of lightning," and recognizable by the transport or "spell that it throws over us." Many expressive theorists, assuming the lyric to be the paradigm of poetry, depart from the neoclassic emphasis on distinct and hierarchically ordered poetic kinds by minimizing other genres except as the occasion for the sporadic expression of lyrical feeling, as well as by applying to all poems qualitative and evaluative terms which are independent of their generic differences. Joseph Warton and other 18th-c. Longinians had gone still farther, by isolating the transporting short poem, or the intense image or fragment in a longer poem, and identifying it as "pure poetry," "poetry as such," or the "poetry of a poem." In the 19th c., there emerged the explicit theory that the essentially poetic is to be found only in the incandescent and unsustainable short poem or passage, originating in the soul unachievable by art and unanalyzable by critics, but characterized by the supreme aesthetic virtue of "intensity." This mode of thinking is to be found in Hazlitt's treatment of "gusto"; in Keats's concept that "the excellence of every art is its *intensity*"; in Poe's doctrine (picked up by Baudelaire) that "a poem is such, only inasmuch as it intensely excites, by elevating, the soul; and all intense excitements are, through a psychal necessity, brief" ("The Philosophy of Composition," 1846); in Arnold's use of fragmentary touchstones for detecting "the very highest poetical quality"; in the Abbé Bremond's theory of "la poésie pure"; and more recently and explicitly still, in A. E. Housman's *The Name and Nature of Poetry* (1933).

Objective Theories: Aristotle, after defining tragedy as an imitation of a certain kind of action with certain characteristic "powers," or effects, showed the way to the further consideration of the tragic poem as an entity in itself, subject to internal requirements (such as unity, probability, progression from beginning through complication to catastrophe) which determine the selection, treatment, and ordering of the parts into an artistic whole. Despite their persistent appeal to Aristotle as exemplar, however, most later critics in effect assimilated Aristotle to the Horatian theoretical frame, aligning the poem to its audience. In the 18th c., however, a radical shift occurred in the approach to poetry, as to the other arts. Ever since classical times the theoretical framework had been a construction paradigm, in which the enterprise was to establish the "art," or what Ben Jonson had called "the craft of making" a good poem, which would also serve to inform critics how to judge whether a poem was good, or well-made. In the 18th c. this often gave way to a perceptual paradigm, in which a perceiver confronts a completed poem, however it got made, and analyzes the features it presents to his attention and "taste," or sensibility. Addison's *Spectator* papers on "The Pleasures of the Imagination" (1712) is an innovative document in the theory of art, above all because, by adopting the general stance of Locke's epistemology, it substitutes for the old view of the *poeta* as a "maker" and the *poema* as a "made thing" the stance of a perceiver to the poem as a given object. Within this altered paradigm, or theoretical stance, two critical models for the nature of a poem were exploited during the 18th c. until they effected a shift, among philosophers of art, from the earlier mimetic or pragmatic theories to an objective theory of poetry-as-such. One of these is the heterocosmic model, in which each work constitutes a unique, coherent, and autonomous world. The other is the contemplation model, in which each work is a self-sufficient object that is contemplated disinterestedly for its own sake.

The figurative model of a poem as its own created world had been inaugurated by thinkers of the It. Ren.—Cristoforo Landino, Tasso, Scaliger—who proposed that the poet does not imitate God's world but, like the God of Genesis, creates his own world; and, it was sometimes suggested, *ex nihilo*, "out of nothing." Such high claims, however, served at first merely as a passing topic of praise within an overall pragmatic view of poetry, used in order to counter the derogation of poets and the charge that their fictions are lies. With this aim Sidney, for example, glorified poetry above all other human achievements by claiming that the poet alone, "lifted up with the vigor of his own invention, doth grow in effect into another nature," when "with the force of a divine breath he bringeth things forth far surpassing her doings"; he at once turns, however, to his basic formulation that poetry is an "art of imitation" that is designed "to teach and delight." The revolutionary possibilities of the concept that the poet is the creator of a new world began to be exploited only when it became necessary to justify poetry against the claim by writers in the age of the "new philosophy" that (as Hobbes put it in "Answer to Davenant") since poetry is "an imitation of human life," the poet may not go "beyond the conceived possibility of nature." Addison's counter-claim, in defending "the fairy way of writing" in *Spectator* 419, is that in such products of the poet's "invention" and "imagination" we "are led, as it were, into a new creation," and that in its non-realistic components, poetry "makes new worlds of its own, shows us persons who are not to be found in being. . . ." The young German philosopher, Alexander Baumgarten, in *Philosophical Reflections on Poetry* (1735), developed this concept that some kinds of poetry are a new creation by translating into poetics the cosmogony of Leibniz, according to which God, in creating this "best of all possible worlds," chose from an indefinite number of "possible worlds," each constituted by "compossible" (mutually coherent) elements, and each ordered by its unique internal laws. In Baumgarten's poetics, the nonrealistic elements in a poem, which he calls "heterocosmic fictions," are justifiable in that they are capable of co-existing in another "possible" world; he also, in an important theoretical move, extends the heterocosmic analogue to account for the "interconnection" of elements in all poems whatever: "The poet is like a maker or creator. So the poem ought to be like a world;" hence each poetic world, since it is governed by its own system of laws, manifests a "poetic" truth that is not one of correspondence to the real world, but of internal coherence. The adaptation to poetry of Leibniz's philosophy of divine creation effected similar conclusions in the Swiss-German critics, Bodmer and Breitinger. As Breitinger summarized this view in his *Critische Dichtkunst* (1740), the poetic imagination finds its originals "not in the actual world, but in some other possible world-structure. Every single well-invented poem is therefore to be regarded in no other way than as the history of an other possible world. In this respect the poet alone deserves the name of *poietes*; that is, of a creator." The consequence, as Bodmer put it, is that "poetic truth," within the distinctive world of a poem, differs from "rational truth" in that its probability consists not in correspondence to the existing world, but "in its coherence with itself." (*Von dem Wunderbaren*, 1740). In England critics who adopted Addison's metaphor of a poem as a new creation achieved parallel results, though in less detail and without the underpinning of Leibnizian cosmogony. In explicit refutation of Hobbes, for example, Richard Hurd (*Letters on Chivalry and Romance*, 1762) affirmed that "poetical truth" is independent of "philosophical or historical truth," on the grounds that "the poet has a world of his own, where experience has less to do, than consistent imagination."

The alternative model—the concept that a poem, like other works of art, is a self-bounded object that is to be contemplated disinterestedly and for its own sake—also had a theological origin, but one quite different from that of the poem as an alternative to God's creation. The historical roots of this concept are in Plato's assertion, in the *Symposium*, that the highest good of life consists in the "contemplation of beauty absolute" (that is, of the Idea of Ideas), as seen "with the eye of the mind"; also in Plotinus' derivative claims, in the *Enneads*, that the Absolute, or One, is "wholly self-sufficing," "self-closed," and "autonomous," and that the ultimate aim of the human soul, impelled by "love," is to "contemplate Absolute Beauty in its essential integrity" and thus to achieve a peace without "movement," "passion," or "outlooking desire." In the early Christian centuries various Church Fathers conflated the self-sufficient Absolute of Plato and Plotinus, however incongruously, with the personal God of the Bible. St. Augustine, more than any other, fixed these ideas in Christian thought, in his reiterated claims that all the good and beautiful things in this world of sense are to be loved only for their "use," but that God alone, as "the Supreme Beauty," and thus self-sufficient, is to be loved not for use but for pure "enjoyment," as His own end and *non propter aliud*, for His own sake [*propter se ipsam*], and *gratis* (free of profit to the self). And in this life, Augustine says, the highest manifestation of love is an "enjoyment" of God which is a *visio*, or contemplation by the mind's eye, of God in His supreme beauty. It was the third Earl of Shaftesbury, in his *Characteristics* (1711), who introduced the theological terms "contemplation" and "disinterested" into the context of a discussion of the way we apprehend beautiful earthly objects, including works of art; but Shaftesbury dealt with such sensible beauties only as ancillary to his Neoplatonic ethical and religious philosophy, which permitted no essential distinction between religious, moral, and aesthetic "contemplation." It remained for Shaftesbury's philosophical successors in Germany, where he enjoyed an enormous vogue, to secularize and specialize the terms "contemplation," "disinterested," and "for its own sake," by transferring their application from God to works of art, and by using these terms specifically to differentiate aesthetic experience from religious and moral, as well as from practical and utilitarian, experience.

The young German thinker Karl Philipp Moritz was the first to propound an unqualifiedly objective theory of art and poetry as such, and in doing so he deployed both the contemplation model and the heterocosmic model of art, in a way that evidenced the degree to which the two were in fact conducive to similar artistic concepts and criteria. In an "Essay on the Unification of All the Fine Arts" (1785), Moritz attacks the reigning views that the arts aim at an "imitation of nature" with the "end" of giving pleasure to an audience. Only the mechanical, useful arts, Moritz asserts, have an "*outer* end." "In the contemplation of the beautiful object [of art], however . . . I contemplate it as something which is *completed . . . in its own self*, which therefore constitutes a whole in itself, and affords me pleasure *for its own sake*." (Moritz's italics) Three years later, in his essay "On the Formative Imitation of the Beautiful," Moritz buttresses these views by adverting to the heterocosmic model of a work of art as its own creation: the "formative power" of the artist dissolves reality in order "to form and create" what nature has left unrealized "into a self-governing, self-sufficient whole." In this way the artist's power "creates its own world, in which . . . every thing is, in its own way, a self-sufficient whole" that has "its entire value, and the end of its existence, in itself."

It is evident that when, only a few years later, Kant published his epochal *Critique of Aesthetic Judgment* (1790), he assumed the perceiver's, instead of the maker's, stance to a work of art; also that he adopted, but greatly subtilized, the contemplation model and distinctive philosophical vocabulary, descended from the Neoplatonists and Augustine, that we have traced in Moritz. According to Kant the "pure judgment of taste" (that is, the normative aesthetic perception) "combines delight or aversion immediately with the mere *contemplation* of the object irrespective of its use or any end"; it is "the one and only disinterested and *free* delight," in that it is "purely contemplative," "without desire," and free of reference to the "external" ends of use or moral good; and it "pleases for its own sake [*für sich selbst gefällt*]." Like Moritz, Kant also conjoins the contemplative to the heterocosmic model: "The [productive] imagination is a powerful agent for the creation, as it were, of a second nature out of the material supplied to it by actual nature," in which, "following, no doubt, laws that are based on analogy," the materials are worked up into "what surpasses nature."

Various of these Moritzian and Kantian concepts of art as such were assimilated by Schiller, the Schlegels, Schopenhauer and others, and became elements in the mainstream of professional aesthetics. In the mid-19th c. similar views emerged among practicing poets and critics, when the concept that a poem, as a sufficient and autonomous object, is to be contemplated disinterestedly for its own sake, became a common tenet among Fr. proponents of *l'art pour l'art*. One source of this view was, through Baudelaire as intermediary, Poe's laudation in "The Poetic Principle" (1848–49), of the "poem *per se*—this poem which is a poem and nothing more—this poem written solely for the poem's sake" and offering a "pure" pleasure "from the contemplation of the Beautiful." Another important source was a popularized version of Kant's aesthetic ideas in Victor Cousin's lectures on *The True, the Beautiful, and the Good*, available in numerous editions after their first publication, twenty years after they had been delivered in 1817–18. "The mere imitation of nature," as Gautier wrote in 1847, "cannot be the end of the artist." The purpose of the modern school of *l'art pour l'art* "is to seek beauty for its own sake with complete impartiality, perfect disinterestedness." This concept of disinterested contemplation, as in the latter 18th c., was often merged with that of a literary work as its own created world. To Flaubert, for example, the relation of an author to his second creation should be like that of God to his original creation, both immanent and transcendent: "An author in his book must be like God in the universe, present everywhere and visible nowhere. Art being a second Nature, the creator of that Nature must behave similarly"—a view that Joyce's Stephen Dedalus echoed, in *A Portrait of the Artist as a Young Man*, in asserting that "the artist, like the God of the creation, remains within or behind or beyond or above his handiwork, invisible, refined out of existence, indifferent, paring his fingernails." In his essay "Poetry for Poetry's Sake" (1901), A. C. Bradley undertook, he said, to salvage the basic truths within the exaggerated claims of art for art's sake. The experience of poetry, he declared, "is an end in itself," and "*poetic* value" is "this intrinsic worth alone," independently of a poem's "ulterior worth" as means to ends outside itself; for a poem is not "a part, nor yet a copy of the real world," but "a world by itself, independent, complete, autonomous," and the reader must "conform to its laws." Poetry and reality "are parallel developments which nowhere meet . . . they are analogues." And the reciprocal of this concept, from the standpoint of the reader, is that the poetic otherworld exists for our disinterested contemplation; as Bradley puts it, the poem "makes no direct appeal to those feelings, desires, and purposes [of our life in this world], but speaks only to contemplative imagination."

The objective conception of poetry-as-such, expressed in one or another idiom, became the dominant mode of thinking for many literary theorists and critics, as well as for many major authors, in the half-century or so beginning in the 1920s. The "Russian Formalists" set up a fundamental opposition between literary (or poetical) language and ordinary "practical," "referential," or "scientific" language. Whereas ordinary language communicates by references to the outer world, literary language is self-focused, exploiting various devices in order to "foreground" the utterance itself, to "estrange" it from ordinary discourse, and to draw attention from outer relations to its own "formal" features, the inter-relationships among the linguistic signs themselves. The loose-boundaried critical movement of Fr. Structuralism, beginning in the 1950's, absorbed some Formalist concepts, but viewed a literary work as primarily a second-order signifying system; that is, it uses language, the first-order system, as its medium, and is itself to be analyzed on the model of the linguistic theory propounded by Ferdinand de Saussure in his *Course in General Linguistics* (1915). Structuralism opposes the views that literature imitates reality, or expresses the subjectivity of an author, or is a mode of communication between author and reader. Instead it regards a work (whether a novel or a poem) as a mode of writing (*écriture*) which, like the linguistic system that precipitates it, is a self-determining structure of inter-relations constituted by a play of specifically literary conventions and "codes." The general aim of structuralist critics, as Jonathan Culler put it in *Structuralist Poetics* (1975), is to "construct a poetics which stands to literature as linguistics stands to language"—that is, as the general laws of a *langue* stand to a specific utterance or *parole*.

Among Am. literary theorists between 1930 and 1960, the most widely accepted formulations were that a literary work is "autotelic," and that we must consider poetry "primarily as poetry and not another thing" (T. S. Eliot); or that the first law of crit. is to "cite the nature of the object" and to recognize "the autonomy of the work itself as existing for its own sake" (J. C. Ransom); or that the essential task of the critic is the "intrinsic," not the "extrinsic" study of literature (Wellek and Warren). The "Chicago Critics," while acknowledging the usefulness of an "integral criticism" that considers poetry, in an inclusive context, as sharing essential features with other human products, themselves advocate and pursue a "differential crit. that deals with a poem as such, in its distinctive internal characteristics. This they do by expanding upon a procedure they attribute to Aristotle: they view each poem as an artistic whole that is formally constructed to achieve a particular "working or power"; the elements, inter-relations, and structure of the poem are systematically analyzed as internal causes of that power—causes that are theoretically separable from extra-artistic causes of a poem in the nature of an individual author, in the audience addressed, or in the state of the language that the author inherits ("Introduction," *Critics and Crit.* ed. R. S. Crane).

The most widespread and commonly applied theory of poetry in the quarter-century between the mid-1930's and 1960 was that named by John Crowe Ransom in 1941 "the New Crit."; it became the reigning point of view in Am. colleges and schools especially after the publication in 1938 by Cleanth Brooks and Robert Penn Warren of the widely used textbook, *Understanding Poetry*. These critics differ in the details of their theory, but share the concept that poetry in the large (with little or no attention to diverse poetic genres) is to be considered as a special mode of language, which is defined by positing for poetry features that are systematically contrary to the abstract, literal, and conceptual nature, the empirical claims, and the referential and practical purposes attributed to the language of "science." A poem thus becomes its own world—a distinctive universe of discourse—which is set against representations of the ordinary world of things, people, and events; and the integrity and boundaries of this world, or poetic "object," are carefully guarded by prohibitions against the "personal heresy," "the heresy of paraphrase" (Cleanth Brooks), and what W. K. Wimsatt and Monroe Beardsley called the "intentional fallacy" (reference to the purpose and state of mind of the author) and the "affective fallacy" (reference to the responses of the reader). The sole end of a poem is the poem itself as a self-sufficient "structure of meanings." The New Critics developed a formidable apparatus for their most innovative and distinctive procedure, the detailed "explication," or "close reading," of individual poems as a totality of "logical structure" and "local texture" (Ransom), or an equilibrium of multiple "tensions" (Allen Tate), or an "organic unity" of ironies, ambiguities, paradoxes, and image-patterns (Brooks). The attempt was often made to reconnect the poem-as-such to the ordinary world by positing as its organizing principle a "theme," which is embodied and dramatized in the poem's evolving imagery and "symbolic action," and is to be judged by such tests as "seriousness," "maturity," "profundity," and the subtlety of the "moral awareness" that the poem manifests. (See Brook's "Irony as a Principle of Structure"; also, the highly influential writings of the Eng. critic, F. R. Leavis, which are in parallel with many of the assumptions and practices of his Am. contemporaries.) But as W. K. Wimsatt stresses in *The Verbal Icon*, such reassertions of the thematic and moral aspects of a poem are to be understood not in an expressive or pragmatic, but in an objective orientation: "Neither the qualities of the author's mind nor the effects of a poem upon a reader's mind should be confused with the moral quality expressed by the poem itself." Similarly with the assertions of Ransom and other New Critics—in opposition to the positivist's claim that valid knowledge is the sole prerogative of science—that poetry is "cognitive" and provides, as Tate says, a "special, unique, and complete knowledge" ("The Present Function of Crit."). It turns out that the knowledge yielded by a poem is not that of correspondence to the world, but that of the concrete and bounded world of the poem itself: "It is sufficient," as Tate puts it, "that here, in the poem, we get knowledge of a whole object." And as in the earlier applications of the heterocosmic concept, the mimetic truth of correspondence is replaced by a truth of coherence that is coterminous with the poem. As W. K. Wimsatt puts this view in *The Verbal Icon*, a poem does not mirror the world but, by the multiplicity of its internal relationships, becomes an object which is itself densely physical, hence isomorphic with the world to which it stands in the relation of an "icon" or (in the term earlier used by A. C. Bradley) an analogue: "The dimension of coherence is . . . greatly enhanced and thus generates an extra dimension of correspondence to reality, the symbolic or analogical."

Resistant, in this century, to the theories of poetry-as-such have been Freudian critics who, whatever the refinements they introduce, continue to treat poetry as primarily a product, under a variety of cunning disguises, of the poet's unconscious desires. Another counter-theory is that of Marxist critics who in recent decades have produced complex and subtle versions of the basic view that literature both expresses and reflects an ideology which, in the final analysis, derives from the structure and conflict of classes attendant upon the distinctive means of economic production in any given era; the special emphasis is on the literary "reflection," in the modern bourgeois era, of the class conflicts, contradictions, crippling intellectual conditions, and human alienation under capitalism. A major new challenge to reigning views was mounted by Northrop Frye's archetypal theory, announced in his *Anatomy of Crit.* (1957) and elaborated in a number of later writings. Frye substitutes for the autonomous single work of the New Critics an all-inclusive autonomous realm, the "self-contained literary universe," which has over the ages been bodied forth by the generically human imagination so as to humanize an inhuman reality by incorporating it into persisting mythical forms that serve to satisfy enduring human needs and concerns. The four radical *mythoi* (structural principles) are the primary genres of comedy, romance, tragedy and satire; but within each genre, individual works inevitably play variations upon many other archetypes, or inherited imaginative forms, that literature shares not only with other "discursive verbal structures" and with myths, but also with ritualized forms of social activities.

Recent Developments: Since the mid-1960's, all traditional theories of poetry have been thrown into considerable disarray by a number of intellectual movements which, whatever their radical divergences, coincide in focusing on the way in which we read, and in the conclusion that there are "no right readings" of any poetic or literary writing, hence that, since the meanings of a text are radically indeterminate, a critic is liberated from his traditional subordinacy to the work he comments on, and in fact achieves the production of meaning—the function of "creativity"—that earlier critics had mistakenly attributed to the author of a work. In *The Anxiety of Influence* (1973) and a number of later books, Harold Bloom proposes that a poet as reader experiences some poem, or poems, of a precursor as an intolerable threat to his own imaginative uniqueness and autonomy. This anxiety brings into inevitable play a variety of psychic defenses which distort drastically the precursor-poem even as it is re-embodied in the poet's own "belated" poem, and so gives this latter the precarious illusion of being "prior" to its poetic predecessor and model, both in psychological time and in imaginative originality. But readings of the later poem, whether by poets or by critics of poetry, are in their turn bound to be "defensive," hence inescapably distortive "misreadings." In essays written during the 1970's, collected in *Is There a Text in this Class?* (1980), Stanley Fish established himself as the most radical exemplar of the international movement of Reader-response Crit. Fish proposes, in what he calls his "affective crit.," that the text of a poem is simply a set of blank signs, an empty stimulus, in response to which a reader, deploying one or another "interpretive strategy," in effect "writes" the text in its formal features, and does not discover, but "creates" all its meanings, as well as its postulated author and his presumed intentions in writing the text. In his later writings Fish stresses the concept of "interpretive communities"; in each such community its members, since they share interpretive presuppositions and habits of reading, are able to agree, approximately at least, in the meanings that they find; but the number of possible strategies and communities is indefinitely large, and since each produces its own reading of a text, the result is an indefinite number of incompatible yet undecidable interpretations.

Most prominent in the 1980's has been Deconstructive Crit., based primarily on the writings, beginning in the latter 1960's, of the post-structuralist Fr. thinker, Jacques Derrida. Derrida views poetry and literature as instances of writing, *écriture*, which like all Western writing are "logocentric," in that they presuppose a "logos" or "presence"—an absolute "ground," or a "transcendental signified"—which exists outside of, and is unmediated by, language, and which functions to organize a language system and to warrant the determinability of any utterance or writing in that language. In the inevitable absence of such a ground, Derrida claims, all writing inevitably deconstructs itself by "disseminating" without limit into an "undecidable" suspension of significations that involve "aporias"—that is, conflicting or contradictory meanings. Am. deconstructionist critics, such as Paul de Man and J. Hillis Miller, have adapted Derrida's views of writing, as well as his standard practice of the deconstructive reading of selected textual passages, to the close reading of individual poems and other literary works, or of passages from such works, in the attempt to show that, by the internal rhetorical, figurative, and counter-logical economy of their textuality, these works are ultimately allegories about their own language, and inevitably disseminate into self-conflicting aporias of undecidable meanings. As Hillis Miller describes the enterprise ("Stevens' Rock and Crit. as Cure, II"): "The deconstructive critic seeks to find . . . the element in the system studied which is illogical, the thread in the text in question which will unravel it all. . . . Deconstruction is . . . a demonstration that [the text] has already dismantled itself." It should be noted that neither Fish's type of Reader-response viewpoint nor Deconstructive Crit. is a theory specifically of poetry or literature, but a theory of reading and writing in general. Deconstructive critics, however, favor, or "privilege," literary texts in their critical analyses on the ground that they show more self-awareness—in de Man's term, they are less "mystified"—about their own fictional and illusionary textual tactics.

The multiplicity, and what seem the unresolvable contradictions, among competing theories of poetry has led to repeated attacks against the validity or utility of such theorizing. Some analytic philosophers, for example, have attacked all such theories as illegitimately grounded on "essentialist" definitions of art or poetry, and as manifesting a variety of logical and linguistic errors and confusions; to them, the only valid crit. consists of verifiable statements about the properties of individual poems or other works of art. (See e.g. *Aesthetics and Language*, ed. William Elton, 1954.) Such "meta-crit.," however, mistakes the historical function of theory in the practice of crit. A profitable theory, although in its own way empirical (by beginning and ending with an appeal to the features of poems), is not a science like physics but an enterprise of discovery—what Coleridge called "a speculative instrument." The definitions of poetry or art from which most theories set out, for example, may or may not have been intended by their proponents to be assertions of the essence or ultimate nature of poetry; in practice, however, they have served as an indispensable heuristic device for blocking out an area of investigation and establishing a point of vantage over that area; they have functioned also as the principles of reasoning about poetry, and the grounds for developing a coherent set of categories and distinctions to be used in classifying, analyzing, and appraising particular poems. The diverse theories described in this article—however contradictory an excerpted statement from one may seem when matched against an isolated statement from another—may in fact serve as alternative and complementary procedures for doing the critic's job of work, with each theory, from its elected vantage, yielding distinctive insights into the properties and relations of poems. Crit. without some theoretical understructure—whether this theory, as in Aristotle or Coleridge, is prior and explicit, or as in Johnson and Arnold, is adverted to only as occasion demands—is largely made up of desultory impressions and of unsystematic concepts that are supposedly given by "common sense," but turn out to have been inherited from earlier critics, in whose writings they were implicated in a theoretical structure. And the history of crit. at the hands of its masters, from Aristotle through Johnson, Goethe, and Coleridge to the present, testifies that the applied, or practical, crit. applauded by impressionists and philosophical analysts alike has been neither purely impressionistic nor *ad hoc*, but most telling when grounded on the principles, distinctions, and coherent reasoning that constitute precisely what we mean by a theory of poetry.

D. Masson, "Theories of Poetry," *Essays Biographical and Crit.* (1856); J. E. Spingarn, *A Hist. of Lit. Crit. in the Ren.* (1899); Saintsbury; A. C. Bradley, *Oxford Lectures on Poetry* (1909); Gayley and Kurtz; Bray; J.W.H. Atkins, *Lit. Crit. in Antiquity* (2 v., 1934) and *Eng. Lit. Crit.*, I, *The Medieval Phase* (1943); II, *The Renascence* (1947); III, *The 17th and 18th C.* (1951); Patterson; S. C. Pepper, *The Basis of Crit. in the Arts* (1946); S. E. Hyman, *The Armed Vision* (1948); Wellek and Warren; Crane, *Critics*; M. H. Abrams, *The Mirror and the Lamp: Romantic Theory and the Crit. Tradition*, 1953 (provides, together with "Kant and the Theology of Art," *Notre Dame Eng. Jour.*, 13, 1981, an expanded treatment of much of the material in this article); Crane; Wellek; Krieger; Frye; Wimsatt and Brooks; B. Markwardt, *Gesch. der deutschen Poetik* (in 6 v., 5 v. completed, 1937–67); B. Weinberg, *A Hist. of Lit. Crit. in the It. Ren.* (2 v., 1961); R. Foster, *The New Romantics, a Reappraisal of the New Crit.* (1962); Sutton; R. Wellek, *Concepts of Crit.*, ed. S. G. Nichols (1963); S. Lawall, *Critics of Consciousness: The Existential Structures of Lit.* (1968); H. Bloom, *The Anxiety of Influence: A Theory of Poetry* (1973); J. Culler, *Structuralist Poetics* (1975) and *On Deconstruction: Theory and Crit. after Structuralism* (1982); G. Webster, *The Republic of Letters: A Hist. of Postwar Am. Lit. Opinion* (1979); S. Fish, *Is There a Text in this Class?* (1980); F. Lentricchia, *After the New Crit.* (1980).

CONVENIENT ANTHOLOGIES OF POETIC THEORY: *Crit. Essays of the 17th C.*, ed. J. S. Spingarn (3 v., 1908–9); *Crit. Essays of the 18th C.*, ed. W. H. Durham (1915); *Eng. Crit. Essays, 19th C.*, ed. E. D. Jones (1916); *Kunstanschauung der Frühromantik*, ed. A. Müller, (1931); *Elizabethan Crit. Essays*, ed. G. G. Smith (2 v., 1937); *Lit. Crit. Plato to Dryden*, ed. A. H. Gilbert (1940); *Lit. Crit. Pope to Croce*, ed. G. W. Allen and H. H. Clark (1941); *Crit.: The Major Texts*, ed. W. J. Bate (1948); *Critiques and Essays in Crit., 1920–1948*, ed. R. W. Stallman (1949); *Crit. Prefaces of the Fr. Ren.*, ed. B. Weinberg (1950); *Lit. Opinion in America*, ed. M. D. Zabel (1951); *Modern Lit. Crit.*, ed. I. Howe (1958); *The Continental Model, Selected Fr. Crit. Essays of the 17th C. in Eng. Tr.*, ed. S. Elledge and D. S. Schier (1960); *18th-C. Crit. Essays*, ed. S. Elledge (2 v., 1961); *Modern Fr. Poets on Poetry, an Anthol.*, ed. R. Gibson (1961); *Modern Continental Lit. Crit.*, ed. O. B. Hardison, Jr. (1962); *Modern Crit. in Theory and Practice*, ed. W. Sutton and R. Foster (1963); *Textual Strategies: Perspectives in Post-Structuralist Crit.*, ed. J. V. Harari (1979). M.H.A.

POST-STRUCTURALISM. See POETRY, THEORIES OF (OBJECTIVE THEORIES).

POULTER'S MEASURE. A meter composed of rhyming couplets made up of a line of iambic hexameter followed by a line of iambic heptameter, thus: "Silence augmenteth grief, writing increaseth rage, / Staled are my thoughts, which loved and lost the wonder of our age." (Fulke Greville, Lord Brooke, *Epitaph on Sir Philip Sidney*.) Employed in the 16th c. by Wyatt, Surrey, Sidney, Grimald, and other Eng. poets, the meter derives its name from the poultryman's proverbial practice of giving 12 eggs for the first dozen and 14 for the second, noted by George Gascoigne in his *Steele Glas* (1576). Despite its temporary popularity, the meter has not proved a satisfactory one for sustained composition in Eng. It has a deadly tendency toward monotony, and the heavy stress accents native to the language lend it an effect of panting effort followed by ludicrous haste. Written out as an iambic quatrain instead of a couplet, a^3 b^3 c^4 b^3, the form persisted as the "short meter" (q.v.) of the Eng. hymns.—G. Stewart, *The Technique of Eng. Verse* (1930); C. S. Lewis, *Eng. Lit. of the 16th C.* (1954); J. Thompson, *The Founding of Eng. Metre* (1961).

PROSE POEM (poem in prose). A composition able to have any or all features of the lyric, except that it is put on the page—though not conceived of—as prose. It differs from poetic prose in that it is short and compact, from free verse in that it has no line breaks, from a short prose passage in that it has, usually, more pronounced rhythm, sonorous effects, imagery, and density of expression. It may contain even inner rhyme and metrical runs. Its length, generally, is from half a page (one or two paragraphs) to three or four pages, i.e., that of the average lyrical poem. If it is any longer, the tensions and impact are forfeited, and it becomes—more or less poetic—prose. The term "prose poem" has been applied irresponsibly to anything from the Bible to a novel by Faulkner, but should be used only to designate a highy conscious (sometimes even self-conscious) artform.

The tendency is to consider Aloysius Bertrand the creator of the p.p.; his *Gaspard de la nuit* of 1842 is the first published collection of indubitable prose poetry, though Bertrand was writing p. poems as early as 1827, and Maurice de Guérin, the other initiator, around 1835. But the actual beginnings are in that 18th-c. France where the Academy's rigid rules of versification were driving many a potential poet with a taste for individuality into prose. Thus came about works like Fénelon's poetic novel *Télémaque* (1699) and Montesquieu's prose pastoral *Le Temple de Gnide* (1725); these, and their many imitators, represent an approach, and encouragement, to prose poetry. Men like La Mothe-Houdar defiantly produced odes in prose, but this was mostly bravado and rhetoric. A greater incentive and more useful model was provided by translations of foreign verse into Fr. prose. The original might be *The Psalms*, Gr. or L. lyrics, Norse, oriental, or other "exotic" folk poems, Eng. preromantic verse, or such works as in the original already are more or less prose poetry, like Macpherson's *Ossian* or the *Idyls* of the Swiss poet Salomon Gessner (1756). In Fr., these emerge as prose poetry, soon to be followed by pseudo-translations which, naturally, take the same form. Best among the latter are the charming *Chansons madécasses* of Parny (1787), purporting to be folk poems of Madagascar. By this time the poetic novels may contain lyrics in prose, e.g., Chateaubriand's *Atala* (1799, publ. 1801), but these are still translations, real or supposed. Minor writers, like Volney and Rabbe, may be stepping-stones, but it is the colorful Bertrand and the limpid Guérin (*Le Centaure, La Bacchante*—unfortunately not publ. till 1861) that write the first fine, admittedly original, pieces which, though neither author is known to have used the term, are p. poems by any name.

The first widely known poems in prose, however, are those of Baudelaire, who also officially christens the genre (*Petits Poèmes en prose*, or *Le Spleen de Paris*, begun 1855, published in full 1869). By owning their filiation from Bertrand, Baudelaire bestowed recognition on a young man who died obscurely in a charity ward. Baudelaire's achievement is to have taken an art-form which still went in heavily for exoticism and verbal genre-painting and given it the variety and scope, or almost, of the *Fleurs du mal*. But he does not always escape prosaism, and often becomes merely anecdotal. Rimbaud is the first, and probably only, poet whose greatest work is his prose poetry: *Les Illuininations* (date of composition uncertain, published 1886) and, somewhat less developed, *Une Saison en enfer* (1873). Here the p.p. is given the sweep of both a boundless consciousness and a creative subconscious, expressed with extraordinary, dizzying collocations of objects and ideas. Where private imagery does not turn to solipsism, stunning effects are achieved in a wholly flexible form sometimes becoming vers libre or even rhymed verse. From 1864 on, Stéphane Mallarmé was working on p. poems which appeared, along with other prose, as *Divagations* (1897). In these dozen or so pieces a revolutionary (but always carefully pondered) use of syntax, creating unusual relationships or isolations within the sentence, and a system of overlapping metaphors (tropes within tropes) produce almost infinite suggestiveness, now and then inscrutability. From the *Illuminations* and the *Divagations* direct paths lead to such important literary phenomena as free verse, the stream of consciousness, surrealism, James Joyce, and, indeed, modern literature's emphasis on private metaphor and *mélange des genres*. Significantly, the verse dramatist Claudel and the experimental novelists Gide and Proust wrote prose poetry in their youth.

By the end of the 19th c. the p.p. is firmly established, and even to list its major European and Am. practitioners would be impossible here. In the early period, however, we must note in Germany the amazing *ex nihilo* manifestation of the above-mentioned Gessner; Novalis and Hölderlin contributed to the genre at the beginning of the 19th c., the young Stefan George and Rilke at the end. Elsewhere in the past century, the p.p. or a reasonable facsimile, made interesting appearances in De Quincey and Beddoes (later in some poets of the Yellow Nineties), in Turgenyev, the Spaniard G. A. Bécquer, the Dane J. P. Jacobsen; two of Poe's short pieces, at least, fall into the category. But assertions and splendors notwithstanding, works like Lautréamont's *Maldoror*, Hölderlin's *Hyperion*, Nietzsche's *Zarathustra*, are not p. poems—unless prose epics, hence barely distinguishable from the poetic novel. The p.p. as such is with us still, but its accomplishments having been absorbed by other genres, it has become the occasional "aside" of writers whose essential utterance takes other forms.

C. Baudelaire, "A Arsène Houssaye," *Le Spleen de Paris* (1869); J.-K. Huysmans, *A rebours* (1884; end of ch. 14 first anthol. of p.p., with comment); F. Rauhut, *Das französische Prosagedicht* (1929); V. Clayton, *The Prose P. in Fr. Lit. of the 18th C.* (1936); M.-J. Durry [review of the preceding item], RHL, 44 (1937) and "Autour du poème en prose," *Mercure de France*, Feb. 1, 1937; A. Chérel, *La Prose poétique française* (1940); *Anthologie du poème en prose*, ed. M. Chapelan (1946); P. M. Jones, *The Background to Modern Fr. Poetry* (1951); "A Little Anthol. of the Poem in Prose," ed. C. H. Ford, *New Directions*, 14 (1953; possibilities and impossibilities of the p.p.: junk, jargon, and a few gems); S. Bernard, *Le Poème en prose de Baudelaire jusqu'à nos jours* (1959); M. Parent, *Saint-John Perse et quelques devanciers: Etudes sur le poème en prose* (1960). J.S.

PROSE RHYTHM. P.r. has been written off as a mere figure of speech and it has been treated seriously by both psychologists and students of literature. Much depends on the definition of rhythm that one starts with. If rhythm means simply, etymologically, "flow," p.r. is a pleasing flow of the sounds of language, and any prose which satisfies the ear is rhythmic. This is sometimes called the rhythm of the flowing line. If, on the other hand, the word has the stricter sense of a series of equal or approximately equal units, the first problem is to find a way of identifying the units. This can be done by grammatical analysis, that is, by observing the length of phrases and clauses: if they seem to fall into more or less equal and repeated patterns, the prose has a recognizable kind of rhythm, sometimes called the balanced style, as is all too common in Dr. Johnson. But this will occur without much regularity; otherwise the prose becomes offensively monotonous or sing-song. Take for example, "Priest falls, prophet rises," or Burke's "Kings will be tyrants from policy when subjects are rebels from principle." To recognize the subtler varieties, such as may occur in ordinary, to say nothing of studied and ornate prose, a trained ear is necessary, and also a careful analysis of the potential elements. And this means breaking down the sentences and paragraphs into phrases, words, and syllables with full regard to their constituents of *time* (duration), *stress* (relative emphasis), *pitch* (rising and falling of the voice in spoken language and an analogous effect in silent reading), and *tempo,* including pauses; for there are considerable differences in rhythm between rapid and retarded speech—the more rapid the speaking or reading, the longer the rhythmic units seem to become.

Another form of measurement is metrical. Owing to the formal arrangements of language (syntax), words and syllables have a natural tendency to come in set patterns ("the course of the river," "human nature," "inevitable development," etc.). The poet adopts these natural patterns, altering them for special effects and sometimes with, sometimes without forcing, molds the language into his metrical scheme. Often the difference between rhythmic prose and poetry is very slight; for example, in Pope's famous line "Most women have no character at all" or in Milton's "Of Man's First Disobedience, and the Fruit" the meter is so "irregular," that is, departs so far from the expected alternation of stressed and unstressed syllables, that without the context one would not recognize the meter at all. Conversely, a great deal of normal prose contains potential, and unintentional, meter which will be noticed only after close examination but which nevertheless is felt and so contributes to the p.r. If, however, the latent meter is allowed to become too obvious or is purposely developed for emotional effect, as in oratorical or pathetic passages, the sense of true prose is destroyed and the reader or hearer resents the trick played on him. The best prose requires therefore a careful balance of these two forces.

In the study of p.r., then, three facts must be taken into account. First, there is this natural tendency of language to assume metrical patterns. This is the most elementary aspect of p.r. Second, the established grammatical or syntactic arrangements of language are often repeated, in the form of parallelism or balance, for rhetorical purposes. Third, there is a psychological factor which both creates and satisfies a desire for rhythmical repetition and which leads us to find or feel, and sometimes to induce where it does not actually exist, a clear sense of rhythm in language. In its extreme form it develops or imposes a sense of rhythm in any prose which is easy to read or listen to, so that we are inclined to say that all good prose is rhythmical.

Great progress has been made recently in the scientific study of speech sounds, going beyond the simple groups of syllable, word, phrase, etc. *This structural analysis* has an elaborate code of symbols, including four degrees of stress and four or five of pitch. Besides the usual phonetic values of vowel and consonant, it embraces juncture, the phonemic, morphemic, and syntactic phenomena, and various formulas. This system may eventually enable us to record and interpret the many variations of speech and so come closer than hitherto to an understanding of rhythms, both in prose and in verse. Yet there will always remain a subjective element, and each reader, each listener will recognize and feel the rhythms according to his native receptivity.

The cadence or *cursus* (clausula) is a special form of prose rhythm. It was invented by the Gr. orators and was, originally, a kind of punctuation for oral delivery, marking the end of a clause or sentence. Cicero adopted the device and used the following clausulae and their numerous resolutions most often:

–⏑––⏓;–––⏓;–⏑⏑–⏓

Zielinski divides Cicero's clausulae into the following classes: *verae* I = cretic (–⏑–) or molossus (–––) + trochee (–⏑) or cretic or ditrochee; *verae* II, which permit substitution of ⏑⏑ for –; *verae* III, which permit substitution of a choriamb (–⏑⏑–) or epitrite (–⏑––) for the cretic; *licitae:* the c. *licita* is a c. *vera* with a 5-syllable word at the end; *malae* and *pessimae,* so called in accordance with their degree of departure from the standard patterns; and *selectae,* which substitute spondees (––) for the trochees of the *verae*. Of these the *verae* and *licitae* comprise 86.8 per cent of Cicero's clausulae, the others 12.7 per cent. Latin prose-writers whose clausulae reflect the Ciceronian pattern include Nepos, Seneca, Suetonius, and Quintilian; among those whose do not are Sallust and Livy. By the 3d c. A.D., the L. clausula had shifted from quantitative to accentual rhythm, and in the latter form it was used during the Middle Ages in three patterns of *cursus:*

planus or plain (–́⏑––́⏓),
tardus or slow (–́⏑––́⏑⏓), and
velox or fast (–́⏑––⏑–́⏑)

Later it became chiefly, with lexical accent substituted for syllabic length, a stylistic ornament; but in the diplomatic correspondence of the Roman Curia it was used, with modifications, as a secret code or signature. Something similar to the classical *cursus* has been noted in Eng., starting from the L. collects of the church service and passing on by aural tradition to the Eng. collects and thence into secular prose. But whether the *cursus* was transmitted to Eng. through the Prayer Book or whether Eng. developed independently its own satisfying cadences has never been fully established. Some patterns recur more frequently in Eng. than others, but they do not correspond closely to the classical *Cursus*. See VERSE AND PROSE; PROSODY.

T. Zielinski, *Das Clauselgesetz in Ciceros Reden* (1904) and *Der constructive Rhythmus in Ciceros Reden* (1914); W. Thomson, *The Rhythm of Eng. Speech* (1907); A. C. Clark, *The Cursus in Mediaeval and Vulgar L.* (1910) and *P.R. in Eng.* (1913); P. Fijn van Draat, *Rhythm in Eng. Prose* (1910); G. Saintsbury, *A Hist. of Eng. P.R.* (1912, 1922); W. M. Patterson, *The Rhythm of Prose* (1917); H. D. Broadhead, *Latin P.R.* (1922); H. Griffith, *Time Patterns in Prose* (1929); B. Tomashevsky, "Ritm prozy," *O Stikhe. Statyi* (1929; an important Russ. contribution based on statistical methods); A. Classe, *The Rhythm of Eng. Prose* (1939); G. L. Trager and H. L. Smith, Jr., *An Outline of Eng. Structure* (1951, 1956); P. F. Baum, *The Other Harmony of Prose* (1952); Norden; W. Schmid, *Über die klassische Theorie und Praxis des antiken Prosarhythmus* (1959); M. Croll, *Style, Rhetoric & Rhythm*, ed. J. M. Patrick, R. O. Evans, *et al.* (1966). P.F.B.

PROSODIC NOTATION. Notation of prosodic aspects of speech is of three kinds, (1) by *diacritical markings* imposed upon ordinary text; normal text in all languages includes some such marks, e.g., "accents," and all marks of punctuation are partially or wholly prosodic; (2) by a distinct *graphic transcription* either of the total phonetic content of a text (*phonetic* transcription conventionally set within square brackets, *phonemic* transcription between slant lines) or of abstracted prosodic features only; (3) by an abstract *schematic symbolism* (usually based upon 1 or 2) representing prosodic elements and values (e.g., use of letters for values, of numbers for position in series, of barring for divisions, etc.); the use of this last is especially to provide concise schematic formulas to represent abstracted patterns of rhythmic or metrical organization of prosodic features.

Of diacritical marks the most commonly used have been the acute accent (ʹ) for primary stress, stress in general, or "ictus," sometimes lengthened (/, the virgule), the grave accent (ˋ) for secondary stress, the macron (¯) to indicate a "long" syllable or element, and the breve (˘) for a "short"; relative length of sounds is frequently indicated by a dot above or after the symbol for the sound, protracted duration by two dots aligned vertically after it. Pauses are indicated by normal punctuation (especially the comma) or by the caret (‸). The caret is used also to indicate an omission. Relative duration of pauses is indicated with the caret by addition of macron or breve or dot(s): duration of pause may be indicated by conventional musical notation for rests. G. Trager and H. L. Smith (*Outline of Eng. Structure*, 1951), followed by many linguists, use diacritically over normal text or transcription, for stress-values the acute accent for primary, circumflex for secondary, grave for tertiary, and the breve for weakest; for degrees of openness of juncture, + for open juncture internal to a stress-group, | for "terminal" juncture after clauses or members with even or level pitch conclusion, || for such juncture with rising pitch, # for completive terminal juncture (with falling pitch), and they then use the names of these signs as designations of the grades of juncture ("plus-juncture," "single-bar-," "double-bar-," "cross-bar-" or "double-cross-"). This is in some ways the best of current diacritical systems for languages like Eng., and is in increasing use; but for abstractive prosodic analysis it has, besides the disadvantages of all merely diacritical procedures, the inconvenience that it cannot easily be generalized to fit all languages and prosodic systems, and that it uses for phonological description signs or symbols which in strictly rhythmic analysis are needed or useful for other values and better reserved for those (e.g., ˘ | ||).

In rhythmic analysis diacritical marking of normal text is less satisfactory for most purposes than some kind of graphic transcription which clearly abstracts the prosodic features relevant to a rhythmic design and presents them in separation from the qualitative phonemic and other nonrhythmic aspects of the speech in which they occur. There has been great variety in the history of prosody in provision of devices for such abstractive notation, and much diversity as to crudity or refinement in them. Perhaps the oldest is the use of letters of an alphabet to represent prosodic values, found in the fragmentary remains of ancient Gr. prosodic (and musical) notation and exploited systematically in the ancient Sanskrit *Chandahsutra* of Pingala (where G = long or heavy, *guru*, L = short or light, *laghu;* Pingala used single letters also to represent systematic combinations of these values, or "feet": M = GGG, N = LLL, R = GLG, etc.); in recent use for Eng., e.g., x = unstressed, a (more often ʹ or /) = stressed, F (*fort*) = stressed, f (*faible*) = weak (P. Verrier, *Métrique anglaise*, 1909), and very often (following G. R. Stewart, *Technique of Eng. Verse*, 1930) S = stressed, o = unstressed, l = light stress, p, P = pause short or long or replacing light or heavy. Less often, numbers (0 or 1 to 3, 4, or higher) have been used, to represent either degrees of prominence (J. B. Mayor; J. Lotz for Gr.) or position of stress or other value (so commonly for Romance verse; for stress-verse by J. Lotz; for prose sequences by M. Croll); numbers (1 to 4 or 6) are commonly used to note levels of pitch. Conventional musical notation has often been adapted for rhythmic analysis of verse. For Eng., occasional and partial use of musical notation begins with C. Gildon (*Complete Art of Poetry*, 1718), and recurs frequently in the later 18th and in the 19th c.; since S. Lanier (*Science of Eng. Verse*, 1880) full musical notation has often been used by writers whose analysis of verse is musical or exclusively temporal (and has therefore generally been avoided by nontemporalists). Systems of arbitrary graphic symbols often variously incorporating musical and other inherited conventional signs have been sporadically used (J. Steele, *Essay . . . establishing the Melody and Measure of Speech . . . expressed and perpetuated by Peculiar symbols,* 1775; W. Skeat, "Versification," § 98, pp. lxxxii-xcvii of "General Introduction" in his ed. of *Complete Works of G. Chaucer,* VI, 1894; W. Thomson, *Rhythm of Speech,* 1923; A. Heusler, *Deutsche Versgeschichte,* I, 1925; MLA Committee of 1923; etc.).

In the system of notation used in the article on *Prosody* in this Handbook, o = the single element or unit, normally a syllable, of weak or unemphatic value when not otherwise marked; ó = a syllable or element of stressed or emphatic value. Where more than two values are required, ó = primary, ò = secondary, ȯ = tertiary, o = weakest; ǒ = value which may be either primary or secondary; **ő** = prominence in excess of adjacent primary value. (Since of contiguous primary values the second must always be phonetically stronger if the two are to be perceptually equal, the sequence ó ó is always phonetically ó **ő** and **ő** is therefore not often required.) The straight comma , is used to indicate the open juncture or break between stress-groups, the caret ʌ for longer pause at more open junctures. (Protraction of pause may be indicated with this caret by a dot under or after it. In metrical sequences, the straight bar | may further be used to separate feet where this is felt to be desirable; the marking of values or stresses should normally suffice for indication of metrical pattern. Caesural breaks are often represented by this straight bar, single or double, or by a vertical dotted line; such breaks too are sufficiently indicated by marks for junctures and pauses.) These signs serve adequately to represent all the values of all the prosodic factors in all languages. Where temporal duration alone is to be noted, as for classical Gr. and L., the macron may be used for long and the breve for short, and o for indifferent or indeterminate quantity; for binary contrast of pitch values, as in Chinese, now commonly o (O) = flat or uninflected, x (X) = inflected; to distinguish levels of pitch, numbers may be used (1 = lowest), or the syllabic sign o placed on a musical staff with lines. When only one of two contrasting values is to be noted, and the place of occurrence of this value alone is to be represented in a schematic indication of a pattern, numbers corresponding to the place of the affected syllables in their series may be used, as by M. Croll for clausular cadences in prose, counting backward from the last syllable (5–2 = ó o o ó o; SP, 16 [1919] 1ff.). For such schemes, J. Lotz has proposed, counting from the beginning for verse, giving the number only of light syllables between the strong or emphatic in series, indicating absence of weak syllables at end or beginning by 0: (thus 2 1 1 0 = o o ó o ó o ó; *Lingua,* 6 [1956], 1ff.).

For rhythmic analysis, it is not necessary or desirable that a notation represent all the variation in the rhythmic aspects of a speech; what is necessary is representation of the rhythinic contrasts relevant to the pattern or meter to be described. The ideal rhythmic notation is therefore always abstractive and, for the total rhythmic variation, only approximative. It should also be remembered that "notational symbols . . . have nothing whatever to do with the problem of good, bad, or indifferent readings; they can, in fact, be used to record readings of any quality or character" (J. W. Hendren, *Time and Stress in Eng. Verse* [1959; Rice Institute pamphlet 46]).

T. S. Omond, *Eng. Metrists* (1921); M. W. Croll, "Report of the Committee on Metrical Notation," PMLA, 39 (1924), lxxxvii-xciv; *Phonetic Transcription and Transliteration, Proposals of the Copenhagen Conference April 1925* (Oxford, 1926; mainly by O. Jespersen). J.C.LAD.

PROSODY is the most general term used to refer to the elements and structures involved in the rhythmic or dynamic aspect of speech, and the study of these elements and structures as they occur in speech and language generally (*linguistic p.*) or in the compositions of the literary arts (*literary p.*). Descriptive study of p., linguistic or literary, may be *theoretical* ("achronic" or "panchronic," concerned with abstracting to the universal or general nature of the phenomena and the principles operating in them), or *historical* (either "synchronic" or "diachronic," and either "comparative" or national); theory and history are here as elsewhere reciprocally complementary. The evaluative *prosodic criticism* related to these descriptive studies is grammatical, rhetorical, or aesthetic, as the value it assesses is one of linguistic correctness, rhetorical effectiveness, or poetic form. A prescriptive p. attempts to provide practical rules for composition and interpretation or delivery. Such precept has always some connection with contemporary descriptive p. and the related prosodic criticism, and is often conflated with them, but it is properly a part, not of these disciplines, but of the arts of poetry and rhetoric, or of grammar and elocution and their pedagogy.

As a part of traditional study of classical grammar, which was both linguistic and literary but concentrated upon poetic texts, p. was the study of "accent" (L. *accentus, adcantus,* = Gr. *prosoidia*), of phonetic properties (chiefly temporal) of syllables and words as relevant to the measure (Gr. *metron*) of rhythm especially in verse, and of meters and the forms of verse generally. In antiquity musical analysis of rhythm, developed notably by Aristoxenus, was applied to verse by writers called *rhythmikoi,* whose procedures differed from those of the *metrikoi,* grammatical or literary metrists like Hephaestion; St. Augustine, *De musica,* represents a late conflation of these. Ancient rhetoric (e.g., Cicero, *Orator*) included treatment of prose rhythm based on these grammatical, musical, and philosophical sources, and medieval rhetoric elaborated these aspects of prose rhythm (*cursus,* etc.). It is within the frame of rhetoric rather than grammar that versification generally is provided for in late medieval times: the Fr. *Seconde Rhétorique* is the art of versification (q.v.). Grammatical and rhetorical elements are often combined with musical in treatments of *ars rythmica* and verse in the late middle ages, when poetry was again in close practical association with music. In the Ren. and after, however, the study of p. was by and large conceived as falling within the province of grammar. Modern *linguistic* study of p. is concerned primarily with the practical functioning of the phonetic elements of speech and with the conventions by which these elements (intensity, duration, pitch, and phenomena of interruption and transition between sounds) operate in linguistic systems, but linguistic p. has also included investigation of verse and of metrical conventions, since wherever a conventional distinction between prose speech and verse exists within a linguistic community, the conventions relevant to this distinction may be considered part of the linguistic system (the *langue* of De Saussure).

Literary p. studies the rhythmic structure of prose and verse, not as exemplifying linguistic norms but as functioning for literary effect in rhetorical processes or constructions of poetic form. Literary p. is not directly concerned with the use which language makes of rhythm for linguistic ends; it is in fact more properly concerned with the use which rhythmic impulse makes of language for its own ends when those are involved with the processes or forms of rhetoric and poetry. But literary p. supposes some understanding of its phonetic materials, and of linguistic conventions along with other conventions in the cultural environment which affect the literary arts, it is part of the task of a literary p. to show how the forms it deals with come to be lodged in the material of a language. Prosodic structures differ from language to language, for languages differ in their selection and combination among universally available phonetic elements; these are always somehow related, but the nature of their relation varies, so that the characteristics of verse do not always remain the same even in a single language throughout its history, and more than one system of versification, and various interpenetrations of verse and prose, can exist in a language at the same time.

It is at times necessary for understanding of verbal rhythms to refer to a broader context of more general or other specialized rhythmic behavior, since the rhythm in a verbal structure may reflect or incorporate that of other rhythmic processes with which the verbal has been associated, or into which it has been assimilated, or which it imitates. Speech is a complex act involving concurrence of the verbal with other physical and mental action, and its rhythm is a property of the speech as a whole, not of its verbal part alone; and the act of speech may be conjoined with other action and so further complicated rhythmically, by the stylized movements of ceremonial activities or by the elaborated rhythms of music or the dance. The rhythm of song or of chant differs from that of words only spoken or recited. It is of course only so much of an external rhythmic context as is somehow registered within the structure of a verbal text that is relevant to literary analysis of the text, yet it is certainly an error in method to assume the reverse and analyze verbal rhythms only in terms of their correspondence with other rhythm, notably the musical. All species of rhythm have generic aspects in common, and there are indeed specific components in some verbal rhythms that are to be accounted for only by musical association or its residual influence; but there are also elements in all literary rhythms which will be ignored or misrepresented in a description based solely on current conventions of musical analysis. It is with the rhythmic structure of dance that the verbal rhythms of verse have most direct affinity; this is not strange, since speech like dance is an organization of bodily movements, including those of the specialized "vocal" organs, and it is an ordering of the physical movements and pressures which produce sounds, that is the basis of rhythm in speech.

The structure of sound in speech is an organization, by relations of similarity and difference, of the elements of speech, a succession of vocal sounds and interruptions of sound by silence occurring in time. The relations in this structure are not of sounds or silences simply or absolutely, but of properties or attributes of sound and of silence. Sounds are differentiated in quality (discriminable character or kind) and in quantity (measurable degree or amount of sonority or magnitude). The rhythm of speech is a structure of ordered variation in the quantitative aspects of the flow of sound in which contrast is balanced by a cyclic recurrence of some identity. Meter (q.v.) is a fixed schematization of the cyclically recurring identity in a rhythmic series. Structured elements may be involved simultaneously in different sets of relations, and so incorporated concurrently into patterns or systems of different kinds. To some of the intrinsic properties and relations of sounds conventional "values" are assigned; all grammatical or strictly linguistic structure, the syntactic as well as the phonological, is conventional structure of this kind. Rhetorical and poetic structures are never wholly thus conventional, and the conventions observed in them are never exclusively linguistic or grammatical. Rhetoric and poetry use the constructs of a phonological system as they use grammar generally, but their own constructions, especially those of poetry, make freer use of intrinsic phonetic properties and relations apart from phonological conventionalization, so far as these are not masked beyond recognition in perception by phonological conditioning of attention. It is the sound as heard, the perceptual "phone" or "allophone" rather than the phoneme as such, that is relevant for literary, as distinct from linguistic, structure of sound.

Vocal sound is the result of vibration produced by constriction of the current of air projected from the lungs (by movements of the diaphragm and other muscles of abdomen and chest) through the larynx, throat, and mouth, and modification of the current and vibrations by varying articulation of the organs in these passages, especially in the mouth. Continuity and interruption or remission of sound depend upon and correspond to the muscular actions and pressures of expiration and inspiration of air and the pauses between them (which though considerable in breathing at rest are neither frequent nor lengthy in continuous speech, in which inspiration normally follows expiration with no interval of rest); it is therefore primarily to the mechanisms of respiratory pressure that most of the massing and grouping of sounds, and in general their quantitative acoustic effects (especially of intensity and duration, but also largely of pitch) are due. Larger and intermediate groupings are determined by action of the diaphragm supported by the muscles of the abdominal and thoracic walls; the smallest aggregatory (and rhythmic) unit, the syllable appears to be the product of a single pressure ("chest-pulse") of the smaller intercostal muscles. Obstruction of the current of air and articulatory modification of vibration and resonance produce qualitative differentiation of sounds, upon which phonemic discrimination of segments of sound is based.

Quality in vocal sound may be generally described as the acoustic effect of articulatory action, broadly including all varieties of constriction and obstruction (vocalic, consonantal, liquid, etc.) or of vibration and resonance (voiced, voiceless; oral, nasal, etc.) as well as distinction of organ, part, or place (glottal, palatal, dental, labial etc.; dorsal, lateral, apical etc.; front, back, high, low, etc.) or mode (open, closed, rounded, unrounded; plosive, spirant, affricate, etc.) of articulation. Each vowel or consonant is a composite "bundle" of several such "distinctive features" (as classified by Jakobson and others), and the relations upon which qualitative structure of sounds depends are relations among these properties or features rather than among the composite sounds or segments (phonemes) as such. Some qualitative differences, e.g. that between voiced and unvoiced sounds, involve accompanying difference in quantity. But qualitative differentiation of sounds, though its figuration (alliteration, assonance, rhyme) may be combined with and even assimilated to rhythmic structure, is never directly a factor in the production of rhythm; rhythm is a structure of quantitative relations.

The properties of sound directly relevant to rhythmic structure are the quantitative properties of intensity, duration, and pitch. Intensity (loudness or volume) and duration are obviously quantitative in perceptual effect as well as physically measurable. Pitch (corresponding roughly to frequency of vibration) has an ambiguous perceptual effect. As used in language, variation of pitch is normally associated with other variation that is quantitative; hence its effect is quantitative, increasing the prominence of the sound altered by its variation.

The various contrasts provided by the prosodic features are used in some languages for lexical distinctions, between words or functional classes of words (e.g. Eng. *contrast,* n. = ó o, vb. = o ó), but their most general linguistic use is syntactic. The mechanisms of this ordering and aggregation of sounds are those of "accent" (of intensity, "dynamic"; or of pitch, "tonic"), of "intonation" (systematic arrangement of pitch) and of "pause" and "timing" (dilation or contraction of sound; transition with "juncture" of various degrees of "openness" between sounds); these mechanisms and their effects may involve accompanying qualitative changes. One of their chief effects is the production of what are usually called (rhythmic) "cadences," i.e. patterns of prominent (strong or emphatic) elements to less prominent (weak or unemphatic) elements. Cadence involves the two aspects of "span" (the number of elements over which a pattern extends) and "direction" (the positional or successional order of the elements). Direction is usually classified as "rising" (o ó, o o ó), "falling" (ó o, ó o o), "mixed" or "rocking" (o ó o, ó o ó), and "level" or "even" (ó ó, o o); these last and other cadence-units (as ó) exhibiting neither "rise" nor "fall," are often called "neutral"; cadence is called "alternating" when emphatic and unemphatic elements succeed each other in a series (especially when the series begins and ends with the same value) and more loosely when equivalence of span is approximated.

Hegel based the treatment of verse in his *Aesthetik* upon a sharp distinction between quantitative and qualitative structures of sound. It is important for analysis to distinguish clearly these two quite distinct kinds of structure; but the distinction is not well drawn in Hegel's often penetrating survey, and he mistakenly conceived the two structures as mutually exclusive alternatives. Though all four properties of sound—quality, pitch, intensity, and duration—are distinct in character and effect, and each produces a different kind of structure or figuration, they do not occur in isolation from each other, and their distinct designs may be combined and interrelated. Rhythmic structure is usually complex, and within it a distinction must be made between primary or constitutive elements which create or establish rhythm and secondary elements whose figuration only supports or supplememts a more basic rhythmic pattern. The primary constitutive factors of rhythm in all systems of versification are relations of intensity or of duration or of pitch; these provide rhythmic structures based upon counting of syllables, on counting or disposition of stresses or tones, and on general quantitative or specifically temporal "measure" or balance.

Patterns of two elements may operate concurrently in a rhythmic structure, the one reinforcing the other in what then may be regarded as a single complex rhythm. Patterns of accentual cadence were thus combined with those of durational elements in some phases of L. verse and of late Gr., and there was concurrence of numerical correspondence of syllables with durational patterns in "Aeolic" Gr. lyric verse; in Romance verse, there is varying concurrence of accentual patterns, more or less regulated, with syllable-counting.

Secondary figuration of adjunct elements may be assimilated into the basic rhythmic structure created by the primary elements. So in all Old Germanic verse alliteration is combined with a primary stress rhythm; in all Arabic and in all the "classical" Persian and Turkish verse modeled upon it some regulated use of qualitative figuration accompanies rhythmic patterning of temporal durations; in Chinese and in almost all Romance verse some "rhyme" or assonance is used with syllable-counting. With syllable-counting, the *lü-shih,* or "regulated" verse of China since the T'ang period, combines a fixed arrangement of pitches or "tones"; in the most elaborate types of traditional Welsh verse the complex qualitative figuration called *cynghanedd* (q.v.) complements a basic pattern of syllable-counting.

Secondary figuration may occur also as free supplementary embellishment or optional incidental design not thus integrated into the basic rhythmic form, as with alliteration in modern Eng. or other Germanic verse, or tone-arrangement in the Chinese *ku-shih* or "old style" verse. Since any entity selected for metrical schematization necessarily occurs in concomitance with other nonschematized entities, and these other entities may themselves be independently patterned or regulated, it is at times difficult to distinguish in a verse-system between elements essential to a metrical scheme and concomitant elements not attended to in native perception of the rhythm as such.

Confusion of essential or primary factors in the constitution of standard verse with incidental secondary characteristics typical of such verse produces "doggerel" (q.v.), i.e. a structure which provides some secondary figuration characteristic of normal verse, but lacks its primary rhythmic form. When secondary elements are assimilated into a primary rhythmic structure it is often not easy to disassociate them from the rhythm or to describe the form of the rhythm without including them. Strictly rhythmic structure is always the basis of verse, and in some languages verse is identical with its rhythmic or metrical structure. But in most languages some additional figuration is characteristic of verse; and even where it is not incorporated into the *discrimen* by which verse is distinguished from prose, it may be as meticulously elaborated as the primary rhythmic structure, and sometimes more strictly regulated (Arabic, Prov., Welsh, Icelandic). The scope of prosodic study has therefore generally been extended to include elements (phonetic, syntactic, semantic) not strictly rhythmical, when these are relevant to the structure of verse. But this extension has not generally modified the traditional conception of the "prosodic" as essentially restricted to the rhythmic.

It is by the dynamic functioning of intensity, duration, and pitch that sounds are aggregated together into the smaller clusters and groups, and then into the larger sequences, that make the (semantically ordered) structure of speech. The phonemes themselves are aggregates, but the smallest structural unit of speech in which quantitative aggregation is felt as the primary factor is the syllable, which may be described acoustically as a single massing of sound between recessions of sonority, usually round a definite peak or center. The formation of syllables is inevitable in any flow of speech-sound, and the syllable therefore occurs as the minimal aggregatory unit in all languages; but there is much variety among languages in the nature of its composition. In most languages the syllabic center is typically a vowel (V), which may or may not have consonant (C) accompaniment before and (less generally) after: CV, VC, CVC, CCVCC, etc. In such languages it is exceptional, but in most not impossible, that syllabic centers be consonantal (*Psst!*); but in some languages, like Japanese, a single consonant may be a syllable. An element of duration or "timing" may operate in syllabic construction. In some languages (Eng., Rus.) syllables vary freely in duration; in some (e.g. Sp.) all syllables are approximately equal in duration; in some ("mora" languages, including ancient Gr. and L.) syllabic duration varies only within a ratio of roughly 2:1.

Where syllables are isochronous the distinct identity of the syllable is never reduced or lost, and equal timing of syllables thus provides for, and appears to induce, syllable-counting in verse, which is then itself a kind of timing. When syllabic duration varies without regulation, as in the Germanic languages or Rus., it seems not to be related to metrical schematization; in these languages variation in time of syllables is absorbed into the contrast of strong and weak stress which is exploited for verse either simply as such or as forming units ("feet") of patterns of "cadence."

As in their construction of syllables, languages differ in their modes of combining syllables into syntactic unities, and especially in the degree of definiteness with which they mark individual units as distinct phonetic entities. The largest units of utterance are marked by pause-boundaries which are true interruptions of sound by silence, but the necessity of maintaining a degree of continuity in the phonetic microstructure of speech prohibits general use of actual silence to mark the limits of the smallest units; the smaller units therefore depend for integrity and distinctness upon internal "culminative" factors rather than upon external "delimitative" effects. In general it may be said that the larger the unit, the more significant will intonation ("melody") be, the smaller the unit the more dependent upon the other prosodic factors for its identity. The smallest unit of aggregation, the syllable, is normally distinguished primarily by the relative prominence of its nuclear center; its borders are often indeterminate.

The next phonetic aggregate beyond the syllable, the phrasal or rhythmic group, is also usually characterized primarily by internal nuclear concentration; it is a sound-cluster spoken with a single pattern or "contour" of accentuation and intonation, the center or peak of which is a phonologically "primary" accent (either "dynamic" or "tonic"). The group-unit may be a single syllable (*Yes!*), or several "words" grouped by a single primary accent; it may stand alone as a sentence, or form part of a sentence in which several groups are combined either by subordinating hypotaxis or in paratactic coordination. The group-unit is the minimal free unit of utterance. No utterance can be made without this unit, and all utterances consist of such units and their extensions.

Syllabic groups are either simple or composite. A simple group includes no accent potentially "primary" other than that of its contour-nucleus; it may however, in a language provided with sufficient grading of stress or variation of pitch, include syllables with accent of "secondary" (or "tertiary") degree, normally incapable of optional utterance as primary. Composite groups include more than one potential primary or nuclear accent, all but one reduced to secondary level, under a single intonation-contour; a composite group is thus a hypotactic inclusion of two or more potentially independent groups under the dominance of the contour and nuclear accent of one.

Within the group-unit, even when it is monosyllabic, there appears a pattern of cadence; the accentual contour is a cadence-pattern. It is at the level of the syllabic group that cadence becomes conspicuous in speech. The *general cadence* of speech, as distinct from the succession of the unitary cadences of its group-units, is the continuous pattern within it of prominent and unemphatic syllables, without reference to group division or group-boundaries. Whenever this general cadence presents or suggests the regularity of alternation or other continuous recurrence, secondary accents rise to greater perceptual importance. Regulation of general cadence by schematization of recurrence within it provides cadence-meter in "stress" languages, notably the Germanic, including Eng. With such meters there can be *interplay* and tension between the continuous scheme of the metrically regulated general cadence and the varying patterns of the successive group-cadences; in languages with metrical schematization of elements other than the natural elements of aggregation, as in the durational feet of Gr. (aggregating by tonic accent) and L. (aggregating probably by stress), there can be *contrast* of these metrical patterns with the "natural" cadence. The unit of recurrence in the rhythm of normal prose seems always to be simply the phonological group as such, without further schematization. Regular serial repetition of a cadence as such, which would make this scheme a unit of recurrence, would compromise the non-metrical character of rhythm in prose, since such schematization of recurrence is what constitutes meter. But in the sporadic figuration which characterizes the further rhythmization of prose (see PROSE RHYTHM) patterns of cadence may have a conspicuous part, especially at the ends of syntactic or rhetorical units, where cadence patterns in systems involving two or more groups are common; (L. *clausulae, cursus*).

Since intonational and delimitative junctures are sufficient to sustain identity without reduction of accent, the larger units of speech have the character of serial sequences of the smaller units rather than of systematic aggregation by nuclear accents; accentually they are sequence-units rather than strict aggregations. A distinction of this kind, between sequence-units created by imposing limits upon *series,* and units which are *systems* by virtue of internal aggregatory structure, is of use in all analysis. But the units relevant for rhythmic structure in verse are not exclusively or even principally the phonetic units that correspond to functional syntactic or rhetorical divisions. These divisions, of words, phrases, *cola,* and sentences or "periods," are indeed present everywhere in speech, and operate to create effects of "balance" and "measure," the ground of rhythm. Relations among lexical and syntactic units, when these are regarded as entities and their masses in any way balanced or "measured" against each other, are examples of the most basic and elementary form of rhythm in speech; it is from this foundation that all the more complex rhythms of verse and meter develop by a more or less natural progression, and to this again that, whenever their impulse is enfeebled or momentarily relaxed, they return.

Metrical rhythm is distinguished from that of prose by having as the unit of cyclic recurrence not the group-entity but an entity constituted "artificially" by abstraction and recombination of prosodic components of the group in some fixed scheme. The metrical schematization of cyclic entities may itself be *serial*—a counting of syllables (syllabics) or of "stresses"—producing units ("lines") larger than the typical group-unit but distinct both from it and from the rhetorical units into which groups are aggregated "naturally"; or it may be *systematic*, an arrangement or ratio of contrasting elements or values, providing units (typically "feet") distinct from the group-unit which may then be ordered by serial count or systematic arrangement into line-units distinct from the larger units of "natural" aggregation; line-units formed in either of these ways may then in turn be ordered together either serially ("stichically") or in some systematic ("strophic") arrangement, which may in its turn be repeated serially or, as in the Gr. choral ode, itself subjected to a further systematic ordering. The selection of elements for metrical schematization and of types of schemes is determined in part by the nature of a language, in part by historical accident; one could not have predicted of L. in its pre-classical stage that its classical verse would adopt Gr. schemes. Once the elements are selected, the multiple contrasts of values of these elements in "natural" speech are commonly reduced to a simple binary opposition for metrical construction (variety of stress-value to "stress" vs. "unstress," pitch variation to "level" vs. "inflected," durations to "long" and "short").

All that is required for a scheme to be maintained continuously in recognizable form, once the unit of recurrence is established, is recurrence of its unit rather than of the scheme that specifies it; there is in the metrical verse of most languages, both at the level of the unit and the line, a good deal of variety in satisfaction of schematic norms ("substitution" etc.). Line-units have in common with the larger units of "natural" aggregation that their terminal sections are their most determinate parts; freedom of variation is more often permitted in the earlier part than at the end, and sometimes schematization is specially or exclusively fixed at or near the end of the line; strophic systematization of lines also seems to enforce determinacy at line-ends (cf. the very general use of end-rhyme).

In general it may be said that where there is fixed schematization of a unit roughly equal to or smaller than a typical aggregatory group (word), the rhythm of the speech is *metrical*; if there is continuous recurrence of a unit larger than the typical group, the rhythm is that of *verse*; where neither of these occurs, the rhythm is that of *prose*. Rhythmically *intermediate* speech, conventionally distinguished in many (especially Oriental) languages, though lacking; the continuous schematization which would make it metrical, and the continuous division by lines which would make it verse, supplements the unschematized rhythm of ordinary prose.

M. Kawczynski, *Essai comparatif sur l'origine et l'histoire des rythmes* (1889); R. Westphal, *Allgemeine Metrik* (1892); P. Verrier, *Essai sur les principes de la métrique anglaise*, II (1909; *livre* 3, ch. v.); C. Jacob, *Foundations and Nature of Verse* (1918); A. Meillet, *Les origines indo-européennes des mètres grecs* (1923); O. Schröder, *Nomenclator Metricus* (1929); "Metrica" in *Enciclopedia Italiana*, XXIII (1934); A. Arnholtz, *Studier i poetisk og musikalsk Rytmik*, I (1938); E. Olson, *General Pros.* (1938); J. C. La Drière, "Prose Rhythm," "Pros.," in Shipley and "Comparative Method in . . . Pros.," *Comparative Literature*, ed. W. P. Friederich (Intern. Comparative Lit. Assoc. 2d Cong. *Proc.*, 1959); A. W. De Groot, *Algemene Versleer* (1946); *Sound and Poetry*, ed. N. Frye (1957, pp. 143–44); *Manual of Phonetics*, ed. L. Kaiser (1957; 215ff., 295ff., 385ff.); J. Lotz, "Metric Typology," *Style in Language*, ed. T. Sebeok (1960); International Conference of Work-in-Progress Devoted to Problems of Poetics. 1st, Warsaw, 1960. *Poetics* . . . (1961); C. Watkins, "Indo-European Metrics and Archaic Ir. Verse," *Celtica*, 6 (1962); L. P. Wilkinson, *Golden L. Artistry* (1963).J.C.LAD.; T.V.F.B.

PSALM. The poetic form of p., at least as it has come down to us in the Western literary tradition, is an invention of the ancient Near East. P.-writing, associated with temple cult, was an important literary activity in Mesopotamia, Egypt, Ugarit (in present-day Syria), and, one may assume, despite the lack of surviving texts, in Canaan. The p.-poets of ancient Israel took over the form from the surrounding cultures, not hesitating to borrow images, phrases, and even whole sequences of lines, but also refashioning the p. to make it an adequate poetic expression of the new monotheistic vision of reality. The collection that constitutes the biblical Book of Psalms is an anthology—or more precisely, a welding together of what were originally four smaller anthologies—that was assembled sometime in the Second Temple period, but that includes poems probably composed over a span of several hundred years, going back to the beginning of the first millennium B.C. There are certain minor shifts in language and poetic structure over the centuries, but far more striking are the continuities of style and convention in the whole biblical literature of psalms.

The term for these poems current in Western languages is derived from the Gr. *psalmos*, a song sung to the accompaniment of a plucked instrument. The two Hebrew terms, which are sometimes used in conjunction, are *mizmor*, simply indicating "song," without the necessary implication of instrumental accompaniment, and *tehillah*, "praise," (the plural, *tehillim*, is the usual Hebrew title of the biblical book). The two predominant subgenres of psalms in the biblical collection are in fact psalms of praise and supplications. Together these make up more than two-thirds of the Book of Psalms. There are other subgenres, such as Wisdom psalms, royal psalms, and historical psalms, but each of these is represented by only a few instances in the traditional collection and none has exerted the postbiblical influence of the supplication and the p. of praise.

Some of the Hebrew psalms are clearly marked for liturgical performance on specified occasions or at specified moments in the temple rite. Others seem intended to be recited by individuals in moments of anguish or exaltation. This double nature of the psalms, alternatively collective and personal, has been a source of their relevance both to the institutional and the individual lives of Christians and Jews ever since. At least some of the psalms, to judge by the orchestral directions set at their head, were framed for musical performance, and most of them exhibit symmetries of form far beyond the norm of biblical poetry in other genres. One encounters refrains or refrain-like repetitions, antiphonal voices, and most common of all, "envelope structures"—poems in which the conclusion explicitly echoes images, motifs, even whole phrases, from the beginning.

This fondness for envelope structures is combined with a recurrent concern about the efficacy and power of language in general and of poetic language in particular. Thus, the typical supplication begins with a foregrounding of the act of supplication ("From the depths I called to Thee, O Lord," etc.) and concludes by recapitulating the initial phrases, usually with the implication: "since I have called to Thee, Thou must surely hear me." The typical thanksgiving p. (the most common subcategory of psalms of praise) begins with a declaration of intent to sing out to the Lord, to tell His praises, and concludes by again affirming the act of praise or thanksgiving, now completed in the symmetrical structure of the poem.

It should also be noted that there is a certain fluidity among the psalmodic subgenres. Every supplication looks toward the possibility of becoming a thanksgiving p., and a few are turned into that retrospectively by the confident affirmation at the end. Even within one subgenre, there are striking differences in emphasis: a supplication may stress sin and contrition, the speaker's terror in a moment of acute distress, a reflective meditation on human transience, and much else.

The beautifully choreographed movements and the archetypal simplicity of style of the biblical psalms have made them a recurrent source of inspiration to later poets. For obvious reasons, the Book of Psalms has repeatedly influenced Jewish and Christian liturgical poetry through the ages. With the resurgence of interest in the Bible after the Reformation, adaptations of psalms became widespread. In France, the versions of Clément Marot are particularly noteworthy. The apogee of psalmodic verse in Western languages was reached in Renaissance England, where the Bible in its new vernacular version became central to the culture. A variety of English poets, from Wyatt and Sidney to Herbert and Milton, tried their hand at metrical versions of psalms. In the signal instance of Herbert, the poet's original production owes something abiding in its diction, imagery, and sense of form, to the model of the biblical psalms.—J. Paterson, *The Praises of Israel: Studies Lit. and Religious in the Psalms* (1950); C. S. Lewis, *Reflections on the Psalms* (1958); C. Westermann, *The Praise of God in the Psalms* (1965); H. Gunkel, *The Psalms: A Form-Crit. Introd.*, tr. J. M. Horner (1967); A. L. Strauss, *Bedarkhei hasifrut* (1970, pp. 66–94); R. Lace, "Le psaume 1—Une analyse structurale," *Biblica*, 57 (1977). R.A.

PUN. A figure of speech depending upon a similarity of sound and a disparity of meaning. For a successful p., the reader must recognize multiple meanings in a context where all these meanings can be applied. The figure is apparently as old as language, possessing irresistible appeal and appearing in all literatures. It is discussed and analyzed in the classic treatises of rhetoric by Aristotle, by Cicero, and in the anonymous *Rhetorica ad Herennium,* where three varieties are discriminated: *traductio, adnominatio,* and *significatio. Traductio* refers to the use of the same word in different connotations or a balancing of homonyms; *adnominatio* is the repetition of a word with the addition of suffixes, prefixes, or with transposition of letters or sounds; *significatio* is closest to the modern p., including *double entendre.* The medieval rhetoricians, Geoffrey of Vinsauf in his *Poetria Nova* and John of Garland in his *Ars Versificandi* made the figure available to such writers as Chaucer and the author of the *Roman de la Rose.* The p. was not looked upon by classical, medieval, or Renaissance writers as primarily a vehicle for humor. For example, the medieval *rime riche,* a form of *traductio,* the use of homonyms in different senses as the rhyming words (e.g., lief-leef [lief-leaf]) was looked upon as a beauty rather than a blemish. The p. could be used for comic effect, but it was also a means of emphasis and an instrument of persuasion. Shakespeare uses it for both serious and bawdy purposes. Like most Renaissance writers, Shakespeare followed the divisions of p. by contemporary rhetoricians into antanaclasis, syllepsis, paronomasia, and asteismus. In antanaclasis, a word is repeated, with a shift in meaning:

To England will I steal, and there I'll steal.
(*Henry V*, 5.1.92)

In syllepsis, a word is used once, with two meanings:

At a word, hang no more about me. I am no gibbet for you.
(*Merry Wives of Windsor* 2.2.17)

In paronomasia, the repeated words are close but not exactly the same in sound:

Out sword, and to a sore purpose!
(*Cymbeline* 4.1.25)

In asteismus, a speaker replies to another, using the first man's words in a different sense:

Cloten: Would he had been one of my rank!
Lord: To have smell'd like a fool.
(*Cymbeline* 2.1.17)

At the same time the p. was esteemed as an adornment for sermons, and Lancelot Andrews can play on *gin* as both *snare* and *engine* or contrivance without comic intent. By the end of the 17th c., word games and excessive ingenuity had brought the p. into disrepute, and by Addison's time, its use seemed a fault. In *Spectator* no. 61, he indicts it as "false wit" and explains it away in the works of "the most ancient Polite Authors" by their being "destitute of all Rules and Arts of Criticism." From the low critical esteem of the early 18th c., the p. has never recovered full respectability. It is negligible as a serious figure of rhetoric in the romantic period, occurring most notably in a far-fetched form as a sort of consciously outrageous comedy, as in Charles Lamb's "Lambpuns," or in Barham's *Ingoldsby Legends,* where in one poem a witch is caught "by a Hugh and a cry." The kind of serious wordplay of Verlaine's

Il pleure dans mon coeur
Comme il pleut sur la ville

would have been thoroughly unlikely in 19th-c. England. Only in the present day, with a revival of interest in the metaphysical poets and greater scholarly interest in medieval and Renaissance rhetoric, has there been any kind of rehabilitation of the p. as a figure of speech and any serious interest in it found in criticism. The allusiveness of modern verse is related to punning, the original context of the quotation standing for the second sense of the word, and here frequently modern poetry makes an approach to the serious wit of the Renaissance (e.g., Eliot's *The Waste Land,* "When lovely woman stoops to folly and . . ." and "Good night, sweet ladies, good night . . ."). However, another influence, the exuberant word-play in Joyce's *Ulysses* and the mass of interlingual puns in *Finnegans Wake* (balmheartzyheat—*Barmherzigkeit*) is working to keep the comic aspect of the p. dominant.

W. Empson, *Seven Types of Ambiguity* (1947); Sister Miriam Joseph, *Shakespeare's Use of the Arts of Language* (1947); H. Kökeritz, "Punning Names in Shakespeare," MLN, 65 (1950) and "Rhetorical Word-Play in Chaucer, PMLA, 69 (1954); W. K. Wimsatt, Jr., "Verbal Style, Logical and Counterlogical, PMLA, 65 (1950); P. F. Baum, "Chaucer's Puns," PMLA, 71 (1956); J. Brown, "Eight Types of Puns," PMLA, 71 (1956); M. M. Mahood, *Shakespeare's Wordplay* (1957). S.F.F.

PURE POETRY is a prescriptive rather than a descriptive term in that it designates, not an actual body of verse, but a theoretical ideal to which poetry may aspire. Any theory of poetry which seeks to isolate one or more properties as essential and proceeds to exclude material considered to be nonessential may be classed as a doctrine of pure poetry. Interpreted in the widest sense, it could be applied to divergent points of view occurring within a broad historical range, such as Sidney's strictures on tragi-comedy and the 18th-c. idea of "sublimity."

Most specifically, the term refers to "La Poésie pure," a doctrine derived from Edgar Allan Poe by the Fr. symbolist poets, Baudelaire, Mallarmé, and Valéry, and widely discussed in the late 19th and early 20th c. In this context, "pure" is equivalent to absolute, on the analogy of absolute music. The analogy is significant in that both the theory and practice of the symbolists were influenced by the relations of poetry and music.

The doctrine was first enunciated in Poe's "The Poetic Principle." For Poe, the essential quality of poetry is a kind of lyricism distinguished by intensity and virtually identical with music in its effects. Since the duration of intensity is limited by psychological conditions, Poe concludes that the long poem is a contradiction in terms and that passages which fail to achieve a high level of intensity should not be included in the category of poetry. Poetry is regarded as being entirely an aesthetic phenomenon, differentiated from and independent of the intellect and the moral sense. The products of the latter, ideas and passions, are judged to be within the province of prose and their presence in a poem to be positively detrimental to the poetic effect.

In their desire to attain in poetry the condition of music, the symbolists were wholehearted disciples of Poe; in elaborating his theory, however, they were far more aware of the problem of language than Poe had been. The relevance of the doctrine of pure poetry to contemporary theory rests almost entirely upon its concern with the symbolic or iconic properties of language. The impetus toward this line of speculation was given in Baudelaire's rephrasing of Poe's idea: The goal of poetry is of the same nature as its principle and it should have nothing in view but itself. The general import appears to be nothing more than an affirmation of art for art's sake, but the technical implications are far reaching. The aim of the symbolists was to confer autonomy upon poetry by reducing to a minimum the semantic properties of language and by exploiting the phonetic properties of words and their marginal or suggestive meanings.

It would not be accurate to ascribe unity of aim to the whole symbolist movement. For Baudelaire, the autonomy of poetic language was incomplete in that meaning involved "correspondances" with an ultimate kind of reality. In his reference to the "supernal beauty" which pure poetry was capable of achieving, Poe had hinted at the possibility of a metaphysical or mystical significance in verbal music. The Abbé Bremond is explicit in claiming a mystical value for pure poetry, which for him is allied to the primordial incantatory element in verse. Mallarmé and Valéry are much more guarded concerning the meaning of poetry, limiting their inquiry to the technical problems of language. Mallarmé's speculations, which were intended for poets, must perhaps remain somewhat obscure to the layman. His conception of pure poetry was that of an absolute, a point at which poetry would attain complete linguistic autonomy, the words themselves taking over the initiative and creating the meanings, liberating themselves, so to speak, from the deliberate rhetoric of the poet. With Mallarmé interest in subject matter in the traditional sense recedes almost to the vanishing point and is replaced by concern for the medium of poetry.

Speculation in this direction reached its limit in Valéry, who eventually found the processes of poetic composition more interesting than the poetry itself. Valéry's contribution to the doctrine of pure poetry focused on the most baffling aspect of poetic language, the relation of sound and sense. In his first exposition of the subject, preface to a volume of verse by Lucien Fabré, it is defined as poetry which is isolated from everything but its essence. Poe's strictures on the epic and on the didactive motive in general are repeated. Valéry acknowledges the debt of the symbolists to Wagner. The aim of pure poetry is to attain from language an effect comparable to that produced on the nervous system by music. This essay gave rise to considerable discussion and debate. Valéry, without abandoning the doctrine, was later to deny that he had advocated pure poetry in a literal sense. It represented for him a theoretical goal, an ideal rarely attainable in view of the nature of language, in which sound and meaning, sonority and idea form a union as intimate as that of the body and soul.

Poe's ideas, as is generally known, had little direct influence on Eng.-speaking critics and poets; the idea of pure poetry was mainly an importation from France. In the 1920's, George Moore brought out an anthology entitled *Pure Poetry.* Although Moore had absorbed the views of the symbolists, his notion of pure poetry actually goes back to an earlier tradition, that of the Parnassians. While the element of verbal music is not neglected, it is not of primary importance. The emphasis is on subject matter. Moore's chief aversions are abstract ideas and the intrusion of the poet's personality. Pure poetry is that which achieves the greatest possible degree of concreteness and objectivity.

It is possible to view imagism (q.v.) as an instance of pure poetry, although the doctrine itself does not employ the term and is quite distinct from the aims of the symbolists. The imagist manifesto was ready to dispense with rhyme and meter, if not with the element of verbal music itself. The qualities of vagueness and suggestiveness valued by Poe and the symbolists as an aid to the achievement of pure poetry were contrary to the imagist demand for the utmost precision in the rendering of the concrete image. The imagist doctrine may be included in the broad category of pure poetry insofar as it locates the essence of poetry in a single feature—the concrete image—and judges the other features of poetry to be superfluous.

As Robert Penn Warren has demonstrated in "Pure and Impure Poetry," the doctrine of pure poetry is hardly tenable in practice. Yet T. S. Eliot regarded it as the most interesting and original development in the aesthetic of verse made in the last century. He found it characteristically modern in its emphasis upon the medium of verse and its indifference to content. In his view, it terminated with Valéry and cannot serve as a guide to contemporary poets.

E. A. Poe, "The Poetic Principle," *Complete Works,* ed. J. A. Harrison, xiv (1902); *Pure Poetry: an Anthol.,* ed. G. Moore (1924); H. Bremond, *La Poésie pure* (1926); D. Porché, *Paul Valéry et la poésie pure* (1926); P. Valéry, *Variété,* 1 (1934); R. P. Warren, "Pure and Impure Poetry," KR, 5 (1943); J. Benda, *La France Byzantine, ou Le Triomphe de la littérature pure* (1945); T. S. Eliot, "From Poe to Valery," HR, 2 (1949); L. and F. E. Hyslop, Jr., *Baudelaire on Poe's Crit. Papers* (1952); C. Feidelson, Jr., *Symbolism and Am. Lit.* (1953); F. Scarfe, *The Art of Paul Valéry* (1954); J. Chiari, *Symbolisme from Poe to Mallarmé* (1956); H. W. Decker, *Pure Poetry, 1925–1930: Theory and Debate in France* (1962).

S.F.

PYRRHIC (Gr. "used in the *pyrrichē* or war dance") or *dibrach* (Gr. "of 2 short syllables"). This may be said to have been the shortest metrical foot in Gr. and L. verse, although it was not recognized as such by Aristoxenus and ancient metricians generally, who felt that feet must be of at least 3 morae or time elements (e.g., the tribrach: ⏑⏑⏑). In Eng. verse the p. foot (2 unstressed syllables) occurs frequently as variant or "substitution" (q.v.) in normal iambic series.—Kolář.

R.J.G.

Q

QUANTITY. See CLASSICAL PROSODY; CLASSICAL METERS IN MODERN LANGUAGES; METER; PROSODY.

QUATORZAIN. A stanza or poem of 14 lines, e.g., a sonnet. The term, however, is now reserved for a 14-line poem similar to or like a sonnet but deviating from its patterns.

QUATRAIN. A stanza of 4 lines, rhymed or unrhymed. It is, with its many variations, the most common of all stanzaic forms in European poetry. Most rhyming quatrains fall into one of the following categories: abab, or its variant xbyb (in which x and y represent unrhymed lines), a category which includes the familiar ballad meter and the elegiac stanza (qq.v.) or heroic quatrain; abba, the so-called envelope (q.v.) stanza, of which Tennyson's *In Memoriam* stanza (q.v.) is a type; aabb, in which an effect of internal balance or antithesis is achieved through the use of opposed couplets, as in Shelley's *The Sensitive Plant.* Less common quatrains are the Omar Khayyám stanza, rhyming aaxa, and the monorhymed quatrain (e.g., Gottfried Keller's *Abendlied*). Quatrains interlinked by rhyme are also to be found, as are those displaying such complications as the alternation of masculine and feminine rhyme and the use of irregular line length. The q. has been used in Western poetry primarily as a unit of composition in longer poems, but the term is also applied to the two component parts of the octave (q.v.) of a sonnet. As a poem complete in itself, the q. lends itself to epigrammatic utterance; Landor and Yeats have shown mastery in the composition of such poems. (See EPIGRAM).

QUINTET. A 5-line stanza of varying rhyme scheme and line length. The most frequent rhyme pattern is ababb as, for example, in Edmund Waller's *Go, Lovely Rose.*

R

READER-RESPONSE THEORY. See POETRY, THEORIES OF (OBJECTIVE THEORIES).

REFRAIN. A line, or lines, or part of a line, repeated at intervals throughout a poem, usually at regular intervals, and most often at the end of a stanza; a burden, chorus, or repetend. (*Burden* usually indicates a whole stanza; a *chorus* is a refrain joined in by a group; a *repetend* need not occur *throughout* a poem.) The r. seems a universal feature of primitive poetry and tribal verse, an accompaniment of communal dance and communal labor. Probably the very beginnings of poetry are to be found in iterated words and phrases. Refrains occur in the Egyptian *Book of the Dead,* in the Hebrew Psalms, in the Gr. idyls of Theocritus and Bion, in the L. epithalamiums of Catullus, in the Anglo-Saxon *Deor's Lament*; they blossom in the medieval ballads, in Prov. fixed forms, in Renaissance lyrics, and in poetry of the romantic period.

A r. may be as short as a single word or as long as a stanza. Though usually recurring as a regular part of a metrical pattern, it may appear irregularly throughout a poem, and it may be used in free verse. In stanzaic verse it usually occurs at the end of a stanza, but may appear at the beginning or in the middle. It may be used in such a way that its meaning varies or develops from one recurrence to the next (Poe discusses this use in "The Philosophy of Composition"), or it may be used each time with a slight variation of wording appropriate to its immediate context (Rossetti's *Sister Helen,* Tennyson's *Lady of Shalott*).

The r. may be a nonsense phrase, apparently irrelevant to the rest of the poem, or relevant only in spirit ("With a hey, and a ho, and a hey nonino"), or it may very meaningfully emphasize some important aspect of the poem—theme, characters, or setting. The r. furnishes pleasure in its repetition of familiar sound; it serves to mark off rhythmical units, and at the same time to unify the poem; and it may be very skillfully used to reinforce emotion and meaning.—F. B. Gummere, *The Beginnings of Poetry* (1908); F. G. Ruhrmann, *Studien zur Gesch. und Charakteristik des R. in der englischen Lit.* (1921). L.P.

RELATIVE STRESS PRINCIPLE: In a paper given in Denmark in 1900, Otto Jespersen identified the principle which was to become one of the axioms of modern metrics: "the effect of surroundings." Castigating 19th-c. metrists for three fallacies handed down from antiquity, the fallacies of long and short (modern meters employ stress or tone), the foot (an artificial distinction which can only lead to unnatural scansions), and two grades of stress (rather than four), Jespersen makes the sanguine observation that "our ear does not really perceive stress relations with any degree of certainty except when the syllables concerned are contiguous"; in meter "the only thing required by the ear is an upward and a downward movement, a rise and fall . . . at fixed places" regardless of "how great is the ascent or the descent."

Hence, "the metrical value of a syllable depends on what comes before and what follows after it." (Boundaries such as line-beginning or pauses therefore allow following "inversions" since the effect of a pause is effectually zero stress.) Syllables which would otherwise be stressed appear weaker between very strong syllables, and weaker syllables such as prepositions gain strength between the weakest syllables, such as articles or enclitics. Subsequent metrists came to see that these two phenomena (later termed demotion and promotion) could be readily employed to bring unusual stress patterns within the rule of a regular iambic meter. So in Pope's line,

On her white Breast, a sparkling Cross she
wore
(*Rape of the Lock*, II,7),

the first four syllables increase steadily in intensity (W. K. Wimsatt's "crescendo foot"), but since the second is greater than the first, and the fourth greater than the third, these really amount, in relative terms, to two iambs. Jespersen noticed precisely this phenomenon, but he also did not neglect the other significant transition, between syllables two and three. Jespersen explicitly rejects the notion of metrical feet.—O. Jespersen, "Den psykologiske grund til nogle metriske faenomener," *Oversigt* (1900), tr. in his *Linguistica* (1933). T.V.F.B.

REPETEND. A recurring word, phrase, or line; loosely, a refrain (q.v.). As distinguished from refrain, r. usually refers to a repetition occurring irregularly rather than regularly in a poem, or to a partial rather than a complete repetition. E.g.: "For a breeze of morning moves, / And the planet of Love is on high, / Beginning *to faint in the light* that *she loves* / On a bed of daffodil sky, / *To faint in the light* of the sun *she loves, / To faint in his light,* and to die" (Tennyson, *Maud* 22.7). R. may be richly studied in the medieval ballads, Poe's *Ulalume* and *The Raven,* Meredith's *Love in the Valley,* Eliot's *The Love Song of J. Alfred Prufrock.* L.P.

REPETITION of a sound, syllable, word, phrase, line, stanza, or metrical pattern is a basic unifying device in all poetry. It may reinforce, supplement, or even substitute for meter, the other chief controlling factor in the arrangement of words into poetry. Primitive religious chants from all cultures show r. developing into cadence and song, with parallelism and r. still constituting, most frequently as anaphora, an important part in the sophisticated and subtle rhetoric of contemporary liturgies (e.g., the *Beatitudes*). Frequently also, the exact r. of words in the same metrical pattern at regular intervals forms a refrain (q.v.), which serves to set off or divide narrative into segments, as in ballads, or, in lyric poetry, to indicate shifts or developments of emotion. Such repetitions may serve as commentary, a static point against which the rest of the poem develops, or it may be simply a pleasing sound pattern to fill out a form ("hey downe a-downe"). As a unifying device, independent of conventional metrics, r. is found extensively in free verse, where parallelism (q.v.: r. of grammatical pattern) reinforced by the recurrence of actual words and phrases governs the rhythm which helps to distinguish free verse from prose (e.g., Walt Whitman, *I Hear America Singing*; Carl Sandburg, *Chicago, The People Yes*; Edgar Lee Masters, *Spoon River Anthology*).

The r. of similar endings of words or even of identical syllables (*rime riche,* q.v.) constitutes rhyme, used generally to bind lines together into larger units or to set up relationships within the same line (internal rhyme). Such r., as a *tour de force,* may be the center of interest in a poem, as Southey's *The Cataract of Lodore* and Belloc's *Tarantella,* or may play a large part in establishing the mood of a poem, as in Byron's *Don Juan.* Front-rhyme, or alliteration (q.v.) the r. of initial sounds of accented syllables frequently supplements the use of other unifying devices, although in OE poetry it formed the basic structure of the line and is still so employed occasionally in modern poetry, as by G. M. Hopkins and in W. H. Auden's *The Age of Anxiety.* Alliteration also may be carried beyond the limits of a single line and may even operate in elaborate patterns throughout a poem (see SOUND IN POETRY) as a counterpoint to other relationships indicated by different sorts of r., such as rhyme, metrical pattern, and assonance (q.v.). The exact r. of sounds within a line serves as a variety of internal rhyme ("Come here, thou *wor*thy of a *wor*ld of praise," Chapman, *The Odyssey*). Another repetitional device used chiefly in a decorative or supplemental function rather than in a structural one is assonance, the use of similar vowel sounds with identical consonant clusters. Such a poem as G. M. Hopkins' *The Leaden Echo and the Golden Echo* will illustrate abundantly how these "supplemental" devices of internal rhyme, alliteration, and assonance may be made into the chief features of the poetic line to support an unconventional system of metrics.

A single word may be repeated as a unifying device or, especially in dramatic poetry, for emphasis. The sections of a poem may be linked by repeating in the opening line of each new stanza the final word of the previous one, as in MacNeice's *Leaving Barra.* This linking device can be carried further into the formal rhetorical figure of climax, as in the following passage where each noun is picked up and repeated in some form.

And let the kettle to the trumpets speak,
The trumpet to the cannoneer without,
The cannons to the heavens, the heaven to
earth.
(Shakespeare, *Hamlet*)

The suggestions of a quality inherent in a single word may be exploited by the intensive r. of the word in every position within a conventional metrical pattern that the poet's ingenuity can devise, as in De la Mare's *Silver,* or a word may be repeated to underline an onomatopoetic effect as in the line, itself repeated at irregular intervals, from Catullus' 64th Ode, "Currite ducentes subtegmina, currite, fusi." The immediate r. of a word for emphasis has an incremental emotional effect, as shown most daringly in *King Lear* with an entire line consisting of a single word repeated ("Never, never, never, never, never!"). One of the dangers of this method is that like all expressions of strong emotion it lends itself to parody rather readily. Almost the same patterns of r. are used by Shakespeare for both serious and comic purposes, the difference in effect lying in context and in metrical subtlety.

O Cressid! O false Cressid! false, false, false!
(*Troilus and Cressida*)

O night, O night! alack, alack, alack!
(*Midsummer Night's Dream*)

The same duality of effect may be observed in the following progression from Shakespeare through Nathaniel Lee to Henry Fielding:

O Desdemona, Desdemona dead! O!O!O!
(*Othello*)

O Sophonisba, Sophonisba O!
(*Sophonisba*)

O Huncamunca, Huncamunca O!
(*Tragedy of Tom Thumb the Great*)

Again it is notable that the effective line lacks complete symmetry, while the unintentionally and the intentionally comic lines are rigidly constructed, a situation which suggests caution in the use of immediate r. A special case of r. is the pun (q.v.), where not similarity but difference is pointed up, and the effect within the context in which it occurs is diffusive rather than unifying. In general, double meanings in poetry will be found more frequently within the "tight" or heavily patterned forms of verse, such as sonnets or heroic couplets, rather than in "loose" forms, such as nondramatic blank verse.

The r. of a phrase in poetry may have an incantatory effect as in the opening lines of T. S. Eliot's *Ash-Wednesday*:

Because I do not hope to turn again
Because I do not hope
Because I do not hope to turn

The remaining 38 lines of the opening section of the poem might well be studied as an example of the effects of phrasal r., containing as they do no less than 11 lines clearly related to the opening 3 and serving as a unifying factor in a poem otherwise very free in structure. Sometimes the effect of a repeated phrase in a poem will be to emphasize a development or change by means of the contrast in the words following the identical phrases. For example, the shift from the distant to the near, from the less personal to the more personal is emphasized in Coleridge's *Rime of the Ancient Mariner* by such a r. of phrases:

I looked upon the rotting sea,
And drew my eyes away;
I looked upon the rotting deck,
And there the dead men lay.

Allusion (q.v.) or quoting is a special case of r., since it relies on resources outside of the poem itself for its effect. Here, as with the pun, the effect of the r. is diffusive rather than unifying, seeming frequently to be an extraneous, if graceful, decoration. Hence, with the exception of a few poets who have used it as a basic technique (T. S. Eliot, *The Waste Land*; Ezra Pound, *Cantos*), its chief use has been humorous, as in Robert Frost's *A Masque of Reason* or in W. S. Gilbert's *Bab Ballads*.

The r. of a complete line within a poem may be related to the envelope (q.v.) stanza pattern, may be used regularly at the end of each stanza as a refrain, or in other ways. The multiple recurrence of a line at irregular intervals as in Catullus' 64th Ode, as cited *supra,* or the line "Cras amet qui numquam amavit, quique amavit cras amet," which occurs ten times in the 92 lines of the *Pervigilium Veneris,* illustrates the effect of a r. of a specific line apart from a set place as furnished by stanzaic structure. Rarely a line may be repeated entire and immediately as a means of bringing a poem to a close, an extension of the method of bringing a sequence of terza rima (q.v.) to a close with a couplet:

And miles to go before I sleep,
And miles to go before I sleep.
(Frost, *Stopping by Woods on a Snowy Evening*)

Lines simply reintroduced once in a poem generally are meant to bear an altered and enriched significance on their second appearance, as:

O all the instruments agree
The day of his death was a dark cold day
(W. H. Auden, *In Memory of W. B. Yeats*)

The r. of a complete stanza within a poem is generally related to the envelope pattern or to the refrain, already cited. In either case, the effect is to reintroduce into an altered situation a unit which has already provoked a response, which will now modify and be modified.

The r. of metrical pattern is one of the most important elements of poetry. Through such r. individual lines are paired as to structure and groups of lines are built and organized into larger units or stanzas. These may be relatively simple like the ballad stanza, resulting from the breakdown of a pair of 14-syllable lines, or complex like the stanza used by Keats in *Ode to a Nightingale.* Undoubtedly part of the interest in a long poem lies in the skillful variation possible in the repetition of a single basic unit, whether the tail-rhyme strophes of metrical romance, the Spenserian stanzas of *The Faerie Queene,* or the heroic couplet in Pope's *Rape of the Lock.* Similarly in blank verse, much interest lies in the variety possible within limits of the regular beat.—C. A. Smith, *R. and Parallelism in Eng. Verse* (1894); B. R. Lewis, *Creative Poetry* (1931); C. P. Smith, *Pattern and Variation in Poetry* (1932); G. W. Allen, *Am. Prosody* (1935); Sister Miriam Joseph, *Shakespeare and the Arts of Language* (1947); J. Greenway, *Lit. among the Primitives* (1964). S.F.F.

RESOLUTION. Term restricted in Gr. and L. metric to the resolution of a long syllable into its metrical equivalent of two shorts, e.g., when an iambus (⏑–) or trochee (–⏑) is replaced by a tribrach (⏑⏑⏑). See CLASSICAL PROSODY and MORA. R.J.G.

REST. A term adapted from music and generally definable as a pause that counts in the metrical scheme. Most writers seem to restrict this definition to situations where a pause seems to compensate (see COMPENSATION) for the absence of an unstressed syllable or syllables in a foot. The standard example is Tennyson's

×× / ×× / ×× /
Break, break, break,
× × / × × / × /
At the foot of thy crags, O sea!

However, others have suggested that a rest may take the place of an entire foot. According to Stewart the variety of metrical pause equivalent to a rest in music seems to be a late literary invention, "hardly begun until after 1920."—Baum; G. R. Stewart, Jr., *Modern Metrical Technique as Illustrated in Ballad Meter, 1700–1920* (1923); W. L. Schramm, *Approaches to a Science of Eng. Verse* (1935). R.BE.

RHAPSODY. Originally a selection or a portion of epic literature, usually the *Iliad* or *Odyssey,* sung by a rhapsode (Gr. "stitcher") or rhapsodist in ancient Greece. The term in literature subsequently meant any highly emotional utterance, a literary work informed by ecstasy and not by a rational organization. It is also applied to a literary miscellany or a disconnected series of literary works. R.A.H.

RHETORIC AND POETICS. From ancient times to the present, r. in the broad sense has meant the art of persuasion, in the narrow sense the studied ornament of speech, or eloquence. Since the time of Aristotle, p. has meant the art of making and judging poetry. Any attempt to describe the relations between these two disciplines runs into many complications, but from Plato to Paul de Man, r. and p. have been closely intertwined. Their relations in a given period seem to depend on two principal factors: (1) how far poetry itself is seen as subject to rule and precept rather than the product of inspiration, as many theorists have preferred to suggest; (2) how far r. is conceived as the art of flattery and deception (Plato) or a way of "making big shoes for a little foot" (Montaigne) rather than the art of discourse (including all those disciplines that prepare speakers to exercise language in the noblest and most effective ways).

In most general terms, r. may be the study of the means of persuasion or an inventory of tropes and figures. P. can be seen as precepts for the production of verse or as an account of the qualities of literary creation and the nature of literature. The changing relations between r. and p. are produced by these alterations.

In Gr. thought there is often an opposition between r. and p., or the techniques of persuasive oratory and poetic activity, which is frequently seen as inspired, not the product of rule or technique. Under the Roman Empire, however, persuasion and proof become less important, and r. comes to be the art of speaking and writing beautifully. Discussion of the poet's craft belongs with r. During the Middle Ages, the study of literature, or poetics, is shared between r. and grammar within the scholastic trivium of the liberal arts, and this tradition of the rhetorical study of classical literary examples lasts until the 18th c., though the rediscovery in the Renaissance of Aristotle's *Poetics* gives rise to a normative p., particularly concerned with the requisites of epic and tragedy. During the romantic period the revolt against r., both as concept and discipline, makes possible the emergence of a theory of poetry independent of traditional r. In the 20th c. r. as the art of speaking has remained in eclipse, but influential movements in literary criticism (New Criticism, Structuralism, Deconstruction) have been concerned with what in earlier times would have been called rhetorical analysis and have led to a renewed interest in r. as a general approach to discourse that would exploit the insights of p. or literary analysis.

R. is said to have been founded by Corax of Syracuse (*fl.* 476 B.C.) to help citizens plead for the restoration of their property after the overthrow of the tyrant Thrasybulus. Tradition holds that the Sophist Gorgias brought these techniques to Greece about 428 B.C., where they were used to train young men in the public speaking necessary to public life in Athens. In Plato's *Gorgias*, Socrates argues that r. is not, as Gorgias maintains, the queen of all the arts, but a knack for humoring the prejudices of an audience. This dialogue, together with the *Phaedrus*, which argues that a proper r. would require knowledge of all the matters speakers or writers treat, sets up the oppositions with which r. has had to contend ever since: show as opposed to substance, mere words as opposed to knowledge of things themselves, tricks as opposed to right reasoning. For Plato, p. does not qualify as a body of knowledge. In the *Ion*, Socrates compels the rhapsode Ion to confess that neither the poet nor his interpreter is master of an art, a rational body of specialized knowledge, but that both are inspired or possessed. This Platonic vision of the poet as ecstatic seer has many echoes in the later tradition of p.—Shelley argues in his *Defense of Poetry* that the finest passages in poetry are not produced by study and have no necessary connection with the will—and frequently works to keep p. and r. apart.

Aristotle's *Rhetoric* established most of the concepts that informed the rhetorical tradition of the next two thousand years. R. involves the discovery of all means of persuasion, the three basic types of which are the appeal to the audience's emotions (*pathos*), the appeal of the speaker's character (*ethos*), and argumentative proof (*logos*). Speeches themselves are classed as forensic, or judicial (arguing the justice or injustice of a past action), deliberative, or political (urging a future course of action), and epideictic, or ceremonial (the celebratory speech of public occasions). Aristotle devotes special attention to the use of topics or commonplaces to discover arguments and to the use of enthymemes, the rhetorical counterpart of the deductive syllogism. While Aristotle regards r. as a matter of persuasion and poetry as a matter of imitation, there are connections between the two: questions of diction important to r. are to be treated in the *Poetics*, and the rhetorical discussion of invention will be relevant to p. Aristotle's own *Poetics*, which investigates literary kinds, identifies six constituents of tragedy (the section on comedy has been lost): plot, character, thought, diction, spectacle, and music. Aristotle's approach is analytical rather than prescriptive (though his reflections on what patterns contribute to a successful tragedy were taken to justify normative p. in later periods); he focuses on elements appropriate to particular kinds of imitation more than on ways of moving an audience, and his work might have served as the basis for an independent tradition of p. had it not been lost until the Renaissance.

The legacy of Aristotelian r. was developed in treatises of Cicero and Quintilian and the *Rhetorica ad Herennium*, attributed to Cicero in the Middle Ages. This Ciceronian tradition divides r. into five parts: Invention (*inventio*), arrangement (*dispositio*), style (*elocutio*), memory (*memoria*), and delivery (*pronunciatio*). The *Rhetorica ad Herennium*'s detailed discussion of style characterizes the high, the middle and the plain style, each suitable for different subjects and purposes, and provides full treatment of the figures of diction and thought that became the center of r. in later ages. The possibility of treating poetics as part of r. thus arose, since r. defines the characters, themes, subjects and figures appropriate to each style.

A favorite example for the illustration of the three styles in the r. of the late Roman Empire was "Vergil's wheel," which aligned with the high, middle, and plain style a type of hero (military leader, farmer, shepherd), and the appropriate animal (steed, cow, sheep), accessory (sword, plow, crook), tree (laurel, fruit tree, beech) and setting (city or camp, field, pasture), as illustrated by Vergil's *Aeneid*, *Georgics*, and *Eclogues*. Tacitus's *Dialogue on Orators* notes a shift from a pragmatic, political conception of r. to a more literary one: "For even the beauty of poetry is now required of the orator, a beauty . . . drawn from the shrine of Horace and Vergil and Lucan." Emphasis no longer falls on the persuasive function of particular elements but upon their appropriateness for certain conventionalized purposes.

Although the author of the *Ad Herennium* was sparing in his use of poetry to illustrate rhetorical principles, Cicero himself was not, but drew freely, for example, upon Terence to show what good r. was. Cicero's most distinguished follower, Quintilian, taught that Homer's writings display all the rules of art to be followed in oratory and that a careful study of the comic poet Menander would be sufficient to develop the whole art of r. The observations about poetry in Horace's *Ars Poetica* bear a striking resemblance to the kind of remarks Quintilian expects of the teacher of r. in the process of *enarratio poetarum*, interpretation of the poets, which is an important component of the orator's education. Quintilian's great innovation was to have outlined the educational program for the ideal orator: r. was to shape the student's entire mental and moral development.

In late classical times and throughout most of the Middle Ages poetry fell under the wing of either r. or grammar. When deliberative oratory disappeared under the rule of the emperors and forensic oratory became highly specialized, demonstrative oratory or declamation became the principal rhetorical study and *elocutio* or style received the major emphasis. Invention and arrangement were either neglected or returned to their original owner, the logician. Some medieval theorists in France associated p. with music, but most medieval manuals of poetry were rhetorics and only the sections on versification made any significant distinction between poetry and oratory. One significant development in the r. of this period is St. Augustine's adaptation of Ciceronian r. and sign theory in *De Doctrina Christiana* for the purposes of expounding the scripture and developing sermons, a form of oratory that did not fall under any of the three traditional kinds.

With the revival of classical learning in the Renaissance came the recovery of the mature rhetorical treatises of Cicero, *De Oratore*, *Brutus*, *Orator*, and the complete *Institutio Oratoria* of Quintilian, bringing with them a revival of the logical components of r., invention and arrangement. One influential book of the early Renaissance was *De Inventione Dialectica* by Rodolphus Agricola (d. 1485). Logic or dialectic, Agricola said, is "to speak in a probable way on any matter"; grammar teaches correctness and clarity, rhetoric style. Similar views were advanced by the Fr. scholar Peter Ramus (1515–72), who insisted that invention and arrangement belonged to logic, because they are functions of reason, and that style belongs to r. Ramus's influential logic text encouraged attention to invention and arrangement in the schools but left r. in a weakened position as the study of style and delivery alone. The demise of traditional r. in the 18th c. can be traced to this separation which reduced r. to a theory of tropes and figures.

In the meantime, however, Ciceronians continued to maintain that r. included both logical and stylistic disciplines, and the study of poetry remained largely rhetorical: dramas, epic poems, odes, elegies were analyzed in terms of invention, arrangement, and style, and also in terms of exordium, *narratio*, proof, and conclusion. The Ciceronian hierarchy of styles (high, middle, plain) took on major importance.

The recovery of Aristotle's *Poetics* in the 16th c. produced some modifications of this rhetorical poetics. Scholars such as Robortelli and Castelvetro began to mingle Aristotle's poetic terminology with the Ciceronian terminology, and their work gradually found its way into p. outside Italy. The *Pléiade* poets, Du Bellay, Ronsard, Peletier, speak of invention, arrangement, and style. Sidney's *Defense of Poesy* is mainly rhetorical. In the next century, however, these logical-rhetorical terms appear side by side with the categories of an Aristotelian p.: Plot (Fable), Character (Manners), Thought (Sentiments), and Diction, as, for example, in Rapin's *Réflexions sur la Poétique d'Aristote* (1674) and in Dryden's *Preface to the Fables* (1700).

In the 18th c. the tradition of rhetorical training linked with the study of classical authors remains strong in the schools, but the rhetorical treatises (DuMarsais's and Fontanier's in France; Campbell's and Whately's in England; even Blair's notable for linking r. with *belles lettres*) are monuments of a discipline reaching its end. The most powerful thinking about language and mind—Locke, Leibnitz, Condillac, Hume, Rousseau—no longer takes place in the domain of r.

The revolt in romantic literature against poetic diction and other codifications of the rhetorical tradition (particularly the hierarchy of styles) accompanied the rise of *aesthetics*, to which serious p. now belongs. Discussion of literature is no longer linked to consideration of rhetorical strategies for affecting an audience or to canons of expression but, as Abrams shows in *The Mirror and the Lamp*, to issues involving creation and imagination. Discussion of rhetorical and stylistic questions survives as a hostility to "artificial" r.; serious treatments of rhetorical figures, such as symbol and allegory, occur in works of philosophical ambitions, from Coleridge to Hegel. P.—reflection on nature of poetry and poetic language—insists on the distinction between art and other discourses previously treated by r. The rise of linguistics, a historical science of language, in the 19th c., deprived r. of another former subject of enquiry.

The 20th c. has witnessed the return of many of the traditional concerns of r., but in different guises, such as stylistics, which tries to characterize different styles in terms derived from linguistics. Of greater literary significance is the work of the Russian Formalists (1915–1930) who, insisting that the "device" is the true hero of the literary work, recreated a rhetorical p., many of whose key terms, such as *ostranie* (defamiliarization) refer to an effect on an audience. Roman Jakobson, who identifies two rhetorical figures, metonymy and metaphor, as the fundamental mechanisms of language, brought this p. to the West where it contributed to Structuralism (see below).

Am. New Criticism, with its focus on the structure and imagery of poems and on the narrative perspectives and strategies of novels, attempted with considerable success to combine rhetorical and aesthetic perspectives. The so-called Chicago School of criticism (see R. S. Crane's *Critics and Criticism*) sought to analyze literature in the terms provided by Aristote's *Poetics*, but was less influential than Northrop Frye, whose *Anatomy of Criticism* mapped literary possibilities in an Aristotelian spirit according to genre, mode, and style.

R. plays a central role in the criticism of Kenneth Burke, who considers literature as persuasion and relates its strategies to those of other discourses. A much neglected aspect of r., its analysis of cultural commonplaces and expectations (topoi and enthymemes) is important for Structuralism: a movement of the 1960's and 70's which, taking linguistics as a model, seeks to work out the underlying systems of norms and conventions that make possible the meanings objects and events have for members of a culture. Structuralists envision a p. that would stand to literature as linguistics stands to language, describing its conventions and rules for the combination of elements. Here and in their study of cultural codes, structuralists such as Roland Barthes and Tzvetan Todorov explicitly link their work with the most ambitious projects of r.

Finally, r. comes to the fore in the "deconstructive" readings of literary and philosophical texts associated with Jacques Derrida and Paul de Man. Emphasizing the figurality of language, deconstruction investigates how rhetorical patterns and processes generate meaning not controlled by an intention. Literature, associated with self-conscious figurality, provides a model for elucidating the dependency of conceptualization and perception on figure. In its generation of meaning through mechanical, rhetorical operations, de Man argues, literature provides a critique of the aesthetic, which posits the harmonious synthesis of sensible and intelligible. He also sees the alternation between views of r. as persuasion and as system of tropes as an indication of the fundamental antinomy of language: the unsynthesizable relation between structure and event.

The term r. frequently appears in Am. textbooks for teaching expository writing as a comprehensive name for grammar, arrangement, and style, but otherwise 20th c. r., like p., is analytical and descriptive, rather than prescriptive, and unlike traditional r., which sought to move or persuade an audience, it concentrates on analyzing *meaning* and contributing to interpretation.

Plato, *Phaedrus, Gorgias, Ion*; Aristotle, *Rhetoric, Poetics*; Cicero, *De Inventione, De Oratore, Brutus, Orator, De Partitione Oratoria*; [Cicero], *Rhetorica ad Herennium*; Horace, *Ars Poetica*; Quintilian, *Institutio Oratoria*; Tacitus, *Dialogus*; Longinus, *On the Sublime*; Augustine, *De Doctrina Christiana*; F. Robortellus, *In Librum Aristotelis de Arte Poetica Explicationes* (1548); T. Wilson, *The Arte of Rhetorique* (1553); Ramus and Talaeus, *Rhetorica e P. Rami Regii Professoris Praelectionibus Observata* (1572); J. C. Scaliger, *Poetices Libri Septem* (2d ed., 1581); Puttenham, *The Arte of Eng. Poesie* (1589); G. I. Vossius, *Commentariorum Rhetoricorum Sive Oratoriarum Institutionum, Libri Sex* (1643); C. C. DuMarsais, *Des Tropes* (1730); G. Campbell, *The Philosophy of R.* (1776); H. Blair, *Lectures on R. and Belles Lettres* (1783); P. Fontanier, *Traité générale des figures du discours* (1821); R. Whately, *R.* (1828); C. S. Baldwin, *Ancient R. and Poetic* (1924); *Medieval R. and Poetic* (1928); I. A. Richards, *The Philosophy of R.* (1936); K. Burke, *The Philosophy of Lit. Form* (1941) and *A R. of Motives* (1950); Crane, *Critics*; Abrams; V. Erlich, *Russian Formalism* (1955); W. S. Howell, *Logic and R. in England, 1500–1700* (1956); R. Jakobson and M. Halle, *Fundamentals of Language* (1956); Wimsatt and Brooks; Frye; Lausberg; A. Kibedi Varga, *Rhétorique et littérature* (1960); H. Morier, *Dictionnaire de poétique et de rhétorique* (1961); Weinberg; G. Kennedy, *The Art of Persuasion in Greece* (1963); J. Dubois et al. *Rhétorique générale* (1970); J. Murphy, *R. in the Middle Ages* (1974); J. Culler, *Structuralist Poetics* (1975); T. Todorov, *Theories of the Symbol* (1977); *Historical R.: An Annotated Bibliog.* ed. W. Horner (1980); D. Rice and P. Schofer, *Rhetorical P.* (1983); W. Trimpi, *Muses of One Mind* (1983); P. de Man, *The R. of Romanticism* (1984).

M.T.H.; rev. J.C.

RHETORICAL QUESTION. Either a word- or sentence-question asked for effect rather than information, one to which the speaker knows the answer in advance and either does not wait for it or answers the question himself: "ti oun aition einai hypolambano; ego hymin ero" (What then do I regard as the explanation? I will tell you—Plato, *Apology* 40b). The device, much more favored in Gr. than in Eng., is found rarely in Lysias, quite frequently in Plato and Isaeus, in a highly developed state in Demosthenes. Used frequently in persuasive discourse, r.q. commands attention from the audience, serves to express various shades of emotion, and sometimes acts as a transitional device to lead from one subject to another. The most famous Eng. example is probably the question at the end of Shelley's *Ode to the West Wind*: "O, Wind, / If Winter comes, can Spring be far behind? R.O.E.

RHYME. Nature and Function. The spelling "rhyme" became common in the 17th c. and is now more usual than the older "rime." The main meaning of the word is: a metrical rhetorical device based on the sound-identities of words. The minor meanings can be summarily disposed of before the main one is elaborated: (1) a poem in rhymed verse (cf. Mrs. Browning's *Rhyme of the Duchess May* which has a "Pro-rhyme" before and an "Epi-rhyme" after); (2) rhymed verse in general (e.g., "Pope's Homer is in rhyme" (3) any kind of echoing between words besides the one specified by the main meaning above (e.g., assonance, consonance, alliteration, etc.); (4) unison or accord (e.g., J. R. Lowell, *Among My Books*: "of which he was as unaware as the blue river is of its rhyme with the blue sky"); (5) a word that echoes another (e.g., " 'Love' is a hackneyed rhyme for 'dove' ") or the sound common to two or more words (e.g., "The meanings of the words are just as important as their rhymes"); (6) a complement to "reason" (in such phrases as: "without rhyme or reason").

As a metrical-rhetorical device in Eng., r. involves two or more r.-fellows. These may be: whole words (*dawn–fawn*); ends of words (ap/*plaud*–de/*fraud*); groups of whole words (*stayed with us–played with us*); or ends of words followed by one or more whole words (be/*seech him*–im/*peach him*). R.-fellows of one sort may of course rhyme with fellows of another sort (*poet–know it*). If a r.-fellow is phonetically analyzed, it will be found to have at least a stem, which must be vocalic (*awe, eye, owe*). It may have an initial, which if it is present must be consonantal (*saw, spy, low*); and it may have a terminal, consonantal (*all, eyes, own*) or vocalic (*ayah*) or both (*awful, eyot, owning*). Both initial and terminal may be present as well as stem (*lawfully, spying, known*). The stem carries the last metrical stress of the line, or possibly the second last

máke of ít–táke of ít.

The sound-identity for a perfect rhyme must begin in each r.-fellow with the stem and continue through the terminal if there is one. At least one of a pair of r.-fellows, two of a trio, and so on must have initials, no two initials being the same (*ill–fill–mill*; but not *ill–till*–un/*til*). Identical initials, however, are legitimate in Fr. at least (see R. HISTORY and RIME RICHE) and have occurred in Eng. When the r.-fellows are monosyllabic, the r. is male, masculine, or single (pala/*din*–harle/*quin*). In Eng. such rhymes far outnumber those involving more than one syllable. Rhymes are said to be female, feminine, or double when the r.-fellows are disyllabic (*master*–di/*saster*). Trisyllabic r.-fellows produce treble, triple, or sdrucciolo rhymes (*Thackeray–quackery*). R.-fellows with still more syllables are so rare in Eng. that no special names are in use for the resulting rhymes. No doubt rhymes of sorts can be concocted from nonce words, as in Lewis Carroll's *Jabberwocky*. But notionally at least r. comes only from sound-identities between real words, given their accepted pronunciation, accentuation, articulation, and usage. R. which conforms to all the requirements is said to be complete, full, perfect, true, or whole. Departures from the norm are licenses, which may or may not be tolerable according to circumstances.

The origin of r. should not be sought locally or linguistically. R. is to be traced rather to the fact that the nunmber of sounds available for any language is limited and its many words must be combinations and permutations of its few sounds. Every language, therefore, is bound to jingle now and then. It will depend on a variety of factors whether the jingles will come to be used deliberately as a device in poetry and how far that device will be carried. Systematic rhyming, however, has appeared in such widely separated languages (e.g., Chinese, Sanskrit, Arabic, Norse, Prov., Celtic) that its spontaneous development in more than one of them can be reasonably assumed. In the rest it may have been introduced like any other device from the outside, and any language that had already acquired r., no matter how, may have learned new applications of it from its neighbors. Men must have been pleased by verbal jingles long before they realized that the jingles had a use in organizing or pointing their verses. R. is indeed only one instance of that animating principle of all the arts: the desire for similarity in dissimilarity and dissimilarity in similarity. Other results within the literary art are: alliteration, anaphora, antithesis and balance, assonance, meter and stanzas, parallelism, and refrains. Perhaps because man is a creature with paired limbs and organs, he takes pleasure in repetitions, not merely simple duplications, but approximations, complements, and counterpoints.

The functions of r. are metrical and rhetorical. From the metrical point of view end- or final r. is a device to mark the ends of lines and link them in couplets, stanzas, or verse paragraphs. It has an organizing effect, therefore, in respect of metrical units longer than the foot. It might be regarded as an ornamental stress falling on and confirming the metrical stresses at the ends of the lines. But middle-and-end r. is sometimes used to mark the ends of the two halves of a line. Such rhyming is sporadic in many ballads, as well as elsewhere. When it is systematic, it simply results from two short lines having been put down as one to save space.

R. in verse is not limited to the ends of lines and half-lines. One word may echo another anywhere in its immediate neighborhood and apart from the metrical scheme. The purpose of such inner, internal, or medial rhymes is then more rhetorical than metrical, as where Browning builds up a seriocomic climax with them in:—

How *sad* and *bad* and *mad* it was—
But then, how it was sweet!

or where Swinburne suggests the darting flight of the bird in:—

Sister, my sister, O *fleet sweet* swallow.

Rhetorical, too, rather than metrical is the practice of Shakespeare and his fellow-dramatists intermingling a good deal of end-r. with their blank verse, generally in couplets, but sometimes in greater complication; they were particularly partial to rhymed couplets for ending a specch or pointing a maxim.

Though r. is primarily a feature of verse, it has been resorted to in prose for occasional effects from the earliest Gr. orators downward. Cicero's discreet use of it was probably what commended it to the mannered stylists of the Renaissance (e.g., Rabelais; Guevara and the gongorists; John Lyly and the euphuists). It can be found in later writers as diverse as Hannah More, Disraeli, and George Meredith, not to mention the practitioners of polyphonic prose.

Though end-r. in verse is primarily metrical, it has also a rhetorical side. "Poetry aims . . . at increasing, by metrical devices, the number of best places for the best words in the best order" (Sir Walter Raleigh, *Six Essays on Johnson*). Of these devices r. is not the least important, and the places which it signalizes are among the very best. It concentrates meaning in "ce mot sorcier, ce mot fée, ce mot magique" (Théodore de Banville, *Petit Traité de Poésie Française*). There is then little point in having good places for words if advantage is not taken of them; and r. is wasted unless its sound cooperates in some ways with the sense. That being so, the poet who has many insignificant words in rhyming places is losing some of his opportunities.

The beauty of r., for the Eng. reader at least, "is lessened by any likeness the words may have beyond that of sound" (G. M. Hopkins, *The Notebooks and Papers*). Even when rhymes are separately unexceptionable, they may be weakened by repetition or near-repetition at no great interval. Such lapses, besides being unenterprising, are destructive of stanzaic patterns. Then again hackneyed rhymes (*breeze–trees*) can hardly yield the pleasure of a mild surprise; and inevitable yoke-fellows (*anguish–languish, length–strength*) still less. It does not follow, however, that bizarre rhymes are *per contra* good in any context, though they may be appropriate in *Hudibras* or *The Ingoldsby Legends*. A last weakness, to mention no more, is to let the r. too obviously dictate the sense. For part of the mastery of r. "consists in never writing it for its own sake, or at least never appearing to do so" (Leigh Hunt, *Imagination and Fancy*).

Languages differ widely in their rhymability, and different conventions have been established as to the acceptable and the unacceptable. Languages which rhyme easily may right the balance by restrictive rules; and those which rhyme less easily may tolerate near-rhymes, though retaining perfect r. as the ideal. Though Gr. and L. poetry normally did without rhyme, it was a recognized figure (*homoeoteleuton, similiter desinens*). It is rarer in Gr. poetry than in L., though not unknown even in Homer and becoming rather commoner in the Alexandrian poets who delighted in all kinds of verbal correspondences. L. poetry seemed to hanker afer r. The earliest remains, which are in accentual verse, frequently jingle. Among modern European languages Sp. and It. run the most readily to r., on account of the relatively small number of ways in which words end. Rhyming is further facilitated in It. by the eliding flexibility of the language. Hence the fluency of the *improvisatori* who can produce extemporary verses in complicated meters with scarcely any cogitation on any subjects suggested by their auditors. Fr. rhymes almost as readily as Sp. and It. But by authoritarian edict many phonetically perfect rhymes are declined on various grounds. Another restrictive influence was the limitation of poets to an exclusive poetic diction, until Victor Hugo "mit un bonnet rouge au vieux dictionnaire." German is less rhymable than any of the Romance languages, but more so than Eng. It has always been ready to accept into art-poetry some of the freedoms of folk-verse and to make a pronunciation in one dialect justify a r. in another. It has also resorted, more often and more successfully than Sp., It., or Fr., to unrhymed measures.

So has Eng., especially in its blank verse. It also has made a considerable use of stanzas which do not require every line to rhyme (e.g., ballad measure, long measure, etc.). Owing to the large number of ways in which Eng. words can terminate, the average number of words to an ending is under three. The number of words which rhyme with only one other is large (*mountain–fountain, babe*–astro/*labe*); and those which cannot be rhymed at all is as large or larger (*breadth, circle, desert, monarch, month, virtue, wisdom,* etc.). The result is that Eng. is more tolerant than any other European language of rhyming licenses. Though Eng. poets vary greatly in the number and the kinds of easements they discover from rhyming rigor, they all allow themselves more merely approximate rhymes than is generally realized, to say nothing of solecisms in usage for rhyme's sake. Several other points are worth mentioning in this connection: first, the anomalies of Eng. spelling which give a sort of sanction to eye or visual rhymes (*cough–plough*); secondly, the fact that so many of the most admired poets came early when the language was different from what it became; thirdly, the respect for ancient precedents and the revivalism in practically every period among poets who harked back to their predecessors for models; and finally, the frequent draughts of Eng. art-poetry from folk-poetry, if not indeed the virtual absence of any barrier between them. Moreover it is the way of art to make virtues of necessities; and so the poets have found reasons for rhyming relaxation which originate in the recognition of the beauty of imperfection and the pleasure of novelty and surprise. They are, by virtue of their calling, verbal experimeters who strain at and overleap the restrictions of the purists; and poetry is the growing end of language, in the matter of r. as in other respects. A.M.C.

For bibliog. see HISTORY (below).

HISTORY. Saintsbury, famous British prosodist, once declared that r. in Eng. appeared no one quite knows how, or why, or whence. Indeed, in origins, in diffusion, and in function, r. is the most mysterious of all sound-pattern repetitions. It is not originally native to any European or Indo-European language. Among Oriental languages, it appears early in South-Semitic and Chinese, whence from either or both it may later have been adapted to the Sanskritic Indian languages and to Iranian. Fragments of Old Latin poems by Ennius certainly show structural r. as a factor in verse side by side with accent and alliteration, but here one suspects acculturation from a language originally from the northern Near East–Etruscan. Not only are the origins of r. mysterious; it is mysteriously complex in its literary suggestions. Obviously, in the ages before silent reading (see Augustine, *Confessions* 3) it was a useful mnemonic device. In addition, it contributes to verse a euphonic factor, a phrase and line segmentalizing factor, a pointing (deictic) semantic factor, and—particularly in modern verse—a factor that underlines irony, litotes, and the unexpected collocations of dissimilars we expect to find in the poetry of dissociation. To trace the history of r. in Western Atlantic literatures is a discursion into the unknown, particularly since early writers integrate it with assonance, consonance, alliteration, and the like under one head. In native North America, it occurs only in one Indian language, where it is probably borrowed from Eng. Most cultures' verse lacks r. either as organizational device or as ornament.

In European literatures, the first mention of anything approaching true r. is in the third book of Aristotle's *Rhetoric*—that remarkable book, long neglected in favor of the *Poetics*—which discusses practical rhetorical devices under the twin heads of *clarity* and *propriety*. Here we are introduced to the notion of homoeoteleuton at the ends, more rarely at the beginnings, of the members of prose periods, as contributing to sound harmony (paromoeosis). Whether or not Aristotle's account derives from Gorgian rhetoricians, or from lost books by Isocrates, or from Near Eastern sources, we do not certainly know. We do know that the later Alexandrian rhetoricians and critics, like some L. writers after them, understood the use of homoeoteleuton in prose.

Verse r., actually homoeoteleuton rather than full r., first appears in hymns of the African Christian Church attributed to successors of Tertullian (A.D. 160?–220?). In these (as in *suscipe: tempore*) only the final inflectional syllable actually rhymed. Full r. seems first to appear in hymns associated with the followers of St. Hilarius of Poitiers (d. A.D. 368?), but was not generally adopted until some centuries later. In Byzantium, Romanus the Melode and Synesius were exploiting its possibilities in hymnology by the 6th c. A.D. The combined evidence of Aristotelian and Alexandrinian homoeoteleuton, the African Tertullian hymns, Hilarian full r., and Byzantinian full r. all points to a South-Semitic, possibly Arabian, source as the diffusion center for r. in the European literatures.

In Western Europe, full r., usually combining end-r. with in-r., seems first to have appeared in Ireland under the influence of early rhymed hymns and among poets writing both in Ir. and in L. Here, the controlling linguistic factor was the early disappearance of Ir. suffixal elements, the development of initial inflection, and the consequent development of end-stress in the word. In Welsh, which was and is a fore-stressed language, r. has always been secondary to alliteration. Very intricate combinations of end-r. with in-r. occur in Ir. as early as the Lorica of St. Patrick (attributed to A.D. 433), and wherever Ir. monks traveled on the Continent of Europe, they seem to have proselytized the use of full r. as ardently as they proselytized their Faith. They are probably responsible ultimately for the intricate rhyming patterns of the goliardic *Carmina Burana*, and eventually, for those of the 9th-c. Ambrosian hymns. From both sources, r. diffused to the Scandinavian countries, where from Bragi onward it alternated with carefully contrived end consonances (*skothendings*) in skaldic verse. In ON skaldic verse, as in Ir. hymns and L.-Ir. goliardic poems, full r. is used as a line-end marker to segmentalize such lovely stanzaic forms as those of the *Pervigilium Veneris* or the Provençal-Minnesänger stanza form abc / abc / dddd and its variants, first found in the *Carmina Burana*.

The introduction of end-r. into West Germanic verse is rather curious. In Old High German, the *Muspilli* shows a degeneration of the original alliterative technique to a point where it is rhythmically unintelligible. Otfried, or someone like Otfried, simply had to introduce end-r. as a structural factor marking line-endings and inducing a new accentual verse structure. That Otfried had uneven success with his new technique merely reveals the relative unfamiliarity of end-r. in the German literature of his day. In OE, ornamental in-r. coupled with end-r. is much more common than one usually supposes. Friedrich Kluge found 28 examples in the *Beowulf* alone. Recent phonemicizations of OE, which construe *ea, eo,* and *io* as mere positional (non-distinctive) variants of *ae, e,* and *i,* add greatly to the frequency of actual full rhymes found in *Beowulf,* the so-called Elegiac poems, the Cynewulfian poems, *Judith,* and so forth. Here we may be concerned with direct or indirect influence from Ir. Yet, although OE full rhymes are ornamental—subsidiary to the primary structural device of alliteration—the *Rhyming Poem* and the *Death of Alfred* in the OE Chronicle (both 10th c.) are so similar to the ON *runhent* (like Egill's ***Höfuðlausn,*** composed at York) that we may suspect a well-developed OE tradition of structural full r. of which these two are the only surviving exemplars. Quite probably it originated in the Scandinavian colonies of Eastern and Northern England. The later evolution of the ME unrhymed alliterative romance in the Central and North West Midlands as compared with that of the rhymed metrical romance (quite similar to the later ON *rimur*) in the North East Midlands and East Anglia adds substance to this hypothesis. Further evidence may be derived from the emergence of such long rhymed poems as *Genesis and Exodus* and *Cursor Mundi* around A.D. 1300, the one from the Central East Midlands, the other from the Northern area.

In ME, the first influx of rhymed verse occurs in the late 12th c. with the *Owl and the Nightingale* and in the 13th c. with Layamon's *Brut* and the lyrics preserved in MS Harley 2254. The first is in form and subject matter a Prov. tenson and may owe its rhymes, as it owes its adapted theme, to direct Prov. influence. The second is curious: it blends the OE alliterative line with full rhymes, assonances, homoeoteleutons, and nunnations (additions of –n), and may very well owe a direct debt to contemporary Welsh verse. The lyrics raise a vexed question: is their use of stanzaic r. to be attributed directly to Prov.-Fr. influence, or to goliardic lyric, or to Saracen influence working through Prov., or to a combination of these possibilities? The earliest troubadour lyrics themselves undoubtedly derive from the goliardic L. verse of the wandering scholars, although later enriched by the intricate erotic rhymed verse of the Arabic Moors. In all probability, particularly when we consider the macaronic verse of the early ME manuscripts, we are to assume a combination of these influences. If *Alisoun* plainly recalls the Prov. influence, *Lenten is come with Love to Toune* recalls, and surpasses, the best of the goliardic lyrics. With Robert of Brunne and the Chaucerians, as with Chaucer himself, the primary influence is undoubted. It is Fr., and Northern Fr. at that. Yet to understand the intrusion of r. into ME verse, certain linguistic facts must also be taken into account. The breakdown of the OE inflectional system enormously multiplied the number of easily rhymed monosyllabic words; the widespread borrowing of Fr. disyllabic and polysyllabic words stressed on the last or next to the last syllable created words easily accessible to end-r. These factors, working in combination, created a verse milieu favorable to r. and relatively unfavorable to alliteration.

The later history of r. in Eng. calls for some preliminary observations. First, languages in which full r. or homoeoteleuton are automatic concomitants of inflection never use r. as a structural factor in verse. Examples are Japanese and certain Bantu languages. Second, end-stress rather than fore-stress facilitates the use of r. A typical example would be that of Italian. Third, when, in any language, rhyming is relatively easy, the poet tends to complicate it by employing *rime riche* (as in Fr.), or highly complex rhymed stanza forms (as in Prov. and Fr.), or by eschewing r. completely (as in the blank verse allegedly invented by Trissino for drama). Eng., greatly influenced in rhyming habit by Continental sources, shows or has shown all three tendencies. *Rime riche* occurs in Chaucer; although the ballade, rondeau, rondel, and triolet have never had the popularity of the sonnet, they have been frequently written and are still being written; blank verse achieved almost immediate popularity in drama; and unrhymed quantitative verse, first introduced by Thomas Watson (between 1530 and 1540), Richard Stanyhurst (1582), William Webbe (1586), and Thomas Campion (1602) was revived even in the 19th c. by Arthur Hugh Clough and the Reverend Rackham—this despite Daniel's brilliant *Defence of Rhyme* (1603). R., in fact, walks a tightrope between ease and difficulty: too easy rhyming or too difficult rhyming produce the same result—the poetic disuse of r.

On these lines, four periods of Eng. rhyming can be distinguished: (1) in the fore-stressed OE, r. was difficult; hence the persistence of structural alliteration; (2) in ME, r. became easier; hence its eventual victory over alliteration; (3) in Early Modern Eng. (roughly 1500–1750) the results of the Great Sound Shift made r. very easy; hence the popularity of such forms as the sonnet on the one hand and blank verse on the other; (4) in the Late Modern Eng. period (roughly from 1830), because of the victorious emergence of the former bourgeois pronunciation as a Received Standard, r. has again become difficult; hence the increasing use of eye-rhymes (based ultimately on the true rhymes of Pope) in the 19th c., and, more lately, the increasing popularity of end-consonance, slant rhymes, assonances, Donnesque rhymes, and, ultimately, through the influence of the Fr. symbolists and Whitman, of "free" (viz. syntactic) verse. H.W.

A. Ehrenfeld, *Studien zur Theorie des Reims* (2 v., 1897–1904); G. Mari, *Riassunto e Dizionarietto di Ritmica Italiana* (1901); Kastner; Saintsbury, *Prosody;* A. Gabrielson, *R. as a Criterion of the Pronunciation of Spenser, Pope, Byron, and Swinburne* (1909); Schipper; F. Zschech, *Die Kritik des Reims in England* (1917); O. Brik, "Zvukovie povtory," *Poetika* (1919); T. S. Osmond, *Eng. Metrists* (1921); H. C. Wyld, *Studies in Eng. Rhymes from Surrey to Pope* (1923); V. Zhirmunsky, *Rifma, ee istoriia i teoriia* (1923); Norden; A. Heusler, *Deutsche Versgeschichte* (3 v., 1925–29); G. Young, *An Eng. Prosody on Inductive Lines* (1928); H. Lanz, *The Physical Basis of R.* (1931); A. M. Clark, *Studies in Lit. Modes* (1945); F.J.E. Raby, *Hist. of Christian L. Poetry* (2d ed. 1953) and *Secular L. Poetry* (2d ed. 2 v., 1957); J. Carney, *Studies in Ir. Lit. and Hist.* (1955); Parry; W. P. Lehmann, *The Development of Germanic Verse* (1956); Navarro; J. W. Draper, "The Origin of R.," RLC, 31 (1957).
See also SOUNDS IN POETRY. A.M.C.; H.W.

RHYME ROYAL. Sometimes called the Chaucerian (and Troilus) stanza. A stanza of 7 lines of iambic pentameter, rhyming ababbcc. In the hands of Chaucer, who used the form in *Troilus and Criseyde, The Parlement of Fowles,* and several of the *Canterbury Tales,* r.r. was an instrument of extraordinary flexibility and power. Ample enough for narrative purposes, the stanza is also suited to description, digression, and comment, and its rhyme scheme is remarkably subtle in its potentialities. The superb hymn which opens *The Prioress's Tale,* the leisurely narrative of *The Clerk's Tale,* and the incisive psychological insights of *Troilus and Criseyde,* all indicate the wide scope of Chaucer's use of the form.

R.r. dominated Eng. poetry in the century after Chaucer's death; it is said to have received its name during this period from its use by King James I of Scotland in *The Kingis Quair,* although some prosodists, e.g., E. Guest (*History of Eng. Rhythms,* 1882) and Schipper trace the name to the Fr. *chant royal.* As late as the second half of the 16th c., r.r. was mentioned by Gascoigne and by Puttenham as the chief Eng. stanza for serious verse, and in this period it was distinguished by being used in Spenser's *Fowre Hymnes* and Shakespeare's *Rape of Lucrece*. Some time before 1619, Michael Drayton revised his r.r. narrative *Mortimeriados* and recast it in ottava rima as *The Baron's Wars*. His action symbolized the end of r.r. as a great Eng. measure; its only important subsequent uses were in Morris' *Earthly Paradise* and Masefield's *Dauber*, in which, however, its traditional flexibility and strength are apparent.—See also G. H. Cowling, "A Note on Chaucer's Stanza," RES, 2 (1926); Hamer; P. F. Baum, *Chaucer's Verse* (1961; notes the Fr. [ballade] origin of the stanza).

RHYME SCHEME. The arrangement of rhyming words, usually at the ends of lines, though sometimes internally, which gives the poem its characteristic pattern. R. schemes may be fixed or variable, simple or complex. The sonnet and the Spenserian stanza, for example, have fixed patterns, but stanza forms not traditionally fixed may be shaped to the needs of the individual poem. Among the more useful r. schemes in Eng. verse are those of the couplet, which often suggests the epigrammatic package of meaning as in Pope, and the quatrain, which allows for some flexibility of arrangement (for example, alternating, abab, as in Gray's *Elegy Written in a Country Churchyard*; enclosing, abba, as in Tennyson's *In Memoriam*; and intermittent, xbyb, as in Coleridge's *The Rime of the Ancient Mariner*). Some r. schemes involve the repetition of whole lines, as in the triolet and the villanelle, and others require the repetition of "rhyming" words, as in the sestina. Because rhyming words must carry a semantic as well as a phonetic value, the r. scheme has a great deal to do with the emergence of meaning aesthetically embodied in the stanza or the poem. S.L.M.

RHYTHM: A cadence, a contour, a figure of periodicity, any sequence perceptible as a distinct pattern capable of repetition and variation. Plato calls it "order in movement" (*Laws* 2.665a); Hauptmann, the 19th-c. music theorist, calls "the constant measure by which the measurement of time is made METRE; the kind of motion in that measure RHYTHM," a distinction not much improved on since. As the principle of organization of temporal events, r. is analogous to symmetry and proportion in spatial arrays; in both planes, r. constitutes the first function of repetition (q.v.). Abstractly speaking, any entity not absolutely unique must be repeated either by itself or among others: if by itself, we speak of *iteration*; if with its opposite or other entities in an ordered design, then we recognize a *pattern*, which is the fundamental principle of all art.

R. is hardly a mere aesthetic phenomenon, however: it is ubiquitous in natural processes (the diurnal and seasonal cycles of light and weather), in the behavior of plants and animals (the cycles of sleep, growth, and reproduction), and in human physiology (the systolic rs. of heart and breath) and activity (language, dance, music, song, poetry). Rs. often seem quite simple, but this is an illusion; most of the rs. we are familiar with are astonishingly complex. Rhythmic patterns characteristically display four features: regularity, variation, grouping, and hierarchy.

Regularity: Rhythmic series are patterns of organization in which markers (such as stress) are deployed at intervals either regular or close enough to reinforce the *expectation* of regularity. Expectation turns out to be a more powerful force in perception than actual stimulus: in reading a text, the mind makes a rapid series of predictions each second about what it ought to see next based on what it has just previously seen (and still holds in short-term memory), and if the expected signal is delayed or missing, the mind often supplies it anyway. In this the mind may seem to sacrifice accuracy for convenience, but in fact some prediction is essential to very rapid processing of large amounts of sense-data. Regularity (spaced repetition) in the data itself is also extremely valuable: there is abundant evidence from experimental psychology, were any needed, that rhythmitization enhances motor behavior, memorization, and learning. In "stress-timed" languages such as Eng., auditors hear stresses at regular intervals regardless of how many syllables actually intervene; this, the much-disputed concept of "isochronism," has led some critics to see Eng. verse as metered by equal timing between beats, as in music.

Variation: Pure iteration of a whole pattern is usually felt to be monotonous, however, though the exact limen at which pleasurable repetition becomes tedious and the reasons for the shift have only recently begun to be investigated. Being reminded of the sketch or shape of a pattern through its permutations is enjoyable, but exact replication without change (which is in any event rare) is wearying. This phenomenon, called "variation," is conspicuous in perception and cognitive processing. The first law of rhythmicity is consequently that a pattern exists so long as it is perceived as such: any variation which supports the pattern will be perceived as constitutive, while any variation which obscures the pattern or modifies it to the point that it is perceived as another pattern is unrhythmical.

Grouping: Since a pure continuum of sound would be entirely undifferentiated, segmentation of the soundstream into discrete units seems central to rhythmic perception. Segmentation however requires demarcation, which is the function of stress in Western music and (most) poetic meters; indeed, the very existence of the beats themselves seems to entail grouping. The most natural groupings seem to be twos and threes, the prime numbers which can be added together or repeated in various combinations to produce every possible larger group. In grammar these give proclitics and enclitics; in verse, binary and ternary meters; in music, double and triple time. Whether or not weak syllables are perceived as grouped after the stress (musical bars) or before (iambic meter) or both (grammar) is uncertain; experiments show that such perception depends in part on the timing of the pauses around the groups (Woodrow). It almost certainly also depends on which semiotic system the auditor perceives is operative. In Western music the accent begins the bar, but this is a mere convention not an absolute; the bar-lines themselves did not appear until the 15th c. Of all possible arrangements of beats in a series, simple alternation is by far the most common and most powerful (all meters tend toward this condition), but of the possible groupings fours (two doubled) are the most conspicuous and perhaps the most stable. Innumerable medieval verses, learned and common, L. and vernacular, sacred and profane run in four-beat r. Interestingly, there is some evidence that the largest number of data the mind can assimilate in one group is about seven, give or take two: the regular four-beat line gives eight. Further, grouping seems to allow catalexis, a principle whereby final elements can be omitted without disruption, indeed to positive effect: ballad meter, for example, originally ran in eight-beat longline couplets folded into four-stress halfline quatrains, but in the most common form the second and fourth lines of the quatrain (couplet ends) are reduced from four stresses to three, an endclipped form that has been greatly preferred over the centuries.

Hierarchy: Patterns on lower levels of rhythmic series are frequently repeated across wider spans on higher levels, melding the whole together to yield "a complex action so integrated that it is perceived as simple" (Kramer). In poetry every repetition of sound whether simple (alliteration) or complex (rhyme, meter) is rhythmic; but the clearest example of hierarchical ordering is dipodic verse (q.v.), where stresses follow weak syllables in usual alternation, but the stresses themselves also alternate regularly, strong and very strong, the principle of alternation being preserved on each successive level.

R. versus Meter: The distinction between r. and m. is old, dating to at least the 4th c. B.C. (Aristoxenus, pupil of Aristotle). Since poetry is of course made up of language, the natural rs. of speech are the threads of which larger rhythmic cadences and meters are woven. It has sometimes been held that the iambic pentameter prevailed in Eng. because Eng. is an iambic langauge, but language taken as a whole is an enormously varied thing, and the claim has never been proven. The relation of meter to the rs. of language is more complex than this. Still, it is evident that the most common syntactic patterns (prepositional phrases, for example) must produce a relatively small inventory of cadences that should appear fairly often. It is these cadences which yield the formulae of literary art-prose known as "prose r." (q.v.). In verse these are meshed with indifferent monosyllables and with special rhetorical emphases and then molded under the pressure of abstract line-patterns to yield regular meters, or else they are iterated systematically (via "formulaic composition" or parallelism, q.v.) to achieve other, more expansive rhythmical effects. In metrical verse the stressing a sentence may take is often not identical to its normal "prose r." (Fowler); in nonmetrical verse, on the other hand, words retain their usual inflections.

The established view is that ultimately meter is simply a subset of r. (Chatman), but this is not exactly true: strictly speaking, meter has no r. Meters provide structure; rs. provide movement within that structure (Weismiller). Without a structure no movement would be possible, but within structure many kinds of movement may be permissible. In these terms r. certainly appears the more complex and interesting phenomenon of the two.

Problems: Rhythmic analysis encounters two problems, one ontological, one methodological. Critics frequently assert that r. is a *felt* phenomenon, a notion that accords with common sense but forces them to treat the poem not as aesthetic object but as aesthetic experience, thus opening the door to all manner of empirical, mechanical, and psychological studies of acoustic perception, psychomotor timing, and reader response. In 20th-c. crit. the general consensus has fallen against such approaches, in part because of notoriously loose terms (r. is surely the vaguest term in crit.), in part because some conspicuous studies led to eccentric results (at the end of his career E. W. Scripture proudly announced his discovery of compound Gr. feet in Eng. verse). The mind is not some Lockean *tabula rasa*, a passive recipient of impressions; rhythmic perception is very much an *active* organization of sense-data, and when critics turn from the poem as object of perception to studying individual perceivers and their acts of perception, they encounter a great wilderness of mostly uncharted terrain. Most of the acoustic and psychological experiments on r. earlier in the century now seem vestigial to poetic analysis on the grounds set forth by the Russian Formalists: "not the phone but the phoneme as such is utilized as the cornerstone of verse" (Jakobson). It is not the sound as heard but the whole system of structural differences embedded in the language which is the proper object of study.

In theory it should be possible to write general rules of rhythmicity which, *mutatis mutandis*, would then be applicable to each kind of rhythmic phenomenon—language, music, dance poetry, perhaps even natural processes. But this remains a so-far unrealized ideal. Historically, theories of r. have nearly always been written in a single field and then extended to other fields which seemed similar. But in practice this has proven to be one of the least productive methods of inquiry. So, for two notable examples, musical rs. have been claimed as (written over) the rs. of poetry (by Sidney Lanier and his followers, the "musical" metrists), as have linguistic rs. (at the hands of the linguistic metrists), without adequate recognition in either case of the essential differentia between these several domains. Whether poetic rs. are merely a subset of the rs. of the language or whether they, like language and dance, simply share "family resemblances" (Wittgenstein) under a common genus so far remains an open question. Modern science has learned amply that r., like other categories of perception, is very much culture-determined. African drum-music at first seems completely chaotic to Western ears unused to extremely rapid shifts of signature and r. And even within one culture researchers have discovered considerable latitude in what auditors recognize as rhythmical.

But this first difficulty entails a corollary problem for critics willing to hazard discussion of poetic r.—analytic precision. In high artverse traditions (the cl. hexameter, the Romance octosyllable and Alexandrine, the Eng. pentameter), meters, being strictly defined, demand and therefore display precision, hence allow minute and exacting analysis. But rhythms, being more diverse and complex, cannot be so accurately described even in stable traditions, much less when a tradition is weak or nonexistent, or when a poet—Whitman is the classic example—revolts against the received prosodic doctrines of the day. Too, r. varies enormously from one reader to another, one performance to another, even one line to the next. Consequently, critics have tended to view rhythmical variation as too evanescent for exact description. What cannot be described cannot be judged. In this respect poetic analysis has had to wait upon developments in modern linguistics not merely for terms but even for the fundamental concepts themselves necessary so we can talk with any precision about the intricacies of verbal structures.

Progress: Still, some progress has lately been made toward a revealing analytic of r. La Drière's influential system, with its hierarchical analysis of cadence and grouping (see PROSODY); developments in colonic analysis in cl. prosody; and the new approach called "grammetrics" developed by Wexler in France and Wesling in America, all focus on the reader's awareness of the grouping of stresses in natural syntactic periods—the word, the phrase, the clause—rather than in the abstract (unsegmented) meter. Traditional prosody treated meter as (and thus limited it to) an organization of phonological elements such as stress or duration. But more recent studies have recognized that verse orders language on every available level—phonological, morphological, syntactic—and though these topics were ignored or treated only indirectly in traditional prosody, they are wholly relevant if not essential to the common reader's experience of verse. In Eng. poetry the meter patterns the stresses, but all the other linguistic and paralinguistic features such as voice pitch, tempo, pausing, timbre, or special inflection are free to elaborate more expansive cadences. The weighting, pacing, and inflecting of a line of verse (as in the wonderful mimetic examples in the *Essay on Criticism*) are our chief sources of delight in the sensuous medium of sound. In the his. of crit. there have been repeated reminders that poetry is too strictly laced if it is to be confined to the metrical, that strictness is not valued by every age, that the expressive power of wider, more varied rs. is not to be disdained—that, after all, to insist wholly on metric is to lose most of Blake, Whitman, the Eng. and Scottish popular ballads, much medieval verse, and a great deal of modern verse as well.

PSYCHOLOGY: H. Woodrow, *A Quantitative Study of R.* (1909); J.E.W. Wallin, "Experimental Studies of R. and Time," *Psychological Review*, 18–19 (1911–12); C. A. Ruckmich, "A Bibliog. of R.," *Am. Jour. of Psychology*, 24–35 (1913–24); P. Fraisse, *Les structures rythmiques* (1956), *Psychologie du rythme* (1974).

MUSIC: C. Sachs, *R. and Tempo* (1953)—hist. of the concepts; G. W. Cooper and L. B. Meyer, *The Rhythmic Structure of Music* (1960); S. D. Winick, *R.: An Annotated Bibliog.* (1974); G. Henneberg, *Theorien zur Rhythmik und Metrik* (1974); G. Read, *Modern Rhythmic Notation* (1978); W. Dürr et al., "R.," *New Grove Dict.*, ed. S. Sadie (1981), v. 15 (excellent survey).

POETRY: A. Rossbach and R. Westphal, *Griechische Rhythmik und Harmonik*, v. 1 of *Metrik der Griechen* (2d ed., 2 v., 1867–68); F. B. Gummere, *The Beginnings of Poetry* (1901), ch. 2; E. A. Sonnenschein, *What Is R?* (1925)—very unreliable; I. A. Richards, "R. and Metre," *Principles of Lit. Crit.* (1925); T. Taig, *R. and Metre* (1929)—much underrated; A. W. De Groot, "Der Rhythmus," *Neophil*, 17 (1932), *Algemene Versleer* (1946); D. Seckel, *Hölderlins Sprachrhythmus* (1937)—valuable bibliog.; E. Olson, "General Prosody: Rhythmic, Metric, Harmonics," Diss., Univ. Chicago, 1938; H.D.F. Kitto, "R., Metre, and Black Magic," *Cl. Review*, 56 (1942); D. L. Sims, "R. and Meaning," EIC, 6 (1956); B. Hrushovsky, "On Free Rs. in Modern Poetry," *Style in Lang.*, ed. T. Sebeok (1960); G. B. Pace, "The Two Domains: Meter and R.," PMLA, 76 (1961); N. Frye, *The Well-Tempered Critic* (1963); P. Wexler, "On the Grammetrics of the Cl. Alexandrine," *Cahiers de lexicologie*, 4 (1964); H. Gross, "Prosody as Rhythmic Cognition," *Sound and Form in Modern Poetry* (1964), "Toward a Phenomenology of R.," *The Structures of Verse* (1979); R. Fowler, " 'Prose R.' and Meter," *Essays on Style and Language*, ed. R. Fowler (1966); A. Cook, "R.," *Prisms* (1967); G. Faure, *Les éléments du rythme poétique en anglaise moderne* (1970); R. Mitchell, "Toward a System of Grammatical Scansion," *Language and Style*, 3 (1970); A. Dougherty, *A Study of Rhythmic Structure in the Verse of W. B. Yeats* (1973); W. Seidel, *Rhythmus: Eine Begriffsbestimmung* (1976); D. W. Harding, *Words Into R.* (1976); Brogan, ch. 5; D. Attridge, *The Rs. of Eng, Poetry* (1981), esp. sect. IV; H. Meschonnic, *Critique du rythme* (1982); W. Mohr, "Rhythmus," Reallexikon, 2d ed., v. III (comprehensive); M. G. Tarlinskaja, "R.—Morphology—Syntax—R.," *Style*, 18 (1984); D. Wesling, *The New Poetries* (1985). T.V.F.B.

RIDDLE. Essentially a metaphor which draws attention to likenesses between unrelated objects, e.g., *Humpty Dumpty*. World-wide and one of the oldest forms of literature, riddles are still used by primitive peoples in times of crisis (harvesting, weddings, etc.) with the idea that solving them may, by sympathetic magic, solve the crisis. They may also be a teaching device, and the oldest recorded are Babylonian school texts. Most riddles, especially the older ones, are in verse, partially perhaps for mnemonic purposes but probably principally because of their original use in magic. Customarily a distinction is made between the literary riddle (*Kunsträtsel*) and the folk riddle (*Volksrätsel*).

The history of riddles is a long one. The Sanskrit *Rig Veda* (final version ca. 1000 B.C.) contains riddles. The most famous Arab riddler was Al-Hariri (1054–1122) whose *Assemblies* was very influential. Hebrew has a long history of riddles, e.g., Samson's exchange with the Philistines at his wedding. The most famous Persian riddles are those in Firdausi's epic the *Shah-Nameh* (10th c.). Gr. riddles stem from the 14th book of the *Gr. Anthology* and from Byzantine literature. The literary r. in western Europe begins its tradition with the 100 L. poetic riddles of Symphosius (5th c.), and under his influence the L. verse r. was cultivated from the *Berne Riddles* (7th c.) and those of Aldhelm (written A.D. 685–705) to the encyclopedic work of Nicolas Reusner, *Aenigmatographia* (1602). The oldest European vernacular riddles are the poetic riddles of the OE Exeter Book (8th c.), many of which are long, ingenious, and of high poetic merit. The earliest in Germany date from the 13th c., the *Warburgkrieg*; in Spain, Portugal, and France from the 16th c. In modern times riddles have flourished in France, particularly in the 17th and 18th c. in Germany in the 19th c., and most of all in Italy. In England they have had no vogue.—F. Tupper, *The Riddles of the Exeter Book* (1910); A. Taylor, *The Lit. R. before 1600* (1948), C. F. Potter, "Riddles," *Funk & Wagnalls Standard Dict. of Folklore, Mythology and Legend*, ed. M. Leach, II (1950). R.P.APR.

RIME RICHE. Rhyming pairs pronounced in the same way without having the same meaning; classified as homographs (written and pronounced alike, as *stare*, the bird, and *stare*, to gaze curiously) and as homophones (pronounced alike but different in spelling, as *stare, stair*). Chaucer, observing Fr. practice, has *seke-seke* (seek, sick), *riche-rubriche, tiraunt-erraunt*, and many other such rhymes throughout the *Canterbury Tales*. Imperfectly naturalized into Eng. verse, r.r. is common and frequent in Fr., *éclaire-crépusculaire*; but rhymes on the suffix are considered weak (i.e., too facile) as *magnifiques-pacifiques, gladiateur-lecteur*. (See discussion of *rime très riche, rime suffisante*, and *rime pauvre* under PERFECT RHYME.)—J. Suberville, *Hist. et théorie de la versification française* (new ed., 1956). S.L.M.

ROMANCE. The r.—the Sp. ballad—is the simplest and most widely used set poetic form in Sp. It usually is written in octosyllabic verse in which the even-numbered lines rhyme with the same assonance throughout the poem and the odd-numbered lines are left free. A few *rs.* are in octosyllabic couplets in consonance. The *r. doble* rhymes all lines in alternating assonance. Other variations of the basic form (even some having a periodic refrain) have at times been popular. The learned and the semilearned—and probably even the illiterate—produce them wherever Sp. is spoken, and scholars collect them by the hundreds. They reflect almost every phase of Sp. life. Since many of them are anonymous and have been transmitted largely in oral form, their origin and complete history cannot be traced. The earliest known written *rs.* date from the early 15th c. In the early 16th c. *romanceros* (collections devoted exclusively to *rs.*) began to appear, the first (1545–1550?) being the famous *Cancionero de romances*, often called the *Cancionero sin año* because it bears no date of publication, by Martin Nucio in Antwerp. The most convenient classification of *rs.*—that summarized by S. G. Morley and adapted from those of Durán, Wolf and Hofmann, and Milá y Fontanals—covers the period from the 15th through the 17th c. It corresponds, with the exception of the *rs. vulgares* to three periods of creation, traditional, erudite, artistic: (1) the anonymous *rs. viejos*, primitive or traditional ballads, usually on historical themes and thought to be among the earliest; (2) the 15th- and early 16th-c. *rs. juglarescos*, minstrel ballads, "longer and more personal, but still supported by tradition"; (3) *rs. eruditos*, erudite ballads, written by known authors after 1550 and based on old chronicles; (4) *rs. artísticos*, artistic ballads, usually lyric, on varied themes, and written by known authors from the late 15th c. through the 17th; (5) the crude *rs. vulgares*, blind beggar ballads, from about 1600 on. Recently, large numbers of orally transmitted *rs.* have been collected in the Americas and abroad by such scholars as Samuel G. Armistead and Joseph Silverman (Sephardic) and Manuel da Costa Fontes (Portuguese) and others.

The *r. heroico*, also called *r. endecasílabo* or *r. real*, is a r. in Italianate hendecasyllables. A r. in lines of less than 8 syllables is called *romancillo.* One variation of the r. is the *corrido* (ballad with guitar accompaniment), especially popular in Mexico. The *jácara* is a r. in which the activities of ruffians are recounted, usually in a boisterous manner.—E. Mérimée and S. G. Morley, *A Hist. of Sp. Lit.* (1930); S. G. Morley, "Chronological List of Early Sp. Ballads," HR, 13 (1945); R. Menéndez Pidal, *Romancero hispánico* (2 v., 1953); Navarro; *Romancero y poesía oral,* vol. 4: *El romancero hoy: Historia, comparatismo, bibliografía crítica,* ed. S. G. Armistead, A. Sánchez Romeralo, D. Catalán (1979). D.C.C.

ROMANCE, MEDIEVAL. See MEDIEVAL ROMANCE.

ROMANCE PROSODY. EARLY DEVELOPMENTS. Although the R. languages are directly derived from L., the evolution of their metrical systems from L. prosody does not show the same continuity. R. versification very likely originated from or developed along with that type of late L. poetry which neglects the rules of quantity (whereby 1 long syllable equals 2 short) and seems to be based on the number of syllables, marked accentual endings and rhyme. The origin of this new "rhythmic" verse has been explained in three different ways: (1) the change of L. pronunciation at the end of the Imperial period consisting in the loss of quantitative differences in vowels and in the replacement of pitch accent by stress accent (Fr. theory); (2) the importance of stress for the structure of L. verse at all times (a theory upheld by most Eng. and some German scholars); and (3) the creation by the early Christians of a syllabic verse with, at first, quantitative cadence in imitation of Syrian meters (the theory of Wilhelm Meyer aus Speyer, newly advocated by some scholars).

Michel Burger (*Recherches sur la structure et l'origine des vers romans*) has offered a more definite explanation of the origin of Rom. verse. He maintains that the transition from L. quantitative meters to accentual verse was a natural and gradual one. At a time when the sense for quantity had vanished, the uneducated when reading classical L. verse disregarded the quantitative metrical scheme and considered only the normal word accent. Thus the Sapphic line *Christe servorum, regimen tuorum* (´– ⏑ ´– – ´– ‖ ⏑ ⏑ ´– ⏑ ´– ⏓) was recited

1́ 2 3 4́ 5 6 7 8 9 1́0 11.

In composing new verse they kept the structure of their models leaving word accents where they had been in L., free in the interior of the verse line and fixed at the end and, to a certain degree, at the caesura. Due to the fact that the ratio 1 long-2 shorts had been lost, the number of syllables in a line necessarily became fixed while the syllables could be arranged in either ascending or descending rhythm. In this new system the last accented syllable of the verse line (originally coinciding with the thesis) marked the end of the verse, the 1 or 2 following syllables being considered as supernumerary. The same happened at the caesura. This is one of the dominant characteristics of all R. verse. Burger believes that the important types of R. verse were already developed before the scission into the different idioms occurred. These types were later further adapted to each individual language and can still be traced back to their L. (quantitative) models: the decasyllable to the iambic trimeter and the Sapphic, the *verso de arte mayor* to the double adonic, the alexandrine to the double iambic dimeter etc.

GENERAL CHARACTERISTICS. R. verse has a definite rhythm indicated by at least one normally accented syllable at or near the end of the verse or of the hemistich. The odd or even number of syllables preceding this accented syllable produces a rising or falling movement and a division into rhythmical groups. Within the line, free distribution of stresses gives to R. verse flexibility and variety which are lacking in Germanic verse. Verse based solely on accentuation in the sense of Germanic prosody, where, between fixed beats, unstressed syllables may be accumulated or omitted, would defy the prosodic features of the R. languages which distinguish less markedly the force and duration of their syllables.

Syllable count is based on the principles of phonetics and euphony which govern the individual languages. In Prov., It., Sp. and Port. the adjustment of the verse line to the required number of syllables is achieved by synaloepha (the blending of two consecutive vowels or diphthongs, one at the end of a word and the other at the beginning of the following word), by elision, or by hiatus. Old Prov. had no strict rules about elision and hiatus. Fr. tolerated hiatus in the Middle Ages but ruled it out completely under Malherbe (17th c.).

It must be noted that the Prov., Fr., Port. and Catalan system of syllable count (i.e., to the last tonic syllable of the line) differs from the It. and the Sp. (Castilian), in which the count is made to one—and *only* one—beyond the last stressed syllable, whether or not posttonic syllables are present; thus, for example, at verse-end, or, in divided verse, at hemistich-end, Sp. *dar, darlo,* and *dárselo* are all counted as two-syllable words. The It. and Sp. equivalent of a Fr. decasyllable is, therefore, considered a hendecasyllable. In much of the medieval Galician-Port. poetry, verse length was determined by the actual number of syllables in the line, regardless of stress location (*ley de Mussafia*). For similar Old Fr. first-hemistich count, see below. The nature of the language, in each case, has largely been the determining factor in the choice of system.

In every Rom. verse there is besides the last tonic syllable which must coincide with the metrical beat, at least 1 additional stress in the interior of the verse line. Archaic meters offer more fixed stresses than modern forms. Thus the Old Fr. octosyllable frequently carried a second stress on the fourth syllable; the decasyllable, likewise, on the fourth, sometimes on the sixth and the dodecasyllable on the sixth. The It. and Sp. hendecasyllable varies its principal stresses which may fall either on the sixth syllable, on the fourth and, usually, eighth syllables, to produce, respectively, the "major" form and the "minor" form. In the Fr. cl. alexandrine a stress on the sixth syllable with a following pause is obligatory, while the romantic poets introduced the *alexandrin ternaire* with accents on the fourth and eighth syllables. The Sp. and Port. alexandrine, a 7 + 7 + syllable verse (Sp. count), had one on the sixth syllable of each hemistich, and the *verso de arte mayor* both a primary and a fixed secondary beat, in each hemistich. Port. sometimes displays more archaic patterns, with beats following at regular intervals, usually placed on even syllables.

Like the Fr. and Sp. med. epic verse, most long verse in early R. poetry is divided by a fixed pause after a rhetorically stressed word. This pause is named after the *caesura* of cl. poetry, which, however, was produced by a word ending within a foot. In Old Fr., the "epic" caesura is one immediately preceded by a hemistich in which the count ends on a stressed syllable; and the "lyric" caesura is one immediately preceded by a hemistich ending with a counted syllable whose vowel is atonic, usually a mute *e*. Ordinarily the caesura in R. verse is emphasized by the syntactic pattern, and sometimes further marked by leonine rhyme or by *rima al mezzo* (a verse-end finds its rhyme at a specified location within the following verse).

In the R. prosody systems, verse time-length is measured by a predetermined number of syllables, and verse rhythm is governed primarily by fixed location of a major stress beat at verse-end, and secondarily by lighter stress(es), in undivided longer verses according to rule, and, with notable exceptions, at the will of the poet in shorter verses and in hemistichs.

The longer lines, such as the alexandrine and the decasyllable (It. and Sp. hendecasyllable) are generally preferred for the most elevated and serious topics or formal occasions, especially those requiring lengthy development (e.g., Fr. cl. tragedy, Dante's *Divina Commedia*, Camões' *Os Lusíadas*), and the shorter are more often—though by no means always—found in poems of light, lyric, or popular tone. Lines of fewer than six syllables, seldom independent except in folk poetry, fables, and the like (e.g., Iriarte's fables beginning "A una mona," "Vio en una huerta," and "Cierto poeta") serve generally as semi-independent hemistichs of longer lines with which they harmonize. Heptasyllables and octosyllables, particularly the latter (either count), are otherwise probably the most widely used, though lines of other lengths are not rare. In Sp., though in the early centuries the hexasyllable equivalent of the *verso de arte mayor* hemistich was frequently favored for certain lyric themes, as in lullabies and *serranillas*, the short verse most commonly used since the late 14th c. has consistently been the octosyllable. The *verso de arte mayor*, following chronologically the 13th and 14th c. *alejandrino*, of which the *cuaderna vía* was composed, was the most highly developed long line in Sp. in the 15th c., but gave way in the 16th c. to the Italianate hendecasyllable introduced by Boscán and Garcilaso, whose poems in the form of *soneto, canción, octava rima, terza rima*, and *versos sueltos*—It. *sonetto, canzone, ottava rima, terza rima, versi sciolti*, respectively—immediately attracted the attention of the best Hispanic poets, and was long to remain the staple of learned poetry in the Iberian peninsula. Until free verse was fully accepted in the 20th c., the hendecasyllable (and its decasyllabic equivalent in Fr. count) was the meter of choice for most "exalted" poetry in It. and Hispanic literatures, and was a strong rival of the alexandrine in Fr., though lines of other lengths and patterns were also frequently so used. In the 18th and 19th c. R. verse forms became increasingly more varied, partly with borrowings, especially from each other, partly with the reintroduction and "modernization" of certain medieval verse forms (e.g., the Sp. alexandrine and the *verso de arte mayor*, both now with strictly regularized syllable count, the former now resembling the Fr. cl. alexandrine, and the latter designed like one type of the It. *senario doppio* or *dodecasillabo dattilico-anapestico*), partly for special purpose, as the 19th c. It. *decasillabo anapestico* used to emphasize patriotic themes, and partly from desire for improvement or greater expressiveness, as in the Fr. alexandrine, in which, affected especially by Romanticism, the bipartite 6 + 6 structure was sometimes replaced by a tripartite 4 + 4 + 4 and by other combinations of less symmetry. Verses of other dimensions have also been practiced in the R. territory, but do not compare in frequency to those mentioned above.

Although basically the same in overall view, since medieval times the various R. measured-verse systems do show individual trends, which, though seemingly minor, clearly produce distinctive aesthetic responses in the reader. One noticeable differentiating feature is to be found in the treatment of vowels in regard to hiatus, synaeresis, and synaloepha; another is in that of verse endings. In Fr., since early in the classical period, the use of hiatus has been rigidly restricted to a very small number of specific exceptions that in any case seldom occur. The halting effect and its impediment to free flow of the verse were thus eliminated. In It., hiatus is generally avoided, as it is in Sp., though in the latter its use was the rule into the late 14th c., after which its frequency gradually waned, though it is occasionally found, sometimes employed for convenience or for historical reasons, or for purposes of emphasis. As for synaloepha, the coalescing into a single syllable of contiguous vowels of separate words, it—with the threat of its cramping and distending effect—is not allowed in Fr. (a final mute *e* followed by a vowel is simply elided). Like synaeresis, the coalescing of contiguous normally independent vowels within a word, synaloepha is used liberally in It., at times almost to excess. In Sp. it is used moderately, controlled by rule, and generally unobtrusively.

Similarly, one may observe that verse-end treatment in the three literatures shows parallel tendencies: in the Fr. system before the advent of free verse, it is expected that masculine (oxytonic) rhymes will alternate with feminine (i.e., those ending with a mute *e* or a mute syllable, originally paroxytonic); in the It. and Sp., in which three stress patterns are possible at verse-end, paroxytones preponderate, whereas oxytones are frequent, especially in octosyllables and shorter verse, and proparoxytones are not at all uncommon. In It., at least, some poems, for special verse-end rhythmic effect, contain deliberately arranged patterns fashioned of two or three end-types repeated at regular intervals throughout the composition, thus kinesthetically reinforcing the auditory power of rhyme. Rhyme itself varies from the Fr. *rime riche*, the preferred Fr. form (in which the consonant immediately preceding the final tonic vowel must also be included in the rhyme) to the assonance (rhyming of vowels only, the last stressed and, if any follow, the last posttonic) overwhelmingly favored in the Hispanic *romance*, including the hendecasyllabic *romance heroico*, and certain other types of poetry.

In fine, the Fr. treatment of the above-noted features produces a sense of smoothly, almost delicately, coursing verse precisely measured, whereas from the It. one may gain the impression of a sturdy and varied rhythmic/arhythmic pulsation, somewhat more pronounced, perhaps, than that of the Sp., which is relatively relaxed and elastic, though full-measure.

The history of the R. strophe is, like that of the verse, essentially one of preservation of established patterns and multiple variations on them. The medieval strophe, often originating in song form, and befitting lyric topics, ranged in complexity from simple epic *laisse* to complicated *sestina* or *chant royal*, and the range thereafter has been fully as broad. The Prov. poets were exceedingly prolific in the production of stanzas and fixed-form poems, and it was a Prov. writer, author of the *Leys d'Amors*, who was probably the first to take an academic interest in prosody as a branch of knowledge worth studying for its own sake. Strophe forms and set combinations of them (such as the sonnet and the *terza rima*) established in or before the Ren. were generally maintained in the modern period, and appear along with numerous new, often *ad hoc* patterns. The Fr. *distique* to *huitain* and beyond continued in use, as did the *iambe, triolet, rondeau*, and *ballade*, for example, while the new strophic inventions and the occasional mixture of strophe types within a poem, and of course blank verse (*versi sciolti*) and other astrophic poetry, helped to prepare the way for free verse. Similar was the history of the Iberian strophe, and of those developed in Italy.

The most primitive strophic form originated in the division of a long line containing interior rhymes into 2 or 3 short ones, hence the Fr. *rimes couées* and *rimes brisées* (aab ccb aab aab), and the cross rhyme (*rimes croisées [incatenate, encadenadas]*). The oldest epics were written in mono-assonanced *tirades* or *laisses*, the oldest Saints' lives in mono-rhymed quatrains (Sp. *cuaderna vía*). Dante's *terzinas*, subsequently used for longer narrative poems, are a three-line chain with a 1-line clausula (aba bcb cdc. . . yzyz). Strophic division was further achieved through the use of the refrain (It. *ripresa*, Sp. *cabeza, estribillo*, Port. *refrão, estribilho*), an echo-like repetition of part of the text and melody. Remnants of original refrains are the Prov. *rims estramps*, It. *chiave*, Sp. *palabras perdidas*, isolated rhymes without correspondence. Later the refrain was extended to two or several lines or repeated in a half strophe at the end of a poem (Fr. *envoi*, It., Prov. *tornada*, It. *commiato, congedo, ritornello*). Strophes of varying length have been used in R. poetry, some of which became popular even elsewhere, thus the It. ottava rima.

One of the oldest forms of refrain poetry is the ballad (Fr. *ballade*, Prov. balada), which probably originated in Provence and in its primitive form was constructed on the theme BBaabBB. In France, it evolved into a 3-strophe poem with a refrain after each strophe and an *envoi* at the end. The It. *ballata* differs from the Fr. in that the first strophic part is divided into two sections and that the *ripresa*, which precedes, is not repeated after each strophe. Of northern Fr. origin is the *rondeau* which depends on the refrain and on the extent of its repetition. Its basic form, A1 A2 aA aa A1 A2, developed into many different types of rondeaux of which the 16th c. variant of 15 lines is now the only survivor. In Spain, the medieval *canción* and the *villancico* are examples of the song form. Unquestionably, the most important of all R. poetic forms is the sonnet which can be briefly defined as two quatrains followed by two tercets. It was developed in Italy by the Sicilian school and brought to perfection by Petrarch. Perhaps the most fitting vehicle of poetic thought ever devised, it has remained in constant favor not only in the R. but in all Western literary languages.

At the end of the 19th c. the traditional syllabic verse was discarded by many Fr. symbolists who replaced it with "vers libre" (free verse). It is a verse based on rhythmical groups corresponding to syntactic units and does not observe any fixed rules. This innovation has been adopted by most It. and Hispanic poets.

E. Stengel, "Romanische Verslehre" in G. Gröber, *Grundriss der romanischen Philologie*, II (1902), 1–96, still remains fundamental; M. Burger, *Recherches sur la structure et l'origine des vers romans* (1957). Other works treating problems of Rom. versification include: P. A. Becker, *Über den Ursprung der romanischen Versmasse* (1890); W. Meyer aus Speyer, *Gesammelte Abhandlungen zur mittelalterlichen Rhythmik* (3 v., 1905–36); Jeanroy, *Origines*; F. d'Ovidio, "Versificazione romanza," in *Opere complete*, IX (1932); T. Gerold, *La musique au moyen âge* (1932); G.Lote, *Histoire du vers français* (3 v., 1949–55); D. C. Clarke, *A Chronological Sketch of Castilian Versification together with a List of Its Metric Terms* (1952) and *Morphology of 15th C. Castilian Verse* (1964); Navarro; L. Alonso Schökel, *Estética y estilística del ritmo poético* (1959); P. Henríquez Ureña, *Estudios de versificación española* (1961); R. Baehr, *Spanische Verslehre auf historischer Grundlage* (1962; tr. and rev. as *Manual de versificación española*, by K. Wagner and F. López Estrada, 1970); M. Fubini, *Metrica e poesia. I. Dal Duecento al Petrarca* (1962); W. T. Elwert, *Traité de versification française, des origines à nos jours* (1965); A. B. Giamatti, "It." and L. Nelson, Jr., "Sp." both in Wimsatt, *Versification*; C. Scott, *Fr. verse art* (1980). T.F.; rev. D.C.C.

RONDEAU. One of the Fr. fixed forms, comparable in its strictness of construction to the triolet (q.v.). The most common type of r., as practiced by Clément Marot in the early 16th c., consists of 13 lines of 8 or 10 syllables each, divided into stanzas of 5, 3, and 5 lines. The whole is constructed on 2 rhymes only, and the first word, or first few words, of the first line are used as a *rentrement* (partial repetition), which occurs independently of the rhyme scheme, after the eighth and the thirteenth lines, that is, after the end of the second and third stanzas. If we allow R to stand for the *rentrement*, the following scheme describes the rondeau: (R) aabba aabR aabbaR. The popularity of the r. diminished toward the first third of the 16th c., and toward the middle of the same century the form disappeared. It was used again at the beginning of the 17th c. by the *précieux* poets, especially Vincent Voiture. In the latter part of the 17th c. and during the entire 18th it was employed to a lesser extent. The r. had a new vogue among some of the romantics, notably Musset, who took some liberty with the arrangement of the rhymes. Théodore de Banville and Maurice Rollinat used the form subsequently.

Aside from an occasional r. in Eng. as early as the latter 18th c., the form did not flourish in England until near the end of the 19th, at which time it attracted the attention of Swinburne, Dobson, and other poets who experimented with the Fr. forms. In Eng. it has, unlike the triolet, often been used as a vehicle for serious verse. In Germany, where it has also been called the *Ringel-Gedicht, Ringelreim,* or *Rundreim,* the r. was cultivated by Weckherlin, Götz, and Fischart. An accomplished r. demands extraordinary skill in managing a natural return of the *rentrement.* Often the *rentrement* embodies a pun or an ambiguity of some sort.—Kastner, H. G. Atkins, *A Hist. of German Versification* (1923); Patterson; M. Françon, "La pratique et la théorie du r. et du rondel chez Théodore de Banville," MLN, 52 (1937; states that triolets, rondels, and rondeaux are a single genre with variations). L.B.P.

RONDEL. A Fr. fixed form, which has had a long and varied history. Its simplest form: AB aA ab AB, reaching back to the 13th c., became known later as the triolet (q.v.). Another early variation was the *rondel double,* which had the following rhyme scheme: ABBA abBA abba ABBA (the capital letters indicate the repeated lines). In the 15th c. the terms "rondel" and "rondeau" (q.v.) seem to have been used interchangeably, and one finds the words *un rondel, des rondeaux.* The rondel best known today is a poem of 3 stanzas and built on 2 rhymes, the scheme being ABba abAB abbaA(B). It is composed of 13 lines in which a 2-line refrain occurs twice in the first 8 lines (lines 1–2 and 7–8) and the first line is repeated as the last line; or it may consist of 14 lines in which case a 2-line refrain appears thrice in the poem. Henley, Gosse, Dobson, R. L. Stevenson, and others have written Eng. rondels.—Kastner; M. Françon, "La pratique et la théorie du rondeau et du rondel chez Théodore de Banville," MLN, 52 (1937). L.B.P.

RULES. Formulations of poetic "r." have commonly been founded on the assumption that literary composition is partly at least a matter of conscious "art" (*technē*) for which one may construct a more or less systematic body of principles and precepts (*technologos; ars*). It is an assumption which, when employed with wisdom and flexibility, has been a basis of much valuable literary theory, criticism, and scholarship. Sometimes, however (as in the 16th and 17th c.), the "art" of poetry has been viewed as a system of highly detailed and inviolable specifications for the subject matter, arrangement, presentation, and style of the various poetic genres; e.g., a play must have five acts; only three actors can be placed on the stage at one time; the established subject matters of the genres cannot be mixed; the pastoral or eclogue must be written in the "simple" style, about shepherds; tragedies must be about kings, princes, and generals; comedies must be about soldiers, servants, farmers, and prostitutes; the "Aristotelian" unities of time and place (limiting the action depicted in a play to no more than two days' duration and usually to a single locale) must be faithfully observed; the time limit of an epic story is one year; etc.

Most 16th- and 17th-c. collections of such r. were in a large degree codifications of artistic practices of classical antiquity, combined with fragmentary citations of various ancient critics; but they were also quite heavily supported by general theorizing about art, nature, the audience, and the poet—from a number of points of view—and particular regulations were frequently defended by different writers on entirely different theoretical grounds. For example, Castelvetro, viewing poetry primarily as designed for the pleasure of a common, ignorant, and unimaginative audience, defends the unity of time on the basis of the impossibility—so he reasons—of making such persons "believe that several days and nights have passed when they know through their senses that only a few hours have passed" (*Poetica d'Aristotele* [1570]); Minturno, however, viewing poetry both as the product of natural and artistic faculties and as a collection of naturally separate genres all designed for the edification of a more general kind of audience, defends the unity of time as one of the standard "intellectual" requirements of artistic achievement for a "good" (hence socially useful) dramatic poem, and does not argue that it is demanded by laws of credibility (*De poeta* [1559]). At the same time, a particular rule could be rejected by one critic on grounds very similar to those on which another had defended it; for example, Pierre de Laudun argued, in his *Art poétique françois* (1597), that strict adherence to the unity of time is unwise, precisely because it tends to force the poet to present impossible and incredible things. (Cf. F. Ogier, *Préface au lecteur* to Schelandre's *Tyr et Sidon* [1628].)

Notwithstanding the volume and earnestness of this earlier theorizing, in the 17th c. a gradual general undermining of the so-called neoclassical r. began, influenced partly by trends toward a more independent "philosophical" kind of criticism, and toward a kind of "circumstantial" criticism by which specific r. of the past were rejected as appropriate only to specific past conditions and circumstances of authorship (see R. S. Crane, in UTQ, 22 [1953], 389–90); and by the middle of the 18th c., especially in England, most of the more notorious r. had been discredited (cf. S. Johnson, *Rambler,* no. 125 [1751]; *Preface to Shakespeare* [1765]). The concentration particularly on the r. of the established genres give way first to more flexible definitions of those genres, then to more inclusive lists of legitimate ones (including, e.g., "heroic plays," comedies of manners, and domestic tragedies), and finally to a shift of interest largely away from genres to aspects and qualities of nature and art relevant to poetry in general. With this shift, however, there was not a general denial of the need for artistic r. The tendency was rather to establish new ones, and they were usually based on the ancient principle that achievement of peculiarly poetic qualities is at least partly an "art," not merely a natural process. Wordsworth, for example, in his Preface to the *Lyrical Ballads* (1800; 1802), while rejecting the "artificial" practices of most 18th-c. poets, announced the presumably innovative r. of "human" subject matter and style by which true poetry could consciously be achieved. Nor was the "neoclassical" principal of guidance by the practices of past masters ever completely abandoned. Rather, rejection of "ancient" examples was commonly accompanied by endorsement of "modern" ones, especially of those who departed from the "neo-classical" r. For example, writers as diverse in theory as Lessing, Herder, Voltaire, and Dr. Johnson frequently cited the example of medieval or "folk" poetry, as well as of such nonclassical authors as Shakespeare and Milton.

Many of the changes which occur from time to time in "accepted" poetic r. thus seem to result as much from changes of taste and prejudice in poetry itself as from changes in theoretical conceptions of it. Even some recent anti-technical approaches to poetry (from which the concept of artistic intention and r. has been virtually eliminated and the central problem is the accomplished "meaning" of poems) tend to imply the highly restrictive modern rule that "true" or "good" poetry must be made—by conscious intention or not—of paradoxical metaphors like those (say) of the Metaphysical poets of the 17th c. It is not inevitable, however, that the r. of poetic art, whether stated or implied, should be so narrowly conceived and restrictive; much poetic theory and criticism exists, ancient and modern (for example, that of Plato, Aristotle, and Longinus, or of Dr. Johnson, Lessing, and Coleridge), whose principles and methods of reasoning, and the "r." which follow from them, may be positively useful to both the critics and the poets of any age, because they are based intelligently and flexibly on aspects of literary achievement and kinds of general theory which have survived the accidental changes of literary fashion and dogma.—Bray; B. Weinberg, *Critical Prefaces of the Fr. Renaissance* (1950) and *A Hist. of Lit. Crit. in the It. Ren.* (2 v., 1961); Abrams.

R.M.

RUNE. A character of the Old Germanic alphabet (or *futhark,* as it is named from the first letters of its series), probably derived partly from Gr. and partly from L. characters. From about the 4th C. A.D. runes were widely used for inscriptions on weapons, coins, memorial stones, etc., and they occur also in Anglo-Saxon, Icelandic, and Norwegian poems, where the individual letters are to be translated into the body of the verse as common nouns. Certain runes (as for example in Eng. the rune-words *wyn, thorn, ethel, dæg,* and *man*) were introduced into native scripts with the advent of Christianity, and served thereafter as regular characters, or, more occasionally, as a kind of shorthand. From early times runes were associated with incantation and magical practices (the word itself meant "whisper, mystery, secret counsel"). The surviving Old Germanic poems which use them as special letters are either gnomic-didactic in character or else they dimly recall more superstitious uses, as when the OE poet Cynewulf signs his works with the runes for his name woven into the verses, so that his readers may pray for him.—B. Dickins, *Runic and Heroic Poems of the Old Teutonic Peoples* (1915); O. von Friesen, "Runenschrift," J. Hoops, *Reallexikon der germanischen Altertumskunde*, IV (1918–19); H. Arntz, *Handbuch der Runenkunde* (1935); R. Dérolez, *Runica Manuscripta* (1954); R.W.V. Elliott, *Runes: An Introd.* (1959). J.B.B.

RUNNING RHYTHM (common rhythm). Term coined by Gerard Manley Hopkins to denote the standard rhythm of Eng. verse measured by feet of 2 or 3 syllables (with only occasional extra unaccented syllables). The rhythm is said to be rising if the stress occurs at the end of the foot, falling if the stress occurs at the beginning of the foot. If the stress occurs between 2 unstressed (or "slack") syllables (as in the amphibrachic foot), the rhythm, according to Hopkins, is "rocking." Running rhythm, in Hopkins' conception, is opposed to sprung rhythm (q.v.).—"Author's Preface," *Poems of Gerard Manley Hopkins*, ed. R. Bridges and W. H. Gardner (3d ed., 1948). P.F.

RUN-ON LINE. See ENJAMBEMENT.

RUSSIAN FORMALISM. See POETRY, THEORIES OF (OBJECTIVE THEORIES).

S

SAPPHIC. An important Aeolic verse form named after Sappho, a Gr. poetess from Lesbos of the 7th–6th c. B.C. The S. stanza consists of three Lesser S. lines

– ⏑ – ⏓ – ⏑ ⏑ – ⏑ – ⏓

followed by one Adonic

or Adoneus, – ⏑ ⏑ – ⏓

Sappho's contemporary, Alcaeus, also used the stanza and may have been its inventor. Catullus (84–54 B.C.?) made an adaptation of one of Sappho's odes (Catullus 51) and composed another in the meter (Catullus 11); with these poems he probably introduced the S. into L. poetry, but it is not certain. Horace (65–8 B.C.) provided the S. model for subsequent Roman and European poets; he used the meter 27 times, second in frequency only to the alcaics (q.v.) among his poems. Horace also makes a single use of the Greater S. strophe, i.e., an Aristophanic (– ⏑ ⏑ – ⏑ – ⏓) followed by a Greater S. line (– ⏑ – > – || ⏑ ⏑ – || – ⏑ ⏑ – ⏑ – >). Seneca (4 B.C.–A.D. 65) sometimes uses the separate elements in a different order, e.g., by arranging a continuous series of longer lines with an Adonic clausula. The S. stanza is today read in two quite different ways. We may stress the long third and fifth syllables ("integer vitae") or the fourth and sixth syllables, which in the Horatian pattern bear the word accent ("integer vitae scelerisque purus"). This second method is suggested by medieval rhyme in, e.g.,

vita sanctórum, décus angelorum.

Late medieval German Sapphics are rhymed.

The stanza was popular with poets and metricians in Italy, France (see CLASSICAL METERS IN MODERN LANGUAGES), Germany, England, and Spain during the Renaissance and, in varying extent, during later periods. Leonardo Dati used it for the first time in It. (1441, cf. HEXAMETER). He was followed by Galeotto del Carretto (1455–1530), Claudio Tolomei (1492–1555), and others. Felice Cavallotti (1842–98) experimented with the Horatian Greater S. Spain's Estéban de Villegas (1589–1669) is the chief practitioner of this meter in his country. In the 18th c. F. G. Klopstock varied an unrhymed stanza with regular positional changes of the trisyllabic foot in the Lesser S. lines; H. von Platen and others in Germany sustained the strict Horatian form. The Victorians, Tennyson and Swinburne in particular, included Sapphics among their many reproductions of classical meter.

Recent examples of the S. ode are in abundance. Translators of Horace and Catullus are constantly attracted by the deceptively simple scheme, e.g.

. . . I'll adóre my Lálage's pléasant láughter,
pléasant discóursing.
(J. B. Leishman)

For an example of original Sapphics today see Ezra Pound's *Apparuit*, one stanza of which reads as follows: "Half the graven shoulder, the throat aflash with / strands of light inwoven about it, loveli- / est of all things, frail alabaster, ah me! / swift in departing."—For bibliography, see CLASSICAL METERS IN MODERN LANGUAGES. Also,

G. Mazzoni, "Per la storia della saffica in Italia," *Atti* dell' Acc. Scienze lett. arti, 10 (1894); C. H. Moore, *Horace* . . . (1902), 42; H. G. Atkins, *A Hist. of German Versification* (1923); G. Highet, *The Cl. Tradition* (1949); Koster; Navarro. R.A.S.

SATIRE, says Dr. Johnson, is "a poem in which wickedness or folly is censured"; and more elaborate definitions are rarely more satisfactory. No strict definition can encompass the complexity of a word which signifies, on one hand, a kind of literature, and on the other, a spirit or tone which expresses itself in many literary genres. The difficulty is pointed up by a phrase of Quintilian (*Institutio Oratoria,* 10.93): "satura [as opposed to other literary forms] tota nostra est"; Quintilian seems to be claiming s. as a wholly Roman phenomenon, although he had read Aristophanes, and was familiar with a number of Gr. forms that we would call satiric, and knew of the tradition tracing the origin of satire to the early (7th c. B.C.) Gr. poet Archilochus. The point is that by *satura* (which meant originally something like "medley" and from which comes our "satire") he intended to specify that kind of poem "invented" by Lucilius, written in hexameters on certain appropriate themes, dominated by a Lucilian-Horatian tone. *Satura* referred, in short, to a poetic form, established and fixed by Roman practice. After Quintilian's day the signification of the term broadened to include works that were "satirical" in tone, but not in form; then, according to Hendrickson, from Gr. *satyros* and its derivatives were appropriated terms which became our *satirist, satiric, satirize,* etc. This confused etymology made for confusion: *satura* was modified orthographically into *satyra* and then, in Eng., into *satyre.* Elizabethan writers, anxious to follow classical models but misled by a false etymology, believed that "satyre" derived from the Gr. satyr-play; satyrs being notoriously rude, unmannerly creatures, "spiers out of . . . secret faults," it seemed to follow that "satyre" should be harsh, coarse, rough:

> The *Satyre* should be like the *Porcupine,*
> That shoots sharp quilles out in each angry
> line. . . .
> (Hall, *Virgidemiarum,* 5.3)

Isaac Casaubon exposed the false etymology of the satire-satyr relation in 1605; but the tradition has remained strong.

The formal verse s. as composed by Horace, Persius, and Juvenal is the only satiric form to have even a remotely determinate structure, and it furnishes exceptions to every generalization ("qui dit satire latine, dit mélange," writes Lejay). Generally speaking, the formal s. is a quasi-dramatic poem, "framed" by an encounter between the Satirist (or, more reasonably, his *persona,* the "I" of the poem) and an Adversarius who impels the satirist to speech. Within this frame, as M. C. Randolph has shown, vice and folly are exposed to critical analysis by means of any number of literary and rhetorical devices: the satirist may use beast fables, Theophrastian "characters," dramatic incidents, fictional experiences, anecdotes, proverbs, homilies; he may employ invective, sarcasm, irony, mockery, raillery, exaggeration, understatement—wit in any of its forms—anything to make the object of attack abhorrent or ridiculous. Complementing this negative aspect of the poem is a positive appeal, explicit or implicit, to virtue and rational behavior—to a norm, that is, against which the vicious and the foolish are to be judged. Thus, though the materials of the s. are astonishingly varied, there is pressure toward order internally from the arraignment of vice and appeal to virtue, and externally from the (often shadowy) dramatic situation which frames the poem.

Formal satires are written in the middle style; they are discursive, colloquial, as befits a form unremittingly aware of its low estate in the hierarchy of genres. Juvenal's occasional self-conscious flights into the grand style, however, sanctioned the "tragicall" s. of later writers, and his *saeva indignatio* contrasts with the tone of urbane mockery characteristic of Horace.

In addition to attacking vice and folly on nearly all levels, the formal satirist has from the beginning felt impelled to justify his ungrateful art. His *apologiae* (Horace, 1.4; 2.1; Persius, 1; Juvenal, 1; Régnier, 12; Boileau, 9; Pope, *Epistle to Dr. Arbuthnot*) are conventional; they project an image of the satirist as a plain honest man, wishing harm to no upright person, but appalled at the evil he sees about him and forced by his conscience (*facit indignatio versum*) to write s. Readers have not always been convinced. While the influence of Roman practice on later satirists in matters of theme, point of view, tone, literary and rhetorical device, etc., has been enormous, relatively few poets have attempted to adapt precisely the Roman form. Boileau and Pope are great exceptions.

The satiric spirit as it is manifested in verse seems to appear (whether as mockery, raillery, ridicule, or formalized invective) in the literature or folklore of all peoples, early and late, preliterate and civilized. According to Aristotle (*Poetics* 4. 1448ᵇ–1449ᵃ), Gr. Old Comedy developed out of ritualistic invective—out of satiric utterances, that is, improvised and hurled at individuals by the Leaders of the Phallic Songs. The function of these "iambic" utterances was magical, as F. M. Cornford has shown; they were thought to drive away evil influences so that the positive fertility magic of the phallus might be operative. This early connection of primitive "s." with magic has a remarkably widespread history. Archilochus (7th c. B.C.), the "first" Gr. literary satirist, composed iambics of such potency against Lycambes that he and his daughters are said to have hung themselves. In the next century the sculptors Bupalus and Athenis "knit their necks in halters," it is said, as a result of the "bitter rimes and biting libels" of the satirical poet Hipponax. Similar tales exist in other cultures. The chief function of the ancient Arabic poet was to compose s. (*hijá*) against the tribal enemy. The satires were thought always to be fatal and the poet led his people into battle, hurling his verses as he would hurl a spear. Old Ir. literature is laced with accounts of the extraordinary power of the poets, whose satires brought disgrace and death to their victims: ". . . saith [King] Lugh to his poet, 'what power can *you* wield in battle?' 'Not hard to say,' quoth Carpre '. . . I will satirize them and shame them, so that through the spell of my art they will not resist warriors' " (*The Second Battle of Moytura,* tr. W. Stokes, *Revue Celtique,* 12 [1891], 91–92). (F. N. Robinson adduces linguistic, thematic, and other evidence to show a functional relation between primitive s., like that of Carpre, and the "real" s. of more sophisticated times.) Today, among the Eskimo, the loss of a duel in s. (the drum-match, in which two enemies alternately hurl verses of ridicule and abuse at each other) may lead to exile and even death. Primitive s. such as that described above can hardly be spoken of in literary terms; its affiliations are rather with the magical incantation and the curse.

When the satiric utterance breaks loose from its background in ritual and magic, as in ancient Greece (when it is free, that is, to develop according to literary rather than "practical" impulsions), it is found embodied in an indefinite number of literary forms which profess to convey moral instruction by means of laughter, ridicule, mockery—forms such as Aristophanic comedy, the Bionean diatribe, the mime, the beast fable, the Theophrastian character, etc., all of which contribute to the developed formal s. of Rome. But the spirit which informs them is too mercurial to be confined to exclusive literary structures; it proliferates everywhere, adapting itself to whatever mode (verse or prose) seems congenial. Its range is enormous: from an anonymous medieval invective against social injustice to the superb wit of some of Chaucer's portraits and the somber power of the Vision of Piers the Ploughman; from the burlesque of Pulci to the scurrilities of Aretino; from the flailings of Marston and the mordancies of Quevedo to the bite of La Fontaine and the great dramatic structures of Jonson and Molière.

By and large the satiric spirit seems to fuse most readily with the comic genres: when s. was prohibited by law in Elizabethan England, and it was ordered that the verses of Hall and Marston be burned, the satirists turned promptly to the comic drama ("comicall satyre") as the form most appropriate for their purposes. But, as in all generalizations about s., the qualifications are important. Juvenal deliberately sought to rise above the prescriptive bounds of the comic; at the end of the scarifying Sixth S. he enforces a comparison in theme and tone with Sophocles. In the modern Age of S. Alexander Pope catches beautifully, when he likes, the deft Horatian tone; but his wit (like that of Dryden in *Absalom and Achitophel*) is also a serious wit, deeply probing and prophetic. The last lines of the *Dunciad* rise to a terrifying sublimity as they celebrate the restoration of chaos, the obliterating triumph of the anti-Logos. Such passages transcend easy generic distinctions.

The private motivations of the satirist we cannot know. The public function of s.—how it works in its social, psychological, cultural dimensions—we understand only obscurely. (Approaches to these problems by way of psychoanalytic theory, cultural anthropology, etc., are promising; e.g., the work of E. Kris and E. H. Gombrich on caricature in Kris, *Psychoanalytic Explorations in Art* [1952].) But the public motivation of the satirist is explicit and self-justificatory; he writes, so he claims, to reform. His audience may be small (a few "right-thinking men") but it must share with him commitment to certain intellectual and moral beliefs which validate his critique of aberration. Ridicule, which in some cultures may kill and in our own kills symbolically, depends on shared assumptions against which the aberrant stands in naked relief. The greatest s. has been written in periods when ethical and rational norms were sufficiently powerful to attract widespread assent, yet not so powerful as to compel absolute conformity—those periods when the satirist could be of his society and apart from it; could exercise the "double vision." Neoclassic poets had available to them as a kind of implicit metaphor the mighty standard of the classical past; witness the success in the period of the mock-heroic genres. These mock not primarily the ancient forms (although there may be affectionate laughter at some aspects of the epic) but present society, which in the context of past grandeur shows contemptible and mean.

The 20th c., like the 19th, lacks such available norms; but unlike the 19th (Byron's *Vision of Judgment* and *Don Juan* and Heine's *Atta Troll* are hardly characteristic of their period) it has a taste for s. Yet though this may be a satirical age, it is hardly an age of great verse s. The alienation of poet from society is notorious; and when the poet has struggled through to the adoption of beliefs and values adequate to his needs, it is a question whether they will serve as metaphors for poetry. Three exceptions (to speak only of poets writing in Eng.) may be noted: Yeats, his vision radically private, and Eliot, his values at the time of *The Waste Land* generally religious, have both written powerful s.; and Auden, his orientation at first social-political, later religious, has demonstrated that a poet writing consciously within the 18th-c. satiric tradition can speak sharply, eloquently, effectively—can speak *satirically*—even to our fragmented society.

J. Dryden, "A Discourse concerning the Original and Progress of S." (1693), *Works*, ed. W. Scott and G. Saintsbury (1882–93), XIII, 1–123; P. Lejay, "Les origines et la nature de la satire d'Horace," in his ed. of Horace, *Satires* (1911); F. N. Robinson, "Satirists and Enchanters in Early Ir. Lit.," *Studies in the Hist. of Religions* . . . , ed. D. G. Lyon and G. F. Moore (1912); H. Walker, *English S. and Satirists* (1925); G. L. Hendrickson, "Archilochus and the Victims of his Iambics," AJP, 46 (1925) and "Satura tota nostra est," CP, 22 (1927); J. W. Duff, *Roman S.* (1936); O. J. Campbell, *Comicall Satyre* (1938); V. Cian, *La satira* (2 v., 1939); D. Worcester, *The Art of S.* (1940); M. C. Randolph, "The Structural Design of the Formal Verse S.," PQ, 21 (1942); I. Jack, *Augustan S.* (1952); M. Mack, "The Muse of S.," *Studies in the Lit. of the Augustan Age*, ed. R. C. Boys (1952); J. Peter, *S. and Complaint in Early Eng. Lit.* (1956); J. Sutherland, *Eng. S.* (1958); A. Kernan, *The Cankered Muse* (1959); R. C. Elliott, *The Power of S.* (1960); G. Highet, *The Anatomy of S.* (1962). R.C.E.

SCANSION. The system of describing more or less conventional poetic rhythms by visual symbols for purposes of metrical analysis and study. Three methods of scanning Eng. verse are generally recognized: the graphic, the musical, and the acoustic. The primary symbols most commonly used in traditional graphic s. are: × or ⌣ representing a syllable which, in poetic context, is unstressed; and / or –, representing a syllable which is stressed. Secondary symbols are: |, representing a division between feet; and ||, representing a caesura (q.v.). In performing s. of a line or group of lines, the reader first marks stressed and unstressed syllables, not according to any preconceived pattern, but according to the degree of sense emphasis transmitted by the syllables. For example:

× / × / × / × / × /
I sometimes think that never blows so red

× / × / / / × / × /
The Rose as where some buried Caesar bled;

× / × / × × × / × /
That every Hyacinth the Garden wears

/ × × / × / / × /
Dropt in her lap from some once lovely head.

(FitzGerald, *The Rubaiyat*)

After ascertaining whether the lines are generally in ascending or descending rhythm, the reader next marks the feet, as follows:

× / × / × / × / × /
I some|times think | that ne|ver blows | so red |

× / × / / / × / × /
The Rose | as where|some bur|ied Cae|sar bled;|

× / × / × × × / × /
That ev|ery Hy|acinth | the Gar|den wears |

/ × × / × / / / ×
Dropt in | her lap | from some | once love|ly

/
head. |

S. does not make rhythm: it reveals it by transferring it from a temporal into a spatial dimension. By giving the reader a visual representation of the metrical situation underlying the words of the poem, s. helps to make clear the function of metrical variations (q.v.): in the fourth line of FitzGerald's stanza, for example, the s. makes visually apparent the substitution of a trochee for the expected iamb in the first position; this variation reinforces the suddenness and the rapidity of the fall of the drops of blood.

The s. of the following stanza also serves to reveal in visual symbols meaningful variations from the expected metrical pattern:

× / × / × / × /
Her lips| were red, | her looks | were free, |

× / × / × × /
Her locks |were yel|low as gold: |

× / × / × / × ×
Her skin | was white | as lep|rosy, |

× / × / × / × /
The Night|mare Life|-in-Death | was she, |

× / / / × /
Who thicks | men's blood | with cold. |

(Coleridge, *Rime of the Ancient Mariner*)

Here the s. of the last line reveals that a spondaic substitution has occurred in the second position, and that the added metrical weight performs the function of reinforcing the sense of the slow, heavy movement of chilled and thickened blood (see METRICAL VARIATIONS).

Total stanzaic structure is often recorded by indicating the rhyme scheme in letters, and the number of feet per line in numbers. For example, the FitzGerald stanza may be represented thus: *a a b* a_5; and the Coleridge thus: $a_4b_3aa_4b_3$.

Some prosodists reject the traditional graphic s. symbols, as illustrated above, and use instead musical symbols. In s. systems of this kind, eighth notes may represent unstressed syllables and quarter or half notes stressed syllables of varying degrees of emphasis. Caesuras are sometimes indicated by musical rests of various lengths. Musical s. has the advantage of representing more accurately than graphic s. delicate differences in degree of stress: it is obvious to anyone that an Eng. line has more than two "kinds" of syllables in it, and yet graphic s., preferring convenience to accuracy, gives the impression that any syllable in a line is either clearly stressed or clearly unstressed. On the other hand, the major disadvantage of musical s. is its complexity; a lesser disadvantage is that it tends to imply that poetry follows musical principles, an assumption not universally accepted.

The third method of s., the acoustic, has been developed by modern linguists working with such machines as the kymograph and the oscillograph. Like musical s., it is a system advantageous in the accuracy of its representations of the empirical phenomena of spoken verse but disadvantageous in its complexity.

Some theorists reject all three kinds of s. and

prefer to mark the rhythmical movements of verse by cadences (q.v.), often indicated by wavy lines or brackets drawn above the poetic line. See also PROSODY, PROSE RHYTHM, RHYTHM.

E. Smith, *The Principles of Eng. Metre* (1923; on the s. of free verse); Y. Winters, *Primitivism and Decadence* (1937; free verse); "Eng. Verse and What It Sounds Like," KR, 18 (1956; articles by J. C. Ransom and others); W. K. Wimsatt, Jr. and M. C. Beardsley, "The Concept of Meter: an Exercise in Abstraction," PMLA, 74 (1959; on the s. of Eng. verse). P.F.

SCHEME. See TROPE.

SCOP. An OE name, like "gleeman," with which it is interchangeably used, for the professional entertainer, a harpist and poet-singer, normally a member of a royal household, who was the shaper and conservator in England of Old Germanic poetic tradition. He was of an old and honored class, sharing with his audience a critical interest in his craft; he commanded a mastery of the complex oral-formulaic materials of Old Germanic prosody (q.v.) hardly comprehensible to lettered societies. His repertory included more than encomiastic court verse: he was also a folk historian; and his narrative celebrations of heroic boldness and sacrifice, mingled with lyrical reflection and secular or Christian morality, have been preserved in later written forms as a central part of the Anglo-Saxon poetical corpus. There are no extant full-length biographies of OE scops, as there are of some of the Icelandic court poets, for instance; but a fictional biography in verse of one Widsith, together with a quasi-autobiographical lyric by a certain Deor, afford glimpses of the bard's social status and of some of his professional techniques. It is likely, however, that the transmission of verse depended less upon the personality and talent of an individual scop than upon the formulaic materials with which he worked, the cooperative appreciation of his audience, and their common familiarity with traditional themes. It is sometimes hard to distinguish between the art of popular and courtly poetry, between the art of a court gleeman and that perhaps of a chieftain who might take up the harp and recite a lay himself; or that of a warrior-singer whose function as a singer would be incidental to his personal knowledge of a battle; or even that of an humble person like Cædmon (Cædman), described in Bede's *Historia Ecclesiastica* (A.D. 721), who had no training as a singer, but who nevertheless developed the art of narrative verse on Christian themes in what must have been, technically, a thoroughly traditional manner.—L. F. Anderson, *The Anglo-Saxon Scop* (1903); R. W. Chambers, *Widsith* (1912); K. Malone, *Deor* (1933, 1962); *Widsith* (1936); D. Whitelock, *The Audience of Beowulf* (1951); F. P. Magoun, Jr., "Bede's Story of Cædman: The Case Hist. of an Anglo-Saxon Oral Singer," *Speculum*, 30 (1955). J.B.B.

SENARIUS. See TRIMETER.

SEPTENARY. A metrical line of 7 feet, usually in trochaic tetrameter:

> mihi est propositum in taberna mori
> (*Confessio Goliae* of Archpoet)

The s. is metrically the same as the heptameter (q.v.) and the fourteener, but the term is now rarely used and best restricted to medieval L. verse and to such vernacular compositions as the Middle Eng. *Orrmulum* and *Poema Morale*, which are predominantly iambic.—Schipper.

SESTET(T), *sestette, sestetto.* (a) The minor division or last 6 lines of an It. type sonnet (q.v.), preceded by an octet (see OCTAVE). Sometimes the octet states a proposition or situation and the s. a conclusion, but no fast rules for content can be formulated. The rhyme scheme of the s. varies. (b) Any separable 6-line section of a stanza, but s. is not generally used to describe an entire stanza. R.O.E.

SESTINA. The most complicated of the verse forms initiated by the troubadours. It is composed of 6 stanzas of 6 lines each, followed by an envoy of 3 lines, all of which are usually unrhymed. The function of rhyme in the s. is taken over by a recurrent pattern of end-words; the same 6 end-words occur in each stanza, but in a constantly shifting order which follows a fixed pattern.

If we let the letters A through F stand for the 6 end-words of a s., we may schematize the recurrence pattern as follows:

stanza 1: ABCDEF
2: FAEBDC
3: CFDABE
4: ECBFAD
5: DEACFB
6: BDFECA
envoy : ECA *or* ACE

Most commonly, the envoy, or *tornada,* is further complicated by the fact that the remaining 3 end-words, BDF, must occur in the course of the lines, so that the 3-line envoy will contain all 6 recurrent words.

The invention of the s. is usually attributed to Arnaut Daniel (fl. 1190), and the form was widely cultivated both by his Prov. followers and by Dante and Petrarch in Italy. It was introduced into Fr. by Pontus de Tyard (ca. 1521–1605), a member of the *Pléiade*, and was practiced in 17th-c. Germany by Opitz, Gryphius, and Weckherlin. In the 19th c. the foremost writers of sestinas were the Comte de Gramont, who wrote an astonishing number of them, and Swinburne, who sometimes varied the pattern, even using rhyme, and who composed, in his *Complaint of Lisa*, a double s. of 12 stanzas. The form has had a certain popularity in the 20th c., and Ezra Pound, T. S. Eliot and W. H. Auden have all written sestinas of distinction.—Kastner; F.J.A. Davidson, "The Origin of the S.," MLN, 25 (1910); A. Jeanroy, "La 's. doppia' de Dante et les origines de la sestine," *Romania*, 42 (1912); L. A. Fiedler, "Green Thoughts in a Green Shade: Reflections on the Stony S. of Dante Alighieri," KR, 18 (1956).

SEXAIN, sixain, sextain, sextet, sestet, hexastich. Names variously and indiscriminately applied to the great variety of 6-line stanzas found in Western poetry. The term "sestet" (q.v.), properly speaking, is restricted to the concluding 6 lines of a sonnet (q.v.), especially an It. sonnet, in distinction to the octave (q.v.), or first 8 lines. The remaining terms are applied interchangeably to such forms as the Burns stanza and tail-rhyme (qq.v.), as well as to the many 6-line stanzas which have no distinctive names. The most familiar types of sexain in Eng. poetry are the following: (1) ababcc, in iambic pentameter (the so-called *Venus and Adonis* stanza, q.v.); (2) ababcc, in iambic tetrameter (Wordsworth's *The Daffodils*; also a familiar stanzaic form in German lyric poetry); (3) tail-rhyme, $aa^4b^3cc^4b^3$ (Chaucer, *Tale of Sir Thopas*); (4) Burns stanza, $aaa^4b^2a^4b^2$; (5) xayaza (Rossetti, *The Blessed Damozel*) The sestina (q.v.) uses a 6-line stanza in which word recurrence rather than rhyme is used as a principle of organization. Six-line stanzas occur more frequently than do 5-line stanzas. Indeed, their incidence ranks only after that of the quatrain and the couplet (qq.v.).

SHAPED VERSE. See PATTERN POETRY.

SHORT METER (S.M. of the hymn books). In effect a variant of ballad meter (q.v.), for if the first tetrameter of that 4343 pattern is shortened, the 3343 arrangement of s.m. results. The form is also similar to the "Poulter's measure" (q.v.) of the 16th c. (if the "Poulter's" couplets are divided at the caesuras), but it is susceptible of greater variety than is found in the monotonous alternations of hexameters and heptameters in the latter. It is most frequently, but by no means exclusively, found in hymnals. S.m. rhymes abcb or abab, and is sometimes written in trochees, but more frequently in iambics, as in Emerson's

To clothe the fiery thought
In simple words succeeds,
For still the craft of genius is
To mask a king in weeds.

L.J.Z.

SIMILE. A comparison of one thing with another, explicitly announced by the word "like" or "as."

Aristotle granted that good similes "give an effect of brilliance," but preferred metaphor to simile because s., being longer, was less attractive, and because the s. "does not say outright that 'this' *is* 'that' . . . the hearer is less interested in the idea." (*Rhetoric* 1410a). As a figure of speech, s. merges with and to some extent overlaps the "prosaic" metaphor of comparison, substitution, or description, differing from it only by the presence of "like" or "as" (see e.g. *Rhetoric* 1406a, 1410a). Not every s. is a metaphor, though some similes can be compressed or converted into metaphors; and only some metaphors can be expanded into similes. At the level of comparison, substitution, or description it is useful to preserve the formal distinction between "metaphor-form" and "simile-form," and to apply the term "submerged s." to figures of metaphor-form which are in fact similes with the word "like" or "as" omitted. For example, "Thou Moon beyond the clouds! . . . Thou Star above the Storm!" is a submerged s. (Many of the more vigorous submerged similes are of the 4-term analogical type A is to X as B is to Y [e.g. "a poisonous resentment"] and are in their origins at least truly metaphorical.) On the other hand, some figures in s.-form may be converted into genuine metaphor, usually by the resonance of the context:

Dull brown a cloak enwraps, Don Juan,
Both thy lean shanks, one arm,
That old bird-cage thy breast, where like magpie
Thy heart hopped on alarm.

Whereas metaphor is a mode of condensation and compression, s. through its descriptive function readily leads to diffuseness and extension, even to the digressive development of the figurative scene, action, or object as an object of beauty in itself. Homer's brief similes (e.g. Thetis rises out of the sea like a mist, Apollo descends like the night, "And with them followed a cloud of foot-soldiers") suggest clearly their origin in metaphor; for, although comparison is explicitly indicated by the word "like" or "as," the two things are not primarily compared but identified, yet without any loss of individual character. Such a use of the metaphor in s.-form may be a natural mark of young and vital speech. (See Bowra, *Tradition and Design*.) Indeed Chaucer's characteristic brief similes are of this kind: "hir eyen greye as glas," "His eyen twynkled in his heed aryght, / As doon the sterres in the frosty nyght." Such similes are also found in Old Fr. romance. But W. P. Ker has pointed out that "similes are not used much in English poetry before Chaucer, or in medieval vernacular poetry before Dante"; that similes, though commonly used by medieval L. writers, are uncommon in Old Eng. and Old Icelandic (*Form and Style*, p. 253).

The true epic s. involves the comparison of one composite action or relation with another composite action or relation. For example, in *Il-*

iad 4.275 the Gr. host led by Ajax is compared to a storm-cloud: "As when a goatherd looks out from a watch-tower of a hill over the sea, and sees a cloud coming afar off over the sea, carrying with it much tempest, showing to him blacker than pitch, coming on driven by the west wind, and he shudders to see it, and drives his flock into a cave, so appeared the march of the Greek warriors." It is to Homer's epic s. that the whole European tradition of extended s. may be traced. In Homer too is to be found an insistently digressive tendency in s. The example cited above has a double reference (for more complex relations see e.g. *Iliad* 13.271–76, 586); but his aim is usually to provide some single common characteristic in the comparison. His favorite source of material for similes is his direct observation of the life around him; he will sometimes, from delight in the material, follow his fancy and develop the picture without much care for the initial comparison (e.g. *Iliad* 4.141–45, 12.278–86). Homer uses his similes for a variety of purposes: for relief, suspense, decoration, magnificence. The Homeric similes—striking, various, self-contained, if not always completely apposite—seldom fail to heighten the narrative and to give pleasure for their own sake.

In succession, Virgil and Dante refined the epic s. in order to develop with precision a multiplicity of comparisons within a single extensive image or action, to "make us see more definitely the scene" (T. S. Eliot, *Dante,* p. 24). This process reaches its culmination in Milton who, as Newton noticed, surpassed all his predecessors in the matter of consistency. Historically, the process may be seen as a process of degeneration from metaphor in the direction of descriptive and logical consistency; from the specifically poetic mode to a discursive mode; from the simple vivid s.-form metaphor discernible in Homer to an extended comparison through imagery, the success of which depends upon the multiplicity and precision of logical, actual, and visual correspondence. (This, in Coleridgean terms, could be described as a movement from Imagination to Fancy.) Homer's success in s. often depends upon violent heterogeneity between the elements of s.—a practice implicitly commended by Quintilian: "The more remote the simile is from the subject to which it is applied, the greater will be the impression of novelty and the unexpected which it produces" (*Institutio Oratoria* 8.3.74; cf. Johnson's dictum: "A simile may be compared to lines converging at a point, and is more excellent as the lines approach from a greater distance"). This striking heterogeneity, often found also in Virgil, may be taken as a mark of the origin of s. in metaphor, being a kind of parataxis or "confrontation" (see METAPHOR). Milton, on the other hand, avoids digressive tendencies in his choice of illustrative material, and chooses his imagery with an almost mathematical subtlety to secure a delicate and complex consistency of internal relations. The organic correspondence of many of Milton's similes with their context and with the whole poem, their exquisite finish, and relentless logical and imaginative consistency, carry them paradoxically out of the field of discursive comparison toward the field of identity and of metaphor, e.g., *Paradise Lost* 3.431–41:

As when a Vultur on *Imaus* bred,
Whose snowie ridge the roving *Tartar* bounds,
Dislodging from a Region scarce of prey
To gorge the flesh of Lambs or yeanling Kids
On Hills where Flocks are fed, flies toward the
Springs
Of *Ganges* or *Hydaspes, Indian* streams;
But in his way lights on the barren plaines
Of *Sericana,* where *Chineses* drive
With Sails and Wind thir canie Waggons light:
So on this windie Sea of Land, the Fiend
Walk'd up and down alone bent on his
prey, . . .

The extended s. is not confined to epic poetry. Jeremy Taylor and Sir Thomas Browne are only two of several 17th-c. prose-writers capable of using s. with perspicuous accuracy and florid invention. Shakespeare had handled extended s. with unerring point and carried it to unmatched depths of implication. But after Milton no poet uses the epic s. with his force or precision. Keats shows craftsmanlike skill in *Hyperion,* his comparison of the fallen gods to Stonehenge being justly celebrated; Byron, through carelessness, misuses the epic s. in *Childe Harold;* Matthew Arnold cultivated the heroic manner rather too sedulously in *Sohrab and Rustum* but not without a few notable successes. Shelley has a curious habit, in passages of transcendent emotion, of accumulating a shower of approximate similes (both in explicit s.-form and in metaphor-form); prime examples occur in *Epipsychidion* 26–34, 115–23 (but cf. *Adonais* 17). The art of extended s. had a vogue in later 19th-c. journalism but has now happily passed out of fashion. And now that power rather than revelation has become the central concern of the public orator, the more grotesque manifestations of extended s. (e.g. "Like a paralytic who finds his arms useless to move his wheel-chair from the murderous flame that would snuff out his life, I am powerless to strain the muscles of coincidence's arm by suggesting any connexion between the mayor's timely affluence and the loss of the Party funds") are seldom heard now even on political platforms.

The distinction drawn by C. S. Lewis (*The Allegory of Love*) between symbolic allegory and "formulated" allegory can be seen to be parallel to the distinction between metaphor and s. Symbolic allegory (e.g. *Roman de la Rose, The Faerie Queene* (in part at least), *Pilgrim's Progress,* Kafka's *Trial*) develops two or more levels of meaning simultaneously. The "formulated" allegory (e.g. Dryden's *Absalom and Achitophel,* Swift's *Tale of a Tub*), in which the "real meaning" is derived by direct substitution from the details and context of the "story," may be regarded as an extension of "submerged s."; for the comparison unfolds in the manner of an extended s., though the primary subject for comparison is withheld and the fact that a comparison is intended is (for a variety of reasons) not explicitly stated. This relation of "formulated" allegory to s. tends to be overlooked because of the habit—to be seen, for example, in Coleridge, Yeats and Fowler—of assuming that all allegory is of the type of "formulated" allegory and concluding that allegory is the contrary term to symbol. See also IMAGERY; METAPHOR.

H. Fränkel, *Die homerischen Gleichnisse* (1921); Ker, pp. 250–59; C. M. Bowra, *Tradition and Design in the Iliad* (1930); J. Whaler, "Grammatical *Nexus* of the Miltonic S.," JEGP, 30 (1931), "Compounding and Distribution of Similes in *Paradise Lost,*" MP, 28 (1931), "The Miltonic S.," PMLA, 46 (1931); I. F. Green, "Observations on the Epic Similes in the *Faerie Queene,*" PQ, 14 (1935); L. D. Lerner, "The Miltonic S.," EIC, 4 (1954); M. Coffey, "Function of the Homeric S.," AJP, 78 (1957); J. Notopoulos, "Homeric Similes in the Light of Oral Poetry," CJ, 52 (1957); K. Widmer, "The Iconography of Renunciation: The Miltonic S.," ELH, 25 (1958). G.W.

SKALD (scald). The word *skáld* had the general meaning "poet" in ON, and still does in Icelandic. In Eng., however, it is applied specifically to the Scandinavian poets of old who were attached to the courts of kings, earls, and other chieftains in the Northern countries, England, and elsewhere. The first skalds were Norwegian. The oldest whose work we know was Bragi Boddason the Old of the first half of the 9th c.; he was the forerunner of a number of other Norwegian skalds, but from the end of the 10th c. and down to the close of the 13th, when the court poetry went out of fashion, the Icelanders dominated the field almost exclusively. Altogether, the names of about 250 skalds have come down to us.—W. Craigie, *The Art of Poetry in Iceland* (1937); *The Skalds,* tr. and ed. L. M. Hollander (1945). R.B.

SKELTONIC VERSE. A verse form (sometimes treated as part of a generic type called tumbling verse, q.v.) named after its originator and principal practitioner, John Skelton (ca. 1460–1529). Its characteristics are: a line that is usually quite short (from 3 to 6 or 7 syllables and of 2 or 3 stresses), though longer lines with the typical skeltonic feel are not uncommon; a rhyme scheme in which a rhyme set may be extended indefinitely, though rhymes are never crossed; the elevation of parallelism to a major rhetorical element.

And if ye stand in doubt
Who brought this rhyme about
My name is Colin Clout.
I propose to shake out
All my conning bag,
Like a clerkly hag.
For though my rhyme be ragged,
Tattered and jagged
Rudely rain-beaten,
Rusty and moth-eaten,
If ye take well therewith
It hath in it some pith.
—Colin Clout

The effect of this highly irregular verse struck a number of generations as "rude rayling," but beginning with favorable comments by various eminent romantics, including Coleridge and Wordsworth, a revaluation has taken place, till skeltonic is much admired by many modern poets.

The traditional roots of the verse form have been variously described as Anglo-Saxon rhyming poems (Guest), as a fine form of native doggerel bent on escaping the dullness of post-Chaucerian poetics (Saintsbury), as an adaptation of rhymed accentual verse of medieval Latinists (Berdan), as a fusion of the Anglo-Saxon 4-accent alliterative line (broken into halves), and the aforementioned Latinists (de Sola Pinto). The most specific suggestion from this later group is Kinsman's, who traces a close relationship from both medieval Eng. and L. poems on the "Signs of Death" to Skelton's *Uppon a Deedmans Hed.* Nelson has advanced a persuasive theory, namely, that the principal forbear of s. is the *similiter desinens* or rhymed prose of the Latins which, combined with *clausulae* (short parallel clauses), enjoyed a vogue from the 11th to the 14th c., and which Skelton himself practiced.—Saintsbury, *Prosody,* I; J. M. Berdan, *Early Tudor Poetry* (1920); R. Graves, *John Skelton. Selections* (1927); W. Nelson, *John Skelton: Laureate* (1939); *John Skelton: A Selection from his Poems,* ed. V. de Sola Pinto (1950); R. S. Kinsman, "Skelton's 'Uppon a Deedmans Hed': New Light on the Origin of the Skeltonic," SP, 50 (1953). R.BE.

SLAVIC PROSODY. A comparative study of Slav. pros. has as its aim both the reconstruction of Common Slav. versification and the description of the individual Slav. prosodic systems which evolved after the breakdown of Slav. unity, around the 10th c. A.D. These systems comprise an oral (declamatory or sung) popular tradition, which to some extent is the continuation of Common Slav. pros., and a tradition of written poetry, which is genetically and structurally connected with the former, but has been subject to various foreign as well as cross-cultural Slav. influences. Whatever metrical system exerted an influence on or was adopted by a given Slav. pros., its needs must be adjusted to the prosodic possibilities of the particular Slav. language implementing it. In recognizing this fact, modern study of versification does not limit itself to an enumeration of ideal metrical schemes but views verse as a structure within which the metrical constants correlate to rhythmic tendencies.

Attempts to reconstruct Common Slav. pros. have so far yielded the following results. Common Slav. had two types of verse: a spoken asyllabic verse, based on syntactic parallelism of the lines; and a syllabic verse, based on a fixed number of syllables in each line and syntactic pause at the end of the lines. Specimens of the first type are found in Slav. folklore in the form of wedding-speeches and sayings and in the imparisyllabic lines found in older Western (e.g. 14th-c. Czech epic poems) and Rus. (17th-c.) poetry. The syllabic type was recitative or sung. Direct descendants of the recitative type are the laments (*tužbalice, plači*) and epic songs (*junačke pesme, byliny*) preserved among the Balkan Slavs and in Northern Great Russia. The laments consisted of short or long lines with a trochaic cadence, which were divided into uniform cola (4 + 4 or 4 + 4 + 4). The epic songs also consisted of long or short lines and were divided into asymmetrical cola: (4 + 6) with a trochaic cadence and (5 + 3 or 3 + 5) with an iambic cadence. The epic verse also had a quantitative clausula. All four types of the recitative verse are very well preserved in the South Slav. area. In the Northern Rus. area the recitative verse changed its structure considerably after the loss of phonemic length and intonation. The asymmetrical verse of epic songs, both long and short, had lost its syllabic pattern just because of its asymmetry, and became a purely accentual verse with a two-syllable anacrusis and a dactylic clausula (which replaced the quantitative one). The symmetrical verse of the laments preserved its syllabic pattern much better. It also developed a new dactylic clausula owing to an additional syllable. Thus it now consists, as a rule, of 9-syllable or 13-syllable lines with a trochaic cadence.

The oldest learned Slav. poetry, that of the Old Church Slavonic-Moravian period, was based on isosyllabism without rhyme and owed its origin to Common Slav. syllabic verse as well as to Byzantine-Gr. forms.

The new political, religious, and linguistic developments which took place around the 10th c. A.D. created the conditions for independent Slav. poetic traditions and prosodic systems. The formation of Slav. states and their subsequent destinies, the adoption of Christianity, and the Schism affected the growth and functions of poetry in the various Slav. countries in different ways. The longest uninterrupted tradition of learned poetry existed among the Western Slavs and, to a lesser degree, in the Catholic Southern Slav. world where it started among Croats and Serbs on the Dalmatian coast during the flowering of the Renaissance in this area. In the Orthodox Slav. world learned poetry developed much later: among Eastern Slavs in the 17th c. and among Balkan Slavs (Serbs and Bulgarians) in the 18th and 19th c., respectively. As a consequence of the breakdown of Common Slav., a new word-prosody developed in the various Slav. languages, which can be formulated as follows: (1) Czech and Slovak; (2) Serbo-Croatian; and (3) Slovenian preserved phonemic quantity. In Czech and Slovak, stress has the function only of delimiting word boundaries, being fixed on the initial syllable of a word. In Serbo-Croatian and Slovenian, stress is concomitant with pitch, which is distinctive but metrically irrelevant, or in the absence of the latter, it delimits the word boundary, falling on the first (Serbo-Croatian) or final syllable of a word (Slovenian). In the Eastern Slav. languages and in Bulgarian, stress has a distinctive function, whereas in Polish it is bound to the penultimate syllable of a word.

Syllabism has been up to now the basis of *Polish* versification. In the 14th-15th c., iso. syllabism of the lines was merely a tendency, which was pronounced in the works influenced by medieval L. poetry. The greatest innovator of Pol. syllabic verse was J. Kochanowski. He canonized the principle of strict isosyllabism, eliminated syntactic parallelism of the lines as a constant, and stabilized the place of the caesura in longer (over 8-syllable) lines. He also introduced a full, 1 rhyme (with a penultimate stress), which was not strictly adhered to by his 17th- and 18th-c. followers. These innovations lent Pol. verse new flexibility: they allowed the use of lines and hemistichs of various length and released syntactic phrasing for expressive effects. The consistent adherence to the syllabic principle accounts for the popularity of the longer lines, especially of 11 (5 + 6) and 13 (7 + 6) syllables, in which the best Pol. lyric and epic poetry has been written. The shorter octosyllable has generally been used in learned poetry without a caesura. In popular verse, this line is divided into hemistichs (5 + 3 or 4 + 4), which entails a breakdown of the line into word groups with an equal number of stresses or a strong trochaic tendency.

The rhythmical measures of the folk song enter at first into Pol. romantic poetry as a form of popular stylization. The impulse for syllabic-accentual pros. was, however, given mainly by the imitation of classical, quantitative meters and by foreign (Rus.) models. Syllabic-accentual meters are used by the romantics in smaller lyric poems and in sections of dramatic works. The great romantics, who introduced masculine rhyme and iambic and anapestic feet (Mickiewicz, Slowacki), used these meters with moderation. Syllabic-accentual verse became the norm with the "positivist" poets (Konopnicka, Asnyk), who practiced it with extreme rigor. Modern poets admit frequent deviations from the metrical scheme. The imitation of classical meters, especially the hexameter, actually led to the introduction of purely accentual meters, based on an equal number of stresses in each line. In our times, these meters, as well as free verse, compete successfully with the traditional syllabic verse.

In *Czech* the 8-syllable line formed the backbone of both lyric and epic Old Czech poetry, with a pronounced trochaic tendency in the former, and syntactic parallelism approaching a constant in the latter. Dramatic works, on the other hand, were based on asyllabism. Syllabic-accentual meters, with a trochaic and iambic cadence, became popular during the Hussite movement with the flourishing of religious songs. But as a consequence of the frequent discrepancy between music and meter, and the general decline of secular poetry, the 15th and 16th c. saw a return to purely syllabic meters, a development which coincided with the Pol. syllabic versification and was partly influenced by it. In this system, quantity served only as an element of variation. However, in the poems and songs of the Czech humanists who imitate classical versification (Komenský, Blahoslav), it becomes the metrical principle.

At the end of the 18th c., syllabic-accentual meters, based on the congruence of foot and word boundaries, triumph in Czech poetry. The poets of the Puchmajer school adhere strictly to the metrical scheme. Later on this rigor is considerably attenuated through the use of quantity, of polysyllabic words, and of heterosyllabic, mainly dactylo-trochaic feet. The romantics (Mácha) make very skillful use of iambic feet, which are contrary to the dactylo-trochaic cadence of the Czech language. Toward the end of the 19th c., the metrical scheme is again rigorously implemented (by the *Lumírovci*) to finally cede place to the modified syllabic-accentual meters and to the vers libre of the symbolists (Březina).

In its early, Štúr period, *Slovak* poetry drew its inspiration from the local folk poetry, which is syllabic. In the last quarter of the 19th c., the Slovak poets (Hviezdoslav, Vajanský) abandoned syllabism for the syllabic-accentual meters of Czech origin, which was strictly adhered to toward the end of that century. Subsequently the syllabic-accentual frame became more flexible, to mark the transition to free rhythms.

Serbo-Croatian popular verse shows striking similarities to that of Czech and Slovak, with the difference that quantity is sometimes endowed with a metrical function (e.g. the quantitative clausula of the epic decasyllable). Dalmatian poetry of the Renaissance owed its verse forms to popular inspiration. The influence of Western (It.) poetry has here been responsible for the introduction of rhyme (and *media rima*), which replaced syntactic parallelism as a constant. Besides the epic asymmetric (4 + 6) and the lyric, symmetric (5 + 5) decasyllable, the most common meters are (8 and 12) syllabic lines (4 + 4 and 6 + 6) with a pronounced trochaic cadence. Modern poetry employs, in addition, 11-syllable lines (5 + 6). Syllabic-accentual meters appeared under foreign (German and Rus.) influence during the 19th c. (Radičević, Zmaj, Kostić; Vraz, Preradović, Šenoa, F. Marković). The division into feet is, as in Czech, dependent upon the arrangement of word boundaries. Quantity serves mainly as an element of variation, although in some positions it may substitute for stress (especially in rhymes).

The meters of modern *Slovenian* poetry, which developed in the 19th c., are syllabic-accentual. The role of quantity as a rhythmic factor is more restricted here than in Serbo-Croatian. In the poetry of Prešeren, the greatest romantic poet, who used primarily the iambic pentameter (with feminine rhyme), the metrical scheme is still rigorously observed. Modern versification (Aškerc, Župančič) has moved in the direction of relaxing the metrical requirements; it also adopted ternary meters and free verse.

Syllabic-accentual meters became the basis of *Rus.* prosody in the 1740's under German influence, following a period of syllabic verse which had reached Russia from Poland, via the Ukraine, in the 17th c. (Simeon of Polotsk, Istomin, Kantemir). From the time of Lomonosov, Trediakovsky, and Sumarokov, binary meters were used almost exclusively in the poetry of the 18th c., especially iambic tetrameter, iambic hexameter (alexandrine) and trochaic tetrameter. At the beginning of the 19th c. the iambic pentameter became widespread in the poetry of Zhukovsky, Pushkin, and others, replacing the alexandrine in dramatic poetry. In the 19th c. ternary meters also became more popular, especially in the second half of the century (Nekrasov, A. Tolstoy, Fet). While in Rus. ternary meters all downbeats, as a rule, are always stressed, in binary meters only the last downbeat in the line has a compulsory stress; stress on the other downbeats is merely a tendency. In ternary meters the excess of constants led in the 20th c. to the admission of a variable number of unstressed syllables (usually one or two) between the downbeats, giving rise to the *dol'niki* in the poetry of the symbolists and acmeists (Bryusov, Blok, Akhmatova, Gumilev, etc.) and, later, to purely accentual verse with a still freer number of unstressed syllables between downbeats (especially in some poems of Mayakovsky). Free verse (*vers libre*), based primarily on phrase intonation rather than on the number of stresses per line, was introduced into Rus. poetry by Blok and Kuzmin, but it was never widely adopted as it was in other Slavic literatures (Czech, Polish, and Serbo-Croatian). Syllabic-accentual meters, especially the iambic, constitute the bulk of Rus. verse up to the present. In addition to the stress and syllabics, in Rus. prosody the arrangement of word boundaries is also free to serve as an element of variation.

Ukrainian and *Bulgarian* learned poetry of the 19th c. (Shevchenko, Botev) is indebted for its verse forms to the popular tradition of the folk song, which shows a strong tendency toward a fixed arrangement of word groups within the short line and a division into hemistichs in the long line. Subsequently Bulgarian and Ukrainian poetry underwent the influence of Rus. syllabic-accentual versification, which became the prevailing norm, with the exception of Western Ukrainian poetry, where purely syllabic verse is still written. In this century, the *dol'niki* (Tychina, Javorov) and vers libre have competed also with the syllabotonic meters.

See especially R. Jakobson, "Studies in Comparative Slav. Metrics," OSP, 3 (1952) and "The Kernel of Comp. Slav. Lit.," HSS, I (1953). The most recent and most comprehensive attempts at a reconstruction of Common Slav. pros.—S. Furmanik, *Podstawy wersyfikacji polskiej* (1947; a clear, though somewhat mechanical survey of the principles of Polish pros.); M. R. Mayenowa (ed.), *Wiersz*, II cz. I (1963), *Sylabizm*, III (1956), *Sylabotonizm*, IV (1957), (*Wersyfikacja*, important ser. *Poetyka, Polska Akademja Nauk*). The most comprehensive v. on two types of Pol. meters.—J. Mukařovský, "Český verš. Obecné zásady a vývoj novočeského verše"; R. Jakobson, "Verš staročeský," 376–429, 429–459, *Československá Vlastivěda*, III (1934; compreh. outlines of the hist. of Czech verse); M. Bakoš, *Vývin slovenského verša od školy Štúrovej* (2d ed., 1949; a synthetic survey of Slovak versification); K. Horálek, *Zarys dziejów czeskiego wiersza* (1957; a brief historical survey of Czech and Slovak verse).—S. Matić, "Principi umetničke versifikacje srpske," *Godišnica N. Čupića* (1930–32; a thorough, though one-sided, study of Serbo-Croatian syllabic meters); R. Košutić, *O tonskoj metrici u novoj srpskoj poezji* (1941; a compreh. study of syllabo-tonic versific., but with a normative bias); K. Taranovski, "Principi srpskohrvatske versifikacije," *Prilozi za knjiženost*, 20 (1954) and "The Prosodic Structure of Serbo-Croat Verse," OSP, 9 (1960; briefer treatment); A. V. Isačenko, *Slovenski verz* (1939; brief survey of Slovenian metrics, with a comparative outlook).—B. V. Tomashevsky, *Russkoe stikhoslozhenie* (1923; a balanced and compreh. work on the structure of Rus. verse); B. M. Zhirmunsky, *Vvedenie v metriku. Teoriya stikha* (1925; clear and well-documented, somewhat controversial study on the structure of Rus. verse); K. Taranovski, *Ruski dvodelni ritmovi* I-II (1953); B. O. Unbegaun, *Rus. Versification* (1956; useful introd. to the hist. and structure of Rus. verse).—V. Jakubs'kyj, *Nauka viršuvannja* (1922; a compreh. study of the principles of Ukrainian pros.)—A. Balabanov, "B' 'lgarski stix," *Iz edin život* (1934); M. Janakiev, *B' 'lgarsko stixoznamie* (1960; up-to-date survey of the hist. of Bulgarian verse). E.ST.

SOLILOQUY. See MONOLOGUE.

SONG. In general, any music of the human voice, most often modulating the words of speech; more specifically, a poem or other formalized utterance and its musical setting, whether composed together or separately, the text before the melody, or vice versa. One might distinguish "s." from what is thought of as "chant" with reference to the smaller melodic range and less sharply defined contours of the latter, and to the fact that one seldom speaks of an accompanied s. as a "chant." It might be observed that we tend to apply the notion of "chanting" to what we consider either primitive or else highly ritualized passages of singing, whether the indigenous singing of non-Indo-European cultures, unfamiliar to Western ears, or, on the other hand, to the prolonged intonation of narrative or scriptural texts. Another useful distinction between s. proper (in its literal, modern sense) and the word's more extended range of applicability can best be pointed out by invoking a distinction between the modern Fr. *chant* and *chanson:* the latter being generally used to refer to what are literally "songs," the former covering the extended senses of "poem," "lyric utterance," "recitation," etc. (Occurrences of such usage apparently as perverse as in *Le Chanson de Roland* and, generically, in *chanson de geste,* however, resulted from their application to long poems which were nevertheless sung to short, interminably repeated, melodic fragments.) At various times, particularly before the development of modern conceptions of literary or musical genres, we may find "s." standing for poems, narratives, and musical compositions almost indiscriminately; but at such times there is almost always a wealth of nomenclature whereby different sorts of forms and functions serve to draw any necessary distinctions. The types of troubadour lyric, for example, are organized with respect not only to verse form (*vers*) but to purpose (*planh, sirventes*) and peculiarities of genesis (*tenso*) as well. In these cases, incidentally, the melodic structure of the music is by and large entailed by the versification, and since both text and melody were generally composed by the troubadour himself, we might almost wish to employ him as the model of the "singer" (in every sense but that of actual performer) in postclassical times.

Up through the Renaissance, "s." continues to refer either to a musico-poetic entity or, at times (and particularly under the influence of antiquity), to a poetic text alone. It is only during the later 15th and the 16th c., however, that modern categories of type of s. begin to be useful. Even assuming (in the 16th c., at any rate) one basic canonical musical language, that of high-Renaissance polyphony, a category of musical types, such as songs of various numbers of parts, those with prescribed accompaniments and those without, etc. may be employed. And categories of subject (amatory, pastoral, satiric, narrative, religious, etc.), poetic form (sonnet, various ode forms, etc.) and function (dramatic lyrics, masque songs, postprandial madrigals, etc.) become necessary, in the light of 16th-c. practice, as descriptive terms.

It is with the notion of s. as *chant* rather than as *chanson,* however, that literary history is primarily concerned. The processes by which more purely literary senses accrued to the word "s." must themselves be studied, of course, against the background of the tangled history of musico-poetic relations. The splitting into separate practices and concepts, in postclassic times, of music, poetry, and dance in no way interfered with the transmission of a literary heritage in which "singing" could now be taken metaphorically as "writing" and the Apollonian lyre as an inspiring muse. The 12th and 13th c., it is true, saw a reunification of music and lyric poetry in the art of the troubadours, trouvères and Minnesänger; even the 14th c. saw an important lyric poet as well as a truly great polyphonic composer in Guillaume de Machaut, and there are cases, like that of the German Oswald von Wolkenstein, of poet-composers as late as the 15th c. After this, however, such names as that of Thomas Campion come to represent the extremely rare exceptions.

But if the 16th c. saw a separation of roles of poet and musician, there nevertheless occurred a temporary identification of *chant* and *chanson.* Short lyric poems of almost any kind, including those like the sonnet whose real heritage was purely literary and intellectual, were written in the conscious knowledge that they were candidates for musical setting. Secular vocal composers turned to plays, sonnet sequences, pastorals, miscellanies, etc. for their texts, and any poem, regardless of its particular literary intention, might end up in a s. book. But even amidst this burst of harmonious musical and literary activity, the notion of *chant* began to crystallize out. An early and significant case is that of the envoy of Spenser's *Epithalamion,* in the lines that seem to summarize so nicely much of the Elizabethan aesthetic (ll. 427–8):

> Song, made in lieu of many ornaments
> With which my love should duly have bene
>   dect. . . .

Here, "song" = "literary composition," pure and simple; and it is thus that "s." comes to designate lyric poems, not necessarily composed as candidates for possible setting at all, throughout the 17th c. The metaphysical lyric, commencing perhaps with Donne's *Songs and Sonnets,* poses a special problem. If we were to contrast the Elizabethan and metaphysical lyric with respect to their musical status, we should have to remark that it is the former that models itself on the *chanson* text, and that the latter tends to approach more and more a formal argument, a quasi-scriptural or philosophical "text" for study, contemplation, exegesis, etc. The metaphysical lyric may be said to be more semantically dense than we would expect the text of a *chanson* to be: the rapidity, that is, with which its highly complex statement moves forward is even greater than the movement of the formal verse itself. The density of a *chanson* text, on the other hand, would be lessened to the degree that its thought progressed less slowly than its own (prosodic) or accompanying (actual) music. Musicians will recognize here a useful analogy to the musical concept of *harmonic rhythm,* which similarly treats of the "density" or rapidity of harmonic change with respect to rhythmic flow.

By and large, it is this rarer semantic density which characterizes the actual s. text throughout the later 17th and 18th c.; and even within the context of the over-all development of lyric poetry, the *chanson* remains a more or less trivial poetic form. In drama, with the possible sole exception of the opening, programmatic lyric in Dryden's *Marriage à la Mode,* nothing approaches the variety and intricacy of purpose to which songs are put by Shakespeare. The development of opera and the exigencies of libretto-writing gradually eclipse in importance, while perhaps never surpassing, the proto-operatic songs of Jonson's masques.

In general, it is only rarely that long or ambitious lyric poems like Smart's *A Song to David* or Blake's *Songs of Innocence* are actually so called, and it is interesting that the title of so important a manifesto as the Wordsworth-Coleridge *Lyrical Ballads* avoids the word almost pointedly. Throughout the 19th c., nevertheless, a greater tendency may be noted to unify *chant* and *chanson,* the German lyric appearing as a *Lied,* for example, and the flourishing of the art-song in eneral as a musical development contributing to this in no small part. In the latter half of the century, however, the notion of *chant* seems to undergo its greatest extended application; with the heritage of the *symboliste* movement and its reverberations in the poetry of many languages up through the present century, "s." comes to be used more and more in perverse and ironic ways, finally coming to name or describe any poem, in verse or prose, and of whatever length. Interestingly enough, it is during this same later 19th c. that an overextended musical sense of "s." begins to develop, in the short instrumental (usually piano) solo piece entitled *chant sans paroles,* and later, simply, "song." See LYRIC; MUSIC AND POETRY.

J. B. Beck, *La Musique des troubadours* (1910); J. R. Noble, *Shakespeare's use of S.* (1923): E. H. Fellowes, *The Eng. Madrigal* (1925); P. Warlock, *The Eng. Ayre* (1926); J. M. Edmonds, "An Account of Gr. Lyric Poetry," *Lyra Graeca,* ed. and tr. J. Edmonds (2d ed., III, 1928); G. Bontoux, *Le Chanson en Angleterre au temps d'Elizabeth* (1936); M. Bukofzer, *Music in the Baroque Era* (1947); *Historical Anthol. of Music,* ed. A. T. Davison and W. Apel (2v., 1949–50); A. Einstein, *Essays on Music* (1956); Beare, *A Hist. of S.,* ed. D. Stevens (1960); C. M. Bowra, *Primitive S.* (1962).

J.H.

SONNET (fr. It. *sonetto,* a little sound or song). A 14-line poem in iambic pentameter (normally iambic hexameter in France) whose rhyme scheme has, in practice, been widely varied despite the traditional assumption of limited freedom in this respect. The three most widely recognized forms of the s., with their traditional rhyme schemes, are the It. or Petrarchan (octave: *abbaabba;* sestet: *cdecde* or *cdcdcd* or a similar combination that avoids the closing couplet), the Spenserian (*abab bcbc cdcd ee*), and the Eng. or Shakespearean (*abab cdcd efef gg*). With respect to the It. pattern (by far the most widely used of the three) it will be observed that a two-part division of thought is invited, and that the octave offers an admirably unified pattern and leads to the *volta* (q.v.) or "turn" of thought in the more varied sestet. The effect of the *abbaabba* octave is truly remarkable. It is actually a blend of 3 brace-rhyme quatrains, since the middle 4 verses, whose sounds overlap the others and echo their pattern, impress the reader with a similar rhyme pattern, thus, ab*baab*ba. Normally, too, a definite pause is made in thought development at the end of the eighth verse, serving to increase the independent unity of an octave that has already progressed with the greatest economy in rhyme sounds. Certainly it would be difficult to conceive a more artistically compact and phonologically effective pattern. The sestet, in turn, leads out of the octave and, if the closing couplet is avoided, assures a commendable variety within uniformity to the poem as a whole. The Spenserian and Shakespearean patterns, on the other hand, offer some relief to the difficulty of rhyming in Eng. and invite a division of thought into 3 quatrains and a closing or summarizing couplet; and even though such arbitrary divisions are frequently ignored by the poet, the more open rhyme schemes tend to impress the fourfold structure on the reader's ear and to suggest a stepped progression toward the closing couplet. Such matters of relationship between form and content are, however, susceptible of considerable control in the hands of a skilled poet, and the ultimate effect in any given instance may override theoretical considerations in achievement of artistic integrity.

Most deviations from the foregoing patterns have resulted from liberties taken in rhyming, but there have been a few novelties in use of the s. that may be mentioned, among them the following: *caudate,* with "tails" of added verses; *continuous or iterating,* on one or two rhyme sounds throughout; *retrograde,* reading the same backward as forward; *chained or linked,* each verse beginning with the last word of the preceding verse; *interwoven,* with medial as well as end rhyme; *crown of sonnets,* a series joined together by rhyme or repeated verses, for panegyric; *terza rima sonnet* (q.v.), with a rhyme scheme corresponding to terza rima; *tetrameter,* in tetrameters instead of pentameters. Meredith's *Modern Love* sequence is clearly related to the s. in its themes and its *abba cddc effe ghhg* rhyme pattern, but whether these 16-line poems should be admitted to the canon is questionable.

Historically, s. beginnings centered about the It. pattern, and it is probable that the form resulted from the addition of a double refrain of 6 lines (2 tercets) to the 2-quatrain Sicilian *strambotto.* In any event (for the origins must remain uncertain) the earliest antecedents of the "true" It. s. are credited to Giacomo da Lentino (fl. 1215–1233) whose hendecasyllables usually rhymed *abababab cdecde.* Although others of Lentino's contemporaries (the Abbot of Tivoli, Jacopo Mostacii, Pierro delle Vigne, Monaldo d'Aquino) used the form and established the octave-sestet divisions (with quatrain-tercet subdivisions), it remained for Guittone d'Arezzo (1290–1294) to establish the *abbaabba* octave, which became traditional through its preference by Dante (*Vita Nuova; Canzoniere*) and Petrarch (*Canzoniere*); and for Antonio da Tempo, in his *Summa Artis Rithimici* (1332), to enunciate the first theoretical discussion of the s. as a type. The sonnets of Dante to Beatrice, and of Petrarch to Laura ("spells which unseal the inmost enchanted fountains of the delight which is the grief of love" [Shelley]) normally opened with a strong statement which was then developed; but they were not unmarked by the artificiality of treatment that stemmed from variations on the Platonic love themes, an artificiality that was to be exported with the form in the 15th and 16th c. as the s. made its way to Spain, Portugal, France, the Netherlands, Poland, and England, and later to Germany, Scandinavia, and Russia; until its use was pan-European and the number of poets not using it negligible. Following Petrarch there was in Italy some diminution of dignity in use of the form (as in Serafino dall'Aquila [1466–1500]), but with the work of Tasso (1544–1595) and his contemporaries (Michelangelo, Bembo, Castiglioni) the s. was reaffirmed as a structure admirably suited to the expression of emotion in lyrical mood, adaptable to a wide range of subject matter (love, politics, religion, etc.), and employed with skill by many writers in the centuries to follow (Alfieri, Foscolo, Carducci, D'Annunzio).

It was the Marquis de Santillana (1398–1458) who introduced the pattern to Spain, although it was not established there until the time of Juan Boscán (1490–1552) and, especially, Garcilaso de la Vega (1503–1536), and Lope de Vega (1562–1635) and other dramatists of the *siglo de oro.* Sá de Miranda (1485–1558) and his disciple, Antonio Ferreira, brought the s. to Portugal, where it is better known in the *Rimas* of Camões (1524–1580) and, more recently, in the exquisite work of Anthero de Quental (1842–1891). Clément Marot (1496–1544) and Mellin de Saint Gelais (1491–1558) introduced it to France, but it was Joachim du Bellay (1522–1560) who was most active, writing (in the Petrarchan pattern) the first non-Italian cycle, *L'Olive*, as well as *Regrets* and *Les Antiquités de Rome* (translated by Spenser as *The Ruins of Rome*). Ronsard (1524–1585) who experimented with the form in alexandrines, and Philippe Desportes (1546–1606) wrote many sonnets and were instrumental in stimulating interest both at home and in England; while Malherbe (1555–1628) put the weight of his authority behind the *abbaabba ccdede* or *ccdced* pattern in alexandrines, which became the accepted line length. After a period of decline (general throughout Europe) in the 18th c., Théophile Gautier (1811–1872) and Baudelaire (1821–1867) revived the form, which soon reached new heights in the work of Heredia, Lecomte de Lisle, Valéry, Mallarmé, and Rimbaud. Germany received the form relatively late, in the writings of G. R. Weckherlin (1584–1653) and, especially insofar as creative achievement is concerned, Andreas Gryphius (1616–1664). There followed a period of disuse until Gottfried Bürger (1747–1794) revived the form and anticipated its use by Schlegel, Eichendorff, Tieck, and other romantic writers. The sonnets of August Graf von Platen (1796–1835; *Sonette aus Venedig*) rank among the best in modern times, while in more recent years the mystical sequence, *Sonette an Orpheus* (1923), of Rilke and the writings of R. A. Schröder have brought the German s. to another high point.

In England the s. has had a fruitful history. Wyatt (1503–1542) brought the form from Italy but showed an immediate preference (possibly influenced by the work of minor writers while he was abroad) for a closing couplet in the sestet. Wyatt did, however, adhere to the Petrarchan octave, and it was Surrey (1517–1547) who established the accepted *abab cdcd efef gg,* a pattern more congenial to the comparatively rhyme-poor Eng. language. This pattern was used extensively in the period, but by no means exclusively for there was wide variety in rhyme schemes and line lengths. It was brought to its finest representation by Shakespeare. A rhyme scheme more attractive to Spenser (and in its first 9 lines paralleling his Spenserian stanza) was *abab bcbc cdcd ee,* in effect a compromise between the more rigid It. and the less rigid Eng. patterns. The period also saw many s. cycles, beginning with Sidney's *Astrophel and Stella* (1580) and continuing in the sequences of Daniel (*Delia*), Drayton (*Idea*), Spenser (*Amoretti*), and Shakespeare; with a shift to religious themes shortly thereafter in John Donne's *Holy Sonnets.* It remained for Milton to introduce the true It. pattern, to break from sequences to occasional sonnets, to give a greater unity to the form by frequently permitting octave to run into sestet (the "Miltonic" sonnet, but anticipated by the Elizabethans), and a greater richness to the texture by employing his principle of "apt numbers, fit quantity of syllables, and the sense variously drawn out from one verse into another," as in his blank verse. Milton's was the strongest influence when, after a century of disuse, the s. was revived in the late 18th c. by Gray, T. Warton, Cowper, and Bowles; and reestablished in the early 19th by Wordsworth (also under Milton's influence but easing rhyme demands by use of an *abbaacca* octave in nearly half of his more than 500 sonnets); and by Keats, whose frequent use of the Shakespearean pattern did much to reaffirm it as a worthy companion to the generally favored Miltonic-Italian. By this time the scope of s. themes had broadened widely, and in Leigh Hunt and Keats it even embraced an unaccustomed humor. S. theory was also developing tentatively during this period (as in Hunt's "Essay on the Sonnet") to eventuate in an unrealistic extreme of purism in T.W.H. Crosland's *The Eng. Sonnet* (1917) before it was more temperately approached by later writers. Since the impetus of the romantic revival, the form has had a continuing and at times distinguished use, as in D. G. Rossetti (*The House of Life*), Christina Rossetti, E. B. Browning (*Sonnets from the Portugese*), and the facile work of Swinburne. Few writers in the present century (W. H. Auden and Dylan Thomas might be named) have matched the consistent level of production found in the earlier work, although an occasional single s., such as Yeats's "Leda and the Swan," has rare beauty.

The s. did not appear in America until the last quarter of the 18th c., in the work of Colonel David Humphreys, but once introduced, the form spread rapidly if not distinctively until Longfellow (1807–1882), using the It. pattern, lifted it in dignity and lyric tone (especially in the *Divina Commedia* sequence) to a level easily equal to its counterpart in England. Following him there was wide variety in form and theme, with commendable work from such writers as Lowell, George Henry Boker, and Paul Hamilton Hayne. Of the later writers E. A. Robinson, Edna St. Vincent Millay, Merrill Moore, Allen Tate, and E. E. Cummings hold a recognized place, although, space permitting, many others might be named who stand well above what Robinson called

> . . . these little sonnet men
> Who fashion, in a shrewd mechanic way,
> Songs without souls, that flicker for a day,
> To vanish in irrevocable night.

During the past century s. themes in both Europe and America have broadened to include almost any subject and mood, even though the main line of development has remained remarkably stable. Structurally, even within the traditional patterns, the type has reflected the principal influences evident in modern poetry as a whole: the sprung rhythm of Hopkins and free-verse innovations have frequently led to less metronomic movement within the iambic norm; substitutions for exact rhymes have supplied fresher sound relationships; and a more natural idiom has removed much of the artificiality that had long been a burden. This adaptability within a tradition of eight centuries' standing suggests that there will be no diminution of interest in and use of the form in the foreseeable future, and that the inherent difficulties that have kept the numbers of truly fine sonnets to an extremely small percentage of those that have been written will deter neither versifier nor genius from testing for himself the challenge of what Rossetti called

> . . . a moment's monument,—
> Memorial from the Soul's eternity
> To one dead deathless hour.

S. Lee, *Elizabethan Sonnets* (2 v., 1904); E. H. Wilkins, "The Invention of the S.," MP, 13 (1915; rewritten and brought up to date in his collected *Studies in It. Lit.*, Rome, 1957); T.W.H. Crosland, *The Eng. S.* (1917); R. D. Havens, "Milton and the S.," *The Influence of Milton on Eng. Poetry* (1922; excellent survey of the s. in 18th- and 19th-c. England); W. L. Bullock, "The Genesis of the Eng. S. Form," PMLA, 38 (1923); G. Bertoni, *Il Duocento* (1930); L. G. Sterner, *The S. in Am. Lit.* (1930); A. Meozzi, *Il Petrarchismo Europeo: Secolo XVI* (1934); E. Hamer, *The Eng. S.* (1936); L. C. John, *The Elizabethan S. Sequences* (1938); W. Mönch, *Das Sonett* (1955; the most comprehensive study to date, with extended bibliog.); J. W. Lever, *The Elizabethan Love S.* (1956); E. T. Prince, "The S. from Wyatt to Shakespeare," *Elizabethan Poetry*, ed. J. R. Brown and B. Harris (1960). L.J.Z.

SONNET CYCLE or sequence. A series of sonnets on a given theme or to a given individual. The effect is that of stanzas in a longer work, but with the difference that each sonnet retains its integrity as an independent poem. When this is not the case, as in William Ellery Leonard's moving *Two Lives* (1925), the sonnet loses much of its force as a type and becomes in fact "stanzaic." At times the sequence will be given added unity by use of repetition, either of rhymes or of lines, between the different poems, as in the "crown of sonnets" (q.v.). From the earliest times the cycle has been used to amplify the limited scope of the single sonnet and to reflect the many facets of the chosen theme. Among the most famous or noteworthy of these cycles may be named Dante's *Vita Nuova*, Petrarch's *Canzoniere*, du Bellay's *L'Olive* (the first non-It. cycle), Camões' *Rimos*, Sidney's *Astrophel and Stella* (the first cycle in England), Spenser's *Amoretti*, Shakespeare's *Sonnets*, Donne's *Holy Sonnets*, Wordsworth's *Ecclesiastical Sonnets*, Rossetti's *The House of Life*, E. B. Browning's *Sonnets from the Portuguese*, George Henry Boker's *A Sequence on Profane Love*, Longfellow's *Divina Commedia*, Arthur Davison Ficke's *Sonnets of a Portrait Painter*, Edna St. Vincent Millay's *Fatal Interview*, and Rilke's *Sonette an Orpheus*. L.J.Z.

SOUND IN POETRY. This subject has attracted much controversy. One reason is our psychophysiological variety. Human beings are divisible into pure verbalizers who can think only in words, pure visualizers who use only visual images, and two larger groups, *predominantly* verbal or visual; a verbalizer unconsciously says words for his thoughts over to himself, as betrayed by his breathing. (Cf. *Science News*, 24 [May 1952], 7–21.) Presumably most poets "verbalize"; poems by exclusive visualizers must depend solely on images, and their sound structure will be conventional or scarcely organized (Blake? Whitman?). Many poets "chant" their verses and, even if they recite in monotone, give full play to vowel and consonant values. Berry (1962) claims that a poet's work matches the physical characteristics of his voice. With Valéry, we may consider a poem on paper as merely an inadequate "musical score."

SOURCE. Human prelanguage may have been a set of predispositions towards fluid utterances partly expressing emotion and need. Poetry, concerned so much with expression, can embody such primitive mechanisms. Expression through sound utterance (now under its own conventions) involves pitch, stress, duration, voice quality, articulatory gesture, phonetic *timbre*, and pattern in time: all can be organized into a formally satisfying poem or chant, or used expressively and decoratively. As music and poetry differentiate, pitch and duration are drawn more into music, articulation and phonetic timbre more into poetry.

A tendency to reduplicative phonetic patterns seems innate in man. They occur in infant babbling; in certain languages; in strong feeling; in spells; in oaths; in proverbial expressions; in oratory; and in advertisements. The chants of modern "primitive" tribes reveal a repetitive structure: refrains, word repetitions, syllable echoes; but these features are already often stylized.

SOUND AS STRUCTURE. Sound effects must be felt against the whole phonology of a language (see TONE-COLOR), the fundamentals of its verse (see ALLITERATIVE METER, CLASSICAL PROSODY, RHYME, CELTIC PROSODY, CYNGHANEDD, and [for syllabic verse] METER, PROSODY); and the particular verse form. Welsh *cynghanedd* crystallized complex phonetic sequences. Legitimate changes rung on structural forms are often exploited musically or expressively. Thus in *pollá d' ánanta kátanta páranta te dókhmiá t' ēlthon* dactyls replace spondees wherever permissible: one reason why the line is appropriate to horses cantering. If *ictus* (metrical beat) was present in classical verse, effects could be achieved by counterpoint with the prose accent, as claimed by W. F. Jackson Knight in Virgil; "reversal of foot" and "ionic foot" are expressive in accentual, and stress-clumping in nonsyllabic verse. The line-internal pause or *caesura* can be expressively shifted. Variation, and grouping, of rhyme-vowels (and rhyme-consonants) has been observed in, e.g., the Eng. Renaissance by Oras.

SOUND AS TEXTURE. The whole body of free sound in verse is available for exploitation. There are periods, usually those in which spoken verse existed side by side with sung verse, as in the Elizabethan or the European Renaissance, when conscious virtuosity in varieties of word repetition, in wordplay, and in sound echoes, is the rule; individuals have also used blatant alliteration etc.; but in civilized verse, alliteration at the expense of sincere expression often defeats the objects of poetry: cf. Poe, Swinburne. Duration-variation may be achieved by grouping sounds either "cloggingly" or "trippingly": contrast the two 5-beat "iambic" lines "Rocks, Caves, Lakes, Fens, Bogs, Dens, and shades of death" (Milton) and "For the ripple to run over in its mirth" (Browning). Classes of vowel or consonant, somber or bright, liquid or harsh, may be grouped (see TONE-COLOR). The tissue of most verse forms a web of sound-patterning, often related to sense and mood; the poet may not have worked for it, the reader may not be aware of it, but the words were chosen, and the reader / listener reacts, under its influence; words first chosen may "attract" others of like sound, which then seem to reinforce their aura. And "le style, c'est l'homme méme" is as true (and untrue) of sound as of any other feature.

FUNCTIONS OF SOUND-MANIPULATION. These may be divided into (overlapping) types, in practice rarely isolated pure. Behind them are (a) associations of sound arrangements with certain sets of words; (b) familiarity with the grammatical function, and hence with any arbitrary use, of sounds as mere labels; (c) traditional and accepted synaesthesias (see ONOMATOPOEIA, TONE-COLOR); (d) vocal / facial emotive expression; (e) instinctive satisfaction in sounds, articulations, and reiterations. Types A-C below are especially concerned with (aspect 1) the *formal structure* of the verse; types D-H, with (2) the *sense*; I-K (also D, H) with (3) the *scene*; L-0 (G) with (4) the *feeling;* and P-R with (5) the *aesthetic flavor.* We start each of these five groups here with its crudest type. Apart from the Emphases (A, D, L) the functions in group 2 are mainly symbolic, in groups 3 and 4 mainly representational. In the face of sound effects under aspect 2 it is helpful to list the words involved in each phonetic theme; under 3 and 4 careful study of the subtleties of sensory metaphor is essential; under 5 an analysis of the patterning is needed for full understanding. Many of our examples here are necessarily too short.

A. (Under aspect 1.) *Structural Emphasis* (i.e. of the form). A rhetorical addition to the formally required sound structure. E.g. gratuitous rich-rhymes; scene-end rhyming couplets in blank verse; alliterative support as in "Against this nearest cruelest of *F*o*es* / What shall Wit meditate, or *F*orce opp*ose*?" (Prior).

B. (Under 1.) *Underpinning*: relatively subtle reinforcement of the verse structure. E.g. unobtrusive sporadically rich rhymes; Milton's compensatory line-end assonance and consonance in his blank verse (Oras, 1953). Sometimes combined with C, as follows.

C. (1.) *Counterpoising*: arrangement of some sounds in opposition to the verse structure. Notice the imperfect rhymes, distractingly echoed by internal rhyme and submerged alliteration, in "viol*et*,— / Solution sweet: meantime the frost-wind blows / . . . sl*eet* / Against . . . St. Agnes' . . . s*et*." (Keats); this compensates for the next stanza repeating this rhyme, in a different place, with "beat" and a second "sleet." Owen's *Exposure* (with a *structure* of dissonant rich-rhymes) has some complicated counterpoising.

D. (2, 3.) *Rubricating Emphasis* (i.e. of words or images). Common; in England richest in Tudor verse. In "The *t*ur*tle* *t*o her make hath *tol*de her *tale*. / So*mm*er is c*ome*, for euery *spr*ay nowe *spr*inges; / The *h*art *h*ath *h*ong *h*is olde *h*ed on the pale; / The *b*u*ck* in *b*ra*k*e his winter *c*ote he flings; / The *f*ishes *fl*ote with newe repaired scale; / The []adder []all her *sl*oughe away she *sl*inges; / The *sw*i*f*t *sw*a*ll*ow pur*s*ueth the *fl*yes *s*ma*l*e; / The *b*usy *b*ee *h*er *h*onye now she minges; / Wi*n*ter is *w*or*n*e, that *w*a*s* the flowers bale" (Surrey) striking echoes rubricate each image (besides cross-links such as *make—brake, tolde—olde, cote—flings—flote—flyes—flowers* and others).

E. (2.) *Tagging*: punctuation of syntax or thought by sounds. Common before the romantics. In "The *b*aiting-place of *w*it, the *b*alme of *w*oe" (Sidney), the analogous nouns in the two parallel phrases are respectively labeled with *b*- and *w*-; in "The pallor of girls' brows shall be their pall" (Wilfred Owen) the metaphor is *primarily* underlined by *p l* / *p l*.

F. (2.) *Correlation*: indirect support of argument by related echoes. Very common. Notice the relevance of the repeated sound-groupings in "Then fare*well*, *w*or*l*d; thy vttermost I see: / Eternal *L*o*u*e, *m*ai*n*tai*n*e thy *lif*e i*n* *m*e" (Sidney); "Five! the finding and sake / And cypher of suffering Christ. / . . . Sacrificed" (Hopkins). Types E and F also occur as pun and nearpun (paronomasia).

G. (2, 4.) *Implication*: more involved interconnection of sound, meaning, and feeling. Almost universal. Wordplay and hidden associations sometimes take part. "With his loll'd tongue he faintly licks his Prey; / His warm breath blows her flix up as she lies; / She, trembling, creeps upon the ground away, / And looks back to him with beseeching eyes" (Dryden) swarms with interlocking echoes too numerous to analyze, but including *f—liliks* / *bl—z* / *fliks* / *l—ks;* cf. "At length himself unsettling, he the pond / Stirr'd with his staff, and fixedly did look" (Wordsworth).

H. (2, 3.) *Diagramming*: the abstract pattern symbolizes the sense. Notice the criss-crossing sound patterns in Dryden's account of the Fire of London: "He wades the Streets, and streight he reaches cross." This has the sounds [e:dz] (*wades*) invading [stri:ts] (*Streets*) and transforming it into [dstre:t] (*and streight*), then in *reaches* (pronounced with [ri:tš—z] or [re:tš—z]) sending their [z] one syllable ahead to leap over in "-s cross" [zkr—s]; thus inspiredly "imitating" the mode of spread of the flames.

I. (3.) *Sound-Representation*: some similarity to the relevant sounds (see ONOMATOPOEIA). Rather rare unless adulterated; its worst excesses are baroque. "The double double double beat / Of the thund'ring DRUM" (Dryden); "Sudden successive flights of bullets streak the silence" (Owen).

J. (3.) *Illustrative Mime*: mouth-movements recall motion or shape (cf. TONE-COLOR). Rare pure. "When *P*éar*se s*úmmone*d* Cuchulain to his *side*, / Wh*at stálked* thróugh the *Post-Ó*ffice?" (Yeats); here a reader's half-conscious mouthing of the words may evoke a looming, slow-striding figure.

K. (3.) *Illustrative Painting*: articulations, sounds, or their patterns, correspond to appearances and nonacoustic sensations. "The horrid crags, by toppling convent crown'd, / The cork-trees hoar that clothe the shaggy steep, / The mountain-moss by scorching skies imbrown'd" (Byron) is chiefly appropriate to the ruggedness, dark tints, and dizzy heights (for analysis see TONE-COLOR).

L. (4.) *Passionate Emphasis* (as from the emotion). E.g. "Ruin seize thee, ruthless King" (Gray).

M. (4.) *Mood-Evocation*: choice of tone-colors resembling vocalizations natural to the emotion. Rare pure. Milton's sonnet of anger and grief on the massacre at Piedmont has all the octet rhymes and one of the two sestet rhymes in [o:], plus resonant octet-rhyme consonants.

N. (4.) *Expressive Mime*: mouth-movements ape the expression of emotion. Chiefly in dialogue. "Out of my sight, thou Serpent, that name best / Befits thee with him leagu'd, thy self as false / And hateful" (Milton): in the succession *s—t / s—p—t / b—st / b—f—ts / s—lf—zf—ls / tf—l* the reader's mouth is made to spit out Adam's hatred.

O. (4.) *Expressive Painting*: sounds, articulations, or their arrangement, correspond to feelings or impressions. Certain repeated sounds express monotony in "And the dull wheel hums doleful through the day" (Crabbe); Shelley's revolutionary fervour is conveyed in the *s, sk,* and *sp* sounds of "Liberty . . . o'er Spain, / scattering contagious fire into the sky, / Gleamed. My soul spurned the chains of its dismay"; for analyses see TONE-COLOR.

P. (5.) *Ebullience*: pure exuberance or pleasure in sound. Seldom alone. "The wealthy crops of whit'ning rice / 'Mongst thyine woods and groves of spice, / For ADORATION grow; / . . . Where wild carnations blow" (Smart) includes the ten interwoven motifs *w—l, th (—)i, kr—s / gr—z, ps / sp, wī, wī'n / īnw, r—s / r—z, w—d, grō, ation.*

Q. (5.) *Embellishment*: superficially "musical." More frequent through the Renaissance (cf. Surrey under D), possibly as compensation for verse not sung. "No clowde was seene, but christaline the ayre, / Laughing for joy vpon my louely fayre" (Drayton) includes the five motifs *n—kl / k . . . l—n, s—n / s . . . n, r . . . l / rl, l—f / l—v, l(—) if—r.*

R. (5.) *Incantation*: profoundly musical or magical. Not infrequent pure, but disappears during the neoclassical period. Adequate analyses impossible here. Enobarbus describing Cleopatra in the barge (*A. & C.* 2.2.191–94); "The *Sounds, and Seas with* all their *finny drove / Now* to the *Moon in wavering Morrice move*" (Milton); "Of perilous seas in faery lands forlorn" (Keats), esp. *v . . . l . . . n / f . . . l—n / f—l—n*; "Shrill music reach'd them on the middle sea" (Tennyson) with *ilm / i / them / themi—l*; "That dolphin-torn, that gong-tormented sea" (Yeats).

SURVEY (Classical, Romance, Eng. and Germanic, Slavonic). *Gr. civilisation* achieved refinements of sound effect. Such writers as Homer, Sappho, Aeschylus, Pindar afford florid sound-patternings. Gr. and L. suffered from excess of like-endings, but other consonances are common, usually parceled out rather as in It. or Fr.: "**Dio**m**ē**dea d' ámbroton ksanthá po*te* **Glaukôpis** éth*ē*ke *the*on; / **gaîa** d' en ***Th*ē**bais hüpédekto keraunothe**î**sa *Dios* bélesin / mántin Oikleídan, polémoio néphos" (Pindar); which also includes such echo-progressions as: *oto / ot / to / oth, po / po / pho, ám / má, deadám / den / éde / eídan, éthēk-eth / édekt—ke.* Demetrius *On Style* writes of imitative words and the virtues of vivid cacophony in Homer; cites musicians who distinguish "smooth" words (vocalic, e.g. *Aías*), "rough" (*bébrōke*), etc.; defends juxtaposed vowels as harmonious; and commends long vowels and lengthened consonants (*Kallistratos*). In the 1st c. B.C. Dionysius of Halicarnassus writes an elaborate analysis of composition, especially sound; double letters like *x* are preferred for sonority, *sigmatism* is condemned, short vowels (especially *e*) are thought ugly; imitative words are illustrated from Homer (e.g. *rhókhthei* "crashes out"); many Homeric examples of sound echoing sense are analyzed, some mainly rhythmical like the famous lines on Sisyphus' stone, but most phonemic.

L. writers (rhetorician-inspired?) use abundant sound-patterning, too rich for a structural code which has been suggested. There is much underpinning, embellishment, painting, sound representation, and mime. Catullus, Virgil especially, Horace, Ovid, even Juvenal, are the great practitioners: "frīgora mītescunt Zephirīs, uēr prōterit *ae*stās / interitūra, sim*ul* / pōmifer *au*tumn*us* frūgēs eff*ū*derit, *e*t mox / br*ū*ma rec*urr*it in*ers*" (Horace) has recurrent motifs in *fr—g* and *ī* (for cold), *fr* / *f—r, fu, rū* / *urr* / *ūr, mu* / *um* / *ūm, pō, cu, terit, in, erit, t—m* / *tm*, etc. Herescu's study concentrates much on patterns in ictus-bearing vowels (italicized in the quotation above), but without "long / short" distinction.

Early medieval L. hymns became accentual and developed rhyme. They also show texture: "Pange, lingua, gloriosi proelium certaminis, / Et super crucis tropaeo dic triumphum nobilem, / Qualiter redemptor orbis immolatus vicerit" (Venantius Fortunatus, c. 600) includes the four themes *p—elí* / *préli* / *pér* / *r—pé, čert* / *ét* /*pér* / *r—č* / *čerìt, up—rkru* / *tr—p* / *ktr—úmpu* /*mpt—r, ór* / *pr* / *p—r* / *rop* / *óbil* / *ptorórbi* / *ol.*

Mediterranean vernacular poets developed a host of rhymed song-forms, etc., some with intricate repetitions like the *leixa-pren.* But rich textures appear too: "Quant l'erba fresqu' e-l fuelha par / E la flors botona el verjan, / E-l rossinhols autet e clar / Leva sa votz e mou son chan, / Joy ai de luy e joy ai de la flor / E joy de me e de midons major; / Daus totas partz suy de joy claus e sens, / Mas sel es joys que totz autres joys vens" (Bernart de Ventadorn, ca. 1150, in Provençal) includes the following in succession: *ler* / *fre* / *elfwe(lh)* / *flors* / *ver* / *lros* / *olsaut* / *levasav* / *laflor* / *jóidemé, edem—dó'm—jó* / *aus* / *aus* / *esens* / *seles* / *saut*; cf., e.g., such diverse poets as Arnaut Daniel in Provençal, Chrétien de Troyes and Guy de Coucy in Fr., Giacomo Pugliese in It., all 1150–1250.

It. Dante's word-classification betters Demetrius'; his onomatopoeia, implication, harmony recall Virgil's: "Ora incomincian le dolenti note / A [f]farmisi sentire: or son venuto / Là [d]dove [m]molto pianto mi percuote" includes "earstriking" *òt* / *to* / *ólto* / *to* / *òt* and at least 13 other motifs, some with stress-shunting in *co, om* /*mo, mi, ián, l—do, le, enti, ent* / *en—t, nt, ol, s—n, ve, m . . . p . . . t.* Later masters are Petrarch, Boiardo, Tasso, Marino, Testi; 19–20th c.: Leopardi, Carducci, D'Annunzio, Ungaretti, Montale, Quasimodo.

In Sp., the few different vowels, never "long," go with a tendency to simple vowel patterns which embellish or underpin a line or neighboring lines. Renaissance masters, preluded by Mena, include Garcilaso, Luis de León, Carrillo y Sotomayor, Góngora: "De *púrpura,* y de *nieve* [-ɛβɛ] / fl*o*rida la *cabeza* [-βɛ-] *coronado*, / *a* d*u*lc*es* *pastos* *mueve*, / sin h*onda,* ni *c*ay*ado* / el *buen pas*t*or, en* ti su h*ato* am*ado*" (León); 19–20th c.: Darío, Lorca, Jiménez. *Portuguese*—Renaissance: Sá de Miranda and the great Camões; 17th c.: Rodriguez Lobo; 18th c.: Bocage; 19–20th c.: Quental, Junqueiro, Nobre, Castro, Pessanha, "Modernists" SáCarneiro and Pessoa, also Mourão-Ferreira and others of today.

Fr. The 15th-c. *Grands Rhétoriqueurs* use a host of conscious echoes and repetitions for embellishment. The 16th-c. *Pléiade* and their followers are rich in deliberate patterning, chiefly for implication, rubrication, painting, or incantation: "Puis tout à coup, avec sa trouppe belle / D'un saut léger en l'onde se lança, / L'eau jette un son, et en tournoyant toute" (Du Bellay) has the succession *tout* / *oup* / *troup* / *léjè* / *anl* / *lan* / *l—jè* / *antour* / *antout*; in 1587 he remarks that *a, o, u, m, b, s, r* "sont une grande sonnerie et batterie aux vers." The Pléiade were influenced by Dionysius; they restored sung verse, and regarded recital as an important test of a harmonious style. Jacques Pelletier had introduced the notion of *harmonie imitative* (chiefly sound-representation); this could be exceedingly crude, as in the punning "La gentille Alouette avec son tire-lire, / Tire l'ire à l'iré, et tirelirant tire / Vers la voute du ciel; puis son vol vers ce lieu / Vire, et désire dire: adieu Dieu, adieu Dieu" (Du Bartas).

Reaction against excess begins with Malherbe, whose echoes are discreet and more logical: "Je crains à l'avenir la *faut*e que j'ai *fait*e" (tagging). In the supreme artist Racine some celebrated lines are richly patterned for correlation or, as in the *afflige* line, for dramatic mood-evocation; usually he produces for implication a quieter sound-scrambling: "Que, sévère aux méchants, et des bons le refuge, / Entre le pauvre et vous, vous prendrez Dieu pour juge" includes the 5 themes *évèr* / *vrév, leref* / *relep, chan* / *jan, p—vr* / *voupr* / *pour, antrelep* / *prandr—d.*

Romantics such as Vigny, Hugo (more bristling), Musset revived wealth of sound (including rich-rhymes), sound-representation and illustrative painting: "J'aime le son du cor, le soir, au fond des bois, / Soit qu'il chante les pleurs de la biche aux abois, / Ou l'adieu du chasseur que l'écho faible accueille, / Et que le vent du nord porte de feuille en feuille" (Vigny) includes the 8 themes: *swa* / *bwa* / *swa* / *bwa, leurdeula* / *ladyeud* / *euy* (3ce); *ôf* / *ôf* and *ab* / *ab* with dissonances; *f . . . euy* / *feuy* / *feuy, ilch* / *ich* / *uch, pl* /*bl, or* / *or* / *or*; and "imitative" vowels. Baudelaire employs rather subtler patterns for mystical correlation and expressive painting. The *symbolistes* meant various things by "music," but their practice often involved elaborate incantation. Mallarmé occasionally has wordplay, perhaps from Poe: "Tristement dort une mandore"; his swan-sonnet in *i* is his best-known example of extended complex patterning, there for painting and implication; but the most intricately interbonded wholes in any language are perhaps his shipwreck and *ptyx* sonnets, partly syllable for syllable, partly in whole lines and rhymes. Verlaine's "music" often depends on short lines with well-focused consonants or vowels. The Belgian Verhaeren's clamant echoings (only onomatopoeic in "Un long appel, qui long, parmi l'écho, ricoche") often amount to word-play. Valéry's exuberant patterns, for painting or emphasis, are sustained but virile: "Harmonieuse MOI, différente d'un songe, / Femme flexible et ferme aux silences suivis / D'actes purs! . . . Front limpide, et par ondes ravis, / Si loin que le vent vague et velu les achève" (© Editions Gallimard 1917 *tous droits réservés*).

Jules Romains and others instituted accord (vowel-less rhymes classified like true Fr. rhymes). Trannoy and Grammont recognize the importance of total vowel-melody in Fr.: e.g. "Voici la verte Écosse et la brune Italie" (Musset) has *a i / a è / é o / é a u / i a i* with satisfying grouping and contrast; Grammont's classification (see TONE-COLOR, as also for the earlier *instrumentalistes* and a modern Belgian critic of sound-suggestion, Delbouille) is more helpful than Trannoy's.

Eng. (see also section FUNCTIONS in this article). In contrast to the simpler syllabic structure of Fr., Eng. fosters strung-out and scrambled patterns, often all-consonant. Alliterative meter (q.v.) persisted to ca. 1400, but Chaucer's occasional patternings could represent ex-classical rhetoric. After a relatively dead period while the phonology underwent rapid changes, Wyatt's songs and Surrey's poems usher in the Renaissance; owing much to It. influence, including Surrey's assonances. Encouraged by Fr. and It. models and a new joy in language, writers produced a wealth of (syntactically) repetitive devices, codified by, e.g., Puttenham. Pun and wordplay mingled with often florid alliteration: Drayton writes one sonnet "Nothing but No and I, and I and No . . ." which is a *pas-de-deux* for these two syllables. Edwardes, Sackville, Greville, Nashe, Raleigh, Daniel, Drayton, employ plangent echoes; Constable, Spenser, Southwell are more subdued: "The sea of *For*tune doth not *ever flow,* / She d*raw*s her *favour*s to the *lowest e*bb, / Her *tides* hath e*qu*al *times to com*e and go, / Her *loom* doth *weave* the *f*ine and *coarsest w*eb," with *weave* assonating with *favours*. Shakespeare, sharing all the rhetorical tricks in his poems and early plays, also develops painting, implication, incantation: "Come, seeling Night, / Skarfe vp . . . pittiful . . . bloodie and inuisible Hand / Cancell and teare to pieces that great Bond / Which keepes me pale. Light thickens, and the Crow / Makes Wing to th' Rookie Wood" (including the seven themes [k—ms—l / sk—f / f—l / v—z—b—l / k—ns—l / k—psm—p—l], [bl—d / nd / bl / nd / b—nd], [pi:s / i:ps], [nd / nd], [k—sm . . . e: / me:ks], [θɪk / đ—k / đ . . . kɪ], [ks / k—sm / θɪk—z / m—kswɪ / đ—kɪw]). Writers like William Browne, Quarles, Herbert, continue repetition and harmony into the next century. Milton in maturity develops expression, correlation, implication, underpinning.

With Waller and Dryden and the heroic couplet forthright rhetoric increases and incantation dies down: "A R*a*ce un*c*on*q*uer'*d*, by their *Cl*ime m*ad*e b*old*, / The Ca*l*i*d*o*n*ians." Pope is richest in correlation and implicatory harmonies: "awakens ev'ry grace, / And calls forth all the wonders of her face"; he often conducts melodiously varied repetition of stressed vowels within alliteration: "Now feels my heart its long forgotten heat"; but "The Sound must seem an echo to the Sense" *may* refer to rhythm. Thomson's rubrication and Johnson's rhetoric are heavy; Dyer, Akenside, Goldsmith, more subtly implicatory: "The spring / Distills her dews, and from the silken gem / Its lucid leaves unfolds"; Gray paints delicately; Collins and Smart are flamboyant.

The commonest rhyme-vowel was and is *ā / ai* (now pronounced [eɪ]), but Pope seems especially addicted to it (25 per cent, less *-r*, of perfect rhymes in *Windsor Forest*, especially "shades"; and assonance everywhere); however, *ee, ī, oh* appear to gain ground through Keats to Tennyson; later short and dark rhyme-vowels increase. Romantics gave jostling variations their head: Keats is lushly incantatory (with some false notes), Shelley passionate, often overwrought: "I stood within the city disinterred; / And heard the autumnal leaves like light footfalls / Of spirits passing through the streets; and heard / The mountain's slumberous voice at intervals / Thrill through these roofless halls; / The oracular thunder penetrating shook / The listening soul in my suspended blood" (Latinesque in its richness and onomatopoeia). Tennyson weaves rather facile spells. Poe, though hailed apostle by Baudelaire and Mallarmé, recalls baroque excess and effect-seeking. Arnold is a milder Gray. Swinburne whips his verses along with consonants. Hopkins' welter of patterns reflects his richly "inscaped" visual world and intensity of response, as well as his interest in Welsh *cynghanedd;* he reintroduced nonsyllabic verse: "Evening strains to be tíme's vást, | womb-of-all, home-of-all, hearse-of-all night" (4 + 4 beats). Housman revived a starker alliterative rhetoric. Owen experimented with florid echoes, some for prophetic emphasis, and introduced vowel-less rich-rhyme (*brutes / brats*) expressing 1914–18 shock and disillusionment. Yeats developed (with arresting rhythms) oscasional richness and rarer "musical" organization of the whole (*Byzantium*); Eliot also, but with much wordplay; both often use thin sounds (abstract vocabulary). Wallace Stevens, another word-repeater, could offer a suave resonance or an untamed clangor. Dylan Thomas used Welsh extravagance eventually subordinated to traceable implications.

German. Simple alliteration survives piecemeal (Luther). The 17th c. has baroque devices. Klopstock and Claudius are subtler. G. sound-echoes, denser than Fr. or Eng., are more florid than It. or Sp. Theorists attend most to vowels. Goethe sets the tone (musical, pictorial): "Ihr seid mir hold, ihr gönnt mir diese Träume, / Sie schmeicheln mir und locken alte Reime. / Mir wieder selbst, von allen Menschen fern, / Wie bad' ich mich in euren Düften gern!" includes (for him) the succession *ihr'uitmihr / traime / / schmaï'elnmihr / teraime / / mihr / lenm—nschen / m / inairen*; the *Erlkönig* is noted for painting, the *Hochzeitslied* for crude onomatopoeia.

Hölderlin is sonorously rich, then starker. Tieck experiments with blatant echoes; Eichendorff is plangently, sustainedly Shelleian: "Und sie sehn ihn fröhlich steigen / Nach den Waldeshöhn hinaus, / Hören ihn von fern noch geigen, / Und gehn all vergnügt nach Haus" (cf. Vigny): note motifs in *fr / fer, n—ch, al, f—n, hön, gn / gen, ehn.* Droste-Hülshoff has bold syllabic effects; Mörike, Storm, fine painting, incantation. C. F. Meyer has dense echoes (implication): "Wolken, meine Kinder, wandern gehen / Wollt ihr? Fahret wohl! auf Wiedersehen! / Eure wandellustigen Gestalten / Kann ich nicht in Mutterbanden halten." George is measured, tableau-depictive; Hofmannsthal is incantatory; Rilke develops from undisciplined floridity to richness organized for bizarre correlations and implications.

Dutch Renaissance masters include Hooft and Vondel; 19–20th c.: Perk, Kloos, above all Verwey (e.g. *De Terrassen van Meudon*), and Mok.

Rus. masters include: Pushkin; symbolists such as Bryusov, Bal'mont (overdone alliteration) and Blok; Svetaeva, Akhmatova, and Pasternak. The postsymbolist formalist movement, which spread to other Slav countries, had much to say on the interaction of sound (i.e. both "verbal orchestration" through phonetic repetitions, and rhythm) with meaning. *Polish* masters of sound include Mickiewicz, Słowacki, Tuwim, and Pawlikowska; *Czech*: Kollár, Neruda, Wolker.

See also, ALLITERATION, ASSONANCE, CONSONANCE, DISSONANCE, EUPHONY, NEAR RHYME, ONOMATOPOEIA, REPETITION, RHYME, TONE-COLOR.

H. Werner, *Die Ursprünge der Lyrik* (1924); A. I. Trannoy, *La musique des vers* (1929); Patterson; M. M. Macdermott, *Vowel Sounds in Poetry* (1940); L. P. Wilkinson, "Onomatopoeia and the Sceptics," CQ, 36 (1942) W.F.J. Knight, *Roman Vergil* (1944); S. Bonneau, *L'univers poétique d'Alexandre Blok* (1946); M. Cressot, *Le style et ses techniques* (1947); M. Grammont, *Petit traité de versification française* (13e éd., 1949); T. Pfeiffer, *Umgang mit Dichtung* (6. Aufl., 1949); A. Spire, *Plaisir poétique et plaisir musculaire* (1949); D. Alonso, *Poesía española: ensayo de métodos y límites estilísticos* (1950); D. T. Mace, "The Doctrine of Sound and Sense in Augustan Poetic Theory," RES, n.s. 2 (1951); D. I. Masson, "Patterns of Vowel and Consonant in a Rilkean Sonnet," MLR, 46 (1951); A. Oras, "Surrey's Technique of Phonetic Echoes," JEGP, 50 (1951); R. Peacock, "Probleme des Musikalischen in der Sprache," *Weltliteratur, Festg. f. F. Strich* (1952); S. S. Prawer, *German Lyric Poetry* (1952); D. I. Masson, "Vowel and Consonant Patterns in Poetry," JAAC, 12 (1953); D. I. Masson, "Word and Sound in Yeats' *Byzantium*," ELH, 20 (1953); A. Oras, "Echoing Verse Endings in *Paradise Lost*," *South Atl. Studies f. S. E. Leavitt* (1953); A. Stein, "Structures of Sound in Milton's Verse," KR, 15 (1953); Wellek and Warren; D. I. Masson, "Free Phonetic Patterns in Shakespeare's Sonnets," *Neophilologus,* 38 (1954); H. W. Belmore, *Rilke's Craftsmanship* (1954); W. Kayser, *Das sprachliche Kunstwerk* (3. Aufl., 1954); H. Kökeritz, "Rhetorical Word-Play in Chaucer," PMLA, 69 (1954); F. Scarfe, *The Art of Paul Valéry* (1954); D. Alonso, *Estudios y ensayos gongorinos* (1955); V. Erlich, *Rus. Formalism: History—Doctrine* (1955); D. I. Masson, "Wilfred Owen's Free Phonetic Patterns," JAAC, 13 (1955); A. Oras, "Intensified Rhyme Links in *The Faerie Queene,*" JEGP, 54 (1955); E. R. Vincent, "Dante's Choice of Words," *It. Studies,* 10 (1955); J. Hollander, "The Music of Poetry," JAAC, 15 (1956); *Sound and Poetry,* ed. N. Frye (1957); *John Keats: a Reassessment,* ed. K. Muir (1958); N. I. Herescu, *La poésie latine: étude des structures phoniques* (1960); D. I. Masson, "Thematic Analysis of Sound in Poetry," *Proc.* of the Leeds Phil. & Lit. Soc., Lit. & Hist. Sec., 9, pt. 4 (1960); F. Berry, *Poetry and the Physical Voice* (1962); C. C. Smith, "La musicalidad del *Polifemo*" [Góngora], RFE, 44 (1962); D. I. Masson, "Sound & Sense in a Line of Poetry," *Brit. J. of Aesth.,* 3 (1963). See also I. Fónagy, "Communication in Poetry," *Word,* 17 (1961); L. P. Wilkinson, *Golden L. Artistry* (1963).

D.I.M.

SPANISH PROSODY. See ROMANCE PROSODY.

SPENSERIAN STANZA. An important stanza in Eng. poetry, composed of 9 iambic lines, the first 8 being pentameter and the last hexameter (alexandrine), rhyming ababbcbcc. The form was invented by Edmund Spenser for his *The Faerie Queene,* and, despite some similarity to ottava rima and to the linked octave used by Chaucer in *The Monk's Tale,* it stands out as one of the most remarkably original metrical innovations in the history of Eng. verse. The stanza is perfectly suited to the nature of Spenser's great poem, at once dreamlike and intellectual, by turns vividly narrative and lushly descriptive, for it is short enough to contain sharply etched vignettes of action and yet ample enough to lend itself to digression, description, and comment. The subtly recurring pattern of rhyme gives the stanza a formal unity, and the final alexandrine is suited to limpidly expressive emotional effects rather than, like the closing couplet of ottava rima (q.v.), to epigrammatic and witty observations.

The Sp. stanza fell into general disuse in the 17th c., although complex variations of it occurred early in the century in the work of Giles and Phineas Fletcher, and although, later, the philosopher Henry More used it in his largely forgotten allegorical narratives. Some poets of the mid-18th c. revived the stanza with enthusiasm; Shenstone's *The Schoolmistress* (1742) and, particularly, James Thomson's *Castle of Indolence* (1748) show a real grasp of its varied possibilities. Beattie's *The Minstrel* (1771–74) provides a transition to the Eng. romantics, who made the stanza one of their principal vehicles. Wordsworth's early *Guilt and Sorrow* is written in this measure, but it remained for the younger generation of romantics to produce poems in the Sp. stanza equal in merit to *The Faerie Queene.* Byron's *Childe*

Harold's Pilgrimage (1812, 1816), with its frequent changes in tone and attitude, utilizes the stanza to advantage; Keats's *Eve of St. Agnes* (1820) revives the rich sensuousness associated with Spenser's stanza as with his whole art; and Shelley's *Revolt of Islam* (1818) and *Adonais* (1821) show their author to be the greatest master of the form since its creator himself. The Sp. stanza has been seldom used since the middle of the 19th c.; an interesting example of a 20th-c. poem in this stanza is the *Dieper Leoensinkijk* (Deeper Life-Vision) of the Dutch poet Willem Kloos, which is also one of the rare examples of non-Eng. Sp. stanza.—Schipper; E. Taboureux, "The Sp. Stanza," *Revue de l'enseignement des langues vivantes,* 15 (1899), 16 (1900); E. F. Pope, "The Critical Background of the Sp. Stanza," MP, 24 (1926); L. Bradner, "Forerunners of the Sp. Stanza," RES, 4 (1928); Hamer. F.J.W.; A.P.

SPONDEE (Gr. "used at a libation" poured to the accompaniment of the 2 long notes). In classical metric, a unit consisting of 2 long syllables:

(– –; *fēcī*)

Meters entirely composed of spondees are rare, but do occur:

Zēu pān|tôn ār|chā, pān|tôn hā|gêtôr
(Terpander, fr. 1)

In the common meters, a s. may replace dactyl, iamb, trochee, or anapaest. In Eng. stressed verse, the s. (′ ′; ámén) is rarer than might be expected, the instance of 2 equally stressed syllables in the same foot being almost wholly confined to compound words or 2 adjacent monosyllables:

The long|day wanes;|the slow|moon climbs
(Tennyson, *Ulysses*)

It is the basis of no Eng. verse, occurring only as a variation. Most Eng. attempts at the foot in classical imitations result in trochees.—Hamer; U. v. Wilamowitz-Moellendorff, *Griechische Verskunst* (2d ed., 1958); P. Maas, *Gr. Metre,* tr. H. Lloyd-Jones (1962). D.S.P.

SPRUNG RHYTHM. Term coined by Gerard Manley Hopkins to describe what he thought to be his most important metrical rediscovery. As Hopkins describes it, "Sprung rhythm . . . is measured by feet of from one to four syllables, regularly, and for particular effects any number of weak or slack syllables may be used. It has one stress, which falls on the only syllable, if there is only one, or, if there are more, then scanning as above, on the first, and so gives rise to four sorts of feet, a monosyllable and the so-called accentual Trochee, Dactyl, and the First Paeon [q.v.]. . . . Sprung Rhythm cannot be counterpointed [q.v.]. . . ." Sprung (or "abrupt") rhythm differs from running rhythm (q.v.) in that it may use rests, monosyllabic feet, and the first paeon (′ × × ×); running rhythm, if scanned from the first stress in the line, will consist of accentual trochees and dactyls only, while s. rhythm can juxtapose monosyllabic feet to produce effects of slowness and weight not possible in running (or "alternating") rhythm.

Hopkins points out that s. rhythm is found in nursery rhymes, and a good illustration of the rhythm is to be found in

One, two,
Buckle my shoe.

Here, line 1 is in s., line 2 in running rhythm. Another example given by Hopkins is

March dust, April showers
Bring forth May flowers,

where, if "showers" and "flowers" are considered monosyllables, both lines are in s. rhythm. These examples will make clear that s. rhythm is essentially a system of overstressing; the poet practicing s. rhythm composes almost as if the spondee were a normal Eng. foot. As has been said of s. rhythm, "Its external distinguishing feature is the free occurrence of juxtaposed stresses without intermediate unstressed syllables."

S. rhythm, by approximating the movements of emotion-charged natural speech, suggests a tone of frank sincerity and intimate emotional involvement. Good examples of the tone most natural to s. rhythm are Hopkins' poems *At the Wedding March* and *Spring and Fall: To a Young Child.*

H. Whitehall, "S. Rhythm," in The Kenyon Critics, *Gerard Manley Hopkins* (1945); Sister M. M. Holloway, *The Prosodic Theory of Gerard Manley Hopkins* (1947); "Author's Preface," *Poems of Gerard Manley Hopkins,* ed. R. Bridges and W. H. Gardner (3d ed; 1948); *A Hopkins Reader,* ed. John Pick (1953). See also P. F. Baum, "S. Rhythm," PMLA, 74 (1959). P.F.

STANZA (It. "station, stopping-place"). A basic structural unit in verse composition, a sequence of lines arranged in a definite pattern of meter and rhyme scheme which is repeated throughout the work. Stanzas range from such simple patterns as the couplet or the quatrain (qq.v.) to such complex stanza forms as the Spenserian (q.v.) or those used by Keats in his odes. The term "stanza" is sometimes restricted to verse units of 4 lines or more, "couplet" and "tercet" being the preferred terms for the shorter forms. The term is also sometimes employed to designate irregular formal divisions found in nonstanzaic poetry (e.g., *Paradise Lost*), but the term "verse paragraph" (q.v.) is here more expressive and less confusing.

Some narrative poetry, particularly of the epic type, is nonstanzaic (i.e., stichic) in structure (e.g., the *Iliad*, the *Aeneid, Paradise Lost, The Ring and the Book*) and thus achieves an effect of linear development in which the narrative line in itself provides the essential structure. Such compositions as Pope's *Rape of the Lock* (in couplets) and Dante's *Divina Commedia* (in tercets, or, more properly, in terza rima) achieve a similar effect. True stanzaic composition, as in Spenser's *Faerie Queene* (Spenserian stanza), Ariosto's *Orlando Furioso* (ottava rima), and Chaucer's *Troilus and Criseyde* (rhyme royal), lends itself to a kind of tension between narrative structure and lyric, elegiac, didactic, or satiric digression. Although the essence of stanzaic composition lies in the regular repetition of the pattern, stanzaic verse often employs variation, not only through metrical substitution but also through irregularities in s. form, as in Coleridge's *Ancient Mariner*, with its subtle rhetorical embroideries on the basic ballad measure.

The term "s." is sometimes applied to independent poems of complex metrical pattern, such as the ballade, the sestina, and the sonnet (qq.v.). Synonymous or analogous terms include the Gr. strophe (q.v.) and the early Eng. batch and stave (q.v.). F.J.W.; A.P.

STAVE (a back formation from the plural *staves*, of *staff*). A group of lines of verse or a stanza of a poem or song, particularly a hymn or drinking song; possibly the term was once restricted to poems intended to be sung. Also, the initial alliterative sound in a verse: e.g., the *s* in the line, "Or snorted we in the *S*even *S*leepers den" (Donne). This special meaning possibly comes from analogy with German *Stab*, meaning *staff*; in German *stabreimender Vers* means alliterative verse. R.O.E.

STICHOMYTHIA. Line by line conversation between two characters in the Gr. drama. It occurs in argumentative passages and is characterized by contrasted statements, repetition of the opponent's words, and angry retort. S. is very frequent in Seneca and is often used by Elizabethan dramatists, especially in plays written in imitation of Seneca's tragedies. Shakespeare employs it in *King Richard III*, 4.4, and in *Hamlet*, 3.4, as does Molière in *Les Femmes Savantes*, 3.5. It is occasionally referred to as "cut and parry" or "cut and thrust" dialogue.—J. L. Hancock, *Studies in S.* (1917); J. L. Myres, *The Structure of S. in Gr. Tragedy* (1950). P.S.C.

STICH(OS) (Gr. "row," "line"). A line of Gr. or L. verse. More precisely a single line (or a poem 1 line long, of which *Anthologia Palatina* 11.312 is an example) is called a monostich, a couplet a distich, and a halfline or section of a verse a hemistich. "Stichic" verse is that which was composed in recurrent and homogeneous lines, whereas in "stanzaic" verse a limited number of lines or cola (often, in the case of personal lyric, in quatrains and generally of varying length and movement) are combined in recurrent groups or stanzas. Stichic arrangement was normal for recitative poetry, whereas that which was sung was generally stanzaic.—J. W. White, *The Verse of Gr. Comedy* (1912); Dale. R.J.G.

STRESS. The vocal emphasis received by a syllable as part of a metrical pattern. S. is held by some linguists and prosodists to be equal to accent (q.v.); it is held by others to be one of the constituents of accent; the term is used by still others to mean metrical accent as distinguished from rhetorical accent. In this latter sense, the term "stress" is often used instead of "accent" to refer to the ideal or normal pattern of accents in a regular accentual or accentual-syllabic poetic line: e.g., "Swift was fond of the four-stress line." The term "stress-unit" has recently attained some popularity as a synonym for "foot," but in fact the two are distinct although they may coincide. Free s. is emphasis which may fall on any syllable of a word according to rhetorical weight; fixed s. is emphasis which falls always on the same syllable of a word regardless of the word's rhetorical context. Four degrees of s. are sometimes discriminated: strong, secondary, tertiary, weak. See ACCENT, METER, PROSODY. P.F.

STROPHE. Originally, the initial component of a choral ode, as in the classical Gr. drama. The s. derives its name from the first of the tripartite divisions of a Gr. choral interlude, which the chorus chanted while moving from one side of the stage to the other; it was followed by the antistrophe (q.v.) of identical metrical structure, chanted in accompaniment to a reverse movement, and then by the epode (q.v.), of different metrical structure, chanted as the chorus stood still.

In later periods the term was extended to apply to a structural division of any irregularly stanzaic poem of intermediate length, particularly of the ode type. It is thus partially synonymous with stanza (q.v.). In the modern period the term "s." has also been applied to the irregular rhetorical unit of free verse, possibly because the original classical s. was free from any prescribed limit of length or meter. The free-verse s. is a unit determined by rhythmic or emotional completeness rather than by metrical pattern.

STRUCTURALISM. See POETRY, THEORIES OF (OBJECTIVE THEORIES).

STRUCTURE. See TEXTURE.

STYLE. How are we to distinguish between what a poem says and the language in which it says it? On the one hand, there is no such thing as a "content" which does exist quite apart from the words; on the other hand the very existence of the word "style" shows that something can be said about the words which does not refer directly to the content. The relation between the two must be described metaphorically; and looking at the metaphors that have been used, we see that they are of two kinds. The first suggest that the relation is mechanical, that s. is something added, more or less at the poet's discretion; if on the other hand we see the relation as closer and more intimate, we are likely to use an organic metaphor.

The first kind is common in Renaissance and neoclassic criticism. Puttenham compares "ornament" (the term had a very wide meaning for him, almost that of "s.") to flowers, to jewels or embroidery, even to "the crimson taint which should be laid upon a lady's lips." Even commoner is the comparison of s. to a garment: says Sir William Alexander (1634): "Language is but the apparel of Poesy, which may give beauty but not strength." The same conception survives into neoclassic criticism: for Chapelain (1668) the essentials of a poem are "l'invention, la disposition, les moeurs et les passions"; diction, s., and versification are unimportant—"de petite consideration." Rosamund Tuve has made an attempt (which has not convinced everyone) to claim that some of these apparently mechanical views are really organic: pointing out that the garment image, for example, was also applied to the body in relation to the soul.

It is possible to find the organic view in Renaissance theory (Ben Jonson uses the body / soul analogy); but it comes into its own only with the romantics. Coleridge states it as well as anybody: images, he says in the *Biographia Literaria,* "become proofs of original genius only as far as they are modified by a predominant passion; or by associated thoughts or images awakened by that passion;" or in several other ways which would give an inner unity to the s. This passage, incidentally, says almost exactly the same as the 17th section of Longinus' treatise *On the Sublime,* the one notable statement of the organic view in antiquity.

After Coleridge there are innumerable statements of the organic view: for Pater, for instance, the process of polishing one's style may seem mechanical, but the result, when successful, is organic—"the house he has built is rather a body he has informed." Two modern statements worth special mention are those of Middleton Murry and Leo Spitzer. Murry, who actually uses the word *organic* ("style is organic—not the clothes a man wears, but the flesh and bone of his body") holds that metaphor is more than an ornament, more even than an act of comparison: in creative literature of the highest kind it becomes "almost a mode of apprehension." This is confined to imaginative writing: in the case of argument and exposition, he is prepared to allow that s. is detachable from content. Spitzer assumes the organic view of s. in his account of the "philological circle": the process of arguing from details of a linguistic structure to its postulated cause, "mental centre" or "inner significance," and then back again to other details. Spitzer regards this process as the same whether the "cause" is the artistic purpose behind a particular poem, or the hypothetical vulgar L. prototype behind the details of modern Fr. and It.: the process applies both to linguistics and to literary study. "The reader must seek to place himself in the creative centre of the artist himself and recreate the artistic organism." This assumes that stylistic details in a poem, like verbal details in a language, are not an inchoate chance aggregation, but part of a related whole: that seems a fair and even a necessary assumption, though many of Spitzer's readers will not follow him in the religious corollaries he deduces from it.

S., then, may be considered as something added, or as part of an organic whole. We need to ask next what it is added to, what it depends on or reflects. There are three main answers to this: that s. depends on subject, or an author, or on period. The first view was systematized in the Renaissance doctrine of the three styles: "to have the style decent and comely it behoveth the maker or Poet to follow the nature of his subject, that is if his matter be high and lofty that the style be so too, if mean, the style also to be mean, if base, the style humble and base accordingly" (Puttenham). The high s. suited epic and, in theory, tragedy; the middle s. verse epistles, "common poesies of love," elegies, and matters "that concern mean men, their life and business, as lawyers, gentlemen and merchants"; the base s. was for satire, and for pastoral, "the doings of the common artificer, servingman, yeoman," etc. Decorum demanded the use of "words, phrases, sentences, and figures, high, lofty, eloquent and magnific" for a poem like the *Faerie Queene*: "Dread sovereign goddess that dost highest sit / In seat of judgement in th'Almighty's stead, / And with magnific might and wondrous wit / Dost to thy people righteous doom aread. . . ." At the other extreme, here is the base s., as used by Donne in a satire: "But he is worst, who (beggarly) doth chaw / Others wits fruits, and in his ravenous maw / Rankly digested, doth those things out-spew / As his own things. . . ." Each s. is bad if applied to the wrong subject: and Puttenham offers examples of such indecorum. Aeneas should not *trudge* out of Troy, Juno should not *tug* Aeneas, for these terms are "better to be spoken of a beggar, or of a rogue, or a lackey" than a prince and the hero of an epic. The theory of decorum has a social basis.

Naturally it is the grand s. that receives most discussion. For the supreme example of its use, we need to move forward to the next age, to the plays of Racine. It is in fact not easy to find the grand s. in Elizabethan literature, for the stylistic practice of the Elizabethans was much less doctrinaire than their theory. Donne and Marlowe mingle the styles and apply them to inappropriate subjects, with daring and successful results. No one does this more than Shakespeare: the language of Cleopatra and Lear, at their finest moments, is full of low terms. For the theory of stylistic decorum runs counter to the great strength of Elizabethan literature, and especially drama—its linguistic flexibility and boldness.

The s. of Racine's plays is discussed by Erich Auerbach as the culmination of a movement toward the grand s. that goes back for centuries. He appreciates the effect that this s. yields in the baroque plays of Racine, but is very conscious of the price paid. Auerbach considers all European literature in relation to the division of styles: this is not really found in Homer, he claims, and it is contradicted by the very spirit of both Old and New Testaments. In the world of Christianity, "sermo gravis" and "sermo humilis" are merged: the effect of Christianity has been to merge tragedy in the everyday, not to isolate it, and so to contribute to the realistic tradition that Auerbach so admires. W. H. Auden, too, rejects the grand s., though for another reason: "All words like peace and love, All sane affirmative speech" have been degraded by their use in a commercial age, "pawed at and gossiped over;" so that the writer of integrity is driven to use "the wry, the sotto voce."

Neoclassic interest in the grand s. almost drove out interest in the others: and the idea that there are three styles (or even more than three, as the Elizabethans often concede) is replaced by the idea that there is only one s., based not on the subject of a poem, but merely on the fact that it is a poem, and must therefore differ from the language of speech or prose. "The language of the age," said Gray, "is never the language of poetry . . . our poetry has a language peculiar to itself." This results in the theory of poetic diction (q.v.), aggressively rejected later by Wordsworth, who maintained, in direct opposition to Gray, that "there neither is nor can be any *essential* difference between the language of prose and metrical composition." Wordsworth's best practice often (though not always) contradicts this; and Coleridge partly reinstated the idea of a special language for poetry in his discussion of Wordsworth's theories. In Coleridge, however, this is not described in terms of choice of words, or any criterion that can be applied mechanically, but it is the result of the poet's "inward vision" and "modifying powers."

So much for subject: next there is the theory that s. reflects the individual author. "Le style est l'homme même": the famous sentence of Buffon seems to sum up this view, though when we look at it in context we see that it is not a view of personality expressed through s. or of "self-expression." For Buffon a fine s. depends on impersonal factors, the truths it presents, the arrangement of the thoughts. In this he is still in the Renaissance / neoclassic tradition (and incidentally is echoed by the demi-romantic Flaubert). It is easy to find assertions in Renaissance criticism that s. is "mentis character," a reflection of the man himself. Puttenham points out that although s. reflects subject, "men do choose their subjects according to the metal of their minds;" and since it is accepted that the personages of a play should speak in character, the extension of this to the poet speaking in his own person needs only a simple analogy. Nonetheless, no preromantic critic sees s. as the man himself in the full sense that this would now be claimed, for this depends on the new emphasis the romantics gave to the individual personality of the writer. The idea that deeper levels of a man's mind are revealed, sometimes even despite himself, in his style, is a comparatively modern one: and its most sophisticated versions (such as that of William Empson) are likely to use the insights of Freud. The traditional view of s. as "l'homme même" was a moral view (as in Longinus and Cicero); the modern version, if not actually psychoanalytic, will certainly emphasize the individual creative act.

The s. of an author can be subdivided chronologically (Shakespeare, Milton, Dryden, Yeats are clear examples); and this division may overlap (it does with Dryden and Yeats, it does not with Milton) with the third way of considering s., as depending on the age. According to this view, it is possible to date a poem by the way it uses language: and there have been attempts (such as that of Bateson) to see a number of main phases of Eng. poetry, depending on the changing state of the language. As an example of period s., we may take the famous perspicuity of the Augustans. The Augustan ideals, as is well known, were clarity, perspicuity, good sense, nature, correctness, and reason: these preferences being based on the growing importance of science, the social influence of the bourgeoisie, the philosophy of Hobbes and Descartes. Obviously it is correct to say that this outlook is reflected in the prose of Addison, Defoe, and Swift, the poetry of Denham, Dryden, and Pope, and that there is therefore such a thing as an Augustan s., of the late 17th and earlier 18th c. What qualifications are needed to this simple view? First, that there is more strain among the Augustan ideals than they themselves always recognized: e.g. between reason and good sense, or between correctness and naturalness. This strain is mirrored in stylistic contrasts, e.g. between the coolness of the prose of Addison and the savage energy of Swift's (yet both are Augustan), or between the language of Pope's pastorals and that of his satires. Further, much of the energy of Augustan writing went into the characterizing of what they did not altogether approve of. "One glaring chaos and wild heap of wit," writes Pope in the *Essay on Criticism,* with a creative fire that in *The Dunciad* was to become an inspired condemning.

Relating s. to period, though prefigured in

such a document as Coleridge's essay on s., is on the whole characteristic of the historical approach of the 20th c. There have been many interesting attempts to discuss the mechanism behind the formation of a period s. F. W. Bateson, for example, emphasizes that social and ethical influences can act on poetry only indirectly through their influence on the language. Promising as this sounds, it issues either in truism or in an utterly unprovable determinism, asserting that the characteristics of a group of poets are "imposed on the poets willy nilly" by the state of the language. Indeed, a theory of "period s." can hardly escape determinism, as we can see in two much subtler critics, Erich Auerbach and Patrick Cruttwell. "At any given moment," says Cruttwell, "there are not more than one or two poetic manners in which success is possible;" and his book (*The Shakespearean Moment*) analyzes those in which it was possible in the 17th c. Cruttwell has not the magnificent sweep of Auerbach's immense learning, but he has the one quality which the attentive reader of Auerbach begins to miss: he recognizes the importance of the creative act. For Auerbach, s. is often (especially in early periods) the reflection of a tension between the author's intent and the pressure of social forces: thus the s. of Ammianus Marcellinus is the resultant of a stoical "respect for the past" in Ammianus being acted upon by the sombre realism, the social violence, and the sensory prominence of gesture found in his material and, behind that, in his age: the author's control, as maker, is almost ignored. And discussing Racine, the s. and the theory behind it, Auerbach offers a "sociological" interpretation of the apparent contradiction (paying tribute to Taine), in terms of an elite with more prestige than function. The determinism of Auerbach is subtler and more specious than that of Cruttwell, but also more rigid; for although Cruttwell offers a less complex version of the social forces at work, he sees these forces not as themselves determining s., but merely as imposing a limit to the kind of creative act possible.

Since 1965 criticism has increasingly rejected aesthetic in favor of scientific and linguistic theories of s. The Marxists (Lukacs, Althusser, Jameson) see s. in relation to economic conditions and the class struggle. Freudians (Lacan, Hollander) see s. in relation to the tensions between ego, super-ego, and libido. Anthropological critics, following Lévi-Strauss, see s. as a reflection of necessary—often binary—social accommodations. More radically, Roland Barthes attempts to show in *S / Z* (1970) that a work of literature (Balzac's *Sarrasine*) is a mosaic of stylistic codes without an aesthetic center. This approach defines an important tendency of "deconstructive" criticism. In one sense it revives the extreme associationalist psychology attacked by Coleridge in the *Biographia Literaria* (chs. V–IX). In another, it announces the post-modern rejection of all myths of essence and hence the emergence of the artist as both the subject of the forces that surround him and the vehicle through which they are arranged into arbitrary and transient images of coherence.

"Longinus," *On the Sublime* (1st c. A.D.); Puttenham, *The Art of Eng. Poery* (1589; esp. Bk. III, chaps. 5, 23); Ben Jonson, *Timber, or Discoveries* (1640; esp. sections CXV-end); Boileau, *L'Art Poétique* (1674); Addison, *The Spectator,* no. 285 (1712; on poetic diction); Pope, *Essay on Crit.* (1711), *The Dunciad* (1728–43), *To Augustus: the First Epistle of the Second Book of Horace Imitated* (1737; a survey of Eng. poetry); G. Buffon, *Discours sur le S.* (1753); Wordsworth, *Preface* to the 2d ed. of *Lyrical Ballads* (1800); Coleridge, *Biographia Literaria* (1817; esp. chaps. 15–22) and "On Style," no. 14 of *A Course of Lectures* (1818); Keats, *Letters* (esp. that to Shelley, Aug. 10, 1820); Bagehot, *Wordsworth, Tennyson and Browning* or *Pure, Ornate and Grotesque Art in Eng. Poetry* (1864); Pater, "S.," in *Appreciations* (1889); R. de Gourmont, *Le Problème du S.* (1902); M. Proust, *A L'Ombre des Jeunes Filles en Fleurs* (NRF ed., v. III, 1919, pp. 156–57; s. as the revelation of personality); J. M. Murry, *The Problem of S.* (1925); P. Valéry, "Situation de Baudelaire," *Variété,* II (1929), 141; F. W. Bateson, *Eng. Poetry and the Eng. Language* (1932) and *Eng. Poetry* (1950); Tuve; L. Spitzer, *Linguistics and Lit. Hist.* (1948); Wellek and Warren, esp. ch. 14, and excellent biblio.); W. H. Auden, dedicatory poem to *Nones* (1952); Auerbach; M. C. Bradbrook, "Fifty Years of Crit. of Shakespeare's S.," *ShS*, 7 (1954); P. Cruttwell, *The Shakespearean Moment* (1954) W. Nowottny, *The Language Poets Use* (1962); R. Barthes, *S / Z* (1970); F. Jameson, *The Prison-House of Language* (1972).

L.D.L.

SUBJECTIVITY AND OBJECTIVITY. This distinction is the result of the 17th-c. Cartesian separation between thought and thing, which along with the rise of science has been baneful to poetry. In the 18th c. it limited the scope of poetry to amusement and morality, and greatly hampered the Eng. poets up to Blake. Blake asserted the power of art, poetry, and the imagination by denying objective reality to God and Nature, or by refusing to admit any distinction whatever between the internal and the external, between the subjective and the objective. The effect of his beliefs is evident in the wholly non-naturalistic imagery of his poetry. Wordsworth and Coleridge posited an ideal correlation between Nature and the human mind, and Coleridge's exposition of "the poetry of nature" (*Biographia Literaria,* chap. 14) illustrates his conception of the fusion of subject and object, or of imagination and observation, by the image of sunset or moonlight upon "a known and familiar landscape." Keats's "What the imagination seizes as beauty must be truth" is his solution of the problem, though he was not always confident of its correctness.

In such Victorians as Tennyson and Arnold the breach between subjective and objective widened. In general there is a discrepancy between the Victorian sensibility and the Victorian beliefs, as witness the exquisite nature poetry, unbased in doctrine, of Hardy amd Housman. Modern poets, bolstered by depth-psychology and myth, have evolved a position akin to Blake's. The hallucinatory vividness of Yeats's "Byzantium," for example, is an assertion of the reality of imagination, a new kind of "willing suspension of disbelief." Yet it is to be remarked that most modern critics have taken subjectivity to mean solipsism and self-indulgence, as in the 20th-c. treatment of Shelley, while objectivity has been equated with honesty and insight. This is a decided shift from Blake's attitude toward free will and the power of the individual.—S. T. Coleridge, *Biographia Literaria,* ed. James Engell and W. J. Bate (1983), I. XII-XIII; J. C. Ransom, *The New Criticism* (1941); Abrams; Wimsatt; A. Gérard, *L'Idée romantique de la poésie en Angleterre* (1955). R.H.F.

"SUBLIME," a Latin-derived word meaning literally "(on) high, lofty, elevated," owes its currency as a critical and aesthetic term to the anonymous Gr. treatise *Peri Hypsous* (*hypsos,* "height, elevation"), formerly ascribed to the rhetorician Cassius Longinus, 3rd c. A.D., but now generally agreed to belong to the 1st c., perhaps around 50 A.D. Whatever his name and origin, its author was certainly a rhetorician and a teacher of the art, but one of uncommon mold. His essay, with its intimacy of tone (it is addressed to a favorite pupil, a young Roman) and breadth of spirit, stands more or less isolated in its own time, but has had a recurrent fascination for modern minds since the 17th c.

The idea of sublimity had its roots in the rhetorical distinction, well established before "Longinus," of three styles of speech, high, middle, and low. His achievement was to draw it out of the technical sphere, where it had to do with style primarily, and associate it with the general phenomenon of greatness in literature, prose and poetry alike. "Longinus" regards sublimity above all as a thing of the spirit, a spark that leaps from the soul of the writer to the soul of his reader, and only secondarily as a matter of technique and expression. "Sublimity is the echo of greatness of spirit." Being of the soul, it may pervade a whole work (speech, history, or poem: "Longinus" pays little attention to *genre* distinctions); or it may flash out at particular moments. "Father Zeus, kill us if thou wilt, but kill us in the light." "God said, 'Let there be light,' and there was light." In such quotations as these "Longinus" shows among other things his sharp eye for the particular passage and his capacity for *Einfühlung* into the actual work: qualities that are rare in ancient criticism and presage the modern spirit.

The distinguishing mark of sublimity, for "Longinus," is a certain quality of feeling. But he will not allow it to be simply identified with emotion, for not all emotions are true or noble. Only art can guard against exaggerated or misplaced feeling. Nevertheless art plays second fiddle to genius in his thinking. There are five sources of the sublime which he enumerates: great thoughts, noble feeling, lofty figures, diction, and arrangement. The first two, the crucial ones, are the gift of nature, not art. "Longinus" even prefers the faults of a great spirit, a Homer, a Plato, or a Demosthenes, to the faultless mediocrity that is achieved by following rules.

The treatise remained unknown, or at least exercised little influence, in later antiquity. It was first published by Robortelli in 1554, then translated into L. in 1572 and into Eng. in 1652 (by John Hall). But it made no great impression until the late 17th c. Paradoxically enough it was Boileau, the archpriest of neoclassicism, who launched the *Peri Hypsous* on its great career and thus helped to prepare the ultimate downfall of classicism. His translation (1672) had immense reverberation, especially in England. The Eng., always restive under the "French rules," instinctively welcomed "Longinus" as an ally. The Augustans duly admired him as "himself that great Sublime he draws" (Pope), but at the same time he was being invoked by John Dennis in support of the thesis that "Passion is the Principal thing in Poetry" (1701) and by Samuel Cobb as a champion of "the Liberty of Writing" (1707). As the 18th c. advanced, the sublime was absorbed into the bloodstream of Eng. thinking not only about literature but about art in general and even external nature. Under it were subsumed all the loftier feelings—"admiration," "transport," "enthusiasm," vehemence, even awe and terror—which literature, art, and nature are capable of inspiring, but for which neoclassicism had no clearly marked place. More and more frequently the sublime was distinguished from the beautiful—and ranked above it. Thus it played no small part in the drift toward subjectivism, the psychologizing of literature and literary experience, the concept of "original genius" unfettered by rules (Edward Young, the Wartons, Robert Wood, ca. 1760–70), and ultimately in the rise of romanticism in poetry and the concurrent establishment of aesthetics as a new, separate branch of philosophy (Kant, Hegel, etc.).

In this development the sublime left its beginnings in "Longinus" far behind; it became an independent concept with an intellectual history of its own. Burke's *Enquiry into the Origin of our Ideas on the Sublime and Beautiful* (1757) and Kant's *Critique of Aesthetic Judgment* (1790) make little use of the *Peri Hypsous.* But its significance is not exhausted by its historical role. Though not greatly in fashion today, it remains a perennially moving plea for greatness of spirit in literature, and it can also provide—coming as it does from a rhetorician—a timely corrective for overabsorption in poetic language and style.

PRIMARY WORKS: "Longinus on the Sublime," ed. and tr., with introd. and appendices, W. Rhys Roberts (2nd ed., 1907; best and fullest ed.); *Anonimo del Sublime,* ed. and tr. A. Rostagni (1947). Tr.: W. H. Fyfe (1927; Loeb ed.); B. Einarson (1945); G.M.A. Grube (1958); D. A. Russell (1965; text and commentary, 1964).

SECONDARY WORKS: T. R. Henn, *L. and Eng. Crit.* (1934; spotty); S. T. Monk, *The S.: A Study of Crit. Theories in 18th-C. England* (1935; definitive); E. Olson, "The Argument of Longinus' 'On the S.'," MP, 39 (1942; repr. in Crane, *Critics;* subtle, overmodernizes "L."); F. Wehrli, "Der erhabene und der schlichte Stil in der poetisch-rhetorischen Theorie der Antike," *Phylobolia für P. von der Mühll* (1946); W. J. Hipple, *The Beautiful, The S., and the Picturesque* (1957); J. Brody, *Boileau and Longinus* (1958); J. Arthos, *Dante, Michelangelo and Milton* (1963). G.F.E.

SUBSTITUTION. In most Gr. and L. verse forms one metrical foot, under certain conditions, might be substituted for another, e.g., in a Gr. iambic trimeter a spondee could replace the initial iambus of each dipody:

⏓ – ⏑ – | ⏓ – ⏑ – | ⏓ – ⏑ –

See also METRICAL VARIATIONS, EQUIVALENCE. R.J.G.

SYLLABLE. Linguistically, the domain of any degree of accent in spoken utterance. The s. is the smallest measurable unit of poetic sound, the fundamental building-block of metrical structure, and, in pure syllabic prosody (see METER), the only constituent to be regarded in the metrically normal line. See also PROSODY, METRICAL TREATMENT OF SYLLABLES. P.F.

SYMBOL. The word "symbol" derives from the Gr. verb, *symballein,* meaning "to put together," and the related noun, *symbolon,* meaning "mark," "token," or "sign," in the sense of the half-coin carried away by each of the two parties of an agreement as a pledge. Hence, it means basically a joining or combination, and, consequently, something once so joined or combined as standing for or representing in itself, when seen alone, the entire complex. This term in literary usage refers most specifically to a manner of representation in which what is shown (normally referring to something material) means, by virtue of association, something *more* or something *else* (normally referring to something immaterial). Thus a literary s. unites an image (the analogy) and an idea or conception (the subject) which that image suggests or evokes—as when, for example, the image of climbing a staircase (the difficulty involved in the effort to raise oneself) is used to suggest the idea of "raising" oneself spiritually or becoming purified (T. S. Eliot's *Ash Wednesday*).

A s. thus resembles what are known traditionally as "figures of speech" (cf. IMAGERY), which themselves comprise "tropes," or departures (turns) from the commonplace modes of signification, and "schemes," or artful elaborations of the forms of words and sentences. A s. is like a trope, in that a simile, metaphor, personification, allegory (qq.v.), and so on, each represent a manner of speaking in which what is said means something more or something else. But a s. is not a trope, and may be distinguished in terms of how it relates subject and analogy in a poem. In the other figures mentioned, what is said (analogy) is distinct from what is meant (subject), and their relationship is based upon a stated or implied resemblance within difference.

A s., on the other hand, puts the analogy in place of the subject (and may thus be thought of as an "expanded" metaphor—and, conversely, recurring metaphors in a given work are often spoken of as symbolic) so that we read what is said (climbing a staircase) as if that were what is meant, but are made to infer, by virtue of the associations provoked by what is said and the manner in which it is expressed, something more or something else as the additional or true meaning (spiritual purification). Thus, an idea which would be difficult, flat, lengthy, or unmoving when expressed prosaically and by itself, may be made intelligible, vivid, economical, and emotionally effective by the use of symbols.

A s., then, may be called, for purely technical purposes, a "pseudo-subject." Nor need the relationship between what is said and what is to be inferred be based, as in metaphor and simile, merely upon resemblance, for many images have become potentially symbolic not through likeness only but also through one sort of association or another—as when the loss of a man's hair symbolizes the loss of strength (Samson) or the rejection of worldly desires (monastic and ascetic practice), not because of any resemblance between them but rather because a primitive and magical connection has been established between secondary sex characteristics, virility, and desire. Of course, an associative relationship may be established having resemblance as its basis when a metaphor or simile is repeated so often, either in the work of a single author or in literary tradition, that the analogue can be used alone to summon up the subject with which it was once connected. Similarly, many interpreters have pointed out that poets tend to use the metaphors and similes of their earlier work as symbols in their later work because of the associative relations thus established. Critics rightly warn, moreover, that symbolic associations of imagery should be made neither too explicit nor too fixed, for implications of this sort are best felt rather than explained, and vary from work to work depending upon the individual context.

The first question, however, which faces the reader of a poem is whether or not a given image is indeed symbolic to begin with. This question may be answered in at least three related ways: (1) the connection between s. and thing symbolized may be made explicit in the work, as with the "Sea of Faith" in Arnold's *Dover Beach*; (2) the image may be presented in such a way as to discourage a merely literal interpretation, as with Byzantium in Yeats's *Sailing to Byzantium,* since no such thing actually exists, or to encourage a more than merely literal interpretation, as with the garden in Marvell's poem of that name, since, although it does actually exist, it is made into something more by virtue of the speaker's reactions to it; or (3) the pressure of implicit association may be so great as to demand a symbolic interpretation, as with Ulysses in Tennyson's poem of that name, since that figure has received such extensive previous treatment in myth, legend, and literature (cf. Homer and Dante). Because there is today a tendency to apply symbolic interpretation rather loosely, it bears emphasizing at this point that an image in a work is not symbolic unless a literal interpretation fails to do it justice; that is to say, a negative test often helps—an image is literal until proved otherwise, and if a literal interpretation can account satisfactorily for its place and function in the work then it is probably not symbolic.

Once the presence of symbols has been established, however, the next question is how to interpret their place and function in the work. This question may be answered in terms of at least three overlapping areas of inquiry: (1) the source of their imagery in experience, whether from the natural world, the human body, man-made artifacts, and so on; (2) the status of their imagery in a given work, whether presented literally as an actual experience (so that it symbolizes something more) or nonliterally as a dream or vision (so that it symbolizes something else altogether); and (3) the way in which their imagery has acquired associative power, whether mainly by virtue of universal human experience (see ARCHETYPE), or particular historical conventions, or the internal relationships which obtain among the elements of a given work (whereby one thing becomes associated with another by virtue of structural emphasis, arrangement, position, or development—this aspect, is, of course, involved to some degree in all works containing symbols), or some private system invented by the poet, or some combination. Regarding the third area of inquiry, examples of universally understood symbols would include climbing a staircase (or mountain) as spiritual purification, crossing a body of water as some sort of spiritual transition, sunset as death and sunrise as rebirth, and so on; examples of conventional symbols would include the transmutation of lead to gold as redemption, the lily as chastity and the rose as passion, the tiger as Christ, and so on; examples of internal-relationship symbols would include the wall as the division between the primitive and the civilized or natural chaos and human order in Robert Frost, the guitar and the color blue as the aesthetic imagination in Wallace Stevens, the island as complacency and the sea as courage in W. H. Auden, and so on; and examples of private symbols would include the phases of the moon as the cycles of history combined with the psychology of individuals in W. B. Yeats, embalmment as an obstacle that cannot be overcome in the attempt to resurrect the spirit in Dylan Thomas (see Olson [bibliog.]), and so on.

In Frost's famous poem, *Birches,* for example, the speaker talks of climbing to the top of a birch tree and swinging on it back down to earth again in such a way that the reader is given to understand that this action means something more than just climbing up and swinging down. That is to say, in the context of this poem the action comes to mean for its speaker a temporary release from the difficulties and responsibilities of daily life (climbing up and away from earth toward heaven) and a subsequent return to those mundane limitations once again refreshed (swinging back down to earth). Climbing, then, stands for his desire to get away, while swinging down stands for his recognition that he must, after all, live out his life on earth where the gods have placed him. Thus this action, which at first seemed to be the speaker's subject, turns out ultimately to be an analogue of his subject (which in no way, of course, diminishes the value and interest of the imagery in itself).

According to the three areas of inquiry outlined above, this symbolic imagery may first be analyzed as coming from the natural world in combination with actions of the human body: earth, heaven, tree, climbing up and swinging down. It is presented, secondly, as literal occurrence. And thirdly, its associative power derives from universal experience—earth as limitation and heaven as release—in combination with internal relationships—the act of swinging from a birch as seen in this context.

Yeats's *Sailing to Byzantium,* on the other hand, is rather more complicated in its symbolism. Here the speaker talks of sailing the seas and coming to the holy city of Byzantium, but, because this cannot be taken literally, what he actually means (again the warning against being too specific in explaining the meaning of symbols must be recalled) is that he wants to divest himself of mortality and its limitations and dwell—probably through the forms of art—in eternity. Notice, however, in the first place, that Byzantium as a symbolic image is derived from man-made artifact (although sailing as transition is not); secondly, that it is presented as a vision and not as something which has literally happened or could literally happen; and thirdly, that, in addition to internal relationships, the associative power of this image depends for its force upon—or at least is aided greatly by—a knowledge of exactly what it meant to Yeats in his private symbology. Thus the symbolism of different writers may be distinguished, characterized, and interpreted. (Even here, however, such categories must be applied flexibly, for Yeats's Byzantium image, although it does indeed have crucial private associations, is also related to the universal image of the "holy city" [e.g., Jerusalem] as fulfillment or redemption.)

Historically, men once tended to see the physical world in terms of spiritual values, not only by way of generating universal symbols (the world as a body, for example, or man's body as a state, and so on) but also of developing—through myth, lore, legend, craft, and learning—special conventions. And it is one of the doctrines of modern criticism that, partly due to the Protestant Reformation, partly to the changes gradually effected in school curricula, partly to the growth of science, and partly to the mere passing of time, not only have many conventional symbols been rendered meaningless to poets and readers alike but also the very power of seeing the physical world in terms of spiritual values has disappeared. Thus symbolism has been called in the 20th c. the "lost" or the "forgotten" language.

Certain 20th-c. poets, following the lead of the 19th-c. Fr. "symbolists" (Baudelaire, Verlaine, Rimbaud, and Mallarmé) each in his own way explored afresh the possibilities of the private symbolism of vision and dreams, and partly under the influence of a renewal of interest in Donne, Blake, and Hopkins, have attempted not only a revival of conventional religious and legendary symbolism, as has Eliot in *Ash Wednesday,* for example, but also have tried, in what they have felt to be a collapse of spiritual values, to invent their own symbolic conventions (Yeats is only the most obvious, with Ezra Pound, Hart Crane, Wallace Stevens, and Dylan Thomas working along similar if less systematic lines). Other poets, such as Frost, William Carlos Williams, and E. E. Cummings, have by and large been content to use natural, literal, universal, and contextual symbols.

The differences of opinion which exist today regarding the nature and function of symbolism in literature are due principally to the variety of ways in which the term is used in the service of different critical theories. This is true for many other terms as well, for a critic's use of any given term is governed by the assumptions he makes about literature and the kind of knowledge he is interested in obtaining. One cannot, therefore, compare and contrast the interpretations of different critics without first realizing what their assumptions and goals are, and consequently how they use their various terms.

Elder Olson, for example, as a neo-Aristotelian, is primarily concerned with literary works in their aspect as artistic wholes of certain kinds. Since he sees artistic wholeness in terms of the over-all effect which a work is designed to have upon the reader—whether doctrinal, as in the case of didactic works, or emotional, as in the case of mimetic works—and since a s. cannot produce such an effect apart from the poem of which it is a part, he regards symbolism as a device which is sometimes used by an author in the service of that effect (to aid in the expression of remote ideas, to vivify what otherwise would be faint, to aid in determining the reader's emotional reactions, and so on).

Other critics, however, having a more general notion of artistic form, are less precise in their definitions. Because Yeats, for example, as a symbolist, is primarily interested in the suggestive powers of poetry, he extends his definition of symbolism to include not only images, metaphors, and myths, but also all the "musical relations" of a poem (rhythm, diction, rhyme, and so on). Because Krieger, Wheelwright, Langer, Cassirer, and Urban, as anti-positivists, are concerned with defending poetry as having epistemological status, they stress in their use of the term its powers of bodying forth nondiscursive meaning, truth, or vision. Because Kenneth Burke, as a student of language in terms of human motives, deduces the form of a literary work from speculation as to how it functions in relation to the poet's inner life, he emphasizes the way in which various elements of that work symbolize an enactment of the poet's psychological tensions. Because the writers in Bryson's anthologies, as social critics, are interested in the uses of symbolism in a cultural context, they focus on the term as referring to the ways in which societal phenomena in general (insigne, designs on currency, structure of public buildings, motion pictures, and so on) serve as indicators of the values of a people.

Thus, if symbolism refers generally to the use of one thing to stand for another, then its specific meanings will vary according to the framework in which this relationship is viewed. A s. is a device of the poetic art when it refers to something in the poem as standing for something else in the poem; it is a power of poetic language when it refers to the way words and rhythms can evoke mystery; it is a function of the whole poem when it refers to the kinds of meaning a literary work can stand for; it is a form of therapeutic disguise when it refers to the ways in which a poem stands for the working out of the author's inner disturbances; and it is an index of cultural values when it refers to the ways in which man's products reveal his attitudes. Since the word is thus capable of such protean meanings—some of them overlapping at certain points—it is obviously best, when using the term, to specify the exact sense intended.

W. B. Yeats, "The Symbolism of Poetry"

(1900), *Ideas of Good and Evil* (2d ed., 1903); H. Bayley, *The Lost Lang. of Symbolism* (2 v., 1912, repr. 1951, 1952); D. A. Mackenzie, *The Migration of Symbols* (1926); H. Flanders Dunbar, *Symbolism in Medieval Thought* (1929); W. M. Urban, "The Principles of Symbolism," *Lang. and Reality* (1939); K. Burke, *The Philos. of Lit. Form: Studies in Symbolic Action* (1941); Langer; C. M. Bowra, *The Heritage of Symbolism* (1943); E. Cassirer, *An Essay on Man* (1944); M. Krieger, "Creative Crit.: A Broader View of Symbolism," SR, 58 (1950); T. Mischel, "The Meanings of 'S.' in Lit.," *Arizona Quar.*, 8 (1952); E. Olson, "A Dialogue on Symbolism," in Crane, *Critics*; Special Issue of YFS, no. 9 (1952–53); Special Issue of JAAC, 12 (Sept. 1953); C. Feidelson, *Symbolism and Am. Lit.* (1953); B. Kimpel, *The Symbols of Religious Faith* (1954); E. Olson, "The Universe of the Early Poems," *The Poetry of Dylan Thomas* (1954); *Symbols and Values* (1954) and *Symbols and Society* (1955), both ed. L. Bryson *et al.*; P. Wheelwright, *The Burning Fountain* (1954) and *Metaphor and Reality* (1962); W. Y. Tindall, *The Lit. S.* (1955); H. Levin, *Symbolism and Fiction* (1956); Frye; P. Kermode, *Romantic Image* (1957); J. W. Beach, *Obsessive Images: Symbolism in the Poetry of the 1930's and 1940's* (1960); *Lit. Symbolism*, ed. M. Beebe (1960); *Metaphor and S.*, ed. L. C. Knights and B. Cottle (1960); B. Seward, *The Symbolic Rose* (1960); *Symbolism in Religion and Lit.*, ed. R. May (1960); H. Musurillo, *S. and Myth in Ancient Poetry* (1951); *Myth and S.*, ed. B. Slote (1963). N.FRIE.

SYNAERESIS. See METRICAL TREATMENT OF SYLLABLES; ROMANCE PROSODY.

SYNAESTHESIA. Term denoting the perception, or description of the perception, of one sense modality in terms of another; e.g., perceiving or describing a voice as velvety, warm, heavy, or sweet, or a trumpet-blast as scarlet. The word occurs in 1891 in *The Century Dictionary*, but in the sense concerned here seems to have been first employed by Jules Millet in his thesis on *Audition colorée* (Montpellier, 1892). S. was popularized by two sonnets (Baudelaire's *Correspondances* [1857] and Rimbaud's *Voyelles* [in MS, 1871]) and Huysmans' novel *A rebours* (1884); but it had been widely employed earlier in German and Eng. romantic poetry, and it occurs in the earliest literature of the West (e.g., in *Iliad* 3.152, where the voices of the old Trojans are likened to the *lily-like* voices of cicalas; in *Iliad* 3.222, where Odysseus' words fall like winter snowflakes; and in *Odyssey* 12.187 in the *honey-voice* of the Sirens). In Aeschylus' *Persians* (line 395), "the trumpet set all the shores ablaze with its sound." Horace writes (*Odes* 1.24.3–4) of a *liquidam vocem.* Hebrews 6.5 and Revelations 1.12 refer to *tasting* the word of God and *seeing* a voice. John Donne mentions a *loud perfume,* Crashaw a *sparkling noyse.* Shelley refers to the fragrance of the hyacinth as *music,* and Heine to words *sweet as moonlight and delicate as the scent of the rose.* Silence is *perfumed* (Rimbaud), *black* (Pindar), *dark* ("Ossian" [Macpherson]), *green* (Carducci), *silver* (Wilde), blue (D'Annunzio), *chill* (Edith Sitwell), *green water* (Louis Aragon). For Milosz the smell of silence is "so old"; for Sartre it is like violets. Dylan Thomas writes of the *light of sound* and *sound of light.* Kipling's dawn *comes up like thunder.* Lorca refers to *green wind* and Mary Webb to the *icy voices* of curlews. S. has been exploited for varied purposes, but attempts to establish it as in itself a sign of illness, degeneration, or decadence seem to be inspired largely by prejudice or ignorance; for s. occurs very widely in language and literature in an apparently universal role among civilized peoples as the metaphor of the senses.—V. Ségalen, "Les synesthésies et l'école symboliste," *MdF*, 42 (1902); I. Babbitt, *The New Laokoön: An Essay on the Confusion of the Arts* (1910; chap. 6); E. v. Siebold, "Synästhesien in der . . . Dichtung des 19. Jhs.," *Englische Studien,* 53 (1919–20); W. D. Stanford, *Gr. Metaphor* (1936); G. Maurevert, "Des sons, des goûts et des couleurs: Essai sur les correspondances sensorielles," *MdF,* 292 (1939); S. de Ullmann, "Laws of Language and Laws of Nature," *MLR,* 38 (1943) and "Romanticism and S.," PMLA, 60 (1945); A. G. Engstrom, "In Defense of S. in Lit.," PQ, 25 (1946); G. O'Malley, "Literary S.," JAAC, 15 (1957). A.G.E.

SYNALOEPHA. See METRICAL TREATMENT OF SYLLABLES; CLASSICAL PROSODY; ROMANCE PROSODY.

SYNCOPATION. See COUNTERPOINT.

SYNCOPE. See METRICAL TREATMENT OF SYLLABLES.

SYNECDOCHE (Gr. "act of taking together," "understanding one thing with another"). A figure often regarded as a type of metonymy, wherein the part is substituted for the whole ("hired hands" for hired men); an individual, genus, or class characteristic for species ("mortals" for humans); material for thing made ("jeans," the name of a cloth, for the pants made of them), or vice versa. Attempting to discover a logic underlying these disparate examples, the Group μ defined s. as the result of a deletion or augmentation of a word's semantic features or "semes"; Todorov sees it as use of a word's signification (its semantic meaning and factual reference) on a different level, as a symbol. Both consider s. the basic trope, from which metaphor and metonymy are derived (see METAPHOR).

Kenneth Burke and Hayden White extend the meaning of the tropes as described in rhetoric to make them represent basic modes of thought and methods of discovery. S. is for Burke any relationship or connectedness, especially of quantity to quality (representation); metonymy is one of its sub-classes, a reduction from quality to quantity, or incorporeal to corporeal. White keeps the two distinct: s. is part for quality of the whole (integration), metonymy being part for whole (reduction).

More commonly, theorists dispense with s. entirely, treating its typical forms as metonymies and denying that some of them are in fact tropes. The purported s. is often literally true: "I see a sail" may mean just that, not "I see a ship," and the close relationship between count nouns and synecdoche—twenty sail, thirty head of cattle—may be based on convenient ways of counting (Ruwet). The use of genus for species ("weapon" for gun) is possibly of stylistic significance, but nothing more. When examined in context, the linguist may find that s. results from deletion of a phrase that if included would result in unnecessary redundancy ("a herd of thirty head" does not require "of cattle"). Few theorists note that whole for part and genus for species substitutions can derive their figural force from an identifying contextual qualification ("an animal that cries," "the gods of blood and salt") or implicit contrast ("what fools these mortals be," as opposed presumably to immortals)—treating the former as periphrasis (q.v.). For additional discussion, see METONYMY.

K. Burke, "Four Master Tropes," in *A Grammar of Motives* (1945); T. Todorov, "Synecdoques," *Communications,* 16 (1970); Group μ, *A General Rhetoric* (1970, tr. 1981); H. White, *Metahistory* (1973); N. Ruwet, "Synecdoques et métonymies," *Poétique,* 6 (1975); N. Sato, "Synecdoque, un trope suspect," *Revue d'esthétique,* 1–2 (1979).

R.O.E.; rev. W.M.

T

TAIL-RHYME (or tailed rhyme or, rarely, caudate rhyme) is the modern Eng. rendering of ME *rime couwee,* from Fr. *rime couée,* which in turn is from medieval L. *rhythmus caudatus* or *versus caudati* (cf. G. *Schweifreim*). The phrase designates a group of lines consisting of (a) a couplet, triplet, or stanza and (b) a following tail or additional shorter line. It could be applied to any such group; but it is generally reserved for a schematic recurrence. The tail may rhyme to a line in the couplet, triplet, or stanza, or to another shorter line after another couplet, triplet, or stanza; or it may be unrhymed to anything; or it may be a refrain, in the same formula throughout (as in Longfellow's *Excelsior* or Tennyson's *Ask me no more*) or in a varying formula (as in Burns's *Holy Fair,* "Fu' sweet that day," "Wi' fright that day," etc.). The most typical tail-rhyme is the romance-six, common in medieval romances and familiar from Chaucer's parody thereof, *The Rime of Sir Thopas.* Its scheme is 8,8,6,8,8,6 syllables, rhyming aabaab. Whittier in *Barclay of Ury* and O. W. Holmes in *The Last Leaf* keep the rhyme arrangement but reduce the syllables to 7,7,6,7,7,6 and 6,6,3,6,6,3 respectively. A similar grouping is Drayton's stanza in *The Ballad of Agincourt,* 6,6,6,5,6,6,6,5, rhyming aaabcccb. Many other arrangements of longer and shorter lines exhibit the phenomenon of tailing.—Schipper; Ker; A. McI. Trounce, "The Eng. Tail-Rhyme Romances," *Medium Aevum,* 1–3 (1932–34). A.M.C.

TANKA (also called *waka* or *uta*). This Japanese lyric form of 31 syllables in lines of 5,7,5,7,7 syllables originated ca. 7th c. A.D, has continued to the present, and may be called the classic Japanese poetic form. Identified for centuries with the court, its diction has been traditional and elevated, and its subjects most often nature, love, laments, or such occasions as travel and felicitations.

The influence of tanka upon modern Western poetry has been vaguer and less extensive than that of haiku (q.v.) and is, therefore, more difficult to assess. The principal obstacles to fruitful understanding of t. have been ignorance—of its language, tradition, and techniques—and the fact that until recently the form has usually been viewed in terms of the exotic and poor translations of one anthology, the *Hyakunin Isshu* (One Poem from Each of a Hundred Poets). The exotic concept of t. merged with the impressionist view of the color print to represent Japanese poetry in terms of delicate, sensitive, coloristic, amoral, and (in theory at least) precise images. Although t. tends to treat separately its different subjects, Western conceptions and imitations of it usually merged nature, love, and the tone of the laments, in techniques borrowed from haiku.

This confusion of genres, in a haze of exoticism, often makes it difficult to distinguish the influence of one form from that of the other. This is particularly true of early Fr. interest (ca. 1905–10) and early Anglo-Am. interest (ca. 1910–15). Although no major European poet has benefited materially from t., a few lesser figures have imitated it or translated translations (e.g., Amy Lowell, Ernest Fenollosa) or devised poetic forms on tanka lines (e.g., Adelaide Crapsey). As a model for experiment, t. was imitated by the imagists and some of their predecessors in France and England, but with less enthusiasm or profit than haiku.

Western estimation of t. probably has suffered from 19th–20th c. Japanese primitivizing of their own culture, a process which has led to a condemnation of the Court tradition of t. and to praise of the imagined greater "sincerity" of haiku. This attitude tended to keep certain of the most influential earlier translators and commentators from tanka; and although excellent Fr., Am., and German translations of this form in recent years have somewhat tempered exoticism and moderated attitudes toward these two genres, t. has not yet become as fruitful a source of poetic theory and technique as haiku and nō (q.v.). See also JAPANESE POETRY.—H. L. Seaver, "The Asian Lyric and Eng. Lit.," *Essays in Honor of Barrett Wendell* (1926); W. L. Schwartz, *The Imaginative Interpretation of the Far East in Modern Fr. Lit. 1800–1925* (1927); E. V. Gatenby, "The Influence of Japan on Eng. Lang. and Lit.," Japan Society (London), *Trans. and Proceed.*, 34 (1936–37); E. Miner, *The Japanese Tradition in British and Am. Lit.* (1958); R. H. Brower and E. Miner, *Japanese Court Poetry* (1961). E.M.

TENOR AND VEHICLE. Because he was dissatisfied with the traditional account of metaphor in what he conceived of as a too exclusively grammatical and rhetorical manner, I. A. Richards coined this pair of terms to improve upon the old theory of metaphor by introducing the notion of "a borrowing between and intercourse of thoughts." Since any metaphor, at its simplest, gives us two ideas, he used "t." to mean purport or general drift of thought regarding the subject of the metaphor, and "v." to mean that which serves to carry or embody the t. as the analogy brought to the subject. Although this was by no means the first modern attempt to analyze the fundamental duality of metaphor—previous writers had already distinguished between "major term" and "minor term," or "thing meant" and "thing said," or "meaning" and "picture," and so on—Richards' distinction and the terms he introduced have gained wide currency among modern critics.

Having traced out t. and v. as the essential ingredients of metaphor, Richards (and the critics who followed him) went on to distinguish between the poetic metaphor and other kinds. In attempting to show that the truly poetic metaphor is never merely decorative or logical or explanatory or illustrative, he claimed that the "transaction" which it sets up between t. and v. "results in a meaning (to be clearly distinguished from the t.) which is not attainable without their interaction." The v., he continued, "is not normally mere embellishment of a tenor which is otherwise unchanged by it but . . . vehicle and tenor in cooperation give a meaning of more varied powers than can be ascribed to either."

Thus, for example, it became very common to interpret the well-known "stiff twin compasses" simile in Donne's "Valediction" in terms of a conflict supposedly set up between the warmth and passion binding the souls of the two lovers together (t.) and the rationality and metallic coldness implied by the mechanical compasses (v.). This analysis was seen as revealing the nobility of the speaker's conceptual powers in recognizing the subtle contradictions and complexities of the experience of love, as well as explaining the cause of our pleasure in this poem in terms of the filling in of such connections between t. and v. which our minds are stimulated to do. A less ambitious interpretation, however, would begin by pointing out that the figure is based on the notion of being separate but joined—a notion which the v. exemplifies and which the speaker is using as part of the argument he is fashioning to console his lady regarding their impending separation (t.). See IMAGERY, METAPHOR.—H. W. Wells, *Poetic Imagery* (1924); K. Burke, "Perspective as Metaphor," *Permanence and Change* (1935); W. B. Stanford, *Gr. Metaphor* (1936); I. A. Richards, *The Philos. of Rhetoric* (1936); C. Brooks, *Modern Poetry and the Tradition* (1939), pp. 1–17; J. C. Ransom, *Poems and Essays* (1955), pp. 159–85. N.FRIE.

TERCET. See TRIPLET.

TERZA RIMA. A verse form composed of iambic tercets rhyming aba bcb, etc., the second line of the first tercet supplying the rhyme for the second tercet, the second line of the second tercet supplying the rhyme for the third, and so on, thus giving an effect of linkage to the entire composition. In t.r., the conclusion of a formal unit is generally signified by the occurrence of a single line which completes the rhyme structure by rhyming with the middle line of the preceding tercet, thus: xyx y.

T.r. was invented by Dante as an appropriate form for his *Divina Commedia*; the symbolic reference to the Holy Trinity is obvious. Furthermore, the intricate harmony which Dante achieves through his mastery of the form gives to the poem a structure at once massive and subtle, a structure which can only be suggested by any passage taken out of context. Most probably, Dante developed t.r. from the tercets of the *sirventes* but, whatever the origins of the form, it found immediate popularity with Boccaccio, who used it in his *Amorosa Visione,* and Petrarch, who used it in his *I Trionfi*. The implicit difficulty of the form, however, discouraged its widespread use after the 14th c., although Monti in the late 18th and Foscolo in the early 19th wrote noteworthy poems in t.r.

The form makes even greater demands on poets who write in a language less rich in rhymes than It. T.r. was introduced into Eng. by Chaucer in his *Complaint to his Lady* and was used by Wyatt and by Daniel. Some of the Eng. romantics experimented with the form, Byron in *The Prophecy of Dante* and Shelley in *Prince Athanase* and *The Triumph of Life*. The latter poet's *Ode to the West Wind* is composed of five sections, each rhyming aba bcb cdc ded ee. In the 20th c. the form has been used, among others, by W. H. Auden (*The Sea and the Mirror*) and, with marked variations, by MacLeish (*Conquistador*). European poets of the 19th and 20th c. who employed t.r. include the Dutch Potgieter and van Eeden and the Germans A. W. Schlegel, Chamisso, Liliencron, Heyse, and von Hofmannsthal.—Schipper; Hamer; Th. Spoerri, "Wie Dantes Vers entstand," *Vox romanica,* 2 (1937); V. Pernicone, "Storia e svolgimento della metrica," in *Problemi ed orientamenti critici di lingua e di letteratura italiana,* ed. A. Momigliano, II (1948); Wilkins.

TERZA RIMA SONNET. A term sometimes used to describe a quatorzain (q.v.) whose rhyme scheme makes use of the interweaving characteristic of terza rima (aba bcb cdc, etc.). Thus a pattern aba bcb cdc ded ee (the form of each section of Shelley's *Ode to the West Wind,* it may be noted) is not unlike the development of the Spenserian sonnet with its couplet ending; but there is an excess of interweaving for so short a poem, and a theoretical demand for a five-part division instead of the normally expected four. Moreover, the principal charm of the t.r.—its cumulative melody—is lost in so short a passage. It is, however, of interest to note that the Sicilian sonnet has been suggested as the source of the t.r. as such. L.J.Z.

TETRAMETER (Gr. "of 4 measures"). A line consisting of 4 measures. In classical iambic (⏑–), trochaic (–⏑), and anapaestic (⏑⏑–) verse the measure is a dipody (pair of feet). There are four classical types: iambic t. acatalectic and trochaic t. acatalectic (8 feet, 16 syllables each) and iambic t. catalectic and trochaic t. catalectic (7 feet, 15 syllables each). A spondee (––) was allowed in the odd iambic and the even trochaic feet. Resolution of a long into 2 shorts was allowed in certain circumstances. A break (diaeresis) was compulsory after the second dipody. The catalectic types are the commoner. The iambic t. catalectic was common in L. comedy; indeed it had rather vulgar associations. The trochaic t. catalectic is one of the oldest and most popular of meters; it was used in drama for excited dialogue, and it was the rhythm of the Roman soldiers' marching-songs and of some of the most famous Christian hymns, e.g.,

pāngĕ, līnguă, glōrĭōsī proēlĭūm cērtāmĭnĭs

Eng. t. (a line of 4 feet; strictly speaking the term is incorrectly used for the Eng. 4-stress line) is less strict than the classical varieties. Usually it is iambic or trochaic, or both, with accentual feet. It was used by Milton (*L'Allegro, Il Penseroso*) and many others, and conspicuously by Scott and Byron in long narratives.—Hardie; Beare. W.B.

TEXTURE. In modern criticism "texture" usually designates the concrete, particular details of a poem as differentiated from abstract or general ideas. The term is derived from the plastic arts, where it normally refers to the surface qualities of a work as against the larger elements of form or design.

In the context of prosody, t. denotes euphony, the actual physical effects of vowels and consonants as distinguished from meter, considered as a temporal and dynamic phenomenon. T., in this sense, is a matter of great subtlety; since the judgment of phonetic qualities is necessarily subjective to a certain degree, t. is not amenable to systematic analysis. Aside from the observation of such well-established devices as assonance and alliteration, the description of t. depends on analogy with nonaural phenomena: hardness, softness; thickness, thinness; darkness, richness, sweetness, harshness. The subject of phonetic t. is further complicated by its interaction with meter; according to Edith Sitwell, it has "incredibly subtle" effects on rhythm and variations of speed.

In the field of poetics, "t." has a much broader reference, including euphony and meter but extending also to the topic of poetic language. It has a special importance in the criticism of John Crowe Ransom as one of two key terms in a general theory of poetry. Ransom has consistently opposed the tendency in modern poetics to create a unitary theory by reducing poetry to a single essence. In his view, poetry is a composite art containing three distinct and irreducible ingredients. One of these comes under the heading of structure; the others under t. The nature or condition of poetry is defined by the relationship of structure and t.

Structure is the argument of the poem, that element which is governed by logic and reason and which, since it belongs to the order of discursive language, may be extracted from the poem in the form of a prose paraphrase. Ransom maintains that without the prose argument there can be no poem, and is therefore opposed to tendencies in modern poetry which would dispense with structure and have the poem consist entirely of what he calls texture.

J. C. Ransom, *The World's Body* (1932), *The New Crit.* (1941), "Crit. as Pure Speculation," in *The Intent of the Critic,* ed. D. A. Stauffer (1941), "The Inorganic Muses," KR, 5 (1943), "Poetry: The Formal Analysis," and "Poetry: The Final Cause," KR, 9 (1947); W. Elton, *A Glossary of the New Crit.* (1948); R. W. Stallman, "The New Critics," *Critiques and Essays in Crit.* (1949); E. Sitwell, "Poetry," in *Cassell's*; Wimsatt and Brooks. S.F.

THESIS. See ARSIS AND THESIS.

THRENODY (Gr. "a dirge sung over someone or something"). The ancient Gr. word for a song of lamentation, a dirge (q.v.), or a funeral song. Although originally a choral ode, it was changed to a monody (q.v.) which was strophic in form employing various metrical systems. Such a poem was not only a lamentation but also an encomium for the dead. From the 6th c. B.C. it became common in Gr. literature whence it spread to other literatures. In modern usage the term may be applied to any lyric of lamentation or memorial, e.g., Emerson's *Threnody on His Young Son,* or even Tennyson's *In Memoriam.*

R.A.H.

TONE. Traditionally, "t." has denoted an intangible quality, frequently an affective one, which is metaphorically predicated of a literary work or of some part of it such as its style. It is said to pervade and "color" the whole, like a mood in a human being, and in various ways to contribute to the aesthetic excellence of the work. Some of the other terms naming the same concept are "Gestalt-quality," "impression," "spirit," "atmosphere," "aura," and "accent." In *Practical Criticism* (1929) I. A. Richards compared t. to social manners and defined it as the reflection in a discourse of the author's attitude towards his audience. Successful management of t., on which the rhetorical effectiveness of a discourse largely depends, consists primarily in the tactful selection of content and in the adjustment of style to suit a particular audience. Other recent critics have analogized t. in literature to a quality of speech. The t. in which something is said may add to, qualify, or even reverse the meaning of what is said, as in sarcasm. Thus the t. of a speaker's voice may reveal information about his feelings, wishes, attitudes, beliefs, etc. presumably on the assumption that vocal tones are used only or primarily to convey attitudes, critics who have adopted this analogy maintain that any indirect expression of attitude in a poem (by choice or words, imagery, slanting, syntax, etc.) is a problem of t. Thus attitudes determine t., and t. reflects attitudes. Since poetry is regarded as a specialization of language for the communication of attitudes, the determination of the exact shading of t. in a particular poem is one of the most important duties of the explicator. The t. of a poem is also a source of value judgments; a poem is deemed poor if the attitudes it expresses are vague, confused, unsustained, unjustified, unmotivated, inappropriate, simple, conventional, or sentimental.—I. A. Richards, *Practical Crit.* (1929); Brooks and Warren; I. C. Hungerland, *Poetic Discourse* (1958).

F.G.

TONE-COLOR. Characteristic auditory quality of a speech-sound or musical instrument (German *Tonfarbe, Klangfarbe*; Fr., Eng. *timbre*). Extended to cover the kinesthetic "feel" of articulation and utterance. The relations of both aspects of tone-color to sound-associations are here examined. (See also ONOMATOPOEIA, SOUND IN POETRY.)

The key to poetic tone-color is phonology. The reader who has, for instance, digested sound spectrograms in their linguistic significance, has a far clearer understanding of the bases of timbre. One such basis is the relation of the *formants* of a given sound to each other and to those of other sounds: *formants* may be crudely defined as pitch zones in which voice overtones are strengthened, owing to the voice-cavity configuration. But a sound may be abrupt or lingering, noise-like or music-like. Jakobson thinks each speech sound in a given language is recognized by its "reading" against a selection from some dozen "either-or" pairs of characteristics. Though their function is linguistic, such features can have aesthetic qualities and natural associations, while in poetry *all* sound qualities come in. When considering the associations of sounds, *articulation* is more important in stops and fricatives, *timbre* in vowels and final nasals or liquids; but the student should be familiar with the "vowel-polygon."

From Plato's *Cratylus* onward the power of sounds has been recognized. A. W. Schlegel connected each vowel with a hue and a feeling-tone; romantics and symbolists made much of universal *correspondances* and synaesthesias; the *instrumentalistes* equated each vowel class with a class of musical instrument; Rimbaud's vowel/color sonnet is suspect, but Ernst Jünger elaborates a nexus of ideas for each vowel. Psychological investigators record synaesthesias, some conflicting; Gestalt theorists invoke *coenesthesia,* basic feelings underlying all pairs of contrasting sensations. Grammont notes associations with emotive expression, percepts, and (metaphorically) abstracts; German writers discuss the general problem, lexical and poetic. Paget and others back articulatory "gesture." Macdermott relates Eng. vowel types predominant in verse passages, to the subject. Imitative and suggestive words have been adduced in all tongues. Wundt distinguishes noise imitation, other percepts suggested by sound, and "metaphors" in which speech sound and object arouse related feelings. Bühler distinguishes objective from relational fidelity (*Relationstreue*) such as that of a fever chart to the fever. The poetic vowel classifications of Grammont and Macdermott are well enough founded to be approximable with Jakobson's linguistic ones. But the most painstaking of the skeptics, P. Delbouille, in a highly critical review of theories, assigns to sound suggestion a very rare derivative rôle.

It is clear that every sound (-collocation) has multiple affinities. The whole picture is distorted by lexical associations. Thus one word (or set) may attract others in *the language* (*swing, sway, swirl, swill, swish, swash, swoop, swat, switch*) and/or *in verse,* where Trannoy speaks of the harmony-generating word: in "Se mêlaient au bruit sourd des ruisseaux sur la mousse" (Hugo), *ruisseaux* is supposed to generate *bruit sourd* since we would expect *bruit clair*: over-simply, since *sur* and *mousse* also echo.

Nevertheless, potential associations are activated in certain milieux. In "And the dull wheel hums doleful through the day" (Crabbe) the monotony is conveyed by the doubled *d-l,* lingering *l*'s and *m,* driving *d*'s, flat British *u*'s. In "Liberty . . . o'er Spain, / Scattering contagious fire into the sky, / Gleamed. My soul spurned the chains of its dismay" (Shelley) the release and ardor are expressed by the swishing *s*'s, leaping *sp*'s, flinging *sk*'s, gay *ā/ai*'s. In "The horrid crags, by toppling convent crown'd, / The cork-trees hoar that clothe the shaggy steep, / The mountain-moss by scorching skies imbrown'd" (Byron), the scene is suggested by the gasping *h*'s, dark *or*'s and *ŏ*'s, rugged *kr*'s, hard-edged *k*'s and *ag*'s, sweeping *mount/m-own'd,* abrupt *-p*'s, dizzy *sk*'s and spiring *trees/steep.* In Mallarmé's swan-sonnet the *i*'s illuminate white bird, frozen winter, spiritual intensity, sterility. Rilke uses *i*-sounds similarly in the unicorn Sonnet to Orpheus, but almost confined to certain lines, set in contrast with *a*-sounds in the first quatrain and *au* in the second, and in modulation with *ei* in the sestet. (Tone-colors can also be used for themselves alone without "program.")

To systematize is possible. Depending on the language (see below), vowels like [e, i, y] tend to be appropriate to height, intensity, sharpness, thinness, delicacy, minuteness, insignificance, pallidity, purity, rarefaction, mobility; but such as [ɑ, ɒ, ɔ] to the opposite notions; like [u, o] to hollowness, roundness, solemnity, gloom, depth, softness, malleability, liquidity; but such as [a, æ, ɛ] to their opposites; like [y, ø, œ] to preciosity, charm, melancholy; but such as [ʌ, ɑ] to their antitheses; rounded vowels generally to interest, rich hue or form; but others to the reverse; vowels like [u, y, i] to mystery, tenderness, cool tints; but such as [a, ɑ, ɒ] to their contraries; short vowels can be brisk or trite, long vowels operatic (diphthongs plastically expressive). *Consonants:—resonants* (nasals, liquids) can suggest harmony, flow, protraction (especially as finals), malleability; *stops:* the opposites; *voiceless:* levity, agitation; *voiced:* the converse; *hissing:* scorn, tenuity; *hushing:* swarm, effusion; *both the last:* speed, harshness; *r*'s: roughness, menace, warmth; *labials:* warm emotions; *velars:* cold emotions; *stops juxtaposed:* obstacle shapes; *fricatives combined with other cons.:* movement shapes. (Cf. Hevner, Macdermott, Grammont, Lockemann, Jakobson.)

But each language differs phonologically, and hence in its aesthetic resources. Thus Gr. words (cf. Norwegian, Swedish, etc.) were probably pitch-accented, L. stress-accented; Germanic tongues have forceful expiratory stress, weak syllables being often slurred, galloped over, or even dropped (today especially in S. England); Romance languages (except European Portuguese) are more evenly stressed and precisely articulated (Fr. especially); weak Rus. syllables are also phonetically reduced. Eng. and Rus. bristle with difficult consonant groups, and in general Germanic and Slavonic contrast in this respect with the simpler syllables of Romance. Danish, and partly Sp., seriously weaken noninitial "stops." L., Gr., early Germanic tongues, It., Finnish, Hungarian, etc., possess double-duration consonants (It. *chi* [s]*sono, hanno*) as well as vowels. In It. and Sp. few syllables end with a consonant, and there are 7 or 5 vowel sounds to England's twenty-odd. Eng., Dutch, German, etc., possess gently "falling" diphthongs (which in Eng. replace most "long" vowels); German, Fr., Dutch, etc., possess rounded front vowels; Fr., Polish, and Portuguese have their nasal vowels. Most Rus. vowels are dull and lax, and so are the "short" vowels in Eng. and other Germanic tongues; Rus. and standard Sp. have no "long" vowels. Many Slav tongues are rich in hissing and hushing consonants, and possess a palatalized set of consonants and (in effect) vowels. Romance languages possess palatal *n* and, usually, *l.* Fr., Portuguese, Icelandic, Welsh, Finnish, etc., lack affricates.

Some Germanic phonologies have perhaps more affinity with the violent, unstable, rugged, distinctive aspects of existence; Romance ones, with the harmonious, steady, smooth, reiterative. If so, the *reverse* aspects should be expressed more easily with less means: hardness and roughness more economically in Romance than in Germanic, e.g. by *a*'s, *r*'s, stops: "un choc d'armures, / Quand a ourde mêlée étreint les escadrons" (Hugo) (helped by the hiatus); fullness, peace, richness more economically in Germanic, e.g. by long sonorous syllables (*Paradise Lost* 4542–50). Languor is expressible by nasal vowels in Fr., by dull vowels and final resonants in Eng.; excitement or movement by acute vowels in Fr., by *sp, sw, sl, st, sh, nce* in Eng. (as in Shelley). Sounds too common in discourse tend to neutralize their effects: e.g. *th-, -s,* [ə], [ɪ] in Eng. Grammatical like-endings bind speech or verse more monotonously together in Gr., L. (German, It., Sp., Portuguese, Slavonic), Finnish, etc.; and paucity of vowel types does the same in Sp. or It., but Eng. and Fr. starkness is partly cluttered up through analytical syntax and particles.

W. M. Wundt, *Völkerpsychologie* (v. 1–2, 1904); A. I. Trannoy, *La musique des vers* (1929); Sir R.A.S. Paget, *Human Speech* (1930); H. Werner, *Grundfragen der Sprachphysiognomik* (1932); K. Bühler, *Sprachtheorie: die Darstellungsfunktion der Sprache* (1934); K. Hevner, "An Experimental

Study of the Affective Value of Sounds in Poetry," *Am. J. of Psych.*, 49 (1937); H. Lützeler, "Die Lautgestaltung in der Lyrik," *Zeitschrift für Aesth.*, 29 (1935); W. Schneider, "Über die Lautbedeutsamkeit," *ZDP*, 63 (1938); M. M. Macdermott, *Vowel Sounds in Poetry* (1940); E. Jünger, "Lob der Vokale" in his *Blätter und Steine* (1942); M. Grammont, *Traité de phonétique* (3e éd., 1946, pt. 3); R. K. Potter, G. A. Kapp and H. C. Green, *Visible Speech* (1947); P. Delattre, "The Physiological Interpretation of Sound Spectrograms, PMLA, 66 (1951); F. Lockemann, *Das Gedicht und seine Klanggestalt* (1952); J. J. Lynch, "The Tonality of Lyric Poetry," *Word*, 9 (1953); W. Wandruschka, "Ausdruckswerte der Sprachlaute," *Germ.-Rom.Monatsschr.*, n.F., 4 (1954); R. Jakobson and M. Halle, *Fundamentals of Language* (1956); P. Delbouille, *Poésie et sonorités: la critique contemporaine devant le pouvoir suggestif des sons* (1961). D.I.M.

TOPOGRAPHICAL POEM. T. poetry was defined in 1799 by Dr. Johnson as *"local poetry,* of which the fundamental subject is some particular landscape . . . with the addition of . . . historical retrospection or incidental meditation." Known to the ancients in verse-geographies and in accounts of voyages, the genre was established in Eng. poetry by Sir John Denham's *Cooper Hill* (1642). Throughout the next century and a half, it flourished luxuriously in Eng. verse, where as many as nine subcategories (hills, towns, rivers, buildings, caves, etc.), each with numerous representatives, may be distinguished. Thomson, Dyer, Crabbe, and a multitude of minor poets wrote t. poetry, but its importance as a separate genre was largely outmoded by the extensive use of descriptive detail for other purposes in romantic poetry, as in Wordsworth's *Tintern Abbey* or *Ode on Intimations of Immortality*. John Betjeman has recently revived t. verse in short works with humorous effect, but no major serious works have appeared.—D. L. Durling, *Georgic Tradition in Eng. Poetry* (1935); R. A. Aubin, *T. Poetry in 18th-C. England* (1936); R. M. Thale, "Crabbe's *Village* and T. Poetry," JEGP, 55 (1956). S.F.F.

TOPOS (pl. *topoi*). A commonplace appropriate for literary treatment, an "intellectual theme suitable for development and modification" according to the imagination of the individual author (Curtius). In his *Rhetoric,* Aristotle used an adapted sense of physical place or t. to represent a rhetorical commonplace, and such *topoi* became the *loci communes* or commonplaces of the Roman rhetoricians, sometimes retaining a degree of their original physical sense by the association, in memory-systems, of specific places at the scene of an oration with specific topics in the speech. Aristotle's use of the term in his *Topics* is not essentially different; in that work *topoi* designate the commonplaces upon which dialectic reasoning bases its arguments and through which the philosopher may effectively communicate with non-philosophers. Ernst Robert Curtius adapted the rhetorical conception to literary use in *European Lit. and the Late Middle Ages*, tr. W. R. Trask (1953). Examples of *topoi* are: the inexpressibility t., in which a poet decries his inability to do his subject justice; the "world upsidedown" (*mundus inversus*) t., in which the world's disorder is shown by fish in the trees, children ruling parents, etc.; and set pieces like the standardized description of an ideal garden (*locus amoenus*). Critics following Curtius have extended the conception of a t. to include traditional metaphors such as the world as stage, the world as book, etc. Curtius distinguished between these "metaphorics" and the other "topics," although in many instances the distinction is difficult to maintain. F.J.W.

TRAGEDY. See DRAMATIC POETRY.

TRAGICOMEDY. The term "t." came from Plautus' facetious reference to the unconventional mixture of kings and gods and servants in his own *Amphitryon* as *tradicocomoedia.* The idea of t. as poetic drama that combined elements of both tragedy and comedy was at least as old as Euripides and Aristotle; Euripides wrote tragedies with a happy ending, e.g. *Alcestis* and *Iphigenia in Tauris,* and Aristotle remarked in the *Poetics* that the popular audience preferred tragedy with a double ending—"an opposite issue for the good and bad personages"—to a single unhappy issue. Moreover, Aristotle admitted that a successful tragedy could be based on a fictitious argument, like that of comedy, although most tragic poets used plots drawn from historic or legendary matter.

T. in modern times stemmed from two sources: (1) classical theory and practice, (2) the "people's choice," namely, the reward of virtue and the punishment of vice. There was some overlapping, but the two branches can be distinguished, the classical one springing from classical tragedy and the popular one from the native mysteries, miracles, moralities, and chronicle plays which freely mingled kings with clowns, tears with mirth. Neoclassical t. developed in Italy under the guidance of Giraldi Cinthio, who wrote several tragedies with a happy ending which he called mixed tragedies (*tragedie miste*). Cinthio distrusted Plautus' *tragicocomoedia,* but admitted that his own *Altile* (1543) could be called a *tragicomedia.* His mixed tragedies combined plots patterned after those of the comic poet Terence with the royal or noble characters of tragedy and attempted the lofty style of Seneca and Euripides. The author justified his violation of the classical prescription for separate tragic and comic genres by citing the authority of Aristotle and the example of Euripides. Popular t., on the other hand, developed as an extension of medieval practice, which more often than not ignored classical prescriptions, and this popular t. appeared as "tragical comedies" or "comical tragedies" or "histories," with serious main plots and comic subplots. The L. school plays of the Christian Terence and vernacular tragicomedies flourished side by side in France, Holland, Germany, and England.

These classical and popular branches grew together before the end of the 16th c. While Cinthio catered to the popular taste for poetic justice, he never admitted comic incidents, sentiments, or diction in his mixed tragedies. One of his successors, Giovanni Battista Guarini, drawing upon still another tradition which lent itself to t., i.e. the pastoral, wrote the best known t. of the century, the *Pastor fido,* and then prescribed formulas for the "new" genre in the critical controversy that followed the appearance of his play. Like Cinthio, Guarini mingled the great personages and lofty sentiments of tragedy with the comic order of plot; unlike Cinthio, he admitted some comic incidents, characters, sentiments, and diction as well. In his *Compendio della poesia tragicomica* (1601), he carefully explained what he was trying to do. Of special interest is his insistence upon a middle style of poetry between tragic grandeur and comic plainness: "In the *Pastor fido* the verse is not turgid, not noisy, not dithyrambic. Its periods are not prolonged, not short, not intricate, not hard, not difficult to understand; they need not be reread many times. Its figures of speech are taken from significant qualities, from proper and not from remote qualities. Its diction is clear but not low, proper but not vulgar, figurative but not enigmatical, beautiful but not affected, sustained but not inflated, pliant but not languishing; and, to conclude in a word, such as is not remote from common speech and yet not close to that of the common herd."

Guarini's own style hardly realized this ideal, but both his critical prescriptions and his "Faithful Shepherd" exerted a widespread influence in France and England as well as in Italy. Jean de Mairet in France and John Fletcher in England, for example, reproduced both the theory and the practice of Guarini. Moreover, leading dramatic poets of both these countries—e.g. Garnier, Hardy, Mairet, Corneille, Du Ryer, Rotrou, Beaumont and Fletcher, Shakespeare, Marston, Thomas Heywood, Massinger, Shirley, Dryden, Davenant—wrote tragicomedies.

When poetic drama went out of fashion, as it did in the 18th c., t. in the old sense disappeared except for an occasional *tour de force* like Rostand's *Cyrano,* and was succeeded in the theater by the prosaic *drame* and problem play. It might be said, however, that the spirit of t., with its mingling of tragic and comic genres, continues in poetry under the heritage of "metaphysical" poetry, which unites wit with seriousness and often employs in one way or another the old device of "tragic king-comic people."—H. C. Lancaster, *The Fr. T.* (1907); F. H. Ristine, *Eng. T.* (1910); W. Empson, *Some Versions of Pastoral* (1935); E. M. Waith, *The Pattern of T. in Beaumont and Fletcher* (1952); M. T. Herrick, *T.* (1955); K. S. Guthke, *Gesch. und Poetik der deutschen Tragikomödie* (1961). M.T.H.

TRIMETER (Gr. "of 3 measures"). Line composed of 3 measures, each measure being in classical verse a pair of iambic feet (⏑–⏑–), or else a spondee followed by an iambus (––⏑–). Developed (probably) by Archilochus of Paros, the t. is the usual meter for invective and for dialogue in Gr. drama. A caesura (q.v.) was obligatory in the inside of the third or fourth foot. Resolution (q.v.) of a short into 2 longs gave Gr. tragedy the possibility of an anapaest (⏑⏑–) in the first foot, a dactyl (–⏑⏑) in the first and third, and a tribrach (⏑⏑⏑) in any of the first 4. In comedy, resolution was more freely allowed. The L. modification of the t., the senarius (q.v.), is the characteristic dialogue meter of Old L. drama. In the senarius of the drama of the republican period and popular verse of later times the Gr. distinction between the even and odd feet was abandoned; spondees were allowed in the first 5 feet, and resolution was carried to its extreme (thus giving the proceleusmatic [⏑⏑⏑⏑] as another possible form). This Roman disregard of the "Dipody Law" (that the alternate feet should not exceed the value of 3 morae or shorts) is thought by some to be explicable only in terms of Roman regard for word-accent. A semiaccentual form of the t. was popular in the Middle Ages:

O tu qui sérvas || armis ista móenia
(*Carmen Mutinense*)

Eng. t. (a 3-foot line; strictly speaking, the term is incorrectly used for the Eng. 3-stress line) tends to be monotonous. Variation is often secured by the use of a dimeter (as in Browning's *A Woman's Last Word*) or tetrameter in a trimeter pattern. See IAMB.—Hardie; J. Descroix, *Le trimètre iambique* (1931). W.B.

TRIOLET. A Fr. fixed form. It is composed of 8 lines and uses only 2 rhymes, disposed in the following scheme: AB aA ab AB (a capital letter indicates a repeated line): "Easy is the triolet, / If you really learn to make it! / Once a neat refrain you get, / Easy is the triolet. / As you see!—I pay my debt / With another rhyme. Deuce take it, / Easy is the triolet, / If you really learn to make it!" (W. E. Henley). The challenge of the form lies in managing the intricate repetition so that it seems to be natural and inevitable, and in achieving in the repetitions a variety of meaning or, at least, a shift in emphasis.

According to O. Bloch and W. von Wartburg

(*Dictionnaire étymologique de la langue française*, 3d ed., 1960), the word "triolet" is not found until 1486, but the poem, as we know it, is much older and, as the simplest form of the rondel (q.v.), can be traced back to the 13th c., e.g., in the *Cléomadès* of Adenet-le-Roi. Subsequently, the form was cultivated by such medieval poets as Deschamps and Froissart. It began to be neglected toward the end of the 15th c. and fell into disuse during the 16th, although it had a brief vogue as revived by Vincent Voiture and Jean de La Fontaine in the 17th c. It was revived again in the 19th c. by Alphonse Daudet and, particularly, by Théodore de Banville.

With the exception of a few religious triolets composed in 1651 by the obscure devotional poet Patrick Carey, there were no triolets written in Eng. before recent times. Introduced by Robert Bridges, the form enjoyed considerable favor in the later years of the 19th c. The modern writers of triolets—Austin Dobson, H. C. Bunner, W. E. Henley and others—recognized, on the whole, the suitability of the form to light or humorous themes.—Kastner; P. Champion, *Hist. poétique du XVe s.* (2 v., 1923); M. Françon, "La pratique et la théorie du rondeau et du rondel chez Théodore de Banville, MLN, 52 (1937; states that triolets, rondels, and rondeaux are a single genre with variations); L. Spitzer, "T.," RR, 39 (1948).
A.P.

TRIPLE METER. (1) Any poetic measure consisting of 3 units, such as a foot of 3 syllables. Hence anapestic, dactylic, tribrachic, cretic, bacchiac feet, etc. are a sort of t.m. (2) Also any larger unit consisting of 3 feet or measures; thus a tripody is a measure of 3 feet. Fr. 12-syllable trimètre is an example of t.m. Spenser's "Iambic Trimetrum" (cf. correspondence with Gabriel Harvey) also employs a variety of t.m., which is more common in quantitative than in syllabic verse, especially L. hymns.
R.O.E.

TRIPLET, tercet. A verse unit of 3 lines, usually containing rhyme, employed as a stanzaic form, as a variation from couplet structure, or, occasionally, as a complete poem in itself. Known to It. poetry as the *terzina* (see TERZA RIMA). "Triplet" is a generic term; "tercet" generally implies the use of rhyme. The sestet (q.v.) of a sonnet is frequently made up of two triplets. The interlinking *sestine* of Dante's *Divina Commedia* are certainly the outstanding example of triplet composition; other noteworthy users of the t. include Donne, who wrote most of his verse epistles in monorhymed iambic triplets; Herrick, whose *Whenas in Silks my Julia Goes* is written in the same stanza form; and Shelley, who employed terza rima in his *Ode to the West Wind* and *The Triumph of Life*. William Carlos Williams has used free verse arranged in irregular triplets in some of the poems of his volume *The Desert Music*. A special use of the t. is exemplified in the heroic couplet writings of the Eng. poets of the Augustan Age. In the poems of Dryden and, to a lesser degree in those of Pope, the heroic couplets are sometimes varied by the interposition of 3 rhyming lines: "A fiery Soul, which working out its way, / Fretted the Pigmy Body to decay: / And o'r inform'd the Tenement of Clay" (Dryden, *Absalom and Achitophel*). The t. has never been used as widely as the couplet or the quatrain (qq.v.).

TRISEMIC (Gr. "of 3 time-units"). Term applied to the principle whereby musical theorists like Aristoxenus (4th c. B.C.) and Aristides Quintilianus (3d or 4th c. A.D.) postulated the existence of syllables equivalent in length to 3 morae. See CLASSICAL PROSODY, and MORA.
R.J.G.

TROCHEE, *choree* (respectively from Gr. "running" and "belonging to the dance"). A metrical unit, in quantitative verse, of a long syllable followed by a short:

$$- \smile;\ \bar{a}n\breve{t}e$$

The rhythm of the trochaic foot was therefore the reverse of the iambic (q.v.), i.e. "falling" instead of "rising." In Gr. and L. verse, where the feet could be varied by the use of spondees or tribrachs (less often by dactyls or anapaests), trochaic measures were used from the time of Archilochus onward, particularly in lyric and drama. (In comedy especially they lent themselves to rapid movement and dancing). Most common was the trochaic tetrameter catalectic, i.e., 7½, trochees or their variations called *septenarius* by the Romans. The term has been adopted into Eng. for the accentual foot of a stressed followed by an unstressed syllable:

ˊ ×; sílvèr

Though common in ME verse, the trochaic base was almost wholly absent from Eng. poetry until the end of the 16th c. when it was employed both in lyric and in dramatic monologues and songs:

Hónour, | ríches, | márriage|-bléssing
(Shakespeare, *Tempest* 4.1.106)

The 4-foot line remained predominant until Blake, whose innovations in length and variation opened up the way for subsequent developments. The 19th c. saw more frequent and broader use, chiefly, however, as substitution in predominantly iambic lines; but by itself it has never been a favorite in Eng., owing no doubt to the difficulty of finding words or phrases to begin the line with a stressed syllable (cf. the variations in Milton's *L'Allegro* and *Il Penseroso*). Used mechanically, as in *Hiawatha*, the trochee becomes monotonous; but in short passages it is often handled with success.—J. W. White, *The*

Verse of Gr. Comedy (1912); Baum; Hamer; Crusius; U. v. Wilamowitz-Moellendorff, *Griechische Verskunst* (2d ed., 1958). D.S.P.

TROPE. Ancient rhetoric in treating elocution or style as the presentation of thought and feeling in "decent and comely order" classified the language so arranged in schemes and tropes. Schemes are figures or patterns of speech which are out of the ordinary; they include figures of thought, which in the 16th c. were called figures of sentence or amplification, and figures of words. Tropes were figures also, but different in nature to the degree that they used words or phrases in senses that were not proper to them. These classifications were easy to maintain as such, but there was much confusion concerning the placing of particular figures. Antithesis was at once a scheme and a figure of thought. Periphrasis was sometimes classified as a trope and sometimes as a scheme. Metaphor, metonymy, synecdoche, and irony were central tropes. In the 16th c. metaphor and metonymy were regarded as tropes of words, and allegory, irony and hyperbole were tropes of sentences. The basis of these distinctions are in Aristotle and Isocrates, and a summary of the ancient teaching on tropes is made by Quintilian (8.6).

Elocution and style from early times were understood to belong equally to the arts of oratory and poetry, but the difficulty of maintaining the distinction in the nature of figures used by arts of different purpose increased with the sophistication of rhetorical practice and teaching and the allegorization of poetry in later Antiquity and the early Christian period. The root of the confusion lay in the doctrine that the orator himself must be moved, for in the extreme this was taken to justify ornament and figures for their own sake, a development of the emphasis of the pseudo-Ciceronian *Ad Herennium.* In the Middle Ages the Venerable Bede's work on schemes and tropes, which became a standard medieval text, initiated a tradition of stylistic rhetoric in England. From his analysis there led such doctrines that neither the Middle nor Low styles permitted the use of tropes, but that the High Style allowed ten of them, which were called "difficult ornaments." The treatment of tropes in the Renaissance went no farther than the extreme stylistic interpretation of Ramus, where schemes and tropes were regarded as the whole of elocution from which even considerations of grammar were excluded. It was not till the 18th c. and Vico that the base of the analysis was radically changed, with the doctrine that tropes belonged to the primitive imagination and were the necessary means of communication.

A special development in the use of tropes in the Middle Ages had spectacular consequences. An elaboration of the liturgy that is associated with the Carolingian Renaissance, and particularly in the rituals of Easter and the days preceding it, has been shown to have given rise to church drama itself. These tropes have been defined as verbal amplifications of passages in the authorized liturgy made to adorn the text, to enforce its meaning, and to enlarge its emotional appeal. One of the earliest examples is in the amplification of the *Kyrie eleïson*:

> Kyrie,
> magnæ Deus potentiæ,
> liberator hominis,
> transgressoris mandati,
> eleïson.

The *Introit* of the Mass at Easter, "Quem quæritis," developed into a completely dramatized form and detached from the Mass became, first, part of the Procession, then of the Matins, and later still was made into a representation of the Visitation. See also METAPHOR; METONYMY; SYNECDOCHE.—A. Sorrentino, *La Retorica e la Poetica di Vico* (1927); W. G. Crane, *Wit and Rhetoric in the Renaissance* (1937); K. Burke, "Four Master Tropes, KR, 3 (1941); D. L. Clark, *John Milton at Saint Paul's School* (1948) and *Rhetoric in Greco-Roman Education* (1957); K. Young, *The Drama of the Medieval Church* (1951); W. S. Howell, *Logic and Rhetoric in England, 1500–1700* (1956). J.A.

TROUBADOUR (from Prov. *trobar,* "invent"). A Prov. poet of the high Middle Ages. The troubadours flourished between 1100 and 1350 and were attached to various courts in the south of France. Their contributions to European poetry, which concern both subject matter and form, were of incalculable importance.

The troubadours made sexual love their almost exclusive theme, and developed the social phenomenon of courtly love, which left its stamp on European culture for centuries. The principal features of the love extolled by the troubadours were: an attitude of subservience and fidelity to a cold and cruel mistress, exorbitant and quasi-religious praise of the lady's beauty, and a requirement that the love be extramarital. Though the love celebrated by the troubadours was sensual, their ideal of "pure" love prohibited sexual intercourse between the lovers—at least in theory. This prohibition had the effect of endowing any casual contact, gesture, or token with enormous erotic significance, and thus bequeathed to later European love poetry a whole vocabulary and grammar of amorous symbol. Most t. lyrics are, thus, amorous in the extreme, but some are satirical or political.

The major genres cultivated by the troubadours, who were at once poets and composers of music, were the *canso d'amor* (see CHANSO), a love song, the *pastorela* (see PASTOURELLE), an account of the attempted seduction of a shepherdess by a poet, the *alba* (q.v.), a lament of lovers who must separate at the coming of dawn, the *tenso, partimen,* or *joc-partit,* debates on the fine points of the code of love, and the *sirventes*, a political invective or satire. These genres were expressed in a variety of metrical forms, some of them, like the *sestina* (q.v.), of extraordinary complexity.

Among the troubadours whose work has come down to us are Guillaume d'Aquitaine, Arnaut Daniel, and Bertrand de Born. Some of the troubadours, such as Sordello, were Italians, although they composed in the Prov. established by tradition.

The t. influence on Dante and Petrarch was immense, in both theme and form. Indeed, the example of the troubadours quickened and formed the lyrical impulse throughout western Europe, as expressed in the poetry of the *trouvères* and *Minnesinger* (qq.v.) as well as in that of late medieval Portuguese and Sicilian poets.

F.J.W.; A.P.

TROUVÈRE. Medieval poet of Northern France, especially Picardy. Contemporary of the troubadour (q.v.), who composed his poems in the *langue d'oc* of the South (or Prov.), the trouvère wrote in the *langue d'oil,* which prevailed and became the Fr. language. In addition to courtly lyrical poetry, which shows the influence of the troubadour in form and sentiment, the trouvère composed *chansons de geste* (q.v.) and *romans bretons.* Notable trouvères include Jean Bodel, Blondel de Nesle, the Châtelain de Coucy, Conon de Béthune and Thibaud de Champagne.—Jeanroy, *Origines; Minnesinger et trouvères,* ed. I. Frank (I, texts, 1952) and J. M. Müller-Blattau (II, music, 1956); R. Dragonetti, *La Technique poétique des trouvères dans la chanson courtoise* (1960).

TRUNCATION (catalexis). The omission of the last (generally unstressed) syllable or syllables in a line of conventional metrical structure. A line lacking one syllable of the normal number is called catalectic; one lacking two is called brachycatalectic. (When no syllable is lacking, the line is acatalectic and when there are one or more syllables in excess of the normal number, the line is said to be hypercatalectic or hypermetrical, q.v.) Truncation is frequent in trochaic verse, where the line of complete trochaic feet tends to create an effect of monotony. The following trochaic lines exhibit t.: "Simple maiden, void of art, / Babbling out the very heart" (Ambrose Philips). T. is also frequently employed in dactylic lines to avoid an effect of excessive bounciness; Hood's second line is truncated: "Take her up tenderly, / Lift her with care." T. in the blank verse of the 17th-c. drama is frequently encountered in passages representing informal utterance: "Good morrow to this fair assembly" (*Much Ado About Nothing* 5.4). The term "initial t." is used to describe the omission of the first syllable of a (generally iambic) line. A line so truncated is also called a "headless (acephalous) line. See also, LINE ENDINGS.

P.F.

TUMBLING VERSE. A phrase first used by James I in his *Reulis and Cautelis* (1585) to apply to 4-foot trisyllabic (anapaestic or dactylic) verse in Eng. which goes back through the alliterative verse of the Middle Ages to the Old Germanic alliterative verse and probably even further to a common Indo-European meter: "I was wery forwandred and went me to rest." The meter was reinforced by the 6/8 dance tune of popular song and was much used in Elizabethan poetry (e.g., Tusser, *Five Hundred Points of Good Husbandry,* 1557). Aside from England the only European country in which this meter was prominent was Spain where, as the *arte mayor* (q.v.), it was used for the most serious poetry. Juan de Mena (ca. 1411–56), the most famous poet to use this measure, employed it in his chief work, *El Laberinto.*—Ker.

R.P.APR.

U

UNITY is the most fundamental and comprehensive aesthetic criterion, upon which all others depend. Plato first among Western thinkers proposed am artistic doctrine of u.; in the *Phaedrus* he perceived an analogy between u. of discourse and the organic u. of a living creature. In the *Symposium* he suggested in connection with the musical scale that u. is a reconciliation of opposites or discords. Organic u. is obtainable by means of conscious arrangement of parts. Aristotle's *Poetics* provides our first great statement on dramatic u. Aristotle emphasizes functionalism; tragedy is superior to epic because of its tighter internal relationships (5.23–24). U. is an ideal relationship of beginning, middle, and end. The ideal tragedy is an imitation of a unified action, large enough to be perspicuous and small enough to be comprehensible. Aristotle's conception of u. is closely related to his artistic requirements of probability and necessity, as they constitute the criteria for the connection of parts (6–9). Thc famous "three unities" of action, time and place were often ascribed to the *Poetics* though he actually sponsors the u. of action only.

Aristotle is concerned with dramatic action; Horace's looser, more informal *Art of Poetry* deals indiscriminately with action, words, metaphor, and poetic or rhetorical devices. The *Art of Poetry* contains the definitive neoclassic statement: "I shall aim at a poem so deftly fashioned out of familiar matter that anybody might hope to emulate the feat, yet for all his efforts sweat and labor in vain. Such is the power of order and arrangement; such the charm that waits upon common things." Horace conceives of u. as an effect of harmony, obtained by skillful "order and arrangement," analogous either to music or more significantly to the harmonious blending of colors, light, and shadow in painting ("ut pictura poesis"). Pope's *Essay on Criticism* in the 18th c. is a classic adaptation of Horace, as Boileau had a little earlier adapted "Longinus." Longinus' *On the Sublime* is the most useful ancient document on lyric poetry. The conception of u. presented in it is relatively romantic, although in its account of arrangement and oratorical "amplification" it has affinities with both Plato and Horace. In his analysis of Sappho's Ode Longinus detects an organic u. derived from intensity of feeling and thought, which manifests itself as a reconciliation of opposing elements, and which artistically declares itself as a process of selection (10).

From antiquity to the end of the 18th c. theories of u. have been primarily theories of dramatic u., with the three unities of "the rules" the dominant issue. The It. Castelvetro has generally been credited or taxed with them in his translation and commentary on Aristotle's *Poetics* (1570). U. for Castelvetro is a quasi-legal consequence of the limitation of a dramatic action to twelve hours; by way of artistic satisfaction, it displays the skill of the poet in doing much with little (Gilbert, *Literary Criticism,* pp. 309–10, 318–19, 354). In general, the larger purposes of the three unities throughout their reign were to foster verisimilitude (q.v.) and to obtain artistic concentration, and for these purposes, as T. S. Eliot has remarked in "A Dialogue on Dramatic poetry" (1928), there is much to be said for them. Under them grew up the great Fr. classical drama of the 17th c., despite the occasional grumblings of Corneille. For whatever reason, the three unities were never entirely naturalized in England, although the "regular" play received due critical respect. Whether because of the whole trend of native Elizabethan and Jacobean drama, or the great counterexample of Shakespeare, or, as Englishmen were wont to maintain, because of the superior independence and originality of the Eng. mind, the unities were only casually observed. Dryden's *An Essay of Dramatic Poesy* (1668, 1684), with its brilliant defense of the Eng. use of subplot (*Essays,* 1.69–71), is a full and fair discussion of the issues. Dr. Johnson was to strike a semifinal blow against the unities by denying their claims to "nature" and verisimilitude ("Preface to Shakespeare," 1765), and Coleridge completely demolished their philosophical and psychological pretensions, as had A. W. von Schlegel, in his lectures on Shakespeare (*Shakespearean Criticism,* I).

Up to the second half of the 18th c. theories of poetic u. for the most part dealt with drama, with some attention to epic (Le Bossu, *Traité du Poëme Épique,* or Addison's *Spectator* papers on *Paradise Lost,* for example) and to narrative poetry in general. Such theories were usually objective, since their subject matter was external action, and analytical, since they were concerned with the known components of recognized genres. With the rise of psychological aesthetics in the 18th c., however, came ideas better suited to lyric poetry, or capable of application to all poetry. New and enlarged conceptions of poetic imagination and a general shift from a mechanical to a vitalist world-view brought forth the romantic organic u., which had various aspects; it appeared as u. of feeling, u. as a vision of a vital, sentient nature, u. as an imitation of the poet's mind in the act of creation, and imaginative u., with the imagination the shaping, unifying, and reconciling power (Coleridge, *Biographia Literaria,* chap. 14).

20th c. theories of u., although they are often direct reactions against romanticism, are nevertheless basically romantic. The concept of u., especially of organic u., was never more important than in the formalist, the psychological, and the mythicist criticism of the period between 1930 and 1960. Thus poetic u. was explained by I. A. Richards in *Principles of Literary Criticism* as a reconciliation of impulses, by Cleanth Brooks and others as a reconciliation of thought and feeling manifested in the interaction of theme with language and metaphor, by the surrealists as a unifying of the total mind by freeing the unconscious, by the Freudians through dream-pattern and Freudian symbol, and by the Jungians by detection of archetypal myth-motifs (T. S. Eliot, *The Waste Land,* Maud Bodkin, *Archetypal Patterns in Poetry*). All such versions of u., however, can be distinguished from their romantic predecessors by their common radicalism and their common effort to banish the subject-object problem of external reference. Since 1968 the concept of u. has lost ground to theories that suggest that the work of art is only an illusion of u.; that it is, in fact, a collection of basically unrelated "codes."

Plato, *Dialogues,* tr. B. Jowett, I and III (4th ed., 1953); S. H. Butcher, *Aristotle's Theory of Poetry and Fine Art* (4th ed., 1911, 1932, 1951); Longinus, *On the Sublime,* tr. W. Rhys Roberts (1907); T. R. Henn, *Longinus and Eng. Crit.* (1934); L. Castelvetro, *Poetica d'Aristotele vulgarizzata et sposta* (1571); H. B. Charlton, *Castelvetro's Theory of Poetry* (1913); R. Le Bossu, *Traité du poëme épique* (1675); *Treatise of the Epick Poem,* tr. "W. J." (1695); J. Dryden, *The Essays of John Dryden,* ed. W. P. Ker (2 v., 1926); S. T. Coleridge, *Biographia Literaria,* ed. J. Shawcross (2 v., 1907); *Coleridge's Shakespearean Crit.,* ed. T. M. Raysor (2 v., 1930); I. A. Richards, *Principles;* M. Bodkin, *Archetypal Patterns in Poetry* (1934) and *Studies of Type-Images in Poetry, Religion, and Philosophy*

(1951); J.W.H. Atkins, *Lit. Crit. in Antiquity* (1934); *Lit. Crit., Plato to Dryden*, ed. A. H. Gilbert (1940); C. Brooks, *The Well Wrought Urn* (1947); S. E. Hyman, *The Armed Vision* (1948); Abrams; Wellek; Wimsatt and Brooks. See also G. F. Else, *Aristotle's Poetics* (1957); R. Barthes, *S / Z* (1970).

R.H.F.

UT PICTURA POESIS. Few expressions of aesthetic criticism have led to more comment over a period of several centuries than *u.p.p.*, "as is painting so is poetry" (Horace, *Ars Poetica* 361). Even with partial explanation (362–65, 1–47, 343–45), the Horatian comparison of painting and poetry was as tentative as the proper Augustan wished it to be. The notion that poetry and painting are alike had had some currency even before Horace, who probably knew—even if he may not have assumed that his audience would recall—the more explicit earlier statement of Simonides of Keos (first recorded by Plutarch, *De gloria Atheniensium,* 3.347a, more than a century after *Ars Poetica*): "Poema pictura loquens, pictura poema silens" (poetry is a speaking picture, painting a silent [mute] poetry).

The views of Aristotle—especially that poetry and painting as arts of imitation should use the same principal element of composition (structure), namely, *plot* in tragedy and *design* (outline) in painting (see *Poetics,* 6.19–21)—furnished additional authority for Renaissance and later attempts to measure the degree and the nature of the kinship of the arts (the "parallel" of the arts) and to determine the order of precedence among them (the "*paragone*" of the arts). Moreover, as Rensselaer W. Lee observed in his illuminating analysis of the humanistic theory or doctrine of painting for which the Horatian dictum served as a kind of final sanction, "writers on art expected one to read [*u.p.p.*] 'as is poetry so is painting.' "

The Horatian simile, however interpreted, asserted the likeness, if not the identity, of painting and poetry; and from so small a kernel came an extensive body of aesthetic speculation and, in particular, an impressive theory of art which prevailed in the 16th, 17th, and most of the 18th c. While a few poets assented to the proposition that painting surpasses poetry in imitating human nature in action as well as in showing a Neoplatonic Ideal Beauty above nature, more of them raided the province of painting for the greater glory of poetry and announced that the preeminent painters are the poets. Lucian's praise of Homer as painter (*Eikones* 8) gave ancient authority for that view, which Petrarch and others reinforced. Among the poets described as master-painters have been Theocritus, Virgil, Tasso, Ariosto, Spenser, Shakespeare, and Milton, not to mention numerous later landscapists in descriptive poetry, the Pre-Raphaelites, and the Parnassians. Painter and critic, Reynolds instanced Michelangelo as the prime witness to "the poetical part of our art" of painting (*Discourse* 15, 1790). Thus a "poetical" or highly imaginative painter could be compared with the "painting" poets.

U.p.p. offered a formula—the success of which "one can hardly deny," René Wellek remarked—for analyzing the relationship of poetry and painting (and other arts). However successful, the Horatian formula proved useful—at least was used—on many occasions as a precept to guide artistic endeavor, as an incitement to aesthetic argument, and as a basic element in several theories of poetry and the arts. Alone and with many accretions, modifications, and transformations, *u.p.p.* inspired a number of meaningful comments about the arts and poetry and even contributed to the [actual] work and theory of several painters, most notably, "learned Poussin." Moreover, like other commonplaces of criticism, the Horatian formula stimulated and attracted to itself a variety of views of poetry and painting that are hard to relate to the original statement.

Another part of the story of the Horatian simile concerns adverse criticism and opposition. In *Plastics* (1712) Shaftesbury warned, "Comparisons and parallel[s] . . . between painting and poetry . . . almost ever absurd and at best constrained, lame and defective." The chief counterattack came in *Laokoön* (1766), with Lessing contending that the theories of art associated with *u.p.p.* had been the principal, if not the only, begetter of the confusion of the arts which he deplored in the artistic practice and theory of the time. R. G. Saisselin has lately shown that the "relations between the sister arts . . . were more complex than a reading of Lessing might lead one to believe" (JAAC, Winter 1961). Since then similar charges have been raised occasionally, as in Irving Babbitt's *The New Laokoön: An Essay on the Confusion of the Arts* (1910), a stumbling block until very recently.

On the other hand, from late in the 19th c. the kinship of poetry and painting appeared in a more favorable light in connection with the arts of the East—in generalizations about the "poetic feeling" of Oriental painting and the pictorial characteristics of Chinese and Japanese poetry and, with the ever-increasing knowledge of Eastern art, in historical and critical studies setting forth the close relationships between Oriental poetry and painting. In China poets were often painters; and critics, particularly in the 11th and 12th c., stated the parallelism of poetry and painting in language close to that of Simonides and Horace. According to Chou Sun, "Painting and writing are one and the same art." *Writing* implied calligraphy, which linked painting with poetry. Thus, a poet might "paint poetry," and a painter *wrote* "soundless poems."

These Eastern views led a number of poets in Europe and America to follow Japanese rules for poems and Chinese canons of painting and even to write-paint "Oriental" poems—"images" directly presented to the eye, "free" impressions in a few strokes of syllables and lines, evocations of mood, lyrical epigrams, and representations rather than reproductions of nature. Yet the poems reflecting the Eastern tendency to regard poetry and painting as "two sides of the same thing" were experimental and specialized works that included only a few of the resources of the two arts. Moreover, the critical analysis of "the same thing," with its "two sides" of painting and poetry, remains at least as difficult as the explanation of the Horatian observation, "as is painting so is poetry."

Today, painters and poets seldom study the Horatian simile and the expanded "texts" of the It., Fr., and Eng. treatises on the humanistic theory of painting, and few artists care whether painting ever had a superior, an elder, or any sister. Oriental theories of the blending, not to say confusion, of art forms are more likely to arouse interest in the kinship and rivalry of poetry and painting. If painting now seems too varied to allow anyone to define it precisely, the same is true of poetry. The relation between poetry and painting was strikingly reaffirmed in the period between 1910 and 1930 by the poets of Futurism, Dada, and Surrealism (e.g., Marinetti, Tzara, Schwitters, Breton) and by the poets of *De Stijl* (e.g. Theo van Doesberg). In New York a close affinity developed between painters (e.g. William Marsden, Marcel Duchamp) and such poets as Mina Loy, W. C. Williams, and Wallace Stevens. In the work of these poets—and in the later work of "Concrete Poets" (see CONCRETE POETRY)—the old concept of *u.p.p.* is revived. Whatever painting is, poetry is the same! Since the Horatian proposition may be useful again, it had best remain unresolved: if poetry and painting *are* the same and were born at one and the same time, they may together fall.—W. G. Howard, *U.P.P.*, PMLA, 24 (1909); and (ed.) *Laokoön: Lessing, Herder, Goethe* (1910; full bibliog.); I. Babbitt, *The New Laokoön* (1910); E. Manwaring, *It. Landscape in 18th C. England* (1925); C. Davies, "*U.P.P.*," MLR, 30 (1935); R. W. Lee, "*U.P.P.*," *Art Bull.*, 22 (1940) and "*U.P.P.*" in Shipley; Wellek and Warren (2d ed., chap. 11); H. H. Frankel, "Poetry and Painting: Chinese and Western Views of their Convertibility," CL, 9 (1957); J. H. Hagstrum, *The Sister Arts* (1958); R. G. Saisselin, "*U.P.P.*: Du Bos to Diderot," JAAC, 20 (1961); W. Marling, *William Carlos Williams and the Painters, 1909–1923* (1982). S.A.L.

V

VEHICLE. See TENOR AND VEHICLE.

VENUS AND ADONIS STANZA. So called from its use by Shakespeare in the poem *Venus and Adonis.* A 6-line stanza in 5-foot iambic lines, rhyming ababcc, it did not originate with Shakespeare, but had been used earlier, e.g., by Sidney in his *Arcadia* and by Spenser in the Januarie eclogue of his *Shepheardes Calender.* Shakespeare employed this form again in *Romeo and Juliet, Love's Labour's Lost,* and other plays. The stanza proved particularly attractive to American poets, e.g., Freneau, *To Sylvius on His Preparing to Leave the Town,* Bryant, *Lines on Revisiting the Country,* and Lowell, *April Birthday at Sea.* R.O.E.

VERISIMILITUDE. The doctrine that poetry should be "probable" or "likely" or "lifelike." Almost all critical theory has in some measure accepted the idea, though differences in strictness and laxness of interpretation are major.

The primary source is the concept of *to eikos* (the probable, the verisimilar) in Aristotle's *Poetics.* It is closely related to his fundamental notion of the imitation of nature. If a poem is not lifelike (at least in some sense), it can hardly be called an imitation. Aristotle's account is perceptive, brief, and left a good bit to the judgment of later critics. He says, in Chapter 9, that the poet describes not historical actions but "the kind of thing that might happen . . . as being probable or necessary." Historical occurrences may *or may not* be probable in this sense, and in tragedy the marvelous or astonishing must be included and the supernatural may be included. He gives some scope, though not very much, in Chapter 15, to propriety of character, as he allows "consistent inconsistency," and a great deal of scope, in Chapter 25, to the impossible so long as it is "convincing," and even some allowance to the improbable, since it is probable that some improbable events will happen. And the writer may depart from representation of common reality in depicting the ideal or in following common opinion. What he insists on is universality and the *apparent* moral and psychological consequentiality of actions. Cicero, Quintilian, Plutarch, Horace accept the idea and tend to restrict it somewhat more than did Aristotle, in the direction of the ordinary and the commonly probable.

In Renaissance thought, theorists from Scaliger through the "querelle du Cid" and later, take the concept very seriously and debate its range and meaning. Propriety of character, where Aristotle himself gave little enough freedom, is interpreted so strictly that stock characters tend to become the exclusive ideal (most notoriously in Thomas Rymer's animadversions against Shakespeare), though in one notable instance Dryden defends the character of Caliban in a brilliant argument, on strict grounds of propriety and verisimilitude (*Essays of John Dryden,* ed. W. P. Ker, I, 219–20). Somewhat more freedom is allowed in the handling of the marvelous (Christian critics being hardly willing to deny supernature a place in serious literature), though there is major disagreement here. Castelvetro, Maggio, Chapelain, and d'Aubignac discriminate between ordinary and extraordinary verisimilitude. Rymer, and later—rather surprisingly—Johnson, take a conservative view with respect to this point, Dryden and Rapin take moderate positions, and Chapelain (who wants a more Christian poetry) a radical one.

It was on grounds of *vraisemblance* that the Academy censured *The Cid* of Corneille. Corneille and Racine accepted the principle of *vraisemblance* or verisimilitude quite genuinely, and the struggle in each of them between the abstracted rules and the pressures of their artistic habits and desires was, for both, fruitful.

Though the term has had much less use in the last two centuries, the idea, as a perennial and inescapable demand, persists in various, often implicit, forms: Wordsworth's turning to the common realities and the language of men, Coleridge's frequent appeals to "good sense," Arnold's "criticism of life," and the New Critics' concern for paradox, irony, "toughness" as giving an adequate, which is to say verisimilar, image of our experiened.—R. M. Alden, "The Doctrine of Verisimilitude," *Matzke Memorial Volume* (1911); Bray; P. van Tieghem, *Petite histoire des grandes doctrines littéraires en France* (1946); Tuve, esp. chap. 9; B. Weinberg, *A Hist. of Lit. Crit. in the It. Renaissance* (2 v., 1961). P.R.

VERS DE SOCIÉTÉ. See LIGHT VERSE.

VERS LIBRE. Rhymed, syllabic verse, mainly the product of the Middle Ages, was not to remain long unchallenged: the *versi sciolti* (q.v.) of the It. Renaissance, prosodic experiments by Antoine de Baïf, alternations of verse lengths in La Fontaine begin a loosening which is climaxed by the v.l. of 19th-c. France. Whitman's free verse may have served as model, but the form appears in the *Illuminations* (1873?) of Rimbaud, who was probably unaware of the *Leaves of Grass* (1855) which, anyhow, seem closer to the *verset* than to v.l. The two v.l. poems of Rimbaud were first printed in the review *La Vogue* in 1886. Gustave Kahn, the editor, published his own v.l. there shortly afterwards, and haughtily insisted that he was nowise influenced by Rimbaud, to whose v.l. he, moreover, denied that appellation. About this time Jules Laforgue, Kahn's friend, produced his—infinitely superior—v.l., to be followed (it would seem) by that of Jean Moréas. These men have claimed, or been credited with, inventing the form; but it is fairer to say the form invented itself through them, the tyrannical structures of Fr. versification eliciting a strong, if gradual, reaction—first in poetic prose, then prose poem (q.v.), then *vers libéré,* and finally v.l. This last can be defined as verse in which neither syllable nor metrical rules obtain, and only rhythm matters. Though rhyme (as opposed to most Eng. free verse) *may* persist, the traditional Fr. regulations for caesura, hiatus, counting of mute *e*'s, etc., are ignored. Consecutive lines may vary greatly in length, or may not, and the only unity generally maintained is one of sense or syntax.

The key problem is rhythm: how can it be defined—or at least demonstrated—in v.l., so as to justify the form's claim to poetic status? According to Herbert Read (following Professor Sonnenschein), we have in v.l. the substitution of the "element of proportion . . . for the element of regularity." Edouard Dujardin, himself an early *verslibriste,* sees it as "a form able to rhythmify or derhythmify itself instantaneously," and so suited to changes of mood in longer, particularly dramatic, poems. Professor V. Černý views v.l. as the spontaneous expression of inner rhythm, fighting "against formalism and, implicitly, for the self-assertion of poetic content" (a characteristically leftist position). One could adduce numerous further descriptions from scholars or practitioners, but it may be safely asserted that v.l. defies precise definition. Whatever is put on paper as free verse and moves us as poetry is v.l.: the rhythm may be simply a question of emotional and intellectual response.

Among other early *verslibristes* should be mentioned Vielé-Griffin, Henri de Régnier, Maeterlinck, and Verhaeren (the first half-Am., the last two Belgians). The movement spread to other countries. It was imported into Italy both by the futurists and the post-symbolist Gabriele d'Annunzio in his plays. In Spain, the "Generation of '98" produced some admirable v.l., especially, perhaps, Juan Ramón Jiménez. The so-called *freien Rhythmen* of Germany go back to Klopstock and the 18th c., and come down through Goethe, Hölderlin, and others; but they have been especially popular in the modern period. Rilke's *Duino Elegies* and the lyrics and dramas of expressionism are the best-known examples. There is probably no occidental literature now without its variety of v.l. The theatre has proved especially receptive to the flexible but effective form. It has also been used frequently in poetry of spiritual (e.g., Francis Jammes, P. J. Jouve) or socio-political (e.g., V. Mayakovsky, Bert Brecht) exaltation. At present v.l. is a vigorous and developing form. An innovation of the 1930s (E. E. Cummings) was the shift of the line breaks away from the natural speech rests, creating an effect of syncopation. See also FREE VERSE.

G. Kahn, "Préface," *Premiers poèmes* (1897);

C. C. Clarke, *Concerning Fr. Verse* (1922; last ch.); M. M. Dondo, *V.L., a Logical Development of Fr. Verse* (1922); J. Hytier, *Les Techniques modernes du vers français* (1923); E. Dujardin, "Les Premiers poètes du v.l.," *Mallarmé par un des siens* (1936); H. Morier, *Le Rythme du v.l. symboliste* (3 v., 1944); A. Closs, *Die freien Rhythmen in der deutschen Lyrik* (1947); P. M. Jones, *The Background to Modern Fr. Poetry* (1951; part two, best introd. to the subject); W. Ramsey, *Jules Laforgue and the Ironic Inheritance* (1953; ch. 9); V. Černý, *Verhaeren a jeho místo v dejinach volného verše* (Prague, 1955; the Communist view). J.S.

VERSE AND PROSE. Words are used (1) for ordinary speech, (2) for discursive or logical thought, and (3) for literature.

Discursive language makes statements of fact, is judged by standards of truth and falsehood, and is in the form of prose. Literature makes no real statements of fact, proceeds hypothetically, and is judged by its imaginative consistency. Literature includes a great deal which is written in some form of regular recurrence, whether meter, accent, vowel quantity, rhyme, alliteration, parallelism, or any combination of these, and which we may call verse. All verse is literary, and philosophical or historical works written in verse are almost invariably classified as literature. We can exclude them from literature only by some kind of value-judgement, not by a categorical judgement, and to introduce value-judgements before we understand what our categories are is only to invite confusion. But although verse seems to be in some central and peculiar way the typical language of literature, all literature is not verse. The question thus arises: what is the status of literary prose? The best way to distinguish literary from nonliterary prose is by what we may call, cautiously and tentatively, its intention. If it is intended to describe and represent facts and to be judged by its truth, it normally belongs in some nonliterary category; if it is to be judged primarily by its imaginative consistency, it normally belongs to literature. We say *normally*, because it is quite possible to look at some works, such as Gibbon's *Decline and Fall of the Roman Empire*, from either point of view.

A subordinate problem also arises in passing: what is the meaning of the word poetry? Aristotle remarked in the *Poetics* that meter was not the distinguishing feature of "poetry." But Aristotle also remarked that the work of literary art as such, whether poem or play or essay, is "to this day without a name," and to *this* day, 2,500 years later, the statement is still true. The word "poetry" has always meant primarily "composition in meter," so that while *Tom Jones*, for instance, is certainly a work of literature, nobody would call it a poem

The first point to get clear about prose is that the language of ordinary speech is not prose, or at least is prose only to the extent that it is not verse. Ordinary speech, especially colloquial or vulgar speech, is a discontinuous, repetitive, heavily accented rhetoric which is as readily distinguishable from prose as it is from regular meter. Any fiction writer who is a close observer of common speech will show in his dialogue a markedly different rhythm from what he himself uses in narration or description. Prose is ordinary speech on its best behavior: it is the conventionalization of speech that is made by the educated or articulate person when he is trying to assimilate his speech to the patterns of discursive thought. Anyone listening to the asyntactic prolixity of uneducated speech, or to the chanting or whining of children, can see that regular meter is in fact a much simpler way of stylizing ordinary speech than prose is, which explains why prose is normally a late and sophisticated development in the history of a literature.

There are, then, at least two ways of conventionalizing ordinary speech: the simple and primitive way of regularly recurring meter, and the more intellectualized way of developing a consistent and logical sentence structure. When recurrent rhythm takes the lead and the sentence structure is subordinated to it, we have verse. When the sentence structure takes the lead and all patterns of repetition are subordinated to it and become irregular, we have prose. Literary prose results from the imitation for literary purposes of the language of discursive thought. Of all the differentia between prose and verse, the only essential one is this difference of rhythm. Verse is able to absorb a much higher concentration of metaphorical and figurative speech than prose, but this difference is one of degree; the difference in rhythm which makes the higher concentration possible is a difference of kind.

This division between prose and verse is however complicated by the various forms of "free verse," which are unmistakably literary and yet are not in meter or any other form of regular recurrence. The naive assumption that any poetry not in some recognizable recurrent pattern must really be prose clearly will not do, and we have to assume the existence of a third type of conventionalized utterance. This third type has a peculiar relation to ordinary speech, or at least to soliloquy and inner speech. We may call it an oracular or associational rhythm, the unit of which is neither the prose sentence nor the metrical line, but a kind of thought-breath or phrase. Associational rhythm predominates in free verse and in certain types of literary prose, such as "stream of consciousness" prose.

A historical treatment of this threefold division of verbal rhythm—discursive, metrical, and associational—would require an encyclopaedia in itself. It will be best if we proceed inductively, confining our examples to the single language of Eng., and look at some of the literary phenomena which may be explained by it. Each of the three rhythms, in literature, may exist in a relatively pure state or in combination with either of its neighbors.

VARIETIES OF PROSE RHYTHM. Prose, we have said, is typically either the language of discursive thought or an imitation of that language for literary purposes. In pure prose the logical or descriptive features are at a maximum, and the stylistic, or rhetorical, features at a minimum. The rhythm of the sentence predominates; all repetition, whether of sound or rhythm, is eliminated as far as possible, and recurring rhetorical devices, or tricks of style, are noticed only with irritation. The aim is to present a certain content or meaning in as unobtrusive and transparent a way as possible. When prose is like this it is at the furthest possible remove from metrical or associative influences. Pure prose has two chief types of rhythm: the more informal and colloquial type which represents the rhythm of educated speech transferred to the printed page, and the more formal type which is thought of from the beginning as something to be read in a book. Let us take a passage from Darwin's *Origin of Species*: "The great and inherited development of the udders in cows and goats in countries where they are habitually milked, in comparison with these organs in other countries, is probably another instance of the effects of use. Not one of our domestic animals can be named which has not in some country drooping ears; and the view which has been suggested that the drooping is due to the disuse of the muscles of the ear, from the animals being seldom much alarmed, seems probable." This passage plainly does not lack either rhythm or readability; there is certainly a literary pleasure in reading it. The pleasure however is in seeing prose expertly used for its own descriptive purposes, and from our confidence that such alliteration as "the drooping is due to the disuse" is purely accidental. Let us compare Darwin's prose with a passage from Gibbon's *Decline and Fall of the Roman Empire*:

"The mystic sacrifices were performed, during three nights, on the banks of the Tiber; and the Campus Martius resounded with music and dances, and was illuminated with innumerable lamps and torches. . . . A chorus of twenty-seven youths, and as many virgins, of noble families, and whose parents were both alive, implored the propitious gods in favour of the present, and for the hope of the rising generation; requesting in religious hymns, that, according to the faith of their ancient oracles, they would still maintain the virtue, the felicity, and the empire of the Roman people." Here, along with the information given about the secular games of Philip, we are aware of certain tricks of style, such as antithetical balance and doubled adjectives. If we are intent only on the history, the tricks of style obstruct our path. But we notice that a specifically literary intention is visible in Gibbon beside the descriptive one. He is suggesting a *meditative* interest in the decline of Rome, and for this meditative interest a certain formal symmetry in the style is appropriate.

We notice also that the more obtrusive stylizing of Gibbon's prose makes it more oratorical, a quality of deliberate rhetoric being present. Another step would take us all the way into oratorical prose, where the formalized style is of equal importance with the subject matter. This is the normal area of all great oratory, as from Cicero down to Lincoln's Gettysburg Address and Churchill's 1940 speeches, the most memorable passages of oratory have usually been passages of formal repetition. Samuel Johnson's letter to Chesterfield provides similar examples:

"The notice which you have been pleased to take of my labours, had it been early, had been kind; but it has been delayed till I am indifferent, and cannot enjoy it; till I am solitary, and cannot impart it; till I am known, and do not want it." With the increase of the rhetorical or symmetrical element in the style, the prose is taking on an increasingly *metrical* quality, and is moving closer to verse. This metrical quality is strongly marked in Ciceronian prose, in the long formal sentences broken in two by an "and" out of which the 17th-c. character books are constructed, in the deliberately symmetrical arrangements of phrases and clauses in Sir Thomas Browne's *Urn Burial* and Jeremy Taylor's *Holy Dying*.

A slight exaggeration of this metrical element would take us into the area of euphuism, which is a deliberate attempt to give to prose the rhetorical features of verse, including rhyme and alliteration as well as metrical balance. Here is a sentence from Robert Greene's euphuistic romance *The Carde of Fancie*: "This loathsome lyfe of *Gwydonius*, was such a cutting corasive to his Fathers carefull conscience, and such a haplesse clogge to his heavie heart, that no joye could make him injoye any joye, no mirth could make him merrie, no prosperitie could make him pleasant, but abandoning all delight, and avoyding all companie, he spent his dolefull dayes in dumpes and dolours, which he uttered in these words." Here we are almost as far away as we can get from anything that we now think of as prose: the predominating rhythm is still the sentence, but the writer has done everything that a descriptive prose writer would try to avoid. Euphuism is of course an intensely rhetorical form of prose: one would expect to find it in sermons, where it has been prominent from Anglo-Saxon times; and in euphuist stories the writer strives for situations where the characters may write letters, lament, or harangue. We notice that the sentence quoted above leads up to a harangue.

Now let us return to the type of pure prose that is more informal and colloquial, designed to suggest good talk rather than good exposition, of which perhaps the greatest practitioner is Montaigne. Let us take a passage from one of Bernard Shaw's Prefaces:

"After all, what man is capable of the insane

self-conceit of believing that an eternity of himself would be tolerable even to himself? Those who try to believe it postulate that they shall be made perfect first. But if you make me perfect I shall no longer be myself, nor will it be possible for me to conceive my present imperfections (and what I cannot conceive I cannot remember); so that you may just as well give me a new name and face the fact that I am a new person and that the old Bernard Shaw is as dead as mutton." As compared with the Darwin passage, there is here some influence of an associational rhythm: we can see the easy use of parenthesis, the imaginary conversation with the reader, and similar signs of the associative process of speech. But everything here is on an impersonal plane, the conscious mind and logical argument being assumed to be in charge. Continuous prose, or writing with a logical shape, assumes an equality between writer and reader. The writer buttonholes his reader, so to speak, when he talks to him continuously. If he wishes to suggest aloofness or some barrier against his reader, or if he simply wishes to suggest that there are greater reserves in his mind than he is ready to display all at once, he would naturally turn to a more discontinuous form.

We find such a form in the series of aphorisms of which many prose works, such as books of recorded table talk, are constructed. Philosophers in particular seem to be fond of it: Pascal, Bacon, Spinoza, Wittgenstein, Nietzsche, are a few random examples. The aphorism is oracular: it suggests that one should stop and ponder on it. Like oratorical prose, it suggests meditation, but the reader is being directed into the writer's mind instead of outward to the subject. In such discontinuous and aphoristic prose the associational rhythm can be clearly heard. Donne's *Devotions Upon Emergent Occasions* provide examples, especially in those passages cast in the form of prayer, where the reader is not being directly addressed: ". . . thou callest *Gennezareth*, which was but a Lake, and not *salt*, a *Sea*; so thou callest the *Mediterranean Sea*, still the *great Sea*, because the *inhabitants* saw no other *Sea*; they that dwelt there, thought a *Lake*, a *Sea*, and the others thought a *little Sea*, the *greatest*, and wee that know not the *afflictions* of others, call our owne the heaviest."

A step further in this direction takes us toward the oracular and associational prose poem of which Ossian is the best known Eng. example, though there is so little intellectual or logical interest in Ossian that there is not much sense of prose left. Eng. does not provide as clear examples of the aphoristic prose poem as German has in Nietzsche's *Also Sprach Zarathustra* or as Fr. has in Rimbaud's *Saison en Enfer*. But it is clear that in the opening of Dylan Thomas's *Under Milk Wood* prose is being as strongly influenced by an associational rhythm as it can well be and still remain prose: "It is Spring, moonless night in the small town, starless and bible-black, the cobblestreets silent and the hunched, courters'-and-rabbits' wood limping invisible down to the sloeblack, slow, black, crowblack, fishing-boat-bobbing sea."

VARIETIES OF VERSE RHYTHM. This subject really belongs to PROSODY, but a few additional suggestions may find a place here. In Eng. such forms as the stopped heroic couplet and the octosyllabic couplet represent the rhythm of metrical verse at its purest, equidistant from prose and from the associational rhythm. The following passage from Pope is typical:

Alike in ignorance, his reason such,
Whether he thinks too little, or too much:
Chaos of Thought and Passion, all confus'd;
Still by himself abus'd, or disabus'd;
Created half to rise, and half to fall;
Great lord of all things, yet a prey to all;
Sole judge of Truth, in endless Error hurl'd:
The glory, jest, and riddle of the world!

The one recurrent sound is the rhyme; assonance and alliteration are kept to a minimum, and even the sentence structure tends to fall into the suggested metrical unit; hence the inevitable and unforced use of antithesis and the regular fall of the caesura. In Dryden and Pope, in the octosyllabics of Marvell, in the simple quatrains of Housman, where a strictly controlled meter makes the words step along in a precise and disciplined order, the predominant sense is one of conscious wit. This sense arises from the technical dexterity displayed in neutralizing prose sense with associative sound, on approximately equal terms.

In blank verse, so easy to write accurately and so hard to write well, we move much further in the direction of prose. For in blank verse there is little place for the metrical absorption of the sentence structure: a long series of blank-verse lines in which the sentence structure closely followed the iambic pentameter would produce intolerable singsong. Hence blank verse tends to develop syncopation and run-on lines, and as it does so a second prose rhythm is set up beside the metrical one. This process may continue until the pentameter approximates prose. The following passage from Browning's *Ring and the Book* has been chosen as less extreme in its approximation than many that might have been selected:

So
Did I stand question, and make answer, still
With the same result of smiling disbelief,
Polite impossibility of faith
In such affected virtue in a priest;
But a showing fair play, an indulgence, even,
To one no worse than others after all—
Who had not brought disgrace to the order, played
Discreetly, ruffled gown nor ripped the cloth
In a bungling game at romps . . .

In such discursive or narrative blank verse as the above the listener hardly hears a definite pentameter at all: what he hears is a rhythm that seems just on the point of becoming prose, but is prevented from achieving the distinctively semantic rhythm of prose by some other rhythmical influence. The rhythm of Jacobean blank-verse drama has its center of gravity somewhere between verse and prose, so that it can move easily from one to the other at the requirements of dramatic decorum, which are chiefly the mood and the social rank of the speaker. In *The Tempest*, especially the speeches of Caliban, and in some late plays of Webster and Tourneur, the barrier between verse and prose often comes near dissolving, and hence the third associational rhythm peeps through, as in this passage from *The Tempest*:

I will stand to, and feed,
Although my last: no matter, since I feel
The best is past. Brother, my lord the Duke,
Stand to, and do as we.

A strong bias toward a prose sentence structure combined with a more elaborate rhyming scheme often produces the kind of intentional doggerel that is a regular feature of satire, as in *Hudibras* or *Don Juan*, or in Ogden Nash. Wordsworth, who stressed the identity of language between verse and prose, sometimes had trouble in keeping the simple flat sentences in the *Lyrical Ballads* from sounding like doggerel. One of Donne's Satire (the fourth) opens as follows:

Well; I may now receive, and die; My sinne
Indeed is great, but I have beene in
A Purgatorie, such as fear'd hell is
A recreation to, and scarse map of this.

Nobody hearing these lines read aloud would realize that they were pentameter couplets: the whole metrical scheme is parody, and as such it fits the satirical context.

In relation to prose, associational writing shows itself chiefly in a change of direction in meaning, away from the logical and toward the emotional and private. In relation to verse, it shows its influence chiefly in an increase in sound patterns. We notice this particularly in stanzaic verse, for the natural tendency of the stanza is to develop elaborate rhyming patterns, often supported by alliteration, assonance, and similar devices. Words tend to echo each other, and an evocative rhythm is superimposed on the metrical one, as in this lovely madrigal from *The Faerie Queene*:

Wrath, gealosie, griefe, loue do thus expell:
Wrath is a fire, and gealosie a weede,
Griefe is a flood, and loue a monster fell;
The fire of sparkes, the weede of little seede,
The flood of drops, the Monster filth did breede:
But sparks, seed, drops, and filth do thus delay;
The sparks soone quench, the springing seed outweed,
The drops dry vp, and filth wipe cleane away:
So shall wrath, gealosie, griefe, loue dye and decay.

A further step in this direction would make the sound-patterns obsessive, as happens occasionally, by way of experiment, in *The Faerie Queene* itself. Edgar Allan Poe, who made the discontinuity and the evocative effect of verse his "poetic principle," shows in such experiments in sound as *The Bells* and in such lines as the famous "The viol, the violet, and the vine" the permeation of meter by associative sound. In Hopkins a similar unifying of metrical and associative rhythms takes place, but in a much more intellectualized context:

'Some find me a sword; some
The flange and the rail; flame
Fang, or flood' goes Death on drum,
And storms bugle his fame.
But we dream we are rooted in earth—Dust!
Flesh falls within sight of us, we, though our flower the same,
Wave with the meadow, forget that there must
The sour scythe cringe, and the blear share come.

This passage illustrates another important principle. As associational patterns increase, and as alliteration and assonance appear beside rhyme, a more vigorous rhythm than a strict meter may be required to prevent the poem from becoming a soggy mass of echolalia. The rhythm in the Hopkins passage is accentual rather than metrical: like the rhythm of music, which it closely resembles, it sets up a series of accented beats, with a good deal of variety in the number of syllables that may intervene between beats. The sixth line of the above passage begins with an accentual spondee, though the prevailing rhythm of the line is anapestic. This accentual rhythm, usually with four main beats to a line, has run through Eng. from Anglo-Saxon alliterative verse to our own day, and often syncopates against the metrical rhythm. Thus "Whan that Aprill with his shoures soote," "To be or not to be, that is the question," and "Of man's first disobedience, and the fruit" are all iambic pentameter lines with four accented beats.

Varieties of Associational Rhythm. It is only in the more experimental writing of the last century or so, with its strongly psychological bias and its interest in the processes of creation, that any serious attempts have been made to isolate the associational rhythm in literature. Owing to this late development, its earlier manifestations have fallen within the normal categories of prose and metrical verse.

The associational rhythm has always been a feature of oracular writing, as in the Koran and in many parts of the Bible, as well as a regular literary device for expressing insanity, as in some of the Tom o'Bedlam speeches in *King Lear*. These uses are solemn or tragic, yet associative rhythms and mental processes have also a close connection with the comic, and, in the form of puns and malapropisms, have been one of the chief sources of humor. The conscious wit that was mentioned as an effect of expertly handled meter is quite distinct from associational wit, which results rather from an involuntary release from the subconscious. The most striking examples of associational rhythm at its purest before our own day are dramatic attempts to render the speech of uneducated or confused people who make no effort to organize their language into prose, such as Mistress Quickly in Shakespeare or Jingle and Mrs. Nickleby in Dickens. This curious duality of the oracular and the comic is peculiar to associational rhythm, and has been illustrated in passages quoted above.

Rabelais is the great progenitor of associational prose, especially in passages depicting drunkenness or other oracular states of mind, as in the fifth chapter of *Gargantua*. But of course in Eng. the tradition of associational prose writing was established by Sterne. Almost any page of Sterne, notably the famous opening page of the *Sentimental Journey*, illustrates the lightning changes of mood and rhythm and the dislocation of the ordinary logic of narrative or thought that are characteristic of associative style. Modern "stream of consciousness" writing is heavily indebted to Sterne. In such passages as this from *Ulysses* we can see the predominance of what we have called the "thought-breath" rhythm of association as distinct from the poetic line and the prose sentence: "Confession. Everyone wants to. Then I will tell you all. Penance. Punish me, please. Great weapon in their hands. More than doctor or solicitor. Woman dying to. And I schschschschschsch. And did you chachachachacha? And why did you? Look down at her ring to find an excuse. Whispering gallery walls have ears. Husband learn to his surprise. God's little joke. Then out she comes. Repentance skindeep. Lovely shame. Pray at an altar. Hail Mary and Holy Mary." The speed of this is andante and the monologue of Molly Bloom at the end of the book presto, but the rhythmical units are the same.

Associational prose develops in two directions, which may be called the disjunctive and the conjunctive. In disjunctive writing, as illustrated most typically by Gertrude Stein, and also found in Hemingway, Faulkner, and D. H. Lawrence, there is a technique of deliberate prolixity, a hypnotic repetition of words and ideas. In dialogue this may express simple inarticulateness or fumbling for meaning: in short, the original naive speech out of which associational writing grows. In more sophisticated contexts it expresses rather a breaking down of the more customary logical prose structures preparatory to replacing them with the psychological and emotional structures of associational prose. In conjunctive writing the aim is the reverse: to pack into the words as great a concentration of association as possible, whether of allusion, of sound (as in punning or paronomasia), or of ideas. The logical culmination of this process is *Finnegans Wake*, where the dream language used shows the influence of Freud's demonstrations of the incredible associative complexity of states of mind below consciousness.

In verse, associational rhythm very seldom predominates over meter before Whitman's time: about the only clear examples are poems written in abnormal states of mind, such as Christopher Smart's *Jubilate Agno*. Whitman's own rhythm shows many formalizing influences, such as that of biblical parallelism, and the relation to prose is also often close. But in Whitman's oracular lines, with a strong pause at the end of each and with no regular metrical pattern connecting them, the distinctive associational rhythm has been fully emancipated. Whitman's natural tendency is disjunctive, and in some later free verse, especially in imagism, this tendency is developed. Thus Amy Lowell:

Lilacs,
False blue,
White,
Purple,
Color of lilac,
Heart-leaves of lilac all over New England,
Roots of lilac under all the soil of New England,
Lilac in me because I am New England . . .

But the prevailing tendency in modern associational verse is conjunctive or evocative, as it is in the erudite literary allusiveness of Eliot and Pound, in the catachresis (q.v.) metaphors of Hart Crane and Dylan Thomas, or in the symbolic clusters of the later Yeats.

In pure prose, where the emphasis is on descriptive meaning, figures of speech are used sparingly, an occasional illustration or analogy being normally the only figuration employed. The more rhetorical the prose, the more naturally figurative the style becomes. In Jeremy Taylor, for instance, there appear elaborately drawn-out similes, and in euphuism similes from natural history (or what then passed as such) are a regularly recurring feature. Verse also, when it steers its middle course between prose and associational rhythm, often finds its figurative center of gravity in the illustrative simile, so prominent in the classical epic. But in verse, words are associated for sound as well as sense, rhyme being as important as reason, and the more intensified the sound patterns are, the greater the opportunities for puns and similar verbal echoes.

Associational writing, when conjunctive, tends to violently juxtaposed metaphor and to a thick figurative texture.

S. Lanier, *The Science of Eng. Verse* (1880); T. S. Omond, *A Study of Metre* (1903) and *Eng. Metrists* (1921); G. Saintsbury, *A Hist. of Eng. Prosody* (3 v., 1906–10) and *A Hist. of Eng. Prose Rhythm* (1912); Schipper; L. Abercrombie, *Poetry and Contemporary Speech* (1914; Eng. Assoc. pamphlet no. 14); Baum; D. L. Clark, *Rhetoric and Poetry in the Renaissance* (1922); C. P. Smith, *Pattern and Variation in Poetry* (1932); O. Barfield, *Poetic Diction* (2d ed., 1952); M. Boulton, *Anatomy of Poetry* (1953) and *Anatomy of Prose* (1954); J. Thompson, *The Founding of Eng. Metre* (1961). N.FR.

VERSE EPISTLE. See EPISTLE.

VERSE PARAGRAPH. Like prose, poetry tends to move forward in units which may be called, by analogy, v. paragraphs. The tendency is particularly strong in narrative and descriptive poetry, where the paragraphs are often indicated by indentation or spacing between lines. Elaborate stanzaic forms like the Spenserian stanza or ottava rima are often developed as v. paragraphs, and in inferior poetry the result is usually monotonous. If a paragraph is defined as one or more sentences unified by a dominant mood or thought, many lyrics could be described as single v. paragraphs, a point especially obvious in the case of the sonnet.

By general consent, the greatest master of the v. paragraph is John Milton. Many of the characteristic effects of *Paradise Lost*—its majesty, its epic sweep, its rich counterpoint of line and sentence rhythms—are produced or enhanced by Milton's v. paragraphs. To sustain his paragraphs Milton employed enjambment ("the sense variously drawn out from one Verse into another"), interruption, inversion, and suspension, or *Spannung,* the device of the periodic sentence whereby the completion of the thought is delayed until the end of the period.—G. Hübner, *Die stilistische Spannung in Milton's P.L.* (1913); E. Smith, *The Principles of Eng. Metre* (1923); J. H. Hanford, *Milton Handbook* (4th ed., 1946); J. Whaler, *Counterpoint and Symbol: An Inquiry into . . .* Milton's . . . Style (1956).

VERSI SCIOLTI. Also, *endecasillabi sciolti.* Hendecasyllabic lines with principal accent on the tenth syllable and without rhyme. They were used as early as the 13th c. (in the *Mare amoroso*) but were first cultivated during the Renaissance as the It. equivalent of classical epic hexameter. Trissino used them in his epic *Italia liberata dai goti,* and his tragedy *Sofonisba.* Despite his lack of success a controversy arose between the advocates of classical austerity and the advocates of rhyme. In the 16th c. rhyme won the day, but in the 18th c. and thereafter, v.s. were used with great success, particularly by Parini (*Il Giorno*), Foscolo (*I Sepolcri*), and Manzoni (*Urania*). Alfieri almost singlehanded made them the standard meter for tragedy. More recently the dramatist Sem Benelli used them in several dramas, and Pascoli adopted them for all but the last of his *Poemi conviviali. Endecasillabi sciolti* are equivalent to blank verse (q.v.) and may have influenced the development of that form in Eng.—F. Flamini, *Notizia Storica dei Versi e Metri Italiani . . .* (1919). L.H.G.

VERSIFICATION, traditionally considered the art or craft of writing verse, as distinguished from prosody (q.v.), the branch of criticism devoted to the theory and analysis of the structures of verse. Verseforms look quite different from the poet's point of view than from the theorist's: the poet learns to think in rhythmical patterns, to know the chances (and dangers) of a rhyme, to discover the freedoms of constraint within a stanza, and so by these to find his way of proceeding; the theorist asks how a meter is related to its language medium, what a form is capable of, what happens to a verseform when transferred into another language, or whether there exist metrical universals. These would seem quite distinct spheres of interest. But in fact there is no clear line to be drawn between v. and prosody: even the poet himself, when explaining his work, must choose terms to describe technique, and those terms inexorably imply a theory. Indeed, poetic praxis itself entails theory, even if unconscious, for performance in a skilled craft implies competence, and competence implies the internalized system of Rules which govern the making.

Such mutual implicature is natural and appropriate. Still, it is sometimes essential to insist on the differences between making and explaining. Unfortunately the literature of traditional prosody is of no help here, for scholars have used the two terms v. and prosody almost interchangeably, with wildly inconsistent results. The final ed. of Robert Bridges' seminal *Milton's Prosody* (1921) is subtitled "An Examination of the Rules of the Blank Verse in Milton's Later Poems," but an earlier edition added "With An Account of the V. of Samson Agonistes"; George Saintsbury's three-volume study of the practice of the Eng. poets is entitled *A Hist. of Eng. Prosody,* but T.V.F. Brogan's survey of the critical and theoretical studies of verseform is entitled *Eng. V.*; and what Clive Scott does for Fr. in *Fr. verse-art* Karl Shapiro and Robert Beum do for Eng. in *A Prosody Handbook.* Yet there are discernible routes of reference which, when traced, will lead to valuable distinctions.

In its primary sense of "composing verse," v. descends to us from L. *versificatio* (n.) < *versifico* (v.), = *versus* + *facio,* as in Quintilian. *Versus* itself is "a turning," particularly the turning of the plow at the end of the furrow (cf. Auden, elegizing Yeats, extolling "the farming of a verse"):

significantly, it is the ending of the furrow that creates, by demarcation, the furrow itself, and not vice versa. So the poet becomes a turner of lines. Words for the making of the thing (*fersian* "to versify" is a regular OE verb, with descendants in *Piers Plowman* and *The Monk's Prologue*) and the thing accomplished (the *O.E.D.* gives as a secondary sense of v. "verse-form or -structure; meter") are old, but the noun of action is apparently recent: the first certain citation of "v." in Eng. is 1603. Late and unstable, the word seems quaint even in the Ren., and in the late 19th c. it took on the connotation of "pseudo-scientific" in the reaction to German Philology, a coloring that lingers still.

"Prosody" derives from L. *prosodia*, "the accent on a syllable," which is of interest because cl. L. verse was in theory quantitative, though the confusion of accent and quantity was literally millennial. In Ren. Eng. *prosodie* denoted "the Art of accenting, or the rule of pronouncing wordes truely long or short," (Henry Cockeram's *The Eng. Dictionarie*, 1623). Early Eng. grammars, following their L. models, ordinarily treated sounds, letters, syllables, spelling, punctuation, and syntax, followed by a concluding section (commonly called the "Prosodia" or "Prosody") treating pronunciation (accent) and usually also verse (quantity). Verse was treated under this rubric because the grammarians conceived verse as *spoken*, hence subject to the rules of pronunciation, and because verse was considered the most important of all uses of language. "Prosody" therefore came to treat the inflections of speech not marked by orthography and the special organization of these in verse. Though "prosody" originally referred to only the former of these subjects, since the Prosodia contained both the term soon came to cover both, as evidenced by Dr. Johnson's definition in the *Dictionary*: "Prosody comprises orthoëpy, or the rules of pronunciation, and orthometry, or the rules of versification." And the word has been preserved, unfortunately, even to the present in *both* senses—for the prosody of speech, a linguistic phenomenon, and for prosody as analysis of verse, i.e. *theoria*. The conflation of the distinction, which arose historically as a mere textbook convenience, has led to more extreme results in modern times, such as the claim that the study of poetry lies entirely within the pale of linguistics (Roman Jakobson). The traditional view, and the view followed in prosody, is that while language is the stuff of poetry, the laws of rhythmical organization evident in verse are simply one manifestation—like others in speech itself, music, dance—of higher laws of rhythmicity itself, as a general and unifying temporal phenomenon. T.V.F.B.

VILLANELLE. A Fr. verse form, derived from an It. folk song of the late 15th-early 17th c. and first employed for pastoral subjects. According to L. E. Kastner (*History of Fr. Versification*, 1903), Fr. 17th c. prosodists such as Richelet reserved the term "villanelle" for one of the rustic songs by Jean Passerat (1534–1602). Although the earlier forms show considerable variation, the v. has since Passerat retained the following pattern: usually 5 tercets rhyming aba, followed by a quatrain rhyming abaa, with the first line of the initial tercet serving as the last line of the second and fourth tercets and the third line of the initial tercet serving as the last line of the third and fifth tercets, these 2 refrain-lines following each other to constitute the last 2 lines of the closing quatrain. If we let a^1 and a^2 stand for the first and third lines of the first tercet, we may schematize the form thus: a^1ba^2 aba^1 aba^2 aba^1 aba^2 aba^1a^2.

Like the older Fr. forms, the v. was employed in 19th-c. Eng. poetry primarily as a light verse form by such experimental dilettantes as Andrew Lang. However, Leconte de Lisle used it in 19th-c. France as a vehicle for philosophical content, and in the 20th c. E. A. Robinson's *House on the Hill* achieved a somber effect. More recently, Dylan Thomas' *Do not go gentle into that good night* restored a majestic seriousness to the v.

VIRELAI (also called *chanson baladée*, and *vireli*). Fr. medieval lyric. Originally a variant of the common dance song with refrain of which the rondeau (q.v.) is the most prominent type. This form developed in the 13th c. and at first may have been performed by one or more leading voices and a chorus. It begins with a refrain; this is followed by a stanza of 4 lines of which the first 2 have a musical line (repeated) different from that of the refrain. The last 2 lines of this stanza use the music of the refrain. The opening refrain, words and music, is then sung again. The v. usually continues with 2 more stanzas presented in this same way. A v. with only 1 stanza would be a *bergerette*. In Italy the 13th c. *laude*, and in Spain the *cantigas*, follow the same form. The syllables *vireli* and *virelai* were probably meaningless refrains which later designated the type.—F. Gennrich, *Rondeaux, Virelais und Balladen* (2 v., 1928). For additional information, see P. Le Gentil, *La Poésie lyrique espagnole et portugaise à la fin du moyen âge, 2ᵉ partie. Les Formes* (1953) and *Le V. et le villancico* (1954); M. Francon, "On the Nature of the V.," *Sym.*, 9 (1955; briefly surveys various schemes and proposes own formula). U.T.H.

VOLTA, or volte. A turn or a repetition (used also of music, dance, etc.). In sonnet development the word was used in Italy to refer to the tercets of the sestet, either because of the repetition of the tercet or, more probably, because of the "turn of thought" which followed the close of the octave. The term would thus be applicable to any point in the thought development, regardless of the sonnet type, where such a turn might occur, as in Shakespeare's Sonnet 18, line 9: "But thy eternal summer shall not fade . . ." or in Keats's *On First Looking Into Chapman's Homer,* line 9: "Then felt I like some watcher of the skies. . . ." It is more than coincidence that both of these occur in line 9, inasmuch as the organization of thought within the limited scope of the form invites (though it does not demand) a division at that point. See SONNET. L.J.Z.

W

WIT. In Aristotle's *Rhetoric,* w. is treated as the ability to make apt comparisons, and also (1389b) as "well-bred insolence." The L. term (*ingenium*) meant unique personal characteristics, or "genius" in the 18th-c. sense of the term. It was used by the rhetoricians to mean "cleverness" or "ingenuity." During the Renaissance it was used in a sense similar to the classical meaning, with perhaps more emphasis on ingenuity and the ability to create the bizarre, the extraordinary, and the unique. Renaissance discussions of *inventio* (e.g. Leonardi, *Dialoghi dell'Inventione*) tended to identify w. with the ability to discover and amplify new subjects; while in discussions of style, particularly during the 17th c., it was identified with the ability to discover brilliant, paradoxical, and far-fetched figures, especially metaphor, irony, paradox, pun, antithesis, etc. (e.g., Baltasar Gracián, *Agudeza y arte de ingenio,* 1642; Emmanuele Tesauro, *Il Cannocchiale Aristotelico,* 1654). Among the many terms used for *w.* are It. *ingegno;* Sp. *ingenio, argudeza ;* Fr. *esprit, ingenuité;* G. *Witz, Geist;* and Eng. wit. (Cf. J. E. Spingarn, *Crit. Essays of the 17th C.,* I, XXIV.)

The high point in the career of w. came in the latter half of the 17th and the first two decades of the 18th c. in the wake of such "witty" poetic movements as It. marinism, Sp. gongorism, Fr. *préciosité,* and Eng. metaphysical style. Thomas Hobbes used the term in *Human Nature* (1650), as follows; "And both Fancie and Judgement an commonly comprehended under the name of Wit, which seemeth to be a Tenuity and Agilitie of Spirits, contrary to the resitness of the Spirits supposed in thou that are dull." And in *Leviathan* (1651): "*Naturall Wit,* consisteth principally in two things; *Celecrity of Imagining* (that is, swift succession of one thought to another;) and *steddy direction* to some approved end." Sir William Davenant's *Discourse upon Gondibert* (1650) associates w. with memory; and Dryden, in the preface to his opera *The State of Innocence* (1684), says, "*The* definition of Wit . . . *is only this: That it is* a Propriety of Thoughts and Words; or in other Terms, Thoughts and Words elegantly adapted to the Subject." In general, authors of the early 17th c. consider w. an essential quality of poetry. Emmanuele Tesauro, for example, believed that the process of divine creation is the defining example of w. and the more w. an author reveals, the more godlike he becomes. Later authors, particularly such rationalists as Hobbes, regarded w. as a psychological faculty.

As the 17th c. progressed, discussions of w. became numerous. Any list would have to include Cowley ("Of Wit," 1656), Dryden (numerous comments throughout the critical works), Flecknoe *Discourse,* 1664), Boyle (Reflections, 1665), Shield (*Essay on Poetry,* 1682), Pope (*Essay on Criticism,* 1711), Addison (numerous *Spectators;* e.g., 58–61), Richard Blackmore (*Essay upon Wit,* 1716), Gay (*The Present State of Wit,* 1711), Corbyn Morris (*Essay towards Fixing the True Standards of Wit,* 1744), and others. It is impossible to reduce the mass of material on w. to any simple form. W. was sometimes contrasted to fancy or judgment; sometimes identified with one or the other faculty. At times it was contrasted to humor, raillery, satire, and ridicule; at times compared to them. "True w." was often contrasted with "false w." (generally, writing which dazzles without appealing to the understanding). As William Empson has pointed out (see bibliography), Pope uses w. no less than 46 times in the *Essay on Criticim,* and with at least six different meanings. At times w. suggests conceited style (argudeza); at times it is quickness at invention in the rhetorical anse of that term; at times it is "Nature to advantage dressed;" and at times it is apt expression. As is natural, the vagueness of the term eventually led critics to suspect its validity. Dr. Johnson attacked Cowley in his *Lives* (1779) for his "heterogeneous ideas . . . yoked by violence together. . . ." Halitt ("Wit and Humour," 1819) contrasted w., which is artificial, with imagination, which is valid. On the other hand Schiller's concept of the *Spieltrieb* (*Uber die ästhetische Erziehung des Menschengeschlechts,* 1793) would seeem to be a revival of the notion that w. (in the sense here of the play-impulse) is an essential ingredient of poetry.

During the 19th c. *imagination* was used to designate the capacity to see resemblances, ability to invent, etc.; and w. became associated with levity. Matthew Arnold rejected Chaucer and Pope from his list of the greatest poets because of their wittiness: they lacked "high seriousness." But T. S. Eliot, placing Donne and Marvell high in the hierarchy of Eng. poets, insisted upon the rightness of "a tough reasonableness beneath the slight lyric grace," and he said that these poets were successful by virtue of their "alliance of levity and seriousness (by which the seriousness is intensified)." The meaning of the term seems not to have come quite full circle: it is not commonly associated with imagination or conceptual power; on the other hand, it is associated with irony, and irony is associated with them.

Crit. Essays of the 17th C., ed. J. E. Spingarn, I (1908; see introd.); M. A. Grant, *The Ancient Rhetorical Theories of the Laughable* (1924); T. S. Eliot, "The Metaphysical Poets," and "Andrew Marvell," *Selected Essays* (1932); W. G. Crane, *W. and Rhetoric in the Renaissance* (1937); C. Brooks, *Modern Poetry and the Tradition* (1939); W. Empson, "W. in the *Essay on Criticism*," *The Structure of Complex Words* (1951); A. Stein, "On Elizabethan W.," *Studies in Eng. Lit.*, 1 (1961); G. Williamson, *The Proper W. of Poetry* (1961); S. L. Bethell, "The Nature of Metaphysical W.," *Discussions of John Donne*, ed, F. Kermode (1962). W.V.O'C.

Z

ZEUGMA (Gr. "means of binding"; cf. Gr. *zeugos*, "yoke"). According to a Gr. rhetorician of the 2d C. A.D., Alexander Numenius, and two of his Gr. successors of undetermined date, the use of a single verb with a compound object (C. Walz, *Rhetores Graeci*, 9 v., 1832–36, v. 8, pp. 474, 686, 709), the construction called *synezeugmenon* by Quintilian, 1st C. A.D. (*Institutes of Oratory* 9.3.62), in whose examples the subject or object or both may be compound. Later rhetoricians very properly extend the definition to the "yoking" together of any two parts of speech by means of any other, normally with no breach of syntax, though some make for confusion by including cases in which the "yoking" word agrees syntactically with only one of the "yoked," thus making z. partly synonymous with *syllepsis*.

Three varieties of z. have been distinguished, as by Johannes Susenbrotus (*Epitome troporum ac schematum*, 1541, ed. 1621, p. 25), according to whether the "yoking" word precedes the words it "yokes," i.e., *prozeugma* ("All fools have still an itching to deride, / And fain would be upon the laughing side," Pope, *An Essay on Criticism* 32–33); or follows them, i.e., *hypozeugma* ("Not marble, nor the gilded monuments / Of princes, shall outlive this powerful rime," Shakespeare, Sonnet 55); or stands between them, i.e,, *mesozeugma* ("Much he the place admired, the person more," Milton, *Paradise Lost* 9.444).—Lausberg. H.R

POETIC GENRES, MODES, AND FORMS: A SELECT READING LIST

The reader who has already consulted some of the entries in the text of this *Handbook* is aware that each is concluded by a short bibliography of important references. The List that follows here is intended as a general reading list providing references for the more common poetic forms, especially of genre and prosody, but it also serves as a supplement to a great many particular entries. In a number of cases important older references not cited in the original entry-bibliographies have been added to the lists below, and every list has been brought up to date. The List should be useful, then, as a first finding-list for the best and most recent work on the topics given. Abbreviations may be located in the General and Bibliographical Lists in the front matter of the book.

ALBA, AUBE: R. E. Kaske, "An A. in *The Reeve's Tale*," ELH, 26 (1959) and MLN, 75 (1960); J. Saville, *The Medieval Erotic A.: Structure as a Meaning* (1972); E. W. Poe, "The Three Modalities of the Old Prov. Dawn Song," *RPh*, 37 (1984), "New Light on the A.: A Genre Redefined," *Viator: Medieval and Ren. Studies*, 15 (1984).

ALLEGORY: D. W. Robertson, Jr., *A Preface to Chaucer* (1962); R. Tuve, *Allegorical Imagery. Some Mediaeval Books and Their Posterity* (1966); P. J. Alpers, *The Poetry of The Faerie Queene* (1967); A. Cook, "A.," *Prisms* (1967); M. Murrin, *The Veil of A.: Some Notes toward a Theory of Allegorical Rhetoric in the Eng. Ren.* (1969), *The Allegorical Epic: Essays in Its Rise and Decline* (1980); J. MacQueen, *A.*, Crit. Idiom Series, 14 (1970); J. I. Wimsatt, *A. and Mirror: Tradition and Structure in ME Lit.* (1970); P. Piehler, *The Visionary Landscape* (1971); I. MacCaffrey, *Spenser's A.: The Anatomy of Imagination* (1976); M. Quilligan, *The Language of A.: Defining the Genre* (1979); P. Rollinson, *Cl. Theories of A. and Christian Culture* (1981); H. Adams, *Philosophy of the Lit. Symbolic* (1983); P. de Man, "The Rhetoric of Temporality," *Blindness and Insight*, rev. ed. (1983); C. Van Dyke, *The Fiction of Truth: Structs. of Meaning in Narr. and Dram. A.* (1985).

ALLITERATION, ASSONANCE, CONSONANCE: P. McClumpha, *The A. of Chaucer* (1888); V. E. Spenser, *A. in Spenser's Poetry* (1898); J. D. Allen, *Quantitative Studies in Prosody* (1968)—unjustly neglected; M. Nelson, "Submorphemic Values," *Language and Style*, 6 (1973); P. G. Adams, *Graces of Harmony. A., A., and C. in 18th-C. British Poetry* (1976)—wider scope than the title indicates; J. A. Leavitt, "On the Measurement of A. in Poetry," *Computers and the Humanities*, 10 (1976); J.T.S. Wheelock, "Alliterative Functions in the *Divina Comedia*," *Lingua e Stile*, 13 (1978).

ASSONANCE: See ALLITERATION, ASSONANCE, CONSONANCE.

BALLAD: See NARRATIVE POETRY.

BALLAD AND HYMN METER: G. R. Stewart, Jr., *Modern Metrical Technique as Illustrated by B.M.* (1922), extended in PMLA, 39 (1924), 40 (1925), and in JEGP, 24 (1925); G. W. Boswell, "Reciprocal Controls Exerted by Ballad Texts and Tunes," JAF, 80 (1967), "Stanza Form and Music-Imposed Scansion," *Southern Folklore Quarterly*, 31 (1967); B. H. Bronson, *The Ballad as Song* (1969); J. Malof, *A Manual of Eng. Meters* (1970); C. Freer, *Music for a King* (1972).

BALLADE: Gleeson White, *Bs. and Rondeaux, Chants Royal, Sestinas, Villanelles, &* (1887); G. M. Hecq, *La B. et ses dérivées* (1891); H. L. Cohen, *The B.* (1915), *Lyric Forms from France* (1922); A. B. Friedman, "The Late Medieval B. and the Origin of Broadside Balladry," *Medium AEvum*, 27 (1958); G. Reaney, "The Devel. of the Rondeau, Virelai, and B.," *Festschrift Karl Fellerer* (1962); N. Wilkins, *One Hundred Bs., Rondeaux and Virelais from the Late Middle Ages* (1969).

BLANK VERSE AND HEROIC COUPLET: R. D. Havens, *The Influence of Milton on Eng. Poetry* (1922); T. W. Baldwin, "Upper Grammar School: Shakspere's Exercise of Versifying," *Wm Shakspere's Small Latine & Lesse Greeke* (1944); G. Hemphill, "Dryden's Heroic Line," PMLA, 72 (1957); J. H. Adler, *The Reach of Art* (1964); A. Oras, *B.V. and Chronology in Milton* (1966);

R. Beum, "So Much Gravity and Ease," *Language and Style in Milton* (1967); A. Ostriker, "The Three Modes in Tennyson's Prosody," PMLA, 82 (1967); D. Sipe, *Shakespeare's Metrics* (1968); J. A. Jones, *Pope's Couplet Art* (1969); W. B. Piper, *The Heroic Couplet* (1969); R. Fowler, "Three B.V. Textures," *The Languages of Lit.* (1971); L. Schädle, *Der frühe deutsche Blankvers* (1972); A. Dougherty, *A Study of Rhythmic Structure in the Verse of W. B. Yeats* (1973); E. R. Weismiller, "Studies of Verse Form in the Minor Eng. Poems," "Studies of Style and Verse Form in *Paradise Regained*," *A Variorium Commentary on the Poems of John Milton*, ed. M. Y. Hughes, (1974–1975), v. 2, 4, "B.V.," "Versification," *A Milton Encyclopedia*, ed. W. B. Hunter, Jr., (1978–1980), v. 1, 8; M. G. Tarlinskaja, *Eng. Verse: Theory and Hist.* (1976), "Evolution of Shakespeare's Metrical Style," *Poetics*, 12 (1983); G. T. Amis, "The Structure of the Augustan Couplet," *Genre*, 9 (1976); B. Bjorklund, *A Study in Comparative Prosody: Eng. and German Iambic Pentameter* (1978); P. Ramsey, *The Fickle Glass* (1979), App.; W. B. Piper, *Evaluating Shakespeare's Sonnets* (1979); O. B. Hardison, Jr. "Speaking the Speech," SQ, 34 (1983), "B.V. before Milton," SP, 81 (1984); G. T. Wright, "The Play of Phrase and Line in Shakespeare's Iambic Pentameter," SQ, 34 (1983), "Wyatt's Decasyllabic Line," SP, 82 (1985); H. Suhamy, *Le vers de Shakespeare* (1984).

BOB AND WHEEL STANZA: Schipper; E. G. Stanley, "The Use of Bob-Lines in *Sir Thopas*," *Neuphilologische Mitteilungen*, 73 (1972); T. Turville-Petre in RES, 25 (1974); H. Kirkpatrick, "The Bob-Wheel and Allied Stanzas in ME and Middle Scots Poetry," DAI, 37 (1976), 3608.

CAROL: R. H. Robbins in MLN, 57 (1942); M. Schöpf in *Anglia*, 87 (1969); R. L. Greene, *The Early Eng. Cs.*, 2d ed. (1977).

CATHARSIS: See DRAMATIC POETRY (TRAGEDY).

CELTIC PROSODY: C. W. Dunn, "Celtic," Wimsatt, *Versification*; J. Travis, *Early Celtic Versecraft* (1973); E. Campanille, "Indogermanische Metrik und altirische Metrik," *Zeitschrift für celtische Philologie*, 37 (1979); E. Rowlands, "*Cynghanedd*, Metre, Prosody," *A Guide to Welsh Lit.*, ed. A.O.H. Jarman et al. (1979).

CHANSONS DE GESTE: W. B. Calin, *The Epic Quest: Studies in Four OF Cs. de G.* (1966); J. Duggan, *The Song of Roland: Formulaic Style and Poetic Craft* (1973).

CLASSICAL METERS IN MODERN LANGUAGES: K. Elze, *Der englische Hexameter* (1867); A. H. Baxter, *The Introd. of Cl. Metres into It. Poetry* (1901); A. Kabell, *Metrische Studien III: Antike Form sich Nähernd* (1960); W. Bennett, *Ger. Verse in Cl. Metres* (1963); D. Attridge, *Well-Weighed Syllables* (1974); T. Herrera Zapién, *La métrica latinizante* (1975); *Die Lehre von der Nachahmung der antiken Versmasse im Deutschen*, ed. H.-H. Hellmuth and J. Schröder (1976).

CLASSICAL PROSODY: B. Snell, *Griechische Metrik*, 3rd ed. (1962); W. B. Stanford, *The Sound of Gr.* (1967); A. M. Dale, *The Lyric Metres of Gr. Drama*, 2d ed. (1968), *Collected Papers* (1969); W. F. Wyatt, *Metrical Lengthening in Homer* (1969); E. Wahlström, *Accentual Responsion in Gr. Strophic Poetry* (1970); L.P.E. Parker, "Gr. Metric 1957–70," *Lustrum*, 15 (1970)—rev. article; A. T. Cole, "Cl. Gr. and L.," Wimsatt, *Versification*; M. Parry, *The Making of Homeric Verse*, ed. A. Parry (1971); W. S. Allen, *Accent and Rhythm* (1973); D. W. Packard and T. Meyers, *A Bibliog. of Homeric Scholarship* (1974); B. Peabody, *The Winged Word* (1975); J. W. Halporn, M. Ostwald, and T. G. Rosenmeyer, *The Meters of Gr. and L. Poetry*, rev. ed. (1980); M. L. West, *Gr. Metre* (1982); *Cambridge Hist. of Cl. Lit.*, ed. P. E. Easterling and E. J. Kenney, v. 2: *L. Lit.* (1982).

COMEDY: See DRAMATIC POETRY.

CONCRETE POETRY: *C.P.: An Internat. Anthol.*, ed. S. Bann (1967); *Theoretische Positionen zur konkreten Poesie*, ed. T. Kopfermann (1974); A. Marcus, "Introd. to the Visual Syntax of C.P.," *Visible Language*, 8 (1974); *C.P. from East and West Germany*, ed. L. Gumpel (1976); J. L. McHughes, "The Poesis of Space: Prosodic Structures in C.P.," *Quarterly Jour. of Speech*, 63 (1977); D. Higgins, "The Strategy of Visual Poetry: Three Aspects," *Visual Lit. Crit.*, ed. R. Kostelanetz (1979); D. W. Seaman, *C.P. in France* (1981); W. Steiner, *Res Poetica, The Colors of Rhetoric* (1982); G. Janecek, *The Look of Rus. Lit.: Avant-Garde Visual Experiments 1900–1930* (1984).

CONSONANCE: See ALLITERATION, ASSONANCE, CONSONANCE.

CONVENTION: J. L. Lowes, *C. and Revolt in Poetry* (1919); H. Levin, "Notes on C.," *Perspectives of Crit.* (1950); R. M. Browne, *Theories of C. in Contemp. Am. Crit.* (1956); N. Frye, "Nature and Homer," *Fables of Identity* (1963); S. R. Levin, "The Cs. of Poetry," *Lit. Style: A Symposium*, ed. S. Chatman (1971); V. Forrest-Thompson, "Levels in Poetic C.," *Jour. of European Studies*, 2 (1972); L. Manley, *C. 1500–1750* (1980); W. G. Thalmann, *Cs. of Form and Thought in Early Gr. Epic Poetry* (1984).

COUPLET, HEROIC: See BLANK VERSE AND HEROIC COUPLET.

DESCRIPTIVE POETRY: See GEORGIC.

DRAMATIC POETRY: G. E. Bentley, *Shakespeare and His Theatre* (1964); S. W. Dawson,

Drama and the Dramatic, Crit. Idiom Series, 11 (1970); H.H.A. Gowda, *D.P. from Medieval to Modern Times* (1972); J. L. Smith, *Melodrama*, Crit. Idiom Series, 28 (1973); A. P. Hinchliffe, *Modern Verse Drama*, Crit. Idiom Series, 32 (1977); J. Baxter, *Shakespeare's Poetic Styles: Verse into Drama* (1980); L. Brown, *Eng. D. Form, 1660–1760: An Essay in Generic Hist.* (1981); G. R. Hibbard, *The Making of Shakespeare's D.P.* (1981); M. Stevens, "Did the Wakefield Master Write a Nine-Line Stanza?" *Comparative Drama*, 15 (1981); C. Freer, *The Poetics of Jacobean Drama* (1981); O. Mandel, "Poetry and Excessive Poetry in the Theatre," *Centennial Review*, 26 (1982); M. Carlson, *Theories of the Theatre: A Historical and Crit. Survey* (1985).

COMEDY: S. Freud, *Wit and its Relation to the Unconscious* (1916); M. A. Grant, *The Ancient Rhetorical Theories of the Laughable: The Gr. Rhetoricians and Cicero* (1924); K. M. Lea, *It. Popular C.*, 2 v. (1934); M. T. Herrick, *Comic Theory in the 16th C.* (1950), *It. C. in the Ren.* (1960); G. E. Duckworth, *The Nature of Roman C.* (1952); M. C. Bradbrook, *The Growth and Structure of Elizabethan C.* (1955); L. Hughes, *A Century of Eng. Farce* (1956); W. Sypher, *C.* (1956); H.D.F. Kitto, *Form and Meaning in Drama* (1956); C. L. Barber, *Shakespeare's Festive C.* (1959); B. Evans, *Shakespeare's Cs.* (1960); G. Williamson, *The Proper Wit of Poetry* (1961); *Theories of C.*, ed. P. Lauter (1964); N. Frye, *A Natural Perspective: The Devel. of Shakespearean C. and Romance* (1965); H. B. Charlton, *Shakespearean C.* (1966); E. Olson, *The Theory of C.* (1968); L. S. Champion, *The Evolution of Shakespeare's C.* (1970); K. J. Dover, *Aristophanic C.* (1972); W. M. Merchant, *C.*, Crit. Idiom Series, 21 (1972); R. B. Martin, *The Triumph of Wit: A Study of Victorian Comic Theory* (1974); A. Rodway, *Eng. C.: Its Role and Nature from Chaucer to the Present Day* (1975); A. Caputi, *Buffo: The Genius of Vulgar C.* (1978); *"An Essay on C." by Geo. Meredith, "Laughter" by Henri Bergson*, ed. W. Sypher (1980); R. Nevo, *Comic Transformations in Shakespeare* (1980); E. Kern, *The Absolute Comic* (1980); D. Konstan, *Roman C.* (1983); R. Janko, *Aristotle on C.: Towards a Reconstruction of Poetics II* (1984); M. L. Apte, *Humor and Laughter: An Anthro. Approach* (1984); E. L. Galligan, *The Comic Vision in Lit.* (1984); Z. Jagendorf, *The Happy End of C.: Jonson, Molière, and Shakespeare* (1984); K. Neuman, *Shakespeare's Rhetoric of Comic Character* (1985); W. C. Carroll, *The Metamorphoses of Shakespearean C.* (1985).

TRAGEDY: A. C. Bradley, *Shakespearean T.* (1904); F. Nietzsche, "The Birth of T.," *Complete Works*, I (1924); H. C. Lancaster, *A Hist. of Fr. Dramatic Lit. in the 17th C.* (1929–42); M. C. Bradbrook, *Themes and Conventions in Elizabethan T.* (1935); H.D.F. Kitto, *Gr. T.* (1939); M. E. Prior, *The Language of T.* (1947); C. Leech, *Shakespeare's T.* (1950); J. V. Cunningham, *Woe or Wonder: The Emotional Effect of Shakespearean T.* (1951, 1964); *Tragic Themes in Western Lit.*, ed. C. Brooks (1956); K. Muir, *Shakespeare and the Tragic Pattern* (1958); I. Ribner, *Patterns in Shakespearean T.* (1960); W. Rosen, *Shakespeare and the Craft of T.* (1960); G. Steiner, *The Death of T.* (1961); E. Olson, *T. and the Theory of Drama* (1961); J. Jones, *On Aristotle and Gr. T.* (1962); R. Y. Hathorn, *T., Myth, and Mystery* (1962); C. I. Glicksberg, *The Tragic Vision in 20th C. Lit.* (1963); *T.: Modern Essays in Crit.*, ed. L. Michel and R. B. Sewall (1963); M. T. Herrick, *It. T. in the Ren.* (1965); N. Frye, *Fools of Time: Studies in Shakespearean T.* (1967); J.M.R. Margeson, *Origins of Eng. T.* (1967); R. B. Heilman, *T. and Melodrama* (1968); C. Leech, *T.*, Crit. Idiom Series, 1 (1969); G. Brereton, *Principles of T.* (1969); L. Michel, *The Thing Contained: Theory of the Tragic* (1970); L. M. Welch, "Catharsis, Structural Purification, and Else's Aristotle," *Bucknell Review*, 19 (1971); H. C. Baldry, *The Gr. Tragic Theatre* (1971); R. B. Sewall, *The Vision of T.*, 2d ed. (1980); T. J. Scheff, *Catharsis in Healing, Ritual, and Drama* (1980); M. S. Silk and J. P. Stern, *Nietzsche on T.* (1981); *T., Vision and Form*, ed. R. W. Corrigan, 2d ed. (1981); O. Mandel, *A Definition of T.* (1982); B. Berke, *Tragic Thought and the Grammar of Tragic Myth* (1982); A. Lesky, *Gr. Tragic Poetry*, tr. M. Dillon (1983), *Gr. T.* (1983); S. Booth, *King Lear, Macbeth, Indefinition, and T.*, (1983); W. B. Stanford, *Gr. T. and the Emotions: An Intro. Study* (1983); E. Faas, *T. and After: Euripides, Shakespeare, Goethe* (1984); J. Herington, *Poetry into Drama: Early T. and the Gr. Poetic Tradition* (1985); A. K. Abdulla, *Catharsis in Lit.* (1985); G. Braden, *Ren. T. and the Senecan Tradition* (1985).

DRAMATIC MONOLOGUE: R. W. Rader, "The D.M. and Related Lyric Forms," *Crit. Inquiry*, 3 (1976); A. Sinfield, *D.M.*, Crit. Idiom Series, 36 (1977).

ELEGY: *Milton's "Lycidas,"* ed. S. Elledge (1966); A. F. Potts, *The Elegiac Mode: Poetic Form in Wordsworth and Other Elegists* (1967); C. M. Scollen, *The Birth of the Elegie in France 1500–1550* (1967); J. E. Clark, *Élégie: The Fortunes of a Cl. Genre in 16th C. France* (1975); C. Hunt, *Lycidas and the It. Critics* (1979); T. Ziolkowski, *The Cl. Ger. E., 1795–1950* (1980); R. J. Ball, *Tibullus the Elegist* (1983); A.W.H. Adkins, *Poetic Craft in the Early Gr. Elegists* (1984); G. W. Pigman, III, *Grief and Eng. Ren. E.* (1985); P. M. Sacks, *The Eng. E.: Studies in the Genre from Spenser to Yeats* (1985).

ENGLISH PROSODY: See METER; SOUND IN POETRY.

EPIC: See NARRATIVE POETRY.

EUPHONY: See SOUND IN POETRY.

FORM: B. Fehr, "The Antagonism of Fs. in the 18th C.," *Eng. Studies*, 18–19 (1936–37); K. Burke, "Container and Thing Contained," SR,

8 (1945), "Psychology and F.," "Lexicon Rhetoricae," *Counter-Statement*, 2d ed. (1953), *The Philosophy of Lit. F.* (1957); I. A. Richards, "Poetic F.," *Practical Crit.*, 2d ed. (1948); W. S. Johnson, "Some Functions of Poetic F.," JAAC, 13 (1955); R. Wellek, "Concepts of F. and Structure in 20th-C. Crit.," *Concepts of Crit.* (1963); *Discussions of Poetry: F. and Structure*, ed. F. Murphy (1964); R. Kell, "Content and F. in Poetry," *British Jour. of Aesthetics*, 5 (1965); J. Levy, "The Meanings of F. and the Fs. of Meaning," *Poetics, Poetika, Poetika*, ed. R. Jakobson et al. (1966), rpt. in his *Paralipomena* (1971); M. Rieser, "Probs. of Artistic F.: The Concept of F.," JAAC, 25 (1966); L. Turco, *The Book of Fs.* (1968); "F. and Its Alternatives," Special Issue of *New Lit. Hist.*, 2 (1971), incl. A. Fowler, "The Life and Death of Lit. Fs."; T. E. Uehling, Jr., *The Notion of F. in Kant's Critique of Aesthetic Judgment* (1971); *Organic F.: The Life of an Idea*, ed. G. S. Rousseau (1972); G. Spencer Brown, *Laws of F.* (1972); R. Duncan, "Ideas of the Meaning of F.," *Claims for Poetry*, ed. D. Hall (1982); L. M. Johnson, *Wordsworth's Metaphysical Verse: Geometry, Nature, and F.* (1982); N. E. Emerton, *The Scientific Reinterpretation of F.* (1984); J. Hollander, *Vision and Resonance: Two Senses of Poetic F.*, 2d ed. (1985).

FREE VERSE: W. C. Williams, "Measure," *Spectrum*, 3 (1959); J. McNaughton, "Ezra Pound's Metres and Rhythms," PMLA, 78 (1963); H. Gross, *Sound and Form in Modern Poetry* (1964); A. Cook, *Prisms: Studies in Modern Lit.* (1967); *Naked Poetry: Recent Am. Poetry in Open Forms*, ed. S. Berg and R. Mezey, (1969)—with authors' statements (*New Naked Poetry* [1976] has none); P. Ramsey, "F.V.: Some Steps Toward Definition," SP, 65 (1968); L. Ern, *Freivers und Metrik: Zur Problematik der eng. Verswissenschaft* (1970); W. Sutton, *Am. F.V.* (1973); J. Kwan-Terry, "The Prosodic Theories of Ezra Pound," *Papers on Language and Lit.*, 9 (1973); D. E. Stanford, "The Experimentalist Poet," *In the Classic Mode* (1978); D. Hall, *Goatfoot Milktongue Twinbird* (1978), ed., *Claims for Poetry* (1982); P. Fussell, "F.V.," *Antaeus*, 30–31 (1978); A. Helms, "Intricate Song's Lost Measure," SR, 87 (1979); C. Hartman, *F.V.: An Essay on Prosody* (1980); H.-J. Frey and C. Lorenz, *Kritik des freien Verses* (1980); *A Field Guide to Contemp. Poetry and Poetics*, ed. S. Friebert and D. Young, (1980); C. Scott, *Fr. verse-art* (1980); A. Golding, "Charles Olsen's Metrical Thicket," *Language and Style*, 14 (1981); C. Miller, "The Iambic Pentameter Norm of Whitman's F.V.," *Language and Style*, 15 (1982); "F.V.," Spec. Iss. of *Ohio Review*, 28 (1982); "Symposium on Postmodern Form," *New England Review/Bread Loaf Quarterly*, 6 (1983); D. Justice, "The F.V. Line in Stevens," *Antaeus*, 53 (1984); R. Hass, *20th-C. Pleasures* (1984); D. Wesling, *The New Poetries: Poetic Form since Coleridge and Wordsworth* (1985), ch. 5; J. Hollander, "Observations on the Experimental," *Vision and Resonance*, 2d ed. (1985).

GENRE: J. Petersen, "Zur Lehre von den Dichtungsgattungen," *Festschrift Aug. Sauer* (1925), 72–116; A. Jolles, *Einfache Formen* (1930); K. Vietor, "Probleme der lit. Gattungsgesch.," DVLG, 9 (1931), "Die Gesch. der lit. Gattungen," *Geist und Form* (1952); K. Burke, "Poetic Categories," *Attitudes Toward Hist.* (1937); E. Olson, "An Outline of Poetic Theory," Crane, *Critics*; "Lit. Gs.," Wellek and Warren; Frye; C.F.P. Stutterheim, "Prolegomena to a Theory of the Lit. Gs.," *Zagadnienia Rodzajów Literackich*, 6 (1964); C. Guillén, *Lit. as System* (1971), chs. 4–5; F. Cairns, *Generic Composition in Gr. and Roman Poetry* (1972); P. Hernadi, *Beyond G.: New Directions in Lit. Classification* (1972); R. L. Colie, *Resources of Kind: G. Theory in the Ren.* (1973); *Theories of Lit. G.*, ed. J. Strelka, *Yearbook of Comparative Crit.*, 8 (1978); H. Dubrow, *G.*, Crit. Idiom Series, 42 (1982); A. Fowler, *Kinds of Lit.* (1982); B. J. Bond, *Lit. Transvaluation from Vergilian Epic to Shakespearean Tragicomedy* (1984); *Canons*, ed. R. von Hallberg (1984); *Discourse and Lit.: New Appr. to the Anal. of Literary Gs.*, ed. T. A. Van Dijk (1984).

GEORGIC: R. Cohen, *The Art of Discrimination* (1964), *The Unfolding of "The Seasons"* (1970); D. B. Wilson, *Descriptive Poetry in France from Blason to Baroque* (1967); J. Chalker, *The Eng. G.: A Study in the Development of a Form* (1969); R. Feingold, *Nature and Society: A Study of Late 18th-C. Uses of the Pastoral and G.* (1977); J. G. Turner, *Politics of Landscape: Rural Scenery and Society in Eng. Verse 1630–1660* (1979); A. Low, *The G. Revolution* (1985).

HEROIC COUPLET: See BLANK VERSE AND HEROIC COUPLET.

HEXAMETER: E. G. O'Neill, Jr., "The Localization of Metrical Word-Types in the Gr. H.," *Yale Cl. Studies*, 8 (1942); W.F.J. Knight, *Accentual Symmetry in Vergil*, 2d ed. (1950); G. E. Duckworth, *Vergil and Cl. H. Poetry* (1969); N. Wright, "The Anglo-Latin H.," Diss., Cambridge U., 1981; W. G. Thalmann, *Conventions of Form and Thought in Early Gr. Epic Poetry* (1984).

IMITATION: T. M. Greene, *The Light in Troy: I. and Discovery in Ren. Poetry* (1982).

INFLUENCE: W. J. Bate, *The Burden of the Past and the Eng. Poet* (1970); H. Bloom, *The Anxiety of I.: A Theory of Poetry* (1973), *A Map of Misreading* (1975)—criticized in F. Lentricchia, *After the New Crit.* (1980), ch. 9; H. Toliver, *The Past That Poets Make* (1981); C. Baker, *The Echoing Green: Romanticism, Modernism, and the Phenomena of Transference in Poetry* (1984).

IRONY: E. Birney, "Eng. I. Before Chaucer," *University of Toronto Quarterly*, 6 (1937); A. R. Thompson, *The Dry Mock: A Study of I. in Drama* (1948); A. E. Dyson, *The Crazy Fabric: Essays in I.*

(1965); D. C. Muecke, *I. and the Ironic*, Crit. Idiom Series, 13 (1970); W. C. Booth, *A Rhetoric of I.* 2d ed. (1974); A. K. Mellor, *Eng. Romantic I.* (1980).

LAI: F. Wolf, *Über die Ls., Sequenzen, und Leiche* (1841)—still the classic study; G. Reaney, "Concerning the Origins of the Medieval L.," *Music and Letters*, 39 (1958); J. Maillard, *Évolution et ésthetique du l. lyrique* (1961); K. W. Le Mée, *A Metrical Study of Five Ls. of Marie de France* (1978).

LIMERICK: G. N. Belknap, "History of the L.," SB, 75 (1981).

LINE: D. Laferrière, "Free and Non-Free Verse," *Language and Style*, 10 (1977)—and prec. art.; M. Williams, "The L. in Poetry," *Antaeus*, 30–31 (1978); D. Levertov, "On the Function of the L.," *Chicago Review*, 30 (1979); M. Perloff, "The Linear Fallacy," *Georgia Review*, 35 (1981); C. T. Scott, "Typography, Poems, and the Poetic L.," *Linguistic and Lit. Studies A. A. Hill*, ed. Jazayery, (1981), v. 4; J. C. Stalker, "Reader Expectations and the Poetic L.," *Language and Style*, 15 (1982); P. P. Byers, "The Auditory Reality of the Verse L.," *Style*, 17 (1983); R. Bradford, " 'Verse Only to the Eye': L. Endings in *Paradise Lost*," EIC, 33 (1983).

MEDIEVAL ROMANCE: See ROMANCE.

METER: Schipper; O. Jespersen, "Notes on M." [1900], rpt. in his *Linguistica* (1933); J. B. Mayor, *Chapters on Eng. M.*, 2d ed. (1901); H. L. Creek, "Rising and Falling Ms. in Eng. Verse," PMLA, 35 (1920); R. Bridges, *Milton's Prosody* (1921); P. F. Baum, *Principles of Eng. Versification* (1922); I. A. Richards, "Rhythm and M.," *Principles of Lit. Crit.* (1925); A. Heusler, *Deutsche Versgesch.*, 3 v. (1925–1929); G. R. Stewart, Jr., *The Technique of Eng. Verse* (1930); J. C. Ransom, "Wanted: An Ontological Critic," *The New Crit.* (1941); A. Stein, "M. and Meaning in Donne's Verse," SR, 52 (1944); R. P. Blackmur, "Lord Tennyson's Scissors," KR, 14 (1952); G. Kellogg, "Bridges' *Milton's Prosody* and Ren. Metrical Theory," PMLA, 68 (1953); V. Hamm, "M. and Meaning," PMLA, 69 (1954); "Eng. Verse and What It Sounds Like," KR, 18 (1956)—symposium; W. P. Lehmann, *The Development of Germanic Verse Form* (1956); Beare; M. Burger, *Recherches sur la structure et l'origine des vers romans* (1957); D. Norberg, *Introd. à l'étude de la versification médiévale* (1958); W. K. Wimsatt, Jr., and M. C. Beardsley, "The Concept of M.: An Exercise in Abstraction," PMLA, 74 (1959); R. Wells, "Comments on M.," S. Chatman, "Comparing Metrical Styles," R. Jakobson, "Closing Statement: Linguistics and Poetics," *Style in Language*, ed. T. Sebeok (1960); J. Thompson, *The Founding of Eng. M.* (1961); G. B. Pace, "The Two Domains: Rhythm and M.," PMLA, 76 (1961); W. B. Yeats, "A Gen. Introd. to My Work," *Essays and Introductions* (1961); P. Maas, *Gr. M.* (1962); B. Snell, *Griechische Metrik*, 3rd ed. (1962); M. Halpern, "On the Two Chief Metrical Modes in Eng.," PMLA, 77 (1962); J. Malof, "The Native Rhythm of Eng. Ms.," *Texas Studies in Lit. and Language*, 5 (1964), *A Manual of Eng. Ms.* (1970); S. Chatman, *A Theory of M.* (1965); K. Shapiro and R. Beum, *A Prosody Handbook* (1965); J. O. Perry, "The Temporal Analysis of Poems," *British Jour. of Aesthetics*, 5 (1965); C. S. Brown, "Can Musical Notation Help Eng. Scansion?" JAAC, 23 (1965); V. Zhirmunskij, *Introd. to Metrics: The Theory of Verse* [1925], ed. E. Stankiewicz and W. Vickery (1966); J. McAuley, *Versification: A Short Introd.* (1966); R. Fowler, " 'Prose Rhythm' and M.," *Essays on Style and Language*, ed. Fowler (1966), "What Is Metrical Analysis?" *Anglia*, 86 (1968); F. Pyle, "Pyrrhic and Spondee," *Hermathena*, 107 (1968); A. M. Dale, *The Lyric Ms. of Gr. Drama*, 2d ed. (1968), *Collected Papers* (1969); H. Kuhn, *Sprachgesch., Verskunst* (1969); G. W. Meyers, "Modern Theories of M.: A Crit. Review," DAI, 30 (1970), 3912; C. L. Stevenson, "The Rhythm of Eng. Verse," JAAC, 28 (1970); D. Crystal, "Intonation and Metrical Theory," TPS, (1971); M. Parry, *The Making of Homeric Verse*, ed. A. Parry (1971); Wimsatt, *Versification*; R. Tsur, "Articulateness and Requiredness in Iambic Verse," *Style*, 6 (1972); W. Sidney Allen, *Accent and Rhythm* (1973); J. Travis, *Early Celtic Versecraft* (1973); D. Attridge, *Well-Weighed Syllables* (1974); J. E. Thiesmeyer, "Prosodic Theory: A Critique and Some Proposals," DAI, 35 (1974), 1064; O. Paul and I. Glier, *Deutsche Metrik*, 9th ed. (1974); G. Nagy, *Comparative Studies in Gr. and Indic M.* (1974); B. Peabody, *The Winged Word* (1975); E. Pulgram, *L.-Romance Phonology: Prosodics and Metrics* (1975); M. G. Tarlinskaja, *Eng. Verse: Theory and Hist.* (1976); R. Tsur, *A Perception-Oriented Theory of M.* (1977); D. Justice, "Ms. and Memory," *Antaeus*, 30–31 (1978); P. Fussell, *Poetic M. & Poetic Form*, 2d ed. (1979); R. Jakobson, "Studies in Comparative Slavic Metrics," "My Metrical Sketches: A Retrospect," *On Verse: Its Masters and Explorers* (1979); P. Barry, "The Enactment Fallacy," EIC, 30 (1980); *M., Rhythm, Stanza, Rhyme* ed. G. S. Smith (1980); C. Scott, *Fr. verse-art* (1980); Brogan; E. Marks, *Coleridge on the Language of Verse* (1981); R. P. Newton, *Vowel Undersong* (1981); D. Attridge, The Language of Poetry: Materiality and Meaning," EIC, 31 (1981), *The Rhythms of Eng. Poetry* (1982); M. L. West, *Gr. M.* (1982); R. Lewis, *On Reading Fr. Verse* (1982); B. de Cornulier, *Théorie du vers* (1982); Reallexikon, 2d ed., esp. "Deutsche Versmasse und Strophenformen," "Reim," "Rhythmus," "Romanische Versmasse und Strophenformen im Deutschen," "Strophe," "Vers, Verslehre, Vers und Prosa."

NARRATIVE POETRY: L. R. Zocca, *Elizabethan N. P.* (1950); R. Scholes and R. Kellogg, *The Na-*

ture of N. (1966); F. Kermode, *The Sense of an Ending* (1967), *The Art of Telling* (1983); P. Alpers, "Mode in N.P.," *To Tell a Story: Narrative Theory and Practice* (1973); J. M. Ganim, *Style and Consciousness in Middle European N.* (1983); E. S. Rabkin, *N. Suspense* (1974); W.J.T. Mitchell, *On N.* (1981); M. Perloff, "From Image to Action: The Return of Story in Postmodern Poetry," *Contemporary Lit.*, 23 (1982); P. Ricoeur, *Time and N.* (1984).

BALLAD: F. J. Child, *The Eng. and Scottish Popular Ballads*, 10 v. (1882–98); R. Menéndez Pidal, *Poesia popular y poesia tradicional* (1922); Ker; G. H. Gerould, *The B. of Tradition* (1932); W. Kayser, *Gesch. der deutschen Ballade* (1936); W. J. Entwistle, *European Balladry* (1939); T. P. Coffin, *The British Traditional B. in America* (1950); A. B. Friedman, "The Late Medieval Ballade and the Origin of Broadside Balladry," *Medium AEvum*, 27 (1958); *The B. Revival* (1961); J. H. Jones, "Commonplace and Memorization in the Oral Tradition of the Eng. and Scottish Popular Bs.," JAF, 74 (1961), with foll. reply; A. K. Moore, "The Lit. Status of the Eng. Popular B.," *ME Survey*, ed. E. Vasta (1965); C. M. Simpson, *The British Broadside B. and Its Music* (1966); J. B. Toelken, "An Oral Canon for the Child Ballads," *Jour. of the Folklore Institute*, 4 (1967); L. Vargyas, *Researches into the Mediaeval Hist. of the Folk B.* (1967); D. C. Fowler, *A Lit. Hist. of the Popular B.* (1968); B. H. Bronson, *The B. as Song* (1969), *The Singing Tradition of Child's Popular Ballads* (1976); D. Buchan, *The B. and the Folk* (1972); J. S. Bratton, *The Victorian Popular B.* (1975); *The European Medieval B.*, ed. O. Holzapfel (1978); *Bs. and B. Research*, ed. P. Conroy (1978); A. Bold, *The B.*, Crit. Idiom Series, 41 (1979); D. W. Foster, *The Early Sp. B.* (1981); *The B. as Narrative*, ed. P. Andersen, O. Holzapfel, T. Pettitt (1982).

EPIC: W. M. Dixon, *Eng. E. and Heroic Poetry* (1912); H. Massé, *Les épopées persanes* (1935); J. Crosland, *The OF E.* (1951); A. G. Brodeur, *The Art of Beowulf* (1959); *Zur germ.-deutschen Heldensage*, ed. K. Hauck (1961); B. Wilkie, *Romantic Poets and E. Tradition* (1965); R. M. Durling, *The Figure of the Poet in Ren. E.* (1965); A. Cook, *The Classic Line* (1966); B. K. Lewalski, *Milton's Brief E.: The Genre, Meaning, and Art of "Paradise Regained"* (1966); W. Calin, *The E. Quest* (1966); N. K. Chadwick and V. Zhirmunskij, *Oral Es. of Central Asia* (1969); R. Finnegan, *Oral Lit. in Africa* (1970) P. Merchant, *The E.*, Crit. Idiom Series, 17 (1971); M. Parry, *The Making of Homeric Verse*, ed. A. Parry (1971); M. P. Hagiwara, *Fr. E. Poetry in the 16th C.* (1972); D. Maskell, *The Historical E. in France 1500–1700* (1973); *Parnassus Revisited: Modern Crit. Essays on the E. Tradition*, ed. A. C. Yu (1973); *E. and Romance Crit.*, ed. A. Coleman, 2 v. (1973); *Heroic E. and Saga*, ed. F. J. Oinas (1978)—surveys 15 cultures; *Europäische Heldendichtung*, ed. K. von See (1978)—34 essays on 9 national poetries; C. Hulse, *Metamorphic Verse: The Elizabethan Minor E.* (1981); A. Fichter, *Poets Historical: Dynastic E. in the Ren.* (1982); J. D. Niles, *Beowulf: The Poem and Its Tradition* (1983); W. Calin, *A Muse for Heroes: Nine Centuries of the E. in France* (1983); W. G. Thalmann, *Conventions of Form and Thought in Early Gr. E. Poetry* (1984).

OLD GERMANIC PROSODY: J. C. Pope, *The Rhythm of Beowulf*, rev. ed. (1966); W. Hoffmann, *Altdeutsche Metrik* (1967); A. J. Bliss, *The Metre of Beowulf*, 2nd ed. (1967); T. Cable, *The Meter and Melody of Beowulf* (1974); P. Hallberg, *Old Icelandic Poetry* (1975); J. K. Bostock, "Appendix on Old Saxon and Old High German Metre," *Handbook of Old High Ger. Lit.*, 2d ed. (1976); A. Kabell, *Metrische Studien I: Der Alliterationsvers* (1978); J. B. Kühnel, *Untersuchung zum ger. Stabreimvers* (1978); R. Frank, *Old Norse Court Poetry* (1978); K. von See, *Skaldendichtung* (1980); S. B. Greenfield and F. C. Robinson, *A Bibliog. of Publications on OE Lit. to the End of 1972* (1980).

ONOMATOPOEIA: O. Jespersen, "Symbolic Value of the Vowel *I*," *Linguistica* (1933); J. R. Firth, "Modes of Meaning," *Essays and Studies*, 4 (1951); H. Wissemann, *Untersuchungen zur Onomatopoiie* (1954); W. T. Moynihan, "The Auditory Correlative," JAAC, 17 (1958); Z. Wittoch, "Les Onomatopées forment-elles une système dans la langue?" *Annali dell'Istituto Orientali di Napoli, Sezione Linguistica*, 4 (1962); I. Fónagy, *Die Metaphern in der Phonetik* (1963); C. Ricks, "Atomology," *Balcony*, 1 (1965); L. B. Murdy, *Sound and Sense in Dylan Thomas's Poetry* (1966); J. D. Sadler, "O.," CJ, 67 (1972); A. A. Hill, "Sound-Symbolism in Lexicon and Lit.," *Studies in Linguistics for G. L. Trager* (1972); J. Pesot, *Les Onomatopées* (1973); E. L. Epstein, "The Self-Reflexive Artefact," *Style and Structure in Lit.*, ed. R. Fowler (1975); F. W. Leakey, *Sound and Sense in Fr. Poetry* (1975); L. Weinstock, "O. and Related Phenomena in Biblical Hebrew," DAI, 40 (1979), 326B; P. Barry, "The Enactment Fallacy," EIC, 30 (1980); M. Borroff, "Sound Symbolism as Drama in the Poetry of Wallace Stevens," ELH, 48 (1981).

OTTAVA RIMA: A. Limentani, "Storia e struttura dell'o.r.," *Lettere italiane*, 13 (1961); R. Beum, "Yeats's Octaves," *Texas Studies in Lit. and Language*, 3 (1961); R. Moran, "The Octaves of E. A. Robinson," *Colby Library Quarterly*, 7 (1969).

PANTOUM: R. Étiemble, "Du 'Pantun' malais au 'pantoum' à la française," *Zagadnienia Rodzajów Literackich*, 22 (1979).

PARALLELISM: J. L. Kugel, *The Idea of Biblical Poetry* (1981); A. Berlin, *The Dynamics of Biblical P.* (1985).

PARODY: *The Brand X Anthol. of Poetry*, ed. W. Zaranka (1981); J. Hartwig, *Shakespeare's Analogical Scene: P. as Structural Syntax* (1984);

L. Hutcheson, *A Theory of P.: The Teachings of 20th-C. Art Forms* (1985).

PASTORAL: D. S. McCoy, *Trad. and Convention: Periphrasis in Eng. P. from 1557–1715* (1965); T. G. Rosenmeyer, *The Green Cabinet: Theocritus and the European P. Lyric* (1969); D. Kalstone, "Conjuring with Nature: Some 20th-C. Readings of P.," *20th-C. Lit. in Retrospect*, ed. R. A. Brower (1971); P. V. Marinelli, *P.*, Crit. Idiom Series, 15 (1971); T. McFarland, *Shakespeare's P. Comedy* (1972); R. L. Colie, *Shakespeare's Living Art* (1974), chs. 6–7; R. Poggioli, *The Oaten Flute: Essays on P. Poetry and the P. Ideal* (1975); H. Cooper, *P.: Medieval into Ren.* (1977); N. J. Hoffman, *Spenser's Ps.* (1977); R. Mallette, *Spenser, Milton, and Ren. P.* (1981); C. Segal, *Poetry and Myth in Ancient P.* (1981); J. Sambrook, *Eng. P. Poetry* (1983)—incl. Gr. and Roman; D. M. Halperin, *Before P.: Theocritus and the Ancient Tradition of Bucolic Poetry* (1983); W. J. Kennedy, *Jacopo Sannazaro and the Uses of P.* (1983); A. V. Ettin, *Lit. and the P.* (1984); D. R. Shore, *Spenser and the Poetics of P.* (1985).

PATTERN POETRY: Addison, *Spectator*, nos. 58, 63; C. Doria, "Visual Writing Forms in Antiquity: The *Versus Intexti*," *Visual Lit. Crit.*, ed. R. Kostelanetz (1979); J. Adler, "*Technopaigneia, Carmina Figurata*, and *Bilder-Reime*: 17th-C. Poetry in Historical Perspective," *Comparative Crit.*, 4 (1982); U. Ernest, "Europäische Figurenge dichte in Pyramidenform aus dem 16. und 17. Jahrhundert," *Euphorion*, 72 (1982); M. Elsky, "G. Herbert's Pattern Poems and the Materiality of Language," ELH, 50 (1983); J. Hollander, "The Poem in the Eye," *Vision and Resonance*, 2d ed. (1985).

PROSE POEM: *The P.P.: An Internat. Anthol.*, ed. M. Benedikt (1976); R. Bly, "What the P.P. Carries With It," *Am. Poetry Review* (May–June 1977); J. Holden, "The 'Prose Lyric,'" *Ohio Review*, 24 (1980); D. Keene, *The Modern Japanese P.P.* (1980); B. Johnson, *The Critical Difference* (1981), ch. 3; S. H. Miller, "The Poetics of the Postmodern Am. P.P.," DAI, 42 (1981), 2132; *The P.P. in France: Theory and Practice*, ed. M. A. Caws and H. Riffaterre (1983)—13 essays on Fr. and Eng.; S. Fredman, *Poet's Prose: The Crisis in Am. Verse* (1983); D. Scott, "La struct. spatiale du poème en prose," *Poétique*, 59 (1984).

PROSODY: See METER.

PURE POETRY: D. J. Mossop, *P.P.: Studies in Fr. Poetic Theory and Practice 1746 to 1945* (1971).

REPETITION: L. J. Richardson, "R. and Rhythm in Vergil and Shakespeare," *University of California Chronicle*, 32 (1930); K. Lea, "The Poetic Powers of R.," *Proc. British Academy*, 55 (1969); P. Kiparsky, "The Role of Linguistics in a Theory of Poetry," *Daedalus*, 102 (1973); E. G. Kintgen, Jr., "Echoic R. in OE Poetry," *Neuphilologische Mitteilungen*, 75 (1974).

RHYME: W. Masing, *Ueber Ursprung und Verbreitung des Reims* (1866); W. B. Sedgwick, "The Origin of R.," *Revue benedictine*, 36 (1924); J. Fucilla, "*Parole identiche* in the Sonnet and Other Verse Forms," PMLA, 50 (1935); K. Stryjewski, *Reimform und Reimfunktion* (1940); F. W. Ness, *The Use of R. in Shakespeare's Plays* (1941); U. Pretzel, *Frühgesch. des deutschen Reims* (1941); W. K. Wimsatt, Jr., "One Relation of R. to Reason," *The Verbal Icon* (1954); F. G. Ryder, "How Rhymed Is a Poem?" *Word*, 19 (1963); M. Masui, *The Structure of Chaucer's R. Words* (1964); M. Perloff, *R. and Meaning in the Poetry of Yeats* (1970); V. Nemoianu, "Levels of Study in the Semantics of R.," *Style*, 5 (1971); F. H. Guggenheimer, *R. Effects and Rhyming Figures . . . L. Poetry* (1972); T. Eekman, *The Realm of R. . . . in the Poetry of the Slavs* (1974); F. Vonessen, "Zur Metaphysik des Reims," *Sprachen der Lyrik*, ed. E. Köhler (1975); A. Roman, "The Informational Strategy of the R.," *Revue Roumaine de Linguistique*, 21 (1976); *Die Genese der europäischen Endreimdichtung*, ed. U. Ernst and P.-E. Neuser (1977); W. E. Rickert, "R. Terms," *Style*, 12 (1978); D. Wesling, *The Chances of R.: Device and Modernity* (1980); B. de Cornulier, "La rime n'est-ce pas une marque de fin de vers?" *Poétique*, 46 (1981), foll. by J. Molino and J. Tamine, "Des rimes, et quelques raisons," *Poétique*, 52 (1982); R. Tsur, *Poetic Structure, Information-Processing and Perceived Effects: R. and Poetic Competence* (1983); D. Billy, "La Nomenclature des rimes," *Poétique*, 57 (1984); W. Keach, "R. and the Arbitrariness of Language," *Shelley's Style* (1985); G. Schweikle, "Reim," "Reimbrechung," "Reimlexikon," "Reimprosa," "Reimvers, altdeutsche," Reallexikon, 2d ed., v. III; J. Hollander, "R. and the True Calling of Words," *Vision and Resonance* 2d ed. (1985).

RHYME ROYAL: T. Maynard, *The Connect. Between the Ballade, Chaucer's Modification of It, R.R., and the Spenserian Stanza* (1934); M. Ito, "Gower and R.R.," *John Gower: The Medieval Poet* (1976); M. Stevens, "The Royal Stanza in Early Eng. Lit.," PMLA, 94 (1979).

ROMANCE: E. C. Pettet, *Shakespeare and the R. Tradition* (1949); B. E. Perry, *The Ancient Rs.: A Lit.-Historical Account of Their Origins* (1967); *Pastoral and R.: Modern Essays in Crit.*, ed. E. T. Lincoln (1969); G. Beer, *The R.*, Crit. Idiom Series, 10 (1970); *Epic and R. Crit.*, ed. A. Coleman, 2 v. (1973); J. Stevens, *Medieval R.: Themes and Approaches* (1973); P. A. Parker, *Inescapable R.: Studies in the Poetics of a Mode* (1976); N. Frye, *The Secular Scripture: A Study of the Structure of R.* (1976); James A. Schultz, *The Shape of the Round Table: Structures of Middle High Ger. Arthurian R.* (1983); *The R. of Arthur*, ed. J. J. Wilhelm and L. Z. Gross (1984).

RONDEAU: W. E. Simonds, "The Three Rs. of Sir Thomas Wyatt," MLN, 6 (1881); M. Françon, "Rondeaux Tercets," *Speculum*, 24 (1949); F. Gennrich, *Das altfranzösische R. und Virelai im 12. und 13. Jahrhundert* (1963); J. M. Cocking, "The Invention of the R.," FS, 5 (1951); G. Reaney, "Concerning the Origins of the R., Virelai, and Ballade," *Musica Disciplina*, 6 (1952), cont. in *Festschrift Karl Fellerer* (1962); N.H.J. van den Boogard, *Rondeaux et Refrains du XIIe siècle au début du XIVe* (1969); F. M. Tierney, "An Introd. to the R.," "Origin and Growth of the R. in France," *Inscape*, 8 (1970), "The Devel. of the R. in Eng. from its Origin in the Middle Ages," "The Causes of the Revival of the R.," *Revue de l'Université d'Ottawa*, 41, 43 (1971, 1973); M. Françon, "Wyatt et le R.," *Ren. Quarterly*, 24 (1971); C. Scott, "The Revival of the R. in France and Eng. 1860–1920," RLC, 213 (1980).

SAPPHIC: E. Brocks, *Die Sapphische Strophe* (1890); G. H. Needler, *The Lone Shieling* (1941); D. I. Page, *Sappho and Alcaeus* (1955); H. Kenner, "The Muse in Tatters," *Agenda*, 6 (1968); R. Paulin, "Six S. Odes 1753–1934," *Seminar*, 10 (1974); E. Weber, "Prosodie verbale et prosodie musicale: La Strophe sapphique au Moyen Age et à la Ren.," *Le Moyen Français*, 5 (1979).

SATIRE: A. B. Kernan, *The Plot of S.* (1965); *S.: A Crit. Anthol.*, ed. J. Russell and A. Brown (1967); M. Hodgart, *S.* (1969); H. D. Weinbrot, *The Formal Strain: Studies in Augustan Imitation and S.* (1969); A. Pollard, *S.*, Crit. Idiom Series, 7 (1970); C. Sanders, *The Scope of S.* (1971); *S.: Mod. Essays in Crit.*, ed. R. Paulson (1971); T. Lockwood, *Post-Augustan Satire: Charles Churchill and Satirical Poetry, 1750–1800* (1979); A. G. Wood, *Lit. S. and Theory: A Study of Horace, Boileau, and Pope* (1984); *Eng. S. and the Satiric Tradition*, ed. C. Rawson (1984).

SCANSION: See METER.

SESTINA: F. de Gramont, *Sestines, précédés de l'histoire de la sextine* (1872); J. Riesz, *Die Sestine* (1971); J. C. Jernigan, "The S. in Provence, Italy, France, and England 1180–1600," DAI, 31 (1971), 6554; P. Cummins, "The S. in the 20th C.," *Concerning Poetry*, 11 (1978); M. Shapiro, *Hieroglyph of Time: The Petrarchan S.* (1980).

SLAVIC PROSODY: V. M. Zhirmunskij, *Introd. to Metrics* (tr. 1966), et al., eds., *Teorija stixa* (1968), *Issledovanija po teorii stixa* (1978); J. Levy, *Paralipomena* (1971)—his coll. essays; E. Stankiewicz, "S.," Wimsatt, *Versification*; *Slavic Poetics*, ed. R. Jakobson (1973); M. L. Gasparov, *Sovremennyj ruskij stix: Metrika i ritmika* (1974), et al., eds., *Problemy stixovedenija* (1976); T. Eekman, *The Realm of Rime . . . in the Poetry of the Slavs* (1974); J. Lotman, *Structure of the Artistic Text* (tr. 1974); I. K. Lilly and B. P. Scherr, "Rus. Verse Theory Since 1960," *International Jour. of S. Linguistics and Poetics*, 22 (1976)—with commentaries—cont. in "Rus. Verse Theory Since 1978," *ibid.*, 27 (1983); J. Mukarovsky, *The Word and Verbal Art* (tr. 1977); E. Etkind, *Materija stixa* (1978); R. Jakobson, *On Verse: Its Masters and Explorers* (1979)—his coll. studies on verseform; *Metre, Rhythm, Stanza, Rhyme*, ed. and tr. G. S. Smith (1980)—7 essays; *Problemy teorii stixa*, ed. V. E. Xolshevnikov (1984)—19 essays.

SONNET: H. Welti, *Gesch. des Sonettes in der deutschen Dichtung* (1884); E. W. Olmsted, *The S. in Fr. Lit.* (1897); L. G. Sterner, *The S. in Am. Lit.* (1930); E. Oliphant, "S. Structure: An Analysis," PQ, 11 (1932); E. Rivers, "Certain Formal Characteristics of the Primitive Love S.," *Speculum*, 33 (1958); M. Krieger, *A Window to Crit.: Shakespeare's Ss. and Modern Poetics* (1964); S. Booth, *An Essay on Shakespeare's Ss.* (1969); B. Stirling, *The Shakespeare S. Order: Poems and Groups* (1969); J. Loader, "A S. in the Old Testament," *Zeitschrift für alttestamentliche Wissenschaft*, 81 (1969); J. Strzetelski, *The Eng. S.* (1970); J. Levy, "The Devel. of Rhyme-Scheme and of Syntactic Pattern in the Eng. Ren. S.," "On the Relations of Language and Stanza Pattern in the Eng. S.," in his *Paralipomena* (1971)—difficult to obtain but important; J. Fuller, *The S.*, Crit. Idiom Series, 26 (1972); P. E. Blank, Jr., *Lyric Forms in the S. Sequences of Barnabe Barnes* (1974); C. Scott, "The Limits of the S.," RLC, 50 (1976); F. Kimmich, "Ss. Before Opitz," *Ger. Quarterly*, 49 (1976); D. H. Scott, *S. Theory and Practice in 19th-C. France* (1977); H.-J. Schlütter, *Sonett* (1979); S. Hornsby and J. R. Bennett, "The S.: An Annotated Bibliog. from 1940 to the Present," *Style*, 13 (1979); P. Oppenheimer, "The Origin of the S.," CL, 34 (1982); H. S. Donow, *The S. in Eng. and Am.: A Bibliog. of Crit.* (1982); *Russkij sonet*, comp. B. Romanov (1983)—introd.

SOUND IN POETRY: C. P. Smith, *Pattern and Variation in Poetry* (1932); K. Burke, "On Musicality in Verse," *The Philosophy of Lit. Form*, rev. ed. (1957); W. B. Stanford, *The S. of Gr.* (1967)—on euphony; E. M. Thompson, "S. Correlations in Verse," *Language Quarterly*, 8 (1969); G. Chesters, *Some Functions of S.-repetition in "Les Fleurs du Mal"* (1975); L. Bishop, "Phonological Correlates of Euphony," *Fr. Review*, 49 (1975); D. I. Masson, "Poetic S.-Patterning Reconsidered," *Proc. Leeds Phil. and Lit. Society, Lit. and Hist. Sect.*, 16 (1976); B. Hrushovski, "The Meaning of S. Patterns in Poetry: An Interaction Theory," *Poetics Today*, 2 (1980); R. P. Newton, *Vowel Undersong* (1981); R. Chapman, *The Treatment of Ss. in Language and Lit.* (1984); F. Ahl, *Metaformations: Soundplay and Wordplay in Ovid and Other Classical Poets* (1984).

SPENSERIAN STANZA: H. Reschke, *Die Spenserstanze* (1918); T. Maynard, *The Connection Be-*

tween the Ballade, Chaucer's Modification of It, Rime Royal, and the S.S. (1934); K.-U. Prausuhn, *Zur Erfüllung der Spenserstanze bei Spenser, Byron, Keats* (1974).

SPRUNG RHYTHM: W. H. Gardner, *Gerard Manley Hopkins (1844–1889): A Study of Poetic Idiosyncrasy in Relation to Poetic Tradition*, 2 v. (1948–1949); W. J. Ong, S.J., "Hopkins' S.R. and the Life of Eng. Poetry," *Immortal Diamond* (1949); *Journals and Papers*, ed. H. House and G. Storey (1959); E. Schneider, *The Dragon in the Gate* (1968), chs. 3–4; H.-W. Ludwig, *Barbarous in Beauty: Studien zum Vers im G. M. Hopkins Sonetten* (1972); R. J. Ventre, "S.R. and Meaning," DAI, 39 (1979), 6151.

STANZA: Schipper; P. Martinon, *Les Strophes* (1912); I. Frank, *Répértoire métrique de la poésie des troubadours*, 2 v. (1953, 1957); W. Pfrommer, *Grundzüge der Strophenentwicklung Baudelaire zu Apollinaire* (1963); L. Turco, *The Book of Forms* (1968); U. Mölk and F. Wolfzettel, *Répértoire métrique de la poésie française des origines à 1350* (1972); F. Schlawe, *Die deutsche Strophenformen 1600–1950* (1972); E. Häublein, *The S.*, Crit. Idiom Series, 38 (1978); H. J. Frank, *Handbuch der dt. Strophenformen* (1980); W. Suppan, "Strophe," Reallexikon, 2d ed., v. IV.

STRUCTURE: See TEXTURE AND STRUCTURE.

SYMBOL: R. Wellek, "The Term and Concept of Symbolism in Lit. Hist.," *New Lit. Hist.*, 1 (1970); C. Chadwick, *S.*, Crit. Idiom Series, 16 (1971); *Symbolism: A Bibliog. of S. as an Internat. and Multidisciplinary Movement*, ed. D. L. Anderson (1975); T. Todorov, *Theories of the S.* (1977, tr. 1982); H. Adams, *Philosophy of the Lit. Symbolic* (1983).

TAIL RHYME: C. Strong, "Hist. and Relations of the T.R. Strophe in L., Fr., and Eng.," PMLA, 22 (1907); U. Dürmuller, *Narrative Possibilities of the T.R. Romances* (1975); A. T. Gaylord, "Chaucer's Dainty 'Dogerel,' " *Studies in the Age of Chaucer*, 1 (1979).

TERZA RIMA: L. E. Kastner, "Hist. of the T.R. in France," *Zeitschrift für französische Sprache und Lit.*, 26 (1904); J.S.P. Tatlock, "Dante's T.R.," PMLA, 51 (1936); L. Binyon, "T.R. in Eng. Poetry," *Eng.*, 3 (1940); J. Wain, "T.R.," *Rivista di letterature moderne*, 1 (1950); M. R. Watson in MLN, 68 (1953); P. Boyde, *Dante's Lyric Poetry* (1967), *Dante's Style in his Lyric Poetry* (1971); J. D. Bone, "On Influence and on Byron and Shelley's Use of T.R. in 1819," *Keats-Shelley Memorial Bulletin*, 32 (1982); J. Freccero, "The Significance of T.R.," *Dante, Petrarch, Boccaccio*, ed. A. S. Bernardo and A. L. Pellegrini (1983).

TEXTURE AND STRUCTURE: T. D. Young, "Ransom's Crit. Theories: S. and T.," *Mississippi Quarterly*, 30 (1977).

TRAGEDY: See DRAMATIC POETRY.

TRAGICOMEDY: C. Hoy, *The Hyacinth Room: An Investigation into the Nature of Comedy, Tragedy, and T.* (1964); D. L. Hirst, *T.*, Crit. Idiom Series, 43 (1984).

TRIOLET: P. J. Marcotte, "An Introd. to the T.," "More Late Victorian T. Makers," "A Trio of T. Turners," *Inscape*, 5–6 (1966–1968); C. Scott, "The 19th C. T.: Fr. and Eng.," *Orbis Litterarum*, 35 (1980).

UT PICTURA POESIS: "U.P.P.: A Bibliog.," *Bulletin of Bibliog.*, 29 (1972); E. L. Huddleston and D. A. Noverr, *The Relation of Painting and Lit.: A Guide to Information Sources* (1978); *Articulate Images: The Sister Arts from Hogarth to Tennyson*, ed. R. Wendorf (1983).

VERSE AND PROSE: D. Winter, "V. and P.," JEGP, 5 (1903–5); T. S. Eliot, "P. and V.," *The Chapbook*, 22 (1921); Ker; A. M. Clark, "Poetry and V.," *Studies in Lit. Modes* (1946); N. Frye, *The Well-Tempered Critic* (1963); P. Habermann and K. Kanzog, "Vers, Verslehre, Vers und Prosa," Reallexikon, 2d ed., v. IV.

VILLANELLE: E. Gosse, "A Plea for Certain Exotic Forms of Verse," *Cornhill Magazine*, 36 (1877); Gleeson White, *Ballades and Rondeaux, Chants Royal, Sestinas, Vs., &.* (1887); R. E. McFarland, "Victorian Vs.," *Victorian Poetry*, 20 (1982), "The Contemporary V.," *Modern Poetry Studies*, 11 (1982).

VIRELAI: N. Wilkins, *One Hundred Ballades, Rondeaux, and Vs. from the Late Middle Ages* (1969).

T.V.F.B.